COMPARATIVE
LABOR MOVEMENTS

COMPARATIVE LABOR MOVEMENTS

JOHN CLARKE ADAMS

ISAAC DEUTSCHER

ALLAN FLANDERS

WALTER GALENSON

VAL R. LORWIN

PHILIP TAFT

KENNETH F. WALKER

edited by Walter Galenson

NEW YORK / RUSSELL & RUSSELL

TABLE OF CONTENTS

INTRODUCTION—WALTER GALENSON

There have been numerous recent attempts to determine the basic forces that shape the labor movement, and upon such foundation to predict the future course of this institution. These efforts are not fortuitous; they reflect the recognition that the future of democracy is closely bound up with the fate of its trade unions. The communists have long recognized, in theory and practice, that trade unions occupy a highly strategic position in modern industrial society, and have everywhere made intense efforts to capture them for the purpose of advancing the political hegemony of communism. Only in very recent years, however, when the industrial strife attendant upon the rapid growth of trade unionism has abated, has the tremendous potentiality for promoting social stability inherent in western trade unionism come to be perceived.

It is not unfair to say that many of those who have been engrossed with these problems have not suffered from excessive factual knowledge when labor movements other than their own were concerned, and their efforts unmistakably reflect this parochialism. There are honorable exceptions. The names of Lujo Brentano, Werner Sombart, Robert Michels, and Selig Perlman immediately come to mind, and it is little wonder that the work of these men has directly influenced generations of students of the labor movement and, indirectly, the labor movements themselves. But even they cannot be said to have had the final word. Additional decades of experience, and the application on a broad scale of more refined tools of quantitative analysis to the universe of data with which they were concerned, have opened new vistas. The time is ripe for additional synthesis of the slowly accumulating capital of raw material available to the social scientist, to the end of providing generalizations that can better explain the past and offer greater hope of peering into the future.

There are different approaches to the problem. Some contend that only through detailed induction, starting at the fundamental unit of labor organization, the factory or the local union, can meaningful results be obtained. Research in "human relations," in which generalization springs from the intensive study of individual situations, represents this point of view. Alternatively, explanations of union or worker behavior have sometimes been sought in sweeping deductive generalization, resting only when absolutely necessary, and there lightly, upon history or empirical fact. In neither case have the results been impressive. It is still necessary to refer students to *Political Parties,* published in 1915, and to *A Theory of the Labor Movement,* published in 1928, if they are to gain any insight into what may be called "theory" in this difficult area.

The present volume had its genesis in the conviction that the most fruitful approach to a study of the labor movement lies in the method of comparative analysis. Hypotheses that grow out of peculiar conditions in one country can then be tested against other bodies of experience, and reconciliation sought in differences among the determining factors. However, the authors do not lay claim to achievement of any such end. Nor will the reader, after having read the essays, be ready to sit down and theorize. Obviously, much more intensive work than this volume represents will be necessary before successful generalization is forthcoming.

Yet theoretical content is not altogether lacking. Though the essays were written by individuals living on different continents, and with widely varying backgrounds, who were accorded considerable latitude in emphasizing what they thought important, there are certain themes that recur. From Australia to Norway, despite tremendous variation in physical, economic, and social environment, trade unions have faced certain problems in common, and their responses are often not dissimilar. Some promising lines of inquiry have been unearthed, and at least a tentative start made in their pursuit.

1. The precise circumstances under which trade unionism first took root varied from country to country, but in all cases it was the product of industrialization. That England was the classic land of trade unionism, and her labor movement the model wherever workers began to organize, lay in early industrial primacy and the thoroughness with which the industrial revolution transformed the English economy. The spectacular rise of German trade unionism, coming at the close of the 19th century, mirrored faithfully the industrial development of that nation, while the continued weakness of French and Italian trade unions reflected the incompleteness of industry's triumph over agriculture in those countries. This is not to say that there were no trade unions prior to the onset of industrialization proper. The printers, the cigar makers, the tailors, the shoemakers, the building craftsmen, were often organized in societies still within the grip of medievalism; but the rise of trade unionism as the major economic institution of our time had to wait upon the emergence of the factory system and the creation of an urban industrial working class.

Now these observations are almost truisms, and they scarcely require further comment. But what is not nearly so obvious, and does merit further consideration, is the precise relationship between the various facets of industrialization and trade union development. Such factors as the period in which the process of industrialization reached its height, the tempo of the process, and the degree to which industry supplanted agriculture as the way in which a country earned its living, all exercised a profound influence on trade union development. Labor attitudes in Germany and Scandinavia, for example, were undoubtedly molded by the fact that industrialization came at a time when the spread of humanitarianism had made impossible the kind of human exploitation so vividly described by the Hammonds in *The Town Labourer* and built into a revolutionary system in *Das Kapital*. One might want to inquire into the significance for French and Italian trade unionism of the relatively smaller units of business enterprise in those countries. For Russia, of course, the timing of the industrial revolution was crucial. As Mr. Deutscher shows, it was the over-whelmingly agrarian character of Russian economic society at the time of the Bolshevik Revolution, and the virtual non-existence of stable trade unionism, that permitted the incredible seizure of control over a huge nation by a handful of determined men. When Russia finally industrialized, it was under the aegis of a powerful political machine which was not able to dispense with trade unions, but rather perverted them for its own purposes. Indeed, it is one of the tragedies of our time that Russian economic backwardness in the first two decades of this century frustrated unmistakable tendencies toward a "normal" course of trade union development.

Among the other aspects of economic history that merit further scrutiny is the role of the medieval gild system as a precursor of the modern labor market. It has been gospel, ever since the Webbs disposed of the question in their *History of Trade Unionism*, that there was little connection, organic or in spirit, between the two systems. The Webbs based their conclusions upon British history, and the long reign of *laissez faire* between the breakup of the medieval system and the rise of trade unions and employer associations provided cogent support for their position. But on the Continent, where mercantilism never entirely disappeared, and where monopolies, official or unofficial, bridged the gap between the two great systems of labor market organi-zation, the case is not nearly so clear. The contemporary labor move-ments of Europe owe much more than is generally realized to the gilds; and conversely, the absence of deeply rooted, preexisting forms of labor organization has been of great significance for "new" countries such as the United States and Australia.

INTRODUCTION

2. Comparative trade union structure and organization provide a promising area for further study, one that may yield real insights into the future. Certain broad lines of development are discernible. Union structure tends almost irresistibly toward the industrial form as economic aggregates become larger and skills are broken down into machine operations. Despite fierce resistance by vested craft interests, they eventually give way, either gradually, as in the case of Britain, or suddenly, in the face of a cataclysm such as that which overwhelmed the German labor movement during the Hitler era. But there are certain puzzling deviations that require more intensive examination. For example, how can one account for the growth in Britain and Denmark of the giant, multi-industrial general workers' union? This form of organization was present at an early stage in the trade union history of other nations as well, but only in the case of these two did it prove a viable form.

The equally controversial issue of trade union centralism constitutes still another field in which interesting results may be forthcoming. There was everywhere an early dispute between the proponents of organization by trade and organization by geographical region, between the "trade" unionist and the syndicalist. The most spectacular of these controversies was that in France, where the importance of the local *Bourses du Travail* still persists. But the ultimate victory of the trade unionist did not finally resolve all problems, for then the principal bone of contention became the relative authority of the national trade union and of the federation of trade unions. Undoubtedly, the fifty to seventy-five years since the formation of the major trade union federations have witnessed a steady trend in the direction of greater central power, but striking differences persist. We have on the one hand, the highly centralized federations of Norway and Sweden, and on the other, the very loosely organized British Trades Union Congress; exploration of the causes of this difference might well throw some light on the future of movements where the problem remains an acute one, as in Germany.

3. When one enters the domain of trade union function and considers collective bargaining and industrial disputes, the method of comparative quantitative analysis is particularly promising. There has always been some interest in international labor statistics, and it has been increasing because of the greater availability of good statistical materials, for which we are largely indebted to the International Labor Office. Numerous theoretical problems can be attacked in this fashion. For example, what has been the influence of trade unionism on the distribution of national income? This is a question that is hardly answerable by reference to the experience of one country alone, but

international comparisons may well yield definitive conclusions on this much disputed point. International comparisons of wage trends, to say nothing of absolute differences in wages and living standards, are few and far between despite the economic policy answers inherent in them.

The best developed area in comparative labor is that of collective bargaining systems. Again thanks to the work of the ILO, there are available careful analyses of the principal collective bargaining systems. Even here, however, there are many things that require additional elaboration. Mr. Walker's description of compulsory arbitration in Australia (Chapter 3) will make clear how little understood Australian collective bargaining is outside the country, despite frequent reference to the "lessons" of Australian compulsory arbitration in support of often conflicting points of view.

4. The determinants of labor ideology have received surprisingly little attention, despite the obvious importance of the subject. Every labor movement has been exposed to numerous hues of political radicalism, yet one doctrine generally comes to the top—and not the same one in every country. Why was it possible in Britain for the Fabian Society to have exercised so decisive an influence on the economic and political thinking of millions of workers, whereas Marxian socialism came up against a stone wall? How is it possible to account for the triumph of social democracy in Germany and Scandinavia, of syndicalism and then communism in France? The problem has been explored adequately only for Russia, where ideology and a plan of action were linked inseparably in Lenin's conception of communism.

The authors of the essays in this volume have endeavored, within the limitations of the space available to them, to indicate some of the possible reasons for the observed differences. For example, the reader will find a brief but cogent explanation for what has been well termed *Le Socialisme sans Doctrines*, the ideology of Australian labor, in terms of the manner in which that country was settled and developed.

5. A final range of problems concerns the future of trade unionism in Western society (their future in the East is all too clear). The crucial question is that of their role in relation to a state which is ever increasing its hegemony over economic life. More than fifty years ago, in *Industrial Democracy*, the Webbs outlined their conception of the part that trade unions would play in a society such as the one that Great Britain has since become, and their version has not been improved upon for sheer depth of insight. We have at the present time, in terms of polar attitudes, the French and Italian trade unions in open and intense hostility to the existing governments—a state of affairs that is nothing new in either country—and at the other the complete absorption of the Russian trade unions by the Soviet state.

INTRODUCTION

In between, trade unions are offering varying degrees of cooperation to their governments, ranging from whole-hearted collaboration in Norway and Sweden to the loyal opposition that is characteristic of nonlabor Britain and Australia. The elucidation of these various relationships is certainly one of the major tasks facing the social scientist.

To summarize, it has been the intention of the authors, by providing a basic minimum of factual information, plus personal evaluation of this material, to indicate the broad lines of trade union history, organization, and function in seven major political areas of the world. The reader should not expect to find a detailed compendium of labor fact; he will find additional material in the bibliography included in the volume, and in the material referred to in the footnotes. The major purpose of these essays is to stimulate further research in comparative labor history and economics, in the belief that such work is crucial for intelligent thinking about what has become the greatest economic institution of our time, the trade union.

Chapter I

GREAT BRITAIN——ALLAN FLANDERS

Growth and Legal Status of Unions

The origins of British trade unionism have been adequately described in the opening chapter of the Webbs' *History of Trade Unionism, 1666–1920*. Subsequent research has not modified their main conclusions. There is no evidence, as they pointed out, to support the view that trade unions grew out of the medieval craft gilds. These bodies, which survive today in the City Companies of London, were dominated by the master craftsmen, and there are no examples of independent journeymen's societies branching off from them. The rise of combinations of workmen in particular trades is to be traced not to any "particular institution" but to "every opportunity for meeting together of wage-earners of the same occupation." In the words of the Webbs:

> . . . there is actual evidence of the rise of one of the oldest of the existing trade unions out of a gathering of the journeymen "to take a social pint of porter together." More often it is a tumultuous strike, out of which grows a permanent organisation. Elsewhere, as we shall see, the workers meet to petition the House of Commons, and reassemble from time to time to carry on their agitation for the enactment of some new regulation, or the enforcement of an existing law. In other instances we shall find the journeymen of a particular trade frequenting certain public houses, at which they hear of situations vacant, and the "house of call" becomes thus the nucleus of an organisation.[1]

Beginnings of organization

The first form of permanent organization among wage-earners was the local trade club of the eighteenth century. They were to be found among hatters, cordwainers, curriers, brush-makers, basket-makers, calico-printers, cotton-spinners, coopers, sailmakers, coachmakers,

---

[1] Sidney and Beatrice Webb, *The History of Trade Unionism, 1666–1920*, page 23. London: Longmans Green & Co., Ltd., 1920. By permission of the Trustees of the late Lord Passfield.

I

smiths, bricklayers, carpenters, silk-weavers, cutlery workers, printers —in short, among skilled artisans in many trades. These bodies sought with little success, mainly by appeals to Parliament, to protect the wage standards of their members, based on custom and apprenticeship, against the growingly devastating effects of unlimited competition. They were not only local and isolated from each other, but virtually illegal. A long series of Acts of Parliament had made it a criminal offense for workmen in particular trades to combine in order to change their wages and conditions. The medieval doctrine that it was the prerogative of the state to regulate such matters still prevailed, although, in practice, the state no longer attempted to do so.

With the Industrial Revolution came the use of power machinery, the factory system, and, politically, the complete triumph of the new doctrine of *laissez-faire*. For the mass of the people this meant a condition of economic and social anarchy. The population grew with an incredible rapidity; workers crowded into towns, which in the main became dirty and melancholy assemblages of factories and hovels; productivity soared; great fortunes were made by some; but the vast majority of the working people became the slaves of the new machines and lived in degrading squalor. The first reaction of the organized craftsmen was to redouble their appeals to Parliament for protection, but they appealed in vain. For:

> . . . the governing classes, who had found in the new industrial policy a source of enormous pecuniary profit, eagerly seized on the new economic theory as an intellectual and moral justification of that policy. The abandonment of the operatives by the law, previously resorted to under pressure of circumstances and . . . not without some remorse, was now carried out on principle, with unflinching determination.[2]

Moreover, with the example of the French Revolution close at hand, their fear and contempt of the new proletariat led them to pass the Combination Acts of 1799 and 1800. These heralded a period of savage repression of trade union activity. Francis Place tells of how:

> . . . the suffering of persons employed in the cotton manufacture were beyond credibility; they were drawn into combinations, betrayed, prosecuted, convicted, sentenced, and monstrously severe punishments inflicted on them; they were reduced to and kept in the most wretched state of existence. . . . Justice was entirely out of the question; the working men could seldom obtain a hearing before a magistrate—never without impatience and insult; and never could they calculate on even an approximation to a rational conclusion.[3]

[2] Sidney and Beatrice Webb, *The History of Trade Unionism, 1666–1920*, page 55. London: Longmans Green & Co., Ltd., 1920. By permission of the Trustees of the late Lord Passfield.

[3] Quoted by C. M. Lloyd, *Trade Unionism*, page 4. London: Black, 1928.

Nineteen printers employed on *The Times* newspaper were condemned in 1810 to terms of imprisonment varying from nine months to two years for "combining and conspiring together maliciously to injure their masters and employers by quitting their work on account of their demands for an increase in wages not being acceded to."

In these conditions trade unionism took root. The Combination Laws were not systematically enforced. Organization among craftsmen persisted often in the form of secret clubs, with fearful oaths and romantic rites. The Lancashire cotton and wool workers, the miners of Northumberland and Durham, and the Scottish weavers, despite their lack of organization, were all involved in large-scale strikes. The workers were learning the lesson that they must rely upon their own strength to improve their lot. But their separate efforts were unrelated, and the absence of communication prevented them even from knowing accurately what was happening to their fellow workers elsewhere.

The struggle for recognition

The first break in the policy of repression was a strange affair, an example of how imperceptibly history can sometimes be made. Francis Place, a tailor of Charing Cross, and Joseph Hume, a radical M.P., managed to steer a bill to repeal the Combination Acts through Parliament as a side-issue, without the government fully realizing what was contemplated; it became law without either a debate or a vote. Its sponsors maintained that trade unionism was only a reaction to repression, so that, if freedom to combine were granted, the new movement would soon disappear. The reverse proved to be true. Encouraged by the repeal, new unions were formed and strikes broke out in many parts of the country. Thoroughly alarmed, the government tried to replace the 1824 Act by a measure more drastic than the Combination Acts. The final result was a compromise. The new Act, passed in 1825, did make it possible for the workers to organize without committing an illegal act, but there was hardly a thing that the unions could do to carry out the purpose of their existence without coming into conflict with the law. Nevertheless, new organizations continued to spring up, and unions of engineers, shipwrights, miners, carpenters, and joiners were formed at this time.

These early trade unions had all the grand ambitions of youth. For the first time the conception of a nation-wide, common purpose gained ground among working people. Efforts were made to form national unions in place of the small local bodies and to set up federations. There was an attempt to establish a general union for the workers in all trades known as "The Philanthropic Hercules," but, although this organization perished soon after it was born, others followed later. The trade unions also directed their attention to more radical methods of improving the lot of their members than the seemingly hopeless process of bargaining with the employers; they aspired to change the economic structure of society, and, under the influence of Robert Owen, looked particularly toward the advantages of cooperative production.

All these new ideas and endeavors culminated in 1834 in the founding of the Grand National Consolidated Trade Union, with Robert Owen as its leader. This organization had a phenomenal growth and recruited a half million members within a few weeks. The employers in the building trades retaliated by insisting on their employees signing "the document," an undertaking to leave or not to join a Union.[4] The legal vulnerability of the unions now became apparent in a series of prosecutions of trade unionists, which resulted in convictions and heavy sentences. The most notable of these was the case of the Dorchester laborers in 1834. For wholly peaceful attempts to build up a union for agricultural workers at Topuddle, six workers were arrested and sentenced to seven years' exile in Australia. The great outburst of indignation to which this punishment gave rise resulted in five of these workers being brought back from Botany Bay in 1838. The Grand National, however, after a series of abortive strikes, broke up. After this collapse of their hopes, the radically minded workers—though not the trade unions as such—concerned themselves with the Chartist Movement and joined in its agitation for an extension of political rights as a prerequisite to their industrial emancipation.

These short-lived and vaguely revolutionary developments had taken place against a background of economic depression. From 1850 on there began a long period of industrial expansion, which gave the trade unions an opportunity to consolidate themselves on a sounder financial basis. In 1851 a number of unions organizing skilled workers in the metal trades formed the Amalgamated Society of Engineers. This was subsequently known as the "New Model," since its form of organization served as a pattern for new national unions in other trades. According to the Webbs, it had a permanent paying membership of 11,000 and a regular income of £500 a week. Such financial stability was without precedent, and the new association became the most powerful trade union in the country. The new form of organization was also characterized by a strongly centralized and businesslike administration. Dues were high by any previous standards, but, in return, provision was made for various friendly benefits. Needless to

---

[4] This was very similar to the American "yellow dog" contract.

say, this form of unionism spread only among the craftsmen and skilled workers, who could afford such payments and who came to be looked upon as "an aristocracy of labor."

The centralization of control within the new unions also made possible greater coordination between them. A group of five powerful leaders, named by the Webbs "The Junta," exercised for a time almost undisputed sway in the trade union movement. They were extreme only in their caution and moderation. Nevertheless, the movement was not static, and a closer unity was growing up from below as well as from above. The strike of the London builders in 1859–60 over a demand that their hours should be reduced to nine per day brought behind them the support of many other trade unions and led to the formation of the London Trades Council. In Glasgow, Sheffield, Liverpool, and Edinburgh similar bodies had already been created as voluntary local federations of trade union branches. In 1868, after one or two abortive attempts from other quarters, the Manchester and Salford Trades Council took the initiative in calling a Trades Union Congress of trades councils and trade unions. Less than 120,000 members were represented, but in six years this number was multiplied tenfold.

The growing power and solidarity of this small trade union movement produced a reaction of alarm on the part of the governing groups. In 1867 a Royal Commission was appointed to investigate the organization and rules of the unions and to inquire into allegations of intimidation, which they were accused of encouraging. "The Junta" now made their outstanding contribution to the cause of trade unionism; they went into action in defense of union rights and secured the assistance of a gifted team of writers and lawyers. The results were historic. Even the majority report of the Royal Commission made recommendations that fell far short of what the employers had been demanding, whereas the minority report, which was in effect acted upon, proposed giving the trade unions legal protection to enable them to safeguard their funds, while leaving them in all other respects voluntary organizations. Between 1871 and 1876 a series of Trade Union Acts was passed, which in their total effect provided: that trade unions could no longer be declared unlawful because their objects were in restraint of trade; that they could protect their funds by taking legal proceedings, if necessary, against defaulting officials; and that they could engage in peaceful picketing in labor disputes. Although they could also acquire a definite civil status by registration with the Registrar of Friendly Societies, this action was voluntary, and generally they were accorded a large measure of freedom from legal proceedings in regard to their internal affairs.

"New Unionism" and political representation

That British trade unionism was now established on firm social, as well as legal, foundations was soon demonstrated by its weathering of the severe trade slump that followed swiftly upon its political success. Membership declined—it was more than halved—but only for a time, and all the larger unions emerged without their resources being seriously impaired. But if the foundations were firm, they were also still extremely narrow, and equally narrow was the prevailing concept of the tasks of the trade unions. The next main phase in their history is concerned with a great widening process in both respects, the discovery by the British trade union movement of its latent possibilities.

In this period there were two main developments within the trade union world—"New Unionism" and political representation—which were closely interwoven, and a third, largely outside it, on which the other two greatly depended. This third development was the revival of socialist ideas. The Marxist Social Democratic Federation and the Fabian Society were founded in the early eighties and Keir Hardie's Independent Labour Party in 1893. Although their political views differed considerably, they all agreed on two things: that the *whole* of the working class should be organized; and that it should, as an *independent* factor, play a decisive part in industry and politics. From working-class and middle-class socialists, then, there came a new impulse to spread trade union organization to the semi-skilled, unskilled and white collar workers. "New Unionism" was the name given to this development. These groups did not have the same possibilities of improving their conditions by exercising some control over the supply of their labor in the manner of the craftsmen. They had, perforce, to resort to more radical action and were attracted more strongly by the socialist concept of an egalitarian society. The Reform Act of 1867 had given the vote to the main body of working-class householders in the towns, and in 1874 the Labour Representation League had secured the return of the first two working-class candidates, both miners, to Parliament. The two established political parties, the Liberals and the Conservatives, were now competing for union support by the passing of social legislation. The idea of building up an independent political representation of labor interests began to appear practical. The new unionism and the new politics went hand in hand.

Just as the formation of the Amalgamated Society of Engineers had proved to be the turning point in the previous period, so did the successful strike of London dockers in 1889 become a signal and a portent for this phase of union development. With the victory of the dockers and the successful organization of the gas-workers, there was a burst of enthusiasm for bringing trade unionism into all those occupations as yet untouched by it. In 1890 the National Union of Clerks came into existence, and shortly after two unions were formed for distributive and allied workers.

Although the growth of unionism among the previously unorganized workers reacted favorably upon the membership of older unions, there was a continual tussle between the old conservative and the new radical forces within the movement. The first victory of the latter was won at the Trades Union Congress in 1890, which committed itself to a program that included the demand for an eight-hour day and a number of near-socialist resolutions. The former retaliated in 1895 when they commanded a sufficient majority at the Congress to exclude the Trades Councils from affiliation. The reason given was that the existing method involved a dual representation of the workers, but, in fact, the Trades Councils were considered to be too closely associated with the new trends. By the end of the century, however, the marked divergence of outlook had largely disappeared. An alliance between a number, but not all, of the trade unions and the various socialist political societies produced the Labour Representation Committee, which in 1906 changed its name to that of the Labour Party.

Expansion, confidence, militancy, and success were now, and for the next two decades, among the main attributes of British trade unionism. Membership grew from roughly two million at the turn of the century to four million by the outbreak of war in 1914. There were several national strikes, notably among the miners, railwaymen, and transport workers. Not all of them achieved their immediate objects but they frequently led to improvements in the machinery for collective bargaining. At the same time the political labor movement was developing and forcing the pace of social reform. Workmen's Compensation came in 1906, Old Age Pensions in 1908, Trade Boards for fixing minimum wages in the "sweated" trades in 1909, and National Insurance in 1911. Judged by present standards these measures did not go far in alleviating the worst forms of poverty and distress, but they established principles, the application of which has since been so greatly extended.

The value of the new Labour Party to the trade unions was particularly demonstrated, however, by the assistance it was able to give them in counteracting two major attacks upon their freedom that came this time from the courts. In 1901 a judgment was given in the case of *Taff Vale Railway Co. v. Amalgamated Society of Railway Servants* that threatened to undermine completely the position that it was thought had been gained by the 1871–76 legislation. It was decided in this case that an employer was entitled to recover damages from a trade union for losses sustained as the result of torts committed by its agents, an interpretation of the law that virtually deprived the trade unions of the power to strike, since the courts had previously been developing doctrines that made most union activity unlawful. The Trades Disputes Act of 1906 removed this liability and fully recognized inducement to breach of contract and peaceful picketing as legitimate adjuncts to the method of collective bargaining. Partly, perhaps, in consequence of this Parliamentary success, the political activities of the unions were next threatened by the *Osborne Judgment* in 1909, in which the House of Lords, as the highest court of appeal, held that it was illegal for a trade union to spend its funds on purposes other than the industrial objects specified in previous Acts. This decision threatened to cripple the new Labour Party, which relied greatly on the unions for financial support, but a sustained agitation brought about the Trades Union Act of 1913, which laid down the conditions under which political objectives could be included in the rules of a union with its members' consent.

The impact of war

The main effect that World War I had on British trade unionism was to enhance its strength and social standing. The cooperation of the trade unions was indispensable for military and industrial mobilization, and wartime full employment greatly improved their bargaining position. The unions voluntarily declared an industrial truce on the outbreak of hostilities. Most of them reluctantly agreed to a suspension of those shop practices that might lead to a limiting of production in wartime conditions on the understanding that they would be restored at the end of the war. At the same time a form of compulsory arbitration was agreed upon for the ultimate settlement of all disputes in the munitions industries in exchange for a government promise to limit employers' profits.

This policy of close cooperation with the government for the prosecution of the war was not accepted so readily by some of the more radically minded trade unionists at the lower levels of organization. Their dissatisfaction increased when it became apparent that profiteering was rife, that the cost of living was rising rapidly, and that wages were not increasing proportionately. The South Wales miners went on strike in the summer of 1915 and proved by their example that a system of compulsory arbitration could not be enforced by penal sanctions. There were many more unofficial stoppages of work organized by "workers' committees," "shop stewards' committees," "vigilance committees," and similar bodies that sprang up in many localities, but especially in the munitions industries. These local organizations formed themselves into a National Workers' Committee Movement, which became an alternative, unofficial leadership in the trade union world. Dissatisfaction with wartime conditions and a definite antiwar spirit contributed much to the growth of this movement, but it also gave expression to a purpose that had been steadily gaining ground in the prewar years. This purpose was summed up by the popular slogan "workers' control."

The dichotomy of attitude that had developed during the war between the official and unofficial leaderships largely disappeared at the end of hostilities. The engineers incorporated the shop steward system into their trade union organization. The demand of the workers to have some voice in the way their industries were conducted had been partly acknowledged in the Whitley Report (a thorough discussion of the report appears on pages 54–57). A considerable extension of statutory wage regulations promised better conditions to the workers in badly paid and poorly organized industries. At the same time there had been an immense growth in trade union membership, especially in the numbers affiliated to the Trades Union Congress, which had risen from 2.2 million in 1913 to 6.5 million in 1920. Thus, it was in a mood of supreme optimism, with a strong belief in the power of the whole labor movement to change the social order, that the trade unions met the great postwar depression that engulfed Great Britain at the end of 1920. They suffered a rude awakening.

Industrial strife on a national scale began with the railway strike of 1919, which for nine days paralyzed the entire railway system of the country. This ended in a victory for the unions and was notable for the publicity campaigns carried on by both sides to gain public support—the government was, at the time, still in control of the railways and therefore in the position of employer. Equally spectacular was the engineering lockout in 1922, but the economic tide had turned and the employers were successful, at least for the time being, in maintaining their claim that the trade unions should have no say in regard to "managerial functions." Though unrest and conflict were widespread, it was the miners who were the hardest hit and who occupied the center of the stage in this stormy era.

In 1921 the miners' first battle against wage reductions and a return to district wage agreements led to the collapse of the Triple Alliance, a powerful alignment of the trade unions of the railwaymen, transport workers, and miners, formed for mutual support in industrial action. It was looked upon generally as a great pillar of strength for the whole movement. The Triple Alliance issued notices for a strike of all their members in support of the miners, but for a variety of reasons these notices were postponed and finally withdrawn on April 14th, a date known afterwards as "Black Friday." The miners continued their dispute on their own, but in the end suffered a heavy defeat.

Black Friday foreshadowed an even blacker event. Five years later the strike called by the Trades Union Congress also in support of the miners and involving one and a half million workers ended in failure. The history of this nine-day General Strike, the most momentous event in the development of British trade unionism, is too intricate a subject for brief comment. It must suffice here to say that it demonstrated two things: the strength of the feeling of solidarity among the organized workers; and the futility of the syndicalist reliance upon "direct action." The government retaliated by passing the Trades Disputes and Trade Unions Act of 1927 (repealed by the Labour Government in 1946), which made a sympathetic strike or a lockout that was designed or calculated to coerce the government illegal, severed the connection between the civil service organizations and other trade unions, and imposed new restrictions on the unions' political activities and their conduct of trade disputes.

From conflict to cooperation

Their failure to resist wage reductions and to stop the wave of victimization that followed the General Strike weakened the trade unions more than the drain on their resources which prolonged industrial conflict had imposed. They now settled down in a new spirit of sober realism to build as best they could upon the solid foundations they had laid in other ways. The employers—at least the more enlightened among them—had also learned their lesson. The constant trials of strength between themselves and their workpeople were undeniably very bad business and were losing them their markets in the world. "Peace in Industry" was the new slogan readily accepted by the government and by most of the leaders on both sides of industry. In 1928 a series of conferences was initiated between the General Council of the Trades Union Congress and a group of leading employers. These conferences, usually known as the Mond-Turner conversations, ranged over a large number of subjects of joint concern, but their immediate outcome was indecisive. Although joint reports were produced, neither of the two main employers' organizations, the National Confederation of Employers' Organisations (now known as the British Employers' Confederation) and the Federation of British Industries, considered themselves bound by the recommendations. The importance of the conferences lay more in the new cooperative approach to industrial relations to which they gave expression.

The development of a common economic policy on the part of the trade union movement had been made possible by its greater integration after World War I. A number of important amalgamations had taken place and loose federations had been replaced by more compact and centralized bodies. Many of the large unions of today were formed at this time. Furthermore the reorganization of the Trades Union Congress in the early twenties had given it a new authority. Its General Council was able to speak in the name of the trade union movement as a whole and was now equipped with a proper administrative staff headed, from 1926 onward, by an energetic and enterprising general secretary, Walter Citrine, who was determined to make the T.U.C. a power in the land.

But labor's disappointments were not at an end. With the failure of industrial action the pendulum had swung to greater reliance upon political action. The return of a Labour Government toward the end of 1929, even though it depended for a majority upon Liberal support, was at first regarded as a great triumph. The Labour vote had risen to 8.4 million as compared with 2.2 million in 1918. Unfortunately this electoral triumph coincided with the outbreak of a world depression. The unemployment figures mounted month by month without the government producing any policy to deal with the crisis. The reckoning came in 1931 and with it the default to the "other side" of some of the leaders of the Labour Party—MacDonald, Snowden, Thomas, and others. In the general election that led to the establishment of the "National" Government, the Labour vote dropped to 6.6 million and its representation in the House of Commons from 289 to 46. The whole of the labor movement was bewildered and cast down as never before.

This shattering defeat had two consequences that helped greatly to prepare the way for the Labour Party's victory in the 1945 general election (when it polled 12 million votes) and the achievements of the postwar Labour Governments. In the first place it brought the political and industrial wings of the movement into closer relationship, since one of the obvious failures in MacDonald's leadership had been his unwillingness to consult with the Trades Union Congress. Secondly, and more important, it underlined the need for working out a constructive socialist policy in place of the somewhat empty propaganda slogans of the past. The Labour Party had to know exactly what it would do, and the Trades Union Congress what it wanted a Labour Government to do when one was formed again. This need was met in various ways. The Fabian Society, which had fallen into a condition of senile decay, was revived with the aid of a New Fabian Research Bureau and contributed much to the formulation of practical policies. The Trades Union Congress in a series of policy statements, of which the two most important were the *Report on the Public Control and Regulation of Industry and Trade* in 1932 and the *Report on Postwar Reconstruction* in 1944, gave the necessary leadership to the trade union movement.

During the interwar years trade union membership reached its lowest point in 1933–34. From then on it increased year by year with the recovery of business and rising money wages. The radically changed conception of trade unionism as a willing and essential partner in the conduct of the nation's economic affairs steadily gained acceptance both within the movement and in society at large. It was World War II, however, that greatly accelerated this development. In some respects it had similar effects to the first, but there were two important differences. This time the trade unions were fully united at all levels in their attitude toward the war. The day after Great Britain declared war on Nazi Germany the annual Trades Union Congress opened at Bridlington. Of the 659 accredited delegates only 490 were able to attend, but of these only two dissented from the resolution pledging full support to the war effort. Consequently there was no appreciable political opposition in the trade union world to the wholehearted cooperation with the government. Of equal significance was the sensible way in which the wartime economy was controlled so as to avoid inflation and profiteering and other of the troubles that showed themselves in 1914–18. Thus the trade unions were able to give reasonable protection to their members and even improve their conditions without industrial conflict developing on any serious scale.

Organization

The way in which the British trade union movement evolved makes it a difficult task to describe its present-day structure. As we have seen, the organization of the trade unions has not been planned or influenced appreciably by the state or by any political party. Nor has theory played much part in its design. The growth of the British unions, as W. Milne-Bailey pointed out, has largely been "a spontaneous, healthy process arising out of the needs of the common people." [5] The result of this organic process is not a neat, tidy pattern, but, as might be expected, a rather bewildering complex of overlapping and interlocking bodies of all shapes and sizes.

---

[5] W. Milne-Bailey, *Trade Union Documents*, Introduction, page 1. London: Bell, 1929.

Unity in diversity

The extent of the diversity of British trade union organization is apparent when the unions are classified according to size. At the end of 1949 there were in existence in the United Kingdom some 700 separate trade unions with an aggregate membership of 9.3 million. These were all organizations, of salaried and professional workers as well as manual wage-earners, known to include among their functions that of negotiating with employers for the purpose of regulating the conditions of employment of their members. Grouped according to their size, the following, decidedly uneven picture emerges:

Size	Number of Unions	Percentage of Total Membership
Under 1,000	407	1.2
1,000— 25,000	248	13.7
25,000—100,000	34	18.5
100,000 and over	17	66.6
Totals	706	100.0

It will be noted that while the 17 largest unions represent two-thirds of the general body of trade unionists, at the other end of the scale more than 400 small unions retain their separate identity although they account for little more than one per cent of the total membership.

Fortunately there is one simplifying factor in this complex structure: the existence of a central body, the Trades Union Congress, which can fairly claim to speak in the name of the whole of the trade union movement. It is true that in 1950 only 186 trade unions were affiliated with the T.U.C. but their aggregate membership was nearly 7.9 million.[6] The unaffiliated unions include only two with more than 100,000 members, the National Association of Local Government Officers and the National Union of Teachers, both of which have a working relationship with the T.U.C. Most of the others of any size, including several teachers' unions, organize employees in national or local government service.

Types of organization

The absence of any kind of uniformity is just as evident when we attempt to classify the unions affiliated with the T.U.C. according to

---

[6] Some of these are in fact federations; for example, those in the cotton textile group, which were counted separately in the previous statistics provided by the Ministry of Labour.

the categories of workers whom they organize. Every conceivable type of organization exists, and no one type can be said to predominate. Theoretically we can distinguish between three main structural forms of union organization: vocational (or craft) unions; general labor unions; and industrial (or common employment) unions. The first group would be taken to include those unions that seek to organize all employees in a single or several related occupations, regardless of the industry in which they were employed; the second, those that open their doors to all workers without distinction as to occupation or industry; and the third those that admit to membership all employees in a particular industry or service, whatever their occupation. This theoretical differentiation has been applied as far as it is possible to the list of unions affiliated to the T.U.C. given in Table 1, but it is too arbitrary to provide more than an oversimplified picture.

Craft unions. The historical approach is more helpful if we wish to understand both the variety in the types of organization and the reasons for their existence. Craft unionism was the first stable form of organization to emerge. Apart from the material advantages that the craft unions were able to bestow upon their members, as a result of their bargaining strength and system of friendly benefits, the loyalties and traditions that they established provided an additional bond. When at the end of the last century new theories of trade union organization began to gain ground, these unions naturally enough showed no inclination to allow themselves to be carved up in response to theoretical arguments. Many but not all of them had been transformed from local into national unions by amalgamation, and it was this process that continued, leading subsequently to the formation of large, multi-craft unions, some of which have also admitted less skilled workers employed in close connection with their trades.

TABLE 1

TRADE UNIONS AFFILIATED WITH THE T.U.C. IN 1950

Employment Groups	Membership (in thousands)
Mining and Quarrying	
National Union of Mineworkers* .... (i)	609
3 other unions	36
Railways	
National Union of Railwaymen .... (i)	421
Railway Clerks' Association .... (c)	86
Associated Society of Locomotive Engineers and Firemen*.... (c)	73
Engineering and Shipbuilding	
Amalgamated Engineering Union .... (ic)	714
Electrical Trades Union .... (ic)	187

TABLE 1—*Continued*

Employment Groups	*Membership (in thousands)*
United Boilermakers & Iron & Steel Shipbuilders' Society*....(c)	83
Amalgamated Union of Foundry Workers ....(i)	78
National Union of Vehicle Builders* ....(c)	55
Association of Engineering & Shipbuilding Draughtsmen......(c)	45
National Union of Enginemen, Firemen, Mechanics & Electrical Workers* ....(t)	36
National Society of Metal Mechanics* ....(c)	34
Shipconstructors & Shipwrights' Association* ....(c)	26
22 other unions	98

Iron and Steel and Minor Metals

Iron & Steel Trades Confederation ....(i)	100
National Union of Sheetmetal Workers & Braziers* ....(c)	38
16 other unions	54

Building, Woodworking, and Furnishing

Amalgamated Society of Woodworkers* ....(c)	198
Amalgamated Union of Building Trade Workers* ....(c)	83
National Society of Painters ....(c)	77
National Union of Furniture Trade Operatives ....(i)	71
Plumbing Trades Union ....(c)	54
Amalgamated Society of Wood-Cutting Machinists ....(c)	31
14 other unions	82

Printing and Paper

National Union of Printing, Bookbinding & Paper Workers....(i)	118
Typographical Association* ....(c)	46
National Society of Operative Printers & Assistants ....(i)	33
11 other unions	65

Textiles

National Union of Dyers, Bleachers & Textile Workers ....(i)	79
Amalgamated Weavers' Association† ....(c)	75
Amalgamated Association of Card, Blowing & Ring Room Operatives† ....(c)	51
29 other unions	72

Clothing, Leather, and Boot and Shoe

National Union of Tailors & Garment Workers† ....(i)	135
National Union of Boot & Shoe Operatives ....(i)	90
National Union of Hosiery Workers† ....(i)	37
8 other unions	37

Distribution and Other Industries

Union of Shop, Distributive & Allied Workers ....(g)	340
Amalgamated Union of Operative Bakers, Confectioners & Allied Workers ....(i)	30
National Society of Pottery Workers† ....(i)	26
12 other unions	81

Agriculture

National Union of Agricultural Workers ....(i)	135

TABLE 1—*Continued*

Employment Groups		*Membership* (*in thousands*)
Other Transport and General Workers		
Transport & General Workers' Union	(g)	1,253
National Union of General & Municipal Workers	(g)	805
National Union of Seamen	(i)	60
11 other unions		64
Civil Service		
Union of Post Office Workers	(i)	147
Civil Service Clerical Association†	(c)	145
Post Office Engineering Union	(c)	50
Inland Revenue Staff Federation	(c)	34
3 other unions		42
Other Public Employees		
National Union of Public Employees	(i)	165
Confederation of Health Service Employees	(i)	52
2 other unions		24
Other Nonmanual Workers		
National Federation of Insurance Workers	(i)	39
Clerical & Administrative Workers' Union	(c)	35
National Association of Theatrical & Kine Employees	(i)	31
National Union of Bank Employees	(i)	29
Musicians' Union	(c)	27
7 other unions		59

Notes: * Unions with no women members
                    † Unions with more women members than men
Classification: (*i*) = industrial
                    (*c*) = craft or vocational
                    (*g*) = general
                    (*t*) = subsidiary of Transport & General Workers' Union
Source: Trades Union Congress, *Brighton Congress Report,* page 14 ff.
London: Trades Union Congress, 1950.

This can be taken as one main line of structural growth, but it should be realized that contemporary British trade unionism reflects all of its stages. There still exist a number of pure craft unions confining their membership to one locality like the London Society of Compositors. The United Patternmakers Association caters to the workers in a single craft but employed in various parts of the country. Typical multicraft unions, which also limit their members to those who have served some kind of apprenticeship, are the Amalgamated Society of Woodworkers, the Amalgamated Union of Building Trade Workers, and the National Union of Vehicle Builders. Both the Amalgamated Engineering Union and the Electrical Trades Union, although formed originally as multicraft unions, now represent a half-way house between craft and industrial unionism. The A.E.U., for example, has accepted male machine operators and laborers into a special class of membership since 1926, and women since 1943.

General labor unions. The second line of structural growth has led to what is perhaps the most characteristic and significant feature of British trade union organization, the existence of two large, general workers' unions, the Transport and General Workers' Union and the National Union of General and Municipal Workers, which together cast more than a quarter of the votes at the annual Trades Union Congress. It is somewhat misleading to describe either of these bodies, but especially the former, as "general labor unions," if this description is taken to imply that they cater only to unskilled workers. The T. & G.W.U. organizes almost all categories of workers employed in overland transport, other than those on the railways, and they represent about one-third of its total membership. Its relationship to road transport is essentially that of an industrial union. On its general labor side, however, it extends into agriculture, quarrying, the manufacture of cement and bricks, power production, engineering and the metal trades, building, textiles, rubber, chemicals, food processing, and several other industries. It also has a special section for clerical and supervisory workers. Most of these industries are also entered by the N.U.G. & M.W., but this union has about one-third of its membership concentrated among the employees of local and other public authorities.

Both of these unions were formed by amalgamations in the early nineteen twenties, but their full history must be traced back to the period of "New Unionism." The dockers' strike in 1889 brought the Dock, Wharf, and Riverside, and General Workers' Union into being, as did the equally successful gasworkers' strike in the same year, the Gasworkers and General Labourers Union. The former body took the initiative in establishing a National Transport Workers' Federation in 1910 and again, under the spirited leadership of Mr. Ernest Bevin, in promoting the amalgamation discussions that resulted in the formation of the T. & G.W.U. in 1922. Between 1923 and 1947 the scope of this union was further enlarged by its power to attract some forty other, mainly small unions into amalgamation, including the Workers' Union in 1929. Similarly it was the old gasworkers' union that changed its name to the National Union of General Workers in 1918 and became the nucleus that attracted other general labor unions and then the main municipal workers' union to form the N.U.G. & M.W. in 1924.

The reasons for the tremendous growth of the general workers' unions, their relative stability, and the great influence that they have exercised on the policy of the trade union movement as a whole would be a particularly rewarding subject for research. Although a thorough investigation of the problem has still to be undertaken there are a few fairly obvious explanations. The exclusiveness of the craft unions led inevitably to the setting up of special unions for less skilled workers, based on lower membership dues and a different approach to the methods of improving the working conditions of their members. There was a strong trend toward amalgamation on the part of these general labor unions, since in their case the old maxim that "unity is strength" had particular application. Most of them had a high membership turnover so that they needed to be broadly based if they were to maintain their effectiveness. When the main amalgamations took place they produced efficient, if somewhat bureaucratic, organizations with considerable financial resources. But their capacity for expansion was due above all to the suitability of their type of organization to meet the consequences of technical change. As Professor Cole has pointed out:

> There has been a great expansion both of light consumers' industries and of clerical and distributive employment. . . . These expanding trades and industries call for only small complements of highly skilled workers. In the main, their demand is for quickness, general intelligence, and a manual dexterity which can be fairly quickly acquired, and is fairly easily transferable from one industry or employment to another.[7]

This "calls for a form of trade union organization based neither on craft nor on industry, but wide enough to cover an extensive range of trades." The fact that the general workers' unions acknowledged no theoretical limits to their domain enabled them to enter freely these fields of employment that most of the other unions were prepared or compelled to ignore.

Industrial unions. Once the evolution of the craft and general workers' unions is understood it is not difficult to appreciate the fate of the doctrine of industrial unionism in the British context. By the time it appeared on the scene as a conscious influence within the trade union world, substantial parts of the territory that industrial unions might be expected to occupy had already been possessed either by stubborn, craft-conscious unions or by the new amorphous general labor unions. The doctrine had its heyday roughly during the period covered by the first quarter of the twentieth century, and was made the subject of passionate advocacy, so much so that for a time its acceptance was taken almost as an implicit characteristic of the progressive, militant trade unionist. As in other parts of the world, it was closely associated with near-syndicalist theory of the social millennium, which found a peculiarly British expression in the doctrines of gild socialism. But its practical influence has been entirely disproportionate to the energy expended on its debate. The strength and

---

[7] G. D. H. Cole, *Fabian Socialism,* pages 156–157. London: Allen and Unwin, 1943.

success of the agitation was great enough to secure the passage of a resolution at the 1924 Trades Union Congress, which, after declaring in favor of reducing the number of trade unions to "an absolute minimum," suggested that "the aim should be as far as possible organization by industry." The T.U.C. General Council was asked to prepare a scheme for the reorganization of the trade union movement accordingly. When the Council presented the report three years later it appeared that the affiliated unions submitting evidence had very different views on the definition of an industry. Furthermore, it was evident that a body such as the T.U.C., composed as it was of all types of unions, was in no position to reach agreement on one particular form of trade union organization. "It was recognised" as the T.U.C. declared in a later report, "that the most which the General Council could achieve would be to remove the main causes of friction in the day-to-day working of the trade unions, and to facilitate negotiations for amalgamations and for various forms of closer unity." [8]

Those British unions that approximate in their structure industrial organizations have in fact little in the way of a common history. The miners, who also participated in the great trade union awakening of "New Unionism," united several of their district unions into the Miners' Federation of Great Britain in 1888, and enrolled, as well as the hewers, many of the less skilled workers in the mines. The Federation sought to organize every worker employed in or about a coal mine, but was not transformed into a national union of mineworkers until 1945. The National Union of Railwaymen was formed in 1913 by the amalgamation of several manual workers' unions then existing; one of them, now known as the Associated Society of Locomotive Engineers and Firemen, preferred to retain its separate identity. Both A.S.L.E.F. and the Railway Clerks' Association (which was established in 1897 and organizes all grades of salaried railway employees) have been strongly opposed to their submergence in the N.U.R. In the railway workshops, the N.U.R. organizes mainly the less skilled workers, while many of the craftsmen belong to one of the several engineering unions; so that even in the unlikely event of the three railway unions agreeing to merge, an appreciable number of railway employees would still remain outside the jurisdiction of the new organization.

Three other strong industrial unions, the Union of Post Office Workers, the National Union of Boot and Shoe Operatives, and the Iron and Steel Trades Confederation, all have dissimilar origins. The Union of Post Office Workers was formed in 1920 from a number of as-

---

[8] *Trade Union Structure and Closer Unity—Final Report,* pages 6–7. London: Trades Union Congress, 1947.

sociations for postmen, telephone operators and clerical workers under the leadership of enthusiastic gild socialists. The National Union of Boot and Shoe Operatives was founded as far back as 1874. Apart from a small local union and an even smaller organization of custom craftsmen, it occupies the whole of the field of boot and shoe production. But this, one of the most successful of industrial unions, was not organized 'on any conscious principle of industrial unionism. The Iron and Steel Trades Confederation, which despite its name now acts as a single union, is the product of an ingenious scheme for avoiding legal difficulties when the law governing amalgamations was severe.[9]

Thus the development of industrial unions in Britain has been one, but only one, of the results of a general process of amalgamation, which has concentrated the main body of trade unionists into a few large unions. Some of them were not created with any conception of industrial unionism as the ideal form of organization and none of them has been completely successful in occupying the whole of its chosen sphere. There is also no obvious trend toward their supplanting other structural types of organizations. If anything, the balance of advantage appears to lie with the general workers' unions, because, for good or ill, their principle of organization is the most flexible.[10]

Nonmanual workers' unions. Some reference must also be made to the developments in trade union organization among nonmanual workers, for it is here that the traditional, theoretical distinctions between the various types of union structure appear to have least relevance. Where the nonmanual workers are strongly organized, as is the case with civil servants, local government officers, teachers, railway clerks, draftsmen, and, to a lesser extent, those employed in the amusement trades, it is usually on vocational lines. Some of these associations, as already explained, constitute the main body of trade unionists that remains outside the ambit of the T.U.C. One noticeable trend in this field of trade union organization is associated with the growth of a union consciousness among workers who originally believed that they had little in common with wage-earners and therefore did not share the same need for protective organization. It finds expression in the gradual transformation of professional associations

---

[9] Under the Trade Union (Amalgamation) Act, 1917 any two or more unions may amalgamate providing in each of the unions the votes of at least 50 per cent of the members entitled to vote are recorded and at least 60 per cent of those voting are in favor. Another method, which avoids the necessity of a ballot in each union, is provided the Societies (Miscellaneous Provisions) Act, 1940. This permits one union to "transfer its engagements" to another if it has carried a resolution to that effect by a two-thirds majority at a delegate conference.

[10] See J. D. M. Bell, *Industrial Unionism: A Critical Analysis*. Glasgow: University of Glasgow, 1949.

into trade unions. An outstanding example of this development, although there are several parallels, is provided by the history of the National Association of Local Government Officers. With the setting up of the National Health Service, which changed the status of most doctors to that of salaried employees, the British Medical Association assumed many of the negotiating functions that are the essential characteristics of a trade union.

There has been a tendency for some well-established nonmanual workers' unions to extend the basis of their organization into related fields of employment. The industries nationalized by the Labour Government have set up separate negotiating machinery for their clerical and administrative employees, and this has helped to promote their organization. So we find the Railway Clerks Association at its annual conference in 1950 deciding to change its name to Transport Salaried Staffs' Association in keeping with its present organizing activities among the clerical employees in road transport.

Role of federations. So far in examining the structural changes in British trade unionism, we have noted mainly the part played by amalgamations in promoting larger organizations and closer trade union unity. We turn now to an equally important feature of the organic process, which has brought about coordinated action in a movement remarkable for its diversity—the growth of industrial federations. Of these, the three most important are the Confederation of Shipbuilding and Engineering Unions, the National Federation of Building Trade Operatives, and the Printing and Kindred Trades Federation. If the reader will consult Table 1 he will notice that there are a large number of unions in each of the employment groups covered by these federations. The need to present a common front to the employers in negotiations made some kind of joint organization essential, and the federal form of organization had the advantage of enabling all the various types of unions to work together. The general workers' unions, for example, affiliate to the federations for that part of their membership which is employed in the industries concerned.

The Printing and Kindred Trades Federation was formed as far back as 1899. All the 16 unions concerned with this industry, including the National Union of Journalists and two small unions that are not affiliated with the T.U.C., belong to it. The Federation has found a fertile field of activity in the Printing Joint Industrial Council, composed of 40 union and 40 employers' representatives, which deals with such matters as apprenticeship selection and training, employment and production, and the strengthening of organization on both sides of the industry. It has little say in wage negotiations, which are conducted mainly by the separate unions, the craft unions reserving to themselves the right to fix their own apprenticeship quotas. An unsuccessful attempt was made in 1949 by the Federation to work out agreed proposals for a new wage structure.

The National Federation of Building Trade Operatives, formed in 1918, is the most highly developed of the federations; it includes all unions with a marked interest in building and construction. This industry has a large number of separate craft unions, the woodworkers, the bricklayers, the painters, the plasterers, the plumbers, and many other crafts all having their own organizations. But national wage negotiations are conducted mainly by the Federation, with its own full-time regional officers and the authority to call out on strike any of its affiliated membership locally without prior consultation with the individual unions. The existence of a National Joint Council for the Building Industry, with a well-defined procedure for negotiation and conciliation, has contributed greatly to the success of the Federation.

The Confederation of Shipbuilding and Engineering Unions is the largest of all the industrial federations with 37 affiliated unions representing over one million and a quarter workers in this complex of industries and trades. For many years it did not include the largest union in the field, the Amalgamated Engineering Union, but with the affiliation of this body in 1947, it became fully representative. It undertakes wage negotiations with the employers' federations in engineering and shipbuilding on behalf of most of its affiliated unions— the nonmanual workers' organizations, for example, the Association of Engineering and Shipbuilding Draftsmen, do not participate—and has put forward proposals for the reform and simplification of the wage structure in the engineering industries.

The industrial federations that exist in cotton and woolen textiles are weaker and looser organizations. In cotton there are still some 150 self-administered, largely autonomous local unions. With few exceptions they are all members of one of six federations, known as amalgamations, each confined to a particular occupation or group of occupations. The largest of these is the Amalgamated Weavers' Association with over 70,000 members. Only the four amalgamations in the weaving section of the industry are members of the Northern Counties Textile Trades Federation, which concludes agreements with the manufacturers' association, the two spinners' amalgamations dealing separately with the employers. All the amalgamations are members of the United Textile Factory Workers' Association, but this body was formed primarily for political action. The T.U.C. General Council has said that it is "satisfied that there is no industry in the country in which it is more essential to secure the greatest possible unification of the administrative and economic policy of the unions" than in cotton textiles.[11]

In the wool textile industry there is one large union, national in scope and catering to a variety of trades, the National Union of Dyers, Bleachers, and Textile Workers. But there are also some twenty other local organizations, many of which cater to skilled workers, managers, foremen, and woolsorters, all with an average membership of less than 1,000. In the woolcombing section of the trade the National Union of General and Municipal Workers has a substantial membership. The National Association of Unions in the Textile Trade links all these unions together mainly for the purpose of negotiating national agreements with an employers' council, although its executive has no constitutional powers to prevent the affiliated unions entering into separate agreements.

The existence of many separate unions does not make the integration of industrial policy an easy matter, even where strong federations exist, but over the years there has been a progressive development toward closer unity of action and the lessening of interunion conflict. This was promoted by the creation of Joint Industrial Councils after World War I. The Staff Side of the Civil Service National Whitley Council, for example, performs some of the functions of a federation of civil service unions; it has a permanent chairman and secretary and publishes a regular monthly bulletin. In the furniture trades, which were in a chaotic state during the interwar years both as regards workers' and employers' organization, the establishment of a Trade Board in 1939 stimulated the formation of the National Federation of Furniture Trade Unions and the British Furniture Trades Employers' Confederation. Shortly afterward a Joint Industrial Council was formed, which established itself so successfully during World War II that the Trade Board could be abolished.

The reluctance of the British trade unions to make a fetish of any particular type of organization has contributed greatly to their strength and sense of common purpose. Flexibility of approach toward the problems confronting it is likely to assist any institution to endure, since the social environment in which it works is always changing. No organizational problem is insurmountable, however complex it may have become, if there is the will to solve it. Where the need for common action arises on the part of several or many unions, large or small, some way can always be found to organize it if there is sufficient goodwill, but goodwill does not flourish when one union is trying to impose its own preference for a particular type of organization upon another.

---

[11] *Trade Union Structure and Closer Unity—Final Report,* page 48, 1947.

The voluntary basis

We have seen how greatly the structural development of British trade unionism has depended upon its voluntary character. But the term "voluntary" may be open to misunderstanding. It does not imply the absence of any form of compulsion in trade union recruitment. In their *Industrial Democracy* the Webbs attacked the "strange delusion in the journalistic mind that . . . compulsory trade unionism, enforced by refusal to work with non-unionists, is a modern device." They pointed out that, on the contrary, it was "coeval with trade unionism itself."

The trade clubs of handicraftsmen in the eighteenth century would have scouted the idea of allowing any man to work at their trade who was not a member of the club. And at the present day it is especially in the old-fashioned and long-established unions that we find the most rigid enforcement of membership. . . . It is, in fact, as impossible for a non-unionist plater or rivetter to get work in a Tyneside shipyard, as it is for him to take a house in Newcastle without paying the rates. This silent and unseen, but absolutely complete compulsion, is the ideal of every Trade Union.[12]

British trade unionism is a voluntary movement in the sense that it has relied primarily upon its own strength and not upon legal sanctions to reduce the number of nonunionists, to obtain recognition from the employers, and to counteract the disruptive influence of seceding unions, in short to establish itself as an effective regulative influence.

What then is the attitude of the British trade union movement toward the "closed shop"? The answer to this question turns on the meaning given to the term. In a statement to the 1946 Trades Union Congress the T.U.C. General Council maintained that:

The "Closed Shop", in the sense of an establishment in which only members of a particular union can be employed, to the exclusion of members of other unions, is alien to British trade union practice and theory. Congress has never consented to the recognition of an exclusive right to organise by one union where other unions have built up their organisation side by side.

Yet at the same Congress Charles Dukes, in his presidential address, said:

The closed shop is nothing new in British trade union practice. It means for us the well-founded claim that workers in an industry or in an establishment

---

[12] Sydney and Beatrice Webb, *Industrial Democracy*, pages 214–215. London: Longmans Green & Co., Ltd., 1920. By permission of the Trustees of the late Lord Passfield.

covered by union agreements should be in their appropriate unions. . . . It exists today in industries where unionisation is so strong that managements are constrained to recognise that the holding of a union card is a necessary condition of employment.

These two views do not conflict but complement each other. Although the British trade unions have always sought to prevent employers from engaging nonunionists, where they were strong enough to do so, they have rarely tried to secure exclusive bargaining rights. The very structure of British trade unionism makes this impracticable, since there are no industries and relatively few establishments where only one union organizes all employees. The craft unions have insisted upon job demarcation; that is, that certain types of work should only be executed by their members, but this has been but one aspect of the device that the Webbs called "restriction of numbers," a means of protecting the craft and the wages and working conditions associated with it.

For Americans accustomed to classify the various forms of union security, the British attitude toward compulsory trade union membership may appear indefinite and a little confusing. It is important to bear in mind that there are few collective agreements stipulating that workers must belong to the union or unions that are signatories of the agreement; the compulsion to join a trade union, where it exists, remains largely "silent and unseen." Since the repeal of the 1927 Trades Disputes Act in 1946, a number of municipalities with Labour majorities have introduced membership of a trade union as a condition of employment, and the Cooperative Movement has maintained a similar provision for some time. But generally, although many employers are willing to express their preference for employees who are organized and would not risk employing a nonunionist at least in certain occupations, they are not prepared to enter into a formal, binding commitment.

This is also true of the nationalized industries. Coal mining under private ownership was about the only industry in the country in which agreements existed providing for the employers' deduction of union dues from the workers' wages. After its nationalization the National Union of Mineworkers sought a national agreement that would extend this practice to all coal fields. The National Coal Board, however, was prepared to continue only existing District arrangements for maintaining union membership; and "in Districts, where there were no arrangements, to tell their officials to do what they could to persuade all workmen to join the Union." Union dues would be deducted from wages only where workmen agreed in writing to this being done. The reasons given by the Board for its attitude in its *Report and Accounts for 1948* are worth quoting:

> There was now only one employer. To grant the N.U.M.'s request would mean discharging all workmen who did not wish to join the Union, regardless of their efficiency and length of service; these workmen would not merely be discharged from their particular jobs, but from the industry, and they would be unlikely to find jobs elsewhere in which they could use the experience and skill they had gained. Further, if a man were expelled from the Union for a breach of Union regulations, the Union would be able to get him dismissed from the Board's service even though the Board had no complaint against him.

In other nationalized industries there has been cooperation between the Boards and the unions to encourage employees to belong to their appropriate organization, but that is all.

The enforcement of trade union membership by employers as the result of a collective agreement might seem to be no more than the logical outcome of the unions' efforts to secure the union shop as a result of their bargaining power, but there is an essential difference between employer and union enforcement, even though the former may in the first place be union induced. At the risk of sounding paradoxical, we might say that the voluntary nature of the compulsion would be greatly diminished. The unions would be assured of their strength regardless of their policies or activities, and there is reason to fear that this would encourage undemocratic tendencies in their own organization. However, the British trade unions are unlikely to change their course and endanger their voluntary basis for a further reason not yet mentioned. Any agreement that stipulates union membership as a condition of employment, without specifying the trade union—and a "closed shop" for *one* union only would usually be rejected on the grounds mentioned in the T.U.C. statement—raises the question of what is a *bona fide* trade union. This is a subject that the British trade union movement has always preferred to leave within its own jurisdiction.

Every voluntary movement must develop its own sanctions and disciplines if it is to maintain its unity and authority. On the whole nonunionism has been regarded by the British trade unions as less of a threat to their success than the development of secession movements. "The splitting-off of a dissident section of a union to form a new organisation is one of the deadly sins against trade unionism," wrote Milne-Bailey.[13] Certainly most unions would be prepared to use every weapon at their disposal to crush a new rival.

The civil service unions have been troubled most by seceding

---

[13] W. Milne-Bailey, *op. cit.*, page 81.

organizations. They cannot in practice use the threat of a strike to prevent such bodies gaining recognition, and the government itself cannot afford to become involved in a discussion of the question of what is a *bona fide* union. It must apply some objective test. Thus the handbook on *Staff Relations in the Civil Service* issued by the Treasury in 1949 states: "To secure recognition an association must show that it is representative of the category of staff concerned. In the Civil Service recognition depends solely on numerical strength." If compulsory trade unionism were made universal either by agreements or by legislation, the same problem would arise. Any dissident body that could obtain sufficient support even among a small section or grade of workers in a particular industry would be able to gain recognition. What has so far been treated as a domestic problem of the trade union movement would become a public issue and a very complicated one. This consequence alone is likely to restrain the movement from pressing any such demand.

One of the inevitable results of the voluntary character of British trade unionism has been its uneven development in the various industries and trades. Unfortunately its untidy structure makes it impossible to compare the degree of organization in each of them. Table 2 is reproduced from the T.U.C.'s own magazine; it provides no more than a rough comparison between the total number employed (including employers and self-employed) and the *estimated* membership of the unions affiliated to the T.U.C. in each of the fields of employment mentioned. The degree of organization among workers eligible to join a trade union is in fact higher than this table indicates. In agriculture, for example, the number of persons employed full time as wage-earners was approximately 640,000, so that about 25 per cent of them were organized. In local government the exclusion of the teachers' unions and of the National Association of Local Government Officers, which are not affiliated to the T.U.C., seriously reduces the percentage of trade unionists shown in the table; their inclusion would raise the degree of organization to a level at least comparable with that in the Civil Service.

However, the main contrasts are plain enough. The workers in coal mining, in the railway service and most of the other forms of transport, in public utilities and the public services, in the printing trades, as well as the majority of skilled workers in any industry, are well organized. Those in agriculture, distribution, catering, and in clerical occupations outside of the railways and national and local government service are poorly organized. In between we have the remainder of the manual workers in manufacturing industries, with considerable variation in the degree of organization. Cotton textiles and boot and shoe-

TABLE 2

DEGREE OF TRADE UNION ORGANIZATION IN VARIOUS BRITISH INDUSTRIES

Industry	Employment end—1947 (thousands)	T.U.C. Membership (Approximate) end—1947 (thousands)	Percentage Organized
Coal	758	598	79
Other mining and quarrying	73	38	52
Public utilities	270	155	57
Transport and shipping	1,438	1,209	84
Agriculture	1,055	163	15
Fishing	35	17	49
Building and civil engineering	1,364	655	48
Manufactures—			
Building materials	590	171	30
Metals and engineering	2,876	1,487	52
Cotton	267	163	61
Wool	178	104	59
Other textiles	207	65	31
Clothing	831	289	35
Food, drink and tobacco	623	195	31
Chemicals	336	120	36
Other manufactures	1,343	544	41
Distribution	2,351	465	20
Consumer services	2,120	456	22
Public services—			
Civil service	680	385	57
Other national government	388	183	47
Local government	1,105	329	30
Totals	18,888	7,791	

Source: "Trade Unions in Industry," *Labour.* Vol. 11, No. 9 (new series) (May, 1949), page 282.

making are highly organized as regards male and female workers. Clothing, furniture, and pottery are near the other end of the scale. Outside of textiles and the public services women are poorly organized. At the end of 1949 about 23 per cent of all female employees in the United Kingdom were members of trade unions, as compared with 54 per cent of male employees.

Trades Union Congress

The Trades Union Congress has a continuous history from 1868, but it became the coordinating center of British trade unionism only after its reorganization in the early nineteen twenties. The main reason for this reorganization was undoubtedly the desire for closer unity of action in the industrial field on the part of the new and larger amalgamated trade unions. It took place at a time of great conflict with the employers over wages, precipitated by the postwar slump. By the end of 1921 the Triple Alliance had collapsed and the General Federation of Trade Unions [14] was obviously not representative enough to meet the needs of the time. Moreover, prior to the slump, there had been an encouraging example of the value of mutual aid. In the railway strike of 1919 a mediation committee, composed of representatives of other unions, had helped to bring about a settlement favorable to the railwaymen. It was natural to hope that if the T.U.C., strengthened by the creation of an executive authority acting as a kind of general staff for the forces of organized labor, could come to the assistance of all its affiliated unions, there would be a better chance of resisting employer attacks on labor standards.

The new constitution that came into operation in 1921, although a compromise that conciliated the craft unions by leaving the autonomy of affiliated organizations untouched, was primarily designed to strengthen the workers' defenses. It divided the unions into 17 trade groups (there have been 18 since 1946) and gave each group representation on a General Council, which replaced the old Parliamentary Committee, roughly in proportion to its membership at the time. Although candidates for the General Council had to be nominated by and from the unions within the relevant group, they were to be elected by the whole membership of Congress on a card vote; that is, with the voting strength of each union proportionate to its affiliated membership. In addition, two seats on the General Council were reserved for women representatives. The powers of the General Council were further extended in 1924 but since then there have been no important constitutional changes in Congress organization.

Thus the T.U.C.'s present constitution still reflects the prevailing concerns and composition of the trade union movement of the early twenties. The powers of the General Council are defined mainly in Rules 11, 12, and 13, which relate to industrial disputes, disputes between affiliated organizations, and the conduct of affiliated organizations respectively.

Rule 11 pledges affiliated organizations to keep the General Council informed of any major disputes in which they may become engaged, either with employers or between themselves. If a peaceful settlement seems likely the General Council cannot intervene, unless requested to do so, but in the event of a breakdown in negotiations or a deadlock, it may give advice to the unions involved. If this advice is accepted and a strike or lockout results, the T.U.C. is under an obligation to organize material and moral support. This rule was the basis of the

---

[14] Established by the Congress in 1899 for the purpose of assisting unions affiliated with it when they were engaged in disputes.

General Council's action in the 1926 General Strike, but that dramatic event also revealed the weakness of the arrangement. Although the Council was able to conduct the General Strike, it had no power to make an agreement to end the miners' dispute, which was the reason for the sympathetic action. This ambiguous position was one factor, although by no means the most important, leading to the collapse of the strike and the subsequent recriminatory exchanges between the miners' representatives and other members of the General Council. Since then this rule has had little practical significance, although in 1932 the T.U.C. opened a fund in support of the striking cotton trade unions.

Rule 12, which gave the General Council powers to deal with interunion disputes, has had a more successful history. At the time when it was adopted, in 1924, this was a serious problem for British trade unionism. The 1920 constitution had provided for the setting up of a T.U.C. Disputes Committee. Between September 1923 and July 1924 this committee held some 40 meetings, largely concerned with accusations in regard to the poaching of members by rival unions. The new rule insisted on the submission of all such conflicts to the Disputes Committee, holding in reserve the threat of suspension or disaffiliation to secure respect for its recommendations. Congress also adopted a number of "main principles" governing "good trade union practice" in order to avoid interunion competition for members, which were extended and improved in 1939. Taking these principles as a basis for advice and voluntary arbitration the T.U.C. has had a great deal of success in settling interunion conflicts without at any time invoking the final sanction provided for in this rule.

Rule 13 empowered the General Council to investigate the conduct of any affiliated organization it considered to be "detrimental to the interests of the trade union movement or contrary to the declared principles of Congress," and, if necessary, to suspend its membership until the matter was fully considered at the next Congress. The final sanction of expulsion was reserved for Congress itself. This has been used only on one occasion, when in 1928 the National Union of Seamen was expelled for its support of a "nonpolitical" (company) miners' union in Nottinghamshire. The union was allowed to reaffiliate again in 1930, after the death of its general secretary, who had been largely responsible for this policy. In short, the General Council has made little use even of its very limited, formal powers. Instead it has sought to strengthen its authority by the cautious development of an agreed basis for common action.

The steady growth in the moral authority of the General Council is one of the most significant features of British trade unionism in the last two decades. As far as the general public is concerned, the T.U.C. has come to be regarded as so representative a body that the limits of its powers are frequently forgotten. Those limits are easily defined by the fact that a trade union in affiliating to the T.U.C. does not yield up any part of its autonomy. The General Council has not extended its authority because any of the individual unions were prepared to place in its hands powers that they previously exercised on their own account. It has done so because the increasing participation of the government in economic affairs has shifted the emphasis from industrial to political action, and the representation of the trade union point of view on any proposed legislation or administrative action can best be undertaken by a central body. Even here it must be recognized that the T.U.C. has no exclusive rights. If the government prefers in certain matters to approach a particular union, or if a union decided to make its own independent representations to the government, the T.U.C. cannot prevent this from happening. All that it can do is insist that if a general trade union view is required on any question no other body is able to provide it, and to try to persuade its affiliated organizations, which it does with a good deal of success, that such a coordinated view is to be preferred to several conflicting ones.

World War II acted as a powerful catalyst in developing the new relationship between the trade unions and the state and further enhanced the authority of the T.U.C. Shortly after the outbreak of hostilities, the Prime Minister directed all government departments to consult with the T.U.C. before taking any action on matters likely to affect the workers' interests. In the following years the complex structure of councils, boards, and committees that were created to advise the government on industrial policy and to assist in the handling of wartime problems was invariably of a tripartite character, with the T.U.C. acting as the custodian of the general interests of the workers on an equal footing with the central employers' associations.

Much of the detailed consideration of policy and administrative problems goes on in the thirty or so special committees composed mainly of members of the General Council and serviced by the permanent administrative staff of the T.U.C. The meetings of the full General Council, which take place not less frequently than once a month, are mainly occupied with approving, amending, or referring back the reports and recommendations of these committees. There are standing committees on organization and on economic questions, on social insurance and industrial welfare, on education and on international affairs. These are composed exclusively of members of the General Council. Other committees concern themselves with the organization and problems of particular groups of trade unionists, such as the National Women's Advisory Committee, the Non-Manual Workers' Advisory Council, the National Advisory Committee for Local Government Service, and are composed of General Council members and of members elected at special delegate conferences or of representatives of unions particularly concerned. On a few subjects, such as colonial affairs and scientific development, the committees advising the General Council also include co-opted experts.

The loss of Lord Citrine as General Secretary of the T.U.C. in 1946 was not without its effect. His personality, his farsightedness and skill in debate at Congress, contributed greatly to the leadership of the movement and often held in check the conflicting pressures of sectional interests within the General Council. Two important problems that had to be faced by the T.U.C., its international affiliations, involving the break with the World Federation of Trade Unions and the setting up of the International Confederation of Free Trade Unions, and the penetration of the communists into positions of influence within the unions during World War II, were brought to a relatively successful outcome. But more important issues were raised by the radical changes in the economic environment of British trade unionism in regard to wages and production policy. They placed a heavy burden of responsibility upon the T.U.C., for which in many ways it was inadequately equipped. The practical limits of the General Council's purely moral authority over affiliated unions were sharply revealed in the attempts it made to give leadership on these issues. There was a notable return to the use of the device originally employed before and after the General Strike of calling in between Congresses special conferences of union executives to enable the General Council to obtain a mandate for urgent policy decisions and to mobilize adequate support from affiliated unions. But this did not alter the situation appreciably. The gap between the T.U.C.'s policy declarations and the practice of many individual unions remained.

One obvious weakness in the existing organization would appear to be that the General Council contains only one member, its general secretary, whose sole concern it is to further the interests of the movement as a whole. It is no criticism of the other members to point out that their first loyalty must be toward their own unions, of which in most cases they are either the general secretaries or full-time presidents. If they are to do the job they are paid to do properly, they can give only a very limited amount of their time and attention to T.U.C. affairs, and the work of the General Council has steadily increased. A resolution was moved by the Amalgamated Engineering Union at the 1947 Congress, which asked for no more than an examination of the proposal "that all, or a number of the members of the

General Council should be engaged full time on General Council business," but it was overwhelmingly defeated.

As yet there is no strong demand within the movement for a further reorganization of the T.U.C., such as existed after World War I. Yet quite apart from any case that may exist for strengthening the influence of the General Council, there are many anachronisms in the rules and standing orders. The statement of objects, which was incorporated as the result of the adoption of an "Industrial Charter" at the 1924 Congress, has been largely outmoded by political developments. Parts of it, such as the demand for a legal maximum working week and a legal minimum wage for each industry or occupation, are actually at variance with Congress policy. Also, the system of election to the General Council no longer provides even a rough equality of representation for the various trade groups. The cotton group, for example, which in 1950 represented a total affiliated membership of 163,506, has two seats on the General Council, whereas the miscellaneous industries and distribution group with one seat includes unions with an aggregate membership of 477,085. These are admittedly the extremes, but there is a clear case for reconsidering the distribution of seats on the General Council, owing to the changes in the distribution of trade union membership that have taken place since their allocation. (At the 1951 Congress it was decided to increase the numbers of seats on the General Council by two, and to allocate these extra seats, one to the miscellaneous industries and distribution group and one to the civil service group. The decision takes effect in the election of the General Council at the 1952 Congress. It will help to modify the grosser inequalities in representation without disturbing existing interests.)

The listing of these anachronisms only serves to underline the reluctance of the greater part of the trade union leadership to propose any reform of the T.U.C. structure. It is probably recognized that to tackle any of these problems would throw the whole of the organization into the melting pot. There is also something of a vicious circle in this reluctance. The smaller unions fear that, with the present constitution, increased powers for the General Council would result in strengthening the position of some of the larger unions, while the latter are content to wield the influence that is theirs at present rather than face the prospect of the creation of a central body that might limit their own autonomy. In any case, the somewhat parochial attitude that prevails in most trade unions, because of their varying histories and traditions, constitutes a formidable barrier to the development of wider loyalties in keeping with the needs of time.

Trades councils

The local counterparts of the Trades Union Congress are the trades councils.[15] They have a long, honorable but checkered history in British trade unionism. Originally they sprang up in some of the main industrial centers about 1860 as federations of trade union locals for mutual support in strikes as well as in organizing and propaganda work, but they also engaged in political activity. One of their number took the initiative in calling the first official Trades Union Congress in 1868 and collectively they played an important part in its early development. In 1895, however, they were excluded from affiliation to that body in favor of a single representation of the workers through their trade unions, and with the growth of the Labour Party, their local political significance dwindled. Only with the General Strike of 1926 did they experience a real revival when the need for this form of local industrial organization was made abundantly apparent. Subsequently the T.U.C. started a campaign to encourage their growth and to bring them into closer alignment with the Congress, so that they might act not only as local coordinators of trade union activities, but also as its own local agents.

In 1950 there were 520 trades councils in England and Wales registered with the T.U.C. Affiliated with them were 15,145 trade union locals paying affiliation fees on nearly 2.9 million members. In Scotland and Northern Ireland the trades councils are not associated with the T.U.C., but remain directly affiliated with the Scottish and Irish Trades Union Congresses.[16] It is possible, therefore, to make only a rough comparison with the total membership of the trade unions affiliated with the Congress, since this includes their Scottish and Irish membership. But this shows that rather less than half of the relevant union membership is linked locally with the trades councils.

This fact already points to the most important feature to be grasped about the organization of trades councils, namely, that they are in

---

[15] These are the British equivalent of the central trades and labor councils affiliated with the American Federation of Labor.

[16] This separate organization of the trade union movement in Scotland and Ireland, though formally independent of the Trades Union Congress, does not confine the authority of that body to England and Wales. The greater part of the membership of the Scottish T.U.C. is drawn from the Scottish branches of all-British trade unions that through their national headquarters are also affiliated with the T.U.C. Although it does include a number of local unions in the textile, building, and printing trades, and among the bakers and teachers, most of these also belong to the T.U.C. The situation in Ireland is more complicated. Apart from the Irish T.U.C., with which a number of all-British unions are affiliated, there is a rival organization, known as the Congress of Irish Unions, which was the product of a split in 1943 and is anti-British.

every sense of the word the most voluntary part of the movement. Most trade unions recommend that their locals affiliate with the relevant trades council, but few instruct them to do so. Where a trades council exists, it is not compelled to register with the T.U.C., but in doing so it accepts certain obligations in regard to its rules and activities. It would, of course, be very difficult for any trades council to function successfully in England and Wales except under the auspices of the T.U.C., and there is no record of any council continuing to operate for any length of time outside this nexus. Almost all the work undertaken by officers of trades councils is voluntary; not more than five or six of the larger councils have a full time secretary. They are not wealthy bodies; only 48 of them had cash assets exceeding £100 in 1950.

It is in their relationship to the T.U.C. that most confusion and controversy has arisen among trades councils. The T.U.C. has done much to encourage and support them. Since 1925 it has arranged a special annual conference of trades councils where their delegates can freely express their opinions by means of resolutions that are not, however, binding upon the T.U.C. At this meeting they elect six representatives to a Trades Councils Joint Consultative Committee, which also includes six representatives of the T.U.C. General Council, and acts as the advisory committee on all matters affecting trades councils. The T.U.C. in addition organizes a special summer school for trades council secretaries and arranges for them to visit its headquarters to gain personal contact with the staff.

Difficulties arise mainly through an unwillingness of some trades councils to accept the role, cast for them by the T.U.C., of being policy-executing rather than policy-making bodies. Policy is made by the Congress, at which the trades councils have no representation beyond appointing one fraternal delegate. Since members of a trade union local may feel frustrated by their incapacity to influence quickly the policy of their own union and, through its delegates to the Congress, that of the movement as a whole, there is a strong temptation to look upon the trades council as providing an easier alternative for getting a resolution passed on national policy even if it has little effect except, perhaps, on local opinion.

The trades councils are the only organizations through which the T.U.C. can make direct contact with the rank and file of the movement to inform them on its common policy and problems. Conversely, a geographical, as distinct from an industrial, breakdown of trade union opinion on matters of economic and social policy affecting the interests of the workers would be helpful to the T.U.C. in determining its attitude to any impending legislative or administrative action.

Unfortunately there has been a marked tendency on the part of some powerful trade unions, or their leaders, to regard any strengthening of the trades council machinery as a threat to their own sovereignty. This shortsighted outlook has so far blocked the acceptance of a suggestion, canvassed at the end of World War II, that the T.U.C. should open regional offices, each with a full-time official in its employ, to work in close touch with the trades councils and trade unions in the area and help them in dealing with local problems. Without some such provision it is clear that the small administrative staff of the T.U.C. can do little to service more than five hundred trades councils in their day to day activities.

Union government

The constitutional problem for British trade unionism has been the same as that which faces every other democratic organization: how to maintain a system of checks and balances that would reconcile leadership with membership control, and responsibility with responsiveness. Unions with different histories have weighted the two sides of the balance differently. The extent of the contrasts can be illustrated with the aid of two examples that probably represent the extremes on either side. In the Amalgamated Engineering Union every full-time officer is elected by ballot of the members for a limited period, and even the general secretary has to stand for re-election every three years. The union executive committee is full-time, so is the union president. It is, therefore, difficult for any one individual to assume a dominating role. An elected national committee meets annually to decide union policy and a special appeals committee, also elected by ballot, is empowered to reverse the decisions of the executive. In the Iron and Steel Trades Confederation, however, the general secretary is not elected; he is appointed for life by the executive, which also appoints all other full-time officials. The executive is elected so as to represent the various grades of workers organized by the union and is part-time. Delegate assemblies, which are not national but regional, are held at its discretion.

Of course the living reality of democratic life in British trade unionism, as in every other social institution, does not depend wholly or even mainly upon the rule book. There are two main elements in the working of every modern trade union, and the relationship between them has a great influence on its vitality and purpose. They are the corps of permanent officials and the active membership. It lies in the nature of things that the official usually exercises a restraining influence on the active members, and they in turn have a stimulating effect upon him. He is conscious of the difficulties of negotiation, of the balance of forces, and the economic facts on which the successful execution of policy depends. They are conscious of their interests and are less hampered by the burden of responsibility. The play of both factors contributes to the success of the union.

There has been a tendency in recent years, mainly in the nonlabor press, to identify the danger of "bureaucracy" with the size of trade unions; the Transport and General Workers' Union has been singled out for special attack. This line of criticism misses the essential problem. It is easy to point to the example of the "new model" craft unions in the nineteenth century that were ruled by the members of the "Junta" far more autocratically than any trade unions are today by one or several of their leaders. In fact the internal democracy of the T. & G.W.U. compares favorably with that of many other British unions and this is partly the explanation of the trouble it has had with unofficial movements within its ranks.

The development of large unions accompanying the enlargement of the scope of collective bargaining must surely be regarded as inevitable. It is true that this has also had certain inevitable consequences that affect the working of internal union democracy. These were simply but aptly stated by Lord Citrine in addressing a conference of works committee representatives in the electricity industry:

Negotiating nationally has necessitated the transference bit by bit of the power formerly possessed by the local members and its being placed in the hands of the representatives who are entrusted to negotiate on their behalf. The individual member or the individual body of members in the locality cannot alone determine whether an agreement shall be accepted or not. Nor is it easy to consult them at every stage. . . . There are many things being discussed during negotiations which it would be quite improper to have reported at a particular stage. There are circumscriptions and limitations upon what can be said in negotiations. The result is that as a rule the unions and the employers have to go to a certain point with their negotiations before they can report them. . . . It may be that the Executive Councils of the unions have not been conducting the negotiations themselves. They may have had to depute some of their officers or members to take part . . . [and] may only know the broad trend of discussions before those discussions are carried to a certain point.[17]

Thus the actual participation of the membership in what is still the main function of a trade union, the making of a collective agreement, may be reduced to little more than registering their collective consent or disapproval for the finished product of lengthy negotiations. It is

---

[17] "National Negotiations in Industry," An address by The Rt. Hon. Lord Citrine, P.C., K.B.E., at Buxton, March, 1949, published by British Electricity Authority, London.

interesting to compare this modern statement with the conclusions that were reached by the Webbs in their *Industrial Democracy:*

> The extreme centralisation of finance and policy, which the Trade Union has found to be a condition of efficiency, has been forced upon it by the unique character of its functions. . . . It is obvious that a uniform policy can only be arrived at and maintained by a central body acting for the whole trade. And thus it comes about that the constant tendency to a centralised and bureaucratic administration is, in the Trade Union world, accepted, and even welcomed, by men who, in all the other organisations to which they belong, are sturdy defenders of local autonomy.[18]

The constitutional checks on bureaucracy in the British unions are, however, relatively strong. Most British unions have annual delegate conferences or the equivalent at which the broad lines of union policy are discussed and decided in unfettered debate. The passing of resolutions contrary to the executive's recommendations is not an infrequent occurrence. The union executives are usually composed entirely of "lay" members, and when they are not, provisions for the periodic election of union officers probably exist.

The most important full-time officer in the majority of unions is the general secretary; only a few unions have full-time presidents. The general secretary's power is certainly considerable because of his role in negotiations and his control of the other full-time officials. He is usually elected. Whether his term of office is for two, three, or five years, for life, or "at the union's pleasure" seems to make very little difference in practice. Rarely does the union change its general secretary before he has reached the retirement age; but most unions impose an age limit of 60 or 65 years. His salary most likely brings him an income in excess of that of most of the workers whom he represents, but only in the case of a few large unions does it rise above £1,000 a year.

However, the last half century has seen the emergence of a new profession, the permanent trade union official. The earlier trade union leader had to stir up a fighting spirit and lead his men into battle. He had to be an orator and to possess, above all, great force of character. He was in close, daily contact with the workers whom he represented. His life was identical with their own, and providing he spoke their mind and remained loyal to their interests he fulfilled his function admirably. Today the trade union official is primarily concerned with conducting negotiations through established machinery

---

[18] Sidney and Beatrice Webb, *Industrial Democracy,* pages 102–103. London: Longmans Green & Co., Ltd., 1920. By permission of the Trustees of the late Lord Passfield.

and with avoiding disputes and especially breaches of agreements. Most of his work is done in the office. He must be a capable administrator; to an increasing extent he must be familiar not only with the circumstances of the industry with which he is concerned, but with the intricacies of economic policy. He must be able to state a good case before arbitrators and win public opinion to his side. In short, to do his job successfully he needs to acquire specialized knowledge and skills, although his long apprenticeship in the hard school of experience is still indispensable. But his power has been increased by the greater complexity of the problems which have to be resolved in determining union policy, and frequently his function is to act as an intermediary between the workers whom he represents, on the one hand, and the employers or the government, on the other.

Clearly the methods by which unions select their officials have become of increasing significance. The method by which they are chosen by ballot at regular intervals and are not appointed for life has the advantage of ensuring that they hold the members' confidence, but it also discourages responsible leadership and takes little account of their qualifications for entering a skilled profession. There is a strong case for appointment by executives or special selection committees and for ensuring that candidates have had the necessary training for union office, though in this case it is more important to ensure that policy decisions are made by "lay" representatives of the members if the growth of a bureaucracy is to be avoided. But the effectiveness of any such constitutional checks is bound to depend on the extent of members' participation in shaping union policy and influencing union administration.

Local branch and workplace

The ordinary member has two possible points of contact with his trade union, the local meeting and his place of work. The local meeting provides him with an opportunity to participate in the government and administration of the union. Where he works, he requires its protection in dealing with his own employer. In some British trade unions local and workshop organization is identical or closely related. The miners are organized in lodges on a colliery basis and lodge officials are dealing constantly with the colliery manager on behalf of their members, although the workers' checkweighman also acts as their on-the-spot representative in other matters. The printers have their traditional chapel organization related to their trades and places of employment, which is the main meeting place of members and the basic unit in their unions' administration. Unions as dissimilar as the

National Union of Railwaymen, the National Union of Tailors and Garment Workers and the Civil Service Clerical Association organize their locals according to their members' places of employment. But this is not the rule. In many cases the union local is a geographical rather than an industrial unit constituted according to the members' places of residence and their convenience in attending the local meeting. It may well include the employees at several different firms and perhaps not all the members of the union at any one of them.

It has been customary for many years for the "good trade unionist" to bemoan the poor attendance at local meetings. The organization known as Political and Economic Planning (P.E.P.) has made a study of this problem admittedly with very inadequate data at its disposal, which was published in July, 1948. In its report it came to the following conclusions:

The proportion of members turning up to branch meetings is on average low. There is a tendency for a nucleus, largely consisting of the officials, to turn up regularly. Many unions have special quarterly branch meetings, and rank and file members may be fined for not attending these unless they present their excuses; similar *ad hoc* meetings may be called on particular issues of importance to the unions, and it is often at these special meetings that voting is taken, whether for election of officers or, for example, on the ratification of a national agreement. A higher proportion of the membership takes part in the meetings where a vote is taken than in the regular routine meetings, but even so, in the majority of branches and the majority of unions only a fraction of the membership participates. . . . The percentage of the membership voting on various issues has been obtained for 16 unions. Percentages vary from 2 to more than 30 per cent, but are mainly between 15 and 25 per cent. The general unions, where votes are collected in a different way, appear to muster a poll of about 50 per cent on most occasions. The printers' unions, where voting is taken in the chapels which are based on place of work, show very high polls.[19]

The fact is that the union local meeting of today is usually so dull that the member not holding any office who has been persuaded to attend may well go home with the impression that he has wasted his time. To some extent this is unavoidable. There is a great deal of routine business to be transacted and important decisions are taken at higher levels of authority. Most unions have an insufficient number of permanent officials, so that they can attend only on rare occasions to speak with authority on the work and policy of the union. Sometimes an outside speaker is invited to enliven the proceedings, but that is little more than a diversion. The T.U.C. has suggested that "the right type of educational work is the thing most suited to revitalize local meetings and keep the member in touch with what is happening

---

[19] *British Trade Unionism,* Six Studies by P.E.P., pages 24 and 26. London, 1948.

in his union and also in the movement generally." The need for members to know more about the agreements which their union has entered into, the reasons for them, and the methods by which they have been concluded is certainly great.

In the past, with a few notable exceptions, the British trade unions have paid more attention to local than to workshop organization. This was understandable fifty years ago, when the locals and district committees were undertaking the main negotiations with the employers and it was an advantage that they were not limited to the employees of one concern. But the general shift from local to national bargaining has not only weakened the members' interest in the local life of their unions, it has also made the link between the worker and his union at his place of employment a decisive factor in establishing the happy mean between bureaucracy and irresponsibility. More recently, full employment, the unions' interest in higher productivity and attempts to extend the principle of joint consultation have combined to shift the emphasis in union activity to the workshop level.

The rules of the great majority of British trade unions do make some provision for the appointment of workshop representatives whose functions and importance vary greatly; in some cases their only job is to collect union dues. The authors of the P.E.P. Report examined the rules of forty-eight unions affiliated with the T.U.C., with a total membership of four and a half million, and found that:

. . . eighteen have collectors, twenty-seven have stewards or similar workshop representatives (including seven in which these stewards are also collectors); while four others, without having either stewards or collectors, have some organisation at the place of work between the member and his branch (for example, the chapel in the printing unions). Of the remaining six societies, some cater for very specialist crafts with few members in any one place or, in addition to having a small membership, are confined to one locality.[20]

But they also pointed out that "organisation on the job is often rudimentary or non-existent. There may be provision for it in the union rules without much being done about it in practice. . . ."

It is mainly in the engineering and allied industries that workshop organization has played and continues to play an important part in union activity. The rules of the Amalgamated Engineering Union or of the Electrical Trades Union, for example, require the appointment of stewards in each working unit, and their range of duties is wide. Piecework prices and such matters which can be satisfactorily settled only at the workshop level are one of their main concerns, but generally it is their job to see that trade union agreements are observed and other conditions established by local custom maintained,

[20] *Ibid.*, page 127.

as well as to inspect membership cards and to prevent, where possible, the employment of nonunionists. In the A.E.U.—but this is an exceptional arrangement—they are not only the agents of the union but are also directly represented on the district committees of the locals. Quarterly meetings of all stewards in each district are held at which reports on the state of membership or changes in wages, hours and conditions within the district are discussed. The National Federation of Building Trade Operatives also organizes monthly meetings of "card stewards" on a district basis from all unions in the Federation. Most of the craft unions have stewards, and in industries where piecework prevails, the unions are compelled to pay some attention to their workshop organizations, although in some cases they prefer to leave these negotiations to permanent officials. Of the major unions, the two general workers' organizations have probably been least inclined to encourage stewards to be more than dues collectors, outside their large membership in the engineering industries, but sections of the membership in both of them, for example the London busmen and tramwaymen in the Transport and General Workers and the London gasmen in the Municipal and General Workers, have a strong and virile representation at their place of work.

In default of a proper examination of the practice of the various unions, which would have to be conducted by the trade union movement itself, it is difficult to get any clear picture of the present state of workshop representation. It is perhaps indicative of the reluctance of some of the more powerful trade union leaders to face the problem that such a report has not yet been produced. This reluctance is partly due to the attempts which have been made by the Communist Party and other political groups to foster unofficial movements among the stewards for their own ends, but also because it is thought that the strengthening of workshop organization might generally undermine the central authority of the trade unions. One of the main purposes of the trade unions has been to settle wages and working conditions on a national basis, to make bargaining as collective as possible. But the risks involved in the growth of any kind of "factory patriotism" have to be weighed against the need for the unions to make their influence felt in the daily lives of the workers. Unofficial movements are the consequence of too great a gap between the top leadership and the active rank-and-file members.

Union finances

The greater part of the income of the British trade unions, about nine tenths, is derived from the members' weekly dues. Entrance fees, where they exist, are small. Special levies have been imposed from time to time, and most union rules provide for this possibility, but their use has been confined to periods of financial stress. Invested funds have become an increasingly important source of income. Some unions pay out the state unemployment insurance benefit to their members and recover from the Ministry of Labour, in addition to the money they have disbursed, a small payment for administration expenses.

Rates of dues contributions vary from union to union according to the types and scales of benefit made available to members, but by American standards they are relatively low. Except in a few craft or professional workers' unions, which have considerably higher rates, dues range generally from sixpence to two shillings a week. Many unions have different scales of contribution for different sections of their membership; it may be optional for the member to choose to which section he will belong, or it may sometimes depend on trade qualifications.

It is mainly the differences in the various welfare or friendly benefits provided (unemployment, sickness, accident, funeral, superannuation) which account for the different rates of dues contributions. The provision of these benefits was a characteristic feature of the nineteenth century craft unions, although some nonmanual workers' unions, formed at a later date, have followed their example. "New unionism," on the other hand, was characterized by its repudiation, by and large, of the provident function, the method of "mutual insurance," to employ the terminology of the Webbs, on the grounds that it weakened union militancy and that the lower-paid workers could not afford high rates of contribution. The rise of the state system of social insurance has reduced the significance of these benefits, but, as might be expected, where they have become an established part of union activity, they continue to be provided as before.

The average union income per member remained remarkably stable after the great changes in trade union organization that took place at the end of World War I, and so has the average expenditure per member on the unions' working expenses, despite the decline in the value of money since 1938. In the last two decades the relatively peaceful state of industrial relations has reduced payments of dispute benefits to a small sum, an annual average per member of about one shilling between 1927 and 1939, and not much more than one penny between 1940 and 1949. Full employment since the early days of World War II has similarly reduced union expenditure for unemployment benefits. This has resulted in an increase in the funds held by the unions from less than £12 million in 1933 to more than £22 million in 1939 and £58 million in 1949. It has been a period of continued expansion in union membership, so that the rise in the funds held per member is less spectacular, though appreciable, from £3.5 in 1933 to £4.4 in 1939 and £7.4 in 1949. Despite this improvement in their financial position, the unions have been disinclined to increase their expenditure on new activities, such as education and research, to any marked extent. Annual political expenditure rarely exceeds one shilling per member and, apart from general election years, usually runs at half that amount or less.[21]

Activities and Policy

The main objectives of the British trade union movement "which bear on the formulation of its economic policy" were clearly stated at the outset of the T.U.C.'s 1944 *Report on Post-War Reconstruction:*

The first of these is unquestionably that of maintaining and improving wages, hours and conditions of labour. This in itself relates to more than rates of wages or earnings measured in monetary terms or other payments and conditions settled by collective bargaining. We are also concerned with what wages can buy—with the cost of living and the general level of prices. We are in fact concerned with increasing the size of the real national income and with the share of it which should accrue to workpeople in terms of goods and services, conditions of work and leisure, as well as opportunities for individual and social development.

Secondly, the Trade Union Movement is concerned with the opportunities which exist for the worker to obtain work. "Full employment" is an aim which the Trade Unions have always pursued. It must be emphasised, however, that the "right to work" which the Trade Unions have sought to establish, is not merely a claim for a job of any kind. We are concerned to ensure that every worker shall be able, within limits determined only by the need to safeguard the reasonable freedom of others, to choose freely work which he prefers and for which he is trained at rates of wages and in conditions commensurate with his skill and the nature of the work.

Thirdly, the Trade Union Movement exists to extend the influence of workpeople over the policies and purposes of industry and to arrange for their participation in its management. The claim to share in the control of industry rests primarily on the simple democratic right of workpeople to have a voice in the determination of their industrial destinies. It is supported by the knowledge that it is only by recognition of this claim that the potentialities, experience and good sense of the workers can be drawn upon and the full productive powers of industry be effectively realised.[22]

There are, it is true, other social objectives which have also frequently

---

[21] The above totals and averages are calculated from the annual Statistical Summary issued by the Chief Registrar of Friendly Societies and relate only to *registered* trade unions in Great Britain. In 1949 there were 417 trade unions on register with nearly 7.9 million members, so they accounted for 85 per cent of the total trade union membership in the United Kingdom.

[22] Trades Union Congress, *Report on Post-War Reconstruction,* page 7. London: Trades Union Congress, 1944.

been made the subject of resolution and representation by the movement. Education, health, housing and social security have been of special concern to trade unionists for many years, and international and colonial affairs have continually received their attention. But the pious resolution is a well-known phenomenon in the trade union world, as elsewhere. The primary purposes of any social institution can only be inferred from what it does. It is not enough to know what are the opinions and aspirations of British trade unionism. If its role in present-day society is to be realistically assessed, we must compare its actual activities with its stated objectives to see what it cares strongly about, what it is prepared, if necessary, to fight for, what relative weight it gives to each of its various objectives when they come into conflict.

Industrial and political action

As in other industrial countries the British trade unions came into being, established themselves on firm foundations, and gradually extended their power and social status mainly as agencies for collective bargaining. That is to say, they succeeded as a form of organization which enabled employees, at first only wage-earners but later also salary-earners, to regulate and thus to improve their wages and working conditions. This success in turn has depended, in the last resort, upon their capacity to withhold their labor collectively, a form of industrial power which is exercised as much in the negotiation of an agreement as in the conduct of a strike.

That the British trade union movement of today also wields considerable political influence, both directly and through its association with the Labour Party, is well-known. When the *Times* correspondent Mr. J. V. Radcliffe, in replying to the traditional vote of thanks to the members of the press at the conclusion of the 1945 Trades Union Congress, told the delegates: "You have no longer any need to thunder; you have only to whisper and Ministers tremble and Field-Marshals bend their knees," he was being amusing, but only because he had extravagantly expressed a recognized fact. "How very far away," indeed, as he said, "are those days when a few top-hatted, frock-coated gentlemen made a promenade of the government offices in Whitehall respectfully carrying resolutions passed by Congress, leaving them at the door, extremely happy if they saw a permanent secretary, and most handsomely flattered if by accident they stumbled across a Minister." Today the trade union movement is represented on some sixty bodies or committees that advise the government; [23]

---

[23] See *T.U.C. Congress Report 1950,* page 526.

and no legislation affecting the interests of workers is likely to be passed without prior consultation with its representatives.

Yet collective bargaining remains not only the chief activity of the British trade unions and the main concern of their members, but also the basis of most of their other activities. Certainly it can be shown historically that the fluctuations in their membership and their fortunes have depended largely upon their capacity to bargain successfully, to secure relative wage advances for their own members or other improvements in their conditions of employment. The prediction of the Webbs in their *Industrial Democracy* that the method of legal enactment would gradually, though not entirely, replace the method of collective bargaining with the advance of what they described as "collectivism" has not so far been fulfilled. Wherever the British trade unions have been strong enough to regulate wages and conditions by direct negotiation with the employers they have invariably preferred to dispense with government assistance. That is why it is not illegal in Britain to employ an adult male twenty-fours a day outside of a few special industries like coal mining; the Factory Acts apply only to the hours of employment of women and young persons. Similarly, in recent years, the unions have strongly opposed the application of any kind of national wages policy, which would involve the government in having a greater say in the outcome of negotiations. Political action has been employed by the unions to support rather than supplant industrial action, as will subsequently be shown.

Development of collective bargaining

The first impression gained by any student of Britain's system of industrial relations is invariably one of bewilderment. In such industries as coal mining, metal manufacture, engineering and shipbuilding, railways, building, cotton textiles, printing, and boot and shoe manufacture, which in May, 1950, accounted for more than 6 million employees or some 30 per cent of the total employee population in Great Britain,[24] the procedures and joint organization for negotiation and the settlement of disputes follow no standard pattern. In all of them trade unionism and organized collective bargaining had come to stay before World War I, at least among manual workers, but at different times and in varying forms, so that their separate traditions became a powerful influence on their union-employer relationships. After 1917, as a result of the recommendations of the Whitley Committee,

---

[24] See "The Employed Population 1948–1950," *Ministry of Labour Gazette,* Vol. LIX, No. 2, (February, 1951), pages 41–45.

to which we will return, the creation of joint industrial councils in many other industries did provide a more uniform type of joint organization, but they rarely replaced other arrangements which had already taken root.

The term "voluntary system," though frequently used to describe the whole of the various arrangements which have been devised to regulate wages and conditions of employment by collective agreements, is in one respect misleading. It cannot be taken to imply the absence of all compulsion, but only the absence of legal compulsion. The employers have not been brought to recognize trade unions and to engage in organized collective bargaining merely by the use of persuasion. Their opposition had first to be broken down mainly by the application of the workers' industrial power. In addition the special circumstances created by two world wars also contributed greatly towards overcoming employer resistance. Once this had been accomplished, however, the advantages of this limited form of industrial self-government were usually recognized alike by both sides. Even so, the struggle has continued over the scope of the bargaining process, both as regards the coverage and the contents of agreements. In most cases it has been the trade unions that have pressed forward toward national regulation and a further limitation of what the employers continue to regard as their prerogatives.

Collective agreements, of one kind or another, were becoming the rule in well-organized industries by the turn of the century. Nevertheless, even today, in certain industries, notably in engineering and iron and steel manufacture, many local conditions of work and certain basic wage rates, are fixed by custom and are not incorporated in written agreements. In Britain a collective agreement as such is not legally binding, although its terms may expressly or by implication become the terms of the individual contract of employment. In practice, despite the lack of penalties, the bargain it expresses is invariably honored by both parties, and frequently it is observed by employers who are not members of the employers' association in question and thus are not formally parties to it. One of the important consequences of this system is that the British trade unions seldom become involved in litigation in matters relating to labor disputes and are probably less dependant upon lawyers than any other national trade union movement.

A brief sketch of the growth of collective bargaining in three industries, coal-mining, building and engineering, may serve to illustrate some of the contrasts and similarities involved in this historical process.

Coal mining. One of the first steps toward union recognition in this industry occurred in 1872 when the colliery owners in the Durham coal field agreed to receive a delegation from the miner's union to discuss their demand for a rise in wages. Previously such demands had been presented separately by trade unionists to the individual owners and hardly a change in wages and conditions had been effected without a strike or a lockout. In the same year a standing joint committee was set up, composed of an equal number of representatives from the Durham mine owners and the miners' association, for the purpose of settling disputes which might arise at any particular colliery, but general wage questions which affected the county as a whole were excluded from consideration. This practice of conciliation spread to other districts, but it was not until 1894 that the first conciliation board was formed in Northumberland to deal with general county wage questions, again to be followed by the establishment of similar boards in other districts, so that before World War I the whole of the country's coal fields were covered by eight of them.

In the meantime the Miners' Federation of Great Britain had been formed in 1888 by the Yorkshire and Midlands miners' associations. One of the immediate purposes of the new organization was to bring about an eight-hour day for all mine workers, a purpose which was accomplished by the passage of the Coal Mines Eight Hour Act of 1908, the first statutory regulation of hours for male labor. This success helped to bring the Durham and Northumberland miners into the Federation. With complete national organization, if only in a federal form, the miners began to think of their industry as a whole and included in their program the demand for a national wages board, which would undertake direct negotiation between the Miners' Federation and the Mining Association of Great Britain, the employers' organization.

When in 1917, for the sake of furthering the war effort, the industry was placed under government control, wages became the subject of negotiation between the government and the Miners' Federation. The mine owners had maintained that national wage rates were impractical because of the varying financial circumstances of the different coal fields, but this obstacle was now overcome by the national pooling of profits under a unified financial policy. For the miners the advantages of this policy were so apparent that they pressed more strongly for the permanent nationalization of their industry, a policy they had adopted in 1912. With the return of private control in 1921, the mine owners were determined to reinstitute the prewar system of district negotiations, and this became the leading issue in the bitter conflicts which then ensued. The seven month national strike in the coal fields in 1926, which led to the General Strike, ended in a complete defeat for the miners and their district unions were compelled to open separate negotiations with the colliery owners in their respective districts.

A modest attempt was made to meet the miners' continued demand for national negotiations by the second minority Labour Government in the Coal Mines Act of 1930, which provided for the establishment of a Coal Mines National Industrial Board. The idea was that owners or workers in any district might refer disputes on which they were unable to secure a district settlement to this board, which could then conduct an inquiry and make a report. Even this cautious proposal was emphatically rejected by the owners. The Mining Association refused to nominate its quota of members to the board and the central employers' associations in solidarity followed their example; the government was compelled to appoint persons willing to serve in an individual capacity. Needless to say, the board had little effect on the industry and soon ceased to function.

It was not until World War II, when in 1942 the newly created Ministry of Fuel and Power took over the operational control of the mines, that a new approach was made to the settlement of wages and conditions "on a national basis by a properly constituted national body." The recommendations of a government appointed Board of Inquiry led first to the establishment of a national minimum wage and, then, in May 1943, to the setting up of a National Conciliation Scheme for the industry, providing both for negotiations and arbitration. A National Negotiating Committee representative of both sides of the industry was formed, but in the event of this committee failing to reach an agreed settlement on any question referred to it, a National Reference Tribunal, composed of three persons not engaged in the industry, was empowered to make a binding and final decision.

The nationalization of coal mining by the Labour Government in 1946 left this machinery intact. It was supplemented, however, by a Pit Conciliation Scheme, adopted by national agreement at the beginning of 1947 "to provide for the speedy settlement of disputes arising in individual collieries." The main point of this scheme is to prevent what are essentially local disputes from becoming the subject of protracted district or national negotiations or, as frequently happens, becoming the cause of unofficial strike action. Such disputes, if they cannot be settled by negotiation in the colliery concerned, are referred, according to a strict timetable, to a joint District Disputes Committee, which, if unable to agree, refers them to an umpire, selected from an agreed panel, for a binding decision.

Building trades. Together with engineering and printing, the building trades were one of the main strongholds of craft unionism in the last century. An important national conciliation agreement was signed in 1904, for the first time, by the unions organizing the bricklayers, stone masons, carpenters and joiners, and the National Federation of Building Trades Employers. But, up to World War I, collective bargaining though widely established was usually local in character and, in most cases, separate agreements were made for individual occupations and there was no formal means of coordinating them. During the war years increases in wages continued to be made on the basis of local agreements, but by the addition of fixed amounts, which were usually the same for all classes of operatives.

The principle of national regulation was first accepted by both sides of the industry in 1919 for hours of work, and in 1920 for wages and other conditions of work, though in the latter case not necessarily on a uniform basis. This agreement resulted in the formation of a National Wages and Conditions Council for the Building Industry, which changed its name to the National Joint Council for the Building Industry in 1926. One of the tasks of this joint body was the "grading" of towns and districts for the purpose of regulating wages and working rules nationally, while allowing for differences in local circumstances. Originally there were 17 grades, but in 1947 they were reduced to 6. "Grading" here is a geographical, not an occupational classification. A uniform rate is fixed for all craftsmen in each grade; and the laborer's rate bears a fixed relationship to that of the craftsman. Nine regional joint committees also exist in England and Wales—there has been an entirely separate Joint Council for Scotland since 1930—but their powers are limited. The most important power is that of introducing "variation amendments," or proposals to alter national rules in so far as they affect a particular region, but they must be ratified by the National Council. A revision of the Council's constitution in 1932 provided a conciliation procedure for dealing with all disputes arising between the federated employers and the unions. Previously it could concern itself only with disputes arising out of the interpretation of its own decisions. Up to 1940 if the two sides of the Council disagreed a special joint committee could be appointed to work out a settlement, or the question could be referred to arbitration by mutual consent. Subsequently this arrangement was changed to provide that if the first alternative of a special committee fails "it shall be the duty of the Council to refer the matter to arbitration."

This high degree of centralized control is remarkable in an industry which has a substantial proportion of its labor force employed by a large number of small firms; and in which, in the interwar years, the growth of a class of speculative builders, usually employing nonunion labor, provided a further obstacle to orderly relations. The machinery did not always work smoothly in the first decade of its existence. In

1924 and again in 1930 the unions, dissatisfied with their wage position and the slowness of the constitutional procedure, gave notice to secede from the Council, but each time agreement was eventually reached and the powers of the Council extended. Since 1924 there has been no national strike in the industry and relatively few local disputes in federated firms. Undoubtedly the provision in the wage agreement for a cost-of-living sliding scale has helped to preserve good relations in recent years.

Engineering. The vast complex of industries and trades known in Britain as "engineering" stands in marked contrast to the building industry in respect to its provisions for collective bargaining. The degree of union organization is probably about the same, about 50 per cent, and weaker than in most of the other basic industries. Both employers and workers are gathered together in single federations for negotiating purposes, the Engineering and Allied Employers' National Federation and the Confederation of Shipbuilding and Engineering Unions. But no permanent joint machinery exists for negotiation, nor anything that can reasonably be described as a system of national wage regulation.

This is best understood if we look at the wage structure. There are no nationally agreed rates for men, although there are for women, and some of the district rates have never been embodied in formal agreements. In some districts agreed rates have been established only for craftsmen and laborers, although semi-skilled workers—the unions prefer to describe them as "skilled machine operators"—form the largest category of workers in the industry. There are, however, national agreements on "national bonus," a method of securing a uniform increase in the various district rates introduced during World War I, on the length of the working week, overtime and payment by results. National and district negotiations take place by the calling of special conferences on the initiative of either side.

The one agreement which lays down a formal arrangement for conciliation in the industry is known as the York Memorandum, an agreement signed in June 1922 and still in effect. This defines a procedure for avoiding disputes and for dealing with questions arising mainly in individual establishments. Disputes if not resolved at the plant level by the shop stewards or at a plant conference may be brought before a local conference between the local employers' association and the local representatives of the union, to be held within seven days unless otherwise agreed. Should the question still remain unsettled either party has the right to bring the matter before a central conference held each month, usually at York. The agreement provides that there shall be no stoppage of work, either partial or general, until the whole of this procedure has been exhausted. There is no provision for arbitration at any stage.

The York Memorandum was largely an amplification of an agreement for avoiding local disputes signed in 1898, and both agreements terminated lockouts in the industry in which the workers were defeated. The leading issues in the 1897–98 lockout were systematic overtime and piecework, but behind them loomed the general problem of "managerial functions." The settlement began with a rather meaningless clause repeated in the following words in the 1922 agreement: "The employers have the right to manage their own establishments and the trade unions have the right to exercise their own functions." In fact, on both occasions the employers successfully resisted the demand of the unions to decide when the working of overtime was necessary. Other issues involved in the 1922 lockout were the employers' demand to have the sole right in deciding who should work a particular machine and the unions' demand to negotiate on behalf of apprentices.

These battles over managerial functions have, of course, a very practical significance for the workers in this industry, although there has also been a more theoretical, syndicalist background to union agitation. For the unions, control of overtime was a means of reducing unemployment among their members, control of the manning of machines was needed to safeguard skilled worker rates and so on. In the thirties and forties the engineering unions gained the substance of many of their earlier demands in individual establishments, although much depended on the strength of their workshop representation. Joint relations in this industry are, however, still influenced by bitter memories among the older workers of past defeats and humiliations and are characterised by a lack of mutual confidence.

Negotiation and grievance procedure

If we now try to broaden the picture to which we have given a little historical depth it will be helpful to distinguish between the collective bargaining procedures used (1) for the negotiation of agreements; and (2) for the settlement of grievances arising either out of the interpretation of agreements or—and this is important in the British context—out of matters not regulated by agreement.

The procedure for the negotiation of agreements is bound to depend on the type of agreement prevalent in the industry, although which is cause and which is effect remains an open question. In the majority of British industries national agreements regulate most of the terms and conditions of employment. But, whereas in building and in railways they do so almost completely, in coal mining they determine only minimum rates of wages, and in engineering, only general wage increases and not district wage rates. National regulation of wages has not meant the elimination of district differentials, although it has tended to reduce them. The building trades are a good illustration of this. In many industries in which wages are regulated by national agreements, provision is made at least for a higher rate in the London area. In industries in which piecework predominates, the negotiation of actual piece rates or work loads has usually to take place in the separate establishments. However, national agreements that determine minimum time rates (a "fall back" wage) and a percentage addition to those rates—often 25 per cent or thereabouts—below which the earning of a workman of average ability on payment by results should not fall, now exist in most of these industries. A further complication arises, as in printing, where various unions in the same industry have separate national or local agreements with the employers.

National negotiations are, then, the main form of collective bargaining undertaken by the British trade unions today. Usually they are conducted through the medium of a permanent joint organization set up for this purpose, although engineering is an important exception. In many cases these joint bodies include all the trade unions with a substantial membership in the industry or complex of industries covered and they all become parties to the same agreements. Frequently there is some provision for arbitration or a third-party decision (by an independent chairman, for example) in the event of the two sides failing to agree. Some industries, for example coal mining, railways and civil service, have their own arbitration tribunals; others agree to resort to the Industrial Court.

Grievance procedure reveals an even greater variety of practices than negotiation. On the whole it is more important in industries in which national regulation is weak, as in iron and steel manufacture and engineering, both of which have well-defined conciliation arrangements for dealing with local disputes. Furthermore, any system of payment by results, even if regulated broadly by national agreement, must continually give rise to disputes of interpretation on actual rates. Thus in boot and shoe manufacture local boards of conciliation and arbitration, as established by an agreement signed in 1895, have contributed greatly to the industry's long record of industrial peace. In many industries, however, there is no defined grievance procedure. A trade union official is called in if the grievance is serious enough, and it is left to him to secure a settlement. Where an agreed procedure exists it may be based on one of three principles or a combination of them. The first might be defined as "reference upwards" which characterizes the York Memorandum procedure in the engineering industry. This is probably the least satisfactory because it leads to delay. Nominally this is also the procedure in cotton textiles, but the officials on both sides are accustomed to secure a local settlement. The second is that of the "neutral committee" successfully developed in iron and steel manufacture. Questions affecting individual plants, if they cannot be settled at the works in question, are referred to a committee composed equally of employers' and workers' representatives from plants other than the one at which the question arose. This particular form of local conciliation procedure may or may not be combined with provision for local arbitration, which is the third principle applied, for example, in boot and shoe manufacture and in coal mining.

The government and the voluntary system

Having described some of the main contemporary features of the voluntary system, we have now to consider the relationship of the state to this method of regulating wages and conditions of employment. The reversal of the Taff Vale decision by the Trades Dispute Act in 1906 gave the unions their full freedom in industrial bargaining. It was followed by the growing, if gradual, acceptance on the part of the government of two main responsibilities: that of supporting the voluntary system, where necessary, both directly and by filling in its inevitable gaps in a way that would not weaken it; and that of helping to bring about a peaceful settlement of disputes without, however, trying to determine their outcome. On the whole the political influence of the trade unions has been used not only to encourage such a development in government policy but also to resist its extension beyond the limits implicit in each of the two responsibilities.

This kind of relationship was already being shaped by events before World War I, but it first found clear expression and official approval in the government's acceptance of the main recommendations of the Committee on Relations between Employers and Employed appointed in 1916, with Mr. J. H. Whitley, M.P., as Chairman. Because what came to be called "Whitleyism" was by no means an unqualified success in the interwar years, the great influence exercised by the reports of the Whitley Committee is often underestimated. In fact it established the main principles on which the institutional pattern of industrial relations in Great Britain has so far been based.

The first of these was that "an essential condition for securing a permanent improvement in the relations between employers and employed is that there should be adequate organisation on the part of both." The acceptance of this principle by the government committed it to a positive encouragement of trade union and employers' organization. The second "was the advisability of a continuance as far as possible, of the present system whereby industries make their own agreements and settle their differences themselves." The emphasis, in other words, was to be on self-government and voluntary agreements. The third principle expressed in various recommendations was that the government should greatly extend its help in the setting up of appropriate permanent bodies for negotiation and for the settlement of disputes, but should not itself participate in them or control their working. Its role was to be that of a midwife rather than a governess, helping in the birth of good industrial relations, but not guiding their course. The fourth principle favored statutory wage regulation in all badly organized industries and trades, but so designed as to encourage its replacement, if possible, by voluntary organization. There was a fifth principle, the one usually associated with the term "Whitleyism," that the scope of subjects considered by joint bodies of employers and workers' representatives should be extended beyond wages and working conditions to all matters of common concern, including "improvements of processes, machinery and organisation and appropriate questions relating to management." This principle found little sympathetic response from either side of industry at the time.

Joint industrial councils. One of the main proposals of the Whitley Committee was that in all industries where both employers and workers were adequately organized the government should help to set up a three tier form of joint organization composed of a national joint industrial council, district joint industrial councils and works committees. In contrast to the *ad hoc* bodies of varying composition already in existence this structure was theoretically designed to provide a standard type of permanent organization with a written constitution and defined functions. This proposal was not only intended to smooth the way for orderly negotiations but was broadly conceived as a means of "promoting industrial harmony and efficiency." The Whitley Committee gave a list of topics which it considered proper subjects for discussion in the councils, including such matters as the better utilization of the practical knowledge and experience of the workers, the statement of the general principles governing the conditions of employment, means of ensuring to the workers the greatest possible security of earnings and employment, methods of fixing and adjusting earnings, piecework prices, technical education and training, industrial research, improvement of machinery, and organization of work and proposed legislation affecting the industry.

The Ministry of Labour sent out a letter to trade unions and employers' associations in October, 1917, explaining the scheme and carefully pointing out that it "indicated no intention to introduce an element of state interference which had hitherto not existed in industry; in fact the councils would be autonomous bodies and would in effect make possible a larger degree of self-government in industry." While offering its assistance to any industry wishing to form a joint industrial council, the government left the employers' associations and trade unions concerned to adapt the scheme to their own preferences and requirements. Between January, 1918, and December, 1921, 73 joint industrial councils were established, and 33 interim industrial reconstruction committees, a less formal type of organization which it was hoped would pave the way for the setting up of a joint industrial council. Many of these bodies failed to survive the period of industrial conflict which ended with the General Strike. According to Professor J. H. Richardson, the chief causes for the breakdown of the councils were "wage conflicts, weakness of organisation of employers and work-people, and divergence of interests between different localities, different sections of an industry and between large and small undertakings." [25]

By 1932 only 51 joint industrial councils remained in existence and only 20 of them had district or local joint bodies associated with them. Some were meeting irregularly and most of them confined their activities to regulating wages and working conditions. The fate of the works committees was even less fortunate. It was estimated that between 1917 and 1922 more than 1,000 works committees were formed, but by 1925, the great majority of them had ceased to function, and those that continued to exist had little or no working relationship with the district and national councils.

World War II produced a new crop of joint industrial councils since organized industrial relations were needed in planning the war economy and were encouraged by the government in many ways. Altogether 56 of them or their equivalents were established or revived during the years 1939–46, making a total of 111 in existence at the end of 1946. By the end of 1950 their number had further increased to 130. The most important fields of employment covered today by a network of joint industrial councils are: public administration, including national government and local authorities; public utilities, gas, water and electricity; and transport other than railways. They also exist, however, in a wide range of dissimilar industries, ranging from bricks, hosiery, and chemicals to flour milling, and cover in all some five million employees. It is noteworthy that in a few industries, mainly printing and boot and shoe manufacture, in which

[25] International Labour Office, *Industrial Relations in Great Britain,* page 137, Geneva, 1938.

joint industrial councils were formed for other than negotiating purposes because alternative collective bargaining procedures were already well developed, they have made some progress in carrying out the broader cooperative functions for which they were originally planned. Whitleyism is usually considered to have found its best application so far in the Civil Service and no doubt the security of employment which exists there has contributed greatly to its success. Even here, however, it has gained but partial acceptance after many set-backs.

Statutory wage regulation. The Trade Boards Act of 1909 was the first, cautious attempt by the state for over a century to intervene in wage determination. The Industrial Revolution and the acceptance of the doctrine of *laissez faire* had led to abandonment of earlier statutes giving local magistrates the power to regulate the wages of artisans in their district. Various Factory Acts had done something to regulate the hours of labor of industrial workers, and to improve the standards of health and safety in the workshops, but wages were regarded as sacrosanct, a matter to be settled by "free contract" between the parties immediately concerned. Only after strong public feeling had been aroused by twenty years' agitation against the appallingly low wages paid to home workers, and those employed in the so-called "sweated" trades, did the claims of humanity make a slight breach in the current tenets of economic theory. Under the 1909 Act, the government was empowered to set up a board to fix minimum wages for timework and piecework in any trade where the prevailing rate of wages was "exceptionally low as compared with that in other employments." Four such trade boards were formed in 1910 and four more in 1914, covering in all about a half million workers.

An important change in this system was recommended by the Whitley Committee and given effect in the Trade Boards Act of 1918. The Minister of Labour could now make an order for a trade board if he was "of the opinion that no adequate machinery exists for the effective regulation of wages throughout the trade." The emphasis was shifted from unduly low wages to the absence of adequate voluntary organization, and the scope of statutory wage regulation was correspondingly extended. Between 1919 and 1921 no less than 37 new trade boards were set up. Recognition had been given to the principle that those workers who could not hope to improve their wages by their own organization were entitled to legal protection, but designed in such a way as to encourage, as far as possible, the growth of voluntary effort. The trade unions were thus safeguarded against a weakening of their own organization, and the better employers, willing to pay higher wages, against the competition of firms prospering on sweated labor.

The trade boards consisted of an equal number of employers' and workers' representatives in the trade, together with three independent members, including the chairman. All members were appointed by the Minister of Labour at his discretion, but the practice developed for him to ask for nominations from trade unions and employers' associations in trades in which there was some degree of organization, and the great majority of the representative appointments have been made in this way. The recommendations of the trade boards only became effective when confirmed by the Minister after time had been given for objections to be lodged. He could refer back their recommendations for further consideration but could not himself fix the rates. Once confirmed, the minimum rates became legally binding upon all employers in the trade, and the Ministry employed a special staff of inspectors to see that they were observed. Employers paying lower rates were liable to fine and imprisonment as well as to the payment of any arrears of wages due to the workers.

Statutory wage regulation was extended to agricultural workers in England and Wales under separate legislation introduced by the 1924 Labour Government, but otherwise after the early twenties it did little more than hold the ground it had gained until the approach of World War II. Few new trade boards were established though large numbers of workers still had neither a legal minimum nor a negotiated wage. Indeed, the Unemployment Insurance Statutory Committee reported in 1938 that there were many cases of persons (mainly those with large families) working for less than they would have received from unemployment insurance. In 1937 the regulation of agricultural wages was extended to Scotland; in 1938 special wages boards, with powers of statutory enforcement, were introduced into road haulage, and the trade boards were enabled to give directions providing for holidays with pay; and in 1938 and 1939 a few new trade boards came into existence, notably in baking, rubber manufacturing and the furniture trades.

It was left to Mr. Bevin, as Minister of Labour in the wartime Coalition Government, to complete the system of statutory wage regulation, both by greatly extending its scope and by strengthening the powers of the bodies undertaking it. This was accomplished under the Catering Wages Act of 1943 and the Wages Councils Act of 1945. The first of these measures provided for the establishment of a permanent Catering Wages Commission with the responsibility of examining the arrangements for the regulation of wages in any branch of the catering industry and of recommending the setting up of a wages board where such arrangements were found to be inadequate. By 1947 five such boards covering all the more important sections of the industry had been formed. The Wages Councils Act renamed the trade boards to "remove the stigma of being associated with the sweated trades" as the Minister explained to the House of Commons, and widened their jurisdiction on wages to the fixing of "minimum remuneration" in place of "minimum rates." This enabled them *inter alia* to make provisions for a guaranteed week and thus protect the workers against the practice of employing them at the prescribed rates on short time. Furthermore, the activities of the wages councils were no longer restricted mainly to questions of pay; they could also advise the Minister on such matters as training, recruitment and working conditions. In fact they assumed most of the functions of a joint industrial council.

The main field of employment that came under statutory regulation for the first time after the passage of the Wages Councils Act was retail distribution, in which eight wages councils have been formed regulating the wages of some one and a quarter million workers. The quantitative significance of this step can be gauged by a comparison: approximately the same number of workers were employed in all the industries covered by the fifty-one other wages councils already in existence in 1947. The catering wages boards, whose composition and powers are the same as those of the wages councils, brought another three quarters of a million workers under legal protection. In 1948 a further Act converted the Road Haulage Central Wages Board into a wages council.[26] Taking agriculture and catering into account, as well as the industries subject to the jurisdiction of the sixty wages councils functioning at the end of 1950, the number of workers whose wages and working conditions are now subject to statutory regulation must be in the neighborhood of four and a half million.[27]

When the trade boards were first formed they were regarded with serious misgiving by many trade unions. It was thought that any form of statutory regulation of wages would tend to weaken trade union organization by encouraging the workers concerned to rely upon authority rather than their own efforts to improve their terms of employment. Experience has steadily diminished these fears. In 1931, when the unions were losing members, a serious clash of opinion developed within the Trades Union Congress on the question whether trade boards were helping or hampering trade union organization.

---

[26] This covers the privately owned sector of the industry. In the part which has been nationalized there is a joint industrial council.

[27] Some of these workers, however, have their wages regulated by collective agreements with individual firms; *e.g.* in clothing and retail distribution.

This led to an inquiry by the T.U.C.'s Trade Boards Advisory Council. No convincing evidence was produced to support the view that the trade boards were responsible for the decline in union membership and it was agreed not to recommend the abolition of any of the existing trade boards. Since then no further opposition has been openly expressed within the trade union movement.

Since the wages councils only fix minimum wages, the trade unions can extend their organization by securing higher rates through collective agreements with the larger and better organized firms in the industry. Their vigilance is also required, in addition to that of government inspectors, to ensure that nothing less than the statutory rates are paid and to claim the arrears due to a worker who has been underpaid. Naturally the efforts of the trade unions are directed towards lifting a trade or industry out of the wages council class. Under the 1945 and 1948 Acts the Minister of Labour may abolish a wages council at the joint request of the organized workers and employers concerned on the grounds that statutory backing for wage agreements is no longer necessary. This has happened in the furniture manufacturing industry after the formation of a joint industrial council.

Other forms of intervention. In supporting the voluntary system the government has increasingly used its influence to aid the trade unions in other ways. One of the means employed has been the "fair wages clause" which was first introduced into government contracts in 1891. In 1909 it was reformulated by a House of Commons resolution to provide that contractors "shall, under penalty of a fine or otherwise, pay rates of wages and observe hours of labour not less favorable than those commonly recognised by employers and trade societies (or in the absence of such recognised wages and hours, those which in practice prevail among good employers) in the trade in the district where the work is carried out." So it remained until substantially amended in October, 1946. The revisions extended its application to subcontractors, made the main standard of fair wages that established by representative collective agreements or by arbitration, and added "conditions of labor" to wages and hours, including the freedom of workers to be members of trade unions. In a series of Acts providing financial assistance to industries from the Public Exchequer, beginning with the British Sugar (Subsidy) Act, 1925, the same principle has been applied. Local authorities also have fair wages clauses which apply to their own contracts.

On one occasion legal force has been given to voluntarily negotiated agreements: the Cotton Manufacturing Industry (Temporary Provisions) Act, 1934. This was an exceptional measure applied to an industry faced, in the words of the Board of Inquiry's report, "with the possible collapse of the whole principle of collective bargaining." Yet it was in a way the precedent for a very significant part of the wartime Conditions of Employment and National Arbitration Order, 1940, which made it obligatory for every employer in any trade or industry in any district to observe terms and conditions of employment not less favorable than those that had been determined by collective agreement or arbitration. The initiative remained with the trade unions (theoretically also with employers' associations) to see that this obligation was fulfilled. There was no system of inspections or prosecutions as with the wages councils. If any employer appeared to be infringing the regulation, he could be reported to the Minister of Labour who had then to refer the question to arbitration. If the award was given in their favor, the workers concerned could then sue their employer for the amount their wage envelopes were short of the recognized remuneration. This arrangement has proved of great value to the trade unions in forcing recalcitrant employers to negotiate.

Conciliation and arbitration. We have seen how in many industries collective agreements lay down the procedure to be followed for the settlement of disputes, both local and national. The government has also gradually extended its provisions for the avoidance of industrial conflict. After a number of abortive experiments in compulsory arbitration before the trade unions had attained proper legal status, the first important step in this direction was taken with the passage of the Conciliation Act of 1896. This allowed the government to inquire into the causes and circumstances of any existing or impending trade dispute, and to appoint a conciliator or arbitrator, the former on application of either party and the latter at the request of both parties to the dispute. The Whitley Committee suggested that a permanent court of arbitration was needed as well as *ad hoc* courts of inquiry, but firmly rejected compulsory arbitration on the grounds that experience with it during the war had shown "that it is not a successful method of avoiding disputes and in normal times it would undoubtedly prove even less successful." The Industrial Court Act of 1919 carried out this recommendation.

Thus after World War I the Ministry of Labour had the authority to assist in the prevention and settlement of industrial disputes by the use of any of three methods: conciliation, voluntary arbitration, or special inquiry, usually in that sequence. It employs a staff of conciliation officers, whose job it is to help both parties to settle differences amicably if their advice or assistance is requested, although generally they do not intervene before an attempt has been made to reach a settlement without their help. Failing agreement the dispute can then be submitted with the consent of both parties to the Industrial Court established by the 1919 Act. The cost of the Court is borne by the government and no charge is made to industry for its services. In practice it consists of a permanent president, appointed by the Minister, and two other members, one from each of the panels representing employers and workers. Despite its name, it is no part of the British judicial system and its decisions are not enforceable. Nevertheless it has gained the reputation of being a genuinely independent tribunal—it is not subject to any form of government control—and only on rare occasions have the disputants refused to accept its findings. In addition to this permanent institution, the Minister of Labour can also appoint single arbitrators or special *ad hoc* boards of arbitration, if this course is likely to prove more acceptable to the contesting parties. The third method, the appointment of a court of inquiry, is only employed as a last resort and does not require the consent of the parties. It is primarily a means of informing Parliament and public opinion of the facts and underlying causes of a dispute. It may be a post-mortem examination of a strike that has taken place or last minute action to avert an impending stoppage. Usually the recommendations of a court of inquiry, although they cannot be enforced, provide a basis for further negotiations and a settlement.

One writer [28] has made an interesting comparison between the results of the Industrial Court's decisions and the outcome of strikes and lockouts in the period 1919–1932, the stormiest years in Britain's industrial relations, which yields the following amazingly close parallel:

1919–1932	In Favor of		Compromise	Total
	Employers	Workers		
Industrial Court awards	540 (35%)	337 (22%)	650 (43%)	1,536 (100%)
Results of strikes and lockouts	2,692 (35%)	1,683 (23%)	3,106 (42%)	7,481 (100%)

The percentage figures certainly suggest that it mattered little to either side whether a settlement was obtained by arbitration or by direct action. Since the arbitrators were usually concerned to find an award that would be sufficiently acceptable to both parties to avoid a trial of strength and thus to anticipate its probable outcome, this is not surprising. It should, however, be realized that after 1920 the use of the Industrial Court was largely confined to particular industries,

---

[28] Duck Soo Chang, *British Methods of Industrial Peace,* pages 167–168. New York: Columbia University Press, 1936.

engineering and shipbuilding, railways and other transport, civil service and public utilities, which together were responsible for 791 awards out of a total of 963 between 1921 and 1932.

The use of arbitration in settling differences between government departments and the Civil Service trade unions on questions of pay and conditions of service merits separate consideration. There is no law forbidding civil servants to strike, but the nature of their employment hardly permits them to do so without serious consequences. At first it was argued that compulsory arbitration was incompatible with the Whitley Council machinery, but in 1925 an agreement was reached to the effect "that failing agreement by negotiation arbitration shall be open to Government Departments on the one hand and to recognized Associations of Civil Servants . . . on the other hand, on application by either party, in regard to certain matters affecting conditions of service." Up to 1936 the Industrial Court was used for this purpose, but in that year a special Civil Service Arbitration Tribunal was constituted on similar lines. Only demands involving employees whose salaries exceed a fixed upper limit—at present it is £1,300—may not be taken to arbitration except with the consent of both parties. The government also reserves the right to refuse arbitration "on grounds of policy"; in fact it has done so only on one policy issue, that of equal pay for men and women. Otherwise the subjects which are arbitrable are defined in the agreement as "claims affecting the emoluments, weekly hours of work and leave." Within these limits the government is pledged to give effect to the arbitration awards subject only to the overriding authority of Parliament, an inevitable constitutional qualification, which is taken to mean that "the Government will not itself *propose* to Parliament the rejection of an award, once made." [29]

After the outbreak of World War II, a general system of compulsory arbitration was superimposed on the voluntary provisions for the settlement of disputes already described. The 1940 Conditions of Employment and National Arbitration Order, often referred to as Order 1305, prohibited all strikes and lockouts connected with trade disputes, with the one proviso that they were legal if the Minister of Labour, having had the dispute reported to him, failed to take action within three weeks to secure a settlement. It also established as a final authority for the settlement of disputes a National Arbitration Tribunal, normally consisting, for the purposes of any particular case, of three appointed members (including the chairman) and two representative members, one from each of the trade unions' and employers' panels. The Tribunal was not intended

[29] His Majesty's Treasury, 1949. *Staff Relations in the Civil Service,* page 27.

to displace or to weaken the established practices of collective bargaining or voluntary arbitration. Under Order 1305 the Minister was obliged to see that any existing joint machinery suitable for settling the dispute was used before referring the case to the National Arbitration Tribunal. Any awards or decisions made as a result of such references by the Minister of Labour, whether under any agreed procedure or by the National Arbitration Tribunal, became legally binding. On one point, however, the power of the Tribunal to make a binding award was challenged by a High Court decision. In what has come to be known as the Crowther case in 1947 it was held that the Tribunal had no power to make an award compelling employers to reinstate dismissed workers. The Lord Chief Justice pointed out that even if employers in deference to an award took men back into their employment, they could not be prevented from giving them notice the next day.

The trade unions first accepted this system of compulsory arbitration as a wartime necessity. They were not, however, in spite of their various criticisms, generally dissatisfied with its working. Many unions, particularly the smaller ones or those with membership in poorly organized industries, were thankful for the opportunity which it gave them to force reluctant employers either to negotiate or to come before the Tribunal and be bound by its award. So it came about that there was no strong trade union demand for the withdrawal of the Order at the end of the war. The Trades Union Congress, though refusing to commit itself in favor of compulsory arbitration as a permanent arrangement, readily consented to its temporary retention in the postwar years in view of the economic difficulties which continued to confront the nation.

Changing significance of strikes

One of the more obvious results of the continued strengthening and extension of the system of collective wage regulation,[30] together with the growing acceptance of the methods of conciliation and arbitration on the part of the British trade unions, has been the decline in the number of working days lost in industrial disputes. The contrast between the extent of industrial conflict before, during, and after the two World Wars reveals the decisive nature of the change.

---

[30] In 1950 the proportion of the total number of workers employed in the industries and services of Great Britain who were covered either by voluntary negotiating machinery or statutory machinery was about 80 per cent. (See: *Annual Report of the Ministry of Labour and National Service for 1950*, pages 115–116. London: His Majesty's Stationery Office, (1951.)

Working Days Lost in Industrial Disputes
(Annual averages in millions)

Prewar Years		War Years		Postwar Years	
1910–1914	16.1	1915–1918	4.2	1919–1923	35.6
1934–1939	1.8	1940–1945	2.0	1946–1950	1.9

In the thirties it was already apparent that the majority of trade unions no longer regarded the strike weapon as an instrument of policy to be deliberately employed on a national scale for bargaining purposes. At the same time the right to strike had lost nothing of its importance; it remained for the trade unions the fundamental condition on which their liberty and influence were based. The prolongation of the life of wartime Order 1305 created a strange situation. On the one hand this Order, as we have seen, entailed the almost total prohibition of strikes and lockouts and actually made it a criminal offence for a worker to "take part in" an illegal strike (and for an employer to "declare or take part in" an illegal lockout). No such drastic limit upon strike activity had previously been imposed in peacetime since the repeal of the Combination Acts. On the other hand, with the repeal of the 1927 Trades Disputes and Trade Unions Act in 1946, the restrictions placed upon strikes and lockouts by permanent legislation were almost negligible.[31]

Order 1305 did not, however, prevent strikes from taking place. During the ten year period 1941–1950, there were more than 17,000 industrial disputes leading to stoppages of work in the United Kingdom, but most of them were strictly local in character and of short duration; the average dispute involved less than 300 workers and lasted about four days.[32] There was in fact little attempt to enforce the law against striking. During the war years there were in all 109 cases of prosecution of workers, involving 6,281 individuals, and 2 of employers for taking part in an illegal stoppage of work. After the war it was not until 1950, when some of the leaders of a gas strike in North London, which was causing the public considerable inconvenience, were brought before the courts, that the Attorney-General made use of his powers. In justifying his previous reluctance to prosecute, Sir Hartley Shawcross told the House of Commons:

The law laid down by that Order . . . is not always easy to apply to all industrial disputes in peace-time. If one prosecutes too soon it may only ex-

---

[31] Striking *in breach of contract* (the individual contract of employment, not a collective agreement) is a criminal offence in certain circumstances for merchant seamen and for employees in public utility industries, gas, water, and electricity, or for any worker whose action causes danger to life or valuable property.

[32] More than half of the recorded strikes lasted less than a day.

acerbate the difficulties and impede the opportunities of settling the dispute by negotiation or arbitration. Prosecution may result in the individuals proceeded against being made martyrs in the opinion of their colleagues, and instead of leading to the observance of the law it may produce even greater disregard of it and so bring the law further into disrepute.[33]

It is generally recognized that the threat of criminal prosecution is about the worst method imaginable for maintaining industrial peace, and to maintain a legal prohibition and not apply it brings the law into disrepute. These considerations no doubt led the government to consider revising Order 1305. Moreover the prosecutions were causing trade union opinion to turn against it. At the 1950 Trades Union Congress, a resolution moved by the National Union of Railwaymen urging "the government to discontinue immediately" the Order, though defeated on the recommendation of the General Council, found strong support, the voting being roughly two and a half million for and five million against. On August 1, 1951, Order 1305 was replaced by a new Industrial Disputes Order (S.I. 1951 No. 1376), after its terms had been agreed to by the British Employers' Confederation, representatives of the nationalized industries, and the T.U.C. General Council. The penal prohibition of strikes and lockouts was abolished, but limited provisions for compulsory arbitration were retained.

The Industrial Disputes Tribunal, which has taken the place of the National Arbitration Tribunal—though similarly constituted—considers "disputes" and "issues" referred to it by the Minister of Labour, and its awards become an implied term of contract between the employer and the workers to whom an award applies. The definition of a "dispute" given in Order 1376 is narrower than given to a "trade dispute" in its predecessor and excludes the Tribunal from considering disputes concerned with the employment or nonemployment of any person or the obligation of a worker to belong to a trade union. The new term "issue" is used for a dispute as to whether a particular employer is observing "recognized terms and conditions of employment" in the district. Employers are no longer placed under a general and absolute obligation in this respect, as they were when Order 1305 was in operation, but since this obligation could then only be enforced by an award of the National Arbitration Tribunal, the trade unions appear to have retained the substance of this support to their voluntary efforts. The other, rather complicated provisions of Order 1376 have been designed "to strengthen the authority of existing voluntary systems of negotiation and arbitration and to uphold the sanctity of agreements and awards." Disputes can only be reported to the

---

[33] *Hansard* (House of Commons Official Report), January 29, 1951.

Minister for action by representative trade unions and employers' associations or by individual employers, and not as previously "by or on behalf of either party to the dispute." The Minister has discretion to stay arbitration proceedings or to refuse access to the Tribunal in the event of a stoppage of work or a substantial breach of an agreement. All in all, Order 1376 may be regarded as a new and extremely important experiment in government intervention in the field of industrial relations. It leaves both sides of industry free to resort to "direct action" but provides them with an alternative, if their voluntary arrangements are inadequate or fail to secure a settlement. It also leaves wide powers of discretion in the hands of the Minister of Labour. How it will work out in practice, whether it will succeed in minimizing industrial conflict, remains to be seen.

Nearly all the "illegal" strikes which have taken place since 1940 have also been "unofficial," that is, they have not been sanctioned or recognized officially by union executives. In recent years the problem why unofficial strikes occur has therefore come in for a great deal of ill-informed comment. Statements about the causes of strikes are much the same as statements about the causes of wars, bound to be wrong if they attempt some universal explanation. It is difficult enough to discover the causes of one particular strike, which rarely are confined to the matters allegedly in dispute. However, there are one or two general observations on the subject worth making.

The problem of unofficial strikes is almost as old as trade unionism itself, and an inevitable consequence of its voluntary character. When a section of membership feels very disgruntled with a settlement which the union has obtained or with the way in which its particular grievance is being dealt with, it can hardly be prevented from resorting to direct action in the hope that its claims may receive more attention. This is no more than the price of democracy and sometimes it may be a healthy corrective to bureaucratic lethargy or indifference. The one occasion on which a Minister of Labour has ventured any information on the proportion of unofficial strikes was before the introduction of compulsory arbitration. In 1937, when the natural increase in militancy which accompanies a trade revival resulted in a wave of strikes, he told the House of Commons that over half of the strikes of the previous year (and possibly a much higher proportion) were unofficial—at least less than a quarter were known to be officially supported.[34]

Undoubtedly Order 1305 was responsible for some increase in unofficial strikes and for straining union discipline. There have been

[34] *Hansard,* July 1, 1937.

cases where the union leaders have not been unhappy about unofficial action since they hoped it would enable them to drive a harder bargain. There have been others where the workers in one or more establishments, knowing that there was no point in agitating within the union for a strike, decided to act on their own account. However, the strikes that have taken place in the postwar years have been concentrated in particular industries as Table 3 shows.

TABLE 3

WORKERS INVOLVED IN STRIKES (PER YEAR) JULY 1945 TO JUNE 1950

Industry	In "Principal"* Strikes		In all Strikes	
	Number (thousands)	As per cent of workers employed	Number (thousands)	As per cent of workers employed
Mining and quarrying ...	89.7	11.1	227.0	28.2
Coal mining	89.7	12.3	226.4	31.0
Other mining and quarrying	†	†	0.6	0.8
Textiles	3.1	0.4	7.2	0.9
Metal, engineering, shipbuilding, etc.	51.4	1.5	103.0	3.0
Iron & steel and other metal	5.5	0.4	25.5	1.9
Engineering	27.9	1.4	50.1	2.6
Shipbuilding and ship-repairing	18.0	8.4	27.4	12.9
Transport	74.3	5.4	95.9	7.0
Railways	3.5	0.5	‡	‡
Road passenger	23.8	8.4	‡	‡
Road haulage	9.3	5.3	‡	‡
Docks	36.5	49.1	‡	‡
Other transport	1.2	0.6	‡	‡
Building, decorating, public works contracting, etc.	3.2	0.3	8.3	0.8
Clothing	2.3	0.4	6.5	1.3
Other industries and services	18.4	0.3	36.7	0.5
All Industries	242.4	1.6	484.6	3.1

* Principal strikes refer to those given in the monthly list of the *Ministry of Labour Gazette.*
† nil.
‡ Not available.
Source: Kenneth Knowles, "The Post-War Dock Strikes," *Political Quarterly,* Vol. XXII, No. 3 (July-September, 1951), page 267.

This would appear to emphasize the need for seeking explanations within the conditions and traditions prevailing within each industry, and the trade unions concerned. The dock strikes have been far and away the most dislocating and disturbing conflicts in postwar Britain and have led on two occasions to the government making use of its emergency powers, and employing troops to load and unload perishable cargoes. Out of eleven million man days lost in the first five postwar years (July 1945–June 1950) the transport workers accounted for thirty per cent, mainly in the big dock strikes, and the miners, traditionally the readiest of all workers to resort to direct action, for a little over a quarter. This may be compared with the ten million working days lost in the last five prewar years (1935 to 1939) when the miners accounted for more than a half and the transport workers for about a tenth.

One of the explanations frequently advanced for unofficial strikes is communist agitation. That the communists have been busy fishing in troubled waters in the postwar years is not open to doubt, but the waters have first to be troubled. This explanation, however much weight may be given to it, only raises further questions. In one sense it is a truism that unofficial strikes reflect inadequacies from the workers' viewpoint in the machinery of negotiation or in union organization, but sometimes a minority of trade unionists want to retain the advantages of national bargaining and collective agreements and yet be free to resort to direct action in violation of agreement when they are personally dissatisfied.

In the case of dock strikes, however, the existence of a strong unofficial movement does suggest that the union concerned, the Transport and General Workers, may have lost the confidence of a substantial section of its dockworkers' membership. Perhaps it is significant that this field of employment has seen the one experiment in Great Britain in which the trade unions have been directly involved in an employing authority. The National Dock Labour Board, composed in equal proportions of representatives of employers and trade unions with an independent chairman and vice-chairman, was set up mainly for the purpose of administering a scheme to provide the dockers with a guaranteed weekly wage.[35] It undertakes to supply the employers with labor and is responsible for registration, recruitment and dismissal, payment of wages, welfare, and discipline. Thus in the eyes of the workers the Board has virtually become the "boss." In a letter to the *Times* (August 6, 1949) Mr. T. Macpherson, a Labour M.P. and a member of the Port of London Authority, bluntly expressed the

---

[35] There are also local boards that have no independent members.

dangers that arise for responsible trade unions in this kind of arrangement:

> The trade union leader duly arrives on the scene and he turns out to be one of the employers—a paid member of the Dock Labour Board. Can you wonder that the docker does not understand it? He finds himself in dispute—rightly or wrongly—with his employer, he pays a trade union official to represent his case, and, lo and behold, when it comes to a fight his trade union leader is defending the bosses' point of view.

After the docks, coal mining has suffered most from stoppages of work. Although there has been a noticeable decline in the amount of working days lost since the nationalization of the industry, the number of strikes remains high. In 1950, coal mining was responsible for 863 stoppages out of a total of 1,338, and in every postwar year this proportion has been well over a half. It is difficult to find any deeper explanation for this fact than the traditional readiness of the miners to resort to direct action; attitudes hardened by decades of bitter experience cannot easily be changed, even by the best negotiating machinery or the new responsibilities of the unions under public ownership. In engineering, shipbuilding, and shiprepairing the chaotic state of the wage structure and the relatively bad union-employer relations in the industries have helped to engender local disputes.

If the causes of unofficial strikes have to be sought in the particular industries in which they have been most prevalent, at least it is apparent that in general the significance of strike action has greatly changed. Whereas a quarter of a century ago a strike, or the threat of it, was a part of union strategy and probably on a national scale, today it is frequently a form of local protest by a group of workers within the union against the decisions of their own organization.

Wages and employment

The main concern of the trade unions in their separate bargaining activities has been to raise, or, in times of depression, maintain the money wages of their members. Collective agreements in Great Britain cover a variety of other matters, including hours of works, piecework arrangements, overtime conditions, payment for holidays, employment of apprentices, training schemes, and provisions for a guaranteed week. In contrast to the American practice, however, they rarely deal with union recognition, security of employment according to seniority or work-sharing principles, or employer-financed welfare benefit programs. In the interwar years the length of the normal working week for most manual workers was 47 or 48 hours, and this has been reduced in the postwar years to 44 or 45 hours, usually spread over a five day week. Two weeks' holiday with pay in addition to the statutory holidays is fairly general now, although in some industries it remains at one week. Since it is impossible to give a brief survey of the diverse provisions which constitute the industrial achievements of the trade unions in the various industries, we will confine ourselves to an analysis of the general movement of wages in the past quarter of a century. Table 4 enables us to make a comparison between wage movements in two periods: 1924–1939, during which there was chronic unemployment; and 1939–1949, when after the outbreak of war full employment was soon established and continually maintained.

TABLE 4

INDEXES OF WAGES, PRICES AND UNEMPLOYMENT IN GREAT BRITAIN, 1924–1949

Year	Average Weekly Wage Rates*	Average Weekly Earnings	Cost of Living		Percent of Insured Industrial Population Unemployed
			Old Ministry of Labour index†	Index for Retail Prices‡	
		1938 = 100			
1924	96		112		10.2
1925	96		118		11.0
1926	96		110		12.3
1927	96		107		9.6
1928	96		106		10.7
1929	95		105		10.3
1930	94		101		15.8
1931	93		95		21.1
1932	92		92		21.9
1933	90		90		19.8
1934	90		90		16.6
1935	91		92		15.3
1936	93		94		13.0
1937	97		99		9.7
1938	100	100 (Oct.)	100	100	11.5
1939	101	—	101	102	9.6
1940	112	130 (July)	118	119	6.4
1941	122	142 "	127	130	2.3
1942	131	160 "	128	139	1.0
1943	138	176 "	127	143	0.7
1944	146	182 "	129	146	0.6
1945	154	180 "	130	148	1.2
1946	167	190 (Oct.)		150	2.4
1947	175	203 "		160	3.0
1948	188	220 "		173	1.7
1949	193½	229 "		178	1.5
1950	197	240 "		184	1.5

* Professor Bowley's index.
† Based on workers' family budgets in 1914.
‡ It is doubtful whether even this index fully reflects the increase in the cost of living.

Source: *London and Cambridge Economic Service*, Vol. XXIX, Bulletin 2 (May, 1951), Page 63; and (for earnings' figures) Ministry of *Labour Gazette*, Vol. LIX, No. 9 (September, 1951), page 345.

The main contrast between the two periods is the relative stability of wage rates in conditions of mass unemployment and their continued upward movement when a shortage of jobs gave place to a shortage of labor. The index for average wage rates shows a fall in the years of the Great Depression, 1929–1933, of some 5 per cent, which had been wiped out by 1937. Over the fifteen year period, 1924–1939, the total increase was no more than 5 per cent. In the full employment period the strongest upward movements in wage rates occurred in 1939–1942 and in 1945–1948, amounting on both occasions to some 30 per cent, an annual average of 10 per cent. Over the ten years 1939–1949 the total increase was more than 90 per cent. The rise in average earnings was greater.

When the changes in the cost of living are taken into account a different contrast is evidenced in the movement of real wages. There is little doubt, despite the inadequacies of the old Ministry of Labour index, that up to 1933 the real wages of the workers who were fortunate enough to have continuous employment were rising. They reaped the benefits of the collapse in world prices for foodstuffs and raw materials, a fact which was not without its influence on trade union policy, since the influence of the unemployed within the trade union movement was negligible. Subsequently when wages were increasing, they lagged behind the rising cost of living. During the early years of the war this became one of the main arguments advanced by the trade unions on behalf of wage claims, but, on the average, wages were soon rising more rapidly than the Ministry of Labour index, that is, than the extent which would be provided for under cost-of-living sliding scale agreements at the time. It was a part of government policy to peg this index, for example by food subsidies. The actual rise in retail prices, however, as measured subsequently by an improved index, was slightly in excess of the rise in wage rates until near the end of the war, when the loss in earnings resulting from decreased overtime and other factors developed a strong and effective trade union pressure for compensatory increases in wage rates in the years 1945–1947.

So far we have dealt with averages for the whole country. Since 1940 there has been a considerable shift in the relationship among various wage rates. In the period August 1939 to March 1950 representative wage rates in coal mining, agriculture, and cotton textiles rose by 185 per cent, 170 per cent, and 114 per cent respectively, whereas those of printers' compositors and railwaymen, to take but two examples of sheltered and strongly organized occupations, only increased by 70 per cent.[36] The wage-leveling effect of full employment is further illus-

[36] A. L. Bowley, *London and Cambridge Economic Service,* "Wage Rates and Earnings," Vol. XXVIII, Bulletin II (May, 1950), page 57.

trated by changes in average earnings in different industries, as shown in Table 5.

TABLE 5

AVERAGE EARNINGS IN SELECTED INDUSTRIES, OCTOBER 1938 AND APRIL 1948

	Average Weekly Earnings Last Pay Week		Percentage Increase 1938 to 1948	
	Oct., 1938	Apr., 1948	Weekly	Hourly
	s. d.	s. d.		
Greatest increases				
Cotton	35 7	96 6	171	177
Pottery, earthenware, etc.	36 10	94 3	156	153
Hemp, rope, etc.	31 2	79 1	154	167
Bolts, nuts, screws, etc.	42 4	105 10	150	164
Other textiles	34 7	86 1	149	165
Tailoring, wholesale	34 5	84 6	146	152
Leather goods	34 10	85 8	146	168
Rubber	51 0	124 3	144	152
Dyeing, dry cleaning, etc.	35 4	85 5	142	141
Woollen and worsted	39 0	94 3	142	143
Smallest increases				
Government industrial establishments	—	119 0	69	82
Tailoring, retail	44 9	78 4	75	84
Local authorities (non-trading).	54 6	96 4	77	85
Electricity supply	68 9	123 2	79	90
Water supply	64 0	116 3	82	90
Printing, publishing, etc.	64 0	118 5	83	90
Docks, harbors, canals, etc.	73 0	135 5	83	78
Tramway, omnibus, etc.	68 7	124 11	84	92
Tobacco, cigars, cigarettes	47 7	88 0	85	97
Pig iron	79 11	149 0	86	85

Source: *Ministry of Labour Gazette*, Vol. XLVIII, No. 11 (November, 1940), pages 281–282; Vol. XLVIII, No. 12 (December, 1940), pages 306–307; Vol. LVI, No. 10 (October, 1948) pages 335 ff.

It will be noted that the greatest increase in earnings took place in those industries where prior to the war they were relatively low, and the smallest mainly in the industries in which they were relatively high. In the same period the earnings of women and juveniles have also increased a good deal more than those of adult males.

Another aspect of this trend toward wage leveling in times of labor shortage and rising money wages is the narrowing of the relative skill differentials in particular industries, illustrated in Table 6. The relative stability of the skill differential in the periods 1885–1914 and 1924–1939 may be compared with its contraction in the periods 1914–1924 and 1939–1950. Salaries have also increased to a smaller extent than wages since 1938.[37]

---

[37] See Dudley Seers, *The Levelling of Incomes Since 1938*, page 60. Oxford: Blackwell, 1951.

TABLE 6

SKILL DIFFERENTIALS IN FOUR INDUSTRIES

(Time rate of unskilled as percentage
of that of skilled workers)

	Building	Shipbuilding	Engineering	Railways
1885	63.6	54	60	50.5*
1914	66.5	55.2	58.6	54.3
1924	75.6	68.8	70.9	68.1
1939	76.3	73.4	75.6	61.5
1950	84.1	81.7	84.7	77.4

* The year 1886.
Source: Kenneth Knowles and D. J. Robertson, "Differences Between the Wages of Skilled and Unskilled Workers, 1880–1950," *Bulletin of Oxford University Institute of Statistics*, Vol. XIII, No. 4 (April, 1951), page 111.

It is not difficult to find an explanation both for the general upward movement of wages and for the changes in the wages structure in conditions of full employment. The bargaining power of the trade unions, and of individual workers, is greatly enhanced and the resistance of many employers to wage increases is diminished since they are more able to pass on added wage costs through higher prices without suffering any reduction in the volume of their sales. Many of them may even be anxious to increase wages in order to attract labor and increase their production. Once wages rise more rapidly than the available results of increased productivity, the wage-price spiral is set in motion with its cumulative effects. The pace of this development cannot be decided theoretically, but as Lord Beveridge pointed out in his *Full Employment in a Free Society:* ". . . there is no inherent mechanism in our present system which can with certainty prevent competitive sectional bargaining for wages from setting up a vicious spiral of rising prices under full employment."

Some of the reasons for the changes within the wage structure are fairly obvious. The fear of unemployment compelled most wage-earners to stay in whatever jobs they had. Some of the more arduous and less pleasant occupations remained among the worst paid, wages varying according to ease of entry, the prosperity of the industry, the degree of organization among the workers and other factors. The greater freedom which full employment gives to wage-earners in their choice of a job changes this state of affairs and tends over the years to establish a closer and more equitable relationship between the remuneration attached to a particular occupation and the sum total of satisfactions and dissatisfactions that it involves. Hence the existence of undermanned industries in postwar Britain. The labor controls, which existed during the war, hampered this change but only to some extent; in a democracy such controls cannot be made so effective as to obstruct strong economic pulls.

It is important to note in connection with both these consequences of full employment the particular influence of what Lord Beveridge calls the "competitive sectional" character of collective bargaining. Unions have lived by securing wage advances and the power and prestige of union officials still depend, at least in part, on their capacity to obtain greater or earlier advances than their competitors. Where any one union is in a strong position, for whatever reasons, to force up the wages of its members, its example is likely to be followed by other unions seeking to maintain the customary wage relationships. This tends to make a wage increase given at any one point in the system spread throughout until it becomes general, thus discouraging the movement of workers into those industries or occupations where they are most needed and intensifying the danger of the vicious spiral.

The shifts in the wage structure from 1939 to 1949 may appear to invalidate this proposition. Certainly they are evidence that trade unions do not bring as complete a rigidity into wage relationships and the labor market as has frequently been suggested. But the effect of maintaining compulsory arbitration throughout the period, after its introduction in July 1940, must be taken into account, since it has restrained the trade unions from using their bargaining power to the full. They have of necessity resorted to arbitration to a far greater extent than in any previous period, and the various arbitration tribunals, although not subject to government direction, have naturally given more weight to the national consequences of their awards than any particular group of employers and trade unions would be likely to do in arriving at a wage settlement.

Postwar wage policy

During World War II the policy somewhat misleadingly described as "wage stablization" depended for its success mainly on the pegging of a very imperfect wage-earners' cost of living index by food subsidies, rationing and price control and on the acceptance by the trade unions of compulsory arbitration. By the latter half of 1947, however, it was evident that this wartime policy was breaking down. The new interim index of retail prices adopted in June of that year provided a truer reflection of the changes in the cost of living: it rose from 101 to 108 points in the six-month period October 1947 to April 1948. Wage increases which were essential in the undermanned industries were stimulating fresh claims elsewhere. Most trade unions were acting on the assumption that restraint was no longer necessary now that the war was over. Many employers were ready to increase wages in order to attract labor to their own firms.

In this situation the Labour Government had to act if the whole of its postwar economic policy was not to be placed in jeopardy. It had previously asked the T.U.C. General Council to consider the subject of wage policy without obtaining any constructive response. To meet the problem of the undermanned industries they had preferred to accept the reintroduction of the Control of Engagements Order supported by limited powers of direction, but this measure was not likely to curb the rising level of wages. In February 1948 the government issued a White Paper, its *Statement on Personal Incomes, Costs and Prices.* This came as a complete surprise to the trade unions. The T.U.C. immediately lodged a protest with the Prime Minister "against this departure from the established practice of prior consultation." The White Paper was a declaration of policy couched in general terms. While stating that "there was no justification at the present time for any rise in incomes from profits, rent or other like sources" and recognizing that there might "well be cases in which increases in wages and salaries would be justified from a national point of view," it declared that "each claim for an increase . . . must be considered on its national merits, not on the basis of maintaining a former relativity between different occupations and industries." Only the case of the undermanned industries was mentioned as an illustration.

The T.U.C. General Council called a conference of trade union executives to consider the White Paper and by a substantial majority the conference agreed that:

. . . the principles of the White Paper relating to wage movements are acceptable to the Trade Union Movement to the extent that they:

(a) recognise the necessity of retaining unimpaired the system of collective bargaining and free negotiation;

(b) admit the justification for claims for increased wages where those claims are based upon the fact of increased output;

(c) admit the necessity of adjusting the wages of workers whose incomes are below a reasonable standard of subsistence;

(d) affirm that it is in the national interest to establish standards of wages and conditions in undermanned essential industries in order to attract sufficient manpower; and

(e) recognise the need to safeguard those wage differentials which are an essential element in the wages structure of many important industries and are required to sustain those standards of craftsmanship, training and experience that contribute directly to industrial efficiency and higher productivity.

The government gave no indication of what it thought of this interpretation of its policy. Taken severally, and without further definition it was obvious that the last four clauses would provide grounds enough for most trade unions to argue that the satisfaction of their wage demands was in the national interest.

But though the trade union movement had only pledged itself to restrict its wage demands to those which were compatible with the terms of its own declaration, in practice it went a good deal further. The attempt was made, and for a time successfully, to hold back as far as possible all wage demands on the grounds of Britain's difficult economic situation. The Ministry of Labour's index of full-time weekly wage rates, which had risen by six points in the year preceding June 1948, gained but another four points during the following two years.

The government proposed no sanctions for the enforcement of its policy other than the threat to use its powers for controlling prices to prevent the passing on to the consumer of any increased wage costs which could not be justified by the principles of the White Paper. This served to stiffen the employers' resistance to wage increases but the burden of restraint fell largely upon the trade unions, or more exactly upon their leadership. The tentative approach to defining the terms of a national wage policy was not followed up. From time to time there were references by government spokesmen and trade union leaders to the justification of wage increases for lower-paid workers but even this one objective remained undefined.

This policy of voluntary restraint, buttressed by the continued voluntary acceptance of compulsory arbitration on the part of the trade unions, was already breaking down under inevitable, internal union pressures when the pound was devalued in September 1949. Devaluation administered a shock to the trade union movement with the result that the T.U.C. General Council after long deliberations produced a recommendation in favor of what amounted to a wage stop until the end of 1950, providing the index of retail prices remained within the upper and lower limits of 118 and 106, but a further conference of trade union executives called to consider this recommendation in January 1950 approved it by so narrow a majority that it could not be put into operation. By June the General Council had had their second thoughts and sent out a statement to affiliated unions recognizing "that there must be greater flexibility of wage movements in the future" but stating that they were "firmly convinced that there is no formula which can be devised as to how this flexibility should operate." Three months later the Congress met and decided by a small majority (3,898,000 to 3,521,000 votes) to refer back the section of the General Council's report containing this modified advocacy of restraint.

Clearly trade union consent is required for the introduction of any control over wage movements. For this reason the Labour Government understandably preferred to place the problems before the leadership of the trade union movement and to leave them as far as possible to work out their own solutions. This has had the advantage of encouraging them to look at wage issues in their full economic context, to give real wages as much significance as money wages and to relate both to fiscal policy. The hope has been that if the trade unions were collectively to adopt their own national wage policy, to which they were prepared to subordinate their individual demands, the dangers arising on account of the competitive, sectional aspects of collective bargaining would be overcome. The example of Norway has frequently been cited to show that this is possible once the unions are prepared to give sufficient authority to their central body. For several reasons there is little promise of such a development in Great Britain. The unions cling stubbornly to their own autonomy in such matters; judging by the debates in recent Trade Union Congresses any attempt to strengthen the powers of the General Council would be decidedly unpopular. Moreover, the conflicting interests of craft, industrial and general workers' unions within the movement would be a serious obstacle to agreement. The author holds the view, developed elsewhere,[38] that a stronger initiative on the part of the government is required if criteria and methods are to be evolved which will permit the merits of competitive wage claims to be judged within the limits set by productivity changes.

Participation in control

The Webbs concluded their *Industrial Democracy* with the observation that "the very fact that, in modern society, the individual . . . necessarily loses control over his own life, makes him desire to regain collectively what has become individually impossible." Unfortunately it is also true that modern society tends to destroy the individual's confidence in his capacity to control his own life and thus to weaken his feeling of personal responsibility for his social environment. This may well prove to be the gravest problem of our time. However, the growth of trade unionism has undoubtedly contributed to the awakening among wage-earners of an awareness of their own dignity and importance, and this has found expression in demands for more than a larger pay envelope and greater leisure. There is a long tradition among British trade unions in favor of the workers having a say in the management and control of the industries in which they are employed, as well as in the determination of their wages and working conditions.

Although theoretical syndicalism of the type that once flourished in

---

[38] See Allan Flanders, *A Policy for Wages*, Fabian Tract No. 281, 1950. London: Fabian Society; "Wages Policy and Full Employment in Britain," *Bulletin of the Oxford University Institute of Statistics*, Vol. XII, Nos. 7 and 8 (July and August, 1950).

France was too rigid a doctrine to gain a hold on the British labor movement, the idea of "workers' control" had found many supporters among the militant trade unionists by the advent of World War I. In 1912 the South Wales miners published *The Miners' Next Step,* which propagated the view that mines should be run by the miners. In the unofficial shop stewards' movement, which became a powerful force in the main industrial centers during the war, the same ideas were current. They seemed no more than the logical outcome of the class struggle, the existence of which the workers' daily experience confirmed. Since it was necessary to get rid of the capitalists, how could this be done if the workers were not prepared, through their trade unions, to take over and run the industries themselves? Only in the intellectual world did this wave of syndicalism find a theoretical expression in gild socialism, which reached the zenith of its influence at this time.

Apart from the failure of the experimental gilds that were set up by trade unionists, mainly in the building industry, two events in the postwar years struck mortal blows at the syndicalist approach, the collapse of the Triple Alliance in 1921 and the General Strike of 1926, although neither invalidated its principles. The syndicalists had preached the gospel of "direct action" for the achievement of their ends and, so far as most industrial workers were concerned, it had failed the pragmatic test.

In the following years, under the leadership of Walter Citrine and Ernest Bevin, the British trade union movement adopted a new approach to the control of industry. Industrial peace and collaboration with the employers were gradually accepted as desirable. Accordingly the unions were urged to declare that the efficiency and prosperity of industry were their immediate concern and on this basis of responsible partnership to stake their claim for a greater say in management. The demand for "workers' control" had not been entirely abandoned but was now being pressed in a different context to the one in which it had been conceived. No longer linked with doctrine of class warfare, it had been placed on a more realistic footing by the unions' acceptance of responsibilities within the existing economic order.

It was not until 1932 that the Trades Union Congress, which had steadily been strengthening its moral authority, attempted for the first time to state on behalf of the whole of the trade union movement, the kind of industrial reorganization it should seek to bring about. The proposals coincided with those which in the Labour Party had found their strong advocate in Herbert Morrison, whose *Socialisation and Transport* was published in 1933. The public corporation was the chosen form for those industries considered "ripe for socialization."

The T.U.C. General Council's Report in dealing with the composition of the boards which were to administer publicly-owned industries suggested that:

. . . members of such a Board should in all cases be appointed by the Government, and should consist neither of technical experts nor of representatives of particular interests, but of persons appointed solely for their ability to fill the position.

This point led to lively debates at both the Trades Union Congresses and the Labour Party Conferences in the next few years. The critics, including Ernest Bevin and Charles Dukes, the leaders of the two powerful general workers' unions, maintained that this did not meet the unions' demand for a measure of direct participation in management. The General Council withdrew their report for further examination and proceeded, jointly with the National Executive of the Labour Party, to draft a statement which recognized the demand of the unions to *nominate* persons for appointment to the public boards. This was given general approval by the annual conferences of both bodies in 1933, although the Labour Party Conference also carried a resolution declaring that the unions should have a *statutory right* to a fifty per cent representation on the boards of nationalized industries.

The next move came in 1943 when the Trades Union Congress instructed the General Council to prepare a *Report on Post-War Reconstruction.* Next year the report was issued and accepted unanimously by the Congress. It recommended that where industries were nationalized the governing boards should include members with a wide experience in the trade union movement, but that these members "should surrender any position held in, or any formal responsibility to the trade unions." Two reasons were advanced for the recommendation: (1) The trade unions must retain their complete independence, their right to bargain and criticize, and this would be endangered if they were previously compromised by the participation of their representatives in the boards' decisions; (2) Control over the policy and direction of a public industry must be exercised ultimately by Parliament as representatives of the whole community, and immediately by individuals unfettered by any other considerations than those of the public interest. At the same time the views of the trade unions on the administration and management of the industries should be taken into account by the formation of consultative councils at all levels of organization, on which they would be directly represented, a proposal which might fairly be described as a belated triumph for "Whitleyism." In privately-owned industry, the same Report suggested that, apart from various measures of public control which should be applied to the whole economy, industrial boards should be set up "composed of representatives of work people and employers in equal proportion and an impartial chairman and other independent members appointed and paid by the Government" whose main purpose would be "to interpret the industry's requirements to the Government and to apply the Government's requirements to the industry."

After the 1945 election victory of the Labour Party, when the first nationalization bills were being introduced in Parliament, no substantial points of difference arose between the Labour Government and the trade union movement. In fact the proposed legislation closely followed the T.U.C.'s own proposals. The first industry to be nationalized was coal mining. Two members of the original National Coal Board, appointed by the government, were trade unionists, and in the Act a statutory obligation was laid upon the Board to establish and maintain joint machinery for consultation with the unions on (1) questions relating to safety, health and welfare; and (2) the organization and conduct of operations on which coal miners are employed and any other matters of mutual interest. The National Union of Mineworkers was wholly satisfied with this type of organization.

Dissatisfaction with the organization of the nationalized industries was first voiced in 1948 both at the Labour Party Conference and at the Trades Union Congress. At the former conference a resolution asking for "workers' participation through their trade unions in the direction and management of nationalised industries at all levels" was supported by three large unions, the Amalgamated Engineering Union, the Union of Post Office Workers, and the National Union of Railwaymen. The resolution was opposed by the National Union of Mineworkers and the Transport and General Workers' Union, and was withdrawn on the understanding that the Labour Party and the T.U.C. would have joint discussions on the subject. At the Trades Union Congress a compromise resolution was accepted which expressed "concern" at the composition of the boards of the nationalized industries and demanded in effect the inclusion of more trade unionists on them.

Obviously the idea of "workers' control" was far from dead. This was strikingly illustrated at the 1949 biennial conference of the Transport and General Workers' Union, where a resolution was carried by 433 votes to 170, despite the opposition of the general executive council, "that trade union representatives should be placed on these boards and executives [*that is, those in the nationalized industries*] with the right of the members to recall such trade union representatives as and when considered necessary." The same conference carried another resolution by 426 votes to 208 to exclude any member of the Communist Party from holding office in the union. The demand for direct representation is being voiced by the communists for their own purposes at the present time, and in some cases, the Electrical Trades Union, for example, the insistence upon workers' control can partly be explained as a result of their influence. A comparison of the two votes at the Transport and General Workers' Conference, however, showed that there is still a large body of vocal trade union opinion in favor of a change in the present method of appointment to the public boards, which is not the product of communist agitation.

At the 1949 Congress the T.U.C. General Council reported the results of their promised investigation into the structure and conduct of the nationalized industries. Apart from repeating the suggestion that a higher portion of the board members should be drawn from the trade union movement, their report was mainly concerned with advocating improvements in the actual working of the consultative machinery. It emphasized that, as far as possible, consultation should always take place *before* policy decisions had been reached by management, that trade unions and management should promote training in the methods and purposes of joint consultation on an extensive scale, and that more attention should be paid to improving the procedures for promotion within the nationalized industries. At the Congress itself there was little debate on the subject and the General Council has subsequently remained unchallenged in its continued rejection of direct representation.

The T.U.C.'s postwar reconstruction proposal for industrial boards in privately-owned industry has also been carried out by the Labour Government in the Industrial Organization and Development Act of 1947. This empowered the responsible minister, the President of the Board of Trade, to set up a development council and assign to it any of twenty functions, if he was satisfied that such a council was needed in the industry and a substantial number of those engaged in the industry desired to see one established. Although statutory bodies appointed by the government, the development councils are independent entities, acting as a bridge between the government and the industry, and are a forum and a clearing house for ideas within the industry itself. Their compulsory powers are severely limited to three. They can raise funds by means of a levy on the industry (subject to a maximum). They can require members of the industry to supply certain information (subject to the consent of the Minister). They can maintain a register of persons carrying on business in the industry (but they have not the right to refuse registration or impose conditions on new entrants). Since the Act has been in force, progress in forming development councils has been disappointingly slow. In the first year the only council to be set up was one for the cotton industry, where there already existed the wartime Cotton Board with similar powers. Since then they have been formed for the furniture, jewelry and silverware, and clothing industries.

Production and joint consultation

The attitude of the British trade unions to production problems has been greatly, if only gradually changed by conditions of full employment. In times of chronic unemployment the trade unions can hardly be expected to display much enthusiasm for new machinery and labor-saving improvements in industrial organization, since they often have good reason to fear that more of their members may become unemployed as a consequence. In the interwar years the employment policies of the trade unions were either directed towards sharing out the available work among a larger number of people (a shorter working week, an increase in the school-leaving age and the introduction of retirement pensions were measures given prominence) or else tended to be sectional, with those unions in a position to maintain them relying upon restrictive practices to protect the employment of their own members. Full employment has not only helped to remove the fears responsible for negative attitudes towards production. It has made their replacement by positive attitudes imperative. In the first place the trade unions have come to realize that any substantial improvement in the standard of living of their members depends upon raising the level of productivity, which cannot be accomplished without their assistance. But also the success of full employment itself depends on the development of new, voluntary incentives to effort when the threat of the "sack" has lost much of its power to coerce.

This is a part of the case for the development of joint consultation in postwar Britain, but not the whole of it. The workers' claim to be consulted by management before decisions are taken which can affect their welfare is fundamentally a moral one. It rests on its own merits regardless of the economic results. The worker's interests in relation to his work are manifold. He is concerned, of course, with how much he gets for it, how long and how hard he has to work, that is, the terms of his employment, which today, in most cases, are regulated by collective agreements. He is also concerned with the way in which he is treated, whether, for example, he is treated with respect as an intelligent, responsible and sensitive human being. Similarly he may be interested in the way in which his work is organized, in the kind of job he is given to do, not only from the point of view of how much it pays, but whether it makes sense, whether his time is being wasted, whether he may take some pride in the result. These are matters where conflicts of interest may arise between management and men that usually cannot be settled by the terms of a collective agreement. Joint consultation may therefore be regarded as a method that enables the trade unions to extend their protective function far beyond what they have been able to achieve in the past by the negotiation of agreements, if only for the reason that the range of interests which can be protected is greatly extended, even though cooperation rather than conflict is its aim.

During the early years of the war the trade unions demanded from the government a more active production policy, in which they could participate. Significantly enough, it was a committee under the chairmanship of the general secretary of the T.U.C. (then Sir Walter Citrine) that worked out the plans for the reorganization of war production. After the Ministry of Production had been formed in 1942, a three level system of organization was adopted to assist the government in this respect. A National Production Advisory Committee was created at the center, with various industrial panels; similarly, eleven regional boards assisted by district committees were established in important towns and localities; and the setting up of joint production committees was encouraged in individual establishments. By June, 1944, as many as 4,565 committees were operating in private firms in the engineering and allied industries. Not all or even the majority of them were unqualified successes but they helped to bring about a more cooperative approach to production problems on the part of management and workpeople. At the regional and national levels a good deal was done to break bottlenecks and to supply the government with industrial advice. Most of this wartime machinery was retained with modifications in the postwar period. The National Production Advisory Council of Industry and the National Joint Advisory Council to the Minister of Labour are two important central bodies assisting the government in the execution of its economic policy. The tasks of the regional boards were adjusted to peacetime requirements. Most of the joint production committees, however, collapsed when the war was over.

In January, 1947, the government brought up the question of reviving the practice of joint consultation at the factory level in privately owned industry at the National Joint Advisory Council to the Minister of Labour. (The nationalized industries, as we have seen, were under a statutory commitment to arrange for consultation at all levels in their organization.) The Council agreed to recommend to employers' associations and trade unions, the setting up of joint consultative machinery, where it did not already exist, subject to the following qualifications:

(a) that such machinery would be voluntary and advisory in character;

(b) that it would not deal with questions relating to terms and conditions of employment which are normally dealt with through the ordinary machinery of joint negotiation;

(c) that it would be left to each industry, through its ordinary negotiation arrangements, to adopt the form of machinery best suited to its own particular circumstances, and to decide, in particular, *whether such machinery could best be established at the factory level or cover a wider area* (author's italics).

Inquiries made by the Ministry of Labour showed that by the end of 1949 in 54 major industries, 26 had agreed to recommend the establishment of joint committees in factory or workshop—13 of these had drawn up a model constitution for such committees—and 17 had decided that initiative should be left to individual firms and workpeople. Eight other industries were of the opinion that the existing joint machinery was adequate for dealing with matters requiring joint consultation, and the remaining 3 had not reached any conclusion.

In most large firms there is some provision for joint consultation but progress has been slow in extending the practice to the greater part of industry. It cannot be said that the employers' associations or the trade unions have put much drive into the campaign; in most cases the initiative has been left to both sides within the individual establishments. The main impetus has come from the government. The regional officers of the Ministry of Labour and the regional boards for industry were asked to take an active interest in the matter and help in the formation of joint consultative committees where there was a desire on both sides to form them and suitable agreements existed. Slow progress on a voluntary basis has raised the question whether the practice should be made compulsory by law in all but the smallest factories, but both the employers' associations and the majority of trade unions are opposed to this course on the grounds that the necessary goodwill cannot be created by legislation.

Political objectives and achievements

The close association between the British trade unions and the Labour Party, which they helped to create, has meant that in the past half century they have relied largely upon that party for the realization of their political objectives. It was not always so. When the Webbs wrote their *Industrial Democracy* (first published in 1897) they contended that when the Trades Union Congress

. . . diverges from its narrow Trade Union function, and expresses any opinion, either on general social reforms or party politics, it is bound to alienate whole sections of its constituents. The Trade Unions join the Congress for the promotion of a Parliamentary policy desired, not merely by a majority, but by all of them; and it is a violation of the implied contract between them to use the political force, towards the creation of which all are contributing, for the purposes of any particular political party. The Trade Unionists of Northumberland and Durham are predominantly Liberal. Those of Lancashire are largely Conservative. Those of Yorkshire and London, again, are deeply impregnated with Socialism.[39]

The resolution passed at the Trades Union Congress in 1899 which led to the establishment of the Labour Representation Committee in the following year (it changed its name to that of Labour Party in 1906) was carried by no more than 546,000 votes to 434,000. Moreover:

The Parliamentary Committee of the Trades Union Congress, including as it did many who were hostile to the entire project, did not itself undertake the arrangements for the Conference, but left them to a committee on which the Socialist societies were strongly represented. Consequently, these bodies, especially the Independent Labour Party, were able to shape the proceedings pretty much as they desired.[40]

Yet between 1900 and 1912 the trade union affiliated membership of the Labour Party rose from 353,000 to 1,858,000, with the powerful Miners' Federation deciding to join the new party as late as 1910. The change in trade union attitude, from a lukewarm interest in independent labor representation in Parliament to a firm commitment in support of one political party, was more than anything else the result of the *Taff Vale* and *Osborne* Judgments, a fact often expressed in the aphorism that the House of Lords made the Labour Party. After the *Taff Vale* Judgment the unions faced the need for legislative action to protect their funds from attack. When in 1906 the Liberal Government was compelled under Labour Party pressure to withdraw its own unsatisfactory measure in favor of the Trades Disputes Act which met the trade union demands in full, they found that they could better rely on a weak party in which their influence was strong than a strong party in which their influence was weak. The reversal of the *Osborne* Judgment by the 1913 Trade Union Act made it possible for the trade unions to spend money on political objects, if they met with their members' consent, and thus provided a legal basis for their relationship with the Labour Party.

---

[39] Sidney and Beatrice Webb, *Industrial Democracy*, page 271. London: Longmans Green & Co., Ltd., 1920. By permission of the Trustees of the late Lord Passfield.

[40] G. D. H. Cole, *British Working Class Politics, 1832–1914*, page 155. London: Routledge & Kegan Paul, 1950.

The reorganization of the Labour Party in 1918 transformed it from a federation, able to act only through its affiliated societies, into a full-blooded political party with an individual as well as an affiliated membership and local organizations of its own in every parliamentary constituency. It also accepted for the first time a socialist objective:

To secure for the producers by hand or by brain the full fruits of their industry, and the most equitable distribution thereof that may be possible, upon the basis of the common ownership of the means of production and the best obtainable system of popular administration and control of each industry and service.

Nevertheless, the effect of the new constitution was to strengthen the influence of the trade unions within the party. The experiences of the war had made a deep impression on trade union opinion and the new generation of trade union leaders had no qualms about supporting so general an expression of socialist aspiration, which could be stretched to cover the various shades of collectivist, cooperative and syndicalist thought.

Up to the General Strike of 1926, however, the main emphasis in the trade union world, at least on the part of those who looked beyond "pure and simple" trade unionism, was upon "workers' control" and its achievement by industrial action. What happened during the short period of office of the first minority Labour Government in 1924 did little to convince the trade unions that they should place their faith in Parliament for the achievement of their ends. Yet it was the lessons drawn from the wage conflicts of the postwar years which subsequently led the British trade unions to become more deeply involved in politics. If in the past they had, as the Webbs suggested, used the method of legal enactment to extend and safeguard their rights and for the same protective purposes as collective bargaining, after the "new approach" had been adopted in the Mond-Turner conversations, political action gradually became the means of extending their influence within the broader field of economic government. The limits to what could be achieved by a readiness to strike in adverse economic conditions, falling prices and mass unemployment, had been painfully demonstrated between 1920 and 1926.

In the lectures that Walter Citrine delivered at the T.U.C. Summer School in 1929 can be found a statement of what became the guiding conception in the next two decades. The development of the economic system, he argued, was toward concentration of ownership and central direction of industry. This emphasis on the regulative as opposed to the competitive principle should be welcomed by trade unions. Without it the control of industry which they had advocated would be impossible; with it their claim to participate in such control would be irresistible. The unions should boldly declare that the efficiency and prosperity of industry was their immediate concern and for this reason demand a greater say in deciding how it was to be conducted. This general approach, however, could be interpreted in two ways, very different in their social significance. The regulative principle could be applied by *capitalist monopolies* conceding a kind of junior partnership to the trade unions in their industries but excluding public influence, a policy euphemistically described as "industrial self-government" in a manifesto of 120 leading industrialists issued during World War II, or by the *government* through measures of nationalization, public planning and control with the cooperation of both sides of industry. Within the trade union world there were forces pushing in both directions. How far it was the unions' association with the Labour Party that prevented them from following the former course may some day be revealed; but the T.U.C.'s 1944 *Report on Post-War Reconstruction* showed a decided preference for public control, and the Labour Party's 1945 election program was drafted on similar lines.

Certainly for the trade unions the postwar Labour Governments brought many substantial gains that could not possibly have been obtained by industrial action. The maintenance of full employment, the completion of the social security system, including measures like the 1946 Industrial Injuries Act, the introduction of the National Health Service, the housing policy, with its insistence that most of the new building should provide homes for workers and let at rents they could afford to pay, the continuation of rationing, food subsidies, utility production and price control, besides the repeal of the 1927 Trades Disputes and Trade Unions Act, are obvious illustrations. The loyalty of the organized workers to the Labour Government was no mere sentimental act, but reflected their satisfaction with the change in their position as compared with the interwar years. Without this loyalty the adoption even for a time of the policy of wage restraint would have been impossible.

The best analysis of the overall effects of Britain's wartime and postwar economic policy on the distribution of income can be found in a study made by Dudley Seers on *The Levelling of Incomes Since 1938*, from which the following statistics are taken to illustrate the progress which has been made toward a more egalitarian society.

TABLE 7
PERCENTAGE INCREASE IN PRETAX PRIVATE INCOME, 1938–1949

Distributed property income	+ 32	
Undistributed corporate profits	+255	
Property income		+ 83
Professional earnings	+105	
Income from farming	+355	
Sole traders' profits	+ 66	
Mixed income		+101
Wages	+147	
Salaries	+103	
Armed forces pay	+214	
Work income		+132
Social security benefits	+157	
War pensions, etc.	+221	
Social income		+167
Total increase		+117

Source: Dudley Seers, *The Levelling of Incomes Since 1938,* page 50. Oxford: Blackwell, 1951.

As we look down the table from property to social income, which means, broadly speaking, looking from the incomes of the rich to those of the poor, the percentage increases become larger for each major group of incomes. When the effects of taxation and price changes are taken into account, the improvement in the position of wage-earners at the expense of property owners is particularly noticeable.

TABLE 8
PERCENTAGE SHARE IN POSTTAX PERSONAL INCOME AT 1938 PRICES

	1938	1949
Distributed property income	20	10
Mixed income	12	10
Total work income		
wages	37	47
salaries	23	22
armed forces pay	2	3
	—	—
	62	71
Social income	6	9
	—	—
	100	100

Source: Dudley Seers, *The Levelling of Incomes Since 1938,* page 55.

This table, it is true, deals only with the distribution of real, spendable incomes. Property owners have benefited by the rise in undistributed profits, which increased 2.3 times in the same period, although their real value has not greatly changed. If these figures are taken as some measure of the results of political action by organized labor, they can well be contrasted with the proposition established by Michael Kalecki that the relative share of manual labor in the national income in Great Britain remained remarkably stable, in the neighborhood of 40 to 43 per cent, over the whole period 1880 to 1935, despite trade fluctuations and the growth of trade unionism and collective bargaining.[41]

Trade Unions, the Labour Party, and the State
Links with the Labour Party

It is a mistake to assume that because today most of the trade unions stand solidly behind the Labour Party they have forfeited their independence or ceased to function as trade unions. The ties between the unions and the Labour Party are exceedingly complex, which may explain the conflicting views sometimes advanced in regard to this relationship. The question frequently asked in other countries is whether the trade unions control the Labour Party or the Labour Party controls the trade unions. In fact neither interpretation would be true. Naturally the trade unions have an influence on Labour Party policy, but theirs is one influence among several and it is not uniform in character. On the whole it is probably more negative than positive: It would be difficult for the Labour Party (or a Labour Government) to disregard any strong and widely held trade union opinion, but policy, except in those matters with which the unions are intimately concerned, is rarely initiated by the trade union wing of the Party. The trade unions for their part are·usually careful not to act in such a way as to injure the Labour Party's prospects, but there is no merging of identities. The Trades Union Congress, which represents them collectively, is very much a separate entity, following political objectives derived from basic trade union purposes. Thus it is not uncommon for the Trades Union Congress and the Labour Party to take a different view upon a subject, although they then endeavor to reach agreement, or at least to avoid any violent conflict in public. All this becomes clearer when we look more closely at the nature of the ties between them.

Not all trade unions affiliated to the Trades Union Congress are also affiliated to the Labour Party. In 1949 the comparative figures were:

	No. of Unions	Affiliated membership
Labour Party	80	4,946,207
Trades Union Congress	186	7,883,355

[41] Michael Kalecki, *Essays in the Theory of Economic Fluctuations*, page 16. London: Allen and Unwin, 1939.

With the exception of the civil service unions other than the Union of Post Office Workers, most of the hundred or so T.U.C. unions not affiliated to the Labour Party are small; the largest, the National Union of Hosiery Workers, has 37,000 members. The total membership of the Labour Party in 1949 was 5,716,947, its individual membership amounting to 729,624. In the same year the trade unions paid £125,828 in affiliation fees out of the total party fees of £144,884, and £148,315 to the General Election Fund out of a total of £156,286. The Labour Party is thus greatly dependent upon the trade unions for its income.

In the past thirty years the trade union membership of the Labour Party has been particularly affected both by changes in the total number of trade unionists and by the 1927 Trade Disputes and Trade Unions Act and its repeal in 1946. Under the 1913 Act trade unionists who had other party allegiances, or for other reasons did not wish to contribute to the political funds of their unions were able to "contract out" of paying the political levy. The 1927 Act reversed this procedure; members of unions who wished to pay the political levy had to "contract in" by signing a written undertaking to this effect. With the repeal of this Act there was, of course, a return to the previous practice. The combined effect of the two factors can be observed in the following table:

TABLE 9

TRADE UNION AFFILIATION WITH THE LABOUR PARTY

	Trade union membership of Labour Party (in millions)	Total membership of Trade unions (in millions)
1920	4.3	8.3
1927	3.2	4.9
1928	2.0	4.8
1934	1.9	4.6
1946	2.6	8.8
1947	4.4	9.1
1949	4.9	9.3

Source: *Report* of 1950 Annual Conference of Labour Party, page 35; *Ministry of Labour Gazette*, Vol. XLIII. No. 10 (October 1935), page 373; and Vol. LVIII, No. 11 (November 1950), page 366.

The table makes it necessary to draw attention to a significant development in the period of "contracting in" when, after, 1933 trade union membership began steadily to increase, while the proportion of members paying political levy declined. In the case of registered trade unions with political funds this proportion fell from 57.7 per cent in 1934 to 41.8 per cent in 1943, after which year it began to increase again, jumping up to nearly 91 per cent in 1947 after the repeal of the 1927 Act.

The practice of sponsoring candidates for Parliament has been a part of trade union practice since 1874, but with the creation of the Labour Party they gradually came under its banner. Today only the National Union of Teachers, which is not affiliated to the T.U.C., follows the practice of sponsoring candidates in all political parties. On the whole the trade union sponsored candidates tend to get the safer seats because the unions are disinclined to spend their members' money on supporting a candidate whose chances are slight. Consequently the smaller the number of Labour M.P.s returned, the larger is the proportion of trade union members, as the following table shows:

TABLE 10

TRADE UNION SPONSORSHIP OF LABOUR CANDIDATES IN GENERAL ELECTIONS

	Number of Labour Candidates	Number returned	Percentage returned	Candidates returned as percentage of total returned
1950 Election				
Trade Union	140	110	78	35
Others	472	205	43	65
		315		
1945 Election				
Trade Union	125	120	96	30
Others	478	273	57	70
		393		
1935 Election				
Trade Union	128	79	62	51
Others	424	75	18	49
		154		
1931 Election				
Trade Union	129	32	25	70
Others	362	14	4	30
		46		
1929 Election				
Trade Union	139	115	83	40
Others	430	172	40	60
		287		

Source: London *Times,* January 31, 1950, and *Report* of 1950 Annual Conference of Labour Party, page 5.

The greater part of the trade union group of Labour candidates is sponsored by the miners, the railway workers and the two general workers' unions. In the 1945 and 1950 general elections they accounted for more than two thirds of the total. The particular interest of these unions in the method of legal enactment and in nationalization is probably the main explanation for their weighty representation.

At the annual conference of the Labour Party the trade unions on the basis of their affiliated membership command an overwhelming majority of the votes. Formally it might seem that policy were entirely in their hands. During the thirties there was a great deal of criticism on the part of the representatives of local constituency parties against trade union domination based on their "block vote." [42] This led to some changes in the Labour Party Constitution in 1937; the constituency party representation on the National Executive was increased from five to seven and they were given the right to elect their représentatives separately. Since then there has been no strong drive for constitutional reform. In practice a great deal of policy making is left to the National Executive and the political leaders of the Party, and on controversial issues the trade unions rarely vote in the same way.

On the National Executive the trade union representation is weaker; they elect twelve out of a total of twenty-seven members, although there are on the Executive five women representatives who are elected by the Conference as a whole. Furthermore, the political leaders of the Party usually have a greater influence on the decisions than the trade union representatives, because of their greater standing in the movement and more intimate knowledge of many of the matters under discussion.

Few of the leading officials of trade unions attempt to enter Parliament today. Many unions have a rule which prevents them from doing so. At present only one member of the T.U.C. General Council is an M.P., and even among the twelve trade union members of the Labour Party Executive only three sit in Parliament.

In practice, then, there is a fairly clear division of function between the trade unions and the Labour Party.[43] The T.U.C. and the Labour Party, although their headquarters are located in the same building, lead a surprisingly independent existence, sharing only a common

---

[42] In a card vote the trade unions' voting strength is based on their affiliated membership; that of the constituency parties only on their individual membership.

[43] After the General Election in October 1951 which led to the return of a Conservative Government, the T.U.C. General Council issued a statement in which they pointed out that: "It is our long standing practice to seek to work amicably with whatever Government is in power and through consultation jointly with Ministers and with the other side of Industry to find practical solutions to the social and economic problems facing this country. There need be no doubt, therefore, of the attitude of the T.U.C. towards the new Government. . . . We expect of this Government that they will maintain to the full this practice of consultation. On our part we shall continue to examine every question solely in the light of its industrial and economic implications."

library. The Policy and Publicity Sub-Committee of the Labour Party Executive includes two liaison representatives from the T.U.C. General Council, and the Economic Committee of the T.U.C. includes two representatives from the Labour Party, but, apart from the National Council of Labour, that is all there is in the way of organizational ties. The National Council of Labour is the most important formal link between the Labour Party, the Trades Union Congress, and the Cooperative Union, and it is composed of eight representatives of each, including the three joint chairmen and secretaries. One of its stated purposes is "to endeavor to secure a common policy and joint action, whether by legislation or otherwise, in all questions affecting the workers as producers, consumers and citizens." It does from time to time issue common declarations of policy, but it largely serves to settle differences of opinion arising between the three main sections of the British labor movement and to keep them informed on each others' activities.

Resisting communist penetration

Tolerance is one of the most firmly entrenched of all British traditions. The idea that anyone should be discriminated against for holding certain political opinions is generally regarded with abhorrence. This is particularly true within the British labor movement, where the term "heresy-hunting" immediately arouses strong emotions of opposition and resentment. Tolerance, however, has its limits and cannot reasonably be carried to the point of self-destruction. An unscrupulous minority must be prevented from exploiting the tolerance of the majority in order to gain the power which will enable it to give its own intolerance full reign. Toward the end of 1948 the T.U.C. General Council decided that the time had come to take more vigorous action than before against the disruptive activities of the communists within the British trade unions. Commenting on the statement *Defend Democracy—Communist Activities Examined*, which the General Council issued after their meeting in November, 1948, Mr. Vincent Tewson, the general secretary, said: "We have been patient, perhaps too patient. But we shall fight this issue through to a finish."

This was not the first time that the Congress had been called upon to tackle this problem. In the late twenties, when the Communist Party acting on the instructions of the Red International of Labor Unions had built up the National Minority Movement and was attempting to establish rival organizations, the trade unions were warned to be on their guard against disruption. The failure of the National Minority Movement led the communists to renew their efforts at infiltration, which were concentrated mainly on the local

trades councils. The development became sufficiently serious for the
T.U.C. to issue in 1935 a circular threatening to withdraw recognition
from trades councils which accepted delegates "in any way connected
with either communist or fascist organizations or any of their ancillary
bodies." The communists then concentrated their efforts on conducting
a campaign to secure affiliation with the Labour Party, a tactic which
also failed.

It was in 1939 that the Communist Party of Great Britain, having
learned something from past failures, set out to capture positions of
influence within individual trade unions in a more gradual and systematic fashion than before. Although its policy continued to twist
and turn in order to conform with the requirements of Soviet Russia,
the new tactic met with greater success. As the T.U.C. has pointed
out in its statement on *The Tactics of Disruption,* the communists
sought influence within the trade union movement from 1939 to 1941
for the purpose of "stopping the war," and from 1941 to 1945 for the
purpose of "winning the war"; from 1945 to 1947 they were concerned
with securing acceptance for the policy of increased production and
from 1947 to the present time with magnifying industrial grievances
in order to impede production by stoppages of work. Throughout all
these changes, the communists have always presented their current
party "line" not as communists but as trade unionists anxious to protect the interests of the workers, an attitude which many militant
trade unionists in their ranks or influenced by their propaganda have
no doubt sincerely held.

The conditions brought about by World War II favored their efforts.
Local meetings were poorly attended by workers exhausted by long
hours of work and the strain of air raids. Many of the younger, able
candidates for union office were away in the armed forces. A small
but well-organized faction working within a union was often able to
capture enough votes to place its own men in key positions. Thus the
picture at the end of 1947 was roughly as follows. Taking the seventeen largest trade unions in Great Britain, each with a membership of
more than 100,000, it was reckoned that the communists and their
supporters had won sufficient representation on the executive bodies
to control or nearly control four of them, to have an appreciable but
not formidable influence on six, while in the remaining seven they
did not count at all.[44]

Since then there has been a steady and considerable decline in their
influence within the trade unions. The decision of the T.U.C. in 1948
to take action against the communists was not the result of any
recent increase in their strength, but was brought about mainly by

---

[44] See London *Times,* February 9, 1948.

the formation of the Cominform and its efforts to hamper economic recovery in Western Europe. Having no executive authority over its affiliated organizations the T.U.C. could do little more than keep them informed on communist activities and ask them to consider whether they could continue to trust communists to occupy important positions of responsibility. This kind of leadership the T.U.C. has given and, on the whole, it has met with a favorable response. But only a few unions have adopted rules to exclude communists from holding office.

The communists are not alone in acting as an organized influence within the trade union movement. Conservatives, Liberals and Roman Catholics all have some kind of organization to advocate their own industrial policy within its ranks. There has never been any suggestion that such activities should be suppressed even within unions that are affiliated to the Labour Party. Admittedly these bodies do not appear to have much effect on union policy, although the Associations of Catholic Trade Unionists, which have grown up in every diocese since 1945, have played an active part in trying to eradicate communist influence, and might be used for other purposes. The main reason why the communists have been singled out for special attention is that, because of their ultimate loyalty to a foreign power, their efforts have been directed towards undermining the industrial and political achievements of British labor. By their incitement and support of unofficial strikes they weaken the machinery of negotiation and impede economic recovery; by their encouragement of any and every wage demand they obstruct the approach to a more responsible wage policy; and by the use of unscrupulous methods and the exploitation of local meetings as a field for political agitation they weaken trade union democracy. Their lack of political success in Great Britain—in the 1950 general election their 100 candidates polled a total of 91,815 votes, and none were elected—has caused them to concentrate their efforts on industrial agitation. Here there are always legitimate grievances to exploit and not a few British communists have good trade union records which they maintain by sacrificing, on occasions, the party line to their union loyalty.

Relations with the state

In all highly industrialized countries the kind of relationship which should exist between the trade unions and the state presents one of the leading social problems of our time. In Great Britain it has been solved up to a point in a traditional, empirical fashion. The relationship, as we have seen, has passed through three successive phases:

hostility, toleration and, finally, partnership. Today the British trade unions are on the whole "with but not of" the state. In other words the partnership has two equally important and only apparently contradictory features: independence and interdependence. This is true in all the three main fields of union activity, in industrial relations, in economic government and in party politics. In the exercise of their primary function, the improvement of the wages and working conditions of their members, the British trade unions have never rejected the assistance of the state, which they have received to an increasing extent, but they have always regarded it as subsidiary to their own efforts. In the design and application of the nation's economic policy, the self-assigned role of the trade unions is a consultative one. They have no veto rights. Formally they can only advise, but their very independence gives them the strength to challenge the government effectively when the need arises. Finally, despite their close association with the Labour Party, they neither control it, nor does it control them. Thus even in this relationship there are both independence and interdependence.

That such a partnership is essential to the survival and development of democracy in the modern world is evident if the possible alternatives are considered. The state and the trade unions might co-exist as independent powers in a condition of open or concealed warfare. This was roughly the position in Great Britain between 1920 and 1926 (although it could be said that some foundations of the present partnership had already been laid). Neither the workers nor the community as a whole gained anything from this. Today it would be an unmitigated disaster, and would lead perforce to one of the other two possibilities: either the state conquers the trade unions, or the trade unions conquer the state. The first course ends in some kind of totalitarian system. Whether the unions are destroyed, as under fascism, or turned into instruments by which the party (which is also the state) controls the workers, as under communism, matters little in terms of democratic freedom and human dignity. The second course, the dream of the syndicalists, commands few supporters today, largely because it is known to be a dream that can never become a reality. The state has social functions other than those which trade unions can perform, and which cannot be dispensed with.

All democratic states have recognized independent trade unionism as an essential social institution, and are accordingly working towards some form of partnership. What is striking about the relationship in Great Britain is how little it has been regulated by legislation. With the repeal of the 1927 Act, which seriously limited the freedom of the trade unions, the control exercised by the state over the domestic affairs and industrial and political activities of the trade unions is slight and is no more than the trade unions themselves desire for the sake of the security of their organization and the protection of their members. In effect, the partnership depends less upon institutional arrangements than upon the way in which they are worked.

The change in the relationship between the trade unions and the state has come about more by a process of learning from experience than by conscious design. The trade union movement, because it answered a profound need on the part of the industrial workers, possessed an inherent vitality which defied suppression. As it gained in power it compelled both the employers and the state to recognize its existence and to come to terms with it. This development was accelerated by the two World Wars in which the bargaining strength of the workers was greatly enhanced. The trade unions know and are not likely to forget that their rights and their achievements have largely been won by their own strength. They will not be willing to surrender their independence, to merge their organization into the machinery of government or to accept any outside control over the exercise of what they regard as their essential functions. At the same time the character of the state has changed partly as a result of their political action. A century ago, when political power was exercised exclusively by representatives of the moneyed and landowning classes, the Marxist (or Leninist) view that the state was simply and solely an instrument for the domination of one class by another appeared plausible. The extension of the franchise, the creation and growth of the Labour Party, the abandonment of laissez faire in favor of a more planned and controlled economy have altered the picture considerably. Class society may not have disappeared, but it is unnecessary to use dubious and jingoistic arguments to persuade the workers that in this state they have something to defend. Thus their organizations, the trade unions, have no hesitation today in cooperating with the government, even though they retain the right to criticize and where necessary oppose it. Moreover they have been accorded a position of influence in the development of the nation's economic policy and have no need to rely purely on defensive action. The fact that Britain has had a Labour Government from 1945 to 1951 made the relationship more cordial and intimate, but it did not alter its basic character.

Yet though the marriage is more than one of convenience, the trade unions and the state live happily together by avoiding any deeper discussion about the nature of their relationship. From time to time awkward questions turn up which make both partners feel a little uneasy about the future. Or perhaps it would be more accurate to say that those who think about the subject at all are conscious that certain problems remain unresolved.

One of them is the attitude which should be taken to compulsory trade union membership. As long as the compulsion exercised on non-unionists came essentially from their fellow workmen, who refused to work alongside men who endangered their own standards, it was no more than a means of self-defense. But the growth in the political influence of the trade unions has raised a new problem, whether the power of the state should be used to enforce trade union membership. The decision toward the end of 1950 of the Durham County Council, which has a strong Labour majority, to insist that all their employees join their appropriate trade union on penalty of dismissal was a minor case in point. In fact the Labour Government condemned this action and used its influence to ensure that the decision was not applied. In view of the repeal of the 1927 Act there was nothing illegal in the local authority's decision, and many—possibly most—trade unionists would see no objection in principle to it since they regard a non-unionist as someone defaulting in a social duty. But it is doubtful whether they have fully considered the consequences of this attitude. Once the state, or any part of it, if only by degrees, makes trade union membership compulsory, it must sooner or later accept some responsibility for the way in which the trade unions conduct their affairs. In that event the voluntary character of British trade unionism and its democratic spirit would be seriously endangered.

A second and more important illustration of an unresolved problem in the relationship between the British trade unions and the state is provided by the future of wage policy. We have seen how the existence of full employment has greatly altered the economic context of collective bargaining and made some form of national wage policy desirable. This situation was met for a time mainly by temporary expedients: self-restraint by the trade unions in pressing wage claims; and the retention of the wartime provisions for compulsory arbitration. The first expedient has largely broken down and the second has been weakened by the restoration of the right to strike. Neither provides an adequate solution to what is likely to be a permanent problem if Britain is eventually to continue its course along the road to democratic socialism. Here the apparent determination of the majority of trade unions to resist any form of state influence on wage movements and wage structures threatens the social achievements which they have helped to bring about. As the author has written elsewhere: [45]

The contents of a collective agreement can no longer be regarded as being

---

[45] Allan Flanders, *A Policy for Wages*, page 15.

only of concern to its signatories. *Laissez-faire* cannot be abandoned in other vital sectors of our economic life and retained on the wages front. Least of all can the trade unions, whose very nature has compelled them to seek an increasing measure of public regulation over the free-for-all scramble of each for himself which characterised economic activity in the last century, now claim that their own preserves should be exempted from the application of those principles which they have urged upon the nation.

In the long run some way will have to be found of making effective the public interest in the outcome of collective bargaining without sacrificing the merits of the voluntary system.

One final example of an unresolved problem which takes us into the heart of our subject concerns the interpretation to be given to that familiar objective, "industrial democracy." There is one view of trade unionism, which at one time was widely accepted in socialist circles, namely, that it is only a reaction against the capitalist organization of industry. According to this view the whole function of a trade union changes in the transition to socialism; it is no longer needed as a form of defense organization on the part of the workers against capitalist exploitation but is required instead for the democratic administration of industry. There have been many variations on this basic theme, ranging from the cruder demands for "workers' control" to the more sophisticated tenets of gild socialism. But even in its most general form it contains a profound error. That trade unionism developed as a consequence of the creation of a propertyless proletariat is an established historical fact. But it meets a social need inherent in industrial civilization. Whether industry is privately or publicly owned it cannot be organized in any other way than in varying degrees of responsibility, which means that some give orders and others have to carry them out. If the interests of the latter are to be respected they need some form of collective organization—a trade union, in fact. This was pointed out very clearly by the Webbs:

> For even under the most complete Collectivism, the directors of each particular industry would, as agents of the community of consumers, remain biased in favour of cheapening production, and could, as brain workers, never be personally conscious of the conditions of the manual laborers. And though it may be assumed that the community as a whole would not deliberately oppress any section of its members, experience of all administration on a large scale, whether public or private, indicates how difficult it must always be, in any complicated organisation, for an isolated individual sufferer to obtain redress against the malice, caprice, or simple heedlessness of his official superior.

For this and other reasons they concluded that however much industry passes under public control:

. . . it is essential that each grade or section of producers should be at least so well organised that it can compel public opinion to listen to its claims, and so strongly combined that it could if need be, as a last resort against bureaucratic stupidity or official oppression, enforce its demands by a concerted abstention from work. . . .[46]

This statement of the case for the existence of independent, protective trade unionism in any democratic state regardless of its form of economic organization, is as valid as when it was written some fifty years ago. The principle also sets limits to the extent to which the trade unions can become involved in the functions and responsibilities of management. Admittedly these limits cannot be fixed theoretically; they are flexible but none the less real.

Does industrial democracy then consist of the combination of collective bargaining and joint consultation, which is statutorily secured within the nationalized industries in Great Britain? Is this the ultimate goal, or a stepping stone to something more? The answer we give to these questions will depend upon our conception of the essentials of democracy. There would be fairly general agreement that democracy is concerned with providing checks upon the arbitrary use of power. The differences of opinion arise on how this is best secured. How far is it something that can be fostered and safeguarded by appropriate forms of social organization? Even the vote can be used to put the enemies of democracy in power, as examples in history show; elections can be managed or their outcome influenced in dubious ways. Experience within the trade union world itself shows that those already holding permanent office are not easily displaced from their positions. Most people will agree today that democracy is incompatible with complete centralization of power in society. This is the powerful social argument in favor of independent trade unionism, of strong local government, of a powerful and energetic opposition to challenge the government in Parliament, and of forms of public ownership which are not identical with state socialism.

Mere decentralization of power, however, within the practical limits of modern society, leads only to anarchy, unless there are certain common principles which enable conflicts to be resolved without a constant reference to a trial of strength. It would appear then that democracy rests upon a state of mind, upon a mass of human attitudes, more than upon any particular form of organization; although the latter may influence the former and we can design our institutions so

---

[46] Sidney and Beatrice Webb, *Industrial Democracy*, pages 824–825, London: Longmans Green & Co., Ltd., 1920. By permission of the Trustees of the late Lord Passfield.

that they encourage the growth of responsible and reasonable attitudes. The same conclusion emerges when we consider that other vital aspect of democracy, self-government. It is not enough to provide institutions for self-government if these are not used because the feeling of public responsibility is weak. There is certainly a danger, or at least a problem in what has been called the *welfare state*, that the people come to regard it as a deliverer of services which entail no particular obligations on their part.

This theme is far too complex to be dealt with adequately here but it has an obvious bearing on the future of "industrial democracy." The moral basis of the demand for "workers' control" and "participation in management" has been the legitimate claim on the part of those who could be hired and fired that their dignity as human beings be respected. Very few industrial workers in Great Britain, or elsewhere, have any desire to take over the technical functions of management, and those who have, usually look for promotion. Their main concern is not to be treated as inferiors, whose interests can be disregarded and who have nothing to contribute beyond their labor to the process of production. There is no reason why genuine consultation, reinforced by strong, independent trade unionism acting in conditions of full employment should not provide for the industrial workers a status fully commensurate with their dignity. But its growth depends upon a new outlook on the part of management and a corresponding, cooperative response from the trade unions. For it is not enough that the interests of the trade unions, as institutions, are taken into account; the ultimate test of the success of joint consultation lies in its effect on the attitudes of all types of employees (not only higher management and the manual workers!) within the individual establishments.

In this may lie the deeper, social significance of the postwar nationalization experiments in Great Britain. The reasons for selecting the fuel and power and the transport groups of industries and services for transfer from private to public ownership were several and not the same in each case, ranging from past inefficiency, the need for integration, monopoly powers, and their significance in investment planning and employment policy. But in the long run the great contribution which nationalization can make may well prove to be in the changes which it pioneers in the field of industrial relations. In this spirit Lord Citrine addressed the 1950 Trades Union Congress:

It is sometimes assumed that the legislation overnight transformed the economics of the industry. Of course, it did nothing of the kind. How could it? It gave the opportunity of building the kind of organisation that could achieve the objects and aspirations that the sponsors of nationalisation have so often and so long advocated. But of itself it only provided the means whereby a building up process could succeed it in order to carry the legislation into complete effect. . . .

We cannot expect any sudden transformation in these circumstances. We had the same personnel both on the side of the officials and on the side of the workers and it is the easiest thing in the world for one to ascribe to the other blame for any shortcomings that may be revealed. That sort of thing will get us nowhere. What we have to do is to try to consolidate the personnel into a single entity directed to the straightforward purpose of achieving the aims that nationalisation sets out to accomplish. . . . We have tried to show that the enlarged responsibilities which have devolved upon so many people require a breadth of mind, require an objectivity, require an experience which can only very partially be obtained in previous employment. We have been trying very hard to inculcate an intensely human outlook in these large and vast industries. It must be remembered that, apart from whether a body is privately or publicly owned, large scale organisation brings its own problems. The problem of size is a very real one and the danger with large organisations is that they become impersonal, a sort of body without a soul. I would dread that development in nationalised industry and my efforts have been directed to trying to personalise as much as possible, as we are doing. I want people to be known not by titles and designations but by names and to be revealed as human beings in their day to day work.[47]

This objective of humanizing industrial organization raises many further problems that are only beginning to receive serious attention in the work of psychologists and sociologists. The trade unions, because they represent more than any other institution the "human factor" in industry, could help greatly in their solution providing they are prepared to take a broad enough view of their tasks. This will depend upon the leadership they receive. Materialistic and idealistic motives are mingled in the spirit that has provided the driving force for their development, but with the accumulation of power the former tend to gain the upper hand. Unless the spirit of idealism that undoubtedly resides within the British trade union movement is summoned and strengthened by a bold conception of what is now at stake, even its present achievements may be endangered by the predominance of sectional and short-sighted attitudes.

---

[47] Trades Union Congress, *Brighton Congress Report,* page 460. London: Trades Union Congress, 1950.

Chapter 2

SCANDINAVIA—WALTER GALENSON

The nations that comprise Scandinavia, Denmark, Norway, and Sweden, are among the smallest in the world, but their modern development has aroused a degree of interest in the West far out of proportion to their size. This is attributable, in no small measure, to the influence attained by the Scandinavian labor movements in the economic and political life of their respective countries, accomplished entirely through democratic means. Since the middle nineteen-thirties, socialist political parties, closely allied with the trade unions, have governed Scandinavia with only brief interruptions. In no other part of the world has a democratic labor movement maintained itself in power so firmly and for so long a period.

Through a skillful combination of traditional collective bargaining techniques and unorthodox government intervention in economic affairs, the Scandinavian labor movement has succeeded in raising worker living standards to a level exceeded only by the American. This is a remarkable achievement when it is recalled that Scandinavia is not richly endowed with natural resources; Denmark has only its fertile soil, Norway and Sweden their waterfalls, forests, and iron ore. All the other ingredients essential for modern industry must be imported. During the second half of the nineteenth century, Scandinavia appeared hopelessly overpopulated, and hundreds of thousands of its people emigrated to the United States to escape a seemingly bleak future. Yet, at the present time, there is an acute and chronic shortage of labor, despite the fact that the population is far in excess of that in 1900. This development, of course, cannot be ascribed entirely to the activities and policies of the labor movement; the fundamental cause was the transformation of the area from one in which agriculture predominated to an essentially industrial society. However, during the past two decades, when further industrial expansion along customary lines appeared to be blocked, it was the labor movement that took over and pioneered new paths, and it is, in large measure, to these efforts that the Scandinavian worker owes his present high levels of housing, medical care, and economic security.

Because of its basic cultural unity, Scandinavia may be treated as a single entity for many purposes. But, at the same time, it must be remembered that we are dealing here with three separate and independent labor movements, each with a unique history and problems. There are many striking differences among the three, and, often, it is precisely the differences that provide an opportunity to draw generalizations from an analysis of Scandinavian labor history.

The Origins and Development of Trade Unionism

The pattern of industrial development

Trade unionism is peculiar to modern industrial society; its rise is attributable to forces activated by industrialization. The growth, structure, and ideology of the labor movement of any country are conditioned by the nature of the industrialization process; that is, by the character of the society in which industry first took root and by the tempo and direction of industrial development. This is not to say that political and cultural factors are not important. On the contrary, they may be decisive in determining the precise lines of trade union growth at a given time. But the dynamic element, in terms of which one may obtain the deepest insight into trade unionism, appears to be the complex of events subsumed under the concept of industrialization.

Scandinavia was relatively late, in the European timetable, in feeling the impact of the economic forces generated originally by the Industrial Revolution. Agriculture was still the predominant activity in 1870, and manfacturing was carried on along handicraft lines. It was not until the final decades of the nineteenth century that the rapid rise of modern industry set in.

There were important differences in the inception and progress of industrialization among the Scandinavian nations. Denmark was the first to experience a quickening of industrial life, a fact that Montgomery attributes to the possibility of capitalistic exploitation of its chief natural resource, fertile soil, at an earlier stage in economic development than was possible in Norway and Sweden, where industry had to wait upon the perfection of the technology of electricity.[1] In 1870, only 55 per cent of the Danish population earned its living in agriculture, compared with 72 per cent for Sweden, with Norway

[1] Arthur Montgomery, *Industrialismens genombrott i Sverige*, page 185. Stockholm: Skoglund, 1947.

somewhere in between. Conversely, 26 per cent of the Danish population was attached to manufacturing and building, compared with 15 per cent in Sweden. This picture of the relative status of the three countries is confirmed by statistics on the urban-rural distribution of the population: in Denmark, about 25 per cent of the population lived in cities and towns in 1870, compared with 17 per cent in Norway and 13 per cent in Sweden.

The period of most rapid growth in Danish industry was from 1880 to 1900. The initial stimulus was due, in large measure, to the drastic decline in grain prices that occurred around 1870 as a consequence of increasing American exports; Danish farmers reacted by switching to animal production, a more intensive and capitalistic form of agriculture, and one that provided a steadier level of employment throughout the year. In consequence, there was greater opportunity for the cities to produce goods that had previously been made in small farm workshops in subsidiary occupations. From 1880 to 1900, the ratio of the agricultural population to total population fell from 51 to 41 per cent, with corresponding increases for the industrial and commercial sectors. The change was hardly a revolutionary one, representing, rather, a steady growth of manufactures based, to a large extent, upon expansion of the old handicraft workshop.

Danish industry continued to grow after the turn of the century, but at a slower rate. The major industries of the nation, in terms of employment, are shipbuilding, construction, and the manufacture of shoes, clothing, and food products. However, the average Danish factory is small, reflecting the handicraft character of much of industry.

Industrialization commenced later in Norway and Sweden, but when it finally began, the rate of change was greater than in Denmark, and the effects upon the economies more striking. Swedish industrial expansion was hampered by falling price tendencies from 1875 to 1895, but the upward price trend beginning in 1895 was accompanied by a rapid growth of manufactures. Technological advance in the transmission of electric power permitted, for the first time, the utilization of large water power resources in the northern part of the country, and required a huge construction program, mainly between 1900 and 1914. The industries most affected by the revolutionary growth at the turn of the century were iron and steel (based upon Sweden's rich iron ore), machinery, and paper and pulp. Foreign demand for Swedish raw materials, iron ore and lumber, helped finance the expansion, though Sweden remained a net capital importer until 1913. The impact of industrialization is illustrated by the fact that the agricultural sector of the population declined from 72 per cent in 1870 to 49 per cent in 1910 and 34 per cent in 1940.

The location of Swedish industry is an important labor relations datum. There is not the same great concentration of industry in limited geographic areas characteristic of most industrial nations. Rather, industrial establishments are to be found scattered among many small cities and towns throughout the country. In 1947, there were 398,000 industrial workers employed in urban areas and 259,000 in rural areas, and of those employed in urban areas, only 106,000 were in Stockholm and Göteborg, the two large cities of Sweden.

Norway was the last of the Scandinavian countries to industrialize, but there the tempo of industrial development was even more rapid than in Sweden. The enormous water power resources of the country were crucial. Great electro-chemical plants were built at Rjukan, Sauda, Odda, and Høyanger between 1905 and 1920, a period that witnessed a doubling in the number of industrial workers. Expansion of the road and railroad networks augmented the need for construction workers. As in Sweden, Norwegian industry is considerably dispersed. The Oslo and Bergen areas combined accounted for only 22.5 per cent of all hours worked in industry in 1947. The typical locational pattern is that of single large plants located at the head of fjords, deep enough to accommodate ocean-going vessels and close to the source of water power. The metal trades, paper, textile, and wood fabrication are Norway's important employers of labor, though the electro-chemical industry (aluminum, zinc, fertilizers) and the merchant marine have an important place in the export trade.

Because of its late entrance into the industrial arena, Scandinavia was able to accomplish within a few decades what it took England a century to achieve. This was due, in no small measure, to technical assistance from England. Scandinavian engineers and workers studied in England, and many industrial pioneers, particularly in Sweden, were British. Scandinavia caught up with Western Europe, industrially, about the time of World War I, and it now ranks as one of the most heavily industrialized areas of Europe, exceeded, in this respect, only by England, Germany, and the Low Countries.

The antecedents of modern labor market organization

In their famous book on trade unionism, the Webbs contended that there was little or no connection between the medieval gild organizations and the contemporary organizations of the labor market.[2]

---

[2] Sidney and Beatrice Webb, *History of Trade Unionism, 1666–1920*, page 23. London: Longmans, 1920.

This may have been true for England, where almost a century elapsed between the introduction of free trade and the foundation of a permanent labor movement. But in Scandinavia, and particularly Denmark, the gild system exercised a profound influence upon the spirit and structure of the labor movement.

The gild system was not uniformly developed throughout Scandinavia, and a recognition of the differences among the three countries is essential to an understanding of their labor history. The Danish gilds maintained effective monopolies of their trades in Copenhagen and the larger cities right up to the time of their dissolution in 1862. At that time, there were 44 separate gilds in Copenhagen and 226 in the rest of the country. In Copenhagen, only a few trades, the dyers, millwrights, and tailors, were not gilded.[3]

The Swedish gilds were less firmly established than the Danish. An important reason, which was equally true for Norway, was that "the cities were few in relation to the broad expanse of the country, and with the existing communications system it was not practically possible to monopolize trade and industrial activity for the advantage of the cities in anything like as effective a manner as the gild system implied."[4] The gild monopolies were abolished in 1846, and, in their stead, trade associations that had the right to enforce "masterwork" requirements were established. This last vestige of the old system was abolished, in turn, in 1864, at a time when its influence was very restricted.

The gilds were least developed in Norway, and exercised a correspondingly smaller influence on subsequent events. In 1839, when there were only 45 gilds in the entire country, the formation of new gilds was prohibited, and the existing organizations were permitted to continue only for the lifetime of any master then holding membership. Subsequent legislation abolished all gilds in 1869, with the sole exception of the Bergen baker's gild, which retained its monopoly until 1894.

In the period of their hegemony, the social structure of the gilds was largely undifferentiated, except with respect to age. Every apprentice could look forward some day to the attainment of independent mastership. But with the decline of gild influence came a widening of the gulf between master and journeyman. The journeyman-master ratio increased, particularly in the building trades (one to twenty in Copenhagen in 1840, one to thirty-five in Stockholm), and most

---

[3] See Bryn J. Hovde, *The Scandinavian Countries*, page 237. Ithaca, Cornell University Press, 1948 and Georg Nørregaard *Arbejdsforhold Indenfor Dansk Haandverk og Industri*, pages 12–15. Copenhagen, 1943.

[4] Montgomery, *op. cit.*, page 122.

journeymen had to resign themselves to a permanent status at that level. Consequently, special journeyman's associations developed within many of the gilds, primarily to provide sickness and death benefits and travel assistance, but also to some extent to represent the wage interests of the journeymen against the masters. There were occasional journeyman strikes, and in a few trades wage lists were negotiated.

As we shall see, the Scandinavian gilds provided a direct organizational base for some employer associations and trade unions. Even in the absence of a direct link between the two sets of institutions, the gilds created a propensity to organize which considerably furthered the growth of the early employer associations and trade unions. In Denmark, the strength of journeyman gild traditions proved a decisive determinant of trade union structure.

The social origins of the industrial labor force

Among the factors that determine the character of a labor movement is one that has received little attention, but which, nevertheless, is of great importance: the social origins of the workers who constitute the original industrial cohorts. While some workers may be recruited from among handicraft workers of the preindustrial era, the major source of labor power for rapidly expanding industry must be agriculture. But the types of agricultural economies from which workers are drawn may differ greatly, and these differences may be reflected in later industrial development.

The agricultural economies of the Scandinavian countries varied considerably because of different natural conditions in the three countries. Denmark, with its flat, fertile land, was well suited to large scale, capitalistic agriculture. A feudal system of landholding prevailed there until the close of the 18th century; it was not until 1788 that the Danish peasant was freed of his bonds to the soil. The breakup of large estates proceeded slowly thereafter, and by 1870 the dominant form of holding was the middle sized farm. However, there continued to be a large number of farmers who could not make a living from their own holdings, and were obliged to work, at least part time, in the service of others. In 1870, there were approximately 2,000 large farmers, 70,000 medium holders, 70,000 smallholders, and 70,000 landless laborers; that is, the dependent group comprised about two-thirds of the total.[5]

It was from the latter group, the smallholders and laborers, that the major portion of the new industrial labor force was recruited. Between 1870 and 1900 there was a net migration of 220,000 workers from

---

[5] Einar Jensen, *Danish Agriculture,* page 95. Copenhagen, 1937.

country to city. These people were not independent farmers fallen upon hard times, nor the surplus children of independent farmers, but rather an habitually dependent group inured to exceedingly unfavorable economic circumstances. They entered upon their new occupations conditioned, if not to the rigorous discipline of the factory, at least to severe restrictions upon the freedom to allocate their working time.

The situation was quite different in Sweden and Norway. There, "the peasants had never become bound because the feudal system had not developed in these countries where there were large sections with isolated farmsteads rather than villages." [6] There were some large farms in the southern portion of the countries, but, even there, the landowners are better described as a yeomanry than as a landed aristocracy. The topography of Sweden and Norway is simply not suited to large-scale farming.

This does not mean that there was no agricultural proletariat in Sweden and Norway. In 1870, 48 per cent of the Swedish agricultural population fell into the class of cottars and landless laborers, and many of the remaining farms were too small to provide their owners with an independent livelihood.[7] In Norway, too, there were large numbers of cottars and landless laborers, though proportionally less than in Denmark and Sweden.[8] However, heavy emigration to the United States acted as a safety valve and prevented an unduly rapid growth in the dependent agricultural population. Between 1850 and 1910 there was a net emigration of a million persons from Sweden, about three-quarters of whom were small farmers, cottars and farm laborers. Norwegian emigration, which had begun earlier than the Swedish, reached its peak in 1882, when in a single year almost 29,000 persons left the country, again, primarily, from the farms, at a time when the total population of the country was under two million. The outward population drain ended only with the provision of employment alternative to farming.

A greater proportion of the workers attracted to industry in Sweden and Norway came from small farms owned by themselves or by members of their families than was true in Denmark. Many had no previous experience in working for others. Their tradition of independence clashed with the requirements of industrial discipline, with important consequences for the labor movements.

There is a qualification to the above statement in the case of

---

[6] *Ibid.*, page 93.

[7] Torsten Gårdlund, *Industrialismens Samhälle*, page 268. Stockholm: Tidens Forläg, 1942.

[8] Edvard Bull, *Arbeiderklassen i Norsk Historie,* page 58. Olso: Tiden Norsk Forlag, 1947.

Sweden. Many small farmers had long been accustomed to supplement their earnings through seasonal employment in such rural industries as brick manufacture, distilling, and sawmills. Lumbering was also an important secondary rural industry (in Norway, as well), but much of it was carried on individually by small farmers rather than on a capitalistic basis.

In sum, the social origins of the early industrial labor force were not uniform among the Scandinavian countries. The Danish workers came mainly from nonproprietors in the agricultural economy, whereas in Sweden and Norway industrial recruits were drawn to a greater extent from an independent yeomanry, the latter tendency being particularly marked in Norway.

Early labor organization

Because of its earlier industrialization the first of the Scandinavian nations to witness the rise of a labor movement was Denmark. The dissolution of the gilds in 1862 left a vacuum in the labor market, but not for long. A number of the journeyman gilds remained in existence as voluntary friendly societies, some of which sought to advance the more general economic interests of their members. But of organic connection between these gild relics and trade unions, the following observation has been made: "Examples of connection between the journeyman gilds of 1862 and the modern trade unions are rare. True enough, the 1862 gilds on many occasions during the rise of trade unionism participated in industrial relations and represented the journeymen against the masters; but often there was enmity between the two groups of unions. . . ." [9]

The more important legacy of the gilds was the organizational propensity with which they endowed the Danish workers. The most stable and best disciplined of the early trade unions, the masons, timberers, carpenters, plumbers, and shoemakers, all had strong gild antecedents. By 1875, all the former gild crafts of any size had perfected trade union organization, though not all survived the depression of 1877–1879. At that time, the only important unions in non-gild trades were the printers and cigar makers, the former for the same reasons that led them to pioneer trade unionism the world over, the latter because of their close relations with the powerful German organizations.

Many attributes of contemporary Danish trade unionism can be traced to gild influence. Union interest in welfare schemes stemmed ini-

---

[9] Nørregaard, *op. cit.*, page 76. In a few instances, the journeyman gilds were captured by socialists and reorganized. See Henry Bruun, *Den Faglige Arbejderbevegelse i Danmark*, pages 475–480. Copenhagen: Nordisk Forlag, 1944.

tially from the necessity of competing with the journeyman gilds. Some
trade unions continued for many years the custom of providing an
escort at funerals, in addition to the payment of death benefits. The
attitude of skilled toward unskilled workers, which has been of crucial
significance in determining trade union structure, also owes its origin
to gild traditions.

The pioneers of Danish trade unionism were three young socialist
intellectuals, Louis Pio, Harold Brix, and Poul Geleff, all of whom
were adherents of the First International. They founded, in 1871,
the International Labor Union of Denmark, but a year later their
organization was dissolved by the authorities and they were imprisoned. A number of local craft unions were established during the
following years, banding together, in 1874, in the Free Trade Union
Central Committee. Upon his release from prison, in 1875, Pio became
chairman of the Committee, but two years later, yielding to police
pressure and bribery, he emigrated to the United States. His desertion, together with the economic crisis of 1877, put an end to the Committee, as well as to many of its affiliates.

An improvement in business conditions, in 1880, gave impetus to
new organization, and, thereafter, the viability of the Danish labor
movement was never in doubt. The decade 1880 to 1890 marked an
expansion in local union organization, while the final decade of the
century saw both further extension and federation. From 1895 to 1900
there was a rate of trade union growth that for Denmark must be
described as phenomenal; for, while before 1895 the largest number of
local unions established in any one year had been 76, in 1890, 684
new local unions came into existence during the five years 1895 to
1899 inclusive. Increasing employer acceptance of trade unionism, as
well as greater tolerance of union activities by the government and
the growing political power of labor, facilitated organization. The most
important cause of union growth, however, was the conjuncture of
six years of good employment conditions and the existence of a hard
core of trade unionism.

The initiative toward national unionism was taken almost invariably by the Copenhagen locals. They were the first, and the strongest,
of the local unions, and possessed the resources to send organizers
about the country. They had strong motives for national unification of
their trades: to protect their wage standards from provincial undercutting, and to prevent the importation of strikebreakers from the
small towns. The serious competition to the national union provided
by regional organization in Norway, where the cities were far distant
from one another in travel time, was lacking in Denmark.

In Sweden, as in Denmark, some of the journeyman gild organizations continued as voluntary societies and played a certain role in the development of trade unionism. In many trades, gild members took the lead in founding trade unions, and there are instances of the transformation of friendly societies into trade unions. Again, however, "the significance of the journeyman gilds and burial societies for the development of the trade union movement was limited mainly to maintaining craft traditions and making the members aware of the importance of organization." [10] The lesser significance of the gild tradition in Sweden may be ascribed to the relative weakness of the Swedish gild system and to the longer interim between the demise of the gilds and the formation of a permanent trade union movement.

In 1885, Swedish trade unionism was where its Danish counterpart had been ten years earlier, and until 1895 it was completely dominated by the craft organizations. Particularly in southern Sweden (Skåne), the Danish trade unions provided important assistance to the struggling Swedish movement. There, the contiguity of the two countries, and the ease of movement between them, rendered it essential for the Danish unions to prevent the importation into Denmark of unorganized Swedish strikebreakers. In 1885, a fourth of the 105 existing local trade unions were to be found in five cities of southern Sweden, which was far out of proportion to the industrial importance of these cities. Nor was the Danish influence limited to southern Sweden, for Danish craftsmen found employment throughout Sweden and carried the gospel of trade unionism with them. The Danes initiated a series of Scandinavian trade union congresses, the first of which was held in 1886, and passed on some of their organizational experience to the Swedes and Norwegians.

The tardy emergence of Swedish trade unionism had important consequences. Before craft unionism had become solidly entrenched, as in Denmark or England, industrialism swept the country and resulted in rapid augmentation of the unskilled labor force. Though craft unionism was by no means eradicated, it emerged far less important, relative to trade unionism as a whole, than in Denmark.

The considerable distance between the major industrial centers of Sweden made regional organization the logical initial form of trade union centralism. The first city central trade council was that established in Stockholm in 1883, and was soon followed by similar organizations in Göteborg and Hälsingborg. By 1890, union centrals existed in every major city of Sweden. The principal function of the city centrals was to provide financial strike assistance to member locals,

---

[10] Tage Lindbom, *Den Svenska Fackföreningsrörelsens Uppkomst*, page 17. Stockholm: Tidens Förlag, 1938.

though they also engaged in political activity in cooperation with the Socialist Party.

The Danish city centrals had been replaced by national trade unions as the predominant form of trade union central organization with a minimum of difficulty, but the Swedish situation was somewhat different:

Stockholm did not occupy the central and dominating place in the trade union movement which Copenhagen occupied in the Danish trade union movement. Sweden was a large country compared with Denmark, and its trade unions were widely dispersed. Great distances separated the various local organizations one from another. Organized links among them were lacking.[11]

Nevertheless, it soon became evident that the national union form of centralization was to triumph in Sweden as well. The first national union, that of the printers, was formed in 1886; its early start was due to the desirability of providing a national fund to assist journeyman printers who moved from city to city in search of work. By 1900, there were 32 national unions, 25 of them having been formed after 1890. As the ease of interurban communication increased, and both the labor and product markets broadened, the functional role of the city trade union central declined.

As in Denmark, the period of most rapid Swedish union growth was from 1895 to 1900. Union membership increased from 15,000 to 66,000 between the two years, three-quarters of the new members belonging to the new factory industry rather than to the older handicrafts. The latter figure, however, was considerably below Danish union membership of 96,000 in 1900, a difference which is more striking when the fact is taken into account that Swedish population was about double that of Denmark.

Norwegian trade unionism got its start at about the same time as the Swedish unions. There was some connection between gilds and trade unions; for example, the Oslo carpenters' local was established, in 1872, by members of the old gild organization, and the unions of shoemakers, bookbinders, bakers, and goldsmiths had similar antecedents.[12] But the relative paucity of Norwegian gilds meant that the great majority of trade unions had no previous organizational basis on which to build.

Though there was some transient organization in the early seventies, it was not until 1880 that durable local unions were established

[11] Lindbom, op. cit., pages 135–136.
[12] Gunnar Ousland, Fagorganisationen i Norge, Vol. I., pages 4–19. Oslo: Tiden Norsk Forlag, 1949.

in Norway. The period 1890 to 1900 was marked by union growth, so that by 1900 there were 250 local unions with a total membership of about 20,000, far below the Danish organizational level. Unionism was confined to a few of the larger cities, and as a result the city central trades councils developed, early, into the most important central organizations. When attempts were made to form national unions, they came into sharp conflict with the city centrals. There was considerable discussion within the young labor movement over the relative merits of the two forms of centralism, and a number of locals, particularly in Oslo, regarded the services which could be rendered by the city organizations as more important than those which the national unions could perform. But the spread of unionism made it more difficult for the city centrals to conduct negotiations and work stoppages effectively, and the national form of organization gained in strength.[13] Nevertheless, in 1900:

> the local unions (in Oslo) had largely allied themselves with the city central trades council . . . Local unions were often more closely tied to city centrals than to national unions . . . The national union form of organization had emerged at the end of the 1890's, but the new unions had not yet established themselves in the consciousness of the membership as the basic organizational structure.[14]

The dominance of the national union may be dated formally from the formation of the Norwegian Federation of Labor in 1899, but the later utilization of the city central by the syndicalists as a political weapon was to keep the issue of structure alive.

The federations of labor

The rapid increase in trade union membership in all the Scandinavian countries during the closing years of the nineteenth century culminated in the formation of central labor federations. The Danish Federation of Labor (*De Samvirkende Fagforbund*) and the Swedish Federation of Labor (*Landsorganisasjonen i Sverige*) were established in 1898, and the Norwegian Federation of Labor (*Arbeidernes Faglige Landsorganisasjon*) in 1899. In all three countries there had been previous abortive attempts at federation, but matters were brought to a head when an inter-Scandinavian labor congress held in Stockholm,

---

[13] "Goldsmiths in Kristiania (Oslo) and Trondheim stood closer to one another than a goldsmith and a brickmaker in the same city. A printer from Ålesund could be used as a strikebreaker during a printing strike in Kristiania, but a dockworker could not thus be used even though he lived in the same city. Therefore the need was greatest for solidarity along craft lines." Edvard Bull, *op. cit.*, page 149.

[14] Ousland, I., *op. cit.*, page 220.

in 1897, resolved that "the national unions in the three countries, and the industrial local unions not affiliated with a national union, shall unite in national federations with a common secretariat in each country."

Though there was virtual unanimity among trade unionists regarding the desirability of federation, agreement stopped there. Practical problems threatened to prevent realization of federation, and, in some cases, kept important national unions out of the federations for considerable periods. Achievement of a satisfactory balance of authority between the federation and the constituent national unions was in every case a critical question. In Denmark, the constitutional committee had recommended that affiliated unions be required to submit to the executive committee of the Federation, for counsel in advance, all new contract demands, and that approval of the demands be made a condition of financial assistance in the event of a strike or lockout. The larger unions balked at ceding this authority to the Federation, and proposed instead that an affiliated union which could finance its own work stoppages be exempt from the duty to consult with the Federation. The constitutional committee, similarly, recommended that when the Federation actually rendered financial assistance to a striking union, it be empowered to conduct all further negotiations with employers, whereas the dissenting unions insisted upon the retention of their freedom to act under any circumstances.

The outcome represented a victory for the proponents of a decentralized federation. The constitution, as finally adopted, required affiliated unions to notify the Federation of demands presented to employers, but they retained complete freedom to negotiate. The Federation was empowered to withhold strike benefits when it disapproved of a strike, but the negative control thus implied was vitiated by decentralization of the strike funds.

Much the same happened in Sweden. Efforts to create a federation that would finance both offensive and defensive work stoppages, and that would have exercised considerable influence in collective bargaining through control of the purse strings, were unavailing. The constitutional convention voted, instead, to limit Federation assistance to lockouts, leaving to each national union the financing of its own strikes. The Swedish Federation of Labor thus began its existence with very limited authority.[15]

Perhaps, because of the relative weakness of the labor movement in Norway, and the greater need of national unions for mutual assistance,

---

[15] For a detailed account of the controversy over centralization in Sweden, see Ragnar Casparsson, *L O Under Fem Årtionden*, pages 30–93. Vol. I, Stockholm, 1947.

the Norwegian Federation of Labor was, from the beginning, the most highly centralized of the Scandinavian federations. The constitutional committee had proposed that each constituent national union be obliged to establish a separate strike fund, and that in addition the Federation be empowered to make additional assessments in support of striking organizations, out of which an amount equal to the total customary strike benefit would be paid. Despite the objections of a few of the wealthiest unions, which feared that they might be required to carry an undue proportion of the burden of finance and opposed the grant of such far reaching authority to the Federation, the measure was adopted. In consequence, the two most important unions at the time, the printers and metal workers, remained independent of the Federation until 1904.

An issue that occasioned controversy, particularly in Sweden, was that of the precise relationship of the projected labor federations to the respective socialist parties. The principal impetus, not only to federation but to initial organization as well, had come from the socialists. However, although practically the entire trade union leadership and the majority of the rank and file were socialists, there was a substantial nonsocialist membership. The ardent socialists wanted to establish an organic connection between the trade union and political wings of the labor movement, but many union leaders feared a possible split in the trade unions along political lines if this were done.

The original Swedish Federation constitution required every local union to affiliate with the Social Democratic Party within three years after its admission to the Federation.[16] The largest national union in the country, that of the metal workers, thereupon refused to join the Federation, and in 1900 obligatory socialist affiliation was replaced by the requirement merely that the Federation work for the affiliation of its members to the Social Democratic Party.

The issue aroused less heat in Denmark and Norway. The strong Danish crafts, with their traditional economic bent, had long advocated complete separation of trade unions and political parties. Consequently, there was little disposition to go along even with voluntary collective affiliation of local unions. The Norwegian socialists attempted to follow the Swedish example, but the majority sentiment was opposed, and the socialists had to content themselves with interchange of executive committee members.

---

[16] This requirement was carried by a two to one vote. The most important union leaders at the convention, Nils Persson, Charles Lindley, Ernst Blomberg and Herman Lindqvist, were opposed to obligatory affiliation, but so great was socialist prestige among the workers that the pure "trade union" argument proved of no avail.

There were other practical problems to be solved. For example, there was that of the precise authority of the new federations in strike and lockout situations, which is dealt with below. Not all difficulties were resolved satisfactorily at the beginning, and the early years witnessed frequent constitutional change. Nevertheless, the actual achievement of federation was a fact, though the federations were far from representative of the entire labor movements of their countries.

Growth of trade union membership

Membership in the Scandinavian labor federations from 1900 to 1950 is shown in Table 1, by five year intervals. In each case there has been a steady increment in membership, with only occasional setbacks due to poor economic conditions, lost strikes or secessions. Danish trade union membership declined in only two periods, 1901 to 1903 and 1920 to 1922, in both instances as a consequence of economic depression. Norwegian Federation membership was more volatile. There was a slight decline from 1908 to 1910, a sharp one after 1920 (from 142 thousand in 1920 to 96 thousand in 1921) and a further drop from 1925 to 1927. It is notable, however, that membership increased substantially from 1930 to 1935, primarily because of an extension of trade unionism to theretofore unorganized industries: lumbering, agriculture, heavy construction, and office work. The Swedish Federation of Labor met its first major setback in 1908–1911, as a consequence of a business depression followed by loss of a general strike. It was almost a decade before recovery from this twin blow was achieved, but, thereafter, membership rose steadily except for a slight setback in the postwar recession of 1921.

TABLE 1
MEMBERSHIP IN THE SCANDINAVIAN FEDERATIONS OF LABOR, 1900–1950,
BY FIVE YEAR INTERVALS (IN THOUSANDS)

Year	Denmark	Norway	Sweden
1900	77	5	44
1905	69	16	87
1910	102	46	85
1915	132	76	111
1920	279	142	280
1925	240	96	385
1930	259	140	553
1935	381	224	701
1940	516	307	971
1945	604	340	1,107
1950	656	487	1,278

Sources: *Denmark:* De Samvirkende Fagforbund, *Under Samvirkets Flag.*
Norway: Ousland, *op. cit.,* Vol. III. *Sweden:* Casparsson, *op. cit.,* Vol. II.

The holding power of Scandinavian trade unionism has been remarkable, a fact that will be more obvious if the Scandinavian trade union figures are compared with those of the United States. Trade union influence expanded steadily; by 1930 the unions were so firmly entrenched that not even the great depression prevented further organization, despite a high level of unemployment.

There have been no rival union movements in Denmark and Norway, nor a significant membership in trade unions independent of the federations. The Danish Federation of Labor now includes about 96 per cent of all organized workers, while the corresponding figure for Norway is of about the same order of magnitude. In Sweden, however, important union organizations still remain outside the Federation of Labor. A syndicalist trade union center, established in 1910, maintains an independent existence with about 23,000 members, mainly in lumbering and heavy construction. The *Tjänstemännens Centralorganisation* (*T C O*), a federation uniting 260,000 white collar employees and foremen in both private industry and government service, is the most important of the independents, though there are smaller groups catering to teachers and the higher civil servants which have considerable membership. While only the syndicalist trade union center is in direct competition with the Federation, there have been numerous jurisdictional conflicts between the Federation and TCO; relations are not good, and it is not inconceivable that the Federation may one day attempt to encroach upon TCO preserves.

The absence of rival unionism on an important scale in the Scandinavian countries has contributed greatly to trade union stability. The trade unions have not been obliged to dissipate their meager resources fighting with each other. Unity is attributable in large measure to the influence of political socialism, for the divisive tendencies that occasionally manifested themselves over economic interests, and led to secession movements, were all counteracted finally through the medium of common political bonds. The opposite danger, that political division may be reflected in the trade union, never materialized in Scandinavia, largely because of continuing socialist predominance in the labor movement, and the relative weakness of syndicalism (except in Norway) and communism.

The degree of trade union organization in contemporary Scandinavia is extremely high. In manufacturing, building, and transportation, it may be estimated at 95 per cent of the labor force in Sweden, and 90 per cent in Denmark and Norway. The possibilities for further trade union growth are limited. With virtually all Swedish industrial workers and about 80 per cent of the white collar workers and government employees already in trade unions, new members must come mainly from the slow increments to the labor force. The curve of Swedish trade union growth, which had a steep slope until the million mark was reached in 1941, has tapered off sharply. The Danish and Norwegian unions have some room for expansion among white collar workers. About half the 180,000 Danish white collar workers (excluding civil servants) are unorganized, while the corresponding percentage in Norway is 75.

The Scandinavian trade unions are thus approaching the practical limits of organization,[17] a fact of great significance for their future. In the past, the necessity of extending organization into ever new fields kept the movement dynamic. New men were thrown to the top, a democratic ferment was at work. But with maturity and the hardening of the union bureaucracy, the opportunities for rapid advancement are limited, and the more cautious administrator replaces the organizer in the leadership hierarchy. There is in trade union maturity an inherent threat to internal union democracy that is already troubling thoughtful Scandinavians.

Trade Union Structure and Operation

The formal structure

The Scandinavian trade unions are basically similar to those of the United States in terms of their structure. The highest governing body of the Scandinavian federations is the congress, or convention, meeting triennially in Denmark and Norway and quinquennially in Sweden. Under the Danish scheme of representation, each national union is represented at the congress by its executive committee, plus a certain additional number of delegates on the basis of membership. However, the small crafts are overrepresented. At the 1946 congress, the General Workers' Union (Laborers) had one delegate for every 2,034 members, compared with one delegate for each 27 gilders. This skewed representation and the large size of the congress, running as high as a thousand delegates, combine to deprive the Danish Federation congress of real policy making authority.

The Federation congress is a more important body in Norway and in Sweden. In both cases they are limited to 300 delegates, apportioned among the constituent unions on the basis of paid up membership. Here, the congress is, in a real sense, the final arbiter of trade union policy, and there is often spirited debate and close voting on disputed issues.

---

[17] Agricultural workers are poorly organized in all three countries, but whether it will be possible to organize workers on the typically small farm is questionable. The Swedish Agricultural Workers' Union, with 46,000 members, has put the upper limit of possible organization at 80,000.

Between regular congress meetings the highest legislative authority is the representative council, which varies in size from 100 members in Norway to 350 in Denmark. Meeting at least once a year, membership in the representative council is proportional to membership in the several unions. Of greater importance, from the point of view of policy, is an executive committee of about 15 members, including the Federation chairman, vice-chairman, secretary, and treasurer *ex officio.* The executive committee is elected by the congress, consists of officers of the principal national unions, and is typically vested with a broad range of authority. The extent to which the authority is exercised by the committee as a whole rather than by the Federation officials, varies among the three federations. Although strong individual chairmen have at times gained dominant positions, it is probably true that, on the whole, the executive committee has managed to keep for itself more power than is consistent with efficient administration. By American standards, the Scandinavian central federation official exercises considerable authority. But this springs from the greater centralization of the Scandinavian labor federations, and the reverse is emphatically true when the positions of national union president in the United States and Scandinavia are compared.

The federations are composed of national unions, whose structures parallel that of the federation, in general. The national union, in turn, consists of local unions, each exercising jurisdiction over a specific geographical area. As a rule, as between the national and local union, the preponderance of authority lies with the former. The bulk of dues payments go to the national union (the 80 per cent taken by the national union in the Danish metal trades is typical), and most trade union funds are held at the national level. Because of the prevalence of industry wide bargaining, local unions have little independence in the negotiation of collective agreements, nor do they usually enjoy the authority to call strikes without the consent of the national union. Even in the handling of local grievances, the national union often becomes involved at an early stage. The relationship between the national and local union in Scandinavia has been summarized as follows:

National collective agreements presuppose a central body which can negotiate and agree on behalf of the membership. This does not mean that the local union is without influence upon collective agreements. On the contrary, the national union is not an independent entity, but rather a federation of locals, each of which influences union leadership and union policies through the congress, while the locals and their members also influence the terms of agreements through referendum voting on the results of negotiation. But the national union is the legally contracting party, which implies that the local's everyday influence upon the national agreement must be limited.[18]

One structural distinction between the Danish Federation of Labor on the one hand, and the Norwegian and Swedish federations on the other, is fundamental. An aspect of this difference can be seen from Table 2, in which distribution of membership among national unions is compared. A single Danish national union, the Laborers' Union, catering to unskilled workers, encompassed 38 per cent of total Federation membership, with the two next largest national unions contributing only 15 per cent between them. The remaining 47 per cent of the members were scattered among 69 small craft unions. By contrast, the Norwegian and Swedish federations had a far smaller concentration within large individual national unions, and a more even distribution

TABLE 2

MEMBERSHIP DISTRIBUTION IN THE SCANDINAVIAN LABOR FEDERATIONS, 1949

	Denmark	Norway	Sweden
1. Total membership	636,000	474,000	1,256,000
2. Number of national union affiliates	72	42	44
3. Average number of workers per affiliated union	8,800	11,300	28,500
4. Percentage of Federation membership in the single largest affiliate	38	11	17
5. Percentage of Federation membership in the three largest affiliates...........	53	32	32

Source: Statistical yearbooks for Denmark, Norway, and Sweden, 1950.

among the smaller organizations. The reasons for this structural distinction among the Scandinavian trade union movements are considered below.

Where industrial unionism does not prevail, national unions in related trades are linked by so-called "cartels," analogous to the departments of the American Federation of Labor. In only a few instances, however, have they assumed any real bargaining function. City central trade councils exist in industrial cities of any size, their principal functions limited to educational, welfare, and political activities. In Denmark and Sweden, the unemployment insurance system operates through the trade unions, with separate government subsidized unemployment funds for each national union. Branches of the funds are associated with the local union, which may also operate its own employment ex-

---

[18] Kaj Bundvad and others, *Tillidsmands Kundskab*, pages 67–68. Copenhagen, 1946.

change. All the federations have established educational societies that operate elaborate trade union schools, study circles, and correspondence courses.

Special mention should be made of the labor press, which is one of the most successful enterprises of its kind in the democratic world. Daily labor newspapers are published in most cities and towns of Scandinavia, controlled and edited by the socialist parties, but financed largely by the trade unions. In Stockholm, the Social Democratic Party publishes a morning paper and the Federation of Labor an evening paper. Most workers read only the labor press, which provides a full coverage of the news as well as more parochial labor information. The Norwegian labor press is almost self-supporting, but that of Denmark and Sweden requires considerable subsidy. In addition to the newspapers, the federations and the national unions publish well-edited monthly journals and a constant stream of pamphlets on special subjects. Socialist trade union publishing houses have been established to issue books of special interest to the labor movement. The result of these activities is that the trade unions are able to present their views on current issues to the membership, quickly and fully.

Craft versus industrial unionism

Craft unions were everywhere the pioneers of trade unionism, and they conceived of federation as loose amalgams of semiautonomous crafts. But this ideal was realized only in Denmark, for in Norway and Sweden, unionism is thoroughly industrial in form. The contrasting histories of trade union development in the three Scandinavian countries provide an instructive chapter in the economics of union structure.

Denmark. Most of the national unions that comprise the Danish Federation of Labor are collateral, if not lineal descendants of the gilds. For example, there is a union of coopers, 320 strong; a gilders' union of 110 members; a glovemakers' union of 150. At the opposite end of the scale is the large Laborers' Union, uniting semiskilled and unskilled workers in a variety of industries, and between the two extremes, industrial or semi-industrial unions in such industries as textiles, metalworking, and ceramics.

There has never been a strong industrial union movement in Denmark. The strength of the craft tradition, and the offsetting separate organization of the unskilled workers, created vested interests among both groups. In 1904, when craft unions began to display an interest in the unskilled workers in their industries, the head of the unskilled Laborers' Union retorted:

This is an honor for the laborers. Not so many years ago the craftsmen considered it beneath their dignity to associate with us. . . . It is very kind of them, but the matter has another aspect, namely, whether the laborers are well served by losing influence over the determination of their own conditions of labor, for it has been shown time and again that small industrial organizations are incapable of securing good wages for laborers as a whole.[19]

There were occasional efforts in the direction of industrial unionism, mainly under syndicalist and communist auspices. A committee established by the Federation of Labor, in 1912, to investigate the desirability of structural change, recommended only the establishment of intercraft "cartels" in related trades; but not until 1938, when a building trades "cartel" was established, was this recommendation acted upon.

Some of the larger craft unions, interested in craft amalgamation as a means of eliminating splinter groups, secured the passage, in 1922, of an amendment to a constitutional provision prohibiting admission to the Federation of a local union which had seceded from an affiliated national union, or which was eligible to join a national union, that read as follows: "The provisions of the present paragraph shall not prevent workers, when they so desire, from combining in cartels and industrial unions." The Laborers' Union, fearing that this would open the door to raiding by the crafts, threatened to secede from the Federation, and was prevented from doing so only by an explicit guarantee that locals leaving it without permission would not be accepted into any other union. In the final analysis, "the amendment had no practical results, and there have since been no noteworthy changes in union structure, which may be said to have become static, although the possibility of merging related trades has been discussed from time to time by the interested organizations. . . ."[20] From 1922 to 1950, the number of Federation affiliates rose from 51 to 72, progress away from, rather than toward, industrial unionism.

The nature of Danish industry and the persistence of gild-inherited craft traditions explain, in large part, the horizontal structure of Danish trade unionism. The small scale of Danish manufacturing has already been remarked; many factories are little more than glorified workshops, specializing in the production of quality products. The large factory typical of the newer industry in Norway and Sweden, which renders collective bargaining on a craft basis impracticable, is rarely to be found in Denmark. Producing primarily for the domestic market, and often shielded by tariff walls, Danish employers have been as willing as the unions to protect their trades from undue com-

---

[19] Oluf Bertolt, *M. C. Lyngsie,* page 27. Copenhagen: Forlaget Fremad, 1944.
[20] *Under Samvirkets Flag,* pages 233–234. Copenhagen. 1948

petition. Forty per cent of the Danish labor market is tightly compartmentalized, entrance being gained only through a formal apprenticeship of four or five years which must be commenced before the entrant has reached the age of 16.

The Danish craft unionist is very much the monopolist so well described by Perlman in *A Theory of the Labor Movement*. But he remains true to this prototype only by virtue of the special circumstances of Danish economic development. His Norwegian and Swedish fellows, despite their initial indebtedness to the Danish organizational example, abandoned craft monopoly for broad industrial unionism.

Sweden. Though the majority of the unions that established the Swedish Federation of Labor were craft in form, there were also some important industrial unions in factory industry. A multi-industrial union of unskilled workers, modeled on the Danish Laborers' Union, was making considerable headway at the time. The issue of structure was early called into question not by trade union theorists, but by the rise of large industrial aggregates, which rendered collective bargaining along craft lines increasingly cumbersome, and led to numerous jurisdictional disputes.

The first major victory for industrial unionism resulted from the serious defeat suffered by the labor movement in the general strike of 1909. The Metal Workers' Union, which until that time had been a staunch protagonist of conservatism in union structure, just as strongly espoused industrial unionism as a means of strengthening the trade unions. Largely because of its influence, the 1909 congress of the Federation resolved on "a successive transformation to pure industrial unions with instructions to the secretariat of the Federation of Labor and the union executive boards to work for merger of smaller groups in an industry with the most representative union in the industry." [21] A committee was appointed to work out the practical details.

The report of this committee, consisting of three printed volumes of a thousand pages, was presented to the 1912 congress. It emphasized the increasing difficulty of bargaining on a craft basis, and the undesirability of a situation in which one craft often, in effect, bargained for others, without the consent of the latter, through a species of wage patterns. The general line of the proposed reorganization was: "trade unions should include all workers employed within the same industry, the scope of an industry should coincide with the coverage of collective agreements, and where suitable, smaller industries closely related in production should be joined in a single union." [22] Specifically, it

---

[21] Casparsson, *op. cit.*, page 406.
[22] Casparsson, *op. cit.*, page 406.

was suggested that the 41 national unions then comprising the Federation be amalgamated into 21 industrial unions.

Because of the strenuous opposition of the craft unions, the committee report was adopted with the important qualification that no union could be obliged to change its form of organization "so long as a majority of the union's members feel that a merger . . . would harm the members and their interests." Thus, what was intended as a radical alteration in union structure was transformed in fact into a statement of intentions, with little force behind it. At the 1917 and 1922 congresses, the majority expressed much bitterness over the failure of smaller craft groups to abide by the spirit of the resolution. The principal advances toward industrial unionism came from the splitting off of industrial groups from the heterogeneous Laborers' Union.[23]

The 1922 congress attempted to force the issue by decreeing that reorganization was to be carried through before the end of 1925. But the printing and building trades, and other crafts, adamantly refused to yield their craft sovereignty, and the Federation executive committee was obliged to present to the 1926 congress a more conciliatory reorganization plan, which was eventually carried out. The principal remaining holdouts are the molders, who have steadfastly refused to join with the metal workers, and the printing trades, which have "cartellized" in preference to outright merger. An industrial union of building workers was formed in 1949, although without the affiliation of a few crafts.

The contemporary Swedish labor movement may justly be described as industrial in structure. Only ten percent of Federation members are in craft unions, and even this percentage may be reduced by half if the scope of collective bargaining is used as the criterion of craft independence. An interesting aspect of structural development in Sweden is that ideological considerations played only a minor role in forwarding it (*cf.* Norway and Germany) and that it occurred within the framework of a single trade union center (*cf.* the United States and England). The industrialization of Swedish trade unionism was based to a large extent on plan, and grew out of the explicit recognition by workers of the inherent weaknesses of craft unionism.[24] The relatively poor resistance of the craft unions may be ascribed to the tardy emergence of trade unionism in Sweden, the consequent lack of strong

[23] The Swedish Laborers' Union voluntarily ceded at least 20,000 members to other unions, and has justly been termed an "organizational nursery." See Paul Norgren, *The Swedish Collective Bargaining System,* page 55. Cambridge: Harvard University Press, 1941.

[24] For an excellent discussion of the causes and results of industrial unionism in Sweden, see Jörgen Westerståhl, *Svensk Fackförenings-Rörelse,* pages 37–58. Stockholm: Tidens Förlag, 1945.

craft traditions, and the preponderance in Swedish industrial structure of "new" factories, unrelated to older handicraft enterprises.

Norway. Evolutionary procedure in Norwegian trade union structure differed from that of the Swedish unions, but the end results were much the same. As in the other Scandinavian countries, the early Norwegian national unions were largely of a craft character, with the unskilled workers organized in a union of their own on a multi-industrial basis. Beginning in 1910, the cause of industrial unionism was espoused by the syndicalists, whose strength was concentrated among the workers in the rapidly expanding mass production industry.

At the 1913 congress of the Norwegian Federation of Labor, when the issue of structure was first taken up for serious debate, the opponents of obligatory industrial unionism carried the day by a small majority. But the tide was running against them. To an increasing extent, the Federation came to represent factory workers rather than handicraftsmen. The 1920 congress, by a large majority, declared itself in favor of national union reorganization along industrial lines. Shortly thereafter, a sharp economic recession reduced trade union membership drastically, particularly in those industries in which the syndicalists were strong. The latter group was also weakened by a three-way division of the political labor movement. Nevertheless, the dominant syndicalists decided to move ahead, and at the 1923 congress of the Federation, all affiliated unions were ordered to accede to reorganization by June 30, 1924.

Considerable progress was achieved by this date. Several industrial unions were formed by craft merger, including one in the building trades. But the bricklayers refused to join in, and were expelled from the Federation, to be readmitted later on their own terms. Other crafts that persisted in maintaining their autonomy were the bakers, molders, bookbinders, and locomotive engineers, and the relationship of these organizations to the Federation was often stormy. The question of structure came up for discussion at every subsequent congress of the Federation, but it soon became evident that little more, in the way of consolidation, could be expected.

At the present time, about 85 per cent of Federation membership is concentrated in 15 industrial unions. The remaining members belong to 27 craft organizations, five of them with less than one thousand members each. Despite the adamant position of the craft unions, it is clear that industrial unionism has been substantially achieved. Judging by the Swedish experience, the triumph of industrial unionism would have been likely even in the absence of the specific political history of the Norwegian labor movement, with its strong syndicalist bent, for the logic of Norwegian industrial structure militated against craft collective bargaining. The addition to the economic undercurrent of the driving force of a powerful political movement made the trend toward industrial unionism irresistible.

The problem of trade union centralization

There are striking differences among the Scandinavian trade unions in the power of the central federation *vis-à-vis* that of the national union. The Danish Federation of Labor, though possessed of considerable authority by American or British standards, is clearly the least centralized of the three, with the Norwegian Federation having the greatest degree of central power, and the Swedish Federation approaching the Norwegian in this respect, during the past ten years. To understand why there should be this divergence among movements so closely related, it is again necessary to sketch the development of each movement separately.

Denmark. Although the Danish Federation of Labor has slowly increased its central authority, every advance has been resisted by the powerful Laborers' Union. The skilled crafts, on the other hand, have been the chief advocates of centralism. Secure in their jurisdictions, and generally able to command a majority vote in Federation congresses, they had little to fear from a strong federation. The Laborers, in a minority and ever suspicious of craft encroachment, were reluctant to yield an iota of their autonomy. The strongest allies of the procentralists have been the organized employers, whose aim it has been to deal with a single labor organization capable of committing its affiliates. The chairman of the Danish Employers' Association recently made clear the attitude of his organization in this respect:

> If the Federation of Labor were in a position to change its organizational structure so as to centralize the power to decree and terminate labor disputes to a greater extent, similar to the prevailing situation within the Employers' Association, we would be able to deal as equals, and the contribution of the central organizations to collective bargaining could be made far more significant than it is today.[25]

The Danish Federation of Labor, unlike the Norwegian, has never been the primary repository of union strike funds, and it therefore lacked the sanction of threatening to cut off strike benefits. Although the Federation may levy special assessments to finance strikes, it does not dispose of large sums of cash, and ordinarily provides a minor part of the total strike benefits, most of which are paid out of strike funds accumulated individually by the national unions. With respect

---

[25] *Beretning om Dansk Arbejdsgiverforenings Virksomhed,* page 97. Copenhagen, 1946–1947.

to financing generally, average annual membership dues are 55 kroner per member, of which only 1.52 kroner per member is paid to the Federation as a per capita fee, the balance being retained by the collecting union.

The Federation was empowered, in 1900, to declare sympathetic strikes binding upon constituent unions, but a disastrous exercise of the power two years later caused it to be revoked. At the present time, no affiliate need become involved in a strike unless it votes itself for participation.

The only determined attempt to expand the constitutional authority of the Federation, after this initial setback, came in 1922, when the craft unions proposed that if a wage movement involved more than one union, as is generally the case, the Federation should be empowered to bargain for the unions concerned and to enter into agreements on their behalf. The Laborers' Union moved the following resolution in opposition:

The congress [of the Federation] shall not have authority to conclude agreements involving wages and other conditions of labor on behalf of affiliated organizations or against their wishes, and the executive committee shall not participate in negotiations over agreements unless the craft concerned is represented.

The Laborers' resolution was adopted to avoid an otherwise certain split in the labor movement, and it put an end to further efforts along the same line. The only concession to the centralists was a grant of authority to the Federation to act for the entire labor movement on a range of such "general" questions as the maximum working day, vacations and cost of living supplements to wages. Nevertheless, the pressure of events increased the need for a common union policy in collective bargaining. The centralized Employers' Association introduced the tactic of the "common settlement," that is, of combining all contract negotiations into one wage movement, and refusing to enter into piecemeal agreements. Consequently, agreements involving thousands of workers were often held up because one or two small crafts refused to accept the general terms. This problem was partly, though not entirely, overcome by the enactment of legislation, with Federation consent, curbing the rights of individual crafts, and affording the Federation greater latitude in promoting general settlements, thus accomplishing by indirection what the affiliated unions refused to do directly.

At the present time, the major functions of the Danish Federation of Labor can be summarized as follows:

1. It represents affiliates in government mediation involving na-

tional agreements. While it cannot commit its affiliates, the expertness of Federation negotiators inevitably has an effect upon the outcome.

2. The Federation can *recommend* the calling of sympathetic strikes.

3. The Federation may withhold strike assistance from an affiliate if it disapproves of the strike. However, the financial consequences of such action are not serious, and the power is rarely exercised in practice.

4. Preliminary collective bargaining conferences among unions in related trades are held under Federation auspices.

Sweden. Until 1941, the Swedish Federation of Labor had much the same status as the Danish Federation. A constitutional amendment enacted in that year, however, greatly strengthened its central authority, and placed it almost on a par with the Norwegian Federation.

The Swedish Federation was conceived originally as a purely defensive organization. It could pay benefits only in the event of a lockout, and then only if the number of workers locked out exceeded five per cent of a union's membership. Otherwise, its only function was to act as a statistical clearing house for affiliated unions. The competence of the Federation expanded slowly, partly through custom and partly through formal constitutional change. It became involved in the organization of areas in which there were no existing national unions. In the general stoppage of 1909, the Federation assumed direct leadership over all the workers involved, but in the bitter reaction to defeat, the defensive character of the Federation was reaffirmed. It was not uncommon, for some years thereafter, for affiliates to remain in arrears for the small per capita tax payable to the Federation, since the latter lacked effective means to enforce collection. The stronger unions, wealthy enough to finance their own strikes, wanted nothing to do with a more powerful central body; this despite the fact that they were closely allied with the socialists and were, theoretically, participants in the class struggle.

The widening of Federation authority did not receive serious consideration until the economic depression of the nineteen thirties and the rise of social democracy to political power. In 1934, the Federation intervened in a building strike to bring it to a close, a political necessity, and thereby incurred the wrath of the participating unions. Nevertheless, the 1936 congress of the Federation appointed a fifteen member committee to examine the entire question anew, and the report of this committee, delivered five years later, served as a basis for broad constitutional changes. The trend toward industry-wide bargaining, and the Basic Agreement reached in 1938 directly between the Federation and the Employers' Association, paved the way for recognition of the more important role that the Federation would thenceforth be required to play.

Under the new dispensation, there was to be preliminary consultation among unions in the same industry in formulating wage policy, under the guidance of the executive committee of the Federation of Labor. The latter was empowered to participate in all negotiations involving affiliates, and to formulate settlements. The union involved might reject such a settlement, but, in so doing, it ran the risk of cutting itself off from Federation strike benefits, which were to be paid during strikes as well as lockouts. No union could call a strike involving more than three per cent of its members without Federation approval, again on pain of losing the right to strike benefits. There were other details, all in the direction of greater centralization, and their adoption by an overwhelming vote of the congress revealed the extent to which the national unions had reversed their earlier stand.

The new situation of the Swedish Federation is evident from the events that have taken place since 1942. During the war, wages were regulated by a direct agreement between the Federation of Labor and the Employers' Association. In 1949 and 1950, on the recommendation of the Federation, all affiliated unions agreed to a "wage stop" in the interest of national economic stability. The influence of the Federation has become so great that "bureaucratization" has become a lively subject of discussion in trade union circles. National unions may endeavor to regain a greater measure of autonomy, but the nature of contemporary Swedish economic policy, with its emphasis upon full employment, calls for a degree of trade union coordination and responsibility that can hardly be achieved under atomistic bargaining.

Norway. The Norwegian Federation of Labor has been highly centralized from the start. At the time of its foundation, the labor movement was so weak that the participating unions were interested primarily in a system of strike insurance. A central fund was established for the payment of both strike and lockout benefits, with the Federation contribution constituting the major part of the total benefit payable.

By virtue of its control of strike benefits, the Federation early assumed an active role in labor disputes. The direct financial hold of the Federation has since been weakened because of the failure of its benefit schedule to keep up with the price level; the Federation still pays what it did in 1905, 6 kroner per week per striker, whereas the average strike benefit is now 25 kroner, the balance coming from the national union. However, the political bent of Norwegian trade unionism, resulting at times in near merger of the socialist and trade union leaderships, offset any consequent weakening of the internal trade union bonds. Moreover, no single union was large or strong enough to impose its will on the Federation by threatening to secede (*cf.* Denmark). The national union was kept relatively weak until recent years by syndicalist agitation for city central trade councils as the basic unit of organization.

The present constitution of the Norwegian Federation of Labor requires that all wage demands that are not of purely local significance be approved by the Federation in advance of submission to the employer. Failure to do so may mean loss of financial assistance, and more important, of the moral and political support which the Federation can provide. The Federation is always represented in government mediation proceedings, and its representatives conduct the proceedings for the unions if more than one union is involved. In the event of a strike involving more than one union, the Federation assumes active strike leadership, and, thereafter, none of the participating unions may settle without its permission. The executive committee of the Federation has become, in a practical sense, the general staff of the trade union movement.

The already considerable authority of the Federation of Labor was further augmented by the process of wage determination that has prevailed in Norway since 1945. All unresolved disputes have, in effect, been subject to compulsory governmental arbitration, and the essence of wage policy has been determined by the Federation, in close collaboration with Norway's labor government, with little discretion left to individual national unions.

Internal union affairs

There are differences only on details among the Scandinavian trade unions on the conduct of their day to day operation. In all three countries, Federation statute forbids denial of trade union membership to qualified workers. The closed and union shop are not formally practiced because of long standing employer insistence on freedom to hire, and retain in employment, competent workers, regardless of union status. However, the high degree of union organization renders the question academic; workers join unions as a matter of course, and the rare individual who refuses to join, on principle, is not bothered. The dues check-off is also unknown, for the unions regard the payment of dues as a matter with which the employer is not properly concerned. Absence of the closed shop and the check-off reflect the degree to which Scandinavian unions have attained security without the necessity of such coercive devices.

Initiation fees are normally nominal. Dues payment varies considerably among unions, depending largely upon the type of union welfare plans in effect.[26] On the average, the incidence of dues payments is higher in Scandinavia than in the United States. The bulk of dues payments remains with the national union, and of the three federations, the Swedish is best off in terms of per capita taxation. During 1949, the income of the Swedish Federation of Labor was 9.3 million kroner (almost two million dollars). The total capital of the Swedish trade unions was 180 million kroner (36 million dollars), a very large sum of money for Scandinavia, and illustrative of the sound financial basis of Scandinavian trade unionism.

All members in good standing have the right to participate fully in membership meetings, and to share in union benefit schemes. The Danish unions, in particular, have gone in for mutual welfare plans, such as sick and death benefits and old age and invalidity pensions. Strike assistance is a matter of right, the payments often equalling the level of unemployment compensation benefits.[27]

By American standards, trade union officials are poorly paid. For example, the chairman of the Norwegian Federation of Labor receives about as much as a medium-level civil servant, and the compensation of other trade union officials is correspondingly lower. As a consequence, the trade unions have been losing good people to the civil and municipal services, which have been opened increasingly to persons with labor backgrounds since the advent of the labor governments; but attempts to raise union salaries have foundered on the rock of rank and file insistence that salaries be no higher than maximum earnings in the trade.

One attribute of Scandinavian trade union democracy that has been increasingly discarded in recent years because of its incompatibility with centralized collective bargaining is the membership referendum on new agreements. Twenty-five years ago it was a strict rule in most Scandinavian unions that no collective agreement be finally ratified until it had been approved by a majority of the workers covered, voting by secret ballot. But with general wage movements replacing individual union bargaining, it became impracticable to permit the members of one of the participating unions to block an agreement favored by a majority of the members of all participating unions combined. Moreover, the percentage of worker participation in

---

[26] In Denmark, the unskilled worker pays 40 øre per week, equal to 0.3 per cent of his wage, and the printer 9.25 kroner, or 5.7 per cent.

[27] The great Swedish metal trades strike of 1945 cost the trade unions about 8 million dollars in strike assistance alone.

referenda on agreements often fell very low, thus enabling organized minorities to exercise undue influence on union policy.

The referendum was eliminated in various ways. Danish unions still adhere to the voting procedure scrupulously, but the rules for tabulating the votes are such as to make virtually impossible the defeat of a contract approved by the leadership. Revision of the constitution of the Swedish Federation of Labor in 1941 obliged every affiliate to insert in its own constitution a provision establishing "the right of the executive committee of the union to make final decisions in questions concerning the termination of collective agreements, the ratification or rejection of proposed agreements and the adoption of measures in the event of conflict." Workers may still be polled in Sweden, but their vote is advisory. Most Norwegian union constitutions retain the referendum, but, since 1945, this right has atrophied as a consequence of compulsory arbitration.

Employer organization

Some knowledge of employer organization is essential to an understanding of the Scandinavian labor market, for Scandinavian employers have united for the purpose of collective bargaining to a degree unmatched elsewhere. They have displayed greater solidarity than the workers, socialist preachments of class consciousness notwithstanding, and it was largely their insistence upon broadening the unit of collective bargaining that forced centralization on the Danish and Swedish trade unions.

The oldest and strongest of the Scandinavian employer associations is the Danish. Preceding national organization in 1898, there was a long history of local and industrial organization. As in the case of the labor movement, the Danish employer associations were rooted in the gild system. There are numerous examples not only of gild initiative in the formation of employer associations, but of the actual transformation of masters' gilds into employer associations. The fact that it proved possible as early as 1898 to unite a large proportion of the nation's employers in a single association attests to the persistence of the corporate spirit in Denmark.

Chronologically, the Norwegian Employers' Association, organized in 1900, came next. But its antecedents were of more recent origin than the Danish, and its membership was relatively smaller. The Swedish Employers' Association was formed in 1902, but not until 1917 and 1918, when it was joined by the bulk of the employers in the machinery and building industries, could it claim to represent Sweden's employers to anything like the same degree as the Danish Association.

The Scandinavian employer associations are built up as federations of industrial associations. Some of the structural differences among them emerge in Table 3, from which it may be seen that employer organization tends to parallel trade union organization, that is, Danish employers are divided by craft,[28] whereas Norwegian and Swedish employers tend to organize more strictly along industrial lines. The

TABLE 3

Structure of the Scandinavian Employer Associations

	Number of Member Associations	Number of Member Establishments	Number of workers employed by members
Denmark (1948) ...	251	23,140	274,300
Norway (1946)	16	4,400	160,000
Sweden (1948)	40	10,700	637,000

Sources: *Denmark: Statistical Yearbook,* 1949, page 183. *Norway:* Galenson, *Labor in Norway,* page 81. *Sweden:* Smith and Åberg, *Arbetsgivare-Arbetstagare* page 55.

Danish Association is the most representative of the three, only a small association of agricultural employers remaining outside its ranks. The Swedish Employers' Association includes only 40 of some 80 national employer associations, the most important of the independents covering ocean transportation, private railways, agriculture, and lumbering. Norwegian employers in the major export industries, paper, lumber, shipping, and whaling are organized independently of the Norwegian Employers' Association.

In every case, the number of workers employed by members of the employer associations is considerably less than total trade union membership. However, this does not provide a true measure of the relative strength of the organizations. Labor organization in the municipalities, the state railways, the postal and communications system, and the civil service naturally has no counterpart among employers. While there are many unassociated employers in manufacturing, the associations include all the larger establishments, by virtue of which their policies have ramifications far beyond their membership ranks.

All the employer associations are governed by annual congresses, smaller central councils meeting three or four times a year, and influential executive committees that tend to become the real policy making bodies. The chief executive officers of the Norwegian and Swedish associations are full-time, permanent officials. The knowledge

---

[28] Structural dispersion in the Danish Employers' Association is overcome by grouping craft associations into large subassociations for collective bargaining. The most important of these subassociations, that in the metal trades, bargains on behalf of 29 separate associations.

acquired by permanent secretariat members of labor law, the strategy of bargaining, the personalities on the union side, and the internal politics of trade unions is impressive. In consequence, Scandinavian employers receive a quality of collective bargaining representation that would be far beyond the means of the individual employer, and at a relatively small financial cost.

Under the Danish scheme of dues payment, each member firm pays annual dues to the Employers' Association equal to 0.5 per cent of its wage bill, plus 0.25 per cent to the strike fund of the local association to which it belongs. Norwegian employers pay a flat one per cent of payroll, while in Sweden, dues are currently 20 kroner ($4) per year for each adult male worker employed and 10 kroner for each female and minor worker. The Swedish plan. protects Association finances from loss during periods of recession, but the Danish and Norwegian plans maintain the real value of contributions without requiring periodic rate adjustments, always a difficult matter politically. Norwegian and Swedish employers are required, in addition to their dues payments, to post guarantee bonds that may be cashed or used as collateral, should the regular strike funds become exhausted.

Strike or lockout benefit payments are subject to considerable variation among the countries. In Denmark, where part of the payment is made by the local associations, there is little uniformity, though the amount is generally fixed at a percentage of the employer's wage bill prior to the stoppage. The usual Swedish benefit is one krone (20 cents) per worker per day, though the rates may be raised in the event of a stoppage of long duration. The Norwegian Employers' Association pays maximum benefits of .05 per cent of the employer's payroll during the preceding year for each day the work stoppage remains in effect, but the payment may be reduced if this formula results in inequitable overpayment. The general rule is that benefits are paid only when a work stoppage is sanctioned by the Association, so that, for example, if an employer suffers a strike after refusing to accept contract terms recommended by the Association, he may be denied benefits.

This is not the only disciplinary means possessed by the employers' association. An employer who continues to work despite a directive to cease operations, or who signs a separate agreement with a union during a general strike, is subject to heavy fine. There have been few breaches of discipline among employers, due in no small measure to the drastic reprisals with which they were met.

Benefit payments to employers are not of the same significance as trade union strike benefits. It is true that they represent emergency payments designed to tide the recipient over a period of stress, and to that extent the two are alike. But trade union benefits are intended to provide the worker with a subsistence minimum which will enable him to remain away from work for long periods if necessary, and the ability of the union to continue benefit payments may be a decisive factor in the outcome of a dispute. Employer benefits, on the other hand, are not of sufficient magnitude to constitute a determining factor in the employer's decision to resist or capitulate. Of much greater importance is the economic picture, the employer's current business opportunities, his inventory and credit position. The benefit sanction, therefore, is not sufficient in itself to ensure the maintenance of employer discipline; the power to fine, moral suasion, and the threat of future economic reprisal are of greater effect.

Bargaining procedure is considered in the following section. Here are pointed out two important elements concerning the role of the employers' association in collective bargaining. First, no local employer association or member firm may enter into a collective agreement without the advance approval of the central employers' association. What has been said of the Swedish Employers' Association is true of all:

In practice, the [constituent] associations have gone far toward entrusting the [Employers' Association] with authority to carry the burden of negotiations right up to the actual signing. An association's officials will always carry the burden of bargaining when its contract is being negotiated; but the [Employers' Association], which has usually, on its own initiative, approached the association weeks before the expiring of its old contract concerning its wishes in respect of a renewal or a new contract, will have put itself in command of the major lines of policy to be pursued. It is only concerning contracts covering a whole industry that the [Association] plays an active role as negotiator, but even as to minor contracts it may have to step in after the local negotiations have failed.[29]

Secondly, until the last decade, the lockout was widely employed by the employer associations. In Denmark, between 1898 and 1946, there was a total of 343,000 striking workers and 330,000 locked out workers.[30] No division between strikes and lockouts in terms of working time lost is available, but the average duration of lockouts has been at least as great as that of strikes.

Collective Bargaining and Its Results

The collective bargaining system

In their broad essentials, the Scandinavian collective bargaining systems are fairly uniform. Industry-wide bargaining, and on certain

---

[29] James J. Robbins, *The Government of Labor Relations in Sweden,* pages 69–70. Chapel Hill, University of North Carolina Press, 1942.

[30] *Under Samvirkets Flag, op. cit.,* page 560.

issues, nationwide bargaining, are practiced. Government intervention, in the form of mediation and quasi-arbitration, is common to the three systems, while contract interpretation disputes are subject to arbitration by governmental labor courts. The principal difference among the countries arises at the point where voluntary methods of conciliation and mediation have failed; beyond that point, the degree of government compulsion is greatest in Norway and least in Sweden.

No useful purpose would be served by separate analysis of each of the Scandinavian collective bargaining systems. I will outline instead the main features of the oldest and best developed of the three, and the one which has served as a model for the others—the Danish system —with appropriate annotations in case of significant deviations in Swedish and Norwegian practice. For the reader interested in greater detail, there are now lengthy descriptions of the three systems available in English.[31]

Danish collective bargaining is based upon an agreement, concluded in 1899, between the Danish Employers' Association and the Danish Federation of Labor, providing, *inter alia*, for mutual recognition of the right to organize. This document firmly established collective bargaining as the predominant method of industrial relations, and is rightly considered the Danish labor constitution.[32] Early rapproachement between the two central labor market organizations, which must be attributed primarily to the strong collective traditions of the country, led to a highly centralized system of collective bargaining. Already in 1910, industry-wide bargaining prevailed in many trades, and, subsequently, such questions as hours of labor, grievance procedure, and cost of living wage adjustments became the subject of uniform nationwide agreements. Organized employers, anxious to avoid the "whipsaw" tactics of powerful unions, sought to standardize bargaining procedure, and since 1936 all agreements between members of the Employers' Association and the Federation of Labor expire on March 1 of every year or, in the case of two year agreements, every other year.[33]

An exact collective bargaining timetable was codified in 1936, by agreement. Notice of intention to terminate an existing agreement, to-

---

[31] *Denmark:* Walter Galenson, *The Danish System of Labor Relations,* Cambridge: Harvard University Press, 1952; *Norway:* Walter Galenson, *Labor in Norway,* Cambridge, 1949; *Sweden:* Paul Norgren, *The Swedish Collective Bargaining System,* Cambridge: Harvard University Press, 1941; James J. Robbins, *The Government of Labor Relations in Sweden,* Chapel Hill: University of North Carolina Press, 1942.

[32] Agreements of similar import were reached in Norway and Sweden in 1935 and 1939 respectively.

[33] This is not true in Norway and Sweden, where contract expiration dates are scattered throughout the year.

gether with the specific changes demanded, must be in the hands of the opposite party three months prior to the expiration date, that is, December 1, and no new demands may be presented thereafter. Informal policy discussions are held within each organization, in September and October, in an effort to secure joint lines of action on each side. Ordinarily, the Employers' Association develops a specific set of recommendations which are followed explicitly by its members. On the side of the union, insistence upon national union autonomy militates against uniform policy at this stage.[34]

On December 1, negotiations begin between the separate national unions and industry associations of employers, lasting for a maximum of six weeks.[35] For trades in which agreement is not reached by January 15 (which has come increasingly to mean all trades) a new phase of collective bargaining begins, involving the two central organizations. The basic questions are segregated, and the negotiators concentrate upon formulation of key bargains, usually wage questions.[36]

One month is allotted to central organization bargaining. If, by February 15, there are still outstanding questions, the final phase is begun under the auspices of a government mediator.[37] As a condition of intervention, the mediator may require the parties to postpone work stoppages for a period of one week. In practice, mediation is always accepted with this condition, and the parties agree to refrain from stoppages until the mediator feels that no useful purpose is served by prolonging the proceedings.[38] Mediation proceedings are a cross between arbitration and bargaining, the mediator attempting to conciliate the parties, and at the same time familiarizing himself with regard to the details of the dispute.

The climax of the bargaining process comes with the formulation of a so-called "mediation proposal," promulgated by the mediator if he

---

[34] The Swedish and Norwegian unions have achieved virtual unanimity of action since 1945, due to the special circumstances of the economic system in which they have been operating.

[35] Neither in Sweden nor in Norway does this preliminary stage ordinarily last so long. In Sweden, when questions of major importance are involved, the negotiators usually invite a government mediator to participate. At this stage he acts in a private capacity and is paid by the parties.

[36] Bargaining is much less centralized in Sweden, and, generally, contracts are signed industry by industry. In 1949 and 1950, however, a uniform wage policy was adopted for all contracts expiring during those years, and there is an unmistakable tendency in this direction.

[37] The mediation phase is conducted in Sweden by a three member commission in important controversies. Denmark and Norway use single mediators only.

[38] The Norwegian mediator has the legal authority to suspend work stoppages for 14 days after he has intervened. There is no specific stoppage delaying provision in the Swedish law, though the parties must meet at the call of the mediator, and will rarely break off negotiations without his assent.

feels that there is any basis for settlement. Ordinarily, he will refrain from issuing such a proposal if either negotiating committee informs him that what he regards as reasonable is not acceptable. At the present time, acceptance of a proposal by the negotiators is tantamount to final settlement, although in the past such proposals were often rejected by a vote of the rank and file on the side of the union.

Government intervention beyond mediation

The Scandinavian systems of industrial relations diverge sharply at this point. In Sweden, both labor and management have been staunch opponents of compulsory arbitration, and thus far they have been successful in avoiding this ultimate exercise of governmental authority. A joint board was set up by the Swedish Basic Agreement of 1939 (the famous Saltsjöbaden Agreement) and was charged with the duty of intervening in any dispute that threatens to disturb vital public services, on the theory that this is the best means of avoiding governmental compulsion. However, there has not yet been sufficient experience under the Agreement to permit a conclusive statement that it is an adequate substitute for government intervention in times of stress.

The Norwegian experience has been precisely the opposite. During the periods 1916–1920, 1922–1923, 1927–1929 and 1945 to the present (1951), government wage boards with compulsory authority were established to decide disputes that did not yield to voluntary collective bargaining.[39] Prior to 1945, government intervention resulted from repeated failure of the collective bargaining system to function adequately, leading to protracted work stoppages. Since 1945, compulsory arbitration has been fostered by the Labor government in order to advance economic reconstruction of the country.

Danish practice has been intermediate between that of Sweden and Norway. In theory, both labor and management subscribe to nonintervention, and before 1933, the government, by and large, confined itself to moral pressure. But in 1933, a socialist government inaugurated a policy of more active intervention, and since then, it has been fairly common for the parliament to enact into law mediation proposals that have been rejected by one of the parties in important disputes. The procedure is entirely *ad hoc;* there is no wage board, and

---

[39] Technically, Norway abandoned compulsory arbitration in 1949. Under the law in effect from 1949 to 1951, only those disputes arising from union or employer demands that are not sanctioned, respectively, by the Federation of Labor or an employers' association are subject to adjudication by a wage board. Both the Federation and employer associations have refused to approve demands that might lead to work stoppages, however, thus retaining compulsory arbitration for all practical purposes.

the parties are often unaware until the very last minute whether the government will intervene, or whether, instead, it will permit threatened stoppages of work to run their course.

Industrial warfare

The countries of Scandinavia have not been uniformly successful in averting work stoppages arising out of labor disputes. Table 4 compares the records of the three countries in this respect; it shows the total of man-days lost due to labor disputes, by five year periods, from 1905 to 1949 (excepting the war years 1940–1944), and the ratio of man-days lost to potential working time of trade union members. In almost every period, time lost in Denmark has been significantly less than in Norway or Sweden. The Norwegian record, on the whole, has been worse than the Swedish.

TABLE 4

LABOR DISPUTES IN THE SCANDINAVIAN COUNTRIES, 1905–1949

	Denmark		Norway		Sweden	
	Man-days lost in labor disputes (thousands)	Ratio of man-days lost to potential working time of union members (percent)	Man-days lost in labor disputes (thousands)	Ratio of man-days lost to potential working time of union members (percent)	Man-days lost in labor disputes (thousands)	Ratio of man-days lost to potential working time of union members (percent)
1905–1909	965	0.66	1,030	1.78	16,225	7.73
1910–1914	1,197	0.58	2,018	2.43	1,825	0.95
1915–1919	1,597	0.37	1,954	1.36	5,399	1.22
1920–1924	5,094	1.05	10,822	7.44	22,395	3.91
1925–1929	4,333	0.93	4,807	3.34	10,171	1.37
1930–1934	641	0.14	8,819	4.03	10,937	1.12
1935–1939	3,087	0.44	3,005	0.64	3,530	0.28
1945–1949	1,935	0.25	277	0.06	11,624	0.87

Source: Walter Galenson, *The Danish System of Labor Relations*, Cambridge, 1952, Appendix A.

There is no simple explanation for these differences. Some factors that may be relevant are: (a) the smaller unit size of Danish enterprise, permitting closer personal relations between employer and employee; (b) the earlier development of collective bargaining in Denmark; (c) greater elaboration in Denmark of institutional devices for avoiding stoppages; (d) the higher absolute living standards of Danish and Swedish workers; (e) the greater strength of the spirit of cooperation in Danish life.

The period of greatest industrial strife was during the years 1920 to 1924, when money wages were reduced sharply as a consequence of the postwar deflation. Not since before 1900 had money wages fallen at all. Since real wages fell on several additional occasions, the Scandinavian experience serves to emphasize the potentialities of conflict inherent in efforts to reduce money wages, in contrast to the much less explosive reaction to reduction of real wages through price increases.

Since 1935, work stoppages have remained at a low level in all three countries. The coincidence of the improvement in industrial relations with the rise of labor to governmental power is striking. It was a socialist government in Denmark that inaugurated government intervention to avoid nationwide work stoppages. The remarkable Norwegian strike record since 1945 can only be attributed to close cooperation between the trade unions and the Labor government. The only serious dispute in Sweden since 1935,[40] the metal trades strike of 1945, represented essentially a socialist maneuver to break the hold of the communists upon this important organization. When the "middle way" of Scandinavian labor relations is held up as a model, the political position of labor must not be forgotten.

In considering the conduct of industrial warfare, there has been much less violence in Scandinavia than, for example, in the United States. The use of strike-breakers has been rare in this century. The percentage of union organization is so high, and union discipline so strong, that picketing is unnecessary as a rule. It is sufficient for a union merely to announce a strike to close an enterprise down. In the early days of the Scandinavian labor movement, blacklisting, eviction from company houses, the use of the police to stop picketing were not unknown. But so unusual was outright violence that the accidental shooting of five persons by the police during a Swedish strike in 1931 caused a revulsion among the workers that embittered labor relations throughout the country for fully ten years thereafter.

A common weapon in Scandinavian industrial warfare, reflecting the degree of organization on both sides, was the sympathetic strike and the sympathetic lockout. The Swedish trade unions, since their defeat in 1909, have been reluctant to embark upon sympathetic strikes, but the Danish and Norwegian unions, and organized employers in all three countries, have acted in concert on numerous occasions. A chairman of the Swedish Employers' Association once remarked that "without the right of the sympathetic lockout, the employers' association would almost cease to exist." [41] It requires highly disciplined organizations to force workers and employers, who have no quarrel with one

---

[40] There were extensive strikes among municipal employees in the spring of 1951, the first significant strike wave since 1945.

[41] Casparsson, *op. cit.*, page 274.

another, to come to the aid of their fellows at considerable sacrifice to themselves. Since the advent of the labor governments, the incidence of sympathetic lockouts has fallen almost to the vanishing point, while the sympathetic strike, never popular among workers, is falling into similar disuse.

The labor courts

The foregoing account of collective bargaining applies only to *new* collective agreements. It is well established in Scandinavia that disputes over the interpretation of *existing* agreements must not lead to stoppages of work. To this end, a labor court has been established in each country, and while such tribunals are not distinctively Scandinavian, their development has proceeded furthest in the Scandinavian countries.

The Danish Labor Court was established in 1910, the Norwegian in 1915, and the Swedish in 1928. The statutes of the Danish court were drafted jointly by organized labor and management, but the Norwegian and Swedish courts had to surmount the initial handicaps of general strikes called by the unions in protest. The courts are all tripartite in form, although they differ in the precise representation accorded to labor, management and the public.[42] Public representatives are usually chosen from the regular judiciary. The labor courts have exclusive jurisdiction over all contract interpretation disputes, and appeal from their decisions can be taken to the regular courts only on the question of their jurisdiction. Procedure is quite formal, though trade unions are often represented by their officials rather than by lawyers. Labor court decisions are enforcible as ordinary judgments at law, even to the extent of checking off amounts from the wages of workers who have been found guilty of contract breach and fined. However, strict contract principles are not followed in fixing damages, the courts possessing the right to reduce or remit damage claims entirely if there are extenuating circumstances, for example, employer provocation that produces an unlawful strike.

The labor courts are now completely accepted by labor as well as by management. Labor has resorted to the courts more than management, and if the individual worker is not always satisfied with court decisions, the administrative burden of union officials is greatly lightened by the existence of the courts. The Danish Labor Court, from 1910

[42] The Danish court has a single public presiding justice and three representatives each of labor and management, the presiding justice being elected by the others for a one year term. The Norwegian and Swedish courts have three public, two labor and two management members, the term of office being three years and two years respectively.

to 1948, handled over 4,000 cases, the Norwegian Labor Court (1916–1940) some 1,650 cases, and the Swedish Labor Court (1929–1939) some 1,970 cases. Employers tend to win a greater proportion of cases than the unions, but this is due largely to the fact that union officials must prosecute, for political reasons, many cases which they know to be unsound.

The ordinary courts have been almost entirely eliminated from participation in Scandinavian industrial relations. But private industrial arbitration flourishes, since the great majority of contract disputes are submitted voluntarily to permanent or *ad hoc* industrial boards. The authority of the labor court is usually invoked only when important matters of principle are involved. This has enabled the labor court to prevent the accumulation of many cases on its docket, to the extent that decisions are ordinarily rendered within a month of the filing of a case, and in the event of extraordinary circumstances requiring greater speed, for example, a strike, within a few days.

Other factors help explain the success of the labor courts. Since only organizations, and not individuals, can appear before a labor court, there is a preliminary sifting of cases, resulting in the elimination of most bad ones. Court personnel has been stable, and application of *stare decisis* has provided a necessary minimum of consistency to the law of collective agreements. There is general agreement that the tripartite character of the courts has made a major contribution toward the prevention of legalism at the expense of practicality.

Some results of collective bargaining

Conditions of labor in industrial employment are almost universally determined by collective bargaining in contemporary Scandinavia. For almost half a century, the trade unions have been equal, and more recently, predominant, partners in the negotiation of collective agreements. It is therefore of interest to examine wage trends to determine how workers have fared under this unusual and highly developed system of industrial relations.

Table 5 shows the trend of money and real wages from 1900 to 1949, by five year intervals, for each country. The reader is warned that for the years prior to 1914 for Denmark and Sweden, and until recent years for Norway, the data are approximate, showing only, in a general way, the direction of wage movements. They are in index form, and since there is no relationship among the base year figures for the three countries, it is not possible to draw any conclusions from the table regarding comparative absolute wage levels.

According to the data, real wages in Scandinavia rose between 240 and 270 per cent from 1900 to 1949, while money wages increased about eightfold. In relating these facts to labor welfare, it is necessary to take into account the elaborate social insurance system of Scandinavia. For example, during the fiscal year 1945–46, Denmark and Sweden devoted 7.6 per cent and 4.1 per cent of their respective national incomes to social insurance payments, while the corresponding Norwegian figure for the year 1947 was 5.3 per cent. Such payments were undoubtedly very small in 1900, and since industrial workers are the chief beneficiaries of social security payments, it is clear that wage changes alone do not reflect the true measure of improvement in their welfare.

There is no question that whatever welfare yardstick one may care to employ, the living standards of Scandinavian workers have gone up substantially over the past half century. Earnings data tend to lose their meaning over so long a period, in view of technological change and altered habits of consumption. But one need only visit the magnificent low-cost housing developments that have been constructed during the last twenty years; compare paid vacation periods for the two periods (three weeks in Norway, and two weeks in Denmark and Sweden, in 1949); and examine the comprehensive systems of sickness, disability, old age, unemployment and invalidity insurance that now prevail, to conclude that life has become easier and fuller for the worker.

Improvement has not been a matter of uniform growth, but has come in waves, judging by the data on earnings. The greatest gains were achieved after the two world wars, under conditions of wage-price inflation and high employment levels. Whether as cause or effect, both these periods witnessed radicalization of the labor movement and an aggressive trade union wage policy.

One of the most interesting aspects of Table 5 is the failure of the Danish real wage index to keep pace with the Norwegian and Swedish indices after 1930, though up to that time the three had moved together fairly closely. The divergence must be ascribed primarily to the different impact of changes in the terms of foreign trade upon the three countries. Denmark exports agricultural commodities and imports industrial raw materials and manufactured goods, whereas Norway and Sweden export industrial raw materials and import agricultural commodities. The relative fall in the world market prices of agricultural goods that took place in the great depression represented a blow to the Danish economy from which there has still not been full recovery. The Danish balance of payments problem at the present time (1951) is much more critical than that of Norway or Sweden. The continued gap between agricultural and industrial prices

exercises a depressing effect upon Danish national product, which is
reflected in real wages.

TABLE 5

INDEXES OF MONEY AND REAL WAGES IN SCANDINAVIA, 1900–1949
(1914 = 100)

Year	Denmark		Norway		Sweden	
	Average hourly earnings	Real average hourly earnings	Average hourly earnings	Real average hourly earnings	Average hourly earnings	Real average hourly earnings
1900	64	81	69	83	70	82
1905	75	93	71	88	77	90
1910	93	104	81	95	96	103
1914	100	100	100	100	100	100
1915	101	87	107	90	114	100
1920	389	149	411	147	380	145
1925	311	147	335	148	261	151
1930	271	164	259	169	279	175
1935	273	161	249	177	270	178
1940	337	144	338	177	338	180
1945	466	160	409	174	443	189
1949	586	192	585	215	571	219

Source: Walter Galenson, *The Danish System of Labor Relations*, Cambridge,
1952, Appendix A.

International comparisons of absolute living standards are exceedingly difficult to make because of varying patterns of living among
countries, and, at best, they can only be very general. The best available evidence indicates that Swedish worker living standards are
slightly higher than Danish, and substantially above Norwegian.[43] It
is probably true that until World War II, the Danish worker enjoyed
the most favorable standards in Scandinavia. A United Nations study
in 1949 concluded that "the purchasing power of hourly earnings in
terms of food is about three-quarters of that in the United States in
the case of the United Kingdom and the Scandinavian countries;
about half of that in the United States in Switzerland, Finland and
Ireland; one-third in France and Hungry; and about one-quarter in
Italy and Austria."[44] Worker housing in Scandinavia is far above the
European average in terms of modernity and space, and compares
favorably with the United States. Clothing comparisons are difficult
to make because of varying climatic conditions. It may be concluded
that, in general, the material conditions of the Scandinavian worker

------

[43] The subject is under intensive study by the trade unions in the three countries, and within a few years it should be possible to reach more definite conclusions.
[44] Economic Commission for Europe, *Economic Survey of Europe 1949*, page
37.

exceed those enjoyed by workers in the rest of Europe, with the possible exception of Switzerland [45] and Great Britain.

The extent to which high worker living standards in Scandinavia may be attributed to the political and economic power of the labor movement is not a question that can be settled by recourse to statistics. The rise in real wages since 1900 was undoubtedly due primarily to industrialization. As Montgomery has pointed out, "there is nothing surprising in the fact that countries which felt the influence of industrialization much later than England should have had a more rapid tempo in wage increases." [46] It will also be recalled that Scandinavia was spared the material destruction of World War I that did so much to undermine the economies of other nations of Europe.

Yet it is doubtful whether in the absence of a powerful labor movement, the Scandinavian workers would have managed to attain anything like their current standards. Since 1930, government economic policy has consistently favored the wage-earner. Through sharply progressive income taxation, almost confiscatory inheritance taxation, subsidies to housing through low interest rates, food subventions and social security measures, a more equal distribution of income has been achieved. Unemployment has been virtually eliminated through fiscal policy measures and direct controls. Trade unions can exact money wage increases from employers almost at will, being restrained mainly by considerations of consequent price effects.

Labor Ideology

Scandinavian labor is homogeneous from an ideological point of view. The trade unions are in close alliance with socialist parties that advocate approximately similar economic and political programs. But the roads over which the three movements traveled to the present ideological unity were not parallel. Danish socialism was, from the beginning, a moderate movement, and extremists were never able to gain a foothold within the main labor current. Swedish labor was more subject to the influence of syndicalism, left-wing socialism and communism, though the bulk of the trade unions consistently supported a moderate social democracy. The Norwegian labor movement, however, deviated sharply leftward for many years, and, for a brief period, was even part of international communism.

The reasons for such differences among people whose cultural back-

---

[45] For a Swedish trade union demonstration that real wages of the Swedish worker substantially exceed that of the Swiss worker, see *Tiden*, 1948, pages 373–375.

[46] Arthur Montgomery, *Svensk Ekonomiska Historia 1913–1939*, page 21. Stockholm, 1946.

grounds are so similar have never been explored satisfactorily. It is usually assumed that there are "psychological" differences to explain the varying reactions; that the Norwegian is more radical and the Dane more conservative by temperament. Actually, a review of some factors in the economic development of the three countries provides a cogent explanation of the observed ideological variations.

The formation of socialist ideology

It was pointed out earlier that the social milieu from which industrial workers came, and the rate at which the industrial labor force was built up, were not uniform in Scandinavia. In general, recruits to the industrial working class tended to come from among farm *laborers* in Denmark, whereas in Sweden, and to an even greater extent in Norway, they tended to be drawn from among the *smallholders*. The rate of industrial expansion was higher in Sweden and Norway than in Denmark, and came at a later date.

Considering the Danish case first, population movement from the country to the city during the years of most rapid industrialization, 1870 to 1900, was steady, but not spectacular. There was no parallel to the explosive population transfers that characterized the industrial revolution in Great Britain, nor was there the pauperization of workers which contributed so basically to the building up of the Marxian theoretical system. In 1901, Denmark was still predominantly rural; 61 per cent of the population lived in rural communities, and perhaps half the remainder in towns with close ties to the land. The Danish farm worker, when he moved to the city, generally improved his living standards. For example, "housing conditions in Copenhagen were much improved during the eighties and nineties. More and more the workers moved out of the old city, and no longer were buildings put up without regard to light and air, as was often the case in the seventies." [47]

Late industrialization was, in part, responsible for this favorable development. Gross exploitation of labor was forestalled by factory legislation. The following description of conditions in Sweden applies equally to Denmark:

England's factories shot up in cities with medieval hygienic conditions; in Manchester, which Engels described, houses were built "like small villages on the naked, grassless clay. . . ." In Sweden, the growth of urban industry in the 1870's coincided with urban hygienic reform. It was of very great sig-

---

[47] Even Marstrand, *Arbejderorganisation og Arbejderkaar i Danmark,* page 142. Copenhagen: Martins Forlag, 1934.

nificance that the expansion of Swedish industry first began when methods of improving city health had already been tried out in other countries.[48]

Moreover, a great many Danish factory workers came from the urban artisan class. They had received a certain degree of protection from the gild regulations, many of which were carried over into trade union agreements. They had had previous industrial experience, they were inured to the discipline of the workshop, and were accustomed to the method of collective negotiation as a means of bettering their economic status.

It is small wonder, therefore, that the Danish workers were not likely recruits for extremist political movements preaching revolution. Though nominally Marxist, Danish socialism was, from the beginning, gradualist. It was nurtured in a political milieu devoid of state repression, and derived much of its support from well-situated craftsmen who had achieved substantial economic results through the method of collective bargaining. After the flight of the original founders, Pio and Geleff, Danish social democracy was under the leadership of men drawn from the upper level of the working class: Peter Knudsen, a glovemaker; Emil Wiinblad, a printer; Thorvald Stauning (who was largely responsible for building the formidable party machine), a cigar maker; and Hans Hedtoft, a lithographer. Dominance by the skilled workers was due in no small measure to the fact that craft unionism was already firmly established when political socialism began to grow. The workers looked upon political action as a means of supplementing union economic power in the daily struggle for better conditions of labor, and not for achieving any social millennium through radical change. Dictatorship of the proletariat has always been an alien concept in Denmark, and the hue and cry over "minister socialism" in France never found an echo in Denmark, where it was accepted as natural that the Social Democratic Party should assume parliamentary responsibility in proportion to its strength.

The ideological history of the Norwegian labor movement is diametrically opposed to that of Denmark. The explosive industrialization of the country, recruitment of industrial workers from small farms without previous experience in steady employment, and the poor working and living conditions they found in the hastily constructed industrial towns, all contributed to the formation of an extreme, radical ideology, matched by few others in Europe. The official history of the Norwegian Federation of Labor, in some striking passages, bears these observations out:

---

[48] Gårdlund, *op. cit.*, page 443.

The young farm boys . . . came from the quiet of the great plateaus and the endless woods, from broad valleys and steep mountains, from the rugged coast and the sheltered fjords. They knew hunger and poverty from childhood. But they did not know the rhythm of industry. And the industry they encountered! The mighty electrochemical industry with its burning hot smelters. Gigantic construction projects, with fantastic dams that changed the landscape, and great water tubes falling from the mountains to the valley below. . . . These boys met the trade unions. But as a rule they met the "rollers" first, traveling construction workers. From them they learned to smoke and drink, to comport themselves differently. Conditions at construction jobs did not permit an orderly life. But they also learned from the "rollers" steadfast comradeship.

When revolutionary agitation swept over the construction projects and the new factories, inspired from Sweden and the syndicalist union that was established there in 1910, it was small wonder that these boys listened to the appeal. The Federation of Labor was too heedful of the Employers' Association and the capitalists. The leaders bargained and bargained. . . . Direct action, that was the way.[49]

Before 1910, Norwegian socialism resembled the Danish movement in many ways. It was mildly reformist in character, interested in extension of the franchise, protective labor legislation, and progressive income taxation, absorbed with "the demands of the day and the realizable possibilities, the tactics of relationships with the Liberal Party, and the possibility of establishing contact with the masses."[50] It belonged to the Second International, though socialism was a slogan and a vague hope for the future.

But the addition of more than one hundred thousand workers to the labor force within the space of a few years, the growth of boom towns with the same frontier atmosphere as in the days of American westward expansion, and the influence of the migrant construction workers, who left "red centers" behind them when they had finished their jobs and departed, completely transformed the movement. The leader of the new generation, Martin Tranmael, had worked for several years in the west and midwest of the United States, and had become impressed with the methods and goals of the IWW. He borrowed ideas from that organization, and adapted them to Norway. His philosophy might be described as a species of syndicalism: the abolition of the collective agreement and the union welfare fund, chief reliance on strike action, boycott and sabotage, and a structural reorganization of the trade unions on the basis of regional syndicates and industrial departments. But in one essential respect Tranmael broke with syndicalism, and thereby avoided the fate of syndicalists in almost all

---

[49] Ousland, III, *op. cit.*, page 636.

[50] See Haakon Meyer, *Den politiske Arbeiderbevegelse i Norge*, page 44. Oslo, 1931.

other countries: he advocated participation in politics, and did not regard parliamentary activity as futile.

By 1919, the conservative socialist leadership of both the party and the trade unions was overwhelmed by the representatives of the new industrial workers. Tranmael declared at the Labor Party congress that year that "the working class must become aware that revolution and dictatorship are absolutely necessary." The Labor Party severed its ties with the Second International, and affiliated with the newly created Comintern. But so unnatural a relationship could not last. The highly individualistic Norwegians (and syndicalism is essentially an expression of individualism and a revolt against the bureaucracy both of the state and the trade unions) would not give the doctrinaire, unquestioning allegiance required by the Comintern. Trouble began almost immediately, and after several stormy years and despite the strongest efforts of the Russians to dominate Tranmael and his associates,[51] the Norwegian Labor Party broke with the Comintern.

The Comintern experience, together with poor economic conditions after 1921 and the tapering off of industrial expansion, served to diminish the revolutionary ardor of the Norwegian labor movement. "Dictatorship of the proletariat" was dropped from the Labor Party program in 1927; socialism through parliamentary means was to be advocated instead. The responsibility of government office, which it attained in 1935, further sobered the Party, and paved the way for its present acceptance of an ideology that is in the main stream of European social democracy.

The Swedish ideological experience was, in many respects, intermediate between that of Denmark and Norway. Labor conditions in most Swedish industrial centers were relatively good; the rate of industrial expansion was slower than in Norway, and decentralization of industry prevented the formation of congested urban areas. There was in Sweden the same group of migratory construction workers that constituted the spearhead of Norwegian radicalism, but its numerical proportion to the total labor force was smaller. Conditions of labor were worst among lumber and heavy construction workers, and in the northern iron mines, and it was among these groups that the radicals made their greatest progress.

In its theoretical aspects, Swedish socialism was to the left of Danish and Norwegian socialism in the first stages. It was strongly influenced by German Marxism, and the orthodox, sectarian character

---

[51] The Russians threw some of their biggest guns into the fray, for the Norwegian party was one of the few in the Comintern that had a mass following at the time. Among others, Radek and Bukharin were sent to Oslo to attempt to convince the Norwegians of the error of their ways

of early Swedish socialism may be attributed to the relatively late development of trade unionism.[52] The absence of the leavening influence of craft unionism is best illustrated by the fact that the first chairman of the Swedish Federation of Labor, Frederik Sterky, was of middle class origin and actually a socialist representative within the unions, a situation almost inconceivable in Denmark. Also contributing to early socialist radicalism was the great conservatism of Swedish society, the late introduction of the universal franchise, and the bitter opposition on the part of large Swedish employers to trade unionism. The triumph of political liberalism and the firm establishment of the parliamentary system came much earlier in Denmark and Norway than in Sweden.

Herbert Tingsten, in a brilliant monograph, has traced the career of Swedish social democracy from 1900, when it first became a political force, to its present position of dominance in the political life of the country.[53] He argues convincingly that the transition from revolution to reformism *par excellence* did not imply a similar change on the part of the majority of the nation's workers, but rather an adaptation of socialist philosophy to the desires of the workers as the party grew from a sect to the true representative of the working class. The influence of trade unionism upon the party was augmented by the rapid expansion of union membership in the 1920's, and with it came a tendency to emphasize short rather than long run objectives. Socialization of industry, which had always been a bone of contention among party intellectuals, dropped quietly out of sight as a central issue in the face of growing preoccupation with "bread and butter" programs.

Syndicalism and communism

The principal threats to social democratic control of the Scandinavian trade unions came first from syndicalism, then communism. In Norway, syndicalists gained full control of the combined labor movement, but the responsibilities of political power diluted their ideology,

---

[52] "The [Swedish] trade union movement arose relatively late; it first began to develop in the 1880's, and then even the factory workers organized. The leadership passed from the bourgeoisie to the rising social democracy, which made no distinction between skilled and unskilled workers. If there had been a strong trade union movement among the craft workers in the 1870's . . . the trade union history of the 1880's might have been different. A well organized, well paid, conservative group of skilled workers could then have developed alongside the masses of poorly organized and completely unorganized factory workers who were more radical and influenced by socialist propaganda." Tage Lindbom, *op. cit.,* pages 65–66.

[53] Herbert Tingsten, *Den Svenska Socialdemokratiens Idéutveckling.* Stockholm: Tidens Förlag, 1941.

which was never very pure. Danish syndicalists captured a few trade unions in 1910, and played some role among seamen and longshoremen. But the Danish labor movement was relatively barren soil for the syndicalists, for living standards were too high, and the avenues of collective bargaining and parliamentary action too promising.

The course of Swedish syndicalism was somewhat different. After the general strike of 1909, the syndicalists seceded from the regular trade unions to establish a union center of their own, the Swedish Workers' Central Organization. This center never developed into a serious competitor of the Federation of Labor; it reached a maximum membership of 37,000 in 1924, and has since dwindled to a membership of 23,000. Nevertheless, as one of the few syndicalist trade unions that has managed to remain in existence over a long period, it is not without historical interest.

Syndicalism in Sweden appealed primarily to workers in construction, lumbering, and mining, to the men who were engaged in heavy work, at low rates of pay, and under poor conditions of labor, often involving constant travel. Of the 33,000 members of the syndicalist center in 1933, 28,000 were in these three industries.[54] It is not difficult to understand, when one reads contemporary accounts of working conditions,[55] why these men should have been attracted by a philosophy which preached direct action instead of collective bargaining, sabotage instead of labor-management cooperation, the revolutionary strike instead of parliamentarianism. Before the advent of communism, syndicalism represented the extreme reaction of the underprivileged against a society which promised them little and gave them less.

In conformance with syndicalist theory, the Swedish syndicalist union center is based upon local syndicates, each embracing all members within a geographical area without regard to trade or industry.

---

[54] Valter Åman, *Svensk Syndikalism,* page 130. Stockholm, 1938.

[55] A Swedish doctor wrote as follows of a visit to a lumber camp in Dalarna during the eighteen nineties: "I had travelled all night and was hungry and frozen in the morning, but when I had to creep in through the low door, the smoke hit me in the face, so that I gasped for breath and drew back, in the belief that I had made a mistake and entered a smoke-house. As soon as more wood was put on the fire and the flame sprang up, I saw men lying side by side around the gigantic bonfire. . . . The patient lay in the further corner of the bunkhouse, and to get to him I had to creep through the heat between the fire and the sleeping men to where he lay, fully clad, with his cap pulled over his head, a coat over him, and a few empty sacks for a mattress. When I lifted him up, I found that both his clothes and his hair were frozen to the wall, which was covered with frost. The diagnosis was double pneumonia, and he was taken to town. . . . I have seen many such lumber cabins through the years, and they were all the same, with the same smoke and heat, ice and darkness." Gårdlund, *op. cit.,* page 373.

The local syndicates are affiliated directly to the national center. Within the syndicate, the workers are divided into sections along industry lines, and these sections in turn are loosely organized into industrial federations. Federations in related industries form industrial departments, for example, building, lumbering, mining. Despite this elaborate superstructure, developed more for ideological than practical reasons, the local syndicate remains the chief repository of trade union power.

The syndicalists oppose the collective agreement in principle. As a means of exercising control over labor conditions, each local syndicate has established a register committee, the function of which is to prepare wage schedules. After approval by the syndicate, these schedules constitute the wages for which members may work. The failure of the register method to provide binding wage rates for definite periods of time enabled employers to cut rates during periods of unemployment, and some of the syndicates have been forced to enter into agreements. The syndicalists have advocated, as a means of enforcing their demands, the sympathetic strike, the slowdown through literal observance of working rules, shoddy work, and ca'canny.[56] But these methods have proved incongruous in a so highly organized society as the Swedish, and, in fact, the syndicalists have practiced collective bargaining.

However, the Swedish syndicalists have remained faithful to the political tenets of their doctrine. Individual union members are permitted to join political parties, though they are discouraged from doing so, but the syndicalist unions abstain strictly from political activity. The leaders profess to believe in the eventual overthrow of capitalism through the revolutionary general strike, and condemn the socialists for compromising with capitalism. As far as practical trade unionism is concerned, however, there is not a great deal of difference between the socialist and syndicalist unions.

Syndicalism was succeeded by communism as the principal left wing ideological challenge to social democracy. Within a few years after the end of World War I, it was clear that a wide gulf existed between Scandinavian socialism, even the Norwegian brand, and Russian communism, and, consequently, separate communist parties, affiliated with the Comintern, were launched. The details of communist policy and organization need not concern us here.[57] The Scandinavian communists loyally followed the Comintern line, with the same splits and deviations as in other countries. Until 1932, they had little

---

[56] See John Andersson, *Syndikalismen*. Stockholm, 1936.
[57] For a history of the Swedish Communist Party, see Ture Nerman, *Kommunisterna*. Stockholm, 1949.

support, but with the severe unemployment that began then, their strength increased. It was only after World War II, however, that Scandinavian communism lost its sectarian character and became a political force. The fiction of communist "activism" in the underground movements of Denmark and Norway, the victories of the Red Army, and war weariness and discontent combined to give the communists a significant parliamentary representation in 1945.[58] Even more important than electoral victories, however, was communist trade union infiltration. However, with the launching of counteroffensives by the powerful socialist machines, communist strength in both the political and trade union spheres fell sharply. By 1951, communists controlled only a few scattered local unions, and their parliamentary representation was small (seven seats in Denmark, eight in Sweden, none in Norway). Except in the event of war or economic crisis, the future of Scandinavian communism is that of a small, conspiratorial sect.

The triumph of socialism in Scandinavia is attributable, in the final analysis, to the peculiar economic development and political atmosphere of the area. At the risk of repetition, it should be emphasized that there has never been in Scandinavia a large, impoverished industrial proletariat to provide the sinews for a national revolutionary movement; that urban worker living standards were for the most part good; and that democratic political institutions had already been established when the numerical expansion of the industrial labor force made possible the growth of socialist power. State repression of labor activities has been minimal for the past seventy-five years. Contemporary Scandinavian socialism is essentially collective bargaining transplanted to the political arena; its strength lies in its ability to augment worker welfare with a minimum of social conflict.

Trade union-socialist relationships

The trade unions and the socialist parties in Scandinavia are two facets of a homogeneous movement. The two are more closely united than is true in Great Britain, for example. Whatever conflict arises between them has its origin more in functional differentiation than in divergence of aim.

Formally, trade union and party are separate organizations. In Norway and Sweden, many local trade unions are affiliated with the socialist party, which means that all members of the local union are

---

[58] The Danish Communist Party had 18 of 148 seats in the lower house, the Swedish Communist Party, 15 of 230 seats, the Norwegian Communist Party, 11 of 150 seats.

automatically party members unless they specifically except themselves. About half the membership of the Norwegian Labor Party and two-thirds that of the Swedish Social Democratic Party comes through such collective membership. While there is no corresponding practice in Denmark, the great majority of those who belong to socialist clubs are trade unionists.

The only country in which the issue of socialist domination of the unions aroused any real controversy was Sweden. So strong was the reaction against formal socialist ties with the early Federation of Labor that in 1909 all mention of cooperation between trade unions and socialism was deleted from the Federation constitution. To soften the blow, the Federation resolved that "the social democratic party is the natural and obvious vehicle for the political efforts of the Swedish working class." [59] However, the constitutional link was replaced by an informal, but effective, joint union-party council that considers all matters of mutual interest; membership in the council is limited to a few of the principal leaders on each side.

Collective membership in Norway was temporarily interrupted by the 1920–1927 split in the political labor movement, but it was subsequently resumed. In Norway and Denmark there is formal machinery for assuring the coordination of policy in the form of mutual representation on executive committees. The trade unions are thus certain that their point of view is represented in party (and government) decisions.[60]

The socialist parties are financially dependent upon the trade unions. The trade unions cover the deficit incurred by the socialist press, and contribute heavily to socialist campaign funds. Despite this, the unions neither control nor dominate the socialist parties.

The aims of contemporary Scandinavian socialism

Danish, Norwegian, and Swedish socialism have gradually approached one another in outlook, so that it is now possible to speak of Scandinavian socialism without tampering with the facts. Closer relations have been fostered by the many inter-Scandinavian labor committees that have been established. But the important factor in cementing relationships is the disappearance of some of the underlying social differences that contributed originally to ideological diver-

---

[59] Casparsson I, op. cit., page 180.

[60] In Norway, there is also a joint trade union-party council of six. This body held 16 meetings in 1949, and discussed, among other things, an export tax on lumber, the employment status of wartime Quislings, price, wage and subsidy policy, and the labor conditions of civil servants. See *Arbeidernes Faglige Landsorganisasjon i Norge, Beretning 1949*, page 15.

gences. The countries of Scandinavia are now industrialized to about the same extent, and there are no significant differences in the rate of capital expansion. Rural-urban migration has all but ceased, and the institutions of the labor market and of political life generally are strong and coherent. With the example of Soviet Russia so close, Scandinavian workers are little disposed to engage in political adventure, and are firmly wedded to the method of economic gradualism.

Lack of clarity among the Scandinavians themselves makes it difficult to be precise about contemporary socialist philosophy. Marxism has all but disappeared as an intellectual force, but nothing as definite or cogent has replaced it. During the depression, when the socialists first gained political power, they were too absorbed with practical measures for the alleviation of unemployment to concern themselves with long range problems. Then came the war, followed by feverish efforts to reconstruct their economies. Now that the most urgent problems have been solved, there is an increasing need for a comprehensive, long term program that will be acceptable to workers and impart dynamism to the socialist movement.

There are several strains of thought on the nature of the future socialist society. Many retain the conviction that the key to true socialism lies in the nationalization of industry; this ideal is strongest among the older members of the trade union bureaucracy. The opponents of "nationalization at any price" argue along different lines. They point out, first, that there is already considerable nationalization in Scandinavia. Among the enterprises run by the government are the railroads, telephone and telegraph systems, radio broadcasting, public utilities (usually municipally owned), moving picture theaters, the sale of alcoholic beverages, and the import and export of certain commodities. Other enterprises, including the airlines and some manufacturing establishments, are partly government owned. A sizeable proportion of the retail trade, particularly in Sweden, is controlled by consumer cooperatives.

Extension of the social sector of the economy, the "moderates" believe, should take place only when there is a demonstrated need for goods and services that private enterprise is unable to provide at reasonable prices. For example, the Norwegian government is undertaking the construction of a steel mill that is uneconomic competitively, but that is important strategically, in that it will make the country self-sufficient in steel. Similar extension of public investment may be necessary to provide employment in depressed areas when excess workers cannot be induced to move, or in order to provide secondary employment for workers engaged in seasonal industries of great importance in terms of the international balance of payments.

However, the principal argument of those who oppose too rapid an extension of the public sector is a political rather than an economic one: the danger to individual liberties implied in complete state ownership.

It is no longer individual freedom in relation to private power groups that is in the foreground, but individual freedom in relation to an increasingly powerful government. The greater the extent to which society assumes control of our mighty contemporary economic machine, the greater will be the disproportion between the individual and the centralized state apparatus where social power is concerned.[61]

On the question of a proposal in place of nationalization as the keystone of socialist policy there is far greater agreement on short run than on long run measures. Economic planning through a system of national budgeting, implemented by strategic direct government controls, is relied upon to assure the one goal to which all socialists subscribe—full employment. Direction of private investment through controls on imports and construction, plus government investment when necessary, will, it is believed, minimize cyclical fluctuation and maximize the national product. It is hoped, in this way, to retain the vital contribution of private enterprise "in utilizing natural wealth, scientific inventions, and labor and technical resources in the interests of increased production," [62] while at the same time the state can coordinate and plan.

There has been no systematic attempt to evolve eventual purposes of economic planning, which is, after all, a means rather than an end. For example, there is considerable difference of opinion on whether there should be further equalization of incomes. One of the leaders of Swedish socialism wrote: "Personally I maintain that there can be no socialist society without a leveling of existing income differentials. . . . We are perhaps all agreed that direct progressive income taxation is the most rational means." [63] Another socialist theorist maintained, however, that "the leveling of incomes has gone so far that a sizeable reduction of the larger incomes will have no perceptible influence upon the living standards of the population as a whole." [64]

Industrial democracy, that is, increased participation of workers in the management of industry, is often cited as a *desideratum,* but the

---

[61] Torolf Elster, *Socialismen under debatt,* page 19. Oslo: Tiden Norsk Forlag, 1950.

[62] *The Postwar Programme of Swedish Labor* (English edition), page 32. Stockholm, 1944.

[63] Ernst Wigforss, *Økonomisk Demokrati,* pages 17–18. Bergen: John Griegs Forlag, 1948.

[64] Elster, *op. cit.,* page 40.

postwar labor-management council movement has not aroused any great interest among the workers. There are also people who believe that the major problem of contemporary socialism is ethical, rather than economic, in character; that the problem of providing workers with a minimum decency standard of living has been solved, in the main, and that the future task of socialism is to raise their cultural level. For example:

> There is today a great social crisis, a cultural crisis, notwithstanding higher living standards, better social security, increasingly more political rights. The reason is that man's intellectual liberation and his will to cooperate have not kept pace with economic, technical and political development. To create intellectually free, independent, thoughtful individuals will more and more constitute the problem upon which the realization of socialism centers. If the social apparatus is permitted to develop further without an accompanying development of the human being, what was intended to be the liberation of mankind will become instead a new slavery, as bad as any history has known.[65]

If anything as definite as a tendency can be said to exist in Scandinavian socialism, it is toward greater collective, in distinction to government, ownership. Consumer cooperatives have strong advocates. The "mixed" corporation, in which the government is the largest shareholder but management remains private, is another alternative to state socialism that is being tried. Offsetting a vague but strong belief, inherited from Marxism, in the desirability of economic collectivism, is fear of a powerful central government. It is not yet apparent how these conflicting ideas will be reconciled.

Labor Government, Labor Party, and Trade Unions

Trade unionism was the earliest form of labor organization in Scandinavia. Political socialism first began to make headway at the beginning of the present century, and within two decades had become the single most important political force in the area. The culmination of socialist progress came with the formation of labor governments in the early thirties. The era of the labor government in Scandinavia is of fairly recent origin, but it is already apparent that this development has had profound effects upon trade unionism.

Trade union wage policy

Though formally dedicated to socialism, the Scandinavian trade unions have been, in fact, dedicated to the philosophy of what Samuel Gompers once described as "a little more." The focus of their activities

---

[65] Elster, *op. cit.*, page 107.

was annual or biennial wage movements, and the gauge of leadership success was the achievement of money wage increases. World War I and its aftermath temporarily rocked the faith of trade unionists in this policy, but the ensuing deflation, and the struggle to maintain the money wage level, led them back to the original road.

Concentration upon wages as the goal of trade union activity does not mean that the unions were unaware of economic realities behind the wage rate. Unions in the export industries have long been aware of the limitations imposed upon them by foreign competition, while the domestic trades have often been cognizant of price-demand relationships. But they operated upon the theory that employers were strong enough to resist trade union demands that would impair their ability to do business. Experience had shown that when entrepreneurs really found it necessary, their staying power exceeded that of the workers. It was appropriate for the union, therefore, to extract as high wages as possible from employers.

The validity of the premises upon which union wage policy was based was challenged by two contemporaneous but distinct events: the achievement of full employment and the advent of the labor government. In much of the Scandinavian discussion of trade union wage policy, the former is emphasized as having created the major problems. Overshadowing full employment, however, there has been the phenomenon of the labor government, devoted to the furtherance of trade union aims and altering the parameters with which the unions must operate. Full employment was, in fact, a postwar phenomenon. In 1939, average unemployment was high. The reorientation of trade union policy had actually begun with the great depression and the rise of the labor parties. But there is no doubt that the cardinal significance of full employment, in the trade union mentality, has sharpened the dilemma of the unions.

A combination of powerful trade unionism and full employment has demonstrated its inflationary propensities in Scandinavia, as elsewhere. Competition for workers disposes employers to pay higher wages, and the unions possess the bargaining power to force the reluctant ones into line. Even when there has been general agreement in the labor movement on the desirability of holding the wage level down, as in the case of the 1949 and 1950 "wage stop" policy of the Swedish unions, the policy has, in part, been circumvented by what is aptly termed a "wage glide," that is, increases in individual wage rates through higher piece rate earnings, through the movement of labor to better paying industries and jobs, and through the payment of above-contract wages to attract workers.

Without labor governments, the Scandinavian trade unions would probably have concentrated upon the maintenance of parity between wages and prices, at a minimum, similar to the policy of American trade unions since 1945. Their argument would be, as it is in Denmark, where the government has rotated between socialists and non-socialists, that they had no means of controlling prices and profits, and that only through money wages could they have protected real wage levels.

The labor governments of Norway and Sweden, out of regard to an equitable distribution of income and to the international competitive position of their economies, have attempted to stabilize prices, to the extent that import prices made stabilization possible. From 1945 to May, 1950, the Swedish cost of living index rose by 12 per cent and the Norwegian index by 9 per cent (compared with 13 per cent for the United States in the same period, and ·considerably more in most European countries), indicating that the policy was reasonably successful. This required considerable self-restraint on the part of the trade unions, which were in a position to secure large money wage increases almost at will, as far as employer resistance was concerned. The Norwegian trade unions went so far as to accept wage determination through compulsory government arbitration.

But restraint and the acceptance of controls were conditioned explicitly upon the coexistence of labor governments able to correct any tendency toward redistribution of income unfavorable to workers through price control, taxation, and fiscal policy generally. The Norwegian trade unions stated frankly that their acquiescence in compulsory arbitration would terminate with the fall of the labor government from power. In the Swedish unions, a vigorous internal debate on the merits of restraint versus aggressiveness in wage policy has been premised implicitly upon trade union ability, through government, to influence prices and profits.[66] Under these circumstances, wage policy becomes merely one facet of national economic policy, in the formulation of which the trade unions participate, and for which they are obliged to accept responsibility.

Consequences of the "new" wage policy

This break with habitual patterns of trade union conduct could not fail to have great repercussions upon trade union stability. The most difficult problem faced by the Scandinavian unions since 1945 has been to reconcile the conviction of its leaders that wage policy must

---

[66] See Gösta Rehn, "Fullsysselsättningen löneproblem" in *Lönepolitiken under debatt*, Stockholm, 1950, and a critique by Erik Lundberg in *Ekonomisk Tidskrift*, 1950, No. 1, page 43.

be coordinated with government economic policy with the insistent rank and file demand for higher money wages. The following quotation from an article by the economist of the Swedish Federation of Labor is in point:

> . . . if the trade union movement accepts a centralized wages policy along general economic lines, it gives up in certain situations one of its most important former tasks. . . . The lasting and uniting task of the trade union movement throughout its long history . . . has been that of increasing wages. . . . The risk involved in [the] necessary reconstruction process is that the movement's objective is too abruptly switched over so that the masses of members find it difficult to conceive the new objective as their own and that the organizations during this period of transition will be exposed to serious troubles. These troubles will arise because the demand of responsibility both toward the interest of the working classes and those of society as a whole, that is, economic stability, in contradiction to the tangible but short-sighted interests of our own group, presupposes a training of the masses which even the advanced trade union movement in England or Sweden is not likely to be able to bring about in so short a time.[67]

The money-wage consciousness of Scandinavian workers has been somewhat weakened in recent years by the practice of adjusting wages on the basis of changes in the cost of living index, thus emphasizing the real wage. The labor press has carried long and frequent articles about money versus real wages, and the publication of index figures is front page news. But the wage inflation of about 100 per cent between 1939 and 1950 has not been sufficient to eradicate money fetishism; had it been ten times as great, as in Finland, the problems of union leadership would be simplified.

Nevertheless, considerable progress has been achieved in altering worker wage concepts. This is particularly true in Sweden, where a wage stop for two successive years did not shake the workers' faith in their socialist leadership, despite communist efforts to utilize the issue. Undoubtedly, the high worker living standards prevailing in Sweden facilitated the task of reconciliation. But even complete success in educating workers to the "new" wage policy will by no means solve the entire problem of union wage policy. There still remains the matter of sectional interests, which is tied up with wage differentials, and even beyond that, the relationship of workers to their unions.

The national union is still sovereign in Scandinavia, though events of the past two decades have served to augment the power of the federation of labor. The process of centralized bargaining has gone furthest

---

[67] Rudolf Meidner, *The Dilemma of Wages Policy in Full Employment* (mimeographed), 1948.

in Norway, and, even there, national unions consistently strive to secure a greater portion of the total wages fund for their own members. A symposium on wage policy conducted by the monthly journal of the Swedish Federation of Labor is instructive in illustrating the persistence of strong sectional tendencies within the trade unions.[68] The strongest proponents of centralized wage bargaining under the auspices of the Federation of Labor were the leaders of the lower wage unions, who hoped thereby to reduce wage differentials. On the other hand, the higher wage trades exhibited hostility to centralization, lest their relative wages suffer.

The fact is that centralization of wage policy, despite the reluctance of some national unions, is essential to the type of economic planning to which the socialists are committed. The achievement of predetermined levels of consumption and investment requires that wages remain within the confines dictated by the availability of consumer goods. The alternative is constant inflationary pressure, and it is recognized that "there is no organization whose very existence is threatened to the same degree by this demand surplus as the trade union movement." [69] It is not surprising that national wage bargaining should have gone furthest in Norway, since it has embarked upon a program of economic planning that exceeds in scope those of its Scandinavian neighbors.

Centralization of wage bargaining does not necessarily imply any specific attitude toward existing wage differentials. Prior to World War II, the Scandinavian unions adopted a so-called "solidaristic" wage policy, the purpose of which was to raise the relative wages of low paid workers. Partly as a consequence of this policy, and partly because of the leveling influence of inflation and full employment, wage differentials narrowed appreciably. While federation wage-fixing authorities might attempt to adjust wages more finely to labor requirements, and maintain a differentiated wage structure, there appears to be a tendency in centralized collective bargaining, because of the political power of the large unions of factory workers, to make uniform bargains in absolute money terms, thus reducing percentage wage differentials.

In postwar Scandinavia, there has been a tug of war between some skilled crafts, seeking to utilize labor shortages as a means of raising their relative wages, and the federations, representing more the interests of lower paid workers and seeking to utilize central bargaining plus uniform cost of living adjustments as a means of reducing

---

[68] The articles have been reprinted in *Lönepolitiken under debatt,* Stockholm, 1950.

[69] Meidner, *op. cit.*

wage differences, or at least to prevent their widening. Considerable internal tension has resulted politically, and economically, because of the reduction of wage differences to a degree that many trade unionists acknowledge endangers the future flow of skilled labor. This is not a fatal defect of centralized wage bargaining, however, but it does call for greater awareness of the function of wage differentials, and more flexibility and less uniformity within the central wage bargain.

Another consequence of the "new" wage policy, with its emphasis on subordination of money wage claims to economic stabilization, is a certain loosening of the bond between the union and its members. When collective bargaining proceeded on a local or even an industry level, and concentrated on wages, there was an immediate connection between union strength and the welfare of workers, and an opportunity for members to participate in the formulation of wage policy. But with centralization, "the relationship between organizational unity and militancy on the one hand and the results of struggle on the other becomes less obvious. Members begin to look upon the trade union movement as an automaton which delivers a certain living standard in return for a specified payment." [70] There are already disquieting signs of diminished worker interest in their unions; for example, in the general wage movement of 1950, in Norway, only 30 per cent of those eligible to vote actually participated in a referendum on the ratification of the settlement, despite great efforts on the part of the leadership to secure a large turnout. This led the labor press to denounce editorially the "spectator mentality" which was creating an "organizational crisis" in the labor movement.[71]

Industrial disputes

A metamorphosis is also taking place in the attitude of the Scandinavian trade unions to labor disputes. The view that political pressure may be a more effective means than economic action of effectuating union demands is gaining currency. Moreover, the unions are beginning to emphasize the identity of maximum output and labor welfare, leading to the conclusion that strikes are, on balance, harmful to the labor movement.

The Danish and Norwegian trade unions have accepted the principle of government intervention as a substitute for economic force. Though they retain the legal right to strike, they have, in practice, refrained from exercising it except in a few instances of internecine warfare with the communists, when a strike seemed desirable for

[70] Anatol Renning in *Lönepolitiken under debatt, op cit.,* page 68.
[71] *Arbeiderbladet,* November 17, 1950, page 4; November 18, 1950, page 4.

tactical reasons. The Swedish trade unions, however, persist in opposing political intervention in labor disputes; Sweden appears to be the last stronghold of a true desire for labor market *laissez-faire* in Europe. In opposing labor government intervention in a serious strike in 1945, the Swedish Federation of Labor issued the following policy statement:

> . . . government regulation of wage disputes . . . is in principle incompatible with free trade union organization, and with the factors which have been, and should continue to be, determining for trade union wage policy. . . . Wage regulation would mean the transformation of the trade unions from independent partisan organizations into negotiating bodies without control over, and responsibility for, wage policy. As the system gained ground, member interest in the organizations would be weakened. Awareness that the union no longer made the final decision in wage policy would reduce the community of interest and the solidarity which have been and remain the unifying force of trade unionism. It is obvious what consequences this would have for the future ability of the movement, perhaps in a different political situation, to protect the economic interests of the members and fulfill its other functions.[72]

But despite subsequent reiteration of the same theme, one may question whether even in Sweden genuine labor market freedom prevails. It is no secret that the 1945 metal trades strike, which evoked the statement quoted above, was primarily in the nature of a socialist counteroffensive against the communists. It is not unlikely that the Swedish labor market will remain free of government intervention, official or unofficial, only so long as the parties refrain from the widespread stoppages of work that in the past constituted the ultimate test of strength between organized employers and workers.

It is not easy for workers to adjust themselves to the changing attitude of their unions toward strikes. Reared in the tradition of class conflict, subject to constant communist calls to direct action to redress grievances, they often resent the condemnation of strikes by their own leaders, particularly when the risks involved in striking have been all but removed. Moreover, regardless of political change, most workers are still in private employment. It requires considerable sophistication to appreciate the underlying shifts that have occurred in economic power.

Even among trade union leaders, there is an uneasy feeling that atrophy of the strike weapon may prove costly in the long run. As long as industry remains in private hands, a change in the political balance of power may lead to a reversion to unrestricted capitalism—one reason for the persistence of the belief, by trade unionists, in

---

[72] Quoted in Gunnar Heckscher, *Staten og Organisationerna*, pages 250–251. Stockholm: K.F.'s Bokförlag, 1946.

nationalization of industry. There is also the question of how far it is possible to go in condemning the use of the strike weapon without endangering political democracy. The Soviet experience has convinced Scandinavian socialists that the right to strike, not as a constitutional maxim but as a political reality, is one of the cornerstones of democracy: "social democracy will never relinquish the principle of trade union independence or deny the ultimate right to strike in state enterprise." [73]

Reconciliation of industrial peace in order to maximize output with the maintenance of freedom of the right to strike will not be easy. It is not inconceivable that the Scandinavian unions may be obliged, quite deliberately, to engage in strike actions at periodic intervals in order to keep that right alive, to cement the bonds of union membership, and to forestall the substitution of "wildcat" strikes for the orderly process of the trade union strike.

Trade unions and the managerial function

As trade union functions in wages and industrial disputes diminish in importance, the unions are becoming more concerned with management problems. It is argued that if workers refrain from striking in the interest of maximum output, they should have a guarantee that industry is being managed efficiently, and a voice in the formation of management policy. The principal avenue for extending worker influence lies through the joint production councils that have been established in most of the larger Scandinavian enterprises. These councils have consultative rather than executive powers. Their purpose is to provide a regular mechanism for the transmission of worker suggestions for improving productive methods to management, and for a return flow of information on the economic, production, and sales problems of the firm to the workers. Employers were by no means enthusiastic about the council idea, but they were forced to accept it under threat of legislative action if voluntary agreement were not forthcoming.

Thus far, the joint councils have not had much success. In Norway, for example, it is estimated that only 10 per cent of the councils established have actually been activated. Employers have been reluctant to provide the councils with vital business information; and there has been some hesitancy even on the part of the union, for, although the councils are explicitly enjoined from dealing with matters that fall within the collective agreement, it is almost inevitable

73 Wigforss, *op. cit.*, page 57.

that they consider such matters, and thus impinge upon trade union functions.

There are other channels for augmenting worker insight into management problems which seem to be preferred by employers and unions. In Norway and Sweden, the central organizations have entered into agreements on time and motion studies, providing for worker participation in such work through time study committees and special shop stewards elected for this purpose and trained at management expense. Industry round-table conferences between top representatives of labor and management have been held to discuss means of raising productivity. Trade unions have sponsored production drives to rationalize work methods.

The appropriate role of trade unions in nationalized industry has aroused surprisingly little discussion in Scandinavia. Thus far, trade unions function similarly in the nationalized and private sectors of the economy. Occasional worker demands for direct representation in the managing boards of public enterprises have been rejected on the ground that such representatives would be placed in an impossible position of dual loyalty.

In general, the era of the labor government has not as yet resulted in severe inroads into management prerogative. To judge by labor attitudes, the best guarantee that this will continue lies in management efficiency. There is little disposition to interfere with the conduct of well-run enterprises, particularly those in the vital foreign trade sector of the economy.

Trade unions and the Socialist Party

A brief account of the formal relationships between the trade unions and the socialist (labor) parties of Scandinavia has already been given. Organizational relationships, however, tell only a small part of the story. Much more intriguing is the allocation of decision-making authority between the two branches of the labor movement in matters of mutual interest. This is a very subtle question, and the participants themselves are not always certain of the answer. Moreover, the balance of power is not stable, but shifts with changes in leadership. A dominant personality may exercise a degree of influence far out of proportion to his hierarchical rank.

It is certainly true that most controversies between the party, which is apt to take the broad, social point of view, and the trade unions, which are more parochial in their interests, are resolved internally, through discussion among the leaders of the two groups. But an occasional dispute breaks out into the open, and it is possible, then, to catch a glimpse of some of the tensions that lie beneath the surface. One revealing incident was the issue of a boycott of German goods, which divided the Swedish Federation of Labor and Social Democratic Party in 1933. The Federation had adopted a resolution calling upon workers to institute a boycott of German products as a protest against the suppression of the German trade unions, with which the Swedes had maintained close relations. Rickard Sandler, the Socialist Minister of Foreign Affairs, stated publicly that if he had been consulted, he would have advised against it, and to emphasize his stand, continued: "So that no one will think that a case of split personality is involved, I will add: if I had been asked my opinion as a party comrade, the social democrat would have expressed his agreement with the Foreign Minister." [74] When the Prime Minister indicated his agreement with this statement, a storm of protest arose in the trade unions. The executive committee of the Federation passed a resolution sharply critical of the Foreign Minister, and it was decided to continue with the boycott. The matter was not of great intrinsic importance to the trade unions, and the warmth of their reaction on this and other issues [75] reflects their feeling of insecurity in relation to the party.

Logically, it is the Socialist Party, rather than the unions, that should play a dominating role. The former is confronted with the more basic policy problems. Trade union wage decisions are only part of the economic data with which the party must deal, but the converse is not true; many party decisions, such as those on foreign affairs, are peripheral to trade union interest. It is almost inevitable that the accession to power of a labor government entails increasing supremacy of the labor party over its allied trade unions.

Personalities may, at times, determine the nature of the party-union relationship. For a number of years, both the Labor Party and the Federation of Labor in Norway were dominated by one man, Martin Tranmael, who, throughout most of his political career, was editor of the Oslo labor paper. Thorvald Stauning, for many years the chairman of the Danish Social Democratic Party, was easily the outstanding figure in the Danish labor movement, though the split in the trade unions between the skilled and unskilled workers, and his identification with the former, resulted in greater union independence of his leadership than was true in Norway. The Swedish socialists, after a brief period during the first years of the federation of labor, were forced into

---

[74] Casparsson, II, *op. cit.*, page 379.

[75] Among them may be mentioned the attempt of the Prime Minister, in 1941, to censor a speech by the chairman of the Federation critical of Germany, and party opposition to the establishment in Stockholm of a second labor daily newspaper by the trade unions, in addition to the one already published by the socialists.

retreat by the "pure" trade union faction, though the two great leaders of Swedish socialism, Hjalmar Branting and Per Albin Hansson, towered above their trade union contemporaries in terms of prestige among the workers.

It was once believed that the bonds between the trade union and the party could be cemented by the participation of trade union leaders in parliamentary activities. Many early trade union leaders were elected to parliament on a socialist ticket, continuing to hold their union office as well. But this dual role proved difficult. Union assemblies often criticized their leaders for devoting too much time to politics and too little to union affairs. While it is still customary for a few of the federation leaders to sit in parliament, active trade unionists, by and large, refrain from such activity. If a trade unionist enters a socialist cabinet—and it is almost the invariable socialist policy to include at least one important union leader—he must either resign or take leave of his union post. It may be that after leaving the cabinet he is able to return to his union, but an internal struggle for power in his absence may result in the end of his union career.

This is one of the reasons why trade unions, despite their greater financial resources, have not gained the upper hand over the socialist parties. Trade union and party careers have increasingly become distinct. A young worker who aspires to union office will, as a matter of course, be active in the local socialist club, but his advancement depends primarily upon his abilities as a trade unionist. The party career man, on the other hand, works his way up through the socialist youth movement into the party bureaucracy, and he is not likely to have intimate contact with the unions. There is occasional crossing over, particularly at the top, from trade union leadership to a minis-terial post, but in general the bureaucracies of the two movements are distinct and separate.

An additional factor of some importance is the practice of combining party and government leadership. The chairman of the Socialist Party becomes the Prime Minister when the party forms a government. The party chairman is thus a national figure, and is vested with the prestige of high public office, whereas the public roles of trade union leaders are more restricted. This alone provides the party with a significant power edge in the event of a controversy with the trade unions.

The logic of power relationships between the party and the trade unions appears to be borne out by the facts, as nearly as one can judge from the outside. But it would be erroneous to conclude that socialist politicians run the trade unions. Party officials scrupulously refrain from interference in internal union affairs, for such interference would be resented. There is a separation of function which is honored by both parties. It is only on the borderline of trade union-party interest that conflict arises, although, as has been noted, wage policy, formerly an exclusive trade union interest, has become a matter of party interest because of its effects upon economic planning. Yet it may be doubted whether even today, the socialists would endeavor to, or could, compel a recalcitrant union to adopt a certain wage policy against its will. The socialists are always aware that political competitors on the left and on the right stand ready to capitalize on worker dissatisfaction caused by political intervention in traditionally trade union spheres of activity.

Trade unions and the state

The ultimate question in considering the future of Scandinavian trade unionism, in an economy increasingly subject to government ownership and regulation, is whether the trade unions can maintain real independence under state socialism, or whether, as in the Soviet Union, they are destined to become mere adjuncts, almost departments, of the state administration.

Even under economic planning, let alone full state socialism, the powers of the trade unions to determine wage policy independently, and to seek to effectuate it through the use of economic force are restricted. "Responsible" unionism must renounce the pursuit of higher money wages as a central policy, and the belief grows that "the strike represents an obsolete point of view, a weapon belonging to a period when capitalists sat with complete power in the central government, in municipalities, and in the economy as a whole. Today a strike may result in greater harm to the labor movement and to socialism than to capitalists. . . ." [76] Stimulation of output to meet governmentally set goals becomes a major trade union task. There is thus a tendency for unions to become administrative and disciplinary arms of the state.

Scandinavian socialists are unanimous on the proposition that the subordination of trade unions to the state might well constitute a fatal blow to democracy. But there has been little consideration of how such a contingency can be avoided, and with what tasks the unions can be invested to prevent their decadence in the face of the withering of their traditional functions.

Many Scandinavians, socialists and nonsocialists alike, have been attracted by the ideal of a society in which each major economic group is represented by an organization independent of government control, though it may have some governmental functions. Policy determination

---

[76] Gunnar Ousland, *Fagorganisasjons problemstilling i dag*. Oslo, 1946.

would then take the form of a species of national collective bargaining among trade unions, consumer and producer cooperatives, farm organizations, with the state as entrepreneur. Decentralization of power would provide a guarantee against autocracy, but, at the same time, the consolidation of interest groups would prevent degeneration into anarchistic chaos. This pluralistic ideal springs from the evolution of Scandinavian society; what has been written of contemporary Sweden applies with almost equal force to Denmark and Norway:

> . . . developments in Sweden have shaped a free organizational system which . . . is completely unique, stronger than any which has existed here or in any other country. Industrial and commercial workers have attained a degree of organization so complete that unorganized individuals within these social classes constitute an insignificant group. . . . Employers have organized, less completely than employees, but nevertheless to such an extent that the collective agreement dominates the entire labor market. Farmers are almost completely organized in an economic movement. . . . The consumer cooperatives have developed into one of the nation's largest entrepreneurs. . . . One may say that Swedish society is largely organized, that is, that most of the interests for which organization is conceivable, are organized.[77]

The trade unions, in this conception, would represent not only the wage interests of workers, but their social and cultural interests as well. Scandinavian trade unions already participate in numerous official and semi-official bodies, including the factory inspectorate, production councils, labor courts, and the administration of apprenticeship and accident insurance. Danish and Swedish unions administer the unemployment insurance system and the labor exchanges. The labor movements have established travel and vacation societies, cooperative building societies, correspondence courses, choral societies, film and radio clubs, and a host of similar organizations. It is in advancing the interests of the worker as a consumer and as an intellectual being, rather than merely as a producer, that many socialists consider the true future of trade unionism.

Others are convinced, however, that this vision of the future is impracticable idealism, incapable of realization in modern industrial society, and that greater centralization in the state, rather than pluralism, is inevitable. But it should be pointed out that Scandinavian trade unions, and other collective organizations as well, have already become integrated with the mechanism of the state to a degree that has few parallels in western democracy, and with no discernible effect on the basic individual freedoms. Few countries permit the citizen as much liberty in expressing his opposition to the state and its institu-

---

[77] Gunnar Heckscher, *op. cit.*, pages 252–253.

tions, and afford him the same degree of protection from arbitrary government action, as do the Scandinavian nations. The strong Scandinavian tradition of political democracy, and the high average level of economic well being, afford a basis for the belief that the solutions to the problems raised in the preceding pages will augment, rather than detract from, the dignity and welfare of the individual.

Chapter 3

AUSTRALIA—KENNETH F. WALKER

Origins and Development

The history of the Australian labor movement falls naturally into three main periods, each of about fifty years. The first period, extending from the first settlement in 1788 to the gold rushes of the 1850's saw the sporadic beginnings of trade unionism, but no enduring organization. In the second period, between the 1850's and the 1890's, the Australian trade union movement took shape as a powerful agency of collective bargaining, with a gradually increasing interest in politics. Throughout the third period, since the 1890's, labor's interests have been represented not only by trade unions but also by a major political party that has been in power for substantial periods in all seven legislatures of the Commonwealth and states.

These periods in the growth of the labor movement correspond broadly with stages in Australia's economic development. The first period, following an introductory phase of subsistence farming, was marked by a conflict between the administration's ideal of a community of independent small farmers and the growth of a pastoral economy appropriate to the geography of the country. By the 1830's, the pattern of development was setting firmly in the form of a pastoral society, with wool as the staple export commodity. In the second period, although wool (and to a lesser extent, wheat) remained the basic industry, the mining of precious metals, especially gold, was an important development, encouraging extensive immigration and sustaining a long wave of prosperity that ended in a severe depression in the 1890's. The third period saw the federation of the six colonies, and the growth of manufacturing industry into a major sector of the economy, especially from the 1920's.

Early unionism

Although trade unions were not firmly established in Australia until the second of the three periods distinguished above, working-class organizations began to emerge in the boom years of the 1830's, especially among artisan immigrants. Most of these early organizations were mutual benefit societies connected with particular trades. In addition to benefit societies, however, organizations of workmen were also formed with the explicit purpose of bargaining with employers over rates of pay. By 1840, at least ten unions were in existence in New South Wales, with a membership of about 400 in a population of 127,000. There were also in the 1830's a number of temporary combinations of workers to win better conditions in particular trades, and some strikes took place.

A sharp economic slump occurred in the early 1840's, and few of the early unions survived. Some restraint was also placed on union activity by the New South Wales Master and Servants' Act of 1840, which provided penalties for leaving a job in breach of contract of service. After presentation of a petition signed by 2,856 workers, the penalties were reduced. This petition is the first recorded instance of organized lobbying by Australian labor.

Thus, in the first period of its history, the Australian labor movement put forth shoots but was unable to establish itself firmly in the ground. However, the germination of the movement had taken place far beyond Australian shores in the "dark Satanic mills" and industrial towns of Britain. "Australia was settled in the Age of the Rights of Man and of the Communist Manifesto. Most of the early settlers had been sweated and soured by industrialism." [1] In the years following the first settlement of Australia in 1788, there was developing in Britain a vast movement of resistance against the traditional power of the employing classes, encouraged by the democratic revolutions of America and France and inflamed by the crudities of early industrial capitalism. The struggles that marked this upsurge of democratic feeling had important implications for Australia, helping to build up the radical element in the population. Some of Australia's early settlers had actually suffered forced transportation for participation in trade union activities,[2] and there were many others of like mind who came to the colonies for other reasons. In addition to men who had been associated with trade unions in Britain, there were dissidents of other types, for example, the "Scottish martyrs," convicted for sedition in 1793; Irish rebels from the Rebellions of 1798 and 1848; participants in the Chartist Revolt; and others. To these were added

---

[1] W. K. Hancock, *Australia,* page 227. London, 1930; First Australian edition, 1945.

[2] The most famous of these were the "Tolpuddle Martyrs," 1834. The transportations are vividly described in the Hammonds' volumes on the town and village laborers in Britain.

large numbers of independent immigrants who had left their home country to escape want and insecurity. Trade union organization was a natural growth among such a population.

The influence of "transplanted Britons" on the development of the Australian labor movement has continued throughout its history. Many of the most influential leaders of the movement, right down to the present time, have been men who brought to Australia experience of the conditions and ideas current in the British Isles. Many Australian unions were started by a nucleus of workers recently arrived from Britain,[3] and at times unions in the two countries have given each other substantial financial assistance.

Advance and retreat, 1850–1890

The gold discoveries of the 1850's set in motion two of the main forces responsible for the growth of a powerful trade union movement in the second half of the nineteenth century. One was the vast wave of immigration that provided large numbers of new settlers sympathetic to trade unionism; the other was the long upswing of economic conditions, creating a labor shortage that gave labor sufficient bargaining power to build a strong organization. Efforts to open the land for settlement by miners stranded by the ebbing tide of gold ended in failure, accentuating the concentration of population in towns, which progressed further than in other new countries such as the United States. This concentration of population doubtless aided trade union organization. Owing to the relative absence of small farming, even in depressions the influence of urbanization was not seriously weakened by the tendency, common in Europe and the United States, for unemployed city workers to "go back to the farm."

The trade unions grew strong first among the skilled workers in the towns, next in mining, and then extended into the pastoral industries. In the 1850's, with labor scarce and wages high, union activity tended to focus upon shorter hours; stonemasons in Melbourne had won the eight-hour day by 1856, and skilled building tradesmen in Sydney and Brisbane also gained this concession about the same time. In many other trades, unions were established for the first time, or union organization was revived; a number of the unions in existence today trace their ancestry, if not their actual beginnings, to the twenty years beginning in 1851.[4]

---

[3] Thus in the 1830's, furniture industry mechanics in Sydney formed a union to keep up the piece rates then payable in London. In 1852, immigrants bound for Australia held a shipboard meeting at which they formed a branch of the Amalgamated Society of Engineers (later called the Amalgamated Engineering Union, of which organization the Australian union remains a branch).

[4] Among the unions founded in various colonies at this time were the Typo-

In mining, union organization began first in the northern coal fields of New South Wales in the 1860's, but was not established in gold mining until the industry had passed out of the stage of individual diggings to large-scale operations requiring capital equipment, financed by corporations. By 1874 the Amalgamated Miners' Association of Victoria had 12 branches, 1830 members, and over £1,000 in funds.

By 1880 craft unionism on the British pattern had been firmly established in most of the skilled trades in building and manufacturing, and industrial unionism was extending from mining into the central sector of the economy—the pastoral industries. Five years later, 100 unions were in existence, with 50,000 members out of a population of 2,700,000.

At this time progress began to be made in building national unions and interunion organizations, both within each colony and on a federal basis. By 1888 the Melbourne Trades Hall Council, which had been founded in 1856, exercised a coordinating authority in all industrial disputes, each member union being required to refer disputes to the Council before they reached "an advanced stage." Councils in other capital cities were founded as follows: Sydney, 1871; Brisbane and Hobart, 1883; Adelaide, 1884; Perth, 1892. The first intercolonial Trades Union Congress was held in Sydney in 1879, there being 39 delegates present, representing 11,000 members.

In addition to these councils, which aimed at including all types of unions, there were also federations of a number of unions concerned with various occupations in individual industries. Thus in 1884 the Sydney Maritime Council was constituted by the various unions in the shipping industry, and in 1875 the unions in the Melbourne building industry formed the Associated Building Trades Union.

This progress in organization was accompanied by improvement in the legal status of trade unions. In all colonies except Western Australia, legislation based on the English Trade Union Act of 1871 was passed by 1890 (Western Australia passed similar legislation in 1900). This legislation gave protection to the funds of trade unions, protected them from prosecution for conspiracy in restraint of trade, and gave union members certain legal rights better enabling them to control their officials.

The primary aims of most unions were to raise wages and shorten hours, but they were also much concerned with checking the immigration of colored peoples. Large numbers of Chinese had entered the country during the gold rushes and following disturbances in the

graphical Association, Amalgamated Society of Engineers, Operative Stonemasons, Carpenters and Joiners, Operative Bakers, Plasterers, Bricklayers, United Laborers, and Shipwrights.

fields, the Victorian and New South Wales governments in 1854 and 1861, respectively, passed legislation restricting the entry of Chinese. Although this reduced the number entering, they continued to land in other colonies and travel overland to the mines, and for another 20 or 30 years there was sporadic trouble over the use of Chinese as strike-breakers and their competition in small "backyard" industries, such as furniture, clothing, and laundry. In Queensland, friction in the sugarcane industry over the use of Pacific Island natives gave further support to the movement for exclusion of colored people from Australia, which culminated in the White Australia Policy of the Commonwealth Government after federation of the colonies. A good deal of the protectionist, anti-foreign outlook that has always characterized Australian labor had its origin in the experience of these years.

The trade union movement also took an interest at this time in various measures of social reform beyond the scope of collective bargaining. Some of these, such as factory legislation and regulation of apprentice training, bore a direct relation to conditions of employment, whereas others were more remote from the unions' immediate industrial interests. Examples of such issues were free public education, payment of members of Parliament, electoral reforms, and old-age pensions. Some, though not all, of this interest in broader social issues was inspired by socialist doctrines that had begun to gain ground among Australian trade unionists, largely under the stimulus of William Lane, editor of the famous *Worker*, a labor newspaper. "Socialism in our time" was Lane's slogan, and in 1893 he led a group of his followers to Paraguay to found an ill-fated socialist settlement, "New Australia."

Against this background of interest in social reform and the reconstitution of the social order, the intervention of labor in politics was discussed, notably at the intercolonial Trades Union Congresses. Direct representation of labor in Parliament was considered at the Second Congress, which urged the establishment of parliamentary committees in each colony to lobby for labor's interests. These were soon functioning effectively in Victoria and New South Wales and before long they had spread to the other colonies as well. Outside the unions, although often with a common membership, Workingmen's Political Associations were formed in the 1870's and 1880's to work for the representation of the working classes in parliament, although most of these associations were almost dormant between elections. From as early as 1850 there had been labor politicians in the colonial parliaments, who, although they did not espouse a comprehensive labor program, stood for working-class interests in general.

The last years of the nineteenth century were crucial years for the

Australian labor movement. They witnessed the formation of the Australian Labor Party, as well as the laying of the foundation for the system of compulsory arbitration within which Australian trade unions have for the most part operated ever since. The drama began with the struggle to extend unionism into the key sector of the economy—the pastoral industry.

After several unsuccessful attempts, unionism was at last established in sheep-shearing in 1886 when the Shearers' Union was founded in Victoria and Queensland with the assistance of organizers drawn from the mining unions. Conflict at once developed over recognition of the union by the employers, who advocated "freedom of contract" and opposed collective bargaining. This stand against unionism in the pastoral industry came at a time when employers were rapidly establishing associations to counter the power of the unions. There were skirmishes in the late 1880's while both parties strengthened their organization, but the unions entered the final decade of the century in fine fettle, inspired by the success of their dramatic intervention in the London dock strike early in 1890, when the sum of £30,000 sent by the Australian unions comprised three-fifths of the total strike fund, and was seven times the amount collected from British trade unionists.

In 1890 the pastoral employers made a determined bid to reestablish "freedom of contract," but although the Shearers' Union was not strong enough to prevent the engagement of sufficient nonunion labor to complete the shearing, it won the dispute by obtaining the support of the Wharf Laborers' and Seamen's Unions, which boycotted the nonunion wool. Later in 1890 the same technique was employed in reverse, the Shearers' Union striking in support of the Mercantile Marine Officers' Association, which was struggling to win the right of collective bargaining. In this dispute over £70,000 was raised in support of the strikers, of which at least £60,000 was contributed by Australian unionists, the rest coming from British trade unionists and the Australian public. After a strike of two months the unions were completely defeated, not only in the maritime industry but in the pastoral industry. Many shearers were condemned under the Master and Servants' Acts and the union's funds were exhausted.

This maritime strike, in which over 20,000 workers were involved, was the prelude to a series of bitter conflicts in various important industries in the next few years over the issue of collective bargaining. In some of these disputes, the machinery and power of the state were used to suppress union activity, and violent incidents occurred, mainly in Queensland.

These shattering defeats having given a sharp check to the growth and power of the unions as agents in collective bargaining, the pressure for direct political action by labor, which had been steadily accumulating for some time, was finally released, augmented by indignation at the part played by the state in the unions' defeat. In its report on the Maritime Strike of 1890, the New South Wales Labor Defence Committee, which directed the strike in that state, emphasized the need for political action:

The rule that unionism must steer clear of politics was a golden rule when there was so much work to be done within our present industrial environments. But that time is drawing to an end, and ere we can radically improve the lot of the worker we must secure a substantial representation in Parliament. This, then, is over and above all the greatest lesson of the strike, that our organization must become a means of education and constitutional power. Already it is half learnt. We have come out of the conflict a united labor party.[5]

In the next few years, the Australian Labor Party was established as a major political party, and within twenty years it had governed in several of the Australian legislatures, including the federal.

Interest in compulsory arbitration, the other turning-point in the history of the Australian labor movement, existed before the 1890's. The subject had been raised at the fourth intercolonial Trades Union Congress in 1886, and from time to time voluntary arbitration had been successfully resorted to in settling particular disputes, such as the Melbourne boot trade dispute of 1884 and the wharf laborers' dispute in the same city in 1886. Government machinery for voluntary conciliation and arbitration of industrial disputes had been introduced in some states without success and when the great disputes of the 1890's showed how industrial conflict could prostrate the community, compulsory arbitration appealed to the Australian middle class as a just solution of the impasse created by the employers' insistence upon the legal right of employer and employee to make individual contracts of employment. By establishing a tribunal to resolve the issues between organizations of employees and employers, the community could give recognition to the principle of collective bargaining without surrendering completely to union assertion of power, and provided machinery which it was hoped would end the deadlocks paralyzing the economy. The intransigent attitude of employers who refused to meet unions in conference did not accord with the ideas of fair play and justice then current in Australia.

---

[5] From The Report of the New South Wales Labour Defence Committee, quoted in J. T. Sutcliffe, A History of Trade Unionism in Australia, page 82n. Melbourne: Macmillan, 1921.

Recovery

The setbacks of the Australian labor movement in its battle with the pastoral employers were quickly overcome, in spite of the depressed state of the economy. In the last five years of the century, 60 new unions were formed, and in the next ten years unions grew rapidly in number and strength under the stimulus provided by the arbitration system. In 1891, at its first organized assault on the polls, Labor had 36 members returned to the New South Wales Parliament, sufficient to give it the balance of power; it also began to gather strength in other state parliaments.

The years of depression and the struggle against the employers also underlined the need for closer bonds within the trade union movement. Individual unions were driven to more urgent consideration of the need for federation with the corresponding unions in other colonies by the problems arising from migration of workers from one colony to another, which weakened union efforts to control competition by workers for jobs and made the enforcement of union discipline difficult. A man could escape disciplinary action by moving to another colony, where he might be accepted as a bona fide unionist, even after acting as a "scab" in his home colony. The more favorable situation enjoyed by those unions that had already achieved intercolonial federation was an object lesson to other unions.

The experience of the great strikes and lockouts also pointed to the desirability of better union coordination. While the union campaigns during this period were magnificent displays of fraternity and co-operation between unions in different industries, there was room for improvement. Various proposals for a more cohesive form of organization had been considered at the intercolonial Trades Union Congresses, some of which did not clearly distinguish between the need for federation or amalgamation of the unions covering the same trade in the different colonies and the desirability of linking unions covering different trades. In 1888 a scheme patterned on the American Knights of Labor was discussed, but a federal organization was preferred. Even this made little headway, however; Queensland, New South Wales and later, Western Australia did adopt a federal form of organization, but so many powerful unions remained outside the federations that both Queensland and New South Wales abandoned it in favor of the earlier (and much looser) labor council form of organization.

Labor and political action

It is possible here to trace the history of labor in Australian politics only in broadest outline. At first, as the party holding the balance of generation; in 1915 the party was governing the Commonwealth and once the party had instituted a strong disciplinary code to control the tendency of members to divide on the issue of free trade versus protection, it was successful in obtaining a good deal of favorable legislation. This period came to an end about 1908, when the older parties joined in coalition, and the political division in Australian parliaments took on the form that has persisted without fundamental change ever since—Labor versus "parties of resistance."

Labor met the new circumstances with confidence and vigor, and in the next few years it reached its high-water mark of power for a generation; in 1915 the party was governing the Commonwealth and five of the six states. However, in 1916 disaster overtook the Labor Party, which split on the issue of conscription for overseas service. Its leaders, expelled from the Labor Party, took office at the head of the nonlabor parties, which accommodated themselves to the change of leadership by a change of name. Labor was defeated in the Commonwealth and all states except Queensland, and did not recover Commonwealth power until 1929. In the states, its fortunes fluctuated during the 1920's, and except in Queensland, the shock of the great depression sent the Labor Party into a long political twilight. The history of the 1916 debacle was repeated to some extent by the emergence of one of labor's leaders as prime minister at the head of a renamed nonlabor coalition.

In the early years of World War II Labor was in power in several states and was regaining its strength in the Commonwealth. Late in 1941 it took office on the vote of two independent members who held the balance of power, and at the election 18 months later won a resounding victory. The Labor Party continued in power until late in 1949, when it lost heavily to the conservative parties, which had been reconstituted and re-named yet again, although it retained a majority in the Senate (the Upper House). In 1951, Labor's fortunes appeared to be on the wane for the time being.

What has the Australian Labor Party achieved during the 60 years since it entered Parliament? In the early period of support in return for concessions, several basic aims had been won—one-man-one-vote, the general eight-hour working day, better factory and mine legislation, free compulsory education, amendments to various acts regulating the relation of employers and employees, and so on. During this period also, Labor made its historic decision on the tariff question, which had threatened to split the party, by coming out in favor of protection, and this became the Commonwealth's established policy soon after Federation. The "White Australia" policy, Labor's interest in which went back to the days when Chinese competed with white men in the gold-diggings, was also established at this time, although not as the result of labor efforts alone.

In 1905 the federal Labor Party defined its objective as follows:

(a) The cultivation of an Australian sentiment, based upon the maintenance of racial purity and the development in Australia of an enlightened and self-reliant community.
(b) The securing of the full results of their industry to all producers, by the collective ownership of monopolies and the extension of the industrial and economic functions of the State and municipality.

This objective was to be translated into reality by a "fighting platform" of nine planks: White Australia, nationalization of monopolies, old-age pensions, a referendum on the tariff question, a progressive tax on land values, restriction of public borrowing, navigation laws, a citizen defense force and amendment of the Arbitration Act. In 1912 the fifth Conference of the party recorded that it had "been able to place to credit (as planks made law) six important items, which in themselves are enough to make all followers of the movement feel a thrill of satisfaction at what had been done." [6] These six planks were White Australia, the tariff question (though not settled by referendum), land tax, navigation laws, citizen defense force (raised through conscription for military training) and old-age pensions. This period also saw the establishment of the Commonwealth Bank, although it turned out to be something less than a people's bank to replace the trading banks, as labor had once hoped.

While still holding the balance of power, the Labor Party supported the "New Protection," whereby industries were to be granted tariffs only if wages and conditions of employment were "fair and reasonable." In the first case heard under the Excise Tariff Act of 1906, which gave effect to this policy, Henry Bourne Higgins, architect of the Commonwealth Arbitration Court, and later its president, ruled that H. V. McKay Pty. Ltd., makers of agricultural implements, had to raise wages by 16 per cent before they could be declared "fair and reasonable." This famous "Harvester" judgment, which provided the basis for the Commonwealth basic wage for a generation to come, was appealed to the High Court, where the Excise Act was declared unconstitutional.[7] When Labor gained power, it was unable to put through a referendum amending the Constitution to make the "New Protection" valid, and thus ended its efforts to put this policy into effect.

Another piece of legislation expressing Labor's policy that was

---

[6] Cited by J. T. Sutcliffe, *A History of Trade Unionism in Australia,* page 148. Melbourne, 1921.

[7] However, for the significance of the Harvester Award, see below, page 209.

ruled invalid by the High Court was the Trade Marks Act of 1905, which gave the trade unions power to insist on a union label on goods to show that trade union conditions prevailed in the factory making them. Labor also attempted, by the Land Tax Act of 1910, to abolish large estates through steeply progressive taxation on unimproved values, but the Act did not have the effect desired, since the nonlabor governments reduced the progression and scale of the tax substantially.

In 1921 the Labor Party recast its aims in a more radical form, stressing nationalization of the principal industries and self-government in industry, although it declared that it proposed to nationalize only those industries that were exploiting the public. The 1927 Congress of the party toned the objective down further. The Great Depression, when in the Commonwealth and New South Wales the attempts of Labor governments to expand credit were defeated by the apostles of "sound finance," focused Labor's attention on the control of banking, and in 1948 the Commonwealth Labor Government attempted to nationalize the banks. Like its attempt to nationalize civil aviation a few years earlier this move was forestalled by constitutional difficulties.

Doubts as to the federal Labor Party's constitutional power to achieve another of its historic aims—the extension of social security through cash benefits and community services—were removed by a referendum in 1946 when the Commonwealth Parliament was given power to legislate on social services. At the same time Labor just failed to win for the Commonwealth control of industry and employment, and by a larger majority, control of interstate transport. In 1948, a referendum to give the Commonwealth power to regulate prices was defeated by a wide margin. Three years before, a referendum had been lost on a proposal to cede to the Commonwealth, for a period of five years, comprehensive powers to meet the problems of postwar reconstruction.

With the constitutional position clarified, Labor set to work building a comprehensive system of social security and community services. Cash benefits such as old-age and invalid pensions, family allowances, hospital and maternity allowances, scholarships for secondary and tertiary education were raised and extended. Grants-in-aid to educational institutions and other agencies of community welfare were increased. An ambitious scheme to provide free pharmaceutical and medical services was planned but could not be carried into operation because of the opposition of the medical profession, which feared ultimate socialization.[8] Before the conflict with the medical profession could be resolved, Labor had been defeated.

---

[8] The medical profession's opposition uncovered a further constitutional check to

When in power in state parliaments, the Labor Party had made some progress toward its objectives, being free of the constitutional fetters against which it struggled in the federal sphere. Family allowances in New South Wales from 1926 and unemployment insurance in Queensland from 1923 are outstanding examples of the party's efforts to break new ground in the social service field. The various state enterprises started by Labor from time to time, many of which were liquidated in the 1930's, were the only discernible result of the party's socialization objective.

Its power in the states, however, did enable Labor on two occasions to effect substantial improvements in the lot of Australian workers throughout the Commonwealth. In 1927, and again in 1947, Labor governments in New South Wales and Queensland legislated a reduction in the standard working week that had considerable influence on the outcome of the cases for shorter hours then before the Commonwealth Arbitration Court. State Labor governments have also been able to raise standards of working conditions and terms of employment by factory legislation; although such legislation has not been initiated solely by Labor governments, the latter have tended to go farther than nonlabor parties. Notable among recent moves was the institution of paid annual vacations by Labor governments in several states.

The achievements of the Labor Party are not to be measured, however, merely in terms of its own legislation. Its influence extended to legislation it did not institute.

Labor politicians have often complained that their opponents have caught them bathing and have stolen their clothes, but many of their own decent democratic garments have been filched from Liberal Party wardrobes. What Labor has done is to determine the standard of democratic fashions and to enforce their rapid adoption. And it was able to do this even before it held office.[9]

Trade union growth and federation

Throughout the Labor Party's history the trade unions have provided the core of its members and leaders and have exerted considerable influence on its policy. While supporting and even leading the Labor Party's political struggle, the trade unions continued to campaign on the industrial front. Table 1 shows the available figures of union membership during the period since the formation of the Labor

Labor's social security objective in 1949, when certain provisions of Labor's Health Service Act were found to be outside the power conferred on the Commonwealth Parliament.

[9] From *Australia,* by W. K. Hancock, page 227. London, Ernest Benn Limited.

Party. Unfortunately, annual figures are not available for the important years when the arbitration system was being established, but all the evidence suggests that membership grew rapidly at that time,

TABLE 1

MEMBERSHIP IN AUSTRALIAN TRADE UNIONS 1891–1948

Year	Total Members	Per Cent of Total Employees
1891	54,888	4.1
1896	55,066	n. a.
1901	97,174	6.1
1906	175,529	n. a.
1911	364,732	27.9
1916	546,556	47.5
1921	703,009	51.6
1926	851,478	55.2
1931	769,006	47.0
1936	814,809	44.1
1941	1,075,680	49.9
1946	1,262,658	59.6
1947	1,339,459	62.9
1948	1,423,150	64.9

n.a.—Not available.
Source: *Commonwealth Labor Reports.*

the form of the legislation encouraging organization among both employers and employees.

What happened in the early days of industrial arbitration was that the officials of a union, having obtained an award which raised wages and improved conditions all round, would go through the country and say to the workers in their craft or industry: "See what we have done for you." The men could not stand out.[10]

Trade union membership as a percentage of total employees continued to grow until 1920, dropped somewhat in the depression of the next few years, then rose again to a peak of 58 per cent in 1927. In the Great Depression membership fell until it constituted a smaller proportion of total employees than at any time since 1913, but climbed again to a record percentage during World War II. Thus the main growth of union membership was in the first twenty years of the period; since then the membership percentage has fluctuated cyclically with economic conditions, without any marked secular trend.

The development of the federal arbitration system to deal with interstate disputes provided a great stimulus to unions to link up with corresponding organizations in other states, so as to gain the benefit

---

[10] From *Australia* by W. K. Hancock, page 181. London, Ernest Benn Limited. See also T. Coghlan, *Labour and Industry in Australia*, O.U.P. 1918; and J. Sutcliffe, *History of Trade Unionism in Australia.* Melbourne, 1921.

of access to the Federal Court, and the proportion of workers covered by awards and agreements of the Federal Court grew steadily.[11]

The growth of interunion organization was slower, especially on a federal level. In the 1890's, the Australian Workers' Union had been formed from a number of unions catering for rural workers, thus establishing a great organization that came gradually to cover almost all unionists in rural occupations and that has always represented the center of conservative policy in the labor movement. The A.W.U. has set great store by political action, and provided the Labor Party with many of its leaders. However, few other attempts at large-scale amalgamation of unions were successful, although organization along industrial lines and confederation of labor into One Big Union dedicated to direct action were primary objectives of the left wing, dominated by the Industrial Workers of the World, during the first twenty years of the century. Industrial unionism has gained a good deal of ground, but mainly as a pragmatic response to the spread of semiskilled industrial work and the policy of extending unionism as widely as possible rather than as a form of organization preferred on *doctrinaire* grounds. The growth of industrial unions, although it has undoubtedly shifted the balance of power within the labor movement, has not arisen from an abandonment of craft organization but rather from a general growth of unionism.

Successive interstate Trades Union Congresses discussed the need for a permanent federal interunion organization, and various plans were formulated,[12] but it was not until 1927 that such a body, the Australian Council of Trade Unions, came into being. Even then the Australian trade union movement was not completely represented, for the Australian Workers' Union refused to participate, nor were Western Australian unions included. (The organization and activities of the A.C.T.U. and its relations with the labor councils in the various states are discussed in the next section.) Throughout their history, Australian interunion organizations have had a struggle to maintain control over the more powerful of their constituent unions, which have always been prepared to follow an independent line when they considered this essential for their own interests. This was probably the basic reason for the defeat of the movement for One Big Union, which reached its peak in the period 1916–1924, although the contentious political doctrine of the I.W.W. tended to confuse the issue. More

---

[11] In 1948, the proportion of Australian wage-earners in private employment working under Commonwealth awards and agreements was 47 per cent. Commonwealth Bureau of Census and Statistics, *Quarterly Business Survey*, No. 4, March, 1948.

[12] An account of the negotiations and discussions is given in J. T. Sutcliffe, *op. cit.*, pages 150–176.

recently, conflict between a left wing led by Communists, and a right wing with a strong Roman Catholic section, has added an ideological aspect to the struggle between the interunion bodies and their constituent unions.

Arbitration and other regulatory legislation

Since the intervention of government in the great disputes of the 1890's that, as has been described, encouraged labor's entry into politics, the relations of trade unions to the state have been defined by three types of legislation:

(a) The laws establishing tribunals for the settlement of industrial disputes.
(b) Other legislation under which trade unions may register and gain legal status.
(c) Coercive legislation controlling stoppages of work in certain industries or in certain circumstances.

Since government machinery for the settlement of industrial disputes was first established, the Commonwealth and states have experimented with various forms and procedures. These experiments cannot be traced here, and attention will be confined to the present position, which varies from state to state. In four states (Western Australia, South Australia, New South Wales, and Queensland) there is a special arbitration court (variously entitled) aided in some states by subsidiary tribunals for particular industries. In Victoria and Tasmania, wage boards exist for particular industries, which, although established originally to determine wages and conditions whether or not a dispute existed, have evolved into agencies for the settlement of industrial disputes. The state tribunals have jurisdiction only within the borders of their state; interstate disputes may be settled under the Commonwealth Conciliation and Arbitration Act. Under this Act disputes over the basic wage for men and for women (that is, the rate paid for work requiring no special skill), standard hours of work, and annual vacations with pay are settled by a Court; other issues are dealt with by Conciliation Commissioners for particular industries (prior to 1947 all issues were dealt with by the Court).

Considerable overlapping and conflict have occurred between Commonwealth and state tribunals, but the Commonwealth tribunal gradually came to assume the leading role. Its paramouncy was confirmed by a High Court ruling in 1926 that its awards must prevail over state awards, and the state tribunals now follow its lead in fixing wages (in some states they are required by law to do so). The state governments are responsible, however, for factory legislation, the Commonwealth being restricted by the Federal Constitution to legislation for the conciliation and arbitration of interstate industrial disputes. The states have also retained the initiative on conditions of employment other than wages, and several important advances, notably shortening the working week and vacations with pay, were first introduced by state legislation.

The legislation governing the working of industrial arbitration tribunals sets certain limits on the organization and activities of trade unions. Under the Commonwealth Conciliation and Arbitration Act, a registering union is required to show that its rules specify the industry it purports to cover, the purposes for which it is formed, and the conditions of eligibility for membership. Its rules may be disallowed if the Arbitration Court considers them tyrannical or oppressive, or contrary to law or an award, or if they hinder observance of the law by members, or if they impose uñreasonable conditions on membership. Its rules must also cover the following:

(a) The election of a committee of management of the organization, and of its branches, and of officers of the organization, and of its branches, under a system of voting which makes adequate provision for absent voting;
(b) The powers and duties of the committees and of officers;
(c) The manner of summoning meetings of members and of the committees;
(d) The removal of members of committees and of officers;
(e) The control of committees of organizations by the members of the organizations, and the control of committees of branches by the members of the branches;
(f) The mode in which industrial agreements, and other documents, may be executed by or on behalf of the organization;
(g) The power of bringing industrial disputes before the Court;
(h) The times when, and terms on which, persons shall become, or cease to be, members;
(i) The mode in which the property is to be controlled and the funds invested;
(j) The yearly or more frequent audit of the accounts;
(k) The conditions under which funds may be disbursed for ordinary and extraordinary purposes;
(l) The keeping of a register of the members arranged, where there are branches of the association, according to branches;
(m) The office of the association and of each of its branches;
(n) The repeal and alteration of and addition to the rules.[13]

Where state legislation establishing industrial tribunals provides for the registration of unions, the requirements run along the same lines, broadly, as in the Commonwealth, although they are less detailed in some states. In Victoria and Tasmania, the Statutes establishing

---

[13] Quoted by O. deR. Foenander, *Industrial Regulation in Australia,* Melbourne University Press, 1947, page 179, from Schedule B of the Act and Clause 6 of Statutory Rules 1928, No. 81, as amended by Clause 1 of Statutory Rules 1940, No. 92.

the Wages Boards, which regulate industrial conditions, do not provide for the registration of unions, although in the practical operation of the tribunals the unions receive full recognition.

The other legislation under which unions may register is of earlier origin than that establishing industrial tribunals, and has the effect of giving a registrant union corporate status and of protecting it from being considered an unlawful combination. Requirements regarding the internal organization of a union vary: some acts, like that of Queensland, lay down specific provisions almost as comprehensive as those quoted above, whereas others are cast more generally.

By far the majority of Australian unions are registered with a federal or state tribunal, and this registration constitutes the only important legal regulation of the internal affairs of Australian trade unions. The force of such regulation, however, is not to be underrated, as the following quotation from a High Court judgment indicates:

It must always be remembered that an "organization" such as the respondent organization is a creation of the Act and simply incidental to its great purposes. Those who become members of such an organization, and particularly those who undertake the duty of managing its affairs . . . take a part more or less responsible in an organization which is not merely a convenient method of obtaining their just rights, but is also a public instrument for effectively administering an important statute of public policy for the general welfare. Such an organization secures rights and privileges, but it also has duties.[14]

The most important of the duties imposed on a union by Australian industrial arbitration laws is, of course, to refrain from strikes. The precise effect of the Australian systems of arbitration upon unions' power to strike and employers' power to lockout is not generally understood and requires explanation in some detail.

Under the Queensland Industrial Conciliation and Arbitration Act, all strikes and lockouts are illegal unless authorized by a secret ballot of a registered union, or if no registered union covers the employees concerned, a secret ballot conducted by the Registrar of the Industrial Court. The South Australian Industrial Code contains a flat prohibition on strikes and lockouts, with a maximum penalty for a strike of £500 fine or three months' hard labor. The Western Australian Industrial Arbitration Act also bans strikes and lockouts, but prescribes a maximum penalty of £100 for a union or employer, and £10 for an individual.

In New South Wales, certain types of strikes "and no other" are illegal. Employees of the government or its instrumentalities may not

---

[14] J. Isaacs, in the High Court, Australian Commonwealth Shipping Board v. Federated Seamen's Union of Australia, 35 C.L.R., at 475-6.

strike, nor may employees in any industry covered by an arbitration award. An award that has been in force for twelve months, however, may be rendered inoperative by a secret ballot conducted by the union according to procedures laid down by the Industrial Arbitration Act. A fine of up to £500 may be imposed on a union if its executives or members join or assist an illegal strike, but the Act provides that the union has a legitimate defense to such a charge if it can show that "by enforcement of its rules and by other means reasonable in the circumstances" it endeavored to prevent its members' joining or aiding the strike. The Act also provides a penalty of a £10 fine or imprisonment for one month for picketing associated with an illegal strike, and penalties for "black bans" (boycotts) on the handling of commodities (£100 maximum fine for a union, £10 or one month's imprisonment for an individual). Lockouts are prohibited in New South Wales, except in response to an illegal strike. In Victoria the system of regulation of wages and conditions by wages boards composed of representatives of employers' and employees' organizations, with an independent chairman, does not directly enjoin unions from striking or from any other direct action, but the Minister may suspend the operation of a wages board determination for up to 12 months if he is satisfied that an organized strike is about to take place. (The effect of this is to free employers from any obligations to pay the wage and provide the conditions prescribed.) The Tasmanian wages board system, however, directly forbids strikes and lockouts on account of any matter in respect of which a board has made a determination, with a maximum penalty of £500 on an organization and £20 on an individual.

The federal system of conciliation and arbitration applies only to unions that voluntarily become registered organizations or are brought under the Arbitration Court's jurisdiction by employers seeking an award. Until 1930 strikes and lockouts by persons or organizations under the Federal Court's jurisdiction were offenses punishable by fine and imprisonment, but after several unions were heavily fined in the late 1920's, a labor government replaced these provisions by much milder ones. Since 1930 officers of an organization render themselves liable to a penalty of £20 if, during the currency of an award, they "advise," encourage, or incite any member of such organization to refrain from:

(a) entering into a written agreement;

(b) accepting employment; or

(c) applying for work or working (Section 78).

The most commonly used method of disciplining an organization under the Federal Act, however, is de-registration by the Court, which means that members cease to be entitled to the benefits of awards.[15] De-registration does not, however, deprive the organization of its status as an association; it retains its property except insofar as this may be subject to an order of the Court on the debts and obligations of the organization.

It will be seen from the above provisions that the degree of compulsion varies from state to state, and in the Commonwealth sphere compulsion is conditional; by seeking registration a union, in effect, binds itself to observe awards and orders of the tribunal, but it is not required to register and Commonwealth arbitration law does not restrain an unregistered organization from strike action.

Other legislation curbing strikes has, however, been in force from time to time in both Commonwealth and state jurisdictions. This ranges from legislation covering general offenses against order and property, some provisions of which might be used to suppress demonstrations, intimidation, or violence by trade unions, to legislation directed specifically at curbing more peaceful trade union action. At the Commonwealth level, the principal statute of the first type is the Crimes Act. Under Section 30J the Governor-General may issue a proclamation that there exists a serious industrial disturbance prejudicing or threatening trade or commerce with other countries or among the states. While such a proclamation is in effect, persons who join or encourage strikes or lockouts in relation to interstate or overseas transport or to any public service provided by the Commonwealth Government are liable to imprisonment for one year and, in addition, to deportation (if not born in Australia). Section 30K makes it an offense punishable by one year's imprisonment to hinder, or to compel or induce persons, by violence, intimidation, or boycott without reasonable cause or excuse, to leave or refuse employment in a public service provided by the Commonwealth or interstate or overseas transport. These provisions have been used against members of the Seamen's Union and of the Waterside Workers' Federation.

Commonwealth legislation directly restraining unions from striking has usually been associated with an emergency, either war or complete paralysis of the national economy through industrial disputes. An example of legislation passed to meet a national emergency created through an industrial dispute was the National Emergency (Coal Strike) Act, 1949, which prohibited the use of union funds, including those of the coal-mining unions, to assist the general strike in the coal industry. (Under this Act the Commonwealth Arbitration Court

---

[15] In 1950 the Court began to use its contempt power to fine unions that failed to obey its orders to comply with awards, although the High Court ruled that it could not go beyond the penalties laid down by the Act for these offenses.

ordered certain unions to pay into Court large amounts they had withdrawn from bank accounts prior to the passage of the Act, and jailed their officials for contempt of court when they failed to comply. The provisions of the Act were so broad as to raise doubt whether shopkeepers in coal-mining districts who gave strikers credit would be committing an offense, although most shopkeepers continued to give credit and none were prosecuted. The Act included a provision rendering it ineffective as soon as the strike was over.)

All the states have legislation controlling riotous and violent conduct, which legislation has at times been used against unions. More important in this connection, however, are the various acts giving state governments extraordinary powers to maintain essential services in emergencies. Thus, for example, the Victorian Essential Services Act, 1948, not only gave the government power to do everything necessary to preserve essential services, but also imposed heavy penalties on strikes by employees of an essential service unless the strike is agreed upon by a majority of voters at a secret ballot held by the Chief Electoral Officer. Penalties are also prescribed for intimidation of employees in essential services and aiding and abetting strikes or lockouts. Not all states have such legislation, which has usually been introduced for short periods only.

One of the most comprehensive pieces of state legislation aimed at directly controlling trade union action was the Industrial Law Amendment Act passed by the Labor Government in Queensland for a few months in 1948. Under the provisions of this Act, all the peaceful means of inducing workers to strike were outlawed, provided such a strike would have been illegal under the Industrial Conciliation and Arbitration Acts, 1932–1947. The strength of the Act lay in the provisions for arrest without warrant, a wide definition of the offenses, and the disposal of cases by summary jurisdiction.

Australian trade unions thus find their freedom of action considerably restricted by legislation, either connected with the working of industrial arbitration tribunals or of a more directly repressive nature. Repressive legislation has generally been used in stoppages threatening to prostrate the whole community, but for the usual run of industrial disputes, the restrictions imposed in connection with industrial tribunals are the more important.

That neither type of legislation has eliminated strikes is clearly shown by Table 2. This is so despite the infliction of severe penalties. The freezing of union funds and jailing of union leaders for contempt of court in 1949 have already been mentioned, but there have been many previous instances. During the Broken Hill Strike of 1908, for example, several leaders were imprisoned for alleged rioting, and in

TABLE 2

Strikes and Lockouts in Australia, 1913–48

Year	Number of Stoppages	Man-Days Lost	% of Stoppages Lasting 6 Days or Less	% of Man-Days Lost by These Disputes	% of Stoppages Lasting 1 Day or Less	% of Man-Days Lost by These Disputes
1913	206	621,400	63.5	7.8	31.7	2.2
1914	337	1,090,395	70.6	7.2	32.2	2.3
1915	358	543,605	70.6	18.4	41.0	5.8
1916	508	1,678,930	66.5	13.4	26.7	3.9
1917	444	4,599,658	61.6	2.0	35.8	7.6
1918	298	580,853	60.0	11.8	24.8	2.6
1919	460	5,652,726	50.0	2.6	33.6	7.2
1920	554	1,872,065	69.5	8.3	41.0	2.7
1921	624	956,617	95.0	19.6	62.0	9.0
1922	445	858,685	87.0	17.9	45.0	5.3
1923	274	1,145,977	91.5	7.4	46.0	2.6
1924	504	918,646	90.0	21.5	51.6	7.7
1925	499	1,128,570	80.0	18.6	51.5	6.5
1926	360	1,310,261	97.0	7.7	51.6	3.3
1927	441	1,713,581	88.0	10.0	48.0	3.2
1928	287	777,278	81.9	12.4	51.7	5.7
1929	259	4,671,478	90.5	2.1	54.5	1.0
1930	183	1,511,241	75.0	3.1	44.4	1.5
1931	134	245,991	68.5	22.9	25.1	5.5
1932	127	212,318	68.5	21.8	37.8	5.7
1933	90	111,956	80.0	34.6	48.0	10.2
1934	155	370,386	69.2	23.3	34.1	4.2
1935	182	495,124	61.0	10.2	27.2	2.8
1936	235	497,248	71.5	19.0	37.9	4.3
1937	342	557,111	79.0	27.2	42.0	7.6
1938	376	1,337,994	83.5	12.2	52.0	5.1
1939	416	459,154	89.5	42.6	55.2	21.2
1940	350	1,507,252	84.2	13.3	57.5	7.5
1941	567	984,174	86.5	29.8	56.0	13.8
1942	602	378,195	90.5	57.2	66.9	28.1
1943	785	990,151	88.0	43.4	58.7	17.0
1944	941	912,752	86.5	43.2	55.6	15.8
1945	945	2,119,641	83.0	17.3	56.5	7.1
1946	869	1,947,844	88.8	18.7	65.2	10.3
1947	982	1,338,728	97.7	46.8	61.4	12.6
1948	1141	1,662,686	95.8	27.3	66.2	11.3

Source: *Calculated from Commonwealth Labor Reports.* The figures include time lost by workers on strike or locked-out or thrown out of work in the establishments where workers were on strike. They do not include time lost by workers in other establishments affected by stoppages.

the Coal Strike of 1909, four union leaders were imprisoned. In the Waterside Workers' Strike of 1928, the union suffered a heavy fine of £1,000, and pickets were wounded by shots fired by police in a disturbance. In 1929 the Timber Workers' Union was fined £1,000 and its leader jailed. When the New South Wales Government opened the Rothbury coal mine in 1929 with nonunion labor, seven miners were wounded and one killed in a clash with police. During World War II striking coal miners were drafted into the army, and troops were used to break strikes on the waterfront.

The problem involved in banning strikes was effectively summed up by the President of the Queensland Industrial Court in 1924:

> The difficulty of enforcing penalties against strikes is partly political, partly practical. The punishment of large numbers of strikers by prosecutions is in
>
> practice a difficult matter. The enforcement of the penalties is usually opposed by one or other political party. In practice the deterrent against strikes is the recognition of the fact that, since arbitration has been on the whole beneficial to the unions, deprivation of access to the industrial tribunals is a substantial loss, and strikes endanger such access.[16]

The attitudes of Australian unions to arbitration, its effects on their organization and activities, and its implications for their relations to the state are considered in various sections below.

Conclusion

The foregoing historical summary raises certain problems concerning the Australian labor movement, some of which are considered in the following sections. It may be useful to consider at this point the question why trade unions became strong and powerful in Australia at a relatively early date, and why the labor movement espoused political action so whole-heartedly.

There was, first, the nature of the people who settled Australia, so many of them having been sympathetic to, if not active in, trade unions and other movements of social reform. It was natural that these people should turn to trade unionism when confronted by an economic horizon limited through poverty of natural resources that made small land holdings uneconomic and even closed mining to the independent prospector in favor of the mining company with equipment and capital. It was no accident that while America was "the land of opportunity," Australia was "the land of equality," where the frugal gifts of nature were at least to be fairly shared.

With its population growth held back by its distance from Europe and limited resources, Australia did not develop an economic climate favorable to the small, independent businessman. The mode of colonization and small population encouraged government enterprise and control, as well as the large corporation. These factors made for a smaller proportion of self-employed people, and greater class consciousness. The relatively early urbanization of the population assisted the organization of workers, as did the absence of foreign immigrants

---

[16] T. W. McCawley, *Industrial Arbitration*. Brisbane, 1924, p. 83.

of different national backgrounds. In an economic environment hostile to individualism and a social environment freed from the restraining forces of tradition and prestige, tendencies that did not develop in Britain and America for another generation flourished early in Australia.

The substantial proportion of the Australian settlers who espoused radical doctrines also assisted the development of a political labor movement in Australia. Government-sponsored immigration (to say nothing of forced transportation) encouraged people to look to the government to develop the country and to solve its social and economic problems. And not only were there social and economic problems to be solved, there were civil liberties to be won, a path to independent nationhood to be blazed. In America, these vital political issues had been decided long before the trade unions became powerful; the unions were faced with only one set of problems and were presented with an awkward obstacle by the hold of the old, established political parties. Australian labor was confronted with a combination of problems, industrial and political, that widened the focus of its policies; and with no political opponents rooted unshakably in the tradition of the country, there was little to hold it back from politics.

Trade Union Structure and Organization

In Australia, as in other countries, industrial unionism developed as manufacturing industry became more mechanized, and a smaller proportion of employees were covered by the craft unionism that grew up in the second half of the nineteenth century from the early unions in certain of the skilled trades. Organization on an industrial basis is the avowed aim of many Australian unions. Nevertheless, compared with the United States, many more unions exist in single industries in Australia. Although the number of unions has fallen in some industrial groups, it has risen in others, and has been relatively stable since 1929.

The membership jurisdiction of trade unions is determined by the industrial arbitration tribunals through which most of them operate, and although in establishing these tribunals it was intended that there should be only one union in each industry, in practice the effect has been to stabilize the structure of the Australian trade union movement in the form that had emerged when arbitration began early in the twentieth century. Confronted by the awkward practical problem of defining an industry, the tribunals agreed to register almost all *bona fide* unions, and set the seal of legality upon existing jurisdictions. Anxious to preserve the liberty of the individual as far as possible, the tribunals have been reluctant to enforce amalgamations against the will of a section of the members, and together with the vested interests of the officials of the various organizations, this has worked to check the growth of industrial unionism.

The typical Australian union is quite small, but there is a wide variation in size, from less than 50 members to over 100,000.[17] Table 3 shows how trade union size has increased since 1912, and reveals that the larger unions have steadily claimed a larger proportion of total membership. In 1912, the 48 largest unions had 71.9 per cent of the membership; by 1930, the 36 largest unions had 70 per cent, and by 1948 the 34 largest unions had 71.6 per cent of the total members. In 1948, only 15.5 per cent of unionists belonged to unions of less than 5,000 members and only 3.5 per cent belonged to unions of less than 1,000 members.

TABLE 3

SIZE OF AUSTRALIAN TRADE UNIONS, 1912–48

Year	Median Size	Number of Unions of 10,000 or More Members	Per Cent of Total Members in These Unions	Number of Unions of 100 or Less Members	Per Cent of Total Members in These Unions
1912	185	7	30.5	147	1.7
1915	203	9	35.3	137	1.4
1920	321	14	45.9	104	0.8
1925	334	21	56.5	105	0.7
1930	367	28	63.5	92	0.5
1935	420	23	56.1	93	0.6
1940	429	28	61.7	90	0.5
1945	443	32	70.2	84	0.4
1948	697	34	71.6	65	0.2

Source: *Commonwealth Labor Reports*. Medians calculated by the author.

Structure and operation

Three levels may be distinguished in the structure of the Australian trade union movement: the plant, the local or state branch, and the federal.[18] The basic unit of organization is the branch, which may cover a whole state, or a large district within a state. Full-time paid officials are rarely found below this level, and it usually forms the smallest unit of formal government (for example, it is the branch that is registered as an industrial organization under state legislation). For the most part, state branches have a great deal of autonomy in matters that do not extend beyond their own states, although the rules of a branch must not conflict with the federal rules, and the federal

---

[17] In 1950, the largest union was the Australian Workers' Union, with 165,000 members.

[18] A substantial number of unions are not federated; in these only two levels are found.

body must have adequate means for controlling actions of a branch that come under the jurisdiction of the federal tribunal.

In each establishment where members of the union are employed there is normally at least one "shop steward" or "shop delegate"; in large establishments, there is one in each main department. Working as ordinary employees, these officials spend relatively little time on union business, although they usually receive a commission on the collection of members' dues, which is generally their main responsibility of office. In some unions, though these are in the minority, the shop steward may negotiate with the management on local matters, and where such negotiation is important, he may be a figure of some standing in the plant. Where there are a number of shop stewards in one plant, they may constitute a committee to deal with management on matters that do not have implications beyond the particular establishment.

Since in almost all industries an arbitration award or agreement covers the majority of plants, such bargaining as does take place at the plant level is generally carried on within this framework. Although different industries vary considerably in the amount and significance of bargaining at the plant level, and there is much more negotiation at this level than is generally recognized, it is unusual for rates of pay and conditions of employment that might be the subject of an arbitration award to be dealt with except by officials of the branch. Unions have generally found that unless centralized control is kept over such negotiations, conditions can be whittled away by unwitting concessions to employers. (Corresponding experience on the part of employers has been one of the main factors in the growth of employers' associations.)

The position is much the same regarding direct action, which in most unions is not usually initiated in a particular plant without the approval of branch officials. Instances of spontaneous stoppages are not uncommon, but these are generally short-lived, frictional disputes rather than major conflicts. Some unions are more successful than others in controlling stoppages by the rank and file. In coal mining, meat slaughtering, and dock work many short stoppages occur through the immediate action of the men on the job, but industries such as textiles, furniture, and clothing rarely experience such stoppages.

The degree of autonomy enjoyed by the state branch of a federal union varies according to whether it operates under a federal or state industrial tribunal. If it operates under a state tribunal it is usually free to follow its own policy in negotiations, including the calling of work stoppages, without the approval of the federal body, although it is common practice for a state branch to advise the federal officials of the existence of an important dispute, particularly if it is likely to lead to a stoppage. If the state branch operates under a federal award, more coordination of policy and negotiation are required in order to present a united front and to ensure that members in one state are not committed to disputes in another state without their knowledge and approval. Instances of a state branch persisting in a line of its own against the policy of the federal body occur from time to time, especially when sharp ideological differences exist in the union, but they are not common.

Some variation exists among federal unions in the extent to which power is centralized in the federal body. In the Australian Meat Industry Employees' Union, for example, each state branch has almost complete autonomy in practice, whereas in the Ironworkers' Association, state branches are much more directly controlled by the federal body.

Although the jurisdiction of a union is decided by the industrial arbitration tribunal when agreeing to register it, demarcation (jurisdictional) disputes are not uncommon, and the tribunals are called upon to make very fine distinctions between the different types of work in the process of marking off the job territory of respective unions. At times, a tribunal will agree to register a second union when those forming it can satisfy the tribunal that they consider their *bona fide* interests are not being advanced by the existing union, which usually opposes the registration. It is not unknown for a union to apply for de-registration of a rival union, or for its exclusion from certain classes of work or certain establishments. For example, in 1950 the Australian Workers' Union asked the Federal Court to de-register the Pulp and Paper Workers' Federation, or alternatively to require the latter union to amend its rules to exclude employees at the mills of Australian Paper Manufacturers at Botany, N.S.W. This application was unsuccessful, as are most of those seeking the de-registration of another union.

Collaboration among unions

Cooperation among Australian trade unions is provided for at each of the three levels of organization distinguished above. In a plant where there are members of more than one union (a common state of affairs), there is often a combined shop stewards' committee that may act as a bargaining agent with management over matters internal to the plant; or it may be unrecognized by management, in which case it is restricted to functioning as a means of consultation among the stewards of the various unions. The diagram on page 199 shows these relationships schematically.

At the branch level, cooperation with other unions is normally effected through the district or state labor council (sometimes known as "trades hall council"), a federation that is open to all unions and includes the majority of them. Unions are represented proportionately to their membership up to a maximum of four or five delegates. These councils, through weekly meetings, formulate policy affecting the trade union movement within their district or state. They also attempt to coordinate and direct the conduct of any disputes of concern to more than one union, by means of disputes committees.

AUSTRALIAN TRADE UNION ORGANIZATION

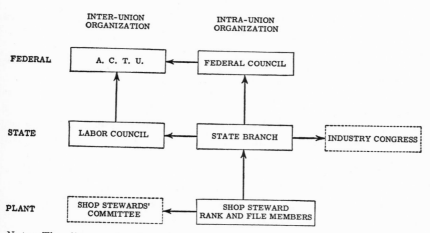

Note: The diagram is schematic only. Arrows indicate the provision of representatives. The dash lines indicate less common bodies.

In addition to the appropriate labor council, the branch may also belong to a narrower state federation of unions that operate in the same industry, or in closely related industries, such as the Council of Coal Mining Unions, the Combined Railway Unions, or the Metal Industries Federation. A relatively small number of unions are linked in these narrower federations, which are usually loosely knit and serve mainly as a medium of consultation.

State labor councils are restricted to issues concerning the union movement within their own states. They have no control over the federal council of an interstate union, and once an issue becomes a federal matter, questions affecting other unions are handled through the Australian Council of Trade Unions (see below). The likelihood of the activities of a state branch of an interstate union becoming of concern to its federal controlling body depends, as mentioned above, on the internal organization of the particular union and especially on whether the state branch operates under a state or federal arbitration tribunal.

At the federal level, the Australian Council of Trade Unions attempts to coordinate policy on issues affecting the trade union movement throughout Australia. Policies are laid down by its biennial congress, to which each affiliated union is entitled to send delegates (one for the first 1,000 members and one for each additional 2,500 members). Each district or state labor council also sends two delegates. Between congresses, the council's policy is carried out by the executive, which consists of two representatives from each of the state labor councils, plus the officers of the council elected by the congress—the president, two vice-presidents, and a secretary. The executive usually meets every three months, and reviews reports from the state labor councils, which for this purpose act as branches of the A.C.T.U.

Between these meetings an emergency committee may meet as required. This latter committee, composed of the officers of the A.C.T.U. plus the full executive of the labor council in the state where the committee meets is not free to make decisions on matters of policy, but is restricted to applying established policy; matters requiring new policy decisions must be referred to the executive for discussion with the unions concerned or for reference to the state labor councils. One of the most important activities of the A.C.T.U., however, is the control and direction of interstate industrial disputes, functioning in the same manner as the Disputes Committees of the state labor councils. The A.C.T.U. Disputes Committee is composed of the president, secretary, vice-presidents and two representatives of each union affected by the dispute.

The staffing of the A.C.T.U. and the state labor councils, like that of most of the individual unions, is extremely modest.

How effective are these arrangements for cooperation among Australian unions? Early in its history the Australian trade union movement developed relatively effective collaboration among unions in negotiations with employers and the conduct of strikes. The great Maritime Strike of 1890 was a triumph of combined union action far in advance of anything then achieved by contemporary trade union movements in other countries, and this tradition has been maintained. Cooperation has been most advanced in the conduct of strikes, where the solidarity of the Australian workers, supported by the generally sympathetic attitude of the community toward trade unions, makes scabbing unusual and facilitates the imposition of successful boycotts.

Fairly effective coordination has also been achieved in the formulation and presentation of claims to employers, especially since the formation of the A.C.T.U., which undertakes the preparation of major cases for the Commonwealth Arbitration Court. The arbitration system has undoubtedly encouraged coordination of this type, particularly with the emergence of the Commonwealth Court as the paramount tribunal, before which issues such as the standard working week and the basic wage for unskilled workers are argued on a nationwide basis.

The extent to which cooperation at these two levels results from the formal machinery of interunion coordination is difficult to assess. Although the labor councils and the A.C.T.U. have not had to struggle with the problems of union jurisdiction as have their counterparts in other countries, their power over the larger unions has been no greater. Disagreements between larger unions and the interunion bodies have at times almost paralyzed council operations and have led to temporary withdrawals and expulsions from labor councils and the A.C.T.U. The latter has been handicapped in its efforts to achieve coordination by the refusal of the Australian Workers' Union to join because it prefers to act independently, and by its failure to persuade the unions in Western Australia to affiliate. The state labor councils are more representative than the A.C.T.U., the Australian Workers' Union being affiliated in most states. More important than the coverage of these bodies, however, is their inability, in the last analysis, to control their constituent unions, which have never been willing to cede autonomy to central organizations. It is true that the disputes committees of the labor councils and the A.C.T.U. are useful means of coordinating the activities of the unions affected by a dispute, and can exert considerable group pressure, backed by the standing they have won as the official representatives of the labor movement, recognized by the government and the community. Nevertheless, they are not always equal to the task of holding a powerful union in line, and such a union may follow an independent policy, even at the cost of expulsion.

Insistence of the powerful unions on following their own policies has defeated all attempts to merge all the existing unions into a single unified organization—One Big Union. In the last twenty years, little has been heard of this historic vision of a completely united union movement. Despite the weaknesses in the cohesion of the A.C.T.U. and the labor councils, no rival central organization or federation has appeared. In a sense the Australian Workers' Union, with its huge, diverse membership, could be regarded as a One Big Union in itself, but it is not a true rival to the A.C.T.U. Although the A.W.U. continues to absorb minor unions from time to time, major unions never consider a merger with the A.W.U. as an alternative to affiliation with the A.C.T.U.

During and following World War II the division between Communists and non-Communists in the labor councils and the A.C.T.U. became so sharp that a complete break appeared possible, but this has so far been averted; and the two factions have devoted their energies to gaining control of the labor councils and the A.C.T.U., particularly the latter, rather than to developing separatist organizations.

Union membership and government

Membership in most Australian unions is open to all those employed in the trade or occupation covered by the union. Almost all the legislation under which unions may register forbids unreasonable restrictions upon entry and admission rules are drawn broadly. The industry is customarily defined in detail in the rules, especially where difficulty has been experienced in the past in distinguishing the union's membership territory from that of other unions. Some unions, particularly those consisting of members of the professions, have strict entrance qualifications, but these rules only demarcate the union's membership territory and do not restrict entry within the professional or occupational group concerned.

The rules of many unions provide for refusal of membership to an applicant, although this always requires the endorsement of the branch executive or committee of management, and very rarely occurs. Persons rejected are usually known to be of bad character, to be scabs, or to have broken union rules on previous occasions. In some unions rejected applicants may appeal to the federal council; persons refused membership in a union registered with an industrial tribunal may appeal to the tribunal.

An initiation fee is usually charged, varying from a very small sum to a substantial amount. Rules always state the maximum entrance fee; a small fee would be two shillings and six pence and a large one ten pounds.

The affairs of a local or state branch of a typical Australian union are in the hands of a committee of management, of which the branch secretary is usually the executive officer. In the smaller unions the officers of secretary and treasurer are often combined, or else the latter is a part-time position. Other members of the committee of management are almost always unpaid, spare-time officers, including the president. It is common for two or three members of the committee to be designated as trustees, to take responsibility for the care and investment of the union's funds. The secretary is always a full-time paid official who may have the assistance of a number of paid organizers and perhaps an assistant secretary. The full-time staff of Australian unions is small, averaging about four or five for a union of 2,000 members, including clerical staff. Very few Australian unions employ any specialist staff on research or educational duties.

The president and secretary of the branch are usually its delegates to interunion bodies with which it may be affiliated, or to the federal council that normally constitutes the supreme controlling body of a federal union. They generally represent the union in negotiations with employers and before industrial tribunals, with most of the work usually falling on the secretary, who is the king-pin in the organization of nearly all unions. He prepares cases for submission to industrial tribunals, transacts the official business of the union, including proceedings arising from breaches of an award, negotiates with employers, addresses rank and file meetings, handles the union's correspondence, and administers any benefit fund the union may happen to possess. If the union publishes a journal, the secretary may edit it, although in the larger unions this would be the responsibility of another officer. Although he is nominally responsible to the committee of management in all these matters, in practice the secretary of a union wields considerable power and may exert great influence on its policies.

Members of the committee of management, as well as the secretary and treasurer, are always elected by the membership, but in some unions all the paid officials are appointed by the committee. Organizers are appointed in some unions and elected in others.

The functions of the committee of management comprise the formulation of policy and the maintenance of discipline over the rank and file. Members are expected to conform to the rules and to pay their dues promptly, failure to do so rendering them liable to fines or expulsion. Offenses listed in the rules vary considerably from union to union and include such things as divulging union business, acting contrary to union policy, making frivolous charges against members, failing to attend a meeting when summoned to explain conduct, wilful breach of arbitration award, collusion with employer to evade awards, continuing to work for an employer who is breaking an award, failure to pay dues or levies (assessments), giving false information about union business to a union officer, and so on.

Annual elections are usually held to choose the committee of management and other officials of the union, but some unions hold their elections biennially. Secret ballots are provided for, usually without preferential voting, although preferential voting is used by some unions. Participation of the rank and file in these elections varies among unions and at different times in the one union. Generally speaking, in Australian trade union circles, 70 per cent of the membership is considered a heavy ballot. Sometimes record votes of over 90 per cent of the membership are recorded, but ballots of less than 30 per cent are not unknown.

Allegations of ballot rigging have been made from time to time, particularly in recent years in relation to the activities of communists. Until recently, neither Commonwealth nor state legislation relating to trade unions placed any restrictions on procedures for the election of officers, but following a Royal Commission on Communism in Victoria in 1949, at which a former communist gave evidence of ballot rigging in which he had participated, the Commonwealth Conciliation and Arbitration Act was amended to facilitate Court intervention to conduct an election where it was satisfied the ballot conducted by the union was unsatisfactory. There is little doubt that election procedure in many unions was open to abuse, and that abuse did occur from time to time through the efforts both of communist supporters and of others. The amendment of the Act was attacked by leftist unionists as unwarranted interference in the internal affairs of trade unions, but it probably stimulated most unions to review their election procedures and to tighten them up.

In the majority of Australian unions, the committee of management and the paid officials remain in office a long time, sometimes from 25 to 30 years, although at times the turnover in office may be quite high within a short period, especially if a factional fight is in progress. In recent years, unions that have become the center of a struggle between Labor Party industrial groups and the Communist Party have experienced rapid changes of leadership.

This tendency for long tenure of office is not necessarily to be taken as proof of a lack of democratic control by the rank and file, however, for the rules of almost all Australian unions make specific provision for removal of officials from office if they do not abide by the union rules, and where the union is registered with an industrial tribunal, members have recourse to the tribunal if they consider that the officials have committed a serious breach of the rules. The Commonwealth Act empowers the Court to order the observance of any of the rules of the union, and failure to comply with such an order is an offense. The Court is reluctant to use its powers under the Act unless there is clear evidence of failure to observe the rules in a manner likely to disturb industrial peace or affect the public interest. As long as the rules are observed and interpreted in a reasonable manner, the Court usually supports the officials against a minority; as far as possible it avoids intervening in factional fights.

Although it is true that a skilful union official can still find ways of imposing his will on the members without going so far as to break union rules, the possibility of appeal to the appropriate industrial tribunal places a check on abuse of power over individual members. Also to be considered is the effect of the tribunals' review of the rules of a union when it applies for registration. For example, the tribunals generally require the union to make provision for an appeal against any disciplinary actions taken by officials against individuals.

Provision for the control of union officials by the members and for the prevention of abuse of their power over individuals may thus be regarded as fairly adequate in Australian unions. Minorities have a reasonable opportunity to become majorities, and they are protected against the more vicious types of persecution. This does not, however, guarantee effective participation in the affairs of the union by the rank and file. It is safe to say that in most unions the members are content to allow the officials to conduct the routine business of the union, and take little interest in policy issues except decision to strike. Such decisions are rarely taken except by a mass meeting of the members concerned, which is normally very well attended. Attendance at other meetings is poor in most unions, however, and decisions are commonly taken on many matters without any direct expression of rank-and-file opinion.

The absence of member participation in routine affairs of the union causes many union leaders concern, especially those who can look back in contrast at the fervor of 50 years ago. The following extract from a union journal illustrates the apathy with which most unions struggle:

> To say the least, members could not take any less interest in their union than that of members of this union. So far this year, members of the Amalgamated Foodstuffs Union have had the opportunity of knowing what is going on, in Brisbane they have had the chance of attending a union meeting on the second Wednesday of each month. . . . Meetings have been held at country towns, but members do not have the interest to attend and hear what the union has been doing. This union has a management committee large enough to make a quorum for the general meetings, but this is not enough, some more should attend and fill the meeting room.[19]

Many Australian unions publish a journal as a service to members. Broadly speaking, these fall into two types: those resembling newspapers and those more like magazines. They appear at intervals varying from one week to three months, and differ widely in style and

---

[19] *The Union Voice*, June, 1950, p. 4.

content in accordance with union policy. By and large, the big industrial unions with widespread membership tend to publish newspaper-type journals at fairly short intervals, and to adopt a more dramatic type of journalism, sometimes of an inflammatory character. The craft unions mostly publish magazine-type journals at monthly or longer intervals, and tend to employ a more staid, often dull, approach.

In most unions, the journal is a fairly heavy item of expenditure, larger in the industrial unions for which the journal is an important means of building solidarity. For example, over one-fifth of the total expenditure of the Coal Miners' Federation in 1949 was devoted to its weekly paper, *Common Cause*, which is distinguished by highly skilled inflammatory journalism. This union has a full-time editor for its paper, an unusual arrangement.

Membership dues vary considerably from union to union, most falling between £1 and £2 per annum, usually paid quarterly. Women and minors, if receiving lower wages, generally pay lower rates. Provision is usually made for levies (special assessments), sometimes with a maximum limit. Generally speaking, the funds of the union may only be applied to the achievement of the objects laid down in the union rules, and this applies to levies as well. Dispute is likely to arise mainly over the use of funds for political purposes. Only New South Wales legislation obliges a union to make payments for political purposes out of a special fund to which members cannot be required to contribute. In Western Australia unions cannot make compulsory levies for election funds. Unions registered under other legislation appear to be free to make political payments out of general revenue, but payments to which some of the members object would be taken into account by the Registrar of the Commonwealth Court if those members applied for registration as a separate organization. This fact sets a brake on any tendency for members of unions registered with the Commonwealth Court to be subjected to levies for objects with which they are not in agreement, although from time to time allegations are made that donations of union funds to various organizations are in reality devoted to political purposes.

Australian unions are not rich. This is indicated by the only published statistics of union finances, those of the New South Wales unions, and by the balance sheets and financial statements of the few unions that publish them in their journals. In 1948, funds held per member in different unions varied from less than one shilling to over £40, the average (New South Wales) being somewhat less than £2. Contributions by members are the main sources of income. Even though the investment income of some unions may be a significant item in their accounts, this is not true of the trade union movement as a whole.

Most unions live within their incomes, year by year, and do not run their funds down except when they become involved in a long stoppage calling for sustenance payments to members during strikes. Payments to members from sick funds and other benefit schemes vary considerably in different years, rising at times to two-fifths of total expenditure, and falling at others to between one-eighth and one-ninth. Meagre information is available on other expenditures of Australian unions. From the published accounts of a small number of unions and from inquiries among trade union officials, it appears that about 35 to 45 per cent of the total expenditure of a typical Australian union goes for salaries, and it may spend from 5 to 20 per cent on the publication of a journal. These figures refer to a year in which the union is not involved in industrial disputes, when strike pay would be so large an amount as to distort the percentages.

Apart from these items, the pattern of expenditure varies considerably among different unions. Local and state branches pay per capita fees to their federal bodies, and these may account for as much as 20 per cent of their expenditures, although usually the proportion is smaller. Fees of various sorts may constitute another substantial item; for example, to officers attending conferences and meetings, shop stewards' commissions, legal fees, auditors' fees. Donations, both political and charitable, may also be a considerable sum. In the half-year ended January 17, 1950, for example, the New South Wales branch of the Printing Industry Employees' Union of Australia devoted £230 to charitable causes, constituting about 2.5 per cent of its total expenditure. It also gave £560 to the Australian Labor Party, which fought a federal election during the period.

Australian union officials are not highly paid, the secretary of a state branch generally receiving between £400 and £600 per annum, and organizers from £300 to £500. Some branch secretaries range as high as £1,000 (the Queensland branch of the Australian Workers' Union pays its secretary £1,000 plus £350 for special expenses), and a few federal officials receive more, but these are exceptions.

Trade Union Functions and Results

Union objectives

Trade union objectives may be conveniently divided into two broad groups: (a) the provision of direct services to members; (b) the improvement of conditions of employment.

Services to members. The first group includes the various benefit schemes run by unions for their members; activities in the field of education, recreation and cultural pursuits, and charitable activities. These types of activity reach back to the earlier stages of trade unionism when a union was as much an association for mutual benefit and communal activities as an organization devoted to advancing members' economic interests. Broadly speaking, these activities are more important in the older unions with craft associations than in the younger unions with more general membership, but the Australian trade union movement as a whole has shown less interest in this field than either the British or the American movements. Attention has been focused more on the winning of economic and political gains, and the emphasis has been on social services to be supplied by the government rather than their provision by the unions. Several factors contributed to this difference: notably the earlier political success of Australian labor, the generally favorable Australian attitude to state intervention, and the fact that many Australian unions were established or built up with the explicit aim of obtaining an industrial arbitration award, which concentrated their members' attention on industrial matters from the start. The small size of many Australian unions limits the scale on which services can be provided for members. The greatest development of trade unionism in Australia came at a time when public education had removed some of the need for union educational activity.

Improved conditions of employment. Despite the importance of the political wing of Australian labor, and deep union interest in political objectives, the betterment of industrial conditions has remained the primary focus of trade union interests. Union objectives under this heading fall into four main sub-groups: (*a*) conditions on the job (that is, wages, hours, sick and annual leave, physical working conditions, and so forth); (*b*) security of employment; (*c*) the security and strength of the union as an organization; (*d*) increased participation by employees in the control of industry.

Conditions on the job. With no significant exceptions, the objective of Australian unions with regard to wages has been the simple one of gaining the highest rate they can get. Arbitration has encouraged this approach to wage demands by creating a situation in which the union has no responsibility for reaching agreement with employers, or for the impact of its demands on the industry, and any restraining influence that might have been exerted by such responsibility is removed. Also, in certain of the arbitration systems, including the federal, the mechanics of obtaining an award have been such as to make it easier for both sides to state their most extreme positions at the outset, even though they recognize that they are not practical bargaining claims;

if they define the ambit of the dispute very widely in the original proceedings, they can apply for a variation of the arbitration award at a later stage much more easily than they can persuade the tribunal that a new award is justified. Single-minded concentration on the highest wage rate has also been encouraged by the strong ethical element introduced into Australian wage determination by industrial tribunals by the notion of the living wage, which has been expressed in various forms in industrial legislation since early in the century, and came into federal arbitration through the ill-fated "New Protection," which attempted to make tariff protection contingent on the payment of "fair and reasonable" wages. The concept of a minimum living standard is hard to make precise, and the difficulty of drawing a line between what is essential and what is merely desirable leads to a continuous stretching of the "minimum" standard. The Australian industrial tribunals' division of wage rates into two elements, the basic wage and the margin added to allow for the special skill required of a particular calling, has encouraged a union approach to wages that is only secondarily related to "ability to pay." Although in practice they are often forced on to the more mundane ground of industry's capacity to pay, the unions strive to maintain their stand on the higher plane of human rights. Thus, in arguing for a 40-hour week in 1946 they stressed the general expectation of a "new" social order after the war, and their demand for a higher living wage in 1949 was supported by a claim that the workers were not receiving a fair share of the national income.

Although this concentration on ethical grounds is the key to an understanding of Australian union wage conduct, it should not be inferred that union leaders never modify their claims according to the economic circumstances of an industry. For example, in September, 1949, the Firemen and Deckhands' Union agreed to a twelve months' postponement of its demand for a rise in wages because the company concerned (Sydney Ferries Ltd.) was experiencing financial difficulties. No doubt, the degree of prosperity prevailing is weighed in the formulation of all wage claims, but it remains a limiting consideration rather than the originating source, and in this respect Australian unionism presents a significant contrast with American, and to a lesser extent, with British trade unionism.

Australian unions have not been sympathetic to the contention that wages should be reduced in periods of general depression, and in the Great Depression they opposed the cut desired by employers, on the ground that it would not relieve the depression because purchasing power would be reduced. In the federal Basic Wage Case of 1949–50 this line of argument was repeated, the unions countering the employers' claim that a wage rise would add to inflation by arguing that higher wages, by preserving purchasing power, would prevent the economy's suffering a severe depression when the boom collapsed. They did accept the pegging of wages in wartime, however, although serious strike pressure developed against its continuance in 1946.

Equal pay for women has been a traditional aim of Australian unions, motivated not only by notions of justice, but by fears of undercutting of wages and competition for jobs. Shorter and more convenient working hours have been an historic goal of Australian trade unions since the struggle for the eight-hour day was waged under the slogan "eight hours to work, eight hours to sleep, eight hours to play!" Their approach has been the same as to wages, with even more emphasis on ethical considerations. As far as possible, they have sought to eliminate work at night and on weekends, by having penalty rates prescribed for work done outside normal hours.

Paid annual vacations and sick leave have also been objectives of Australian unions, although the pressure for these items on the "fringe" of wages and hours has varied among unions at different times, becoming more general in the late 1930's. Paid long service leave became an objective among the coal-mining unions shortly after World War II and spread gradually to other unions. Australian unions have not shown as much interest as American unions in winning private pension plans from employers; their social outlook leads them to look to the government to provide this as a social service, and some unions even oppose private plans on the ground that they tend to tie the worker to a particular employer.

Security of employment. Concern with security of employment is expressed in various methods of sharing the available jobs, in practices designed to limit entry to the trade and to control the rate of work, and in resistance to technological change and mechanization. The simplest of these policies is keeping output down so that there will be more work to go around. Officially this is denied by union leaders, but it nevertheless occurs, usually through informal organization on the job. The view generally accepted by Australian workers (and of course not restricted to Australia) is summed up by the coal miners' saying about coal stocks: "When there's coal on the grass, we're on the grass."

Antipathy to increasing production underlies the opposition of many unions to the extension of wage incentive plans. Other objections are raised, too, such as the wearing out of older, slower workers, the prevalence of rate-cutting, the replacement of collective bargaining by individual bargaining, and the breaking down of skilled jobs, but the basic obstacle is the fear of overproduction. This fear extends, naturally, to all improvements in methods and to mechanization. It is both general and specific, relating not only to the possibility of general unemployment but also to the danger of unemployment for a specific group, in particular the skilled workers. Although technological change is steadily weakening the monopoly power of the skilled worker, the unions that oppose incentives do not see why they should help the process along by accepting the extension of incentives and methods engineering.

Some unions have not opposed wage incentive plans, which have operated successfully in a number of industries for a long time. The official policy of the union movement, however, has been to oppose incentive plans, especially those involving the setting of rates by time study. In the years following World War II, the wider use of wage incentives was advocated by employers and the nonlabor parties to raise productivity and as an alternative to increases in time wages. The Labor Government did not press the unions directly to accept incentives, but in 1949 the Prime Minister (Mr. J. B. Chifley) announced that he favored judicious application of wage incentives "with proper safeguards" and raised the matter with the Federal Labor Advisory Committee. The A.C.T.U. was requested to investigate incentive payments, and circularized its member unions for their opinions. This inquiry, it was reported, indicated that about 60 per cent of the affiliated unions opposed any form of incentives and 40 per cent were in favor of incentive plans that preserved the union's right to negotiation over rates. The 1949 Federal Conference of the A.C.T.U. decided by a small majority to continue opposition to wage incentives, confirming decisions of previous conferences.

In addition to trying to make more work, or at least seeing that the amount of work does not decline too rapidly, Australian unions may try to keep down the numbers among whom the work is to be shared. The most highly developed practice is the limitation of the proportion of minors or apprentices that an employer is permitted to engage. This limitation serves at once to achieve the twin objectives of reducing competition from lower paid labor and of restricting the numbers entering the trade. In the more highly skilled trades, it is doubtful whether these restrictions are very important in practice since employers rarely wish to engage the numbers permitted, but in other trades where youthful labor can more readily be used in a wide range of operations, it is undoubtedly significant.

A third trade union objective related to security of employment is the fair sharing of such employment opportunities as may exist at any one time. The general union solution to this problem is the seniority rule, usually expressed as "last to come, first to go." Unions usually seek to have seniority adopted for promotion as well as for retrenchment and re-employment. As might be expected, unions in industries that experience violent fluctuations in employment in a short period lay greater stress on the sharing of job opportunities through seniority.

Union security. Seniority is attractive to unions, not only because it appears to be fair, but because it provides an objective basis for choice among workers and prevents any possibility of discrimination against unionists as such. It is thus a common union objective toward another major goal, the maintenance of the security and strength of the union as an organization. More important than seniority in this connection, perhaps, are the objectives of preference in employment to unionists and compulsory unionism (union shop).

Union interest in preference to unionists originated in employer discrimination against unionists. Even when this has been overcome, however, unions have sought preference as a means of strengthening their organization and increasing their power. Compulsory unionism has also been persistently sought by the Australian union movement, both in industrial awards and by legislation.

In some industries where the uncertainty of employment is particularly great, unions have attempted to gain complete control of hiring, which goes further than compulsory unionism, usually involving strict application of seniority by the union.

Australian unions have also fought for the right of union officials to enter plants at reasonable times for the purpose of collecting dues, posting notices, interviewing members, and inspecting time and wages records. Australian unions have not shown much interest in the "checkoff" (collection of union dues by the employer), fearing victimization of members, and preferring to maintain contact between members and officials in collection of dues.

Increased participation. In the broadest sense, any collective bargaining constitutes a limitation upon managerial functions; but an important practical distinction may be drawn between restrictions on management's freedom to determine conditions of employment and participation by a union in other functions of management, including the day-by-day internal direction of the operations of an enterprise. Increased participation in the control of industry in this latter sense is a union objective that arises from union attempts to gain more security of employment for the membership and to maintain a strong organization.

Efforts to spread employment opportunities by seniority or control of hiring, or to control the amount of work so as to maintain jobs for members, imply some interference with managerial direction of the enterprise. Australian unions all desire to participate in managerial decisions on the hiring, promotion, layoff and dismissal of labor, and especially where employment opportunities are directly affected (as in certain seasonal industries), in decisions on the speed of work. For the most part, however, they have been less concerned with managerial decisions that do not bear so directly upon employment. They have always been ready to fight the case of an individual member whom they consider to have been unjustly disciplined, and in certain industries where disciplinary action is frequently taken (such as railways) the unions spend a great deal of time on this type of work. In some industries they have also attempted to influence management's choice of foremen. For example, in January, 1950, the Ship Painters' and Dockers' Union fined two of its members employed as foreman and charge-hand in a ship repair yard, directed them to abandon their employment in these capacities, and refused to permit its members to work under them. (The Company resisted and was upheld by an industrial tribunal.)

For the most part, however, Australian unions have not attempted to win any real measure of control over the general direction of individual businesses. The move for "workers' control" of industry, always popular with the left, has never become a major practical goal for Australian unions, although it has found some expression in the official objectives of the Labor Party in the following form: "The organization and establishment of cooperative activities, in which the workers and other producers shall be trained in the management, responsibility and control of industry."

In this connection it is significant that in marked contrast with the United Kingdom, the cooperative movement has never developed in Australia to any great extent. The Australian labor movement has not displayed the same strain of cooperation that has been so characteristic of British labor, and was also apparent in lesser degree at certain stages of the history of labor in the United States. Although attempts have occasionally been made by employer groups to encourage profit-sharing in Australian industry, the practice has not become widespread and unions take little interest in it. Some union leaders oppose profit-sharing on the ground that if the firm can afford to share profits it can afford to pay higher wages, which would be better for the worker because they could not be so easily given and withdrawn with fluctuations in profits that are beyond employees' control. The growth of employee stock ownership schemes in Australia in recent years does not appear to have excited any attention from the unions.

Australian union attitudes to paternalism on the part of employers are also relevant in this connection. Although there are some notable examples of paternalism, it is less widespread than in Britain, and the majority of Australian unions are somewhat hostile to it, on the ground that it tends to bind the worker to an individual establishment. In some industries in which unions and management compete continuously for worker allegiance, unions have even taken exception to management-organized recreation for employees and have developed their own rival recreational activities. But this extreme attitude is not common, and in many industries recreational activities organized or subsidized by management are well patronized and appreciated. On the whole, however, the factory is not so generally regarded as a natural center of social and community life as in Britain.

Quantitative data on the objectives of Australian trade unions regarding conditions of employment are available since 1913 in the statistics of "causes" of industrial disputes involving a stoppage of work. Although the ostensible "cause" of a dispute recorded in the official statistics does not always reveal the true underlying factors, the figures serve to indicate the type of issues on which Australian unions have been willing to fight. Questions of wages, working conditions, and "the employment of particular classes of persons" have been together responsible almost equally for about three-quarters of the total disputes, although they accounted for a smaller proportion (61.8 per cent) of the time lost. Wage questions caused the greatest loss of time (35.9 per cent), the main issue being the raising of wages, which was responsible for 22.9 per cent of the total time lost. Next in importance as a source of lost time was "the employment of particular classes of persons" (14.8 per cent) and working conditions. Disputes over hours of work were negligible in number, but accounted for 11.1 per cent of time lost. Disputes over the employment of nonunionists have been relatively unimportant, while disputes on "other union questions" amounted to approximately 5 per cent of disputes and time lost.

In interpreting these figures, it must be remembered that they relate to a period when unionism was already well established and was relatively free to concentrate on improvements in conditions of employment. If figures were available for an earlier period, they would probably show much more concern with issues relating to trade unionism; even in the published figures, more days were lost over such issues up to 1919 than later.

Negotiation and arbitration

Negotiation with employers is a universal technique of unions under capitalism; in the Australian environment two unusual features are compulsory arbitration and the importance of government as employer.[20]

---

[20] In June, 1947, government employment constituted 24.7 per cent of total employment. *Monthly Review of Business Statistics,* October, 1950.

Union attempts to negotiate directly with governments over conditions for their employees have always met with resistance, government usually delegating its function as employer to a board, commission, or other instrumentality responsible for the work performed by the employees concerned. For example, the Commonwealth Government does not interfere in the direct negotiations between Commonwealth public service unions and the Commonwealth Public Service Board, nor do the state governments intervene in negotiations between their railways commissioners and railway unions. Both state and Commonwealth Governments, however, influence the conditions of employment in government undertakings by broad policy rulings, and by legislation. Gradually, the unions succeeded in having arbitration tribunals set up for government employees (employees in "industrial" government enterprises such as railways were covered first, and members of the civil service later), thus limiting governments' freedom of decision on conditions for their own employees. In addition, governments have, on occasion, given their instrumentalities directives on such matters as preference to unionists in government employment.

Compulsory arbitration has had a profound influence on Australian union methods of operation by the limitations it has placed on trade union freedom of action. Attitudes of Australian unions to arbitration have always been mixed. Even in the years when support for arbitration was gradually developing among various sections of the community, some elements within the labor movement remained opposed, holding that if the unions did not yield any of their freedom of action, they would make more progress toward both their industrial and their social objectives. Ideological perspectives, as well as practical judgments, have influenced union attitudes on this issue, and opposition to arbitration has always been centered on the politically left sections of the labor movement. Nevertheless, disappointment with the results achieved by arbitration has been quite widespread, and whether unions would do better without arbitration has been hotly debated within the union movement. On one side, there are opinions such as that expressed by the Secretary of the Newcastle Trades Hall in 1947, that "over the years the Arbitration Courts, as at present constituted, have given 99 per cent of their decisions in favor of the employer." [21] Against this, other union leaders have pointed out that a number of unions "have been born out of, and have grown strong as a result of, arbitration, and would as quickly fade and die if the arbitration protection were withdrawn and they were forced out of the enervating atmosphere of the Court into the hard work-a-day world of industrial and economic strife

---

[21] *Newcastle Morning Herald,* January 9, 1947.

where the ability to hurt is the most cogent argument." [22] A more balanced view was expressed by the New South Wales Labor Council in 1930:

> On a rising market arbitration prevents the workers from obtaining full advantage of their economic power due to the keen demand for labour. On a falling market arbitration obstructs employers from obtaining the full advantages of their economic power due to the scarcity of jobs and the weakness of the trade unions through abnormal unemployment.[23]

Opposition to arbitration has at times become strong enough to lead unions to pass resolutions advocating withdrawal from the system. Even the A.C.T.U. Congress resolved in 1934 "to repudiate compulsory arbitration, to call on Trades Unions to withdraw from the Arbitration Courts, and to adopt a policy of direct negotiations with the employers for industrial agreements." [24] In practice, however, the union movement has not been prepared to embark on this course. When in 1944 the national secretary of the Federated Ironworkers' Association, a prominent communist, returned from a visit to the United States proposing the replacement of arbitration by collective bargaining, and the wider use of incentive payments, a storm of protest arose.

In effect, then, the Australian unions support and operate through the arbitration system despite their disappointment with the gains it has brought the workers. "Their support has been based on the purely utilitarian ground that arbitration on the whole is more profitable to the union than are strikes," [25] and by no means implies that they have forsaken direct action. As the general secretary of the Printing Industry Employees' Union of Australia said in 1935, "nobody representing the unions accepted the Arbitration Court, or the policy of arbitration, as the last word on the subject; it was simply a means to an end and should be used accordingly." [26] A certain amount of direct action, in the unions' opinion, is necessary to ginger up the arbitrators, and they have steadily resisted the restraints imposed by arbitration on direct action. Strong unions have always been prepared to strike against an award if they thought they would gain their objectives by doing so.

As this pragmatic attitude to arbitration implies, the trade union idea of a good arbitrator is one who gives them what they want. This

---

[22] J. Hooke, *Is Arbitration Enough?*, symposium organized by Workers' Educational Association, page 1. New South Wales, 1946.

[23] N.S.W. Labor Council, *Report on Arbitration,* unpublished, 1930.

[24] A.C.T.U. Congress, *Proceedings,* unpublished, 1934.

[25] T. W. McCawley, quoted in *Economic News,* Queensland Bureau of Industry, Vol. 16, No. 1 (January, 1947), page 1.

[26] *Labor News,* February, 1947.

was blatantly expressed by two Labor members of the Federal Parliament when it was debating the amendment of the Conciliation and Arbitration Act in 1947:

Mr. Williams (Labor, N.S.W.) said he hoped the Government would appoint trade union leaders as conciliation commissioners (who were to have arbitral powers) . . . "I feel sure that men would be selected who would represent the workers," he said. . . . Mr. James (Labor, N.S.W.) said he hoped all the conciliation commissioners would be trade union leaders. "I hope the unions have the right to select them, and that if they do not do a good job for Labor the unions will sack them," Mr. James said.[27]

Unions have been critical of regular judges as arbitrators, alleging that their social position and background make them unsympathetic to labor and that their training predisposes them toward unnecessary legalism. As one union secretary wrote:

I never forget my first experience in an Arbitration Court. It was before a Full Bench sitting. The judges were arrayed in wigs and gowns, and there was a full exhibition of Court conduct and paraphernalia. My own impression was that it was an awe-inspiring spectacle designed to force its attitude and decisions, rather than to serve out justice in respect of claims put forward on behalf of workers. These men, on a minimum wage of £2500 per year, were proposing to impose judgment on workers striving, at that time, not to improve—but to prevent a reduction in their meagre basic wage allowance. And that is the kind of impression gained by any layman, and the opinion held by almost every worker in industry.[28]

The fact that most unions operate through the arbitration machinery does not mean that they never conduct direct negotiation with employers. The normal procedures within the arbitration and wage-fixing systems provide for the registration of an agreement with the arbitration tribunal, which may then be enforced as an award, and even when arbitral procedure is used in making an award, most of the terms incorporated in the award have already been agreed to by the parties in conference. In addition to such negotiations over the provisions of agreements and awards, unions continually negotiate with employers over minor matters not included in awards. Federal awards provide for boards of reference, with equal representation of employers and employees and an "impartial" chairman, to deal with disputes arising from the operation of the award, and similar arrangements operate under the arbitration systems of some states.

Almost all these negotiations, however, are conducted under the

---

[27] *Newcastle Morning Herald,* April 17, 1947.
[28] J. A. Ferguson, *Is Arbitration Enough?* symposium organized by Workers' Education Association, page 2. New South Wales, 1946.

shadow of an industrial tribunal, or even at its direction and within the framework it lays down. With the sole important exception of the metal mining industries of Broken Hill, very little collective bargaining occurs in complete independence of an industrial tribunal of some sort. This has at least three significant implications for the nature of negotiations. First, a premium is placed on the capacities of union officials as quasi-legal advocates. Although tribunals are not bound by the more stringent legal formalities, most of them follow general judicial procedures and in an attempt to make their work orderly and systematic, they tend to make their decisions consistent with precedent and to build up codes of rules and interpretations. Advocacy before industrial tribunals has become rather professionalized, and competence in this sphere has become a crucial qualification for union office. Thus a specialized legalistic approach to industrial disputes has been encouraged in both the employer and union organizations. The fact that most negotiations with employers are regarded by both parties merely as a phase of proceedings before a tribunal encourages a carry-over of attitudes and approach from the more formal to the less formal setting.

The second result of the setting in which negotiations with employers take place is that throughout negotiations the parties do not direct their energies solely toward the goal of gaining as much as possible from the other side with the minimum sacrifice in terms of a work stoppage, but continually have in mind the possible effect of their actions upon the tribunal. As noted earlier, with some tribunals, including the federal, for procedural reasons the parties' initial claims and counterclaims are cast in the most extreme terms, far beyond those they are willing to accept. Relations are thereby exacerbated, and each party entering upon negotiations is reminded afresh of its opponents' ultimate, long-range goals and the divergence of these from its own. The responsibility for reaching agreement, and for the terms of agreement, is removed from the parties, who are thus freer to remain intransigent and emphasize points of difference rather than agreement.

Third, the close relation of negotiations with the process of obtaining an award from a tribunal has encouraged the growth of employers' associations. These associations are grouped into state federations that are linked in federal organizations, the two main ones being the Associated Chambers of Manufacturers and the Australian Council of Employers' Federations. No statistics of the proportion of employers in associations are available, but from Table 4 it will be apparent that these associations grew very rapidly in strength in the 1930's, though employers in the key industries had been strongly organized much earlier. The possibility that a concession to a union by a few employers might encourage a tribunal to incorporate it in an award makes these associations anxious to "hold the line" by retaining firm control of negotiations, and they strongly discourage their members from dealing individually with unions. As with unions, a certain professionalism has developed among the "industrial officers" of employers' organizations, with an emphasis on legalistic interpretation of awards and a policy of no concessions. Although the development of employers' associations along these lines cannot be ascribed entirely to the arbitration system, it appears to have played an important part.

TABLE 4

EMPLOYERS' ASSOCIATIONS IN AUSTRALIA, 1922–39

Year	Number of Associations	Total Members	Number of Associations with over 1,000 Members	Per Cent of Total Members in These Associations
1922	467	51,700	10	38
1923	480	70,000	14	37
1924	469	77,900	16	44
1925	480	103,400	18	56
1926	478	113,600	20	62
1927	485	122,700	20	61
1928	505	127,200	22	62
1929	527	135,300	25	66
1930	534	134,700	25	66
1931	547	132,400	22	65
1932	549	129,600	21	62
1933	521	132,200	17	60
1934	505	134,900	20	63
1935	500	136,200	19	63
1936	506	168,400	20	65
1937	511	169,700	24	67
1938	506	175,700	27	68
1939	514	177,000	30	67

Source: *Commonwealth Year Books*. Figures not available for other years.

Negotiations between employers and unions have gradually become broader in reference, partly as a result of the growth of employers' associations and partly owing to the working of the arbitration systems. The arbitration tribunals' practice of setting a minimum wage for unskilled labor, irrespective of the industry in which it is employed (known as the Basic Wage), a standard working week, and certain other "standard" conditions such as annual leave and sick leave, has had the effect of widening the bargaining unit from a single industry to almost the whole economy, now that state tribunals follow the lead of the Commonwealth Court on most of these matters. Thus what might begin as negotiations between a single union and an employers' association may end up as a case between the entire union movement on the one side and the entire set of employers' associations on the other, with all the state and Commonwealth governments also taking part, either as employers or "intervening" in the public interest. Although the original parties are heard during the proceedings, the major part of the case for the unions is usually conducted by the A.C.T.U., and the employers' federations usually arrange for joint representation. Important cases, such as the Forty-Hour Week Case of 1946–7 and the Basic Wage Case of 1949–50, may last fifteen months.

Procedures ·for bringing matters before a tribunal are specific. They vary in formality and complexity, being simplest for the wages boards. The Federal procedures were probably the most complex until 1947, when a substantial proportion of the Court's responsibilities were taken over by conciliation commissioners and procedures considerably simplified. Negotiating practices, however, vary widely among industries, some of which adhere to formalities, whereas others supplement these by informal dealings.

Industrial warfare

Australian unions make use of almost all the traditional techniques of industrial warfare. The ultimate weapon is the general strike, but this has rarely been used by Australian unions, although some big strikes, such as the Maritime Strike of 1890 and the New South Wales Rail Strike of 1917, extended very widely. (In 1912 Brisbane suffered a general strike.) At other times, something like the effect of a general strike has been achieved by a long stoppage in a strategic industry, particularly coal mining.

The "rolling strike," or "sectional strike," is a technique of striking individual plants successively, so that only a small proportion of the union's members are drawing strike pay at any one time, although the effect on the individual employer is as severe as a strike throughout the industry. The "sympathy strike" is one by employees not directly concerned in a dispute, who nevertheless strike to display their belief in the justice of their fellow-workers' cause, in the hope that their own employer may put pressure on the employer in the original dispute. This type of strike is fairly common in Australia. The "sit-down" strike, in which strikers do not leave the plant, is aimed particularly at preventing strike-breakers from carrying on the strikers' work and has been effectively employed in the gas industry; otherwise it is is rarely used. The "regulation" strike is the process of carrying out every working rule and procedure to a literal extreme, thereby rendering operations almost impossible. It is confined to government instrumentalities, but not frequently employed.

Akin to the "regulation strike" is the "go-slow," a deliberate reduction in the customary speed of work. In a period of acute labor shortage, when much overtime is being worked, a ban on overtime is a powerful weapon. Doubt as to whether an overtime ban constituted direct action led industrial tribunals to insert a clause in most awards requiring an employee to work a "reasonable amount" of overtime at the employer's direction.

A new strike technique was tried soon after World War II in the metal trades, the "mass resignation." The whole of a union's members employed in a workshop would leave, and no other members of the union would apply for employment. Obviously workable only in an acute labor shortage, this maneuver was ruled by the federal arbitration tribunal to be a strike.

In most industries where strikes occur, unions are so strong that picketing is unnecessary. In other trades, or at times when mass unemployment has weakened the unions and provided a body of potential strike-breakers, pickets are used. Picketing, however, is not a normal feature of a strike in Australia, and it is hardly ever used for publicity purposes. Australian unions have made almost no use of publicity as a technique for capturing public support, although employers and government are doing so with increasing frequency.

One of the most widely used weapons of industrial warfare is the "black ban" (boycott), often more effective in gaining a union's objective than a strike. Thus the Waterside Workers' Federation placed a ban on handling goods for Dutch ships during the Indonesian War. This ban effectively stopped Australia sending aid to the Dutch, without committing the union to such a major conflict as a strike. The "black ban" is often used for nonindustrial objectives, as was the Waterside Workers' ban referred to above, or the ban by the Building Workers' Industrial Union on certain luxury buildings in Victoria in 1950.

Strike-breaking is relatively rare in Australia, and violence in industrial disputes is almost unknown. As noted earlier, clashes did occur in the early days of unionism, and in the early days of arbitration. Strike-breaking by the New South Wales Government as late as 1933 led to a fatality. Nevertheless, industrial warfare proceeds almost entirely unstained by violence or bloodshed.

Techniques of industrial warfare commonly used by Australian employers may be briefly listed. The weapon corresponding to the strike is the "lock out," which is by no means unknown, although rarely admitted to be such. Another weapon, used more often than is admitted, is black-listing of militant unionists so that they cannot obtain employment. During big lock outs, employers' associations sometimes give financial assistance to member firms that are financially embarrassed, raising "fighting funds" by levies. These funds are also used for publicity designed to gain public support.

To what should the relative peacefulness of Australian industrial warfare be attributed? What weight can be given to the effect of arbitration, that bold endeavor to bring law and order into the industrial jungle? First, there is the foundation of general peacefulness and social unity characteristic of Australia—a country that has never known civil war, has no tradition of violence, and has inherited much of the British habit of compromise. Second, there is the sheer strength of the union movement and Labor Party, supported by a middle class that bears no hostility to organized labor, and even favors it. Third, perhaps some weight should be given the traditional laziness of the easy-going Australian character. The influence of these factors has probably been as great as that of arbitration, the main contributions of which were to strengthen the union movement and to establish collective bargaining beyond all doubt.

Trade union achievements

In describing the extent to which there has been progress toward the objectives of Australian trade unionism it is not possible to make a precise assessment of the effect of trade unionism because of the difficulty of distinguishing it from the effects of other factors. Since knowledge of how events would have gone in the absence of the unions must necessarily be subject to inference and conjecture, the influence of trade unionism can only be traced indirectly.

Conditions on the job. Australian statistics of wages are based on minimum rates laid down by arbitration awards and registered agreements; they understate the true wage levels in good times and overstate them in bad times. The size of the error is not known, but it seems possible that it ranges up to ten per cent. The figures of money wages and real wages (money wages deflated by a cost-of-living index) shown in Table 5 thus include an element of uncertainty. Broadly, however, they indicate that while money wages almost trebled between 1911 and 1948, real wages rose by only 36 per cent, and were below their 1911 level until 1921.[29] Table 5 also shows that the average nominal weekly hours of work (that is, exclusive of overtime) fell by 18 per cent between 1941 and 1948, from 48.93 hours to 39.96 hours. In the fourth column of Table 5, the index of real wages has been adjusted to allow for this shortening of hours, and thus adjusted shows a rise of 75 per cent between 1914 and 1948 (the unadjusted index rose 43 per cent in this period).

---

[29] Procedures adopted in construction of the official index give it a downward bias, the size of which is not accurately known.

TABLE 5

WAGES AND HOURS IN AUSTRALIA, 1901–1948

	1. Index of Money Wages (1911=100)	2. Index of Real Wages (1911=100)	3. Index of Hours of Work (1914=100)	4. Column 2 Corrected for Changes in Hours (1914=100)	5. Column 4 Corrected to Allow for Unemploy- ment (1914=100)
1901	84.8	—	—	—	—
1910	95.5	—	—	—	—
1911	100.0	(100)	—	—	—
1912	105.1	—	—	—	—
1913	107.6	—	—	—	—
1914	108.1	94.8	100.0	100.0	100.0
1915	109.2	84.2	99.7	89.1	88.1
1916	114.4	86.7	98.8	92.6	95.1
1917	122.6	87.2	98.3	93.6	94.8
1918	127.0	84.6	97.9	91.2	93.7
1919	137.0	80.8	96.9	88.0	89.6
1920	162.7	84.1	96.2	92.2	94.0
1921	182.6	108.7	94.5	121.3	117.4
1922	180.1	111.2	94.8	123.7	122.3
1923	180.5	108.5	95.4	120.0	121.6
1924	184.0	112.4	95.4	124.3	123.4
1925	186.1	112.5	94.9	125.0	124.3
1926	191.4	114.1	93.1	129.3	141.9
1927	194.6	117.1	92.9	133.0	134.9
1928	196.3	117.2	92.5	133.6	130.0
1929	197.2	115.1	92.7	131.0	126.9
1930	193.9	119.8	94.0	134.4	118.3
1931	175.2	121.0	93.0	137.2	108.6
1932	163.9	119.0	93.0	135.0	104.4
1933	158.4	118.7	92.7	135.1	110.3
1934	159.0	117.3	92.7	133.4	115.7
1935	161.2	116.9	92.5	133.3	121.4
1936	163.8	116.2	92.2	132.9	127.3
1937	170.7	117.8	92.0	135.0	133.5
1938	179.9	120.9	91.6	139.2	138.5
1939	184.6	121.1	90.5	141.2	139.0
1940	188.9	119.0	90.0	139.5	139.9
1941	199.7	119.4	89.6	140.6	146.6
1942	216.4	119.6	89.2	141.5	151.8
1943	230.9	123.1	89.1	145.7	157.1
1944	232.6	124.6	89.1	147.5	158.9
1945	233.9	125.2	89.1	148.2	159.6
1946	240.0	126.3	89.0	149.7	160.9
1947	259.8	131.8	86.9	160.0	172.4
1948	291.4	135.7	81.7	175.2	188.2

Source: *Commonwealth Labor Reports*. Columns 4 and 5 computed by the author. Throughout, the figures relate to male wage-earners. The index of real wages is obtained by dividing the index of money wages by the "C" series of cost-of-living index numbers of retail prices.

These figures indicate the changes in the position of a wage-earner in employment; throughout the period, some workers were unemployed (the proportion ranged from 0.9 per cent in 1948 to 29 per cent in 1932). To indicate the position of the wage-earning group generally, the last column of Table 5 presents the index of effective wages adjusted not only for the shortening of hours but also for the proportion of unemployment. It will be observed that this adjusted index shows an even greater rise in real wages in the years of high employment, but is much lower than the other indices over a considerable part of the period.

These improvements in wages are not startling compared with other countries. For example, real hourly wages in the United States doubled between 1914 and 1939 [30] (in Australia the rise was only 36 per cent) and in Britain real hourly wages rose by approximately one-half.[31] Hours of work in United States manufacturing fell by 29 per cent between 1909 and 1939, compared with the fall of 18 per cent in Australian industry as a whole. In the United Kingdom, hours fell by about ten per cent.

The principal factor responsible for these different rates of improvement in wages and hours appears to be the variation in the rate at which productivity has risen in the countries concerned. For the most part, rises in real wages matched increases in productivity; in the United States, for example, where real hourly wages doubled between 1914 and 1939, productivity per man-hour also doubled,[32] and in Britain where real hourly wages rose by about 50 per cent, productivity per man-hour increased by the same proportion.[33] In Australia, as shown in Table 6, real wages have also moved closely with changes in productivity.

The close correspondence of changes in real wages to changes in productivity, in countries of widely different economies and industrial relations, suggests that the activities of Australian trade unions have not exercised a decisive influence on the general level of real wages, although they have probably played a part.in ensuring that the general level of real wages has not lagged unduly behind productivity. It is worth noting, however, that although international comparisons show that in most countries only ten per cent of the rise in productivity during this century was taken out in the form of shorter hours, in Australia the proportion was nearer one-third.[34] This difference is very likely due to the emphasis Australian unions have laid on shorter hours.

---

[30] *U. S. Monthly Labor Review,* September, 1940.

[31] A. L. Bowley, *Wages and Income in the United Kingdom Since 1860,* page 30. Cambridge, 1937.

[32] *U. S. Monthly Labor Review,* September, 1940.

[33] Colin Clark, *Economic News,* July-August, 1948.

[34] *Ibid.*

TABLE 6

REAL WAGES AND PRODUCTIVITY IN AUSTRALIA, 1913–44

Year	Index of Weekly Real Wages (annual averages) 1913=100	Index of Real Output per Man-Year (1913–4=100)	Index of Hourly Wages (Dec. 31) (1913–4=100)	Index of Real Output per Man-Hour (1913–4=100)
1913–4	100.0	100.0	100.0	100.0
1916–7	88.9	94.0	—	95.3
1919–20	82.9	80.5	89.8	83.0
1922–3	114.1	102.2	116.3	109.2
1925–6	115.4	112.7	120.7	120.5
1928–9	120.2	118.8	125.7	130.4
1931–2	124.1	126.5	131.6	138.6
1934–5	120.3	128.9	128.9	142.0
1937–8	120.8	117.5	133.9	130.6
1940–1	122.1	111.6	133.3	123.7
1943–4	126.3	121.6	139.0	126.6

Column 1 relates to calendar years, that is, 1913, 1914, 1915, and so on.
Source: J. E. Isaac, *Economic Analysis of Wage Regulation in Australia*, 1920–47. Unpub. thesis, University of London. Based on data from *Commonwealth Labor Reports* and Colin Clark, *Economic News*, Oct./Dec., 1946.

The information available on labor's share in the national income before 1928–29,[35] together with that published for later years, shown in Table 7, suggests that labor's share of the national income has not risen to any marked extent since early in the century. Although the long-run stability of labor's share in the national income probably results from the interaction of a number of factors, it would appear that the improvements in real wages and hours that labor has enjoyed cannot be attributed to a "squeezing" of nonlabor groups by the economic power of the trade unions.

Account must also be taken of the transfers of income arising from the financial operations of the government, through taxation on the one hand and social service benefits on the other. Unfortunately no comprehensive statistics of the net benefit derived by wage-earners through these transfers are available. The data indicate that the net benefit represented about five per cent of wage-earners' incomes in 1938, and about seven per cent in 1943–44.[36] Although figures are not available, this benefit has undoubtedly grown from almost zero at the beginning of the century and represents considerable progress toward the union goals.

Even before taking these transfers into account, however, the distribution of incomes in Australia is one of the most equalitarian in the

[35] J. E. Isaac, *Economic Analysis of Wage Regulation in Australia,* Unpublished thesis. University of London, 1948.

[36] The estimate for 1938 is from J. Nimmo, "The Australian Consumption Standard," in *Australian Standards of Living,* Institute of Pacific Relations, 1939, page 174. The estimate for 1943–44 is based on calculations by the author.

TABLE 7

SOURCES OF PERSONAL INCOME, AUSTRALIA, 1929–48

	Labor Income (Including Pay of Defense Forces) (Per cent)	Entrepreneurial Income (Including Farmers) (Per cent)	Property Income (Per cent)	Status Income (Pensions and Other Social Service Payments) (Per cent)
1928–9	58.6	24.4	13.8	3.2
1929–30	62.0	19.9	14.6	3.5
1930–1	64.1	15.4	15.5	5.0
1931–2	60.5	18.8	14.7	6.0
1932–3	59.2	21.1	14.4	5.3
1933–4	57.7	23.9	13.8	4.6
1934–5	58.7	22.6	14.2	4.5
1935–6	57.3	24.9	13.6	4.2
1936–7	55.2	27.0	13.8	4.0
1937–8	56.3	25.9	13.8	4.0
1938–9	59.4	21.5	14.9	4.2
1939–40	58.0	23.5	14.6	3.9
1940–1	62.3	20.0	14.1	3.6
1941–2	65.7	17.5	12.6	4.2
1942–3	66.9	18.0	11.0	4.1
1943–4	66.7	18.2	10.9	4.2
1944–5	66.9	17.4	11.3	4.4
1945–6	66.2	18.1	10.5	5.2
1946–7	59.8	23.2	10.9	6.1
1947–8	56.7	28.3	9.5	5.5

Source: From "The Composition of Personal Income," by H. P. Brown, in *Economic Record* (organ of the Economic Society of Australia and New Zealand), Vol. XXV, No. 48 (June, 1949), page 35.

world, according to calculations for various years by Colin Clark, using the Pareto formula.[37] Since figures are available for odd years only, no precise statement can be made about the trend, but the evidence suggests a tendency to greater equality.

It has been argued that, through the operations of wage-fixing tribunals, prompted by the trade unions, wages in Australia have been insufficiently flexible, thus adding to unemployment.[38] This view neglects the fact that wages affect spending power; the relative price of labor is not the only factor determining the amount of unemployment, which is also affected by the total amount of spending in the community (which, in turn, is determined by a number of factors). Also, it is generally recognized that wages fell more swiftly in Australia during the Great Depression of the 1930's than in other countries where arbitration was not practiced, especially if allowance is made for the fact that the actual wage rates being paid at the peak of the boom were substantially above the minima prescribed by awards, so

[37] Colin Clark, *Review of Economic Progress*, Vol. III, No. 2 (February, 1951).
[38] F. C. Benham, *The Prosperity of Australia*, Chapter VI. London, 1928.

that the official figures, based on award rates, understate the extent of the decline. Altogether, it seems unlikely that Australian trade unions have been sufficiently powerful to keep wages at a level so high as to contribute to unemployment, although this might have happened in a few individual industries.

Differences in the wage rates of skilled and unskilled labor (margins for skill) have been for the most part considerably lower in Australia than those prevailing in Canada, the United States, and to a lesser extent, the United Kingdom. Among the several factors responsible for this, the nature of Australian trade unionism is undoubtedly significant. Although, as in other countries, Australian unionism began in the skilled trades, it was firmly established among the less skilled workers much earlier than in Canada and the United States and had developed strong industrial and general unions early in the twentieth century. This helped to weaken the tendency, so marked elsewhere, for the wages of skilled labor to be kept up relative to the wages of unskilled labor by the bargaining power derived from the greater union strength of the skilled.

The industrial character of Australian unionism, and its relatively complete penetration of the entire field of industry at an early stage, have also helped to increase uniformity of wage rates among industries; the differences among average wage rates in the various industrial groups have been falling steadily over a long period. (In 1891, the mean deviation of wage rates in the fourteen industrial groups from the general average was 16 per cent, in 1939 it was six per cent, and four per cent in 1946.) [39]

In setting women's wages, Australian industrial tribunals have followed two distinct principles. For jobs for which men and women compete, women receive the full male rate; for "women's work" on which men are not usually employed, the rate for women is based on an estimate of their needs, which until 1950 was approximately 54 per cent of the male basic wage. In 1950, the Commonwealth Arbitration Court set minimum rates for "women's work" at 75 per cent of the male rate, thus confirming permanently the rate legislated by the Commonwealth Government under its temporary wartime powers as an expedient designed to attract female labor into certain essential industries. During World War II the principle of paying women the full male rate for men's work was modified by the establishment of a special tribunal, the Women's Employment Board, which was required to set women's wages according to their efficiency relative to men. (In practice the Board generally awarded 90 per cent of the male rate.)

---

[39] Calculated from figures in Commonwealth Bureau of Census & Statistics, *Labor Report,* No. 35 (1945–46), page 68.

Over the years, industrial tribunals, at the instance of the unions, have steadily restricted normal hours of work by placing bans or penalty rates on work at night and on weekends. Penalty rates are paid for shift work, and for both day work and shift work the awards usually specify permissible starting and finishing times. Through such provisions, unions have succeeded in gaining a good deal of control over the arrangement of working hours.

Paid annual leave, except in a few specially arduous occupations, was not generally awarded by industrial tribunals before 1935, when the Federal Court granted one week's paid vacation to the printing industry and followed this practice in most industries thereafter. Legislation by labor governments in New South Wales in 1944 and in Victoria in 1946 gave all employees two weeks' paid annual leave, and this rapidly became general, with unions in some trades pressing for three weeks.

Paid sick leave has been provided in a few awards for thirty years or more, but until the late 1930's, the Federal Court's approach to the problem of sickness absence was to add a "loading" to the wage rate to compensate for pay lost through sickness. In 1941 the metal trades were granted one week's paid sick leave, and this soon became general, although it was not until 1945, following the passage of the New South Wales Annual Holidays Act, that the New South Wales Industrial Commission reversed its earlier decision not to grant both annual and sick leave in the one award.

Long-service leave was granted to coal miners in 1950, and this probably marked the beginning of a general extension of this benefit beyond the narrow field of industry (mainly public utilities) in which it had previously been established by agreement between unions and management. Superannuation and similar schemes have not spread widely, being restricted mainly to large monopolies following a policy of paternalism. (The principal exception is coal mining, for which the union succeeded in winning a government financed pension scheme.)

Security of employment. Australian unions have undoubtedly succeeded in increasing the security of the individual worker's employment. Weekly hiring has replaced daily hiring in almost all trades, the employment of casuals being either forbidden or subject to penalty rates. By taking action under arbitration awards in cases of allegedly unjust dismissal without notice, unions have also placed a limit on the exercise of arbitrary authority by the employer. (Some of the legislation establishing industrial tribunals forbids discriminatory dismissal of union members, and where this is not provided for in the legislation, it is included by the tribunal in awards wherever it appears necessary. It is unusual, however, for an award to place any other restrictions on the employer's right of dismissal, provided the necessary notice is given.) Competition from lower-paid apprentices, minors, and females has been restricted by the limitations placed on their employment in the skilled trades. Homework has been prohibited.

Where the unions have fought determinedly against the extension of wage incentive plans, they appear for the most part to have been successful. But wage incentives are more widespread in Australia than is generally realized; in September, 1949, 17 per cent of manual workers in Australian manufacturing industries were on piece-work or bonus payments based directly on output. Another 16 per cent were receiving other types of bonuses. For all industries taken together (but excluding rural and government employment) the corresponding figures were 13.8 and 15.0 per cent. (In Britain in April, 1947, 26 per cent of manual workers were being paid under some system of payment by results, while surveys in 1945 and 1946 in the United States indicated that about 30 per cent of manual workers in manufacturing industry received incentive payments.) [40]

Australian unions have not succeeded in establishing seniority widely. Only a few awards prescribe seniority (the principal industries concerned being gas and railways), and apart from these industries seniority exists only in a few trades or establishments by virtue of individual unions' control of the supply of labor and the exercise of strong bargaining power.

Union security. Registration with an industrial tribunal gives a union rights that guarantee its basic security as an organization. Employers are required to negotiate with it as the collective bargaining agent of their employees, its members are protected from the grosser forms of discrimination against unionists, and union officials are given rights of entry to the factory on union business, which in some awards is defined to include examination of time and wage records. Many awards also require the employer to provide a notice board on which union notices may be posted.

Industrial tribunals in Australia have been reluctant to grant preference in employment to unionists. Under the Commonwealth Conciliation and Arbitration Act, preference can only be awarded "other things being equal" (that is, if there is no other basis for an employer preferring one employee to another), but even with this limitation few Commonwealth awards include preference clauses. Although preference has been more widely granted by state tribunals, it has usually been similarly qualified by the proviso that other things should be equal as between applicants for employment.

---

[40] Department of Labour and National Service, *Bulletin of Industrial Psychology and Personnel Practice,* Vol. VI, No. 1 (March, 1950), pages 13–17.

Compulsory unionism has never been gained in Australia to any great extent. As would be expected from their attitude to preference, tribunals have nearly always refused to grant a union shop and labor governments have not legislated for compulsory union membership. The most notable exception to the general rule is the scheme for decasualization of labor in the stevedoring industry after World War II, which provided exclusively for the employment of union members as wharf laborers.

The powers of trade unions are not limited to those conferred upon them by award, however, and some unions have been able, under favorable conditions, to establish much greater control than that granted by awards over the hiring, transfer, promotion, and dismissal of labor in certain industries and establishments. In the furniture manufacturing industry in New South Wales, for example, the union has an arrangement with employers that amounts to a closed shop. In some of the largest works in the heavy engineering industry, complete seniority has been established by unofficial agreement.

Sometimes powers wider than a tribunal is willing to grant in an award may be incorporated in an official agreement filed with the tribunal, which binds the parties in the same way as an award. For example, in August, 1947, Rubery, Owen and Kemsley, a subsidiary of the British firm of that name, filed such an agreement with the Federal Court, in which the company undertook to enforce a union shop, and the union agreed that in the event of a dispute, its members would remain at work pending a secret ballot. The union also undertook to supply all labor, although the company had the right to employ labor from other sources if the union could not meet its needs.

Finally, the promotion appeal system in the Commonwealth and state public services and some state enterprises may be mentioned. Under this system, any employee may appeal against the promotion of another, and his case is heard by a tripartite committee on which the union has one of the three votes. Although only a small proportion of appeals are won, the administration tends to give a good deal of weight to the possibility of appeal when deciding promotions, and the union in this way exerts a considerable influence on the decisions.

Increased participation. The degree of participation achieved by unions in managerial decisions directly affecting employment opportunities and security has already been discussed. Participation in the general management of individual businesses has not developed far, owing to lack of interest among unions and to opposition from employers. Even during and after World War II, when in Britain, Canada, the United States and some Continental countries there was considerable growth of joint consultation at the plant level between management and workers, no corresponding development took place in Australia. Although employers' associations and unions collaborated with considerable success in meeting the problems arising from the organization of particular industries for war, this collaboration did not lead to the establishment of joint machinery in the individual plants. Profit-sharing has also failed to develop on any scale, although employee stock ownership began to grow after World War II.

The fact that there was little joint consultation machinery in Australia at a time when development of such institutions took place in most industrial countries confronted by similar economic conditions and labor problems can be variously interpreted. It could signify that adequate opportunities and machinery already exist for exchange of viewpoints and discussion of common problems, and it is true that much more informal consultation goes on than is generally recognized, particularly in the small plants that comprise so much of Australian industry. But if this interpretation were correct, industrial relations in Australia would have a very different character. Apart from the loss of time through disputes, which is higher than in many countries, all first-hand observers agree that antagonism between management and unions is "in the air" in Australia. A more plausible explanation is that the arbitration system, by focussing the attention of unions and management on their differences, instead of on their common ground, provides a less favorable background for consultation at the plant level than collective bargaining.

But this is not a complete explanation. Also influential has been the practice of industrial tribunals of consistently limiting the intrusion of unions into managerial functions. Provided that the employer observed the stipulated conditions of employment, and imposed no undue hardship or inconvenience upon his employees, the tribunals have refrained from regulating the internal direction of the business and have restrained unions from venturing beyond issues directly related to conditions of employment. Finally, it is possible that the very success of Australian unionism in achieving legal regulation of managerial functions directly relating to the conditions of employment removed an important area of consultation and cooperation that, in other circumstances, has provided a natural foundation for further growth.

Ideological Influences

The Australian labor movement has been a pragmatic and pluralist movement, concerned little with ideologies but much with practical results. Doctrines have been borrowed and modified according to immediate objectives; their function has been to rationalize, not to originate, practical policies. The movement has produced no significant theorists, nor have intellectuals played a leading part in it; if anything, the movement is anti-intellectual. These characteristics, which contrast sharply with European labor movements, have been well summed up by Metin in his famous description of Australian labor as *Le Socialisme sans Doctrines.*[41] It would be almost as true to say that Australian labor has had too many doctrines, for it has been influenced by several streams of thought, and presents a confusing picture of shifting doctrinal positions and emphases. The most important influences have been Chartism, the teachings of Henry George, nationalism, and non-revolutionary and revolutionary socialism. At different periods, each of these doctrines has achieved wide vogue among Australian labor according to its appropriateness to the situation in which labor found itself.

Chartism was the earliest major ideological influence upon Australian labor, gaining strength as the number of Chartist sympathizers in the population increased in the 1830's and 1840's. Chartist emphasis upon electoral reform and the achievement of political democracy was well suited to the circumstances that produced the "Eureka Stockade," [42] where the old cry of "No taxation without representation" was raised. Labor profited from the broad impact of Chartist thought upon the community, which helped to produce a social environment sympathetic to the efforts of the working class to advance its interest by union organization and political activity. For its own program, labor drew upon Chartist advocacy of adult suffrage, other electoral reform, and its emphasis upon free public education.

While the appeal of Chartism to Australians in the middle of the nineteenth century may be traced to the pressure for political democracy arising from a large population that owned no property and saw little prospect of owning any, the attractiveness of the doctrines of Henry George may be attributed to increasing preoccupation with the problem of land distribution as the decline of alluvial mining drove the miners on to the land. In the 1870's, while futile attempts were being made to "unlock the land" from the grip of the squatters with their vast holdings, Henry George became a prophet of much renown, and he toured Australia with great success. Universal prosperity, to be achieved by taxing the unjust gains of the big landholder, was a particularly attractive prospect to Australian labor at that time. Henry George's doctrines are still advocated in Australia, but their influence on the Labor Party waned in the twentieth century. Labor's

---

[41] A. Metin, *Le Socialisme sans Doctrines.* Paris, 1901.

[42] Armed resistance by miners on the Ballarat gold fields to the imposition of license fees by the Victorian Government in 1854.

federal land tax, the fate of which was described above, was a monument to the impact of the "single tax" on Australian labor.

The roots of Australian national feeling go back to the earliest conflicts between the British Colonial Office's aims for the colonies and those of the local population, sharpened by class antagonism summed up by the disparaging nickname of "currency" applied to the colonials by the English-born gentry. Throughout her history, Australia's sons have been ready to assert their country's independence of, and superiority to, the mother country, and this adolescent, self-conscious struggle for independence fused naturally with class hostility to the large landowners, who retained their connections with Britain. "Australian nationalism is the child of Australian democracy . . . it was impossible to disentangle the passions of class and of nationalism, so inextricably were they intertwined." [43] Labor's national feeling was sharpened by its concern over competition from Chinese and Polynesian labor, and it claimed that it was more truly Australian than the employing classes. The protectionist section of the labor movement, which was centered in Victoria, was also able to claim that its economic doctrines were more consistent with Australian nationalism.

Australian nationalism came to a head in the last twenty years of the nineteenth century. By 1881, 63 out of 100 inhabitants were Australian born, and by far the majority regarded Australia as their home. The issue of free trade versus protection was being vigorously debated, and Federation was under way. Henry Lawson and other writers were interpreting Australia to Australians. It is no wonder that official pronouncements of the emergent Labor Party should often strike a nationalist note sharpened by attacks on the class distinctions and traditions of property and prestige characteristic of the Old World. The influence of nationalism upon labor at that time is indicated by the fact that the earliest official objective of the federal Labor Party, announced in 1905, included as its first item, "the cultivation of an Australian sentiment, based upon the maintenance of social purity and the development in Australia of an enlightened and self-reliant community." White Australia was, of course, the primary expression of this aim in practical policy, and in the re-definition of its objective in 1921, the nationalist aim was dispensed with. But in its emphasis on Australia's independent role within the British Commonwealth, Labor's foreign policy shows its strain of nationalism to the present day. Some of this may be attributed to personalities such as Mr. W. M. Hughes in World War I and Dr. H. V. Evatt in the 1940's, but some goes deeper, an example of which was the long hesitation before committing Australia to the international monetary proposals formulated at Bret-

---

[43] W. K. Hancock, *op. cit.*, page 53.

ton Woods. Labor's attitude on this issue was no doubt partly inspired by its memories of the financial difficulties that arose through overseas commitments in the Great Depression, and particularly of the budget cutting, wage reducing recommendations of British financial experts who visited Australia. Suspicion of the machinations of "international financiers," "overseas monopolists," linked with antagonism to "imperialist exploitation," runs deeply in Australian labor.

The anti-imperialist quality of Australian labor's nationalism is the key to the paradox raised by the significant strain of internationalism also discernible in its policies. This line of thought sprang from the socialist doctrine of world working-class solidarity, and until this ideal became identified with the international policies of the Communist Party, Australian labor had no difficulty in reconciling it with its insistence on Australia's freedom to develop her own economic and political institutions.

Socialist doctrines began to have substantial influence on Australia in the 1880's and have continued ever since to exert a strong ideological effect on the movement. A wide variety of socialist doctrines have been and are still espoused, ranging from the revolutionary doctrines of communism at one extreme to the experimental, pragmatic state interventionism of Australian practical politics at the other. Conditions in Australia were favorable in several respects to the acceptance of socialist doctrines. Early urbanization, a limited horizon of economic opportunity, the absence of a property-owning middle class—all these assisted its growth. Also important was the dominant role of the government, not only in colonizing the country, but also in developing it by means of state railways and other utilities that had proved unprofitable to private enterprise. Australians were thus given practical illustrations of the working of state enterprise that served at least to remove their worst fears of socialization. Australians were also accustomed to highly centralized governments, centralization being encouraged by the mode of colonization, by the long distances separating the rural population, and by the absence of any need for fortified outposts to ward off hostile natives. Thus the notion of central planning met with little resistance from entrenched local government. Altogether, although it is an exaggeration to suggest that "the doctrine of the class struggle might almost have been written to rationalise the spirit of Australia," [44] socialist teachings fitted naturally into the social and economic environment.

The socialism that first gained currency in the Australian labor movement was nonrevolutionary, relying on gradual transformation

[44] L. Ross, "Australian Labor and the Crisis," *Economic Record,* pages 204–222. (December, 1932), Vol. VIII.

of the social order by constitutional means. It had a utopian idealistic quality, of which Lane's experimental socialist "New Australia" in Paraguay was the most extreme manifestation. Lane's doctrines, which became influential through his editorship of *The Australian Worker,* the principal labor newspaper in Queensland, were drawn from Marx, Bellamy, and Henry George with more than a dash of the religious flavor characteristic of much British socialism. The nonrevolutionary socialism of the last decades of the nineteenth century fused naturally with the upsurge of national feeling that occurred at that time; Australia was to shake off the outworn capitalist society of the Old World and, untrammelled by tradition, build an independent socialist commonwealth that would accord with the Christian ethic. The brave slogan "socialism in our time," was not backed by the destructive ruthlessness of more revolutionary socialists. Reliance was placed more upon the good sense and goodwill of men, once they had seen the vision of the new society, to embrace it willingly; education and propaganda were to bring the vision before them. The approach is well illustrated by the following extract from an editorial in *The Australian Worker,* although it belongs to a slightly later period (1909):

If ever the day comes when bullets are needed to back up ballots, we shall be there with our little gun. If on the other hand, capitalism will permit us to achieve the revolution bit by bit, a little today and some more tomorrow, and will allow us to quietly overthrow its system and dispossess it, we shall be glad to leave the gun at home and call ourselves piecemeal if not peaceful, revolutionists.

Thus, for example, the 1889 manifesto of the Australian Labor Federation, which was organized by Lane, began intransigently with the Federation's aim of a socialist community, but then proceeded to state "The People's Parliamentary Platform," which listed a series of measures falling far short of "socialism in our time" but possessing the invaluable advantage of appealing to nonsocialist voters, both labor and nonlabor. Andrew Fisher, afterward Labor Prime Minister, told *The Australian Worker* some years later: "No party worthy of the name can deny that its objective is socialism, but no socialist with any parliamentary experience can hope to get anything for many years to come, other than practical legislation of a socialistic nature." [45] And although the party's official objective had a socialist flavor, with its reference to "securing of full results of their industry to all producers," and to "collective ownership of monopolies and the extension of the

---

[45] L. Ross, "Socialism and Australian Labor," *Australian Quarterly,* Vol. XXII (March, 1950), pages 21–35.

industrial and economic functions of the State," the fighting platform included only proposals for nationalization of monopolies and the extension of social services.

Revolutionary socialism, at first associated with the Industrial Workers of the World, and later with the Communist Party, has undoubtedly had greater impact upon the organization of the Australian labor movement than on its doctrines. The great body of Australian labor consistently rejected revolutionary ideologies, but many unionists have been prepared to support revolutionary leaders because they advocated a militant day-by-day industrial policy for the union. The strength of the revolutionary socialists in the Australian labor movement has never been their doctrines, but their organizing skill, their ruthlessness, and the appeal of the immediate practical gains they have won for the rank and file of the unions.

The greatest triumph of the socialist train of thought in Australia was in the addition, in 1921, of a new section to the Labor Party Objective, the "Methods." These included socialization of "all principal industries," the government of nationalized industries by boards on which the workers would be represented, establishment of an elective Supreme Economic Council by all nationalized industries, and the setting up of labor education bureaus for training workers in the management of nationalized industries. But even these steps toward collectivism were to be taken explicitly by "the constitutional utilization of Industrial and Parliamentary machinery," and the Party Congress added a declaration that "The Party does not seek to abolish private property, even as an instrument of production, where such instrument is utilized by its owner in a socially useful manner without exploitation." Six years later most of the more radical items in the Methods were dropped and the industries to be nationalized were listed specifically. (The list, which has remained unchanged since 1933, is as follows: banking, credit and insurance, monopolies, shipping, public health, radio services, sugar refining.)

The Great Depression stimulated interest in social reform, including socialist programs, but focused attention on changes in the monetary and banking system. This concentration on monetary matters was regarded by thorough-going socialists as a retreat from the fundamental issues of social organization, and although labor's attempt to nationalize the banks in 1948 was one of its most ambitious acts of socialist policy, it was rooted more firmly in bitter memories of the depression than in doctrine, and conceived more as a practical measure of anti-depression policy than as the instrument of an ideology. Even so, rank-and-file support for bank nationalization was not strong, probably because memories of the depression were dimmed by years of prosperity.

One of the important forces working actively within the labor movement against revolutionary socialism is Roman Catholicism. Although Australia is predominantly Protestant, and there is no clear-cut geographical division between Catholic and non-Catholic sections of the population, Roman Catholics comprise twenty per cent of the people, and have always been particularly influential in the labor movement. Some of Australian labor's antagonism to Britain and to international entanglements may be traced to its Irish Catholic element, and more recently this section has led the struggle against communism.

But the reluctance of Australian labor to embrace socialism, particularly of the revolutionary type, goes deeper than the power of Catholicism. Australia has been called "the land without a middle class," and it is true that the absence of a large section of small property holders has favored the growth of the labor movement. At the same time, it has made the labor movement an amorphous mass, including within its ranks many people who, while prepared to support further government intervention in favor of their own interests, are not sufficiently underprivileged to entertain ideas of transforming society, let alone by force. Perhaps the absence of wide differences in income and privilege is the heart of the matter. Although the horizon of economic opportunity in Australia was narrow enough to develop class consciousness, the very successes of labor have blunted the edges of its ideology. Its democratic, nationalistic fervor in the nineteenth century captured the imagination of the Australian people, but with its first aims achieved, it has sought uncertainly for a social ideal that could accommodate and appeal to the diverse elements it endeavors to unify.

For the most part the Labor Party program since 1911 has been a collection of loosely related measures designed to improve the economic position of employees rather than to provide a consistent pattern of social reform. There have been three foci of policy that have served to draw the movement together at different times. The first was the issue of conscription for war service in World War I, which led to expulsion of a number of key leaders and split the Labor Party. The sections of the movement opposed to conscription were unified by a conception of the relation of the citizen to the state that extended beyond the narrow confines of immediate economic gains for employees. The second focus was anti-depression policy, which also raised issues involving the whole fabric of social organization. The third focus was the vision of social welfare through social services, a concept with a history stretching back to the benefit funds of the early trade unions, but given new impetus and significance by the insecurity arising from depression.

The first of these unifying conceptions, the anti-imperialist, anticonscription, pacifist ideal, appears to have lost its force during World War II. Australia has become so directly involved in world conflict that the issue of conscription is no longer likely to divide the community as it did in World War I.

The second and third policy issues provide the foundation for labor's nearest approach to a social ideal acceptable to all the elements within the movement, as well as to the "swinging voter." This is the concept of the "Welfare State," protecting the citizen from insecurity of employment through a guarantee of full employment, and from personal insecurity through comprehensive noncontributory social insurance. Although this concept is broad enough to embrace all the divergent elements with which labor is concerned, it has the drawback of being so broad that it tends to overlap with the policies of nonlabor parties. If Australian labor is to maintain its identity as a distinctive social and political force, it must give definite content to the vagueness of the Welfare State.

The Future of Trade Unionism

Rather than speculate on the details of possible events affecting the future of the Australian labor movement, it is more profitable to attempt in this section to place the Australian labor movement in historical perspective, and to delineate the major trends that seem likely to shape its development in the future.

As described above, the origins of the Australian labor movement in the social conditions and reformist theories of Great Britain in the Industrial Revolution provide an important clue to its nature and development. Historically, the Australian labor movement appears as a stream diverted from the main flow of social reform in Britain, the accumulated pressure of which carried it forward over the unresisting terrain of the new society. Although the men who built up the Australian trade unions drew on the theory and experience of British unionism, before the end of the nineteenth century the Australian labor movement had outstripped the British in power, organization and technique; it gained political power long before the British movement, and until very recently could lay claim to considerably greater influence upon the community.

It would be wrong, however, to regard the Australian movement as a small replica of the British, more successful, because it met easier going. Developing as they did from the same origin, and sharing a common social and cultural background, the Australian and the British labor movements present many similarities. But under the influence of its physical, economic, and social environment, the Australian movement developed uniquely.

The crucial factors molding the Australian movement into a different pattern from the British appear to have been establishment of the arbitration system and the Labor Party's early achievement of political power. Each of these events, one in the industrial and one in the political sphere, marks the point at which the period of rapid early advance culminating in a strategic victory gave way to a long period of stability and relatively slow progress. In the industrial sphere the rapid growth of unionism in the thirty years following the discovery of gold met a crisis at the end of the nineteenth century in the determined assault of employers on the principle of collective bargaining. Eventually, the right to bargain collectively was guaranteed by the state in the legislation establishing industrial tribunals; the unions had won a strategic victory—but at the cost of submitting to arbitration and foregoing direct action (at least in theory). On the political side, the Labor Party gained early power, but at the cost of having to retain the support of middle-class voters by watering down the more radical parts of its platform. Both these strategic victories were critical for Australian labor; they represented significant shifts in power and in the relationships of employer and employee, and endowed labor with a new status in industry and politics. They were also critical in the sense that they were won only on terms that introduced certain stabilizing elements into the situation, which tended to slow down any rapid movement toward further change in labor's position.

The establishment of collective bargaining through the arbitration system and the achievement of political power placed the Australian trade unions in three distinct relationships to the state. In the first place, unions are associations formed for the purpose of negotiating conditions of employment for their members and of rendering certain services to them. Their position as such is legalized by the various state Trade Union Acts. Where they are registered as industrial organizations under legislation establishing industrial tribunals, they are to a considerable extent, both legally and historically, creations of this legislation. They are not simply voluntary associations dealing with their own contracts and employers, but are restricted to a certain role designed to give effect to the aims of the arbitration system. (In practice, as indicated above, Australian unions have never fully accepted this role, and have sought to preserve their freedom of bargaining and direct action, even challenging the power of the state when they consider themselves strong enough.) In their third role, the unions are political bodies seeking, through the A.L.P., to gain the power of government and to use it in their interests.

The contradictions of these three roles become acute when labor gains political power, for conflict then arises between the aims of unions and the government's need to placate the middle-class voter in order to stay in power. Many examples of this conflict could be given. When the unions press their demands by direct action against the orders of industrial tribunals, they put a Labor Government in the position of using the power of the state against them or of over-riding a tribunal and in effect abandoning arbitration for direct legislation on conditions of employment and industrial matters generally. (In the federal sphere, constitutional limitations would prevent this except for measures directly related to defense.)

In full employment brought about by a vast wave of investment, such as that arising from Australia's development and immigration after World War II, the need to control inflation presents a Labor Government with the acute problem of persuading the unions to moderate or even forego their wage demands at a time when their bargaining power is at a maximum. It is this type of issue, rather than any more *doctrinaire* policy, such as the nationalization of banking, that provides the greatest threat to the solidarity of political and industrial labor in Australia.

The situation is complicated by the peculiar position of the Commonwealth Arbitration Court. As the body responsible for setting the federal basic wage on which all other wages are founded, this Court is an extremely powerful instrument of social policy. For all practical purposes, its decisions, unless overruled by the Commonwealth Government under its defense power, are superior to those of any parliament; both Commonwealth and state governments appear before the Court as intervenors or as parties when the basic wage and standard hours are being decided. Government economic policy is thus only indirectly linked with the determination of wages, and it is doubtful whether the link could be made any more direct (except in wartime) without amendment of the Commonwealth Constitution. It is likely that this separation of the government's executive powers from the determination of wages has not been altogether unwelcome to Australian Federal Labor Governments, for it removes from them responsibility for decisions that would highlight the conflict between their general economic policy and the wage and hour demands of the unions.

The possibility of a constitutional amendment that would give the Commonwealth power to legislate directly over industrial matters should not be overlooked, since a referendum on this point was only narrowly lost in 1946 (a majority of voters, but not of states, were in favor of the proposal). If this occurred, important changes might be made in the whole machinery for dealing with industrial relations and wage determination, and the Federal Government might assume more direct responsibility for wage policy.

Whether this happens or not, Australian unions have shown neither the inclination nor the capacity to abandon their traditional role dedicated to the defense and advancement of the interests of a particular group of workers by the established technique of squeezing more out of the employer. If this approach is allowed free rein in conditions of over-employment, when the demand for labor is far in excess of the supply, a rapid rise in prices can hardly be avoided (although many other factors may contribute), and governments of all complexions are almost certain to be driven to attempt to curb union demands in some way.

Such attempts are not likely to be successful unless unions can be given a fuller appreciation of economic issues as they affect the community in general and their own industries in particular. At present, Australian unions, and even the interunion bodies representative of large sections of the union movement, are not organized or equipped for a broader approach. The arbitration system does not encourage the development of more responsible attitudes, but rather the reverse. The intimate connection of many Australian unions with the Labor Party tends to make some of them machines for getting candidates into Parliament rather than organizations capable of taking a broad and informed approach to the problems of their industries. Employers and their associations, by failing to take unions into their confidence, miss opportunities to provide some of the information needed for a full understanding of the various factors affecting industry.

If unions are to be expected to modify their behavior in accord with certain economic policies, they will naturally demand a voice in the determination of those policies. Thus the problem is not merely one of giving industrial labor more information about economic policy and the problems it is designed to meet, but rather of giving it a share in the formulation of that policy, and in its execution. The social and economic power that now reposes in trade unions could be a valuable aid toward the achievement of economic goals broader than the advancement of the interests of a single group of workers.

If this line of development were projected to its logical conclusion, trade unions would become, not merely protest movements designed to win better conditions from employers, but organizations representing the full range of employees' interests in the conduct of the industry on which their livelihood depends. Unions would have an interest in, and some responsibility for, all matters affecting productive efficiency and the general operation of the industry. Wage and other demands, instead of being made in a vacuum, would be negotiated against the background of a comprehensive program for the development of the industry in accordance with a general policy for the economy as a whole. Conflicts of interest would still arise between workers in different industries, and between wage-earners and other sections of the community, and some machinery would be needed for settling these as swiftly and as smoothly as possible. A reshaped arbitration system might serve a useful purpose, with more chance of success than under present circumstances. Strikes and lock outs would still occur, no doubt, but they should be fewer and shorter because unions would be participating more effectively in the decisions affecting their own members.

Such a development does not depend on Australia becoming more socialist. Nor is it an inevitable course of events; it is rather a sociological prerequisite for success by any government, labor or nonlabor, in curbing union demands under expansive full employment. It is more likely that governments will not succeed in controlling union demands and that inflationary pressures will explode into a depression, for attitudes entrenched and embittered by generations of experience of job scarcity are not likely to change quickly.

Failure to develop methods of integrating the policy of particular unions with considerations of general economic welfare could have unfortunate consequences for democracy in Australia. If a union, through direct action, can enforce its will on the community, even overriding parliamentary decisions in the process, other groups in the community can follow its example and successfully resist the will of the majority, as expressed through government policy. Several examples of such resistance occurred shortly after World War II in retail trade, milk supply, and medical services, and to the extent that such defiance of government policy through direct action spreads, society becomes a collection of irresponsible, egotistic groups defeating democratic parliamentary procedure.

The response of Australian labor to the challenge of full employment thus carries vital implications for the future of the country. From Australia's experience, other industrial nations may learn much that will help them solve the industrial relations problems of full employment.

Chapter 4

GERMANY——PHILIP TAFT

The Origins and Development of Trade Unionism

Germany, in the early nineteenth century, was slowly breaking the rigid gild restrictions that hampered her industrial growth. The rate at which the changes were being achieved differed in the several states, for the German gild system was the most severe in all Europe and was strongly entrenched and "before 1840 large enterprises of the factory type were extraordinarily rare." [1] Capitalistic enterprises were occasionally subsidized by government during the eighteenth century, but the more significant type of industrial arrangement was the loose congeries of home workers, mainly in the textile trades, organized around a merchant capitalist who performed the marketing services for the group. The heads of the different German governments frequently provided financial aid for these establishments.

In most instances, government economic aid in the eighteenth century was provided to agglomerations of home workers rather than to the promoters of new factory industries. Some differentiation took place among home workers. The more capable retained their independence, bought their raw materials, and sold their finished product to the jobber-entrepreneur. The less prosperous were in a position similar to that of the English and French cottage workers, receiving their material from an entrepreneur and working on it for a piece-wage.

There were a good many trades of this sort in Berlin. . . . They had been created by government and by hothouse methods . . . in order to provide the luxuries appropriate to an ambitious capital, or goods for export to meet the needs of a mercantilist policy, eager for a favorable balance of trade.[2]

Germany had suffered both from the march of Napoleon's armies across her lands and from the Continental System forced upon Europe

[1] J. H. Clapham, *The Economic Development of France and Germany,* page 85. Cambridge: Harvard University Press, 1921.

[2] *Ibid.,* pages 86–87.

243

by the conqueror as a means of undermining England's economic supremacy—a system that had stimulated industries unable to survive peacetime competition. Freed from the restraint imposed upon it by the Continental System, English industry was able to regain its supremacy in the markets of the world. The rulers of Prussia were impressed and not only sought advice from English industrialists and engineers, but, in 1821, established the *Gewerbe Institut* (Industrial Institute) for the purpose of spreading the new industrial knowledge and encouraging experiment and invention.

Despite these steps, industry grew at a slow pace. The dislocations of the Napoleonic Wars left their mark upon economic life. The absence of the spirit of individual initiative and the scarcity of capital were limiting factors. Lack of industrial freedom and the political division that cut Germany into a multitude of states, each with its own laws and tariffs, hampered progress. The creation of the Zollverein in 1834 aided the growth of industry. However, the rules and conditions governing labor were decidedly backward, and constituted a drag upon progress. Gild restrictions were still widespread in the 1830's, and freedom of entry into trades (*Gewerbefreiheit*) far from universal. The workers themselves were not always anxious for the establishment of a free labor market. The growth of capitalistic enterprises in the 1840's created both hardship and discontent among the old gild masters who saw themselves squeezed down to the status of daily wage-earners. These conditions naturally led to unrest among those affected by the economic innovations, but did not result in widespread violent demonstrations, such as the Luddite riots in England. Yet the German craftsmen also regarded the machine and mechanical power as evils menacing their positions as skilled artisans.[3]

Another kind of agitation, one closely linked to modern socialism, also arose. Wilhelm Weitling, a tailor, after leaving his homeland, associated himself with secret refugee societies in Brussels, Paris, and Switzerland. Weitling joined the League of the Just, a society of German political refugees, and soon achieved a position of leadership. Despite his need to earn a living by working long hours at his trade, Weitling was able to translate into German the work of the Christian Socialist, Hugues Félicité Robert de Lamennais. Influenced by the revolutionary theories current in Parisian radical circles in the late 1830's, Weitling developed into a militant communist. At the request of the League of the Just, he wrote *Die Menschheit, wie sie ist und wie sie sein sollte* (*Mankind as it is and as it should be*). The book was an "attempt to integrate the workers' movement in its broader aspects

---

[3] A. Sartorius von Waltershausen, *Deutsche Wirtschaftsgeschichte, 1815–1941,* pages 142–144. Jena: G. Fischer, 1923.

with the new program of communism, or socialism, interchangeable terms at the time."[4] Weitling's communism was based upon moral principles, and he demanded absolute equality for all people. The evils afflicting mankind he ascribed to the use of economic and political power for selfish ends, and, as a remedy for the abuses suffered by the poor, believed in a thoroughgoing revolution that would sweep tyranny and oppression from the earth.

Weitling left Paris for Switzerland in 1840, and there resumed his revolutionary and literary activity. Two years later he published his *Garantien der Harmonie und Freiheit,* which was regarded by Franz Mehring, the leading socialist historian and biographer of Marx, as having come closer to reconciling the labor movement and socialism than the works of any of his predecessors.[5] Weitling worked out an elaborate system of communism to be brought about by violent revolution. He was the first German socialist theoretician to emphasize the role of the proletariat in the unfolding of the historical revolutionary drama. However, in the latter part of his life he was an inactive spectator on the political scene.

First organizations of labor

Although Weitling influenced the early worker and radical groups of German labor, the first organized effort at the setting up of a trade union movement in Germany was made by Stephan Born, a socialist journalist. A number of local unions had been established, and in the turbulent year of 1848, Born tried to weld the disparate organizations into a fighting movement. Born's efforts, and the fevered circumstances under which they were made, resemble the attempt of Robert Owen to establish the Grand National Consolidated Trades Union, in 1834, in Great Britain. Both attempts met only with ephemeral success, and both showed symptoms of confusion of aim, but, in a sense, they were pioneer efforts on the part of workers to build economic organizations able to defend themselves against a nascent and aggressive capitalism. Stephan Born succeeded in organizing the Fraternity of Labor at a convention in Berlin in the summer of 1848. A set of demands that have a modern ring were presented by the convention to the Frankfort parliament: establishment of minimum wages and maximum hours and the setting up of works' councils of labor and employer representatives to determine conditions; regulation of apprenticeship; government aid for the sick and needy; and abolition

---

[4] Carl Wittke, *The Utopian Communist,* pages 39–41. Baton Rouge: Louisiana State University Press, 1950.

[5] Wilhelm Weitling, *Garantien der Harmonie und Freiheit,* Introduction by Franz Mehring, page xiii. Berlin: Vorwärts, 1908.

of restriction upon labor and its right to organize. A central committee was elected and a journal, *Das Volk*, established.[6]

In the same year, another congress of labor took place in Frankfurt under the leadership of Karl George Winkelbach, who wrote under the name of Karl Marlo. More closely linked to the past than the movement initiated by Born, the emphasis of this meeting was on the alleviation of the restrictions upon freedom of entry into trades and the establishment of the right of free movement of workers through the country. The movements initiated by Marlo and Born for a time flowed together, but the tide of reaction that swept Germany, after 1848, swallowed the first attempts of German labor to gain a foothold in the economy.[7] Born, a revolutionist by temperament, participated in the rising at Dresden and was forced to flee. By the middle of 1854 the Fraternity of Labor had ceased to exist.[8]

The trade unions and the socialist movement of Germany could not be permanently repressed. The conditions that were to make Germany a great industrial power in the twentieth century were already being prepared in the middle of the nineteenth. The two decades that followed the collapse of the revolution of 1848 witnessed a feverish railway boom, the ending of the remaining medieval restrictions, the development of the coal industry on an extensive scale, and the creation of a modern banking and financial system, all of which helped to facilitate Germany's economic expansion. In the 1860's "the German iron industry took a leap forward,"[9] and her textile industry began to increase its use of power-driven looms for the weaving of yarn. The transition from home work to factory operations was at first slow, but accelerated as experience demonstrated the advantages of mechanized production. During the 1850's and 1860's, Germany laid the basis for the growth of her chemical and electrical industries which were to contribute greatly to her industrial preeminence in the following decades.

During this early period, the labor movement was feeble and inactive. The leaders of the revolution of 1848 were in exile and scattered over Europe and the United States, and the watchful police were on the alert against any recrudescence of radical activity. Ordinary trade union activity came under the ban, and only the propaganda of

---

[6] Max Quarck, *Die erste deutsche Arbeiterbewegung.* Leipzig: L. C. Hirschfeld, 1924.

[7] Alfred Weber, *Der Kampf Zwischen Kapital und Arbeit,* pages 63–67. Tübingen: J. C. Mohr, 1921.

[8] Karl Zwing, *Geschichte der deutschen freien Gewerkschaften,* pages 19–23. Jena: Verlagsbuchhandlung, 1926.

[9] Clapham, *op. cit.,* page 286.

Schulze-Delitzsch was permitted. The latter was a leader of the Progressive Party, a middle-class reformist group, favoring a constitution guaranteeing expansion of suffrage, freedom of speech, press and assembly, and *laissez faire* in economic matters. This party sought to win a following among the workers, but, in contrast to a policy of militant economic and political action advocated by the emerging socialists, Schulze-Delitzsch advocated self-help, which meant that through systematic saving, labor could solve its economic problems. Workers, in his opinion, should pool their savings and set up cooperatives for the advancement of credit or the purchase of raw materials.[10] The self-help program gained a considerable following and a large number of loan and credit associations were organized. The fatal weakness of this movement was that it failed to arouse the enthusiasm of the modern factory worker with his scant opportunity to save. In contrast to the small tradesman and artisan for whom the gospel of self-help might have had meaning, the German industrial worker could scarcely accumulate the means needed for these enterprises. Consequently, Schulze-Delitzsch's program failed to make many converts among the part of the labor force that is of predominant importance in a modern workers' movement.

Independent politics

As was noted above the 1860's saw the German economy make important advances. Increased investment led to the expansion of manufacturing, land and water transport, and the building of a machine tool industry. These changes caused an increase in the number of wage-earners, and a demand for the removal of the restraints upon the right of the workers to form unions. Beginning with Saxony in 1861, the German states gradually relaxed their prohibition on the right of workers to organize associations. This, of course, did not eliminate all legal difficulties faced by organizations of labor. The associations that arose in the 1860's were nonpolitical, aiming at the education of the members in technical and cultural subjects. Not all were content with the limits set by the sponsors of these groups; some members favored adding political and social questions to the subjects to be considered by the educational societies, and, as a consequence, the movement divided between those who advocated concentration upon nonpolitical problems and those who wanted to concentrate upon controversial political problems. The nonpolitical standpoint had the wholehearted support of the Progressive Party and Schulze-Delitzsch,

---

[10] Herman Schulze-Delitzsch, *Capitel zu einem deutschen Arbeiterkatechismus,* pages 110–138. Leipzig: Ernest Keil, 1863.

who feared that political discussion might be a prelude to political action.[11]

The final disassociation of German labor from the latter view is due in large measure to Ferdinand Lassalle, who had been active in the campaign for the broadening of the franchise. His gifts as a writer and speaker and the personal courage he exhibited on numerous occasions inevitably attracted attention to him. At the time Lassalle became identified with the workers' movement, neither issues nor policies were as yet clearly defined, and an invitation by a Leipzig committee arranging a congress of labor gave Lassalle the opportunity to state the program upon which his fame rests.

Lassalle issued his "Open Letter" in which he attacked the philosophy and program of the Progressive Party and presented one of his own. First, he denied the desirability of German labor cooperation with the Progressive Party which had, in his opinion, shown itself incompetent and impotent in the struggle for constitutional freedom and political rights. Instead of tagging along behind other political parties, labor must establish an independent political party based upon universal, equal, and direct suffrage. Cooperation should be accorded by the workers only when the Progressive Party supported the demands of labor. Otherwise, the workers must refuse to give any political aid.

Having disposed of "collaboration with bourgeois parties," and after sounding a call for independent political action by labor, Lassalle next turned to an examination of the policies that would raise the living standards of the workers. The ideas of Schulze-Delitzsch were attacked. The meager savings of the underpaid worker could never be pooled into a fund large enough to enable the producers' cooperatives to compete with private enterprise. As for consumer cooperatives, another of Schulze-Delitzsch's proposals, these could never afford the permanent relief needed by labor, serving at best only as a temporary palliative. The basic problem of the worker arose out of the "iron law of wages," which was, in fact, an adaptation of the Ricardian theory of wages for socialist ends. Wages, argued Lassalle, could never rise above the subsistence level, for if they rose above the amount needed to supply the most elementary needs of the worker and his family, the laboring population would increase, and as a consequence of the increase in the supply of labor, wages would again be pushed down to the subsistence level. Thus, Lassalle harnessed the theoretical spokesman of early nineteenth century capitalism, David Ricardo, and the

[11] August Bebel, *My Life,* page 47. Chicago: The University of Chicago Press, 1913.

intellectual defender of the declining landed interest, Thomas Henry Malthus, to the newly fabricated socialist chariot.

The situation was, however, far from hopeless. Lassalle had trotted out the "iron law of wages" only to show the inefficacy of the traditional remedies. The answer lay in the promotion of producer cooperatives; but to be effective they had to be promoted by the state. The "iron law of wages" could be overcome only by the workers becoming their own employers. The difference between wages and profits would then disappear. It was the task of the state to provide the means by which this program could be brought to fruition, and thereby to enable the workers to unite together in cooperative production. The aid of the state was essential, but this would not be forthcoming as long as the state was controlled by the rich and powerful. Therefore, universal suffrage must be introduced in order to make the state responsive to the will of the working masses. Labor should organize into a General German Workers' Association to carry on a peaceful campaign for the universal and secret ballot throughout Germany.

Trade Unionism up to World War I

Lassalle's program was of extreme importance to the future trade unions. Not only did one of his associates, Johann Baptist von Schweitzer, launch the first modern German trade union movement, but the emphasis of Lassalle and his followers upon the autonomy of the labor movement and its divorce from middle class liberalism stimulated independent action and class consciousness in the ranks of labor, attitudes that proved indispensable to the formation of an independent movement of labor.

The educational societies, already under attack by Lassalle, were also challenged from another quarter: the followers of Marx. August Bebel, who was to become the chief parliamentarian of the future social democracy, and Wilhelm Liebknecht, an admirer and student of Marx, urged the workers' educational societies to cast off their non-political integument and become active participants in the social and political struggle of Germany. Their purpose was accomplished at the Chemnitz congress of labor educational associations, when Bebel became head of the League of Workers' Associations, and eventually gained an endorsement for the International Workingmen's Association (the First International).

Bebel and Liebknecht were anxious to win over the adherents of Lassalle, who, since the latter's death in 1864, had been led by von Schweitzer. On the basis of their philosophy, the followers of Lassalle could not approve of trade unions, for according to their view, unions were unable to overcome the "iron law of wages." On the other hand, Bebel and Liebknecht, as faithful followers of the exiled Marx, could only regard the program for government-financed cooperation with impatience and distrust. Despite their ideology, the followers of Lassalle began to accept the view that unions, even if they could not solve the basic social problem, might be effective in eliminating some industrial evils. This view gained increasing support with the rise, in the 1860's, of local unions as distinct from worker educational associations. In some instances regional unions extending beyond the local area were founded. The oldest interlocal labor organization was the General Tobacco Workers' Union, formed under the leadership of Friedrich Wilhelm Fritsche in 1865. The printers formed a union in the following year, and the tailors and the woodworkers organized nationally in 1868.

With the increase in the economic organization of labor the unions began to demand concessions, and to refuse arbitrary changes in the terms of employment. As a consequence, strikes increased both in number and in the places and industries affected. In 1868, a number of strikes took place in different parts of Germany. Cigar makers, ribbon workers and painters struck in Berlin, as did the weavers in Hanover.

The spread of union organization convinced the heads of the Lassallean wing of the socialist movement of the need to win the support of these organizations. Von Schweitzer and Hans Fritsche, the leader of the cigar makers' union, tried to gain the support of the Lassallean General German Workers' Association for the calling of a national convention of unions. Many of the delegates attending the Hamburg convention of the Lassallean organization were reluctant to approve such a venture. Under the prodding of von Schweitzer, the delegates agreed that even though the strike could not change the basis of production, it was a means of stimulating class consciousness, of eliminating police interference with labor organizations, and of aiding in the abolition of many social evils. However, Fritsche's proposal that authority be granted to the executive to call a congress for the establishment of a central group of trade unions was rejected. Facing the possibility of a split in their ranks over the issue, the delegates granted von Schweitzer and Fritsche the authority to call a labor congress on their own responsibility. This congress opened in Berlin on September 26, 1868. The declared objective of the congress was to encourage the formation of unions in every trade. Existing organizations were asked to send delegates, and the unorganized were also invited to send representatives. About 142,000 workers were represented by 206 delegates from 110 locals. Berlin, Hamburg-Altona, Elberfeld-

Barmen, and Brunswick, sent the largest delegations, but many other localities were represented. After a four-day session, the convention decided to set up ten broad unions, some industrial, others quasi-industrial in character, and prepared a set of rules the affiliates were to follow. The executive committee was given extensive power over the subordinate groups and it, alone, had the right to authorize the use of the strike. This aspect of the movement aroused the opposition of some trade unions, among them the printers, who favored a decentralized and federative type of organization and not a highly centralized one.[12] The trade union movement launched under the aegis of the Lassalleans was not supported by the Marxist wing of socialism. Bebel and Liebknecht went their own way, and, in 1869, organized the Social Democratic Labor Party at Eisenach.

Socialist domination of the trade union movement led to another split. It forced both liberals and Christian proponents of trade unionism to launch movements of their own. As a matter of fact, the liberals had been trying to gain the right of suffrage for the workers for a number of years. In the 1860's, Max Hirsch, a liberal journalist, had visited England and observed its trade unions. English unionism, at the time, was dominated by what the Webbs called the "New Model" union: organizations of skilled workers that accepted liberal economic doctrines and that sought to gain concessions through maintaining a monopoly in the labor market and by providing friendly benefits. Hirsch, in a series of letters, extolled the virtues of that type of trade unionism, and challenged the hegemony of the socialists over the young German movement. Under the leadership of Hirsch and Franz Duncker, a publisher, a labor convention held in Berlin, during 1868, set up the German Trades Association (*Verband der deutschen Gewerkvereine*). The Hirsch-Duncker unions repudiated the class struggle and emphasized peaceful collaboration with the employer through collective bargaining and the trade agreement. Antimonopolistic in view, the movement advocated competition in business and profit sharing for labor. It pioneered in the development of conciliation and arbitration procedures. In contrast to the socialist unions, the Hirsch-Duncker organizations emphasized their national character, and declared themselves neutral in religion and independent in politics. Equality before the law and a greater share of the national income for workers were among their aspirations, as well as the extension of labor legislation to protect the worker against accidents, and increased security for the ill, the industrially injured, and the aged.

---

[12] Gustav Mayer, *Johann Baptist von Schweitzer und die Sozialdemokratie*, pages 226–253. Jena: Gustav Fisher, 1909. Franz Mehring, *Geschichte der deutschen Sozialdemokratie*, Vol. I, pages 248–251. Stuttgart, 1896.

Closely related to the Hirsch-Duncker unions of manual workers were the unions of white-collar workers organized in the *Gewerkschaft der Angestellten* (GdA). At their peak the white-collar unions reached a membership of 300,000, and, in 1920, the various unions influenced by the Hirsch-Duncker outlook united in the *Gewerkschaftsring deutscher Arbeiter-Angestellten und Beamtenverbände* (Federation of Unions of German Workers, Employees and Civil Servants).

It is clear why the liberals sought to segregate their followers within the ranks of labor. They opposed the philosophy and ultimate goal of the socialists, and believed that both the interests of the country and of the workers themselves would be harmed if the labor movement were tied to socialism. The differences between the followers of Lassalle and Marx were not as great, each believing that it was necessary to abolish capitalism. But the personal and ideological differences between the latter two groups kept them, for a time, apart. Each promoted its own trade union: "None of the political factions of the Labour Party would renounce the formation of its own special union, hoping thereby to obtain an accretion of power." [13] However, sentiment gradually developed for unifying the two socialist economic organizations, for conflicts between the unions of different political persuasion tended to interfere with the carrying out of purely economic tasks.

No essential economic difference existed between the Lassallean and Marxist unions, and the division between them reflected only a cleavage over political issues. On the political plane, the differences steadily narrowed, and finally, at the Gotha congress in 1875, the two wings of German socialism, the Marxists or Eisenacher group and the Lassalleans, united in one party. The program evolved at the congress was a compromise, although Franz Mehring believed it to be a compromise more in form than in substance. This view was not shared by Marx, who was convinced that the Gotha program departed from the true gospel, and, in a letter to his followers, including Bebel and Liebknecht, sharply attacked the concessions made to the views of Lassalle.[14] For the trade unions, the Gotha congress was important, since it enabled the unions dominated by the socialists to pool their strength and avoid the debilitating effect of interunion rivalry.

The remaining division of the economic organizations of labor upon ideological or political grounds was decried by some union leaders. An unsuccessful effort was made to unite all workers, irrespective of their political or social ideas, into one organization. Sponsored by a leader of the woodworkers' union, York, a group of unions met in

---

[13] Bebel, *op. cit.*, page 121.
[14] Mehring, *op. cit.*, page 356; Karl Marx, *The Critique of the Gotha Program*, pp. 3–23. New York: International Publishers, 1938.

Erfurt in 1872, and decided that since all workers under capitalism were exploited, regardless of their beliefs, it was therefore necessary to eliminate issues that divided workers by declaring the neutrality of the trade unions on questions of ideology.[15] The death of York ended the agitation for political neutrality, but the close alliance of the main body of trade unions and the socialists repelled many workers who favored the economic organization of labor but refused to affiliate with unions espousing doctrines antagonistic to their religious or political views.

The unification of the two socialist groups came immediately after the Franco-Prussian war. Germany's forward rush as an industrial and mercantile country may be dated, for practical purposes, from the successful issue of the war with France in 1871.[16] The victory of Sedan climaxed a series of triumphs which gave the German people a consciousness of great and expanding power. At the same time industry began that spectacular rise that was to make Germany the continent's foremost industrial nation. The mineral, metal, iron, steel, electrical manufacturing, and chemical industries made giant forward strides, accompanied by the growth of cities and the industrial labor force.

German labor, exclusive of government workers, agricultural laborers, and domestic employees, had under the *Gewerbeordonung* of 1869, the legal right to combine "for the purpose of obtaining more favorable conditions of wages and work, particularly by means of suspension of work." [17]

Nevertheless, the unions of the 1870's and 1880's faced serious opposition both from the authorities and from employers. Some of the antagonism can be attributed to the employer reaction to strikes, which were on the increase in the 1870's. More formidable opposition came from the government through the use, by Bismarck, of the antisocialist laws to hit not only at the socialists, but at the trade unions as well. According to one source, there were 26 national unions with 1,300 local groups and 49,000 members in 1877. Most of these organizations fell by the wayside as a result of government oppression. During their existence many of these unions maintained strike funds, published journals and furnished their members travel aid.[18]

Even before the expiration of the antisocialist laws, the trade unions

---

[15] Zwing, *op. cit.*, page 46.

[16] William Harbutt Dawson, *The Evolution of Modern Germany*, page 37. London: T. Fisher Unwin, 1909.

[17] Quoted in *ibid.*, page 107.

[18] Paul Umbreit, *Der Krieg und die Arbeitsverhältnisse*, page 21. New Haven: Yale University Press, 1928. Adolf Braun, *Die Gewerkschaften vor dem Kriege*, pages 29–31. Berlin: J. H. Dietz, 1925.

were regathering some of their lost strength. Beginning in 1882, local unions again appeared in a number of places, and these locals began reaching out for wider unity with other unions in their craft. The government again endeavored to suppress them, but the right of non-political labor organizations to combine was upheld by the courts. The unification of a group of local unions was possible only by excluding political discussion and activity from the affairs of the organization. Several national unions were formed during the 1880's, but the exclusion of political issues did not meet with the approval of socialist-minded leaders and rank and file members. Divergence of opinion arose over the desirability of forfeiting the right of the unions to promote their political interests for the advantage of a national union. In a broad sense, the politically-minded workers favored confining the movement to the local union, for they regarded the union as, fundamentally, recruiting stations for the political labor party. For them, trade union activity was a labor of Sysiphus, incapable of permanently altering the degraded position of the workers. The proponents of national unionism had a different view; essentially "trade-union minded," they believed that the economic organizations of labor could bring the workers permanent and significant gains. The unions could not, in their opinion, be regarded as auxiliaries of a labor party, but had to be strengthened and supported so that they could effectively achieve their objectives.

The General Commission of German Trade Unions

The expiration of the socialist laws in 1890 allowed the Social Democratic Party to function without hindrance from the authorities. At the same time the trade unions escaped from the many restrictions hampering their growth. But many issues had to be decided, the form of their organization being among the most important. After an early attempt to unite all workers suffering from capitalist exploitation without regard to their political affiliations had remained abortive in 1872, a new start, under more favorable auspices but on a narrower political basis, was now made. At the initiative of the leaders of the metal workers' union, representatives of a number of unions met in Berlin in November, 1890, to decide upon a course of future action. The conference decided to call a convention of trade unions and to prepare an organizational plan. The General Commission of German Trade Unions to lead the movement was set up, and Karl Legien, who was to head the trade unions until his death in 1920, was appointed chairman of the Commission. It was authorized to conduct agitation in behalf of unionism, to support workers engaged in strikes and lockouts, to issue a journal, and to gather statistics on wages and other issues of concern to labor. Investigation revealed that there were in Germany, in 1890, 53 national unions with 3,150 local branches and 227,733 members, plus an added 73,467 members organized locally.[19] The General Commission called a convention at Halberstadt, which opened on March 14, 1892.

One of the important questions that came before this meeting involved local versus national central unions. If the proponents of each view were to be classified, it would appear that those who favored the setting up of national unions were essentially trade unionists who wanted to construct powerful and independent organizations of labor able to formulate and articulate their views on major issues, although they might also be sympathetic to socialist political action. The localists were divided. There were some who feared the growth of a strong bureaucracy within the trade unions, a bureaucracy that could dominate and overwhelm local affiliates. These views had an anarcho-syndicalist flavor, and their more extreme proponents subsequently withdrew from the standard trade unions to set up an organization of their own. While this controversy within the German trade unions possessed some characteristics peculiar to the country, similar disputes over the relative merits of centralization and local autonomy were not uncommon elsewhere. It took several decades of bitter experience to convince many American trade union locals of the need to endow their central organizations with wide powers. Because of the suppression in Germany of many union activities during the years 1878–1890, the period of the antisocialist laws, solutions to these problems could not be evolved slowly as in the United States.

One aspect of the controversy was, however, peculiar to Germany: the opposition to the formation of national unions on purely political grounds. These opponents of national organizations feared that national unions would not limit themselves to economic activity, but would instead become concerned with political questions, a province that, in their opinion, should be reserved for the Social Democratic Party. However, victory went to those who favored the national type of organization.

There was also considerable discussion over the issue of craft versus industrial unions. The convention avoided a doctrinaire approach to this problem, and while amalgamation of allied trades was suggested as desirable, each group was allowed to decide the question on the basis of its own experience.

The General Commission was not given much power over its affili-

---

[19] *Protokoll der Verhandlungen des ersten Kongresses der Gewerkschaften Deutschlands,* pages 15–16. Hamburg: C. C. Legien, 1892.

ates. It was instructed to carry on propaganda on behalf of trade unionism, to collect statistics and information on strikes, and to publish a journal. A per capita tax was levied upon all affiliates, and the accumulated funds could be used by the executive to support serious strikes. At the beginning, there was strong objection by some unions to the attempt of the General Commission to influence policy. The opposition came from socialists who felt that such activity usurped the province of the Party, and from trade unionists who disapproved of the General Commission's views on such questions as craft versus industrial organization. With time, the desirability of allowing the General Commission a wider latitude was recognized.

From the beginning of the new era in 1890, the basic unit of the German trade union was the craft, amalgamated, or industrial union with a nationwide jurisdiction. The national union was usually directed by a salaried staff, elected at regular conventions. Locals in a particular area formed councils for organizing purposes, while city central organizations made up of the locals of various crafts and industries were also established. At first the city centrals directed many of the functions of their affiliates, including strikes, but they were gradually displaced in this respect. The so-called Free Unions, those supporting the General Commission, were closely tied to the Social Democratic Party, although the leaders of the unions supported, on the whole, the more moderate or revisionist faction within the party.

The syndicalists refused to remain within the free trade unions because they rejected the centralizing tendencies. To them, local autonomy and the absolute right of the local group to control its policies and destiny was a sacred and inviolable principle. In 1897, the syndicalists set up the Free German Trade Union Federation (*Freie Vereinigung deutscher Gewerkschaften*), which became, in 1919, the German Free Labor Union (*Freie-Arbeiter Union*). Emphasis was placed upon local autonomy, with the federative principle followed in the trade and industrial superstructure. Syndicalist union membership reached a high point of over 200,000 in 1922. In philosophy and outlook the syndicalists were closely related to the General Federation of Labor of France during its heroic period prior to World War I, and to the Spanish Anarcho-Syndicalist National Federation of Labor.

Christian labor organizations

The free unions, as the organizations under socialist influence were called, did not have the field to themselves, although they were, numerically, the largest of the German trade union groups. Their socialist leadership and their close relation to the Social Democratic Party made it difficult for trade unionists opposed to the philosophy of socialism, because of their religious beliefs, to affiliate with the free unions. Criticism of modern industrialism from the Christian point of view had been initiated in the 1860's by the Bishop of Mainz, Wilhelm Emanuel von Ketteler, who had been influenced by Lassalle, and sharply attacked liberal capitalism with its emphasis upon competition and the maximizing of profit. He drew attention to the seamier side of an expanding industrialism: its exploitation of the young and the weak and the inevitable increase in moral and economic problems. For Ketteler, the "fundamental characteristic of the labor movements of our day, that which gives them their importance and significance and really constitutes their essence, is the tendency everywhere rife among workingmen, to organize for the purpose of gaining a hearing for their just claims by united action." [20] However, he argued that Christianity alone could direct unionism in the most fruitful directions. His views made a deep impression on Catholics who favored reform of many economic institutions and the formation of trade unions, but were outside the socialist orbit and could under no circumstances be drawn into it.

An attack upon modern industrialism from the religious point of view was also made by the evangelical social movement, the pioneer of which, Johann Wichern, introduced the concept of social Christianity. On the whole, the emphasis was upon aiding individuals in need rather than on the sponsoring of a mass movement: personal benevolence rather than social reform.[21] The followers of Wichern extended their activity to sponsoring social reform. They helped to prepare the ground for Christian trade unions, but the evangelical social movement came under the influence of Pastor Stöcker and was led by him into the morass of antisemitism.

Even before the agitation initiated by Bishop Ketteler, Father Adolph Kolping had protested against the social and spiritual void that surrounded the modern worker. Deprived of the opportunity to meet with his fellows and the chance for a technical education, he was in constant danger of being lured into the radical camp. Kolping was mainly interested in infusing the modern industrial worker with renewed faith in religion. He helped to organize journeymen's clubs to which both Catholics and Protestants were eligible. Yet, these groups were closely tied to the Catholic Church. They aimed at the material and moral uplift of the worker and the elimination of all possible conflict between employer and employee through peaceful adjustment

---

[20] Quoted from von Ketteler in Philip Taft, *Movements for Economic Reform,* page 423. New York: Rinehart and Co., 1950.

[21] Paul Göhre, *The Evangelical-Social Movement in Germany,* translated by Janet and E. Kay Shuttleworth, page 9. London: Ideal Publishing Co., 1898.

of differences. Saving and industriousness were encouraged and producers' and consumers' cooperatives approved.[22] Bismarck's *Kulturkampf* at the end of the 1870's led to an attack upon these organizations and their complete isolation from non-Catholic workers. As a result, many either dissolved or transformed themselves into purely religious organizations.

The Papal Encyclical, *Rerum novarum,* stimulated renewed interest and support of labor organizations among Catholic workers. While the encyclical devoted much space to an attack upon socialism, it recommended trade unions as a proper instrument for the protection of labor against the abuses of capitalism. Moreover, the workers' associations established for the advancement of religious, cultural, and material welfare were not held to be an adequate substitute for trade unionism. Recognition of this shortcoming indirectly led to the formation of Catholic trade unions. These unions were not, at the outset, fighting labor organizations. Instead they aimed to promote peaceful solutions of industrial problems by labor and management.[23] However, the Christian unions not only sought to spread spiritual and religious doctrines, but were actively concerned with raising the material and social values of labor.

The religious groups that favored trade unionism as a means of raising the worker's level of living and surrounding him with a protective code were faced with a dilemma because of their hostility to the free trade unions. The formation of a trade union with a Christian ideology in the Ruhr by a group of coal miners represented a pioneer attempt to build unions that were, ideologically, nonsocialist. A coal miner, August Brust, launched a Christian trade union in Dortmund, in 1894. It was an interdenominational organization, and it aimed at improving the moral and social conditions of the miner, and promoting peaceful relations between employer and employee. It sought to secure for the worker a just wage that would reflect the value of the labor and, at the same time, maintain the dignity of the worker. The organization declared itself loyal to the nation, and forbade any discussion of religion or politics at meetings.

The example of the miners was subsequently followed in other industries, and, eventually, the leaders believed that a unified organization of Christian trade unions was desirable. As a result, the first congress of Christian trade unions was held at Mainz in 1899, and an executive committee was set up to direct organization, to promote common interests, and to collect statistics of concern to the affiliated

---

[22] Theodore Böhme, *Die Christlich-nationale Gewerkschaft,* page 37. Stuttgart: W. Kohlhammer, 1930.

[23] Böhme, *op. cit.,* pages 43–44.

unions. The congress declared that its affiliates were to be interdenominational, but based on Christian principles. The organization was to remain nonpolitical and was not to affiliate with any political party. The congress advised the merger of unions in the same or allied trades and recommended the formation of city centrals to promote the general interests of labor. Unions were urged to seek to raise the moral and material level of their members, and were advised to organize and carry on friendly activities. In view of the common interest of capital and labor, peaceful methods of settling differences were recommended, and the strike was to be used only as a last resort. The organization sought to support each of its affiliates in the effort to promote the general interests of labor by seeking legal recognition of the trade union, promoting conciliation as a means of settling labor disputes, mutual support in cases of unusual need, and the publication of statistical information on wages and living conditions of workers in particular trades. A more closely knit organization was established at the fourth Christian union congress in 1902, and a permanent secretariat was established to direct the work. Adam Stegerwald was appointed to head this group.[24] Christian solidarity was to be the bond between employer and employee, and an antidote to class war.

The interdenominational character of these unions was not approved by those Catholics who believed that the craft groups (*Fachabteilungen*) within the workers' Catholic associations were adequate and a more desirable form of organization. Leading the fight against the interdenominational unions was the *Verband der Katholischen Arbeitsvereine* (Union of Catholic Labor Societies). The fight took on considerable virulence, and was only resolved at the annual conference of German Bishops at Fulda in 1919, at which the interdenominational unions were approved, and the craft groups entered into the ranks of the interdenominational unions.

In November, 1920, the convention of the General Association of Christian Trade Unions held at Essen demanded political equality of all German citizens, establishment of a popular regime (*Volkstaat*), and avoidance of a class state. Popular sovereignty was declared to be the only basis of a mature political nation. The convention also favored the principle of the solidarity of vocations and classes, and the collaboration of worker and manager. Works councils were endorsed as agents of peace and concord in industry, which would, in time, put an end to labor disputes. Christian trade unions were urged to participate in the works councils so as to avoid "putting the works councils on the socialist footing of class war." However, the "Christian trade unions," according to their official organ, "certainly reject and oppose

24 *Ibid.*, pages 52–61.

all purely individualistic economic systems, but it does not follow that we share the socialist theory." Christian trade unionism described itself as a "vocational and corporate movement, not a class movement. Its object is to transform and revive industrial life by introducing moral principles." [25] The Christian unions favored collective bargaining and arbitration, and opposed the class war, but not strikes for limited demands. They were able to increase their membership steadily, but, like the free trade unions, they initially suffered great losses as a result of World War I. Beginning in the late years of World War I, the Christian trade unions profited from the widespread movement of workers into unions and more than doubled their membership. In 1920, the *Deutsche Gewerkschaftsbund,* the partnership of the almost equally strong Catholic *Gesamtverband der Christlichen Gewerkschaften,* comprising manual workers, and two other *Gesamtverbände,* comprising chiefly Protestant white-collar workers and civil servants, reached a total of 1,250,000. The postwar economic disturbances, however, resulted in a membership decline to about half this level by the mid 1920's.

Growth of the free trade unions

However, by far the most influential trade union center and the one having the largest membership remained that of the free trade unions, the General Commission. The free unions did not make any substantial gains until 1895, and Zwing believes it was due to their great faith in political action that German labor only gradually learned to recognize the need for building trade unions for day-to-day struggles.[26] But this is scarcely an adequate explanation. There is apt to be much more opposition from employers to the formation of unions than to a political party, and, consequently, the period of preparation is likely to be longer and the gains in membership slower. Unions trench upon the employers' interests and prerogatives immediately, and demands for concessions are likely to be met with severe counter measures, including the blacklisting of union members. Nevertheless, beginning in 1895, the free trade unions made continual progress, and as Table I shows, with the exception of slight losses in membership in 1901 and 1907, membership rose steadily until the outbreak of World War I. In the years when the free unions suffered an overall loss of membership, the economy was depressed and the number of unemployed higher than normal.

---

[25] International Labor Office, "The Programme and Organization of Christian Trade Unions of Germany," *Studies and Reports, Series A, No. 21.* Geneva: I.L.O., 1921.

[26] Zwing, *op. cit.,* pages 80–81.

In the first years of its existence, many affiliated unions called on the General Commission for aid during strikes, but such requests were refused because of lack of finances. As a consequence, a resolution was introduced at the convention in 1899 that the General Commission set up a strike fund to be supported by regular contributions. It was, however, rejected.[27] It was believed that the support of strikes was essentially the task of the individual union, and that the General Commission should furnish aid only when a serious struggle for survival was taking place.

TABLE 1

MEMBERSHIP IN THE GERMAN FREE TRADE UNIONS, 1891–1914

Year	Number of National Unions	Total Membership
1891	62	277,659
1892	56	237,094
1893	51	223,530
1894	54	246,494
1895	53	259,175
1896	51	329,230
1897	56	412,359
1898	57	493,742
1899	55	580,473
1900	58	680,427
1901	57	677,510
1902	60	733,206
1903	63	887,698
1904	63	1,052,108
1905	64	1,344,803
1906	66	1,689,709
1907	61	1,865,506
1908	60	1,831,731
1909	57	1,832,667
1910	53	2,017,298
1911	53	2,339,785
1912	50	2,553,162
1913	49	2,573,718
1914	48	2,075,759

Source: Zwing, op. cit., page 82.

The major organized industries were mining, the metal trades, textiles, the wood industries, and the building trades. Paper, leather, and clothing industries were also well organized. The large mass unions divided themselves into sections or divisions so as to facilitate the handling of their administrative and trade problems.

[27] *Protokoll der Verhandlungen des dritten Kongresses der Gewerkschaften Deutschlands,* pages 69–71. Hamburg: C. C. Legien, 1899.

Unions and the party

The free unions and the Social Democratic Party were closely related ideologically and through personalities. Active socialists were leading trade unionists, and the trade union head, Legien, was a member of the Social Democratic Party. With the growth of their influence, the trade unions began to feel increasingly the need to evolve independent policies more suitable to their needs. There prevailed among socialists wide differences of opinion on the role and significance of the trade unions. The parliamentary leader of German social democracy, Bebel, believed that the importance of the trade unions was declining, and at the Cologne congress of the Party, he argued that the entrance of the government into social insurance welfare legislation would limit the range of trade union activities.[28] The Erfurt program of 1891 containing the Party program and views on many issues warned against the tendency of the trade unions to divide the better-paid worker, the aristocracy of labor, from the exploited mass. The groups within the Party that regarded the trade unions as "political schools of socialism" were unenthusiastic about the centralizing tendencies within the trade union movement. Some leaders of the Party feared that the General Commission would develop policies independent of the Party, and at the Party convention of 1893 Legien had to deny the charge that members of the General Commission planned to adopt the policies of Samuel Gompers. At the same convention, Legien also criticized Bebel for espousing the view that the growing concentration of capital would inevitably weaken the influence of the trade unions.[29]

Nevertheless, Legien, as head of the free trade unions, insisted, at the Gotha congress in 1898, that the trade unions had the right to devise their own social and political policies, and that they were in no sense obligated to accept the policies of the Social Democratic Party. He asserted that the field of general social policy must never become a Party monopoly, and the membership of workers in the trade unions who did not belong to the Party compelled the trade unions to exercise independence in such matters. Moreover, he emphasized that the trade unions were the most effective instruments for achieving the shorter work day and for enlarging the right to organize.[30] The early conventions of the free trade unions devoted

[28] Paul Kampffmeyer, *Changes in the Theory and Tactics of (German) Social Democracy*, pages 149–150. Chicago: Charles H. Kerr and Co., 1908. Karl Kautsky, *Das Erfurter Programm*, pages 206–225. Stuttgart, 1892.

[29] *Handbuch der Sozialdemokratischen Parteitage von 1863 bis 1909*, pages 190–191. Munich: G. Birk & Co., 1910. *Protokoll über die Verhandlungen des Parteitages der Sozialdemokratischen Partei Deutschlands*, page 215, 1893.

[30] *Protokoll über die Verhandlungen . . .*, page 194.

considerable time to discussing the relations that should obtain between the Party and the trade unions. Those who favored the freeing of the unions from the tutelage of the Party rejected the view of many socialist leaders that the trade unions were, in any sense, an inferior type of organization, or that the activities of the unions were in any way of less importance than those of the Social Democratic Party; or that the trade unions needed the guidance of the Party on the appropriate policies to follow.[31]

The greatest doubt of the efficacy of the trade unions came from the left wing of the Social Democratic Party. Rosa Luxemburg, an eminent theorist and a leader of the left wing of German Social Democracy and international socialism, contended that the power of unions to improve the conditions of labor was already severely limited. She was convinced that

> . . . we are not moving toward an epoch marked by a victorious development of trade unions, but rather toward a time when the hardships of labor unions will increase. *Once industrial development has attained its highest possible point and capitalism has entered its descending phase on the world market, the trade union struggle will become doubly difficult. . . . Trade union action is reduced of necessity to the simple defense of already realized gains, and even that is becoming more and more difficult. Such is the general trend of things in our society. The counterpart of this tendency should be the development of the political side of the class struggle.* (Luxemburg's italics.)[32]

This view was held by virtually all of the orthodox Marxists, and it was only the non-Marxist or revisionist wing of the Party that valued highly the work of the trade unions.

The mass or general strike was another issue that aroused serious differences within the Social Democratic Party and was regarded by union leaders as an undue interference in their internal affairs. The issue first came up at the Dresden congress in 1903 and was discussed in several subsequent Party conventions. The proponents of this strike tactic were members of the left wing, the leaders of which were Karl Liebknecht, Rosa Luxemburg, George Ledebour, Klara Zetkin, and Karl Radek. The notion that the mass strike was a desirable tactic received ostensible confirmation from the Russian Revolution of 1905, when a series of extensive strikes created a crisis and temporary reform of the government. Rosa Luxemburg attempted to apply the lessons of the Russian mass strikes to Germany; she believed that the

---

[31] Zwing, *op. cit.*, pages 119–120; Sigfried Nestriepke, *Die Gewerkschaftsbewegung*, Vol. I, page 413. Stuttgart: Ernest Heinrich Montz, 1921–1923.

[32] Rosa Luxemburg, *Reform or Revolution*, page 18. New York: Three Arrows Press, 1937. The pamphlet is a translation (the 1908 edition) of *Sozialreform oder Revolution* first published in 1899 during the controversy over revisionism.

peaceful tactics evolved by the trade unionists were only a passing historical phase, and that the organized and unorganized workers would from time to time be drawn into extensive mass strikes that were likely to shake the foundation of the economic system.[33] The Jena congress of the Party, in 1905, declared that in the event of an attack upon the universal franchise or upon the right to organize, the use of the mass strike would be justified.[34]

The free unions did not look with equanimity upon such ideas; the 1905 trade union convention in Cologne warned its members that the mass strike was promoted by people without experience, and that such an issue should not even be discussed, since it tended to weaken the trade unions and to divert them from their day-to-day activities.[35] Only seven votes were cast against this view. At the Mannheim Social Democratic congress in the following year, the question was again raised. By then, the reactionary Russian government had gained control of the situation and faith in the mass strike among German socialists had consequently declined. In discussing the question, Bebel pointed out that without the support of the trade unions and their leaders, the mass strike was impossible. He alluded to the Russian experience, emphasized the difference in the political and cultural level of the two countries, and warned against mechanical comparisons or the assumption that the same tactics were applicable under different circumstances.

Legien opposed any attempt to determine tactics in advance and warned against doctrinaire discussions on the question. A resolution was adopted declaring that in the struggle for the improvement of conditions of labor, the trade unions were of equal importance with the Party, and that on questions involving the common interests of the Party and the unions, the heads of the respective organizations were to seek, through consultation, a common policy.[36] With this resolution, the German Social Democratic Party explicitly recognized the trade union movement as an equal rather than as an appendage. It is true that the free unions continued to be close in outlook and sentiment to the Party, but the notion, inherent in Marxist doctrine and explicitly stated by Marxist theorists, especially those on the left, that the trade unions were an adjunct or school for the Party was rejected. The vote was a clear demonstration of the growing power

---

[33] Rosa Luxemburg, *The Mass Strike,* Translated by P. Lavin, pages 53–61. Detroit: The Marxian Educational Society, no date.

[34] *Handbuch der Sozialdemokratischen Parteitage von 1863 bis 1909,* page 306. Karl Kautsky, *Die Politsche Massenstreik,* pages 124–129. Berlin: Vorwärts, 1914.

[35] *Protokoll der Verhandlungen des fünften Kongress der Gewerkschaften Deutschlands,* pages 30, 215–229. Berlin: C. C. Legien, 1905.

[36] *Handbuch der Sozialdemokratischen Parteitage,* pages 309–310.

of the trade unions, and their ability to cut themselves loose from the direct control of the Party. Nevertheless common tradition and the political climate of the German Empire tended to reaffirm the close working relation between party and unions, even if the trade union leaders viewed with alarm the philosophy of some of the party leaders.

Structural groupings of unions

German unions, similarly to those in the United States, England and Scandinavia, began as local organizations. Both craft and industrial groups existed from the beginning, but the German unions showed a tendency to evolve toward the industrial or quasi-industrial forms of organization. Unions such as the metal workers and transport workers contained a wide variety of trades. In the case of the metal and wood workers' unions, the basis for organization was the material that the workers used, and in the case of the transport workers, the service, the transferring of persons or goods, was the basis upon which the jurisdiction was determined.

The local union (*Ortsverein*) was the basic unit; it conducted agitation, collected statistical materials, and administered local beneficiary activity. An executive committee usually headed the local, and, depending upon size, one or more salaried officers were employed. A structural form resembling the regions or districts in the United States was sometimes organized. The district unions carried on their activity on a broader basis, and directed campaigns of organization and for the improvement of job conditions. Some unions also established provincial or regional organizations. There existed also city centrals, or *Gewerkskartelle*, whose function was to unify the various unions in a single geographic area. These groups clashed initially with the national unions over their assumed authority to intervene in trade issues, and as a result their functions had to be more clearly defined. They were finally limited to promoting the common economic interests of their members, to supervising labor reports, and to protecting the interests of labor in the elections to the conciliation service and works' councils. In addition, they supported the organizational drives of weaker unions, and aided in local strikes.

Conflict between the local central organization and the national trade union was by no means peculiar to Germany. Similar differences arose in the United States whenever the city centrals or state federations sought to intervene in trade questions. In Germany, the city centrals played a somewhat more active role than those in the United States, particularly in workers' education. This phase of their activity was undoubtedly due to the influence of socialism and of the socialists, who placed great emphasis upon labor education. The proliferation of labor legislation during World War I and under the Weimar Republic increased the importance and the amount of the city centrals' activities, and selection of members to conciliation boards and to works' councils became an important function.

German national unions showed a tendency toward amalgamation of independent unions into larger groups. Several factors favored this trend. Smaller unions frequently sought to join a larger one after a strike or lockout had seriously depleted their funds or membership. Thus, an independent union of metal chiselers amalgamated with the metal trades' union after a severe strike during 1907. Workers belonging to different unions but working for the same employer or for members of the same employers' associations, would fail to see the necessity for more than one labor organization. In this way, the unions of cigarmakers and tobacco workers came together. Technical change, by wiping out the boundaries between trades, promoted amalgamation; this process is best seen in the steady absorption of formerly independent unions into the metal workers' and the wood workers' organization.

The 62 national organizations existing in 1891 were reduced to 49 in 1923, not counting the organizations newly established in the period that also merged with some other union.[37] During this same period some groups withdrew from larger unions because of jurisdictional difficulties or other complaints, but the trend within German trade unions was toward larger organizations. According to Umbreit, the membership of the free trade unions in 1913 stood at 2,548,763. More than 20 per cent of the total, 528,968 members, were in the metal workers' union; 326,631 members were in the building workers' union; 200,855 members were in the transportation workers' union; 188,120 were in the woodworkers' union; and 184,196 in the general factory workers' union. These five large unions thus contained 1,448,770 members, or more than 56 per cent of the total free trade union enrollment. German trade unions did not resist amalgamation as have the labor organizations in the United States, and the result was a few large unions that grew larger in time.

Beneficiary activities

A wide variety of beneficiary activities was carried on by German unions. As a rule, benefits were paid by the central organizations, though some locals occasionally added contributions. Members in good standing were offered travel aid, unemployment benefits, sickness

---

[37] Johann Fiedler, *Die Konzentrations bewegung der Gewerkschaften*, page 1. Leipzig: Hölder-Pichler-Tempsky, 1924.

insurance, disability, and mortuary benefits. As in the United States, not all unions provided either the same range or the same amount of benefits. According to Zwing, in 1892, ten unions operated unemployment compensation systems, and by 1916 the number of unions providing this service reached 34. The establishment of systems of unemployment insurance was opposed in certain sections of the trade union movement on ideological grounds. It was argued that since unemployment is caused by capitalism, the costs should be borne by the capitalist state, and not by the workers themselves. Closely allied to this view was the one that expressed the fear that support of the unemployed might cause the workers to lose their revolutionary élan. Those who supported union unemployment funds believed that the union membership would remain more stable if unemployment benefits were paid, since the unemployed would have an inducement to stay on the rolls, and that the income thereby provided to the idle worker would reduce the probability of the unemployed undercutting the wage levels of the employed workers. The issues were debated at a number of trade union conventions, but the principle of union unemployment insurance systems was always approved.[38]

Support of traveling members was an old custom inherited from the practice of the medieval gilds. (In the United States this type of expenditure was not usually made by the unions on a formal basis, but many of the unions in the 1890's, and even later, informally supported "wandering" brothers.) Sickness insurance was paid by some unions in addition to the aid received from the state, and death and invalidity benefits were established by the printers as early as the 1870's. The beneficiary activities of several unions were established before Bismarck's welfare schemes, and after the latter were organized, the union programs were essentially a supplement to those of the state.

Employers' associations

Employers' associations that were devoted to nonlabor activities, such as the improvement of product and marketing, arose in Germany between 1850 and 1870. Joint activity by employers in labor problems was a later stage of development and grew up in the first instance as a defensive move against organized labor. Closer union of employers frequently followed a strike movement in their industry. Among the first employers' associations organized (1869) to deal with labor were the *Deutsche Buchdruckerverein* (the German Master Printers) and the *Verein deutscher Glacé handschuh fabricanten* (the Association of Kid Glove Manufacturers), an old trade association

---

[38] Zwing, *op. cit.*, pages 89–92.

transformed into an employers' group for the handling of labor issues. Employers' organizations were, however, not widely established in industry until after the expiration of the antisocialist laws in 1890, when the unions increased their membership. At the outset, the majority of employers' organizations were local or regional in makeup.

With the growth of a militant trade union movement, the conviction that only a unified employers' group could create an effective force capable of meeting the campaigns of the unions grew among employers. A strike of weavers in Crimmitschau, Saxony, in 1903 was the catalytic agent that led to the establishment of a broad employers' organization. The employers affected appealed to the Textile Association of Saxony for aid, and the latter not only provided help, but induced the Central Federation of German Manufacturers to furnish additional assistance. The latter organization had hitherto not concerned itself with labor questions, but in January, 1904, it sponsored a belligerent employers' association, the *Zentralstelle der Arbeitgeberverbände* (the Central Administration of Employers' Associations) as an agency for combating labor.

Division in the employer ranks soon arose, however, and the handicraft trades established the *Vereinigung deutscher Arbeitgeberverbände* (the Union of German Employers' Associations). Employers producing semi-manufactured goods and raw materials organized, at the same time, the *Hauptstelle deutscher Arbeitgeberverbände* (the General Administration of German Employers' Associations). The chief objective of both new groups was opposition to the demands of the unions through a common front among employers. Both built up defense funds to indemnify their members against losses suffered during strikes and lockouts. The General Administration of Employers' Associations limited itself to defending its members against organized labor. It was a militant opponent of unionism, and refused to engage in any form of collective bargaining. The Union of Employers' Associations, while it, too, opposed organized labor, adopted at times a more conciliatory attitude. Gradually, the two central organizations of employers came closer together and out of their cooperation grew a merger into the *Vereinigung der deutschen Arbeitgeberverbände* (Federation of German Employers' Associations) which became the primary defender of the political and economic interests of German employers.

The federation was a congerie of associations, some organized on a trade or horizontal basis (*Fachverbände*), others including only employers in a single branch of industry, and a third category of intertrade groups (*Gemischtgewerbliche Verbände*) including employers in several branches of an industry. Local and regional groups were also established. Among their customary practices were the blacklisting of strikers and the supplying of strikebreakers, the operation of employment offices, propaganda in behalf of the employer viewpoint during labor disputes, and the promotion of legislation favorable to the employer. Up to World War I, the employers' associations remained aggressively opposed to the unions and used their entire arsenal of weapons to defeat the claims of organized labor.[39]

Favorable to the employer and, in fact, instruments used against the free trade unions were the "yellow" or company unions, formed in 1905. During a lockout of metal workers in Augsburg, the employers announced they would only rehire nonunion members. At the same time, they encouraged the formation of "plant societies." The spread of this movement, especially through Bavaria, led them to call a convention in 1910, at which they set up a League of Plant Unions, dedicated to promoting harmony between employer and employee. At the outset of World War I, these groups achieved a membership of over 150,000.[40]

Union strike machinery

In their campaigns for improvement of wages and working conditions or in resisting attacks upon them by employers, German unions were frequently forced to resort to strikes. When employers began to organize, strikes and lockouts tended to be of longer duration. Quite early, the workers, and especially their officers, discovered that strikes had to be financed and that enthusiasm, while indispensable, was, for the purpose of financing, less important than coin of the realm. Informal methods of financing were not certain or satisfactory, and the fifth convention of the free trade unions, in 1905, decided that both the direction and financing of strikes were, in the first instance, the task of the single national union; that all unions had the duty to arrange their dues and other income so as to be in a position to finance their labor disputes; and that in the event of a strike or lockout of unusual severity, one in which the union's resources were inadequate, the entire movement would have the duty to help finance the workers involved. The General Commission was, under these circumstances, authorized to appeal to its affiliates for financial aid for those on strike, and was thereupon to have a voice in the direction and settlement of the dispute. Unions were not, as formerly, to appeal directly to those not involved in the dispute for financial aid.

Quite early in the history of German trade unionism, a tendency developed to require the approval of the central national executive

---

[39] W. Kruger, "Employers' Associations in Germany," *International Labour Review* (Sept. 1926), pages 313–344.

[40] Hans Alexander Apolant, *Die Wirtschaftesfriedliche Arbeitnehmerbewegung Deutschlands,* pages 31–32. Berlin: Julius Springer, 1928.

before allowing a local to call a strike. The wood workers' and the printers' unions were among the first to impose such rules upon their members. Some unions also required the approval of more than a simple majority of those involved for the calling of a strike. In order to prevent hasty action, the national officers had to be given a certain period of notice before a strike could be called. Failure of a local to abide by the rules for the calling of strikes usually led to a denial of strike benefits. Since not many locals were able to build up a sufficiently large treasury to free themselves from the necessity of support by the central union during a strike, they were ordinarily compelled to follow the rules.

TABLE 2

STRIKES AND LOCKOUTS IN GERMANY, 1890–1913

Year	Number of strikes and lockouts	Number of workers involved	Man-days lost
1890–1891	226	38,536	*
1892	73	3,022	*
1893	116	9,356	*
1894	131	7,328	*
1895	204	14,032	*
1896	483	128,808	*
1897	578	63,119	*
1898	985	60,162	*
1899	976	100,779	*
1900	852	115,761	1,234,025
1901	727	48,522	1,194,553
1902	861	55,715	964,317
1903	1,282	121,593	2,622,232
1904	1,625	135,957	2,120,154
1905	2,323	507,964	7,362,802
1906	3,480	316,042	6,317,675
1907	2,792	281,030	5,122,467
1908	2,052	126,885	2,045,585
1909	2,045	131,244	2,247,512
1910	3,194	369,011	9,037,575
1911	2,914	325,253	6,846,240
1912	2,825	479,589	4,776,818
1913	2,600	248,986	5,672,034

Source: S. Nestriepke, op. cit., page 395.
* No figures available.

Unlike the Socialist Party, the trade unions could not regard every strike as a gain, in the sense that a strike would tend to reveal the class character of society and of the state. Even where a strike did not endanger the safety of the union, it drained the strike fund. In common with unions in the United States, the German unions recognized that local unions were, at times, likely to call strikes either without adequate cause or before they had exhausted all possibilities for peaceful settlement. Therefore, to protect the union and the strike fund provided through contributions of all locals, centralization of strike permission was essential.

The increase in the number of strikes from 1890 to 1913, and the number of workers involved in them, shown in Table 2, was due, primarily, to the increase in the number of organized workers. The number of strikes rose steadily from 1896 to 1904, though there was no corresponding straight line increase in the number of workers involved.

The number of workers involved in strikes during the entire period was largest in 1905; the number of strikes was greatest in the following year. A decline in business activity reduced the number and intensity of labor disputes in the following three years, but a revival of industrial activity thereafter again resulted in an increase in the number and intensity of labor disputes.

Wages and collective bargaining

The available evidence indicates that the money wages of German labor rose steadily from the 1890's to World War I. No over-all figures on wage changes are available, but sectional figures tend to substantiate this conclusion. Wages of Ruhr miners increased from 3.71 marks per day, in 1893, to 6.54 marks, in 1913, or 76 per cent during the intervening period; wages of masons in Berlin rose from 0.525 marks per hour in 1893 to 0.82 marks in 1913–1914, or 56 per cent; the printers enjoyed a somewhat smaller increase, and the weekly wages of the unskilled workers increased, between 1893 and 1913–1914, by 34 per cent in Berlin, 43.3 per cent in Mannheim, and 40.4 per cent in Rostock. Unskilled railroad workers on the Prussian railways did even better; between 1895 and 1914, their daily wages rose 63.6 per cent.[41]

Collective bargaining was first introduced in the printing industry in the 1860's and 1870's. During the next decade, local unions in other industries entered into arrangements with their employers, but only in the 1890's did they become widespread. There were several reasons for the slow progress made in this direction. Unions had not achieved sufficient power in many industries to be able to force agreements upon the employers. The views of many socialists were also an obstacle: Collective agreements were regarded as a form of social compromise, as instruments that limited the worker's ability to use his

---

[41] Waldemar Zimmermann, *Die Veränderungen der Einkommens und Lebensverhältnisse der deutschen Arbeiter durch den Krieg*, pages 296–305. New Haven: Yale University Press, 1932.

power at opportune moments.[42] The opposition to collective contracts
vanished as the unions became stronger, and at the third trade union
congress, held in 1899, the collective agreement was described as
"evidence of equality between employer and employee." Subsequent
discussions were not concerned with the desirability of collective agreements but with whether they should be subject to legal regulation.

The number of collective agreements, establishments, and workers
covered steadily increased. In 1904, there were 575 collective agreements in effect.[43] The agreement figures for the years 1907 to 1918
are shown in Table 3.

TABLE 3

NUMBER OF COLLECTIVE AGREEMENTS, ENTERPRISES AND WORKERS COVERED, 1907–
1918

Year	Number of agreements	Number of enterprises	Workers covered
1907	5,324	111,050	974,564
1908	5,671	120,401	1,026,435
1909	6,578	137,214	1,107,478
1910	8,298	173,727	1,361,086
1911	10,520	183,232	1,552,827
1912	12,437	208,307	1,999,579
1915	11,677	186,120	1,488,191
1918	7,819	107,503	1,127,696

Source: Zwing, op. cit., page 114.

The contracts covered wages and method of wage payment, hours of
work, and other working conditions; procedures for settling disputes
during the term of the contract were defined. The number of workers
covered by collective agreements rose steadily and reached almost two
million before the outbreak of World War I. Collective agreements,
in the main, regulated the conditions of employment in small and
medium-sized industrial plants operated by employers with relatively
moderate resources, subject to competition in the product market.
Heavy industry fought the establishment and recognition of unions by
the encouragement of "yellow" unions, the use of strike-breakers during
labor disputes, refusal to bargain, and by demands for more repressive
labor legislation.

World War I and its Aftermath

The war period

In common with the majority of socialists, the free trade unions—
and the others also—supported the Fatherland at the outbreak of the

[42] Nathan Reich, *Labour Relations in Republican Germany*, pages 63–65. New
York: Oxford University Press, 1938.
[43] Umbreit, *op. cit.*, p. 33.

war. In turn the government initiated a conciliatory policy—the *Burg-frieden*. Nevertheless, all of the three trade union groups suffered severe losses in membership and in income during World War I. Between June 30 and December 31, 1914, the free unions suffered a loss of over 1,300,000 members. Several causes contributed to the decline: unemployment that followed the declaration of war; the calling of thousands of members and union functionaries into the armed services; the increased employment of women, who were not as responsive to the appeals of the unions and who were excluded from membership by a number of organizations; and the shifting of workers from their customary employment to war employment. For example the upholsterers' union had only 1,857 of its 5,368 members working at the trade, and the woodworkers' union found 20,000 out of its 112,000 members employed outside of its jurisdiction.[44] To meet this problem there was an attempt made to allow workers who shifted to war work to retain their membership in their old unions.

From the beginning, all union groups supported Germany's war effort. Such an attitude was in harmony with the profession of the Christian and Hirsch-Duncker unions, while the free trade unions followed the lead of the majority socialists. However, as the left wing of the Social Democratic Party became more vigorous in its demand for the abandonment of the prowar policies, the trade unions felt themselves endangered by the possibilities of a similar division. The demand of a left-wing journal in June, 1915, that the Party cease supporting the war led the General Commission to reaffirm its prowar policies and to denounce the sowers of disunion. The position of the heads of the free labor unions was subsequently approved by a conference of trade union officers. However, the unions faced sharper attacks after the left wing of the Social Democratic Party had split away in 1917, and formed the Independent (*Unabhängige*) Social Democratic Party. A conference of the new Party vehemently attacked the leadership of the trade unions and attempted to become a rallying point for an opposition. In Leipzig, unions with a membership of 10,000 withdrew from the pro-war city central labor union, and organized another under their control. It required considerable effort by the General Commission to keep control of this and similar situations.

From the beginning, the unions sought to discourage strikes by their members. However, as the war continued, and the cost of living rose continually to higher levels, strikes increased, as can be seen from Table 4.

---

[44] Nestriepke, *op. cit.*, II, page 24.

TABLE 4

NUMBER OF STRIKES AND LOCKOUTS IN GERMANY, 1915–1917

Year	Number of disputes	Workers involved	Man-days lost
1915	66	2,221	6,511
1916	142	14,639	36,555
1917	193	66,634	152,802

Source: Nestriepke, *op. cit.*, Vol. II, page 38.

While the increase in the number of disputes between 1915 and 1917 was not quite three-fold, the number of workers involved and the man-days lost rose in much greater proportion. Discontent spread, and some of the disputes, especially those in the armaments industry, took on a distinct political coloring.

Despite loss of membership, the unions attempted to widen their legal rights, and the three central organizations cooperated with this end in view. Demands for the strengthening of the right to organize and the elimination of restrictions upon organization by government workers grew. In June, 1916, an act was passed explicitly giving unions the right to discuss political and social issues without facing the danger of being regarded as political groups.

Revolutionary upsurge

As the conflict continued, strikes in protest against the continuance of the war increased. In January, 1917, strikes occurred in Leipzig and Braunschweig, and in April of 1917 a strike of Berlin metal workers estimated to involve between 200,000 and 300,000 workers took place.[45] On November 9, 1918, a general strike broke out in Berlin and the Kaiser abdicated. In the stormy events that followed, the Berlin workers played an important role; Richard Müller, a leader of the Berlin metal workers, was also one of the *revolutionäre obleute,* revolutionary chiefs, in Berlin. Supported by the workers in heavy industry, the *obleute* had planned an uprising for November, 1918, when they hoped to set up a socialist republic. Their plans were frustrated by the unexpected mass uprising on November 9, which eventually led, instead, to the establishment of a moderate government dominated by the majority socialists.

The Revolution of November 9 caught all wings of German labor by surprise. With the spread of the revolt, soldiers' and workers' councils were formed at the front, in barracks, on ships, and in factories. An executive council of soldiers' and workers' councils was

[45] Ossip K. Flechtheim, *Die Kommunistische Partei Deutschlands in der Weimar Republik,* pages 24–25. Offenbach: A. M. Bollwerk Verlag, 1948.

organized in Berlin, and this body appointed six People's Commissars, three from the majority socialists and three from the more radical independent socialists, to govern the country. As a protest against the government's hesitant policies, the independent socialists withdrew from the People's Commissars in December, 1918, placing the majority socialists in complete control. During the three months in which the People's Commissars governed the country, November, 1918, through January, 1919, a significant body of labor and welfare legislation was placed upon the statute books. The eight-hour day was introduced, civil service employees were granted the right to organize, the duty to provide for the relief of the unemployed was imposed upon the municipalities, employees were protected from arbitrary dismissal by employers, and demobilized workers were reinstated in their former employment. Nevertheless, a large number of independent socialists and all members of the extreme revolutionary *Spartacus* group opposed the government and advanced the slogan "all power to the workers' councils." In contrast, the majority socialists demanded a parliamentary republic, a demand supported by the first general congress of Workers' Councils held in Berlin, December 16–20, 1918. A resolution favoring a parliamentary government and the election of a Constituent Assembly on January 19, 1919, was approved. The elections to the National Assembly in January gave the moderate parties a majority. A government based upon the Social Democratic Party and the Center Party was formed.[46]

However, on November 15, 1918, long before the political course that Germany was to take in the future had been established, the trade unions, following up their, by now, well-established policy of collaboration with state and employers, took a decisive step toward the reshaping of Germany's social and political institutions. Under the leadership of Legien, for the unions, and Stinnes, for the employers, they concluded an agreement on a so-called *Zentralarbeitsgemein-schaft* (central working committee between employers and trade unions). At the outset the employers made the greatest concessions. They recognized the trade unions and endorsed complete freedom of association. Employers agreed not to encourage or support company unions, to allow labor an equal voice in the administration of the employment offices, to engage all demobilized workers, to determine the conditions of work through the collective agreement with differences to be decided by boards of conciliation, and to establish the eight-hour workday. It was also agreed that a joint council of employer

---

[46] See Arthur Rosenberg, *A History of the German Republic,* translated by Ian F. D. Morrow and L. Marie Sieveking, pages 1–124. London: Methuen & Co., 1936.

and employee representatives be created to seek solutions to common problems.

The advantages which the employers received from this agreement, which was subsequently approved by the provisional government, were equally, if not more, substantial. At a time when the victorious left seemed to be able to reorganize the state according to its own ideas, the unions put their authority behind the maintenance of much of the traditional social structure. It is true that they did not renounce their goal of socialization, but for the immediate present social relations were to be continued as before and guaranteed by the free collaboration of employers and trade unions.

Measurably strengthened by the moderation of the trade union leaders, the National Assembly was able to establish the Weimar Republic, which was to be the government of Germany until its overthrow by Hitler. In 1920, the German trade unions saved the Weimar Republic from an attempt by a formation of freebooters to overthrow it. Armed soldiers occupied Berlin, and Wolfgang Kapp, a nationalist politician, proclaimed himself head of the state. The government, deserted by the army, was forced to flee, but it was saved when the three central groups of trade unions, under the leadership of Legien, called for a general strike. After the strike had swept away the counter-revolutionary conspiracy, the trade union leadership played with the idea of establishing a government primarily based on the support of the various union movements and the working class parties.[47] But the mutual distrust between the USDP (Independent Socialist Party) and the Social Democratic Party was too far advanced and the traditional patterns of organization of German society proved to be too deep-seated to allow more than some minor governmental reshuffling.

The German Federation of Labor

The Nuremberg trade union congress of July, 1919, decided to reorganize the free trade union movement. During World War I, the General Commission had acquired more influence over the labor movement, and in place of the former loose federation, the *Allgemeine Deutsche Gewerkschaftsbund* (General German Federation of Labor) was set up. The organization was empowered to bring together the national unions for the promotion of their common interests, and was charged with collection of labor materials, promotion of labor protective laws and workers' education, settlement of jurisdictional differ-

---

[47] Theodore Leipart, *Carl Legien: Ein Gedenkbuch,* pages 116–119. Berlin: Allgemeine Deutschen Gewerkschaftsbund, 1949.

ences, support of affiliates in unusually serious labor disputes, and the promotion of relations with foreign labor groups. An executive committee of 15 was established to head the organization, and conventions were to meet once every three years.[48]

The form of organization and the role of the works' councils aroused controversy. The convention urged all unions to broaden their ranks and to accept as members helpers and apprentices. Industrial unionism was approved as desirable under modern conditions, and cooperation among closely-allied unions recommended. The development of the works' councils presented a problem for the unions, since attempts were being made by the more radical groups within the labor movement to oppose the influence of the trade unions in the plant by strengthening the power of the works' councils. The convention of 1919 therefore declared that the works' councils could be effective only if they were closely tied to the trade unions and served as an instrument for the achieving of union aims. Richard Müller, a leader of the left wing, wanted a more radical position taken on this issue; he introduced a resolution affirming the right of the works' councils to intervene in all the details of plant management. Such a view was rejected, but the right of the works' councils to a voice in all questions affecting labor was affirmed. The congress, however, emphasized that the task of dealing with economic problems in the plant fell directly and exclusively upon the trade unions.[49]

The Nuremberg congress also dealt with the relations of the Social Democratic Party to the free unions. At the Mannheim congress in 1906, it had been resolved that the executives of the unions and the Social Democratic Party were to work together on issues affecting their common interests. As a result of the split within the Social Democratic Party during World War I, many trade unionists joined the Independent Socialist Party. Consequently, the trade unions, to avoid becoming involved in a controversy between political socialist groups, had to declare their political neutrality. In deference to its socialist faith, however, the congress proclaimed itself a class and not a narrow trade organization.[50]

The form of organization was still an important issue. Should industry or craft unions be promoted? At the Leipzig congress in 1922, the industrial form of organization was endorsed, and a committee was appointed to investigate and advise on methods of building in-

---

[48] *Protokoll der Verhandlungen des Zehnten Kongress der Gewerkschaften Deutschland,* pages 63–64, 516. Berlin: Allgemeinen Deutschen Gewerkschaftsbundes, 1919.

[49] *Ibid.,* page 59.

[50] *Ibid.,* pages 301–318.

dustrial unions out of existing organizations. The committee could not agree, and the executive committee drew up a program for the unions which, in modified form, was adopted by the 1925 convention. Industrial organization was endorsed as an aim, and a plan for realizing it presented. But the effectuation of the proposals through amalgamation was left to the individual unions.[51]

Works' councils

During the short revolutionary period, works' councils arose in many industries. The institution had been known in Germany for many years, but part of its current popularity was gained from the example of revolutionary Russia where the soviet, originally a workers' and soldiers' council, had been able to seize power. In Germany, works' councils had been suggested to the National Assembly in Frankfurt in 1848. Factory regulations were to be drawn up in each establishment by the employer and a representative of his employees. Such rules were to be effective when approved by a district committee that was to be chosen by the factory councils in the area. Nothing came of these suggestions as a result of the collapse of the Revolution, but it was not entirely erased from the consciousness of labor.[52] With the rise of trade unions, the works' councils came to be regarded as a possible offset to their influence. Employers were required, under an amendment to the Industrial Code enacted in 1891, to post factory rules. The law also provided that factories employing 20 or more workers elect works' committees. These committees were to be consulted on factory rules, but acceptance of their advice was not obligatory. In 1905, the election of workers' committees in mines employing 100 or more workers was made compulsory in Prussia. At the outset of World War I, the several thousand existing works' councils were not very important, and the trade unions were by far the more effective representative of labor.

As the war continued, increasingly severe controls were needed over the labor market. The Auxiliary Service Act, which contained many features objectionable to labor, included concessions on the position of the works' councils. Works' councils or committees were now made compulsory in all plants employing more than 50 employees, but the functions even of these councils were not too important. In addition,

---

[51] *Ibid.*, pages 272–298.

[52] Marcel Berthelot, *Works' Councils in Germany*, page 3. Geneva: International Labor Office, 1924; C. W. Guillebaud, *The Works' Council*. New York: The Macmillan Company, 1928; Boris Stern, "Works' Council Movement in Germany," *Bulletin of the United States Bureau of Labor Statistics, No. 383* (1925), page 3.

conciliation boards, composed of three representatives of employers and three of workers, were set up with chairmen appointed by the War Board. These boards were to decide any differences that could not be settled directly by the parties. The Legien-Stinnes agreement gave the works' councils recognition and a voice in settling labor conditions.[53] Soon thereafter, on December 23, 1918, the government issued an order making works' councils compulsory in establishments employing 20 or more workers. These councils, in cooperation with the employer, were to be charged with seeing that the terms of collective agreements were observed.

Article 165 of the new constitution defined the position of the works' councils. Workers were given equal rights with employers:

. . . to cooperate in the regulation of wage and labor conditions, as well as in the whole economic development of production. . . . For the purpose of safeguarding their social and economic interests, the wage-earning and salaried employees are entitled to be represented in Workers' Councils for each establishment, as well as in Regional Workers' Councils organized for each industrial area, and in a Federal Workers' Council.

The regional and federal councils were to join with the representatives of the employers to form regional and national economic councils in order to facilitate economic cooperation between the two groups— the national economic council could submit bills involving economic questions to the federal government, and the latter had then to introduce such measures regardless of its wishes.

Article 165 was the basis for the Works' Council Act of February, 1920. Councils were to be elected by the employees by a secret vote in establishments employing at least 20 workers. Those employing between 5 and 19 workers could elect shop delegates only. A council was to be composed of at least 3 members, when the number of employees did not exceed 49, and a council of 30 members was to function in establishments employing 15,000 or more workers. All workers above the age of 18 were entitled to vote. The expenses of the council, as well as the salaries paid to the councilors for time lost from work, were to be borne by the employer. Unions had the right to send a representative to meetings of the council to act in an advisory capacity if their members were employed in the plant.

Works' councils were obligated to promote efficient production and amicable labor relations in the plant. Appeal to a conciliation board was allowed in disputes that could not be settled directly. In cooperation with the employer, the works' councils were to establish working rules, aid in safety work, and cooperate in the administration of

---

[53] Umbreit, *op. cit.,* pages 262–290.

welfare schemes. Protection of the right to organize and enforcement of collective agreements were other tasks allotted to the councils. Management alone had the responsibility for carrying out decisions, and the works' councils had no authority to interfere in the operation of the business. Works' councils could appoint several members of the boards of directors of all companies, and had the right to receive information on issues affecting labor, including wage records. Periodic reports might be asked on prospects for future employment, and large employers might be required to present balance sheets to the councils.[54]

The works' council law was regarded by employers as allowing for too drastic interference with management prerogatives, but it did not satisfy the longings of the left wing socialists and the communists, who wanted much greater power for the councils. On the other hand, the unions felt that they could not allow the works' councils to develop into an independent force. Article 8 of the works' council law protected the position of the trade unions by recognizing the "right of the economic associations of wage-earning and salaried employees to represent the interests of their members," and by allowing trade union representatives to be present at council meetings. The dominance of the trade unions was challenged by the more radical elements of labor, who saw in the councils a means of undermining the more conservative influence of the unions and of gaining control of a potent economic weapon. As an instrument in the tug-of-war between the left wing and the trade unions, there was established the central committee of works' councils at Berlin, with which 26,000 councils in and around Berlin were affiliated. Not only did it seek to weaken the influence of the trade unions, but it attempted to enlarge the political influence of the councils.

The trade unions had no intention of permitting such a program to succeed, and took steps to frustrate the left wing's influence. As a first step, the free trade unions entered into an arrangement with the Federation of Salaried Employees (AfA) to set up a joint works' council committee, and urged that analogous committees be set up on a local basis. Although the law had provided for separate worker and white-collar representation, common candidates for the works' councils were to be supported by both organizations. At the first congress of the works' councils in Berlin in October, 1920, the issues were vigorously debated. Heinrich Brandler, the leader of the Communist Party, demanded that the works' councils be converted into revolutionary organs, but the trade unionists insisted that the "activity of these

---

[54] Guillebaud, *op. cit.*, pages 16–18; Berthelot, *op. cit.*, pages 27–39; Stern, *op. cit.*, pages 9–12.

councils is confined to reforming the economic system." [55] The trade
union view was accepted, and the resolution adopted by the congress
declared:

The Works' Councils find their support in the Trade Unions, which remain
as before, the chief protagonists in the economic sphere, in the struggle between
Capital and Labor. The Works' Councils must base themselves on the Trade
Unions because they can only accomplish their task if they are certain of the
support of the Trade Unions. The development of the Trade Unions into
powerful industrial unions is exclusively a matter for the Trade Unions themselves.[56]

The Leipzig congress of the free trade unions, in 1922, declared
that the trade unions had always sought the expansion of labor's right
for an equal voice in the determination of conditions in the plant,
but that the realization of these aims depended upon the power of
the trade unions. Therefore, the unions were urged at their conventions
to prepare lists of candidates for election to the works' councils.[57] The
next convention, in 1925, again emphasized that the works' councils
could only win a voice in the determinations of the conditions of work
if they were supported by the unions.[58]

On the whole, the Christian trade unions were less fearful that their
position would be usurped by the works' councils, since, in contrast to
the free trade unions, their membership was not likely to be attracted
by radical propaganda. Nevertheless, the Christian unions urged their
members to eschew political discussion in the works' councils and to
use them as a means of raising production and protecting the economic
interests of the worker.

The various union groups gained control over the works' councils
by putting forward lists of candidates for representatives. Members
were urged to support their respective lists, and no member of the
free unions was allowed to be a candidate on another slate. Eventually,
the majority of the councils were controlled by the free trade unions,
as may be seen from Table 5.

Where a firm operated more than one plant, it was permissive to
organize either a joint council representing all plants or a united
council which was a delegate body representing the individual councils
operating in the single plants. As distinct from the above groups,
central works' councils were set up in an effort to devise a common
policy in plants and enterprises controlled by a combine or cartel.

[55] Quoted by Bertholet, *op. cit.*, page 44.
[56] Quoted in Guillebaud, *op. cit.*, page 44.
[57] Salomon Schwarz, *Handbuch der deutschen Gewerkschaftskongresse*, pages
183–193. Berlin: Allgemeinen deutschen Gewerkschaftesbundes, 1930.
[58] *Ibid.*, pages 193–195.

These latter organizations had no statutory position, and, consequently, the employer could refuse to bear the cost of their operation. The result was that they were financed by the trade unions and a possible rival to the latter's position was thereby prevented from arising.

TABLE 5

NUMBER OF WORKS COUNCILS CONTROLLED BY VARIOUS POLITICAL GROUPS

	Total	Social-ist unions	Catho-lic unions	Demo-cratic unions	Com-munists	National Social-ists	Other	Unor-ganized
1930 ...	156,145	135,689	11,333	1,561	2,374	—	1,025	4,163
1931 ...	138,418	115,671	10,956	1,560	4,664	710	1,282	3,565

Source: W. Woytinsky in *Internationales Handwoerterbuch des gewerkschaft-swesens*, Berlin, 1932, page 1590.

Employers, especially after the subsidence of the revolutionary wave, sought ways to limit the authority and effectiveness of the trade unions. Gradually employers began to realize that the works' councils were to be a permanent part of industrial relations and attempted to adapt them to their own purposes. Sometimes, especially in the first years, efforts were made to corrupt works' councilors, but more often attempts were made by employers to acquaint the workers' representative with the economic problems of the enterprise and, thereby, moderate his hostility. Even though "the majority of works' councilors retained their socialist ideology, with its negative attitude toward private enterprise, in the day-by-day practice of the Works' Council they found a *modus vivendi* with management, ideological differences notwithstanding." [59] The limited capacity of the works' councils to deliver concessions to the workers in the plant led to some disillusionment. In some plants, moreover, it was difficult to get workers to serve as councilors, for fear that they be victimized by the employer. An increase in the reluctance of workers to serve as councilors was noted after the onset of the economic decline in 1929 when the ill will of the employer might have meant the loss of employment. The tendency was especially evident in plants with few workers, and frequently, especially when unemployment was on the rise, the works' councils did not function in these establishments.

Since works' councils are again a serious issue in German political and economic life, their performance in the 12-year period of the Weimar Republic is more than an academic question. It is necessary, however, to recognize that the councils arose in a period of revolution, then passed through a disastrous inflation. The hope that the works' councils would become "enterprise minded" was not borne out. That

---

[59] Reich, *op. cit.*, page 197.

works' councils "have signally failed to show either the capacity, or, for the most part, the desire to cooperate with the employer in increasing the efficiency and productivity of industry, is universally admitted and not least by their own spokesmen." [60] The works' councils, like the trade unions, showed an unwillingness to accept innovation. It was difficult for councils to accept with enthusiasm changes that adversely affected their constituents. The works' council movement, as it took legal form, was based upon a community of interest between the worker and the enterprise as a productive unit. While the theory may be correct, it was difficult to distinguish the enterprise as a productive unit from the enterprise as a private property. Consequently, changes regarded, rightfully or wrongly, as adversely affecting the worker group were likely to be resisted despite the theoretically common interest.

Employers also showed little fidelity to the theory of common interest in practice. The requirement that the works' councils be furnished with information on the state of business and production was generally evaded, so that a trade union writer concluded that the information furnished by the employer is "so scant and devoid of substance that it is hardly possible to derive from it any knowledge of the affairs of the enterprise." [61] Nor did the employers show any more enthusiasm for the provisions of the law that required works' councilors to be appointed to the board of directors of corporations; the purpose of this provision was evaded by transferring many problems to specially appointed sub-committees. Thus the works' councilors were deprived of learning about many important issues. At the demand of the unions, legislation was enacted in 1931 that would have prevented the practice of withholding vital information from the workers' representatives by giving single members of boards of directors, including works' councilors, the right to have certain kinds of information, and to discuss important problems. There was not sufficient time to discover whether these changes met the problem; Hitler came to power soon thereafter and the works' councils were destroyed with the other democratic institutions of republican Germany.

Thus the works' councils of the Weimar Republic corresponded neither to the hopes of their supporters nor to the fears of their foes. They did not become agents of economic and social change, nor did they break the trade union monopoly in labor representation. Their members in the boards of directors remained isolated; without the necessary

---

[60] Guillebaud, *op. cit.*, page 238.
[61] Statement of Clement Nörpel, Quoted in Reich, *op. cit.*, page 208.

knowledge in the intricate field of corporate business and finance they proved, even with willing and cooperative employers, unable to profit much by their attendance. In the end, when they were discarded, they had dwindled into mere cogs in the legal machinery set up to guarantee workers some protection against dismissal, a fact that in itself epitomizes the discrepancy between early expectations and the eventual social reality.

Collective contracts

Collective bargaining had a long history in German industrial relations. However, it was vigorously opposed by many employers, especially those in heavy industry. Some concessions were made to labor by the Auxiliary Service Act of 1916, and even more substantial recognition was given to labor by the agreement with the employer groups in November, 1918. The Weimar Republic gave legal sanction to collective bargaining, which influenced the growth of this institution in subsequent years.

The collective agreement assumed even greater importance than it otherwise would have had through the right of arbitrators or the Minister of Labor to impose terms of employment upon employers reluctant to accept conditions regarded as reasonable and proper. In addition, the Minister of Labor could extend the terms of a collective contract with individual firms to an entire industry, if the collective agreement were of major importance in the determination of working conditions. The argument was raised that employers who entered into voluntary labor agreements under which their costs were increased should not be placed in a disadvantageous competitive position. Therefore, labor contracts applied not only to employers signatory to the agreement, but to all others in the same industry if the contract were extended by the Minister of Labor. Contracts were limited to a specific geographical area and time period. With the encouragement received from the government, the number of collective contracts increased considerably during the Weimar Republic, as indicated by Table 6.

An innovation developed in German collective bargaining due to the inflation in the early 1920's, when, because of the rapidly declining value of money, a revision of wage payment was necessary at short intervals if equity and industrial peace were to be preserved. The clauses governing wages were embodied in a special contract and were negotiated separately from the other terms in the agreement. This is similar to the provisions in American labor contracts which are made for a specific period of time, but permit the reopening of the wage clause.

TABLE 6

NUMBER OF FIRMS AND WORKERS COVERED BY COLLECTIVE AGREEMENT, 1920 TO 1931

Year	Number of enterprises	Number of workers
1920	*	5,915,725
1921	363,546	8,629,966
1922	551,989	11,071,574
1923	717,957	12,290,352
1924	*	*
1925	567,196	10,070,264
1926	582,198	9,458,784
1927	559,486	9,315,784
1928	647,495	10,625,248
1929	722,105	10,573,271
1930	*	*
1931	804,788	10,113,222

* No figures available.
Source: "Die Tarifvertrage fur Arbeiter in Deutschen Reich am 1 Jan. 1931," *Reichsarbeitsblatt, Sonderheft 58,* (1933), page 6.

Collective bargaining, because of the support it received from government, expanded much more rapidly than union membership. While trade union membership rose between 1913 and 1925 from 3,024,000 to 4,902,000 or by about 64 per cent, the number of workers covered by agreements increased by about 500 per cent in the same period. Some of the increase in the number of enterprises covered by collective contracts was due to government extension of contract rather than to trade union power. In the United States, where the government has merely protected the right to organize, the number of workers covered by labor contracts is only slightly greater than the number organized in unions. In contrast to pre-Hitler Germany, the emphasis in the United States is upon voluntary organization and not upon extension of the terms of employment by administrative order to nonunion firms.

Under the German system, a distinction was made between two kinds of collective arrangements, collective contracts and factory rules. A collective contract was an agreement between an employer or an association of employers and an association of employees over wages and other terms of employment. The normative parts of a collective contract were "all those which may be incorporated in the individual labor contracts—concerning wages, hours of work, holidays, and so forth—while the remaining clauses determine the legal rights and duties of the parties to the collective but not to the individual contracts; they prohibit militant action, disciplining measures, and so forth." [62]

Factory rules, on the other hand, were collective arrangements be-

---

[62] *Conciliation and Arbitration in Industrial Disputes,* page 254. Geneva: International Labor Office, 1933.

tween employers and workers in a single enterprise. Usually these arrangements regulated issues such as starting and stopping time, thus concretizing the collective contracts usually concluded between employers' associations and the corresponding unions. However, while terms of employment for a particular individual covered by a collective contract with a union could never be legally below those specified in the agreement, the same rule was not applicable to the factory rules. Terms less favorable than those in the works agreements could theoretically be concluded with individual workers. However, the factory rules, except in the absence of a controlling collective contract, were generally of secondary importance only.

Labor disputes and their settlement

The growth of collective bargaining and its encouragement by the state led to the expansion of conciliation and arbitration. A system of mediation and arbitration had first been organized in 1891. The law then authorized the setting up of labor courts with equal representation of labor and management, the chairman to be appointed by the municipal authorities. At first the courts could only intervene at the request of both parties, but later they were allowed to urge the parties to submit differences to them. The four judges, two representing labor and two management, who with the chairman made up the court, were appointed for indefinite periods, up to six years. These courts had no jurisdiction over disputes arising out of collective agreements; they decided only conflicts arising out of individual employer-employee relations, the most frequent issue being the payment of back wages or payment for dismissal without notice.[63] The courts were reasonably successful in carrying out their tasks.

World War I increased the need for methods of settling disputes, and with the enactment of the Auxiliary Service Act in 1916, the role of mediation and arbitration in settling grievances increased. The nation was covered by a network of conciliation boards headed by a chairman appointed by the War Office. The permanent members were selected by the trade unions and employers' association. The boards could intervene at the request of one party, and they dealt with many kinds of disputes involving wages and working conditions. If a dispute had not been placed before a commercial court, either party could ask for the intervention of a conciliation committee. The award was not binding upon those not participating in the hearings, but as these

---

[63] Frieda Wunderlich, *German Labor Courts,* pages 25–27. Chapel Hill: The University of North Carolina Press, 1947.

boards derived their influence from the war authorities, their decisions could not be disregarded with impunity.

The system was a useful method of settling disputes, and when the enabling legislation, the Auxiliary Service Act, was repealed, the arbitration and conciliation machinery was retained and even expanded. Arbitration boards were set up by provincial authorities in cooperation with the Reich Minister of Labor to deal with local disputes. Arbitrators, who were either full-time or part-time officers, were appointed by the central government to handle disputes extending beyond the local area. The Minister of Labor was able to intervene directly or through an agent in disputes of national importance. Arbitration boards were made up of two representatives from each side, and an impartial chairman. Efforts were made to get uniformity in decisions although it was not essential that boards or arbitrators follow precedent. However, the Reich Minister of Labor had the authority to remove either boards or arbitrators, and, therefore, his directions on important issues could not be ignored.[64] Moreover, in particularly important cases, the Minister of Labor, with the agreement of the parties concerned, sometimes appointed an outstanding personality as *ad hoc* arbitrator.

The arbitrators, who were in effect conciliators as well, intervened at the request of either one of the parties, or upon their own initiative, if the dispute was of importance. Once arbitration had been undertaken, the parties were obliged to attend. As a first step, the arbitrator or the chairman of an arbitration board sought to bring about an agreement. If the impartial board member failed to bring about a settlement, a hearing was held with all members of the board participating. Hearings were informal and at their close another effort was made to bring about a voluntary agreement. Failure to achieve a settlement led to the issuance of an award by the majority, although, for a time, the vote of the chairman of a board could overrule the majority decision. An award was made if the two sides were competent to conclude an agreement. Syndicalist and anarchist unions were not regarded as competent to conclude agreements since the principle of direct action which they espoused was held to be inconsistent with collective agreements.

The first object of the system was to encourage voluntary agreement, and if such were concluded, it was signed by the parties. Otherwise, an award was made. The right to make awards binding was initially given to the authorities in certain types of cases during demobilization. In 1923, the government decided to use "means of compulsion if an award is just, and its enforcement will be to the economic and

---

[64] *Conciliation and Arbitration in Industrial Disputes,* pages 239–250.

social advantage of the undertaking or occupation." [65] Consequently, an order was enforceable, even if one of the parties rejected it, if it was held that in the interest of the community or even in the interest of a single industry no suspension of work should be allowed. Only arbitrators and the Minister of Labor could declare awards binding. Specific criteria of what constituted "interest of the community or an industry" were never published. Once an award was declared binding, its terms were automatically imposed upon the parties to the proceedings. The award was usually in writing, but German practice did not require an opinion explaining awards.

During the first year of the operation of the system, 1924, a new currency system was established after several years of inflation. The need to redefine wages brought a large number of cases before the various agencies charged with arbitration. The number declined from 18,575 in 1924 to 5,043 in 1926. As a result of the improvement in business in 1926, the unions pushed for higher wages and the number of cases rose to 8,436 in 1927 and 8,037 in 1928. The number dropped to 7,109 in 1929 and 4,017 in 1930, and rose again to 6,898 in 1931. The drop was due to the depression that engulfed the German economy in the late 1920's and the rise in 1931 was due to efforts of business firms to reduce wages.

Of the total number of cases that came before the mediatory and arbitration authorities, about 30 per cent were settled informally, and without a hearing; another 10 per cent were settled during formal hearings; and in another 50 per cent of cases an award was made by the mediation boards. Refusal of one of the parties to accept the award inevitably led to the initiation of proceedings for making it compulsory. Considerable opposition arose to the compulsory aspects of the system, especially among employers who maintained that the parties thereby evaded their responsibility and allowed the government too much power. Employers, especially after the beginning of the crisis in 1929, sought to limit compulsory imposition of terms to industries vital for the maintenance of public order and security. Moreover, they insisted that industries in which compulsion was, if necessary, to be exercised, should be clearly defined. The unions were more reconciled to the system, although there was opposition to it even among them. Those who argued for compulsion believed that its abolition would allow powerful and centralized industries to destroy collective bargaining, and would thereby enable such industries to return to individual agreements with their workers.[66]

---

[65] *Ibid.*, page 265.
[66] *Ibid.*, pages 268–275; Reich, *op. cit.*, pages 138–151.

Union membership

The development of union membership showed two distinct phases: Startling gains in the first years of the Weimar Republic were followed by a steep decline after currency stabilization.

The gains in membership achieved by the unions in the 1919–1920 period were unprecedented and may be compared with those made in the United States during the later 1930's. The membership of the free unions was 1,453,877 on September 30, 1918, and was almost double that number at the end of the year. Gains continued until the high point of 8,144,981 members was reached in June, 1920. Slightly more than 80 per cent of the membership was enrolled in the 12 unions shown in Table 7.

TABLE 7

MEMBERSHIP IN THE TWELVE LARGEST GERMAN TRADE UNIONS, 1913 AND 1920

Unions	1920	1913	Increase
Metal workers	1,647,916	556,939	1,090,977
Agricultural workers	695,695	19,077	676,618
Factory workers	643,800	210,569	433,231
Transport workers	568,080	229,585	338,495
Textile workers	491,480	141,487	349,993
Building workers	470,749	326,631	144,118
Miners	450,320	104,113	346,207
Railroad workers	428,174	—	428,174
Wood workers	379,381	195,441	183,940
White-collar workers	376,400	32,384	344,016
Public workers	288,274	52,996	235,278
Clothing workers	143,590	49,978	93,612
	6,583,859	1,919,200	4,664,659

Source: Umbreit, *op. cit.*, page 195.

The greatest gains were made by the agricultural workers, the white-collar workers and the railroad workers, the latter having organized during World War I. It was, of course, to be expected that the well-organized skilled workers would gain the least proportionally.

Between 1923 and 1925, the unions suffered severe losses in membership. Aside from the Hirsch-Duncker unions, whose membership constituted an unimportant part of the total, the membership of both the free and Christian trade unions fluctuated widely in the decade of the 1920's. The relevant data on union membership are given in Table 8.

The loss of membership after 1923 was a direct consequence of currency reform with its tighter wage schedules, its unemployment, and its mounting employers' aggressiveness.

TABLE 8

MEMBERSHIP IN GERMAN TRADE UNIONS, 1918–1931

(*in thousands*)

Year	Free trade unions	Christian trade unions	Hirsch-Duncker	Total*
1913	2,574	343	107	3,024
1919	5,479	858	190	6,527
1921	7,568	986	225	8,779
1923	7,138	938	185	8,261
1925	4,156	588	158	4,902
1927	4,150	606	168	4,924
1929	4,906	673	169	5,748
1931	4,418	578	181	5,177

* This does not include the syndicalist unions.
Source: *Encyclopedia of Social Sciences*, Vol. 15, page 14. New York, 1935.

Labor setbacks

One of the most cherished gains of German labor, the eight-hour day, was temporarily lost during the employer offensive. German industrialists, led by heavy industry, began to snipe at the eight-hour day almost as soon as it was installed, but some felt it would be unwise to impose a longer workday by legislation without the support of the trade unions.[67] The demand for longer daily hours of work was based upon Germany's alleged inability, because of impoverishment caused by the war and by the need to raise reparation payments for the victorious powers, to afford the luxury of so short a workday. Acting under an enabling act of December, 1923, which gave it plenary power in economic, financial, and social matters, the government by decree permitted a working day in industry of more than eight hours. Employers took advantage of the severe decline in business to force the longer work day upon labor, and in an agreement with the three trade union centers, the North Western group of the Association of German Iron and Steel Industrialists abolished the eight-hour shift. Not until 1927 was the eight-hour day restored in this industry.[68]

The offensive of industry and the loss of membership by the unions encouraged the communists to fish in troubled waters. Communist influence in the free trade unions, in the mid-1920's, was quite substantial, although not as great as in the works' councils. In the election of delegates to the convention of the metal workers' union in 1923, the communists won one-third of the seats. A similar proportion of delegates at the convention of the textile workers was under communist influence. The communists, in an offensive against the leadership of

---

[67] Hugh Quigley and R. T. Clark, *Republican Germany: A Political and Economic Study*, pages 283–284. New York, 1928.
[68] *Ibid.*, pages 286–289.

the trade unions, called a conference of trade union representatives at Weimar, in November, 1923, under the slogan "save the trade unions." The Executive Committee of the Communist International regarded the slogan as an error, and while it advised communists to remain in the trade unions, it insisted that the main effort must be made among the unorganized and in winning control of the works' councils. According to the Comintern, only by changing their character and basing themselves upon the works' councils could the unions save themselves from destruction.

The heads of the Federation of Labor did not remain idle in the face of this attack; they denounced the attempt of the Communist Party to seize the trade union movement, and demanded that the city centrals that had sent delegates to the communist-directed Weimar conference repudiate their actions. In addition, a number of individual unions refused to seat communist delegates to their conventions. To counter this policy, the communists withdrew from the free unions and set up independent organizations of their own.[69]

In 1925, in response to a change in the international line of communism, many communist-influenced organizations tried to rejoin the free trade unions. But again in 1927, when Moscow abandoned the united front strategy, the Red Trade Union Opposition (RGO) was more or less officially given the task of splitting rather than conquering the unions and of promoting dual unionism. This change in tactics, while contributing to the weakening of the unions in the depression period, did not win the hoped for mass support for the communists. By and large, the trade unions were able to keep their organizations intact, though at the price of a deepening malaise among the rank and file.

Wages

The available evidence indicates that real wages declined very substantially during World War I, with the skilled workers suffering a much greater deterioration in their position than the unskilled.

As can be seen from Table 9, the first effect of the November Revolution was a substantial increase in real wages, but from the end of 1919 to 1924, the situation was reversed. Whereas up to 1919, the primary influence upon the workers' real income position had been the growth of trade unionism and the influence of the socialists upon government policy, the latter phase was predominantly determined by monetary causes. Beginning in 1920, prices outran money wages. Between 1920 and 1922, the index of real wages for skilled workers had dropped to

---

[69] Flechtheim, *op. cit.*, page 90–91; 112–115.

TABLE 9

INDEX OF REAL WAGES IN GERMANY, 1913 TO 1919

(*1913 = 100*)

Year	Government workers		Ruhr Miners	Printers
	Skilled	Unskilled		
1913	100	100	100	100
1914	97.2	97.2	93.3	97.2
1915	79.7	80.8	81.3	77.3
1916	69.2	73.8	74.4	60.6
1917	63.9	74.2	62.7	49.4
1918	83.3	99.8	63.7	54.1
1919	92.2	119.8	82.4	72.3

Source: Constantino Bresciani-Turroni. *The Economics of Inflation*, page 304. London: George Allen and Unwin, Ltd., 1937.

64, and in the next year to 58. Unskilled workers fared somewhat better; their real wages going to 86 in 1922 and 72 in 1923.[70] Professor J. W. Angell places the index of real wages for all labor at 75 in 1922 and 65 in 1923.[71] The reduction in real wages as a result of the catastrophic rise in prices led to difficulties in collective bargaining. At first it was agreed that the wage clauses could be reconsidered every two or three months while the other terms in the contract were to remain in effect for longer periods. Unions demanded cost-of-living adjustments, but this demand was resisted by employers. The executive board of the German Federation of Labor advised its constituent unions to seek guarantees of a given level of real wages from their employers as a means of meeting the constant and rapid decline in the value of money.[72]

In the summer of 1923, wage fixing on the basis of the cost-of-living index compiled by the Reich Statistical Bureau became well established. Many trade unions sought to compel the employer to accept automatic increases in money wages with rises in the cost of living, but the resistance of employers to the automatic formula compelled frequent negotiations with the labor unions, which were seeking to retain a constant real wage in the face of the inflationary rises that spread throughout the German economy.[73] But this method proved inadequate to achieve a stable real wage. Even the weekly fixing of wages based upon an index of prices failed to protect the workers' real

[70] J. H. Richardson, "Aspects of Recent Wage Movements," *International Labour Review*, (Feb. 1928), page 181; James W. Angell, *The Recovery of Germany*, page 256. New Haven: Yale University Press, 1929.

[71] *Ibid.*, page 256.

[72] Fritz Sitzler, "The Law of Collective Bargaining in Germany," *International Labour Review* (Oct. 1922), pages 513–514; *Ibid.* (Aug. 1923), page 224.

[73] Fritz Sitzler, "The Adaptation of Wages to the Depreciation of the Currency in Germany," *The International Labour Review* (May, 1924), pages 643–660.

wage, because the depreciation in the value of money was so rapid that wages received in a particular week had a smaller purchasing power the following week. Consequently, an agreement between the unions and employers, in August, 1923, set weekly wages for the coming week on the basis of anticipated prices in that week, so that the money wage received would be sufficient to purchase a given level of living. If the actual wage were either higher or lower than the wage assumed in the agreement, an adjustment was made in the wages for the next week. The constant rise in prices provoked widespread discontent, and the number of strikes, and workers involved in them, was very high between 1920 and 1923.

One of the more unstabilizing results of the inflation was the wide variability in money wages. According to the Reich Statistical Bureau, wages of miners were 47.7 per cent of the prewar level in January, 1923, 86.2 per cent in March, 47.6 per cent in July, and 81.2 per cent in October. Even greater variation of wages in the metal industry was reported.[74] There was also a tendency for wage differentials between skilled and unskilled workers, and between those of men and women, to become narrower.

Germany revalued her currency in October, 1923. A decree issued on October 15, 1923, established the *rentenmark* which, with other measures, halted the inflation and brought with it, for a time, a relatively stable price level.

Strikes

Germany soon faced serious labor difficulties; the number of workers involved in strikes during 1924 was the second highest of any year of the 1920's and the number of man-days lost was the highest in German history. (See Table 10.) Strikes in the chemical and mining industries in 1924 were due to employer efforts to lengthen the work day. The demand for the lengthened work day, as already noted, was based upon the assumed need of Germany, because of its reparations obligations, to use its resources more intensively. The same reason was given for maintaining a real wage below the prewar level. These views were not accepted by the unions that, instead, sought to recover some of the ground they had lost during the inflation. Many employer attempts to impose longer hours, or deny their employees higher wages, were defeated. According to Preller, average hourly wages rose during 1924 from 57 pfennig to 72.5 pfennig.[75]

Labor gained from the stabilization of the currency. According to

---

[74] Bresciani-Turroni, *op. cit.,* page 311.
[75] Preller, *op. cit.,* p. 319.

Angell,[76] average real wages of German labor went from 65 in 1923 (1913=100) to 81 in 1924, 97 in 1925, 96 in 1926, and 98 in 1927. Not until 1928, when the index was 104, did average real wages of German labor go beyond the level of the prewar year of 1913. The sharp recovery of real wages was in part a reaction to the low levels to which they had sunk during the inflation. Moreover, as soon as the new currency had been established, real wages ceased to be predominantly influenced by monetary forces. German industry improved both as a result of rationalization—increased efficiency due to technological change—and the influx of foreign capital which enabled industry to expand. Favorable conditions in the labor market strengthened labor's bargaining position, and increased productivity enabled industry to meet its higher wage bill without trenching upon profits.

TABLE 10

STRIKES AND LOCKOUTS IN GERMANY, 1920 TO 1932

Year	Number of disputes	Number of establishments affected	Number of workers involved	Man-days lost
1920	3,807	42,268	1,429,116	16,755,614
1921	4,455	55,237	1,489,454	25,874,452
1922	4,785	47,501	1,823,921	27,732,832
1923	2,046	24,175	1,606,501	12,477,712
1924	1,973	28,430	1,618,011	36,197,888
1925	1,730	25,162	753,647	16,934,820
1926	358	2,836	92,456	1,251,366
1927	853	10,403	485,658	7,148,250
1928	743	7,864	719,850	20,355,365
1929	435	8,584	179,667	4,254,877
1930	356	3,416	213,201	4,030,717
1931	478	4,744	167,572	1,893,723
1932	657	2,632	127,720	1,137,890

Source: Quoted from the *Statistiches Jahrbuch für das Deutsche Reich,* Vol. 45 in Reich, *op. cit.,* page 152.

The development of wage policy was essentially the function of the separate trade unions, and the German Federation of Labor had little to say about this area of activity. However, at their Breslau convention, in 1925, the free trade unions denounced the systematic efforts of employers to lower real wages and urged German trade unions to fight for a just wage. Resolutions urging the setting of wages and the making of agreements on a national rather than a local basis were also introduced at several conventions, but they were merely referred to the constituent unions for consideration.[77]

Industry expanded during the 1920's and, for technical and financial

[76] Angell, *op. cit.*, p. 256.
[77] Schwartz, *op. cit.,* pages 259–260.

reasons, the cartel and the large industrial agglomeration became very powerful in German economic life. At the end of 1928, German industry stood at the peak of its power. Yet there were serious *lacunae* in the rosy picture. Unemployment rose in 1926—1,750,000 workers found themselves without jobs in the summer of that year. The wave of unemployment temporarily receded, but in the winter of 1928–1929 it was again higher, reaching the unprecedented level of 2,600,000 workers.

Some movement to the left was noticeable in the elections to the Reichstag of 1928. A socialist, Herman Müller, became Chancellor. Renewed controversy over wage policy began when the employers' organizations insisted that wages could not be increased because they would adversely affect capital formation, which must now be nourished from internal savings rather than from capital imports. The unions rejected this view and demanded higher money wages to compensate for a rise in the cost of living. A number of large-scale strikes and lockouts took place over these issues in 1928, the cumulative effect of which is shown in Table 10.

Economic depression

The German economy faced increasing difficulties in 1929 and, with the spread of unemployment, attacks upon the wage level began again. On the ground that the cost of living had been lowered, employers demanded the lowering of wages. This was the basis upon which an arbitration board ordered a reduction in the wages of Berlin metal trades workers in 1930.

The economic crisis also brought with it an attack upon the social insurance system. Employers, through their organizations and their spokesmen in parliament, demanded a reduction in the employers' contribution to the unemployment fund and other funds for social security. Their main argument was, as in the case of wages, that costs had to be lowered to stimulate exports and that internal capital formation had to replace capital imports. The free unions and the Christian trade unions believed that only through the maintenance of social insurance benefits, especially to the unemployed, could the wage level of the employed be protected from undermining by the millions of idle workers. Moreover, they feared the effect of a cut in social expenditures upon the mood of the unemployed, lest a reduction in social services should drive them into the arms either of the communists or Nazis. The controversy came to a head in the latter part of March, 1930, when the moderate coalition government split over the question of increasing the federal government's contribution to the unemployment

insurance fund. Writing in behalf of the German Employers' Organization, two directors informed the government: "The employers base
themselves on the fact that a further increase of the contributions to
unemployment insurance is incompatible with the state of the economy
and also with the need for lightening the burden of economy as
emphasized by the Reich Government in its program." [78]

When Herman Brüning succeeded to power as Chancellor, he slashed
the social expenditures of the government. Wages and other prices fell,
and by March, 1932, the trade unions reported 6,128,000 workers
without jobs, which was believed to be an underestimate by 600,000.
Of the idle, 30.2 per cent were supported by unemployment insurance;
27.3 per cent received emergency relief; 29.9 per cent received ordinary
relief; and 12.6 per cent received no government aid.[79] In addition to
the unemployed, one-fourth of those working were engaged only on
part-time work. The impact of unemployment fell most heavily upon
workers in the younger age groups, especially those between the ages
of 18 and 21.[80]

Weimar trade union policies in retrospect

Together with the Social Democratic Party, the trade unions had
been the main architects of the Weimar state. The Legien-Stinnes
agreement, officially terminated in 1924, had opened the way for at
least a limited understanding between the two main social forces:
entrepreneurs and workers. During the Kapp Putsch the workers had
proved to be the main defenders of the Republic. The comprehensive
social insurance legislation, with 35 million workers insured in health
benefit funds, as well as the system of collective agreements, including
those officially extended to nonparticipants in collective bargaining,
had brought the majority of the salaried and wage-earners under this
system of "collective labor law." This system embraced equally the
government system of compulsory arbitration, the labor courts which
enforced it in individual cases, the labor offices, the government employment agencies, and the autonomous system of unemployment
insurance under joint administration of labor and employers.

The system rested on the active participation of the trade unions,
which had helped to construct it and had an important share in its
administration. The unions not only wanted to keep this system intact,

---

[78] Quoted in W. M. Knight-Patterson, *Germany from Defeat to Conquest*, page
461. London, 1945.

[79] *Protokoll der Verhandlungen des Ausserordentlichen (15) Kongresses der
Gewerkschaften Deutschlands*, pages 41–44. Berlin: Allegemeinen Deutschen
Gewerkschaftsbundes, 1932.

[80] Preller, *op. cit.*, pages 457–458, 473.

but, further, to extend it from the social welfare and labor sphere into the economic sphere proper. Here, with the exception of the not very important works' councils and the never fully implemented economic council legislation, the influence of the unions had been very limited; it did not extend beyond their potential political influence with the state or city administrations, the Reich Railway, and other public corporations with holdings in the field of transportation or public utilities. Conscious of this weakness, the free unions developed, in 1928, a comprehensive program of economic democracy which at the Hamburg congress, in 1929, was given official sanction. Instead of economic control on the plant level via the dead-end street of works' councils, labor now demanded its share in already existing or future supra-enterprise organizations which controlled the market and regulated production, sales, and prices.

But German labor in the years of depression, 1930 to 1932, did not have the power to press its economic program. Moreover, its program of economic organization was not accompanied by an equally farsighted work-creating program, but, under the influence of the social disaster caused by the earlier inflations, took a "neither inflation nor deflation" position. Aside from demanding work relief, the unions had no policy to meet the ravages of depression. Labor had to spend its main energies in fending off, not always successfully, attempts to turn the system of collective labor law, which was, as German labor thought, created for the defense and improvement of its standards, into an anti-labor weapon. Labor participation in social self-government could not prevent reductions in jobs; and wage, unemployment relief, and social insurance cuts. It even had to tolerate decrees permitting entrepreneurs to fix wages below those laid down in freely negotiated collective agreements. And having become a part of the official social administration machinery, labor, although without influence on major economic policies, was now held equally responsible for the ensuing social consequences of the economic debacle. This was the situation when the unions had to face the onslaught of the Nazi movement.

On January 30, 1933, the Papen-Hitler government came to power. It was the beginning of the end for the German trade union movement. The free unions pleaded for calm, and the head of the liberal Hirsch-Duncker unions joined the Nazis. The democratic unions did not rush to the Nazi bandwagon, and in the last elections for works' council representatives, held in April, 1933, the free unions polled 73.4 per cent of the vote. The free unions did, however, disassociate themselves from the Social Democratic Party and the International Federation of Trade Unions. This gesture did not save them from destruction, for a totalitarian government cannot tolerate independence in any sphere of activity, let alone one as important as labor organization. After proclaiming May 1st, the traditional socialist holiday, as a "holiday of national labor," the Nazi government ordered the occupation of the headquarters and offices of the unions. Leaders and subordinate officers were arrested and all property belonging to the organizations of labor seized. Many union officials were hurried off to prison and concentration camps; some were tortured and killed. At one blow, the great unions built up over 50 years, encouraged and strengthened by the Weimar Republic, were destroyed.

German Unionism Since 1945

In the place of the trade unions, the Nazis established the German Labor Front, a section of the National Socialist Workers' Party. While the trade unions were suppressed and their leaders hounded out of public life, their influence upon the German worker was not entirely erased. As the belief that the Nazis were to be defeated spread during the war, the free trade unions began to occupy a more significant place in the consciousness of the German worker. Underground work was extremely difficult, but some trade unionists managed somehow to retain contact with one another. Persecution of former officials was not infrequent, and some were periodically hustled off to jail or to a concentration camp. A leading trade unionist, Wilhelm Leuschner, was a participant in the abortive plot on the life of Hitler during the summer of 1944. He was executed with a number of other conspirators. There was a widespread belief that the trade unions would have to play an important role in the revival of German democratic life in the postwar period, but continual organized activity was extremely difficult and risky.[81]

General Eisenhower, in a radio broadcast upon the entry of Allied armies into the Rhineland, assured German labor that it would be allowed to establish free trade unions. In February, 1945, a meeting of trade unionists had taken place in Aachen with the approval of the Allied military authorities. This was made known by radio to the Germans still living under the Hitler regime. With the collapse of the Nazis, meetings to establish trade unions were held in many places and local unions set up. The organizers were limited in their activity by the regulations of the military occupying officers, and all organizations had to be approved.[82] Unions arose simultaneously in many

---

[81] *Bericht des Deutschen Gewerkschaftbundes Ortsausschuss Hamburg, über Wiederaufban und Tätigkeit der Hamburger Gewerkschaften im Jahre 1945–1947* pages 11–15. Hamburg: Freie Gewerkschaft, no date.

[82] *Die Gewerkschaftsbewegung in der Britischen Besatzung Zone,* pages 16–24. Koln: GMBH, 1949.

parts of Germany, and the first steps toward centralization were the formation of area federations, then zonal federations.

Soon after the liberation of Hamburg, a campaign to reestablish a trade union movement in that city was organized. At a conference in May, 1945, presided over by a former trade union officer, Adolph Schönfelder, an executive committee of 36 persons, 15 of whom had belonged to unions prior to 1933, was formed. In contrast to the unions existing prior to the rise of Hitler, the new organizations emphasized their nonpolitical and nonreligious outlook. All workers were welcomed, and questions of political and religious affiliation were held to be private matters.[83]

The establishment of unions in Hamburg led to emulation elsewhere. At the beginning of 1946, a conference of trade union representatives from Schleswig-Holstein and Hamburg set up an executive committee for that area. During March, 1946, the first trade union conference for the entire British zone was held at Hamburg, attended by 74 representatives. The delegates faced a tremendously difficult task. The once proud German labor movement no longer existed, and lacking funds and trained personnel, had to begin rebuilding at the "grass roots." Among the many problems facing the delegates was that of uniting all of the organizations. Unions had arisen independently and the difficulties of communication and travel in the early postwar years made fusion impossible. Nevertheless, the conference came out for a single union, and declared that the most important task of the unions was to represent the *economic* interests of labor. An executive committee headed by Hans Böckler was chosen.[84]

The leaders of the new trade unions were convinced that the division among the pre-Hitler trade unions contributed to the catastrophe that overtook the entire German labor movement on May 2, 1933. Therefore, they insisted that the new unions must not be divided on political or religious grounds. A determination to avoid the errors of the past was evident in the universal desire to prevent the competition that existed before 1933.[85]

The Eastern zone unions, the *Freie Deutsche Gewerkschaftsbund* (Free German Trade Union Association), seemed to have subscribed to the tenet of a united union movement with still greater alacrity. But the similarity is only superficial. While West German trade union unity was determined by the consideration that diversity of political creeds should not prevent the successful representation of the common

---

[83] *Bericht des Deutschen Gewerkschaftsbundes Ortsausschuss,* pages 29–36.

[84] *Ibid.,* pages 39–48.

[85] Adalbert Stenzel, "Die Gewerkschaftliche Organization der Angestellten", *Gewerkschaftliche Praxis* (March, 1949), pages 86–87.

economic interests of all workers and salaried employees, East German trade union unity derived from an attempt to streamline all union activity under the supervision of official communist authorities. Moreover the slogan of trade union unity was also thought useful as a weapon for easy penetration of the West German labor movement by East German emissaries.

Thus, at the first stage, the organizational patterns of postwar trade union organization were determined primarily by the varied policies of the occupation powers. Soviet-zone trade unions were designed from the very beginning as a centralized instrument for labor domination by the communist administration. In Western Germany, British policy early permitted individual trade unions to integrate into an all-zonal trade union federation; while in the United States zone of occupation the reestablishment of trade unions at the local level was, relatively early, followed by the building up of trade unions at the state but never at the zonal level. In the French zone, developments similar to those in the United States zone took place at a slower pace.

The program of the various Western trade unions echoed to a large extent the old demands for economic democracy and socialization of basic industries contained in the programs of their predecessors during the Weimar Republic. However, the actual functions of the unions in the pre-currency reform period remained rather narrowly circumscribed. With a wage freeze, and with money wages being of only secondary importance, the principal union function, the conclusion of collective agreements, remained without much importance. Emphasis during this period was, therefore, more on the rebuilding of organization and on support for all endeavors to revive German democratic institutions. Between 1946 and 1948, whether it were on a city or state-wide basis, West German public administration owed much of what little organized public support it had to the trade unions.

Sudden changes intervened with the currency reform in the summer of 1948. For the unions, this period brought increased tasks and new difficulties. Their treasuries were empty, but their members expected that they would now effectively represent their interests. There was coincidentally rapid progress in the economic and political integration of the Western zones. When the economic council for the combined economic area was set up in 1947, trade union representation had to transcend zonal and state lines. Therefore, a trade union council was constituted, in 1947, as an informal coordinating body of all West German trade unions. Mergers between individual industrial unions on a zone-wide basis went on increasingly; the next logical step was to unify the unions in the several Western zones. This movement was accelerated by Allied and German resolution not to wait any longer before merging Western Germany into a new federation. With the founding of the *Bundesrepublik Deutschlands* in the spring of 1949 and the elections to the Bonn parliament in August, 1949, the reestablishment of full West German trade union unity was no longer to be delayed.

The West German trade unions had by the end of their amalgamation become the most important mass organizations of Western Germany. The greatest union membership, 2,700,000, was achieved in the British Zone. In the United States Zone, the three state federations in Bavaria, Hesse, and Würtemburg-Baden had an aggregate membership of 1,700,000; while the unions in the French Zone established regional federations with a total membership in 1949 of about 400,000. By 1949, total union membership in the Western Zones reached 4,800,000, or 40 per cent of the labor force.

Soon after the end of hostilities, unions were also organized in the Soviet zone, and in February, 1946, the first general conference of the Soviet zone unions took place. The conference established the Free German Labor Federation and claimed a membership of 3,277,578. The organization proclaimed itself the sole representative of manual and white-collar workers, and declared that upon German labor rested a responsibility to aid in the reconstruction of Germany on the basis of the Potsdam agreement.[86] The affiliated unions were advised to enter into collective bargaining agreements, to aid in the establishment of a 45-hour week and a system of social insurance, welfare, and protective legislation. Eighteen industrial unions were set up. All workers in an enterprise were to belong to one union and were to be united with similar groups in other enterprises in nation-wide industrial unions. The most important administrative functions, among them finances, were centralized with the federation rather than the industrial unions. Top leaders were appointed from the ranks of the Communist Party with the addition of a few collaborators from the pre-1933 union hierarchy.

The Berlin trade unions had originally been organized as a part of the F.D.G.B. However, the help and assistance granted to noncommunist unionists by the Western occupation powers and the growing resentment against F.D.G.B. methods and procedures were soon felt. Despite communist control, the opposition gradually gained in influence and at the Berlin trade union conference in 1947, 75 opposition delegates were in attendance. This was only a prelude to events in the following year for, with the increased resistance to communist domination, the opposition elected 280 delegates to the conference. This number was

---

[86] *Geschäftsbericht des Freien Deutschen Gewerkschaftsbundes,* pages 18–23. Berlin: Die Freie Gewerkschafts, 1947.

large enough to control the proceedings, and an attempt was made to revoke the mandates of a large number of non-communist delegates. As a result, the opposition withdrew and organized the *Unabhängige Gewerkschafts Opposition*, or U.G.O.[87] The Provisional Executive Council of the U.G.O. declared that the "duty of trade unions is to represent the social and economic interests of the wage-earners in the economy, in the state, and in society. They proclaim their independence from the state, from all employers—private and public—and from all political parties." The autonomy of affiliated unions was approved, democratic rights of free speech, press, assembly were endorsed, and a more equitable distribution of income demanded.[88] The U.G.O. worked with the unions in the Western Zones, and in July, 1950, the Berlin independent trade union opposition merged with the German Federation of Labor.

During the split between U.G.O. and F.D.G.B., the official relationship between the West German unions and the F.D.G.B. of the Eastern zone continued. Altogether there were nine inter-zonal conferences held between the representatives of the two. However, the last conference, held near Lindau in August, 1948, was adjourned *sine die*, before the agenda could be taken up. Western delegates had insisted on admitting a delegation from the Berlin U.G.O., and when the request was refused by the F.D.G.B., the meeting was adjourned. A number of subsequent F.D.G.B. requests for a resumption of four-zone conferences were ignored by the West German union leadership. While it had been clear, since at least 1946, that the F.D.G.B. was neither a democratic nor an independent trade union organization, West German union leaders had for a long time tried to prevent a final rupture between Eastern and Western trade unions. They remained sincerely interested in any move which could prevent the final partitioning of Germany, and may also have thought that preservation of organizational ties would lead to a quicker elimination of communist control once four-zone unification was agreed upon by the occupying powers. As long as this possibility existed, Western union leadership avoided official contacts with the U.G.O., the anti-communist opposition union in Berlin, so as not to give the F.D.G.B. a pretext for severing contacts with Western unions. Only after the Soviet blockade of Berlin had destroyed all hope for a four-power agreement on German unification were the West German unions willing to terminate their official relations with the F.D.G.B.[89]

---

[87] *International Free Trade Union News,* September, 1948, page 2.
[88] *Ibid.,* October, 1948.
[89] Markus Schleicher, "New Life in Trade Unions in Germany," *International Free Trade Union News,* July, 1949, pages 2, 8.

The German Federation of Labor

In April, 1948, the trade unions of the American, British, and French zones selected a committee to devise a program for combining the labor organizations of the three zones into a common organization. At a conference in February, 1949, it was decided to call a convention for the launching of a unified trade union movement in Western Germany.[90] The convention held in October, 1949, established the German Federation of Labor (*Deutsche Gewerkschaftsbund*) or D.G.B., for the German Federal Republic. In attendance at the convention were 487 delegates representing almost 5,000,000 members. Hans Böckler, a metal worker who had headed the unions in the British zone, was elected to the top office of the Federation. The D.G.B. was made up of both manual and white-collar workers, and it aimed to help create an economy that would abolish social injustice and economic need. The Federation was to pursue a policy which would protect the rights of the individual and assure him a proper share of the social product; to seek an equal voice, or the right of co-determination of the worker, in all economic and labor questions of the economy. It advocated the socialization of basic industries, especially the coal, iron, steel, chemical, power, and credit industries. The convention was of the opinion that events between 1918 and 1933 had demonstrated the limitations of formal political democracy unless it were also supported by the democratizing of industry. The trade unions sought representation upon corporate boards of directors. They insisted that the economic policies of great corporations cease to be the exclusive province of a few managers, and that all pertinent information be made public. The D.G.B. endorsed technical improvement so that productivity could be increased, but insisted, in return, that such increases be translated into higher living standards. An assurance of maintenance of real wages was sought, and limited price control suggested as one means.

The struggle for the improvement of the standard of living and conditions of labor was declared to be a main task of the trade unions. Regulation of wages and working conditions was to be the joint task of the union and the employer, but protection by other methods was to be accorded those in an exposed position in the labor market. Reconstruction of the social insurance system and protection against the exploitation of women and young workers were demanded. Equal pay for equal work was announced as a guiding principle, and opposition registered to all measures restricting the right to organize. How-

---

[90] *Protokoll Grundungskongress des Deutschen Gewerkschaftsbundes,* pages 64–82. Cologne; G.M.B.H., 1950.

ever, the affiliated trade unions were advised that the strike was to be the last means used, and required approval by at least 75 per cent of those voting in a strike ballot. If a strike were called in disregard of this provision, the union was not to be obligated to finance support of the strikers and was required to seek the return of the strikers to the job.[91]

TABLE 11

MEMBERSHIP IN THE GERMAN FEDERATION OF LABOR AND THE GERMAN
UNION OF WHITE-COLLAR WORKERS, MARCH 31, 1951 (EXCLUDING BERLIN)

Trade union	Membership	Per cent of total membership*
Metal	1,418,441	26.0
Public services, transport traffic	695,013	12.7
Mining	590,897	10.8
Railway	419,410	7.7
Textile and clothing	417,309	7.6
Chemicals, paper, ceramics	418,607	7.6
Building, stone and earth	389,285	7.1
Food, beverages, restaurants	253,759	4.7
Woodworking	193,320	3.5
Post and telegraph	176,240	3.2
Printing and paper	124,920	2.3
Gardening, agriculture, forestry	104,610	1.9
Leather	101,852	1.9
Commerce, banking, insurance	69,406	1.3
Education and science	56,825	1.0
Art, professions	39,463	0.7
(*Total*) Federation of Labor	*5,469,357*	*100.0*
White-Collar Workers	291,548	5.1
Grand total	*5,760,905*	*100.0*

* These percentages are given for the 16 Federation unions in percentage of the Federation total, while the corresponding percentage for the White-Collar Union is computed as a proportion of the combined Federation-White-Collar total.
Source: Deutscher Gewerkschaftsbund, *Mitgliederstand am 31 Maerz 1951.*

The D.G.B. is made up of 16 industrial organizations, the membership of which is shown in Table 11, as of March 31, 1951. Since the D.G.B. functions, in principle at least, along industrial lines, it could not tolerate separate white-collar or civil servant organizations within itself. However, in so far as the latter groups are concerned, dual unionism exists in the form of the Union of White-Collar Workers (*Deutsche Angestellten Gewerkschaft*) with about 300,000 members, and the revived Association of German Government Employees, the latter more a professional organization than a trade union. Otherwise, jurisdictional conflicts between affiliates of D.G.B., which are not infrequent due to the existence of a number of catch-all unions, are taken care of by D.G.B. arbitration boards.

[91] *Ibid.,* pages 318–339.

The Federation is directed by a president, two vice-presidents, and eight additional full-time officers, all elected by the D.G.B. convention. In addition, there is an executive committee composed of the chairmen of the 16 affiliated unions; if issues concerning individual districts are discussed, the district chairmen are invited to join the meeting of the executive committee, which between conventions conducts the business of the organization.[92] The charter provides for a system of distribution of functions between the Federation and the individual unions, with the broad issues of social, economic, and cultural policy reserved for the Federation, and the more specific areas, such as collective bargaining, particular industrial disputes or relations with individual union members, left with the industrial unions.

While this delimitation leaves much room for uncertainty, the wording of the charter is very clear as to the seat of financial authority. The Federation has only three derivative financial sources: (a) 15 per cent of all dues collected by the affiliated unions; (b) the quarterly DM 0.15 per capita contribution to the DM 10 million solidarity fund administered by the Federation and (c) such special assessments as the enlarged executive board, consisting of a majority of representatives from the industrial unions, may be willing to vote for Federation purposes out of the purses of the affiliated unions.

In the practice of the last two years, Hans Böckler, the forceful president of the D.G.B., backed up by the work of its Research Institute in Cologne and working harmoniously with the leaders of the big industrial unions, exercised a strong leadership in union affairs. However, whether his successor, Christian Fette, who was elected at the second D.G.B. Congress in June, 1951, will be able to play the same role, or whether leadership will fall to the heads of the three or four most powerful industrial unions, is still an open question.

The D.G.B., like its predecessors in the Western zones, is politically neutral. This neutrality means that the unions are not organizationally committed to any political party, but rather represent an independent force pursuing their own social and economic objectives. These goals, which go beyond the mere protection of the immediate interests of the worker, cover a broad field of economic and social activity. Since these ends can be reached only through political action, union "neutrality" is, however, in the long run only conditional. The unions are not neutral toward any political organization that, though following a catch-all approach to all social groups, aims, in reality, at the destruction of the democratic state and, with it, of free trade unionism.

---

[92] Albin Karl, "German Trade Union Movement—Its Structure and Operation," *International Free Trade Union News* (March, 1951).

This attitude dominates the unions' rejection of the Communist Party and neofascist groups.

There are altogether about 28 major union functionaries among the 402 members of the Bundestag, 20 of them sitting with the Social Democratic Party and some 8 with the Christian Democrats. The unions, hitherto, have not supported any political organization through financial subsidies. In most issues of domestic social and economic policy, the policies of the socialists and the D.G.B. are almost identical. However, in matters of foreign policy, such as the Ruhr authority and the Schumann Plan, the D.G.B. has taken a line which deviates from the socialist policies and is more favorable to the government.

Employers' associations

Upon coming to power, the Nazis dissolved the employers' associations, and replaced them with economic associations that occupied a place in relation to the employer that the Labor Front did in relation to the worker. The collapse of Nazi power did not witness an immediate revival of employers' organizations; the occupation authorities were not sympathetic to such ventures, as leading employers were politically suspect because of their reputedly close ties with the Nazis. Gradually, the hostility was relaxed, and employer associations were organized in all the Allied zones. At the beginning, they were limited to single industries, and, in the main, confined themselves to offering suggestions and advice on social and political questions. With the relaxation of the "wage stop" in November, 1948, the employer associations began to occupy themselves with collective bargaining. As a result, their number increased. In general, a tendency was shown for the employer organization active in collective bargaining to avoid political activity, a separate group being formed, under these circumstances, for the promotion of social and political policy. In some instances, however, the same employers' group may perform both economic and political functions. Both kinds of organizations exist, with employer groups in homogeneous industries showing a preference for combining the two functions in one body.

The growth of organization among employers soon led to a merger of groups in different industries. Some opposition to this tendency was shown by the American occupation authorities, but the British showed no hostility to this development. The inter-industry employer groups have attempted to influence social and political policy.[93]

The trade unions early showed pronounced hostility toward the

---

[93] D. F. MacDonald, *Employers' Associations in Western Germany*, Berlin: Office of Military Government, Manpower Division, 1949.

revival of the employer groups.[94] However, the necessity of finding a partner able to bargain collectively on a supra-enterprise level soon broke the ice.

Collective bargaining

In 1946 the occupation authorities issued rules for the reestablishment of labor courts, works' councils, and the conciliation and arbitration of labor disputes. In general, the patterns established under the Weimar Republic were followed. It was not possible, at first, to win many economic concessions through collective bargaining, since only a few and relatively unimportant issues were subject to negotiation.

At the beginning, the unions faced not only difficulties arising from lack of office space and equipment, and availability of communication and transportation, but also the controls set up by the Allied authorities. A serious obstacle for the trade unions was the regulation of the major terms of employment by the occupation governments as a means of holding down wage increases which might have fed the fires of inflation. The freezing of wages removed this major question from the area of collective bargaining, although the regulations did permit the elimination of sub-standard wages, defined as wage rates of less than 0.50 marks per hour, and the equalization of the wages of women workers with those of men, providing similar conditions and productivity obtained.[95]

The stabilization of the currency on June 20, 1948, drastically curtailed the fluctuation in the value of money and increased the importance of wage bargaining. Wage increases could now, within limits, be translated into a greater amount of goods, and this tended to stimulate collective bargaining, especially after the abolition of the "wage stop." The government's right to extend collective bargaining contracts to employers and employees not covered by an agreement was re-established in 1949. Extension of a contract to firms not participating in direct negotiations with a union is allowed only if 50 per cent of the workers in an industry are already covered and if the public interest so demands. However, neither the Allied legislation nor hitherto issued German legislation provides for arbitration awards binding on the parties without their express consent. This deviation from Weimar law and practice is supported by both employers and trade unions. The memory of the salary cuts through official fiat, after 1929, are still fresh in the minds of the trade unions, and, at

[94] George Philip Dietrich, *The Trade Union Role in the Reconstruction of Germany,* Berlin: Office of Military Government, Manpower Division, 1949.
[95] Matthew A. Kelley, "The Reconstitution of the German Trade Union Movement," *Political Science Quarterly* (March, 1949), pages 42–44.

least as long as a free market economy lasts, the unions expect more
from the exercise of their own strength than from a reliance on govern-
ment-determined arbitration awards.[96]

Works' councils

Works' councils were spontaneously organized and they received
legal standing from the occupation authorities in April, 1946. Right
from the beginning, the unions in the Western zone favored giving the
councils a voice in the formation of "production policy along with
matters directly affecting conditions of employment such as hiring,
firing, promotions, welfare, safety and recreational measures, and the
like." [97] Others looked upon the works' councils as a means of improving working conditions in the plant rather than as an instrument for
labor control of industry. Among trade unions, "the exercise of codetermination, where accepted by employers, has resulted in joint
undertakings not unlike those engaged in under labor-management
cooperation in certain industries in the United States." [98]

Some of the *land* or provincial constitutions, followed by some
implementing legislation, granted the works' councils the right to a
voice in the making of economic decisions by the enterprise, but this
right was suspended until a decision had been made whether this
question was to be under the jurisdiction of the central or *land* governments. In the end, both the central and *land* governments were
authorized to legislate on this issue, but Federal legislation was to
supersede the enactments of the *lander* on this question whenever a
conflict arose.

Unified works' councils are chosen by all employees in the shop,
irrespective of their affiliation or nonaffiliation with an organization
of labor. However, unions are allowed to endorse a list of candidates
in the council elections. Moreover, works' councils are required to
cooperate with the unions and thereby the organizations of labor can
exercise a significant influence over the councils. As in the pre-Hitler
period, the negotiation of collective agreements is lodged with the
unions, but the works' councils have considerable authority in the
administration of agreements and in the handling of grievances.[99]
Trade union influence over works' councils was difficult to establish
during the period before currency stabilization when unions had little

---

[96] E. Buehrig, *Gewerkschaften und Schlichtungswesen*, pages 16–17. Cologne:
Bundesverlag, 1950.

[97] Matthew A. Kelley, "Communists in German Labor Organizations," *Journal
of Political Economy* (June 1949), page 223.

[98] *Ibid.*, page 223.

[99] Paul Fisher, *Works Councils in Germany*, pages 10–11. Office of the United
States High Commissioner for Germany, Office of Labor Affairs, 1951.

to offer. But since then, the old union-works' council relationship, with the council as the extended arm of the union, has reasserted itself.

Codetermination and economic democracy

A voice in policy making (*Mitbestimmungsrecht*) within industry has been one of the demands continually repeated by leaders of the revived German unions. The desire for more active participation in the making of policy was often expressed by the unions under the Weimar Republic. It served as the very foundation of the already mentioned demand for economic democracy,[100] elaborated by the trade unions just before the economic crisis.

With the re-establishment of labor organizations in 1945, the issue of economic democracy, or codetermination, reappeared. At first, it manifested itself in the demand that works' councils be consulted on personnel decisions. Union representatives in the American and British zones, in a joint statement issued early in 1947, demanded that economic self-government supplement political self-rule, and that the regulation of economic processes not be left to a management bureaucracy, but rather be shared by all groups. The statement suggested the formation of joint councils of employer and labor representatives for the working out of a program for allocation of economic resources and price setting. The desire of labor for codetermination was supported by both the Social Democratic Party and the Christian Democratic Union. The second general meeting of Catholics at Bochum in November, 1949, approved codetermination "in social, personnel and economic affairs as a natural right" which should be promptly realized.[101]

The wide political and labor support of codetermination forced this issue to the attention of the federal government in the form of a demand that codetermination be applied immediately to the coal and steel industries.[102] It was the view of the late leader of the German Federation of Labor, Hans Böckler, that totalitarianism could be prevented in Germany only by the extension of democracy from the political to the economic sphere. The German trade unions regarded their right to participation in policy decisions in industry as the only guarantee for Germany's future democratic growth, and the steel

[100] Wirtschaftsdemokratie, *Ihr Wesen, Weg und Ziel,* edited by Fritz Naphtali, Berlin, 1928.

[101] *Herder Korrespondenz Orbis Catholicus* (October-November, 1949), page 31.

[102] I am indebted to L. Bruck for making available to me in advance of publication a series of articles on this question to appear in the *International Free Trade Union News.*

workers and coal miners were ready to strike for the establishment of this principle. The view of the *Bundeskanzler* that strikes should be called only over issues that arise within the framework of the collective agreement, and that codetermination is a legal and not an economic issue, was rejected. Böckler pointed out that under the law regulating the right to organize and the making of collective contracts, the workers had the right to intervene, through united action, in any economic question.[103]

The rising opposition to the key demands of German labor was a threat to the moderate policies and cooperation that the German unions had followed. Having gained the right of codetermination in two major industries as a consequence of Allied decree regulations, German labor sought assurance that these rights would be maintained. Since the unions were uncertain whether the federal government and industry would be willing to confirm its originally Allied-imposed prerogatives, the unions began to think of using the strike weapon. On October 12, 1950, a conference of works' council chairmen representing 130,000 steel workers voted to use available trade union methods to prevent the restriction of codetermination. As a next step, the Metal Workers Industrial Union held a referendum on whether a strike was to be called for the enforcement of codetermination, and received an overwhelming vote of affirmation. A strike vote among the miners yielded similar results.

On January 25, 1951, representatives of the trade unions and the employers in the steel and coal industries met under the chairmanship of Chancellor Adenauer and agreed to grant labor the right of codetermination. The Chancellor promised to submit to the federal parliament legislation necessary to implement the agreement; and upon this promise the unions in the coal and steel industries called off their planned strikes, scheduled for February 1, 1951, to enforce codetermination. As specified in the agreement, codetermination means equal representation of the unions and stockholders upon the supervisory boards (*Aufsichtsräte*) of the steel and coal companies. The unions were also given the right to propose the appointment of one member to the individual management boards of the coal and steel companies.

While the agreement rightfully attracted widespread attention, it, in fact, only recognized relations that had existed in the major segment of the steel industry since 1947. At the beginning of 1947, 24 decartelized steel companies had been established, and the unions were allowed equal representation on the boards of directors of the companies. These boards, made up of eleven members, had five trade union representatives. Under the new arrangement, the board of directors of eleven

---

[103] *Die Quelle* (January 1951), pages 3, 49–50.

members will have five representatives of labor and five of management. Two of the representatives on the labor side are to be chosen by the works' councils, two (and this is the most important and most controversial point, only very reluctantly granted by industry), will be selected directly by the competent union, continuing a practice introduced in 1947. The fifth labor representative, also to be union-proposed, analogous to the fifth management representative, shall be a quasi-public representative picked from outside union or employer ranks. The eleventh man, the umpire, so to speak, is to be elected by the other ten by a majority of at least three from each group; if the ten fail to agree on the eleventh member, a complicated procedure with mediation committees and possible appeals court intervention is invoked, with the ultimate possibility of his selection by a stockholder's meeting.

The German Federation of Labor has disavowed any desire to infringe upon the functions of management. It argues, however, that in view of the importance of labor in the economy the right to choose supervisory organs should not be the exclusive right of management. In the years immediately following the collapse of the Nazi regime, employers in the steel industry were very favorable to codetermination, and the head of the Kloeckner Steel Works wrote to the trade unions: "We at Kloeckner's think that the reorganization of the steel industry must be effected in order to respond to changed conditions, and that, in this connection, it is above all necessary to establish the actual equality—that is, the equality of rights as well as the responsibility of capital and labor." [104] With the passing of time, German employers became more opposed to this scheme, and they were particularly anxious to prevent the appointment to joint committees of anyone not connected with the enterprise. This would have meant the exclusion of "outside" trade unionists or experts from the boards of directors.

Codetermination is basically an attempt to give to labor a voice in the making of industry decisions. It is undoubtedly influenced by the socialist views of pre-Nazi German labor, but it carries an implied recognition that nationalization does not solve the labor problem. Codetermination focuses upon problems that have not interested American labor, except for some small segments of it. American unions have so far sought to gain influence only over these areas that directly affect the workers' wages and working conditions. Influenced, in part, by the experiences during the Great Depression, but also cognizant of the role that industry played in the rise of Hitler, German labor would like to keep a closer watch on business policies. German unions, in

---

[104] Quoted from *Gesetzvoschlag des Deutschen Gewerkschaftsbundes zur Neuordnung der deutschen Wirtschaft* (May 22, 1950), in Bruck, *op. cit.*

common with the remainder of the German community, are hospitable to overall economic planning, and they may regard a voice in industrial decision-making as one of the steps that will promote planned economic activity. There is also a possibility that codetermination is a partial substitute for socialism which has lost, because of the Nazi and Soviet experience, some of its glamour.

The German unions have worked hard to have codetermination accepted both by industry and government and, equally important, to bring it under their control. The earlier codetermination legislation, which found expression in the Hesse 1948 law, had concentrated codetermination rights exclusively in the hands of the respective works' councils. This the unions could not allow, since it would not only possibly have revived the antagonism between works' councils and unions, but also, as the Weimar experience had conclusively shown, because isolated works' councils without union guidance would not be able to utilize their prerogatives in the interest of the community as a whole.

It would be foolhardy to forecast developments in the field of codetermination. It will suffice to note that as industry acquires confidence, its will to resist the encroachments upon its historical prerogatives grows. The cold war has strengthened the bargaining position of German industrialists, who have already shown signs of their intent to challenge the system of codetermination. German employers demonstrated, during the Weimar Republic, their ability to reduce to impotence the desire of workers to secure certain kinds of industrial information. Whether they can frustrate the present aims of German labor only the future can reveal. However, it is necessary to remember that the German unions are embarking upon an Herculean task at a time when their cadres have been depleted and when many of their leaders are lacking in adequate experience.

Whatever the outcome of codetermination, the rise of a democratic labor movement in Germany has been one of the most significant developments of the postwar era. Relatively stronger than before the rise of Hitler, it is also free from the taint of the other totalitarianisms. It is well disciplined and shows promise of being a bastion for the defense of civil and human rights, a means for the improvement of the economic and social position of the German worker, and a barrier against dictatorship, of the right or of the left.

Chapter 5

FRANCE—VAL R. LORWIN

History of Trade Union Development

A series of revolutions and wars have been the natural frontiers in time that have shaped not only the forms of government, but the growth of the economy, and the life of workers' organizations in modern France. The workers who marched against the Bastille, in 1789, and the Tuileries, in 1792, were not an industrial proletariat; they were artisans and handicraftsmen; the first steam engine had not yet been introduced in France. But, in this case, as in others of the "century of revolutions," these workers who did the heavy manual labor of revolution did not collect its rewards.

The revolution swept aside the gilds and corporations that had long regulated economic life but, harnessed to the state, had lost their vitality. In 1791, the National Assembly gave each citizen the right to "practice any trade or craft which he pleases." It condemned the gilds as "a source of abuse because of the length of the apprenticeship, the servitude of the journeyman, the expenses of entrance: they hurt the public in restricting commerce." The journeymen made use of their new-found freedom in a series of strikes, caused by rising prices. This alarmed the master workmen, who gave forth a cry echoed down to our day: "Is this the time, when the prices of everything should go down, for the workers to make such demands?" The National Assembly, in response and in the name of the new individualism, passed the Le Chapelier Law. This law, identifying the new combinations with the abolished gilds, prohibited workmen's associations under "any pretext or in any form." Members of the same trade or occupation, entrepreneurs, storekeepers, workers, or journeymen were forbidden, if assembled, to name officers, keep records, deliberate or pass resolutions, or adopt regulations "on their pretended common interests." Specifically, it declared that "all gatherings of artisans, workers, journeymen, or laborers against the free exercise of industry and of work to which all persons have a right under any condition agreed upon by private contract" were "seditious assemblies."

A few days after the passage of the law, Le Chapelier informed the Assembly that it might be necessary to make an exception to the new law for the chambers of commerce, employers' organizations. "Certainly you understand well," he said, "that none of us intends to prevent the merchants from discussing their common interests." The Assembly voted agreement.

Napoleon's legislation continued the discrimination against workers' collective action. Every workman had to have a workbook (*livret*), without which he could not be employed. Essentially a police measure, this was justified as "guarantying workshops against desertion, and contracts against violation." The Penal Code punished workers' "coalitions" with imprisonment. Employers' coalitions were to be punished with fines and shorter prison terms, but only if they tended "to force down wages unjustly and abusively." In disputes over wages, the employer's word was to be taken. This was, except for a brief moment in 1848, the spirit of French legislation until 1864. Enforcement of these prohibitions on labor organization varied from severe repression, jail sentences, and fines, to indulgence and tolerance, depending upon the political aims of the workers' organizations, and the temper of the government, at the particular time.

The beginnings of the Industrial Revolution in the first half of the nineteenth century were later, and on a smaller and slower scale, than in England, but accompanied by the same harrowing abuses. Textile production was the one branch of industry where factory conditions tended to prevail; although, even in textiles, domestic work and small workshops remained important. The workday was 13, 14 or 15 hours. Women and children were employed in large numbers, for a fraction of men's meager wages. Factory hygiene was miserable. Housing in industrial cities, such as Lille, Rouen, and Nantes, was filthy, crowded, dank, and unlighted. A series of crises and periodic unemployment made the workingman's budget a matter of "almost constant anguish."

The first ameliorative legislation was not passed until 1841; and this applied only to workplaces employing over 20 people. It forbade the employment of children under 8 years of age, and set an 8-hour maximum workday for children of from 8 to 12, a 12-hour day for those between 12 and 16, and prohibited night work for children under 12. In parliamentary discussion, however, the manufacturers had succeeded in eliminating provisions for a paid inspectorate; inspectors were to be former manufacturers, serving without pay. So "it was not surprising that the law was only very inadequately applied."[1] The law was not recast until 1874.

---

[1] Henri Sée, *Histoire Economique de la France,* Vol. II, *Les Temps Modernes,* page 191. Paris, 1942.

Preunion organization

Despite the restrictive legislation, some workers' organizations did spring up in the first half of the century.[2] Those who sought to organize were largely artisans, employees of small shops, and home workers. Hatters, printers, bronze foundrymen, carpenters, stonemasons, painters, plumbers, shoemakers, tailors, jewelry workers, and weavers were among the first crafts to organize. Except for the Lyon silk weavers, none of these could be called industrial workers. They were, in most cases, the crafts least touched by industrial concentration, and they were better off than the workers in larger-scale industry.

The forms of organization, in this "preunion" period, were essentially of three kinds: *compagnonnages,* mutual aid societies, and "resistance societies." (The lines of distinction were sometimes blurred.) The *compagnonnages,* descendants of the gilds abolished by the Revolution, had the oldest roots. They were secret societies of journeymen workers, with admission based on tests of technical skill. Restricted to bachelor workmen, they helped their members travel, learn, and work across the country in the "tour of France" that was a living tradition during much of the nineteenth century. With a strong corporate feeling of solidarity within each group, they were constantly embroiled in bloody rows among themselves. They exercised a control over the supply of labor in a number of skilled trades, and until 1830 they were the only effective workingmen's organizations.

The mutual aid society, like the English friendly society, insured its members against work accidents, illness, and unemployment. Such associations had already begun to take form under the Old Regime, and despite the Le Chapelier law they continued to exist. By 1823, the printers of Paris alone had 30 such societies with 2600 members, but that was almost one-fourth of all the mutual aid societies of Paris then in existence. The authorities showed some justified suspicion that the societies might go beyond mutual aid, and might fight for their members' economic interests against employers.

The resistance societies that developed secretly or openly after the Revolution of 1830 aimed to defend the worker not so much against ill fortune as against the employer. They fought against the wage cuts

---

[2] For general history and description of the unions before World War I see: Lewis L. Lorwin, *Syndicalism in France,* 2nd edition. New York: 1914; and the article "Syndicalism" in *Encyclopedia of the Social Sciences;* Edouard Dolléans, *Histoire du Mouvement Ouvrier, 1830–1936,* 3d. edition, 2 Vols. Paris, 1948; Paul Louis, *Histoire du Mouvement Syndical en France,* 2 Vols. Paris, 1947 and 1948; Jean Montreuil (Georges Lefranc), *Histoire du Mouvement Ouvrier en France des Origines à nos jours.* Paris, 1947; and Maxime Leroy, *La Coutume Ouvrière,* 2 Vols. Paris, 1913.

made possible by the introduction of machines and the flocking of workers to the cities. The Paris copper smelters' society, for example, was founded in 1833 "to resist peacefully any abusive and unjust reduction" in wages. Like a mutual aid society, it proposed to aid aged and infirm members. But, in addition, it proposed to pay two francs a day (a normal day's wage) to any member unemployed because of his refusal to accept an unjust wage cut, or for any other reason judged in the interests of the craft. On this basis it recruited more than a thousand members. At Lyon, the society of the silk weavers (actually not the proletariat of the industry, but the working subcontractors) united to obtain a reasonable wage for their labor. They waged a spectacular strike in 1831. This began with a sort of collective agreement for the setting of wages in the silk industry, and turned into a confused insurrection, after employers refused to be bound by the new agreement.

The Revolution of 1830 gave a momentary impetus to organization. The workers, who in the "Three Glorious Days" of the Paris revolt overturned the Restoration Monarchy, naively assumed that they had obtained a new economic liberty, as well as political freedom. They soon discovered that they had obtained little of either. There was a brief flourishing of workers' organizations, and then, following the 1834 law against any associations of more than twenty persons (directed chiefly against republican clubs), a period began when organization, economic or republican in purpose, had to be secret.

The 1840's, sometimes cruelly called the "Hot-Air Forties," were a decade of great social questioning and striving. Humane socialist thinkers were at work. From these men Marx was later to take many ideas, although he ridiculed their lack of "scientific" spirit. Cooperation was being eagerly discussed as a road to social. emancipation, and workers' cooperative production and credit societies were being launched. There was a new ferment of labor organization, and the monarchy showed a considerable but uncertain tolerance, broken by prosecutions, fines, and imprisonment. The printing trades were, as often happens, in the lead in organizing. The Paris typographers founded an organization that soon included about half of the workers in the trade in Paris; and in a joint commission with the employers it set wage rates in what was in effect a collective agreement.

In February 1848, after a year of economic crisis, the government of Louis Philippe was swept away. As in 1830, the political leaders of the opposition were quite unprepared for their sudden victory, but this time the people of Paris insisted on the proclamation of the Republic. The provisional government included one socialist, Louis Blanc, and one worker. The workers expected more than this, for unemployment was widespread, but they were willing to give the government a chance. "The people put three months more of misery at your disposal," they hopefully declared to the provisional government in February. The government's one speedy response was to organize "national workshops" to create employment. The work projects chosen were, however, crude, discouraging, and largely useless, and the whole program was placed under the direction of an enemy of the scheme. In June, with 40,000 enrolled in Paris in the "workshops," the government suddenly closed them down. The workers demonstrated in confused protest. "When the bourgeoisie takes fright, it quickly becomes cruel," remarks one of the best social historians of France.[3] The alarmed government let its Minister of War, General Cavaignac, take over the handling of the workers. In a tactic that was to be used again in 1871, he let the workers throw up barricades, then slowly and systematically cleaned them out, and killed or dispersed the rioters. At least 3,000 workers were killed in the fighting of the "June Days," and the working-class movement was crushed.

George Sand said at the time, "I no longer believe in a Republic which begins by killing its proletarians." These "June Days" left a deep impression on French workers. In it they saw, as later they felt they saw repeated in other struggles, the crushing by force of their demands for simple economic justice; the alliance of bourgeoisie and government; the indifference of bourgeois politicians; the appeal to the army against the people; the betrayal of a revolution they had made. When the assembly voted a large credit to aid workers' producer cooperatives, it was too late, and three years later, the workers of Paris did not rise when Louis Napoleon overthrew the Republic.

The Second Empire

The two decades under the "little Napoleon" marked a speedup in the tempo of industrialization and a promising growth in union organization that came to a tragic halt in 1871. France moved from an essentially artisanal stage toward that of an industrial power. The old system of the little workshop and the home worker was not wiped out by the factory, however, and for a long time the two systems of production were to exist alongside of each other. The number of establishments with power-driven machinery increased from 6,540 to 22,850, while the machinery in industry increased from 76,000 horsepower to 336,000. Railroad trackage was built up from 3,685 kilometers to almost 18,000 kilometers. The iron and steel industry, long

---

[3] Georges Duveau, introduction to Edouard Dolléans, *Victoire des Obscurs*, page 5. Paris, 1936.

somnolent behind walls of protection, was pushed into greater activity by the Anglo-French treaty of 1860 and the winds of competition it let into France. The joint stock company, favored by new legislation, for the first time assumed importance as a form of organization and a source of capital.

In this period we find the "last generation of employers of working class origin." [4] The new lines of class were being frozen. Paris showed the change in the dwellings of the citizens who set the pattern for so much of the national life. As a result of the renovation of the city by Baron Haussmann and the enrichment of the middle classes, bourgeoisie and workers ceased, to a marked degree, to inhabit the same tenements, or even the same *quartiers*. Many workers' families moved into suburbs almost totally working class in character, and the bourgeoisie moved into luxurious neighborhoods. The visible breach was enough to make the economist Chevalier declare, "There are now two hostile temperaments (*natures ennemies*): the bourgeois temperament and the proletarian." [5]

The latter years of the Empire saw the first great advance in the legal status of labor organizations. The laws against strikes had never fully prevented them, as the figures on the many prosecutions for "coalitions" show. Anxious to rally workers' support to offset the loss of support among many of the propertied, the Empire made a number of concessions. In 1864, it repealed the old ban on strikes, although it did not formally grant the right of either assembly or association. Two years earlier it had permitted a delegation of freely-chosen Paris workers to go to the London Exposition of 1862. The delegates were impressed by the strength of the English unions, by their legal rights, and by the better wages and the organization of work in England. The visit led to the French participation in the founding of the First International in 1864. By 1870, the French sections of the International—some political groups, but most trade union sections—numbered perhaps 200,000 members, and were the most important component of the International. In the general, though uncertain, tolerance of the "liberal Empire," there was a great growth in workingmen's organizations. In Paris, practically every trade had its local union or *"chambre syndicale"* by the time of the Franco-Prussian War. There, and in several other large cities, the unions of various trades were forming the first city-wide federations, when the Franco-Prussian War halted the movement of organization and federation.

---

[4] Georges Duveau, *La Vie ouvrière en France sous le second Empire*, page 415. Paris, 1946.

[5] Michel Chevalier, *La Rive Gauche* (July 25, 1863), cited by Georges Duveau, *op. cit.*, page 412.

The existing organizations were swept away by the war's after-math, the uprising known to history as the Paris Commune, and its suppression by the Provisional Government of the newly-declared Republic. The Commune [6] was unprepared and spontaneous, a mixture of many motives: patriotic ardor to continue the war against the Prussians; a vague desire for a "social" (rather than a conservative) republic; a desire for local autonomy, particularly the autonomy of Paris; and an accumulated series of avoidable minor grievances. Tragic blunders were committed on both sides, and violence done which has not yet been forgotten. It was 1848 again, only far worse, because many on both sides remembered the June Days of 1848. Thiers, who had taken fright in 1848, was now head of the Provisional Government at Versailles, and he avenged himself on what he called the "vile multitude." When the purposely deliberate recapture of Paris was complete, when 17,000 Communard prisoners had been shot out of hand, Thiers telegraphed to the prefects in every department: "The ground is strewn with their corpses; this frightful spectacle will serve as a lesson," and affirmed to the National Assembly, "The cause of Justice, of Order and Civilization has triumphed." [7] Most of the victims of the fighting and the prison condemnations and deportations were workers; many active workers fled abroad. As in 1848, says the monarchist Beau de Loménie, the authorities "magnified at will, after the event, the peril which society, they insisted, had just escaped." [8]

The Third Republic

In the period between the Commune and World War I, the modern trade union movement took firm root. The government of the Third Republic gave its legal blessing, and even some support to the move-ment, although, many times, it took repressive measures. The period was, on the whole, prosperous, though its prosperity was unevenly distributed within French society, and the slow improvement in the workers' standard of living was interrupted by a number of slumps. Industrialization continued, at first more slowly than under the Empire, then with an acceleration at the turn of the century. New

---

[6] The word "commune" is derived, not from communism, but from the medieval Commune, the chartered town. Its opponents blamed the Commune on the International, although it actually played only a small role in the direc-tion of the event. Karl Marx and the International, after some hesitation, took the credit, and the legend was created.

[7] Cited by Dolléans, I, page 386, *op. cit.*

[8] Beau de Loménie, *Les Responsabilités des dynasties bourgeoises,* Vol. I, *De Bonaparte à MacMahon,* page 135, Paris, 1943.

processes enabled France to exploit the iron mines of the areas of Lorraine that it had retained, and steel output went up from 383,000 tons in 1880 to 4,630,000 tons in 1913; in the textile industry, power-driven machinery increasingly displaced hand looms. France pioneered in one important industry, automobiles. But the traditional luxury trades continued to be important, and capitalist organization and large factory units replaced the small workshop only in the heavy industries. The growth of the urban population was greatest in the Paris region, at the time still an area of predominantly small and middle-sized workshops. The surrounding rural populations were flowing into the great iron and steel centers of Lorraine, and into smaller centers of industry elsewhere. It was a period of considerable rural emigration, and it became fashionable to deplore *"l'exode rurale."* The needs of industry also stimulated the beginnings of the great twentieth century immigration to France, mostly from Belgium, Luxembourg, and Italy. For, under the Third Republic, there took place what a British historian has called that "great and distressing historical event—the rapid decline of the proportion of Frenchmen to other Europeans." [9]

After the Paris Commune and the decimation of workers' leaders, France had enough vitality to start re-forming a union movement, slowly and cautiously at first. By 1876, there was held the first of a series of "workers' congresses" which preceded the formation of any definitive national organization. Five years later there were already 500 local unions (*chambres syndicales ouvrières*), of which 150 were in Paris; there were some 60,000 members in all.

The unions were tolerated, but not legal. However, the government of the Third Republic, in the hands of republicans after 1877, wished to gain the support of workers, and some of its leaders not only wanted that support for themselves, but also saw the value of stable, peaceful unions. The law of 1884 granted freedom of association. It required the unions, like other associations, to register their statutes and lists of officers with the government. Many unions denounced the law as a "police measure" because of its registration requirements, but most complied, in at least a perfunctory fashion. Unions were now legal, and the State and the unions were to live together, even if quarrelsomely.

The period of the late 1870's and the 1880's saw the founding of a number of competing socialist parties. The splitting and resplitting of the socialist organizations (four splits in the years 1880–82; five national socialist parties by 1899) went on for a generation before

[9] D. W. Brogan, *France under the Republic, 1870–1939,* page 418. New York, 1940.

they were unified in 1905. This fragmentation made impossible the orderly relations and division of work between trade unions and socialist political parties that came to characterize the workers' movements of the prewar period in most western European countries. In the bitterness of internecine warfare, in the "incapacity of socialist fraternities to fraternize," that distinguished left-wing politics, the new and none too strong unions were torn apart. They became suspicious of socialist parties and politicians. When the anarchists, after a period of "propaganda of the deed" by bomb-throwing, went into the trade unions in large numbers, early in the 1890's, they carried their contempt for socialist politics with them, and fortified the unionists' hostility to socialist parties.

Local unions of the various trades and crafts were springing up all over the country. The first national union was created by the hatters in 1879, to be followed by the printers' national union two years later, and, in 1883, by a federation of the miners of the south. The first overall national organization, the National Federation of Labor Unions, was founded in 1886. It was almost immediately taken over by one wing of the socialist movement, the Guesdists, who of all the socialist parties in France were the most Marxist by doctrine and by personal ties. By 1889 the government stated there were 140,000 members in 1,000 local unions, now coming to be known as *"syndicats."*

Despite the new national unions, the local union was the essential unit of trade union life. Meanwhile there developed the institution of the *Bourse du Travail.* Like the word *syndicat,* this term has no exact equivalent in English. The *Bourse du Travail* had some of the functions of a labor exchange (which is what the term literally means), of a workers' club, and of a central labor union. It gathered information on the supply and demand for labor, and posted available jobs and rates. To coordinate, and if possible control, the employment market, was its first ambition. It aided traveling unionists, either with jobs or small cash grants. It offered a library and evening courses, vocational and cultural. As time went on, it took on more and more the character of a federation of local unions.

What made it unique was the combination of these functions, and the development of a philosophy of labor action which, in its original vision, combined practical day-to-day action for the economic protection of workers with the ideal of the "total" emancipation of the working class.[10] The program of the *Bourses* was bound up with the

---

[10] The *Bourses,* however, generally received government subsidies, chiefly from municipalities. All through their existence they debated the virtues and difficulties of ridding themselves of dependence on these subsidies.

life and work of one of the most extraordinary and devoted men in the history of French labor, Fernand Pelloutier.

Pelloutier and the *Bourses*

Pelloutier, as a young journalist in St. Nazaire, was early attracted to the socialist party of Guesde. He tried to win the Guesdists over to the idea of the general strike; failing, he left the socialist party and political action, came to Paris, and, at first under the influence of the anarchists, threw himself into labor organization. From 1895 on, he was the moving spirit of the federation of the *Bourses du Travail*, which had been created by 14 *Bourses*, in 1892, and numbered 65 at his death, in 1901. Consumed by a terrible illness much of this time, and dying at the age of 33, he left behind a solid organizational work, and a generous statement of social purpose.

Pelloutier said of the *Bourses:*

[they] associate themselves with all the demands which can—in ameliorating, no matter how slightly, the immediate lot of the proletariat—liberate it from demoralizing worries about the day's bread. . . . They demand the shortening of working hours, the fixing of a minimum wage, the respect for the right of resistance to exploitation by the employer. . . . They work to save their members from the anguish of unemployment and the insecurity of old age.[11]

Along with these immediate demands, he sought, as did most spokesmen of the workers of that day, "the social revolution." This he saw not only in the abolition of private property and the dethronement of the bourgeois state, but in the education of the worker to assume his responsibilities as a free individual in a free society. He wrote:

Partisans of the suppression of private property, we are also that which the politicians (including socialist politicians) are not . . . men truly without god, without master, and without nation, the irreconcilable enemies of all despotism, moral or collective, that is to say of laws and dictatorships, including that of the proletariat, and the passionate believers in the cult of the individual.[12]

Labor Federation

The number of organized workers [13] increased steadily:

1890	140,000	1902	614,000
1892	288,000	1905	781,000
1895	419,000	1910	977,000
1900	491,000	1912	1,064,000

[11] *Histoire des Bourses du Travail*, page 17. Paris, 1946.

[12] *Ibid.*, page 14.

[13] These are the official figures based on union declarations to the Ministry of Labor (Bureau of Labor in the Ministry of Commerce before the establishment

In 1894 there were 2,178 local unions, with some 400,000 members. The original National Federation of Labor Unions was dying. It had become an adjunct of the Guesdist socialist party, and it was split on the question of the general strike. The next year a new national organization was set up, the *Confédération Générale du Travail*, the CGT (General Confederation of Labor), which proposed to federate both national unions and *Bourses du Travail*, and which, with splits, mutations, and changes of orientation, was to remain the major labor federation of France. For its first years, its existence was precarious, and the Federation of *Bourses* exercized a far greater influence. But, in 1902, the amalgamation of the CGT with the Federation of *Bourses* was made firm, and the CGT entered upon six or seven years of what is often called the "heroic period" of its history.

As its statutes took shape, the CGT was set up in two sections, the section of industrial or craft unions (for example, printers, textile workers, and so forth) and the section of the *Bourses*. Every local union was supposed to belong both to the national union of its industry or trade and to its local *Bourse*. The departmental federation (*union départementale*) later took the place of the local *Bourse* as the important regional grouping in the CGT structure.[14]

The life of the union movement was, for the most part, in its local unions and in its *Bourses du Travail*. Except for the locals of a few well-knit national unions, the local unions jealously guarded their autonomy of action. Of the slender dues they irregularly collected from their members, they paid an exceedingly small per capita tax to the national union and the Confederation. This distribution of dues income reflected the distrust of central authorities and of officialdom which is so profound in French life. It was partly a consequence of the important role of the anarchists in the trade union movement, in the 1890's and the 1900's. But, mainly, it was a result of poverty, both of the workers and their organizations, and the failure of most unions to develop either systems of benefits or collective bargaining relations. Only the printers had regular sick benefits and strike benefits; only the printers and the miners practiced real collective bargaining.

The average nominal membership of the local unions of the CGT,

in 1906 of the Ministry of Labor). While these figures, like all statistics on union membership in France, must be used with the greatest caution, they are the best, because the only, approximations available. Cf. critical notes on membership data at a later period in David J. Saposs, *The Labor Movement in Post-War France,* pages 121–122. New York, 1931, and Henry W. Ehrmann, *French Labor: from Popular Front to Liberation,* page 288, note 2. New York, 1947. On membership concepts, see *infra,* pages 373–374.

[14] There are 90 departments in metropolitan France. The department is thus much smaller than the American state. It has comparatively little autonomy, being administered chiefly by a prefect appointed by the central government.

in 1904, was 168; perhaps half of the average monthly dues of one franc (then 20 cents) per member was actually collected. The result was an annual income for the local union of about 1,000 francs, not enough to maintain paid officials, or develop insurance benefits, or build strike funds, or leave much, if the locals had been willing, to maintain a strong national union, let alone a strong confederation. The CGT's total resources were about $3,000 for the year 1906.

The discipline within the national unions and the CGT was loose. On paper, Paris dominated both. The headquarters of almost all the national unions and the CGT were there, and most of the national officials and members of the national representative councils were selected from among the Paris members, to save traveling expenses from the provinces. But the unions disregarded the decisions of the CGT executive and even the CGT conventions when they disagreed with them. There developed an acceptance of a double standard of union morality that plagued the CGT, a divergence between speeches of officials and conduct of the organizations, between talk and action. The trade unions' weak position in the economy, their minority status, and their financial instability went hand in hand, and all led to, and in turn flowed from, the concept of the union's role in society. This concept came to be known as revolutionary syndicalism, or simply "syndicalism," which was largely a French contribution to trade union philosophy.

Syndicalist philosophy of early 1900's

The philosophy of syndicalism was the romantic and extreme statement of the place of labor and labor's own organizations in society. It was equally hostile to the capitalist employer, the state, and the political parties, even those calling themselves socialist. Like the socialists, the syndicalists took the class struggle to be the basis of economic life and of social development. "The class struggle opposes the workers in revolt against all the forms of exploitation, material and moral, by the capitalist class," said the Charter of Amiens, the declaration of the CGT convention of 1906, and the classic statement of the revolutionary syndicalist position.[15] The union (*syndicat*) was the necessary grouping of the workers for the struggle against the capitalist class. It was by the action of the unions alone that the real transformation of society, the disappearance of wage slavery and of the employer class, would come. Then the unions would drop their belligerent role and become the essential basis of the reorganization

---

[15] For the Declaration of Amiens, see Appendix A to Saposs, *op. cit.;* for French text, see Louis, *op. cit.,* Vol. I, pages 262, 263.

of a free, classless society. The state, now the ally and arm of the exploiting employer class, would disappear. Society, though its future outlines were seldom even sketched by the syndicalists, would then be organized in some loose, federative way around the workshop, the local union, and the *Bourse du Travail*, with the national unions and the General Confederation of Labor in some vague role of coordination. "Society is built on the image of the workshop," said Lagardelle, echoing Proudhon. "The free workshop will make the free society." [16]

The method by which this revolution would take place was the general strike, the supreme manifestation of "direct action." The syndicalists were not so sure as the Marxists that historical inevitability was working in their favor, that capitalism was bound to disappear of its own contradictions. An effort of organization, and at least an historical moment of violent struggle, were necessary; the proletariat's concerted refusal to work, at some decisive moment, would sweep aside the old economic and political order. The idea of the general strike had been bruited about among European radicals at least since the 1830's, but in no country and no labor movement did it take on the determining role which it did among the French syndicalists before the First World War. Georges Sorel, who was the leading theoretician *after the fact* of the syndicalist movement (and not at all the founder of its doctrine), said the general strike was one of the great "social myths" by which men are moved. [17] Most of the syndicalists took the idea more literally. Every strike, they said, was a preparation for the general strike; any strike might—these things could not be foreseen—turn into *the* general strike. The strikes that were constantly taking place, therefore, were more important as rehearsals for the general strike than for what they could win for the workers immediately. It was not necessary, it was not even possible, for *all* the workers to be organized. A conscious organized minority (i.e., the CGT) would give the lead, and at the decisive juncture the hitherto torpid masses would follow, by a "sudden leap of awareness," in the face of which the employer class, the state, and even its troops would be powerless.

The state was as much the enemy as were the employers, in syndicalists' eyes. The apparatus of political democracy and universal suffrage was a trumpery, and parliamentary action at best a diversion. The state blinded the working class with the notion of patriotism, while using its troop to shoot down strikers, and training the workers

---

[16] Hubert Lagardelle, *Le Socialisme Ouvrier,* page 314. Paris, 1911.

[17] Sorel's *Reflections on Violence,* which appeared in 1906 (the year of the Charter of Amiens), is available in English translation. The most recent edition, Glencoe, Ill., 1950, has an excellent critical introduction by Edward A. Shils.

to be cannon fodder in imperialist wars. The political parties who claimed to represent the workers only turned the workers' energies from the real struggle. The socialist parties were run by bourgeois intellectuals and professional people; only the unions were pure working-class organizations. Honest socialists were impotent to help them, and less honest ones climbed to office on the backs of the workers only to betray them. The syndicalist creed has conventionally been described as "anti-political," and so its founders proudly called it. Actually it was opposed to political parties, but very much concerned with political ends. In the name of the primacy of "economic action," it reached out for all the political tasks which in other industrial countries the unions left largely to the political parties.

It had no use for intellectual refinements in the analysis of class relations or the role of government, for intellectual constructions of the future society it sought to achieve, or for the leadership of intellectuals, who were felt to be bourgeois theorists who knew neither the hardships nor the needs of the workers. Among the active syndicalists, said Griffuelhes, secretary-general of the CGT, "there is a sentiment of brutal opposition to the bourgeoisie; . . . these unionists want passionately to be led by workers." [18]

On the eve of World War I, the CGT claimed 600,000 members; the actual figure was lower. At no time in the prewar period did the CGT include a majority even of the organized workers, and only a minority of workers were organized. Out of some 10 million workers in France just before World War I, of whom 5 million were in industry and transportation, only a little over a million were members of any unions, and less than half that number were members of the CGT. Within the CGT, probably no more than half subscribed to revolutionary syndicalism. The system of representation in the CGT conventions favored the syndicalists. It gave one vote to every local union, whatever its membership. A large number of small, weak unions were among the ardent syndicalist unions, but so were the building trades and metal workers. A number, though not all, of the largest and most solid unions, notably the textile workers, railwaymen, and printers, generally opposed the revolutionary syndicalist doctrines. These "reformists," as they were called, had had some experience in collective bargaining with employers; or they believed that the unions should work with the Socialist Party; or they had no confidence in the general strike; or they opposed the antimilitarist incitement of the CGT.

Having said that most French workers did not adhere to syndicalist unions, we still must ask why this revolutionary doctrine became the

---

[18] Dolléans, *op. cit.,* Vol. II, page 126.

official doctrine of the CGT, and why it flourished in France, Spain, and Italy, and hardly took root elsewhere. Not only was its importance great in its day, but the syndicalist outlook has stamped the French labor movement ever since. Let us examine the major reasons for its success. None of these taken alone makes sense as an explanation; they need to be seen together as a living pattern of the French unions in relation to the national economy and the political scene early in the century.

The state of the economy. The French economy, in contrast with the German or English or American, seemed comparatively static, in terms both of technical change and of entrepreneurial attitudes. As far as workers could see, the economy held out no prospects of a rising standard of living through evolutionary changes.

Employer attitudes. French employers, with few exceptions, resisted both ameliorative legislation and collective bargaining. The notion that the "authority" of management must be protected against any union encroachments was an article of faith for most employers. The revolutionary language of the CGT helped frighten employers away from the bargaining table. But the arbitrary character of shop regulations and the resistance of employers to unions were major reasons for labor's revolutionary attitude. Cause and effect went hand in hand.

The role of the state. The state seemed to be the arm of the employing class, and parliamentary action of little avail. The French government had, before World War I, developed no social services to compare with these of imperial Germany or liberal England. Troops had fired many times on strikers, and on peaceful demonstrators. The state had alternated between repression and attempts to domesticate the unions, between subsidies to the *Bourses du Travail* and closings of the *Bourses* when they got out of hand. Its ambivalence created more bitterness among workers.

Socialist Party—trade union relations. The disunity of warring socialist sects had, for a generation, created turmoil among the unions. The domination of socialist politics by middle-class and professional men (only one national leader of the socialist parties of the Third Republic was a worker) aroused the criticism of trade unionists. The increasing moderation of socialists, as they began to win municipal power and seats in Parliament, left place for a revolutionary movement; and syndicalism was a reformulation of the socialist faith in revolutionary terms.

The failure of socialist parliamentary efforts to enact social legislation added to the impatience of the unionists with both socialist politics and the parliamentary process. To the growing moderation of the socialists was joined the reproach of "betrayal." After the socialist

Alexander Millerand entered the bourgeois cabinet of Waldeck-Rousseau,[19] "Millerandism" was heatedly debated in French and international labor and socialist circles for 15 years.

Class consciousness. Social distinctions were coupled with economic distinctions to make the more reflective and active of the workers feel that they had little in common with the bourgeoisie. *"Ouvriérisme,"* the cult of "of-by-and-for" the proletariat, was strong among French workers, and particularly among the self-taught worker-intellectual leaders who stated the syndicalist philosophy before the "bourgeois intellectuals," like Georges Sorel, took it up.

The state of the unions. The syndicalist doctrine appealed to unions that were poor, weakly organized, and had not succeeded in developing either benefit features or collective agreements. If most workers were still unorganized, that did not matter so much, the syndicalists said; what mattered most was the militant minority, the élite. When the moment of the general strike came, the others would take their places with their own class. Far nobler than a treasury able to pay strike benefits was the practice of "solidarity," workers' helping striking workers; it developed the revolutionary consciousness which was the all-important requirement. Syndicalists were fond of pointing out that the Belgian, German, or English unions were dues-collecting and benefit-administering machines; the CGT would not have its will to action paralyzed by bank deposits or property holdings. The general strike, by its nature, did not need mass membership or financial staying power; when all the workers folded their arms, capitalist society would quickly collapse.[20]

The revolutionary tradition in France. The general strike fitted in with a habit of thinking in apocalyptic terms, nourished in France by the tradition of the French Revolution, and by the succession of revolutions (1830, 1848, 1870) by which political change had come during the nineteenth century. "The people have always been by nature

---

[19] This step was all the more debatable because another member of the same cabinet was General de Gallifet, "the butcher of the Paris Commune."

[20] John Bowditch, in "The Concept of *Élan Vital:* A Rationalization of Weakness," *Modern France: Problems of the Third and Fourth Republics,* pages 32–43, Princeton, 1951, shows the parallel in this decade between the revolutionary syndicalists' reliance on an élite to carry along the mass of French workers, and the similar reliance by a number of influential army officers on the moral superiority of the French soldier, the superiority of the offensive and the *"furia francese,"* to compensate for German material advantages and numbers. "That two groups so widely separated as the revolutionary syndicalists and aristocratic army officers should each have seized upon the mystical concept we have labeled *élan vital,"* shows "the willingness of important elements of France to turn their backs on the age in which they lived and to employ myths . . . as a means of escaping from rather +han coping with their problems," page 43.

millennary," said Montégut.[21] "The Revolution was for the people the great judgment of the nations which was to precede the reign of a thousand years, and since then they await the appearance of the promised Messiah with a constancy which the cruelest denials cannot shake." The Revolution appeared as "eternal, and invincible as God, whose place it had taken," to workers who no longer nourished the millennary hopes of religion.

Finally, the national character. It is characteristic of Frenchmen to talk of the French national character.[22] On the slippery terrain of national character, we may follow a French syndicalist, Griffuelhes, secretary-general of the CGT. The French working class, he said, "has all the faults which characterize the Latin: the lack of follow-up or tenacity in its action, which is made up of waves of wrath which a little nothing activates and a little nothing appeases. It is not very persevering, "not that it is incapable of endurance, but that it attaches more importance to the effort of an hour, a day; for this effort it gives itself entirely, its action is like fireworks which explode in brilliant colored clusters which leave only a trace, all memory and regrets. Then if the effort succeeds, and gets results, everyone takes note of it, not dreaming that in order to maintain it action is still needed." [23]

Frenchmen are individualists, and individualism in France often verges on anarchy. Frenchmen like to speak of themselves as *"Frondeurs,"* rebellious to authority. "Our impulsive and rebellious temperament does not lend itself to high dues," said the commission organizing the 1902 CGT convention, in an explanation which French unionists have often repeated with a mixture of despair and pride. Another national quality strong in the labor movement, is the devotion to general ideas and to resounding phrases. This puts a premium on abstract theory as against empirical achievements, and it emphasizes oratory as against administration in union leadership. The ideas, once formulated and propagated, themselves constitute a force working in the same direction as the conditions that breed them.

The doctrine of the general strike, the loose structure and the floating membership of the CGT, the verbalized rancors against social injustice and all the rulers of society, the occasional but unsustained sacrifices, are the expression of this national temper. In the most recent period, it has been the Communist Party rather than the trade

---

[21] Montégut, Emile, in *Revue des Deux Mondes,* August 1871, pages 881–882.

[22] National character we take to be the complex of education and traditions within the social and economic and political setting that constitute France, and of course not a matter of "race" or blood.

[23] Griffuelhes, *Voyage révolutionnaire: Impressions d'un Propagandiste,* page 7, Paris, [1910].

unions themselves that has harnessed these rancors and this apocalyptic vision of social change in a new kind of CGT, more disciplined and less taken with liberty.

The period between 1871 and World War I was poor in labor and social legislation. The "opportunist republicans" who governed during most of this period had two principles: "One: No reform until the time is ripe for it. Two: The time is never ripe." [24] The legislation that was passed was generally received with hostility and suspicion by the CGT. In 1892, the government provided the first voluntary conciliation and arbitration services. In the decade before World War I, legislation provided for the eight-hour day for miners, for one day's rest in seven for all workers, and a ten-hour day for women and children. The first general system of old-age pensions was voted by a 1910 law, which the unions denounced as a "colossal swindle," and, by their opposition, rendered largely inoperative. Hostility between the government and the labor movement was kept alive by the government's opposition to its own employees' efforts to organize. The government was slowly forced to yield, step by step, but not without a long series of strikes and dismissals of union members, which sustained the bitterness of feelings. Until the war, most of the government employee unions did not seek affiliation with the CGT, but the CGT actively upheld their right to organize and to strike.

The antimilitarist campaign opposed the CGT most violently to the government. The labor movement had, by the end of the century, broken with the Jacobin and Paris Commune tradition of patriotism. The CGT first attacked the army as a strike-breaking agency and a breeder of the patriotism that obscured the class struggle. It called upon recruits to refuse to do their military service, or at least to refuse to fire on strikers, and to use their time in the army to propagandize against the military. As international crises began to succeed each other, the CGT became haunted by the imminence of war. Its answer was the threat of the general strike. Its special convention at the time of the Balkan crisis in 1912 declared, "In case of a military adventure the duty of each worker is to not respond to the order of mobilization and to rally to the organization of his class to carry on the struggle against his sole adversaries: the capitalists."

World War I

In August, 1914, there was no general strike and no opposition to mobilization or the war. Workers, like other Frenchmen, marched off shouting "On to Berlin!" The behavior of the CGT and its leaders,

---

[24] Albert Guérard, *France: A Short History*, page 205. New York, 1946.

in 1914 and during the war, became the subject of a great deal of soul-searching; and it was one of the issues on which the organization was to split. Since even the most powerful socialist parties and the best-organized trade union movements of Europe did the same *volte-face* in 1914, there is perhaps nothing too surprising in the CGT leaders' behavior. The groups of the Left had vastly overestimated the hold of revolutionary and pacifist sentiments on the masses, and underestimated the depth of nationalist feeling, the helplessness of individuals in the face of events, and their own unpreparedness for action, national or international, against war. They had deceived themselves with the sonority of resolutions in national and international labor and socialist congresses, and with the numbers of socialist votes in elections and deputies in parliaments.

The CGT, after two decades of earnest discussion about a general strike, had no plans whatsoever to carry out its truculent resolutions. Had it tried, it would have been overwhelmed. The government had ready a list of several thousand union and radical leaders whom it was prepared to throw into jail at the moment of mobilization. At the last minute, it decided it was unnecessary to use the list. Later on, speaking of 1914, Merrheim, active, honest, and courageous leader of the antiwar group in the CGT, said, "We were completely carried off our feet, bewildered. . . . At that moment the working class, roused by a powerful current of nationalism, would not have left to the agents of the government the job of shooting us: it would have shot us itself." [25] Dumoulin, CGT secretary, questioning himself in the trenches, answered, "Fear is not syndicalist, socialist, nor any other 'ist'; it is human. At the CGT we were afraid of the war, we were afraid of the repression, simply because we were human beings like everyone else." [26]

The war marked the collapse of revolutionary syndicalism as the dominant ideology of the trade union movement. No halfway approach to the war was possible, and the CGT collaborated, as much as it was allowed to, in the organization of production. Leon Jouhaux, who had been elected CGT secretary-general in 1909, as a revolutionary syndicalist, became a familiar figure on government committees. The CGT also dropped its prewar opposition to collaboration with the Socialist Party.

The union structure was shaken from top to bottom. Membership dropped precipitately at first, and the union cadres were disorganized

---

[25] Dolléans, *op. cit.*, Vol. II, page 222.

[26] Georges Dumoulin, "Les syndicalistes français et la Guerre," reprinted in appendix to Alfred Rosmer, *Le Mouvement ouvrier pendant la guerre*, page 530. Paris, 1936.

as a consequence of mobilization, censorship, the obstacles to union activity, and the disorganization of industry which prevailed until France realized it was in for a long war. Slowly union membership picked up, from perhaps 35,000 in 1915, and 78,000 in 1916, to almost a half million by the end of the war, and over a million in 1919. The Metal Workers' Union alone rose from 7,000 members in 1915 to a claimed 204,000 on the eve of the armistice—five times its prewar figure. As the cost of living mounted more rapidly than wages, as the reports of great profits circulated, and as war-weariness grew, strikes began, among the metal trades and munitions industries, and among clothing workers. The winter and spring of 1917 were a low point in morale, with spontaneous mutinies on the western front, and strikes in Paris and elsewhere. In 1917 the government instituted compulsory arbitration. But in the spring of 1918 there was another wave of strikes, particularly in the munitions industries. These were strikes over wages and working conditions. But they also reflected the steady growth of an antiwar minority in the CGT, led by the Metal Workers' Union. By the end of the war, spurred on by the Russian Revolution and by the hundreds of thousands of new industrial workers in the CGT, this group was almost as strong as the Reformists (now including Jouhaux and other former revolutionary syndicalists), who were in control of the CGT's machinery.

The character of the working class underwent its most rapid change during the war and the immediate postwar years. David Thomson has summed it up:

Only the urgent demands of the war between 1914 and 1918 made France develop her industries on a massive scale, and produced a second industrial revolution, violently carried through in the worst conditions. . . . The silent French revolution of 1914–18 was the displacement of the pre-war industrial worker, technically skilled, alertly intelligent and politically individualist, by the operatives of mass production, herded into the big towns, and including among their ranks many foreign immigrants.[27]

Paris and its suburbs showed this change most of all. Hitherto essentially an area of small and middle-sized workshops, the region, chiefly the suburban belt, was transformed by the wartime speedup of industrialization, the growth of the chemical industry, and the new automobile industry. Paris had been a city of immigrants from the French provinces, but after the war it became also an area of immigrants from other European countries and North Africa. Throughout France, immigrants took up much of the country's heavy and dirty

---

[27] David Thomson, *Democracy in France,* page 45. London: Oxford University Press, 1946. Published under the auspices of the Royal Institute of International Affairs.

work, in the coal and iron mines, in foundries and steel mills, on the roads and in building, and, chiefly as seasonal workers, in agriculture. By 1936, there were almost two and a half million declared aliens (and probably many more undeclared) in the country: mainly Italians, Poles, Spaniards, Czechs, and Belgians.

The Interwar Period

Postwar unrest

The pressure of industrialization, and the addition of hundreds of thousands of immigrants to the working-class population, notably in the key region of Paris, would have affected the trade unions under any circumstances. These factors were combined with the spirit of postwar disillusionment, and, most important, with the emotional impact of the Russian Revolution. The wave of unrest and of vague expectation of tremendous changes that ran through the working class of France, as of other countries suddenly freed from the clutch of war, frightened the government into action. For a generation, the CGT had been demanding the eight-hour day; in 1919, the principle was enacted into law, and its application left to negotiation between management and labor. The first general legislation on the status of collective agreements was passed in 1919, and the agreements were made enforceable at law.

The internal fight which came to absorb the CGT's energies prevented it from making effective use of these concessions. The issues were: the wartime cooperation of the leadership with the government, the responsibilities for the failure of the big strikes of 1919 and 1920, and the degree to which the French trade unions would place their destinies in the hands of those who had just made the Bolshevik Revolution in Russia. Partly, it was the renewal of the old disagreement between reformists and revolutionaries. Now the reformists were in control of the CGT machinery, while the minority controlled the powerful metal trades and building trades unions, was strong among the railroad workers, and dominated the Paris region unions. But that minority was an uneasy combination of revolutionary syndicalists, anarchists, and communists, who agreed on little but their opposition to the majority leadership.

Cooperating during the war with the government and with the production effort, the CGT leadership had dropped, for all purposes but the oratorical, its old intransigence toward government and employers and the spirit proudly affirmed before the war that "the CGT is illegality in permanence." A number of government employee unions had affiliated. The CGT had acquired a new stake in society. Jouhaux might still affirm, "We are revolutionaries in the surest sense of the word," [28] but before the war the explanatory phrase had not been necessary. The new spirit was shown in the famous "Minimum Program" adopted in 1918 just after the war's end. In addition to demanding a voice in the peace conference, and the immediate restoration of individual liberties, the CGT called for a program of social insurance legislation and the establishment of a national economic council. For the first time, it called for nationalization of industry, instead of the old syndicalist demand of the "mines to the miners" and "the factories to the workers." But to avoid the evils of the state's bureaucratic control, it asked that nationalized industries be under the "autonomous control . . . of new collective organisms administered by representatives of producers and consumers." [29]

The spring of 1919 saw a wave of strikes which some writers at the time thought was a "concerted attack upon the structure of bourgeois society." Far from launching a "concerted attack," many of the striking unions insisted on their autonomy to the point of declining CGT offers of assistance. There were strikes all over the country and in most trades, including some which had never struck before. Many of the strikes, as well as many of the collective agreements signed under the 1919 law, concerned methods of applying the principle of the eight-hour day. A large percentage of the strikes, helped by favorable trade conditions, were successful in gaining objectives that were strictly economic. It was not so with the most spectacular strike of 1919, that of the Paris region metal workers. The Metal Workers' Union had succeeded in signing the first agreement of its history with the Paris region employers' federation. A dispute over the application of its provisions led to the strike. The union ranks were swollen with new recruits, and they swept aside the district and national organizations of the union and tried to run the strike through an "Action Committee" based on improvised plant strike committees. Asked whether the union should continue or break off negotiations with the employers, one of the Action Committee spokesmen said, "We've got to make the Revolution. If we don't succeed, then we can resume the economic bargaining." [30] Such a strike could do neither, and it ended in total failure.

In 1919 France in some ways was at the great moment the advocates of the general strike had always talked about. But, now that it had come, it only threw a lurid light on the confusions among the new industrial proletariat and the controversies within the labor movement.

---

[28] Leon Jouhaux, *Le syndicalisme et la CGT*, page 15. Paris, 1920.

[29] The program is given in full in Leon Jouhaux, *op. cit.*, pages 205–213.

[30] Dolléans, *op. cit.*, Vol. II, page 306.

The left minority accused the national leadership of letting slip by the long-awaited revolutionary situation, of lacking "the essential; faith in the working class and its destinies." [31] But Merrheim, who had been the leader of the anti-war movement, who had reluctantly abandoned the minority for fear of splitting the CGT, told the CGT convention of 1919, "No, comrades, we have not assassinated the Revolution. And, when one speaks of the Revolution, of a 'revolutionary situation'—my greatest sorrow is to have found in France a revolutionary situation without having found any revolutionary spirit in the working class." [32]

Division in the CGT

In the name of the officially revolutionary doctrines of the organization, and spurred on by the government of the new Russian state and the Communist International, the minority attacked Jouhaux and the CGT leadership, boring from within the organization. The debates became even more acrimonious after the failure of the great railway strike in 1920, and the collapse of the general strike which the CGT, under pressure of the minority, called to support the railroad workers. Late in 1921 the CGT was split. The reformists retained the organizational apparatus, and the opposition set up its own organization, the CGTU (Unitary General Confederation of Labor, *Confédération Générale du Travail Unitaire*).

The Socialist Party had already split in 1920. A majority went over to the Comintern, leaving most of the leaders and a minority of the members to reform their ranks as the "French Section of the Workers' International," commonly called the SFIO. The Communist Party took a large share of the working-class following, while the SFIO held more of the old socialist following among the government workers and teachers, liberal professions, lower middle class and peasants.

The painfully united trade union movement had thus enjoyed twenty years of existence; the united Socialist Party fifteen. The split in the political wing of labor's organizations was to be permanent; the trade unions were to reunite again during the Popular Front, split on the Nazi-Soviet Pact and the war, reunite in the underground, and split again in 1947. The splits and reunifications alike reflected more faithfully than in any other country the succession of world political upheavals since 1914.

In the 1920's France enjoyed some of the few years of prosperity the country has had in this century. Following the feverish wartime expansion in the heavy industries, and the rebuilding of devastated

[31] Pierre Monatte, *La vie ouvrière,* July 23, 1919.
[32] Dolléans, *op. cit.,* Vol. II, pages 315–316.

plants, the modernization of industry made little headway. Investors preferred to put their money into French and, especially, foreign government bonds. But thanks in part to the reconstruction of the devastated areas, there was no postwar economic crisis; employment was high, real wages increased modestly, and the work week decreased.

The unions, following the debacle of the 1920 general strike and the CGT split, had again become organizations of a small minority of French workers.[33] In 1922, after the split, the CGT claimed 373,000 members. The CGTU began with a somewhat larger number and with greater strength among industrial workers. But it was soon torn by divisions and its membership was alienated by the hopeless strikes and unrealistic policies then pursued by the Communist Party. Some of the most sincere revolutionary syndicalists had been attracted by the Russian Revolution to the Communist Party, only to leave it, disillusioned, a few years later. After attacking the reformist "politicians" in the CGT, they soon attacked with equal fervor the communist "politicians" who rapidly took over control of the CGTU and affiliated it with the Red International of Trade Unions, the trade union arm of the Third International. In 1924, the anarcho-syndicalists withdrew to set up a "third CGT" faithful to the 1906 Charter of Amiens. Gradually, other minorities left to return to the CGT, or drop out of the trade unions, leaving the CGTU a declining organization entirely under communist control.

The CGT rebuilt its torn structure, but its chief gains in membership came not from industrial workers, but from the affiliation of the majority of independent civil service unions in 1927, whose important role has remained a characteristic of reformist unionism since then. The government workers were the best organized group of workers in France, and the steadiest dues payers. After 1927, about half of the members of the CGT were members of civil servants' unions.

About a third of the membership of both the CGT and the CGTU, in the late twenties, was to be found in the "sheltered" and regulated industries of a public utility character. And in these fields, especially coal mining, took place most of what collective bargaining there was in industry. The printing trades were the only unregulated private industry in which unionism and collective bargaining flourished. In the purely private industries, notably metal-working, textiles, and the

---

[33] The best study of French unionism during the 1920's is the comprehensive and analytical work by David J. Saposs, *The Labor Movement in Post-War France.* New York, 1931. Also useful is Marjorie R. Clark, *A History of the French Labor Movement, 1910–1928.* Berkeley, 1930. For both the 1920's and 1930's see Adolf Sturmthal, *The Tragedy of European Labor,* New York, 1943, and André Philip, "France," in H. A. Marquand, ed., *Organized Labour in Four Continents.* London, 1939.

building trades, union membership had dropped, not only well below the brief 1919 peaks, but even below those of 1913.

The CGT turned its back on its violent prewar syndicalist past, although its leaders still paid it the tribute of revolutionary phraseology. It sought written collective agreements in industry, although stoutly denying that this meant "class collaboration." It lobbied in Parliament in behalf of social legislation, and for its civil service membership. In Parliament, it worked not only with the Socialist Party, but also with the Radical Socialists [34] who were in the government in various coalitions, during much of the period between the two wars, while the socialists were, until 1936, never in it. The chief product of this activity was the passage in 1928 of the first comprehensive social insurance legislation in France, to take effect in 1930. This included old age insurance, maternity benefits, invalidity benefits, and health insurance. The CGT, whose opposition had made ineffective the old age insurance law of 1910, now threw much of its energies into participation in the administering of the 1930 law. One reason for the law's passage was the obviously unfavorable comparison between the position of most French workers and that of the workers in the "recovered provinces," Alsace and Lorraine, which retained the German social insurances. Another reason was the rise of Catholic social action among employers and workers, which stressed protection of the family and, in 1932, promoted the first law requiring the payment of family allowances.

Catholic unionism

Catholic social doctrine had, in the late nineteenth century, produced noteworthy appeals to sentiments of social justice and charity. But these were for the most part set in a corporatist view of society, and couched in accents of political reaction. The great Catholic leader Count Albert De Mun said, before the 1884 law on trade union association was voted, that it would not be a "remedy against the division of employers and workers," but "the definite organization of the war between the two." [35] After some false starts with various forms of paternalistic organization ("mixed unions"), the first Catholic trade unions had been permanently established, in 1887, among white-collar workers in Paris. Catholics who saw the value of independent labor organization had to work, in the first decade of the century, against

---

[34] This is the conventional English rendering of the untranslatable name of this middle-of-the-road party, which represented essentially the "middle middle-class," the professional classes and farm owners.

[35] Quoted in Paul Vignaux, *Traditionalisme et Syndicalisme, Essai d'Histoire Sociale (1884–1941)*, page 34. New York, 1943.

a flurry of activity by "yellow" (company) unions which drew much Catholic support.[36]

In 1913 the white-collar workers' organizations became a national union, the first and still most powerful of the Catholic national unions. Organizing industrial workers was more difficult, but, by 1919, it was possible to establish a national center, the CFTC, the French Confederation of Christian—or, more properly, Catholic—Workers (*Confédération Française des Travailleurs Chrétiens*). Its chief strength was in white-collar employment, especially banking and retailing, and in industries with a large percentage of women workers, notably the textile centers of the North, Roubaix and Tourcoing. It also had an important membership in Catholic Alsace.

Drawing their inspiration from the principles of social justice set forth in the encyclical *Rerum novarum* of Leo XIII in 1891, the Catholic unions rejected the class struggle doctrines of the other confederations, and sought collaboration with employers through collective agreements and joint commissions. They were not, in principle, against strikes, but called them as a last resort, and often opposed strikes called by the CGT or GCTU. Despite their moderation in action, they were fought by employers, most bitterly by some Catholic employers. The powerful Catholic textile employers of the Roubaix-Tourcoing area [37] appealed to the Vatican for condemnation of the CFTC, and it was only after five years of study, in 1929, that Rome gave the anxious Catholic unionists the assurance of its support, and rebuked the employers' attack.

Nominally Catholic, France was, except for a few regions, a country of workers who had been "dechristianized" since the mid-nineteenth century. For a long time to come, Catholic unionists and priests engaged in Catholic labor action were to have the feeling of being "on mission" to a heathen land. The slow advance of Catholic unionism among the industrial workers was to be quickened by the establishment of the Catholic Workers' Youth movement, the JOC (*Jeunesse Ouvrière Chrétienne*) in 1927, but that did not show results in industrial worker support and leadership until later. By the end of the 1920's, the CFTC had fewer than 100,000 members.

---

[36] Jules Zirnheld, founder of the Catholic trade union movement in France, describes how one ecclesiastic spoke of his "dear workers" who "counted on the interest and affection of the nobles, the clergy, of Catholics and patriots." A national leader of the "yellow" union movement publicly thanked the benefactors of the organization as "all good Frenchmen and big industrialists." *Cinquante années de syndicalisme chrétien,* page 144. Paris, 1937.

[37] "Strong in their virtue and their fortune, charitable and authoritarian . . . leaning on a system of company welfare work and a technique of anti-unionism." Vignaux, *op. cit.,* page 41.

The economic crisis came later and with less force to France than to most industrial nations, but it persisted stubbornly. In the autumn of 1932, there were still fewer than 300,000 unemployed. The low birth rate had over many years created a chronic shortage of manpower. The blow fell hardest on foreigners, to whom France had been so hospitable for many years. Their employment opportunities and their numbers in the country were drastically cut by government action; the French labor movement, traditionally internationalist in its outlook, approved. Thus, France did not know any such army of seemingly permanently jobless as was the undoing of Germany.

The deflationary policies of the early 1930's did not reduce budgetary deficits (tax receipts fell faster than did expenditures), nor did they stimulate the confidence counted on to help revive economic activity. In fact, they enhanced the severity of cabinet crises, shook confidence in the institutions of the country, and led to a virtual abdication of Parliament, which acknowledged impotence by giving the cabinet power to legislate by decree-law. Unemployment grew, and reached its high point in early 1935, when about 850,000 were out of work and millions were working short time. Industrial production then was 72.5 per cent of 1929. France had no system of unemployment *insurance,* only unemployment *assistance*—that is, a dole—of the most meager proportions. As deflationary policies emphasized the ills they sought to cure, more and more of the civil servants and lower middle class felt the pinch. The protected farm market finally felt the impact of world depression. Thus, there was laid the base for the Popular Front, the electoral combination of the Radical Socialist, Socialist, and Communist Parties, representing a voting coalition of middle class, farmers and workers.

The fascist threat and the Popular Front

As Hitler took power across the Rhine, the shadow of fascism spread across the country worried by unemployment and wage-cutting, the fall in farm prices, and the depression of trade. How close France was to fascism in early 1934 is hard to say. Several native French fascist leagues were functioning aggressively, but they were neither united nor well-led. Their opportunity seemed at hand when Parliament and the nation were shaken by one of the big financial scandals that occured periodically in the Third Republic. On February 6, 1934, the fascist leagues and the communists rioted against the government and the institutions of the Republic, massing in confused, but alarming, combination around the Chamber of Deputies.

It was the leaders of the CGT who took the counteroffensive in

behalf of Republican institutions.[38] The CGT called a general strike
for the day of February 12, "as a warning and a manifestation of
strength and decision." The CGTU and the Communist Party
hesitated, then reversed their stand of February 6, and joined in the
general strike. For the first time since the split a dozen years earlier,
reformist and communist labor organizations acted together. For the
first and only time in their history the French unions staged a completely successful general strike. Its objectives were clear-cut, and
its appeal was broad, not only to workers but to all classes, to defend
"the fundamental liberties without which life is not worth living."
The success of the February 12 strike, which the workers credited to
the common action of the unions, prepared the way for the reunification of the CGT and the CGTU. "Anyone who resisted the plea for
unity would have seen the disaffection of the masses," [39] said Leon
Blum, leader of the Socialist Party. Meanwhile the international
communist line switched from its fight on the "social fascists" (that
is, Social Democrats), and insistence on "unity from below" against
reformist labor leaders, to its Popular Front phase of 1935–1939. The
Franco-Soviet alliance of 1935 was one of the major products of, and
reasons for, the new line—a belated response to the German threat
to the Soviet Union.

Unity had been the theme of endless talk and empty resolutions
since the 1921 split. Now, with the enthusiasm of their new line, the
communists yielded so on every disputed point that the reformists could
hardly resist the unity demand. The reunification was agreed upon
by the two confederations in 1935, and consummated at the "unity
convention" of Toulouse early in 1936. In the CGT, reunited "without
victors or vanquished," there were about a million members, of whom
three-fourths came from the CGT, and one-fourth from the CGTU.
The communists urged "democratic centralization" in the CGT structure, but the reformists managed to retain the old loose "federalist"
structure. For the time being, the reformists, with their greater
numerical strength, controlled most of the national unions and departmental federations. But they had no effective way to enforce the CGT's
prohibition on internal factional organization, nor did they really face
the issue of how to prevent the communists from organizing within the
trade unions to take them over. Instead, the declaration of political
independence in the hallowed Charter of Amiens of 1906 was reaffirmed,
after having been invoked by both sides. This, as Ehrmann puts it,[40]

---

[38] On the period from 1934 to 1940, see the richly documented and thoughtful
volume by Henry W. Ehrmann, *French Labor: from Popular Front to Liberation.*
New York, 1947.

[39] *Le Populaire*, Feb. 25, 1935.

[40] Ehrmann, *op. cit.*, page 35.

was "masking the real issues behind an apparent emphasis on trade union independence," and it "proved to be a 'paralyzing abstraction,' " which left the rank and file unprepared for the political fights that were soon to rock the CGT.

In the 1936 national elections, the new Popular Front coalition scored a sweeping success. Within its three parties of the so-called Left, moreover, there was a considerable redistribution of power. The radical socialists lost ground, the socialists emerged as the largest single party in the Chamber of Deputies, and the communists not only got a million and a half votes, but, for the first time, got seats in proportion—72 instead of the 10 they had had in 1932. The hope and enthusiasm generated by this Popular Front victory exploded within the nation's factories in the sit-down strikes. In June, 1936, about 2,000,000 workers went on strike. The communists later took the credit, and their enemies, as so often, were willing to give them the credit. But the strikes were not the work of the communists; they were almost entirely spontaneous. The CGT itself had neither the membership nor the organization to call, let alone direct, such a movement. The strikes were a demand *for* organization; not the work *of* an organization. The strikers' demands were less for wage increases than for recognition of the unions and for collective agreements and an end to the discharge of union activists. With remarkable discipline and good spirits, they polished their machines and sang (*Tout va très bien, Madame la Marquise*, almost as often as *The Internationale*), while they waited for the new government to act.

Leon Blum, first Socialist Prime Minister in French history, had invited the CGT to take part in the Popular Front cabinet, but this it had refused.[41] Now he had to act speedily, and not by military force, to get the strikers out of the plants, to get production going, and to quiet the fears of the rest of the nation. He summoned representatives of the employers' confederation, the CGPF,[42] and the CGT and got them speedily to sign a broad general agreement of unprecedented scope. Only a combination of government pressure and fright before the great unknown of the sit-downs induced the CGPF representatives to sign the Matignon Agreement, by which they agreed to bargain collectively, to respect the right of their workers to join unions, and to allow the election of shop stewards. They also accepted a general wage rise averaging 12 per cent; the figure was set by the arbitration of Blum himself. The government immediately introduced legislation

---

[41] The Communist Party also refused, retaining a freedom of action which helped frustrate the government.

[42] The General Confederation of French Manufacturers, *Confédération Générale de la Production Française*, founded in 1919. See *infra*, pages 380–382.

to foster collective bargaining and carry out the Matignon agreement, to introduce the basic forty-hour week (without reductions in pay), and—perhaps most popular of all the Popular Front laws—paid vacations in industry. Parliament acted with an unwonted speed in which alarm at the sit-down strikes showed perhaps more than an awakened social conscience. In fact, with the exception of the law on compulsory arbitration, all the important labor legislation of the Popular Front was passed in these few days of June, 1936.

The 1936 legislation laid an obligation upon employers and unions to bargain collectively. The government intervened by convoking for negotiations the "most representative organizations" of employers and workers, regional or national, for the branch of industry or commerce concerned, and by helping them reach an agreement. Agreements were required to cover a wide range of issues, including provision for the election of shop stewards. The government could "extend" agreements negotiated by the "most representative organizations" to cover those employers and workers in the same industry and area who were not represented by the parties to the agreement itself. By extension, the government gave the force of public regulation to agreements arrived at by "the most representative" unions and employer associations. Compulsory arbitration was introduced, and the CGT, breaking with tradition, supported its introduction.

The membership of the unions leaped in 1936 as those of no free labor movement ever had. From about one million members before the sit-downs, the CGT soon reached the figure of 5 million. In mass-production industries, membership multiplied ten or twenty times in less than a year. The union structure bulged at the seams, as the chronically understaffed CGT sought to absorb the millions of recruits, untrained in union rights or responsibilities, to cope with strikes, to find shop steward candidates, and to play its part under the new labor legislation. Suddenly and for the first time, the CGT was really a mass movement. The Catholic unions also grew greatly, from about 100,000 to over 400,000. In most negotiations, however, it was the CGT which represented labor. The collective bargaining law placed emphasis on the role of "the most representative organizations" of workers and employers. The government interpreted the law to mean that more than one union might be "most representative" in any given bargaining unit; the American concept of the exclusive bargaining agent was rejected. The CGT, while no longer denying the *bona fides* and independence of the CFTC, as it had previously done, nevertheless succeeded generally in preventing recognition of the "representativity" of the CFTC unions, and in shutting the CFTC out of the signing of most collective agreements, except in the field of clerical employment.

Employers' organization, hitherto never strong or disciplined on its labor relations side, also underwent change.[43] The employers replaced the CGPF president, Duchemin, for not having held out stoutly enough at the Matignon conference. The CGPF strengthened its central organization, and changed its name from the General Confederation of French *Production* to the General Confederation of French *Employers* (*Confédération Générale du Patronat Français*). This indicated the more important role of industrial relations, and especially the place now offered small and middle-sized firms and commerce, hitherto almost absent from the organization, alongside the big industrialists.

Collective bargaining. The first results of the Matignon Agreement and the accompanying legislation were a flowering of collective agreements, from a handful in existence at the beginning of 1936 to over 2,000 by the end of the year, and 5,700 by March, 1938.[44] But most employers did not really accept the principles of Matignon, which they felt had been forced on them by the government under the menace of the sit-downs. Under the most favorable of circumstances, the change in attitude that was needed to make collective bargaining work would have taken a long time, and it would have required strength and responsibility on the union side, and a continuation of government support for genuine collective relations. Neither of these conditions was present, and French employers made no such effort of adjustment to living with trade unions as did American employers after the mid-thirties.

The government tried to get agreement between the CGPF and the CGT on basic issues of industrial relations, but the CGPF preferred to hold back. This forced the government to legislate, prolonging the duration of collective agreements, and setting up arbitration procedure by legal compulsion instead of negotiation. The procedure was designed to let the parties reach decisions themselves or through arbitrators they chose themselves, but it was not long before the great majority of cases were left to the decision of the third party or "super-arbitrators," named, usually, by government authorities. The last CFTC convention before the war declared:

---

[43] There is little published material on employer organizations. On this period, see René Duchemin, *Organization syndicale patronale en France*. Paris, 1940; and C. J. Gignoux, *Patrons, soyez des patrons*. Paris, 1937.

[44] The fullest general account of French labor relations is that by Pierre Laroque, technician and theorist of "the new order" of collective bargaining, *Les Rapports entre patrons et ouvriers*. Paris, 1938. See also Joel Colton, *Compulsory Labor Arbitration in France, 1936–1939*. New York, 1951. There are no comparable works on the post-Popular-Front period.

. . . the collective agreements tend to be reduced to the uniform repetition of the legally obligatory clauses; conciliation and simple arbitration are too often treated as pure formalities; solutions are expected only from the "super-arbitrators." . . . In conflicts, the representatives of the parties themselves prefer not to accept their responsibilities, they unload them on a third party. . . . One cannot remain free except by accepting responsibility.[45]

Meanwhile the industrial atmosphere was being embittered by the firing of shop stewards, who had no special protection against arbitrary dismissal. The unions, increasingly racked by political differences, did not have the power to compel employers to respect their newly won rights. Nor did the CGT realize the implications of its new role, of its acceptance of compulsory arbitration, of its reliance on the state, and its place in government institutions,[46] that went with its sudden, unprecedented, and brief power under a friendly government.

What remained after this vast, but short, experiment of the Popular Front were chiefly a mass of interesting precedents in negotiation, mediation and arbitration; the myths on both sides about the forty-hour week; the rancor of employers at forced concessions; the nostalgic memories of workers for the easy victory of the sit-downs, and their permanent gain of the paid vacations.

Collapse of the Popular Front. The economic program of the Popular Front made less headway than its social reforms. The Bank of France was nationalized, as were the railroads and aircraft production, but the flight of capital out of France continued. The modest public works program was abandoned in the face of the continuing budgetary deficit. The forty-hour week did not by itself significantly reduce unemployment, nor increase purchasing power. Moreover, it was applied by management as a *maximum* forty-hour *plant* week, rather than as a *basic* forty-hour *work* week. Worst of all, in the face of German rearmament, in France alone of the great European powers, production was hardly rising; by 1938, it was still 25 per cent below 1930 levels. This failure of production to recover was, in part, due to the "week of two Sundays," as the forty-hour week was called; in part, to what the eminent conservative, Paul Reynaud, called the weakening of "the creative spirit and the willingness to take risks" in French industry; in part, to the disturbed social atmosphere, caused by labor-management recriminations and the price rises which rapidly consumed all the wage gains of labor.

The Popular Front's social components were soon split. Farmers were reasonably satisfied by the stabilization of farm prices, and no longer needed to support the rest of the Popular Front program. The middle classes were increasingly alarmed by the unrest of labor. But

---

[45] Quoted by Vignaux, *op. cit.,* page 72.
[46] Cf. Ehrmann, *op. cit.,* especially pages 57–59.

in any event the Popular Front was doomed by events abroad, by the rising tide of Nazism, the war in Spain, and the fascist encirclement of France. "It was a sign of the increased tempo of the age that the retreat that every Left majority in the Chamber made about two years after its election was made by the Blum Government in less than a year." [47] A second Blum Government in 1938 was only the briefest interlude in the drift to the right.

Within the CGT, the semblance of unity of 1936 did not last long. Issues of foreign policy soon came to dominate, and to divide, its councils. French labor was confused and torn, like the rest of French society, by the Nazi threat. By the time of Munich, it was the communists who were the chief and most vociferous, though not the only, spokesmen for a bold line against Germany. Many of the leaders on the noncommunist side were steeped in the sentimental pacifism that French labor had dropped only momentarily in 1914. Or they remained the prisoners of vague general formulas of international action by Geneva, or wishful illusions about imminent American aid.

The general strike of 1938 turned the gradual decline of the labor movement into a near-collapse. When the Daladier Government, which had signed the Munich agreement, promulgated the "Reynaud decree-laws" weakening the forty-hour week, the communists pushed the CGT into calling a one-day general strike, on November 30, 1938. Nominally, it was a protest against the decree-laws, but these were so complex that few workers understood how they would affect them. Actually it was a communist protest against the government of "the men of Munich," but in that political aim it had the support of only a minority of French workers. On neither issue could the strike attract general support as in February, 1934. The noncommunist leaders hoped that somehow the government would allow them to save face while cancelling the strike call. But Daladier was glad to use the occasion presented him to break with the CGT and the communists. To smash the strike, he used the power of requisitioning workers, under the recent National Service Law; this law had been passed amidst manifestations of national unity on all sides, and it called for consultation of government with the organizations of labor and management. The railroad and local transport workers obeyed their orders of requisition, and the strike was a dismal failure. The sequel was the mass dismissal of strikers and shop stewards, and a swift drop in CGT membership. The 5 million of the heyday of the Popular Front dwindled to some 2 million in 1939. And, as is natural in a declining movement, internal dissensions mounted in bitterness.

---

[47] Brogan, *op. cit.*, pages 717–718.

The CGT split of 1939

When the war broke out, all the various attitudes of Frenchmen toward the war, from defeatism and apathy through relief to rare enthusiasm, were represented in the CGT, and persisted. Only the communists changed, suddenly dropping four years of super-patriotic anti-Hitlerism to become apologists for the Hitler-Stalin pact and once again opponents of all "imperialist wars." The government banned all communist organizations and publications, and proceeded to make large-scale arrests. In the CGT there was a split clear down the line of the organization. The CGT executive excluded from its ranks not only the leading communist trade unionists, but all those who refused to condemn the Hitler-Stalin Pact.

The rebuilding of the CGT after the expulsion of the communists moved slowly. The mobilization of 5 million men disrupted union activities. The strict wartime regulation of wages, hours, and working conditions left little scope for the unions and little inducement for workers to maintain membership or pay dues. The membership of industrial workers which the CGT had built up in 1936, and in which the communists had been strongest, was not recovered. By the beginning of 1940, the CGT itself claimed only 800,000 members.

Had the communists been allowed to continue publishing, and thus publicly defending the Russian policy right after the Nazi-Soviet Pact, they might have discredited themselves more thoroughly among workers, and for longer. Later, however, the communist underground propaganda against the "phoney war" began to have a certain effect. This occurred less because of its intrinsic appeal than because of the indifference and hostility that government and employers were showing toward workers' interests, and the government's abridgements of civil liberties in the presumed interest of repressing the communists, while it openly tolerated high-placed defeatists and fascist sympathizers. During the first nine months of the war, the noncommunist labor leaders struggled in vain for recognition of the place of unions in the national effort. Almost everywhere, the government excluded labor, and in many cases management, from consultation, and operated by bureaucratic decision. It even suppressed the compulsory arbitration legislation at the outbreak of war. Not only did it outlaw strikes, but it practically halted contractual relations between management and labor. The unions had no part in wages and hours regulation or manpower policies. A stingy management of industrial production created flagrant inequities between civilian workers and draftees doing the same jobs. Employers emasculated the new wartime shop steward legislation. They could get troublesome workers out of the way by having them shipped off to the army. Only after the Battle of France was raging, did the CGPF finally sign with the CGT an agreement for wartime collaboration.

"In the struggle for independence which republican France must sustain, there is no room for selfish interests or for class actions or doctrines," said the joint declaration.[48] But it was far too late; in a few weeks France was no longer republican or independent.

World War II and Its Aftermath

The occupation and Vichy

Night did not close in completely on France after Parliament's abdication to Pétain and the German occupation of much of the country. For all its hatred of democratic institutions, the new order was only a partial and halting despotism, not all-pervading. The shadowy government at Vichy was able to order the slogan "Liberty, Equality, and Fraternity" erased from all public buildings, but none of the French fascist movements and parties attracted more than slight membership or support. Trade union life was choked, and the government sought to turn habits of worker association into corporatist channels. But, as compared with Germany or even Italy, trade unionists managed to carry on a great deal of independent activity, legal, semi-legal, and illegal.

To the extent that Vichy had a philosophy, it had no place for free economic association, any more than it had for free political activity. The régime, as a monarchist said at the time, "allowed only one free vote to remain, that of the stockholders' meetings of joint stock companies." [49] In 1940, it promptly dissolved the national trade union centers, the CGT and the CFTC, and the CGPF. But when it came to implementing its own ideas on labor, it bogged down in doctrinal quarrels and intrigues for power.

The cornerstone of the new structure was to be the Labor Charter (*Charte du Travail*), promulgated in October, 1941. The Charter banished the class struggle, and forbade all political or religious interests on the part of the unions. Union membership was to be obligatory, and there was to be only one union for each trade or industry in each locality. The chief function of the unions was to help set up the "social committees" (*comités sociaux*) which were to be the chief organs of corporate labor policy.

The social committees were to be organized in pyramidal form from

---

[48] *Le Peuple*, June 6, 1940, cited by Ehrmann, *op. cit.*, page 231.

[49] E. Beau de Loménie, *Les Responsabilités des Dynasties Bourgeoises*, Vol. I, page 16, Paris, 1943.

the plant level up through local, regional, and national levels, with a tripartite composition of (*a*) employers, (*b*) manual and white-collar workers, and (*c*) foremen, technicians, and supervisory personnel. Most of the functions formerly in the domain of union action, or union-management negotiation, were theoretically assigned to the social committees. Strikes and lockouts were prohibited. Representatives of the government were to supervise unions and social committees at every echelon.

Many of the best brains and leading spirits of industry, finance, and the top bureaucracy served Vichy. Not surprisingly, the clearest phase of Vichy policy was its organization of industry for the allocation of materials, and for the control of price and production policy, through industry committees (*comités d'organisation*). These committees were, in general, effectively run, and accepted by industry and business, even if with some well-founded complaints against concentration of power in the hands of the "trusts." Business found its supplies and its markets organized, its profits generally guaranteed, and its labor difficulties extinguished.

The "corporation" was to have been created by the linking of the industry committees with their economic activities, and the social committees with their labor functions. But the relations between the two were never defined. The industry committees, far more potent, went their way undisturbed. The social committees were never even organized at the higher echelons, so that there was no meshing of the two.

Like most other Frenchmen, trade union leaders and rank and file members had been stunned by the defeat in 1940. Many naturally assumed that Britain would soon be conquered too, and that the new order was firmly implanted over most of the continent. For these and other reasons, some union leaders accepted posts in the Vichy government. René Belin, assistant general secretary of the CGT, and leader of the violently anticommunist, pro-Munich *Syndicats* [50] group, became Minister of Industrial Production and Labor. His attitude and that of the union leaders who followed him was defended in 1950, by an able friend, as chiefly an attempt to prevent the communists from working with the Germans to get concessions based on their stand against the war: "In the feeble state of the union movement then, these union leaders saw only one possibility: to utilize to the maximum what remained of the French government, to make use of it against the social reaction which was threatening and against the probable maneuvers of the Communists." [51]

---

[50] So named from its organ, the weekly paper *Syndicats*.

[51] Georges Lefranc, *Les Expériences syndicales en France de 1939 à 1950*, page 36, Paris, 1950.

Even after the Labor Charter was promulgated, it was only the top "confederal" structure of the CGT and the CFTC that was fully swept away. A number of trade union leaders were able to continue in posts in local or national unions or departmental federations. Some of these leaders held aloof from all participation in the organisms of the Labor Charter, while others participated but bided their time, and yet others participated while carrying on active work against the occupation and Vichy.

Resistance

A resistance grew up slowly. As the first shock and utter confusion of the defeat gradually lifted, the French spirit and the values of the French labor tradition reasserted themselves. Then, with the Russian, and then American, entry into the war, it became reasonable to hope for victory against the Nazis. Finally, the drafting of men for forced labor in Germany after 1942 drove many able-bodied citizens to the *Maquis* (literally, wild, bushy land) and created a resistance of military significance.

As early as November, 1940, nine CGT reformist leaders and three leaders of the CFTC published the "Manifesto of the Twelve," which protested the dissolution of the two confederations, reasserted that "trade unionism has been and remains founded on the principle of liberty," including "the right of workers to be represented by representatives of their own choosing," and the "right to belong to the organization of their choice, or not to belong to any organization," and spoke out plainly against racial and religious persecution, suppression of opinion, and the privileges of wealth. In a reconciliation of some elements of traditional Catholic social doctrine with the CGT's outlook, the Manifesto offered the ambiguous formula: "the free union, within the organized 'profession,' [52] under the sovereign state." Not yet attacking the still vague and inchoate ideas of Vichy, it said, "It is not necessary to choose between trade unionism and corporatism. Both are equally necessary." Gradually, many CGT reformists came around to fuller and franker opposition to the Labor Charter and the Vichy regime. A number went into the various underground resistance movements, particularly after Léon Jouhaux was arrested and taken to Germany as a hostage.

The communists had, perforce, been in opposition to Vichy but did not throw themselves into the resistance to Germany until the invasion

---

[52] The term *profession*, so common in French, and often translated as "profession," has no English equivalent. It refers to a branch of economic activity, which may be a trade or an industry, or an occupation. Generally it does not refer to the liberal professions unless qualified by the adjective.

of Russia. Until then, they were still urging: "Neither Berlin nor London," [53] attacking de Gaulle, and telling workers: "Get it straight that it is not in the victory of one imperialism over another that our common salvation lies." [54] Immediately after June 22, 1941, they brought their energies and a functioning clandestine organization into the struggle against the Germans, praised de Gaulle, and put aside the social revolution in favor of a rediscovered patriotism and appeals for unity with all classes against the occupant.

As one product of the new international situation, the reformist CGT and communist labor leaders agreed upon a reunification, by the Le Perreux agreement of 1943. This stipulated a 5:3 ratio in the executive of the underground CGT,[55] and in the departmental federations and national unions, the proportions between the two wings as of September 1939 were to be reestablished. The work of reunification went forward, not without some recriminations. An interlocking of legal and illegal organizations developed. The CFTC and the reunited CGT both recognized de Gaulle's leadership of the resistance, and sent representatives to London and Algiers to work with the Free French movement. Both were prominent in the underground National Resistance Council, in which were represented groups from extreme right to left, and later in the departmental Committees of Liberation.

Urban workers bore much of the brunt of the occupation. They suffered from food shortages, and they were the least able to pay the black market prices for all the necessities available only on the black market. Wages were set at lower levels, and far more successfully controlled, than prices. Wages were kept low to encourage French workers to go to Germany; the exceptions were in the interest of German production in French factories. Bombings took their toll among workers in factories and among their families living near railroad marshalling yards or bridges. Forced labor in Germany presented the greatest hazard—not only of expatriation and exploitation, but of death by bombing. Since many workers had been active in left-wing politics, and were active in the resistance, they were numerous among the political deportees, and among the victims of Nazi and Vichy torture and execution squads.

---

[53] A. Rossi, *A Communist Party in Action: An Account of the Organization and Operations in France,* Chapter VIII, note 46. New Haven, 1949. Despite its title, this well-documented study covers only the period between June 1940 and late 1941. The same author's *Les Communistes français pendant la drôle de Guerre,* Paris, 1951, covers the "phoney war" period.

[54] *L'Humanité,* June 20, 1941. Cited in Lefranc, *op. cit.,* page 115.

[55] The *Syndicats* wing, of which Belin had been the leader, which had about a third of the votes in the last prewar convention, was not represented at Le Perreux.

A good part of the resistance was the resistance of workers. There was a considerable amount of slowdown on the job and sabotage. Most notably the railroad workers, especially after D-Day, contributed intelligence on enemy movements and sabotaged installations and equipment. Like others, the workers found a revival of patriotism and a hope for the future in the resistance. In August 1944, as the Allied armies came close to Paris, the CGT and CFTC called out their followers in a general strike to speed the liberation of the capital: "Let us unite, ever more closely with the entire nation, and reconquer our freedom." [56]

Labor's position at the liberation

As in the other western European nations, at the liberation, labor in France held a position of new esteem and power. It was, as the CGT-CFTC call had said, "united more closely with the entire nation." Its activity and its losses in the resistance had been conspicuously greater than those of any other class. To symbolize that position, one CGT leader, Buisson, had been president of the Algiers Consultative Assembly, and another, Saillant, succeeded Bidault as head of the National Resistance Council when Bidault entered de Gaulle's government. Perhaps labor received recognition even beyond its sacrifices and achievements. For the country, striving to heal the national self-esteem lacerated in the years just past, fostered a myth of its own quasi-total resistance, in which a large part of the historical record was that of labor's sabotage and strikes, its deportees and its maquisards.

The other élites of the nation were gravely compromised, whereas labor had scant responsibility for the régime which had just ingloriously disappeared. Financial and industrial leaders and their political spokesmen in the center and right parties, and much of the ecclesiastical hierarchy, the upper bureaucracy, and the military were low in repute and in self-confidence. The writing of the time was all "social" and at least vaguely socialist. The reforms which had been discussed in the years of self-criticism after 1940, and put forth as the program of the National Resistance Council, were, for the most part, reforms which the CGT had preached between the wars, and it was assumed that labor would have a leading role in implementing them in a reborn France.

Under the provisional governments of de Gaulle and his successors, France nationalized its coal mines, its gas and electric power production

[56] Cited in *La Voix du peuple*, January 1946, *XXVIe congrès confédéral de la CGT, rapports confédéraux*, page 33.

and distribution systems, the 34 largest insurance companies, the Bank of France and the 4 largest deposit banks. This "revolution in the ownership and direction of French industry and banking," [57] supported by labor, was the work of overwhelming majorities in the Constituent Assembly, in the first year after the war's end. The government also greatly broadened its health insurance and old age insurance programs and unified their administration. At the plant level it instituted joint committees to promote labor-management cooperation, and reinstituted the system of shop stewards. It created a National Economic Council representing all the major economic interests of the country, as a "fourth house" of the legislature, with advisory powers.

The unions named representatives to the boards of directors of the nationalized industries, banks, and insurance companies. Workers were given a large share of control, through elected representatives, in the administration of the social security program. The National Economic Council chose Léon Jouhaux as its president. There were labor members on the National Credit Council, and CGT members and chairmen on committees of the Monnet Planning Commission.

In this political climate, workers flocked to the CGT,[58] and its membership soared to new heights, exceeding those of 1936. By 1945, it claimed 5¼ million members, and, by 1946, over 6 million, with less of a gap between facts and claims than at many other periods. The CFTC, likewise, went beyond its prewar peak, and soon claimed a membership of 700,000. It politely declined the CGT's insistent suggestions to unite with it, but declared itself willing to continue concerted action as in the resistance.

A new organization appeared in the CGC (*Confédération Générale des Cadres*), the General Confederation of Technicians and Supervisory Employees. Many of the *cadres* had joined the CGT under the impetus of the liberation. After a year or two, they observed that the CGT was not the best defender of their interests in an inflationary situation; most dropped out of the CGT and many went into the CGC. Both the CGT and CFTC contested the *bona fides* of the CGC at first and tried to exclude it from government wage commissions, but abandoned that attempt by 1946.

Employers' organization resumed more slowly. In the hectic days soon after liberation, there were many who feared trial and severe punishment, loss of industrial properties or worse, for real or fancied collaboration with the occupation. For almost two years the only

---

[57] David H. Pinkney, "The French Experiment in Nationalization," *Modern France,* page 355. Princeton, 1951.

[58] The Vichy labor legislation was abolished by an Algiers decree shortly before the liberation of Paris.

over-all national representation of employers was through a "Committee of Fourteen," chosen by the de Gaulle government as a device for getting some consultation of employer opinion.[59] In 1946, employers set up a new organization to replace the pre-1940 CGPF; this was the National Council of French Employers, the CNPF (*Conseil National du Patronat Français*). They disavowed the weaknesses of the Committee of Fourteen, pointing out that it had not been selected by the employers themselves, and never had a mandate to represent their interests. In theory, the CNPF was only a loose coordinating council of area employer associations handling labor relations and national trade associations handling price and production questions. Its constitution provided that no organization be considered bound by any decision for which its representatives in the CNPF did not vote. Actually, the membership of the CNPF was soon more inclusive and its discipline far tighter than that of the CGPF before the war. Charges of employer collaboration with the Germans and Vichy were met by the naming of a president who, as a political deportee in Germany, was beyond reproach. In a fairly short time, just as the weight of the coalition governments moved well to the center and right, the CNPF came to assert itself in national life.

Other employer organizations included the Association of Small and Middle-sized Enterprises, with the special concerns indicated by its name, which was also a constituent of the CNPF. A Catholic employers' association, whose members were likewise in the CNPF, played no important role. Finally, there was the Young Employers' Association (*Centre des Jeunes Patrons*), with bolder and more experimental notions about social policy than those of the CNPF, but without great weight in the making of employer policy. These smaller organizations did not carry on any direct industrial relations.

Employers and trade unions could not engage in collective bargaining, for the system of wartime government wage controls was continued, with the government machinery supplemented by consultative tripartite wage commissions. One of the first acts of the government was to grant an overdue wage increase, and within the first year of liberation wage rates were raised about 60 per cent. But for some time the workers' interest was less in the rate of wages than in the price and supply of food. The de Gaulle government, preoccupied at first with the war, paid more attention to military and foreign policy and prestige than to economic problems. It let the irretrievable early months after liberation slip by—when bold measures were expected, and when almost anything might have been accepted—without any

---

[59] There were also employer representatives on the various industry wage committees which had consultative status in government wage-fixing.

fundamental reforms of the tax system, any blow at black markets, or even the currency contraction planned in Algiers. It did not offer sufficient price inducements for deliveries to legal channels to over-come farmers' habits, well developed and morally sanctioned during the occupation, of selling in the highest (that is, black) market. Nor did it take measures of compulsion to assure those deliveries, or punish black marketers. Following a practice as old as the French Revolution, it fixed food prices but failed to assure their supply. The result was that black and grey markets flourished, to the great disadvantage of urban workers and modest rentiers and pensioners.

Industrial production recovered from the war's destruction and German looting. For the year 1945, as a whole, production was still only 45 per cent of 1938 levels, but by the end of the year it was at 66 per cent of 1938. Tremendous efforts were put forth by the railroad workers in the repair of the shattered railway network and the depleted, overaged, and damaged rolling stock; the miners made efforts in overcoming shortages of pit props and equipment. Thus, they broke the two worst bottlenecks. The production of consumer goods, how-ever, was at extremely low levels, and food shortages were still acute. In the winter of 1946, the Paris radio was saying:

The nation is now asking in its prayers to be given its daily bread. It no longer asks for grandeur, a large army, or good institutions. Whether it is a question of bread, meat, or fats, we must import without delay, at any cost, the amount we need until such time as French agriculture can meet our re-quirements.[60]

Communists take control of CGT

In the year following liberation, the trade union movement took on a new political complexion.[61] The immediate reasons for this were many. The Communist Party, during the resistance, had prepared for the day when the CGT would resume its liberty. It had trained people who moved swiftly, and where necessary with force, into the key posts in local and national unions and departmental federations. It also moved into the purge commissions which were to eliminate the collaborators from the labor movement, and used them to eliminate some of the potential opposition. Many of the most aggressive anti-communists, especially those of the *Syndicats* faction, had disqualified themselves by their activities under Vichy. Others were also eliminated, whose offense was that they were anticommunist, or had been com-munists who had quit the party after the Nazi-Soviet Pact.

---

[60] Broadcast of February 10, 1946.
[61] See Val R. Lorwin, "The Struggle for Control of the French Trade Union Movement," *Modern France*, pages 200–218.

The communists and the liberal Catholics had the most conspicuous records in the resistance. The communists had had the greatest number of victims, and of these they made constant display, with inflated figures, as "the party of the fusillade victims" (*le parti des fusillés*), while they identified their prewar CGT opponents with anti-national and anti-working class behavior. The demonstrative nationalism of the communists since mid-1941, and the uneasy consciences of the non-communists about their own pacifism (and in many cases their acceptance of Munich), made the latter hesitate for several years even to mention the communist position in the two years of the Nazi-Soviet pact. In addition to the aura of the resistance, the communists basked in the aura of the Red Army, fortunately for them unseen in France, and the revived prestige of Russia.

The communists were the only party to come out of the clandestine period with a functioning party machinery. In the confused and critical months right after liberation, when the political lines of the Fourth Republic were being drawn, they had the inestimable advantage of knowing what they wanted, while their rivals were divided and uncertain; and of being concerned with the realities of power, while their rivals were lulled with talk and abstractions. The Communist Party also devoted great attention to the press and propaganda, far beyond the capacities and resources of other groups, and they worked through a host of busy front organizations of women (hitherto hardly organized), youth, farmers, small and medium-sized businessmen, prisoners and deportees, writers and artists.

They knew how to utilize the positions they had gained when de Gaulle took their representatives into the government. They put party comrades into jobs in the ministries. They placed other comrades in the bureaucracy of nationalized industries; these in turn were often able to make hiring dependent not only on a CGT card but also on Communist Party membership or endorsement.

In the CGT the noncommunists, whom for convenience we may here call reformists,[62] were divided and unorganized, and they were willing at first to essay the "unity" which the communists had preached, but without self-deception, since Russia's entry into the war. The socialists were the only party that offered potential competition to the communists for mass support among the workers. The socialists, however, had to rebuild their party organization; in the resistance they had dispersed their efforts in a number of underground groups. The socialists had neither the toughness nor the unity of purpose of the communists. They did not accept the communist offers of unity of action,

---

[62] The noncommunists also included some who were not of reformist outlook, such as the remnants of old-style revolutionary syndicalists, and Trotzkyites.

but they allowed the pervasive vague talk of socialism, and their
own position in the government, to blur their realization of how
rapidly opportunity was slipping away from them. When the first
party conventions were held after the war, the socialists had a third
of a million members, while the communists had a million. In the labor
movement, and especially among industrial workers, the proportion
of communist superiority was even more pronounced.

By April, 1946, when the first postwar CGT convention was held,
the communists controlled all the major industrial unions, and practically all the major departmental federations, with the Paris region,
more than ever, their stronghold. They made their top labor leader, the
able Benoît Frachon, co-secretary general with Léon Jouhaux, and
they made voting both at CGT conventions and at the National Committee (see infra, page 368) strictly proportional to membership represented. They permitted the reformists a far higher percentage of places
on the executive organs of the CGT than their following gave them.
Their maximum advantage lay in keeping the CGT nonpolitical in
appearance. In this they failed because of working class discontent
and the change in Soviet foreign policy and, hence, in the international
communist line. Until the spring of 1947 the communist leadership
moderated its wage demands, put the brake on strikes, and stressed
"the battle of production." Said the executive report to the 1946 CGT
convention, "The emancipation of the working class is inseparable from
the independence of the country, itself inseparable from its economic
recovery." [63] Perhaps the communists expected to take power by
parliamentary means, and felt that their efforts to maintain work
discipline and rule out strikes would establish habits essential to a
communist-run France.

For a time they risked their leadership by holding this line. The
communist Minister of Labor, a leader of the metal workers' union,
denounced the printers, when they struck for higher wages, as saboteurs
and Trotzkyites. In mid-1946, in opposing a wildcat strike of the Post,
Telegraph, and Telephone Workers, the communist leadership brought
on a split in this powerful union, the first split in the postwar CGT.
In May, 1947, an independent union called a strike which spread
through the Renault works, the most important plant in all France.
After first denouncing the strike, the CGT leaders concluded they were
in grave danger of being "outflanked on the left." Suddenly reversing
themselves, they swung into action as leaders of the strike. In a short
while, the party leaders also briskly reversed their position, and left
the government on the issue of wage increases.

---

[63] *La Voix du Peuple,* January 1946. *XXVIe congrès confédéral de la C.G.T.,
Rapports Confédéraux,* page 52.

Two months later, the full change in the communist international line came with the Soviet stand against the Marshall Plan, and both the Communist Party and the CGT were in all-out opposition. They made up for lost time in pushing overdue wage claims. In November and December, they called a series of strikes, amounting, in all but name, to a general strike against the economic recovery of France and against the government.

1947 strikes and schism

The strikes of November-December, 1947, were perhaps the bitterest in French experience, and the stakes in the country and in the labor movement, the highest. As the miners, railwaymen, dockers, metal workers, gas and electricity workers, and building trades went out, over 2 million workers struck. The communist leaders of the CGT not only demanded wage raises, but also attacked the Marshall Plan, then still only a plan, and called for the return of the communists to the government on their own terms. How far they planned to go if the strikes had been successful is hard to say. The union leaders who opposed the strikes later argued plausibly that they had saved France from the fate of Czechoslovakia.

The strikes failed. The autonomous rail workers' union, the reformists still within the CGT, and the Catholic unions came out against them. The government, after two weeks of the stoppages, showed a new firmness, and took measures to protect and encourage those ready to work, and to repress sabotage. Quickened by want in strikers' families, the common sense of French workers asserted itself to reject a political strike against economic recovery. When the rail workers went back, it was clear that the strike movement was lost.

The strikes precipitated the long-brewing schism in the CGT. There had already been smaller splits since 1946. The first had been that of a small anarcho-syndicalist group which had formed the National Confederation of Labor. Sizable groups of rail and postal workers had broken away to form autonomous unions. The reformists within the CGT had been loosely organized around the publication and distribution of their weekly journal, *Force Ouvrière* (Workers' Force, FO), successor to their underground *Resistance Ouvrière*. Their national leaders had postponed the break as long as they could. Most of them had lived through two splits already, and they had both sentimental and practical fears of the consequences of another, as well as a knowledge of the weaknesses in their own fighting potential. For Jouhaux and the circle around him were now mostly public figures or union office managers. They were no longer the tireless organizers and fighters who would be needed to rebuild an organization almost from scratch, in the teeth of the CGT backed by the most powerful party in France. They knew how different would be their task from what it had been in 1921, when it was they who had kept the name and the apparatus of the CGT, or in 1939, when the opposition they expelled was also proscribed by the government.

The reformist leaders had little choice, however. The FO lower-echelon leaders had reached their breaking point under the violence directed at them by local strike leaders; now they faced the top leaders of FO with the choice between splitting or remaining impotent in the CGT while their following melted away. In December, 1947, therefore, the FO group seceded from the CGT and by April, 1948, it held its first convention. Claiming to be the true heir of the old CGT, and clinging to the tradition-hallowed name, it called itself the *Confédération Générale du Travail—Force Ouvrière*.

The loss of the strikes, and the schism, gravely weakened the CGT and cost it perhaps two million members. But its organizational framework remained intact. Although its preoccupations became more and more political, it continued to be the major organization among industrial workers. FO failed to win over the majority of those industrial workers who dropped out of the CGT, or the many who, though dissatisfied, remained within it. The FO leaders were handicapped by the lack of financial resources, by their lack of organizational drive, and by the primarily civil-service and white collar base with which they had started. They also suffered because, while asserting their non-political character as the basis of their being, they were regarded as tied to the Socialist Party and to the government. In a real sense they were prisoners of government economic policy, or lack of policy. Their limits of action were set by the precarious position of the Third Force governments, whose life was threatened by the communists on the left and the Gaullists on the right.

While the CGT was demanding wage increases, FO, the CFTC and the CGC formed a "price-reduction coalition" which appealed to workers' judgment and patience, and pointed out that only price stabilization could raise their real wages. The government had hailed the formation of FO as the great watershed in post-liberation politics. But, soothed by a few months' seasonal halt in price rises, it let its friends wait for satisfaction instead of pushing the measures needed to halt inflation. When prices resumed their upward movement in the summer of 1948, and the government still held back on wage increases, the FO-CFTC-CGC "price-reduction coalition" collapsed. A series of rapid cabinet crises over the wage-price issue shook the government.

In a few months—but only after the CGT's crippling coal strike—wage increases, larger than first contemplated, had to be granted.

The 1948 coal strike was less far-reaching than the strikes of the year before, despite CGT attempts to extend the tie-up from the mines to the rails and docks and other vital points. But in one way it bit deeper. The CGT called out the mine safety and maintenance men, a threat to the nation's mines and to miners' future livelihood unprecedented even in the coal strike under the occupation. This forced the government to use police and troops, and a series of bloody fights took place.[64] Like the 1947 strikes, this strike was no success in any ordinary trade-union terms. In long-run international communist strategy, the 1947 and 1948 strikes may have served their purpose. They slowed down the recovery of France. They weakened the confidence of her European partners and of the United States in French stability and the capacity of France to play its central role on the continent. They contributed to the further erosion of the social fabric, and many workers were confirmed in their old feelings of hostility to government.

The nation's recovery continued (with United States aid) despite the setback of the coal strike. By 1949, the industrial production index stood at 123 per cent of 1938, although this represented hardly any improvement over 1929. After 12 years of inflation, prices were comparatively stable during most of 1949 and early 1950, but this was also a period of comparative industrial stagnation and some increase in unemployment and partial unemployment. The unemployment was still statistically slight,[65] but it caused concern among workers, always very sensitive to questions of personal security, who had no system of unemployment insurance. And they were assailed by CGT and Communist Party arguments that the Marshall Plan was aimed at pauperizing French workers and throwing them out of work so as to weaken their will to resist a war of anti-Soviet aggression.

National income and wage structure in 1948–1950

The economic position of wage-earners, as compared with other elements in the population, became clearer with the passing of the days of scarcity. The wage-earners' share of national income was 48.5 per cent in 1949 and 47.3 per cent in 1950.[66] The official estimates of

---

[64] To the delight of the communists, it was a socialist Minister of the Interior who, as in 1947 ordered out the troops.

[65] 149,000 unfilled employment requests in December, 1949. Unemployment was, however, greater than this number. There is no official figure of unemployment.

[66] *Rapport sur les comptes économiques de la nation,* 1951, by the Minister of Finance and National Economy. National accounts data have made great progress

the distribution of shares of national income are given in Table 1.
Wage-earners' shares were roughly the same, in 1949 and 1950, as the
48 per cent at which they were estimated in 1938. There had thus
been no redistribution of national income as between wage-earners and
other classes.[67] The work week was longer;[68] workers were putting
forth a greater effort for the same fraction of national income. They
were still bearing a disproportionate share of the tax burden of the
country, because of the government's inability or unwillingness to raise
taxes from farmers, manufacturers, distributors, and self-employed
professionals. Withholding taxes on wages and salaries were among
the few collected in full, and the largest share of tax revenue still came
from indirect taxes bearing most heavily on wage-earners.

TABLE 1

DISPOSABLE INCOME IN FRANCE BY DISTRIBUTIVE SHARES, 1949 AND 1950

	1949		1950	
	Billions of francs	Per cent	Billions of francs	Per cent
Wage and salary earners*	3,325	48.5	3,630	47.3
Entrepreneurial income and distributed profits †	2,920	42.5	3,380	44.2
Undistributed corporate profits	610	9.	650	8.5
Total	6,855	100.	7,660	100.

* Total pensions are ascribed to the wage and salary earners' group.
† Before depreciation allowance. Distributed profits include not only dividends
(estimated at only 100–150 billions) but also entrepreneurial income of sole proprietors, income in kind (farm owners), and rents. "In all these categories," it is
pointed out, "the concept of income of enterprises is inseparable from that of personal income."
Source: Based on Ministre des Finances et des Affaires Economiques, *Rapport
sur les comptes économiques de la nation*, February, 1951.

in recent years in France, but they are still only the roughest approximations, and
are particularly likely to understate entrepreneurial shares, and hence overstate
wage-earners' shares, in national income, because of gaps and errors in the raw
data upon which the estimates must be based. As the Minister's statement points
out, "The superficial accuracy implied in the use of specific numeral values
hides a good deal of real uncertainty in the basic figures. . . ." The distinguished
economist Alfred Sauvy remarks ("La Situation Economique," *Droit Social*, December 1950, page 399), "The lack of basic materials obliges the specialists to
reconstitute the national income by means of several available fragments, like
Cuvier reconstituting the skeleton of an animal on seeing several bones." He
discusses some of the opposition to the development of national income statistics, including the vote against such research by the employer group in the
National Economic Council. However, M. Sauvy suggests, "the metric system
and smallpox vaccination had their adversaries too."

[67] Within the entrepreneurial groups there had been a decline in corporate
dividends and an increase in the share of sole proprietors and farmers.

[68] 44.6 hours in October, 1949 as compared with a 1938 monthly average of 39.4
hours. This is a scheduled work week, not hours actually worked.

Within the working class there had been a tremendous redistribution of income. The chief differences were the greater share going to the heads of large families and the relative cut in real income of the bachelor or childless worker; the gain in the position of the worker in the provinces as compared with Paris; the improvement in the wages of women as compared with those of men; and the general narrowing of occupational wage differentials.[69] Money and real wages in 1950 and before the war are compared in Table 2.

TABLE 2

INDEXES OF MONEY AND REAL WAGES OF MALE WORKERS IN FRENCH INDUSTRY
AND COMMERCE, APRIL, 1950, COMPARED WITH OCTOBER, 1938
(*October 1938 = 100*)

	All France	Paris	Provinces
1. Hourly wage rates	1,110	928	1,135
2. Net full-time weekly earnings plus family allowances			
A. Single or childless worker	1,342	1,034	1,437
B. Worker * with wife and two children..	1,794	1,363	1,926
3. Consumer prices	1,756	1,556	1,789
4. Real hourly wage rate	63	60	63
5. Real earnings, including family allowances			
A. Single worker	76	66	80
B. Workers* with wife and two children..	102	88	108

* Wife not working, therefore receiving allowance for "single wage" in family.
Source: Wage data from *Institut national de la statistique et des études économiques. Statistique Générale de la France.* Consumer price data based on *Institut d'observation économique.* This unofficial source has furnished the best available cost of living data, in the absence of an official cost of living index.

As a result of enlarged family allowances, while the average single or childless worker in industry or commerce, in Paris, had a money income in April, 1950 only 10.3 times that of October, 1938, the father of two children had an income 13.6 times that of 1938. In the provinces, the same categories of workers had incomes, respectively, 14.4 and 19.3 times their 1938 incomes; those with larger families had, of course, bettered their incomes even more.

The narrowing of the differences between Paris and the provinces could also be seen in the officially determined wage minima. Whereas rates in the lowest nonagricultural wage areas had been more than 50 per cent below Paris, before the war, the official wage zones set a maximum differential of 40 per cent in 1944, 25 per cent in 1945, and by May, 1951 the government had reduced the zone differential in minimum wages to 15 per cent. Actual cost of living differences had

[69] See especially "Taux, Masse et Disparité des Salaires en 1949," *Etudes et conjunctures; économie française,* Institut National de la Statistique et des Etudes Economiques (Nov.-Dec. 1949) pages 58–74; and Alfred Sauvy, "Les Salaires français," *Revue Economique* (Dec. 1950), pages 513–22, as well as periodic surveys in the Ministry of Labor's *Revue Française du Travail.*

also been narrowed—but not to the same extent [70]—by more rapid price increases in the provincial cities than in Paris.

The differentials between wage rates for men and women had been reduced. Women's wage rates before the war had been estimated at 70 per cent of men's wage rates. In 1946, equal pay for equal work was proclaimed by decree; in mid-1949 women's rates were 93 per cent of men's rates. The differentials between primarily male and female occupations had been reduced in the process of improvement of the relative position of the lower skilled categories, in which most women were to be found. The gap between unskilled workers, and skilled workers, technicians and supervisory employees had been greatly narrowed as a result both of inflation and the expanded family allowances.

Some employer organizations denounced the government for the heavy burden of "social charges." Before the war, payments for family allowances and social insurance added only 15 per cent to the direct wage bill; by 1951, they added 33 per cent. But since the total wage bill (direct wages plus social charges) had not gone up in relation to national income, it was clear that, in effect, workers as a group were paying for the increases in their family allowances and social insurance themselves, out of reduced direct wages. Given the low wage levels in France, there was no question of the need of those who were now getting a larger slice of total wage-earner income. But the changes within the wage structure probably increased social tensions and the vulnerability of workers to extreme political appeals, and decreased incentives to greater responsibilities in the production process. The real incidence of social and indirect wage changes made "the working class function as a vast mutual aid association in which . . . it was the poor who were helping out the poorer." [71]

The government had, at the end of 1946, enacted a law to permit the resumption of collective bargaining on all issues except wages. But since wages were the issue of overwhelming concern to workers, the rebirth of collective bargaining under the 1946 law was stillborn. The government reaped most of the harvest of worker discontent during these years. It had removed retail price controls on practically all commodities by early 1948. The unions' demand for a return to full freedom of bargaining gathered weight, until by late 1949 the govern-

---

[70] While Paris prices are reported by various sources, and indexes are computed, data on prices in the provinces are almost totally lacking.

[71] Michel Collinet, *Lettre aux Militants*, November 20, 1950, page 2. A more bitter comment, not infrequently heard, is that worded by an FO local leader thus, "We are getting paid less and less for our work, and more and more for being 'Father Rabbit.'"

ment introduced the bill which became the collective bargaining law of February 1950 (discussed *infra*, pages 378–380).

Workers who had in their minds equated a return to free collective bargaining with a great improvement in their wages were disappointed. The first experiences under the new law showed that the unions were in no state to win large gains against the weight of well-organized employer associations, the conservatism of the government (the largest single employer of French labor), and labor's own divisions, apathy, and fatigue. The inequality of the bargaining partners alarmed even the conservative press and the clergy, who saw in it a cause of further embitterment of workers. Moreover, it began to be clear to the more thoughtful union leaders that any durable improvement in workers' standards would have to come from changes in the redistribution of national income which only governmental action could produce. Money wage rises were the most transitory of gains, and direct controls on prices *qua* prices were ineffectual.

The elaborate bargaining structure envisaged by the law reduced itself in the first year's practice largely to the negotiation of simple wage accords, rather than the full-fledged collective agreements which called for clauses on many issues beyond those of wages. Workers' eyes were chiefly on wages, and employers were reluctant to negotiate on the issues of interest to union leaders, such as trade union activity in the shop or broadening of the rights of elected workers' representatives covered by legislation. Despite the theory of agreement by "most representative" organizations, both the government and private employers reacted to CGT politics by bargaining often with the other, numerically often least representative, unions. By the end of the first year of the law's operation, the Minister of Labor announced that some 740 wage accords and 77 collective agreements had been signed.[71a]

After the outbreak of the Korean war, prices moved forward rapidly as the effects of world price inflation began to affect French production, but before any impact of increased rearmament was felt. Prices rose by more than 12½ per cent between September, 1950 and March, 1951, and continued to rise. Wages kept pace for a time, but it appeared that improvements of gross deficiencies in workers' standards of living would have to be postponed indefinitely. With the rigidities of the French economy, the needs of rearmament seemed likely to impinge upon the most broadly approved social claims.

Faced with a resumption of the inflation chronic in France since World War I, and pessimistic about the government's possibilities of holding any line on prices, the unions launched insistent campaigns for automatic adjustment of wages to rises in the cost of living, in

[71a] Assemblée nationale, *Débats*, March 16, 1951, pages 2081–2082.

the government-fixed minimum wage, and in wage agreements. A number of agreements signed in early 1951 included some type of provision for reopening wages in the light of price rises; generally, they did not include automatic escalator clauses.

The French working class had since the war improved its position less than that of almost any other western European country. The economy had operated in low gear for most of the twentieth century. The government was unable, or for political reasons unwilling, to repress tax frauds and tap new sources of revenue among the prosperous sections of the farm population and the business community. Lack of public confidence in the currency restricted the government's ability to attract private savings or undertake deficit financing. Private investment was at low levels and little risk capital was available.

The overcrowded, high-cost apparatus of distribution had become even more sluggish with the host of new entries in the period of shortages. Labor organizations were weak, and their energies had been diverted down the paths of communist politics or in pursuit of money wage increases which had proven, as a Catholic unionist said, "vain and fragile." The country had not yet recovered from the destruction of life and values and work habits caused by two wars within one generation on its own soil.

There were, however, factors of strength. France did not stand alone; she had friends and allies. In addition to continuing help from overseas, there was the potentially hopeful plan for international integration of the coal and steel industries, a creative idea which France had given to Europe. In the absence of adequate private investment, the government was now directing an active investment policy, although its Monnet plan stressed basic production at the expense of investment programs of more direct and tangible interest to workers (for example, housing). Many farms were modernizing the equipment with which to work a rich land. There was a stir of new ideas among a significant minority of employers on social problems as well as on production methods. Labor and management were both becoming aware of France's need for higher productivity. The workers of France had shown that in a crisis, despite all their pent-up wants and grievances, they could resist the appeals to catastrophic action. Democratic trade unionists were re-thinking their ideas, abandoning old romantic notions, and seeking a more creative role in a society which greatly needed their contribution.

The Structure and Functioning of French Unions

The structure of French trade unions was the product of two major influences: One was the syndicalist and federalist practice which shaped the formal structure of the unions of all three national centers; the other was the communist, centralizing force in the most important of the three centers. The first influence had its source in the trade union movement itself, and in the state of industrial relations, but in many ways looked backward to a pre-industrial era. The second had its source outside the trade union movement, in the Communist Party.

The structure of the contemporary labor movement is the heritage of the generation before World War I. The unions had grown up in an economy of small concerns and decentralized product markets. They had been organized chiefly from the ground up, by local initiative, rather than by national organizations working from the top down. In their formative period, the most dynamic and articulate element had been the *Bourses du Travail*, which represented local autonomy as against the centralizing agencies of unionism. All parts of the labor movement were starved for funds, but the national organizations were the last to receive a share of dues. The *Bourses* usually had some municipal subsidies on which to operate, making it possible to avoid facing squarely the problem of dues. The local union was largely independent *vis-à-vis* its national union, and the national union *vis-à-vis* the confederation. The small and ill-paid staffs in national union and confederation offices were subject to jealous control by representative bodies. The voting system in the CGT emphasized the principle of "federalism" or decentralization by giving the same vote (until the 1920's) to the smallest organizations as to the largest. At the base was a fluctuating membership, largely of an elite of skilled workers, egalitarian and individualistic in outlook, skeptical toward authority, with a "platonic loyalty to labor organization." [72] Nor did the unions build up benefit features, or compulsive devices, such as the closed shop, to maintain a passive loyalty over periods of disaffection or loss of interest. In short, a loose union structure [73] corresponded to the syndicalist doctrine, itself both a cause and a consequence of these practices and attitudes.

In the last generation, changes in the economy and in the political interests of labor demanded a more coherent and centralized structure. Labor has had to deal with larger employer units, producing for wider markets, and organized in more vigorous associations. Labor's relations with government have become of the essence of its functions, and in France, government is almost always the central government. After World War II, the government nationalized and concentrated the administration of a number of industries most important to the unions.

[72] Saposs, *op. cit.*, page 159.
[73] To all these statements there were of course some exceptions, most notably, the printers' union of the CGT.

It took over a central role in investment planning and in wage determination. Labor was called on for representation in various functional councils, industry-wide and national. International political and economic relations interested labor more directly. For the CGT, after the war, there was the additional and prime factor of centralization in Communist Party control.

These factors were partially, but very imperfectly, reflected in the union organization. Inherited structures and traditional attitudes among the rank and file resisted the trend toward centralization and bureaucratization. In the non-communist unions, the national unions and the confederation offices continued to struggle for more financial support. They were handicapped by the open rivalries of groups and *tendances*, and the lack of strong leadership in many of the central posts. Finally, employer associations insisted on decentralization of collective bargaining to an area basis.

Local and national unions

The local union (*syndicat*) of workers in one trade or industry remains the basic unit of organization. It is usually city-wide but may cover either a larger geographical area or, in some big employer units, a single plant. If city-wide or larger in coverage, it is divided into sub-locals (*sections syndicales*) for the various employer units covered. Some building trades locals in large cities are divided into craft sub-locals. The locals of one national union may coordinate their action on a regional basis through a council (*union intersyndicale*). The significance of the local union may be clearest from two facts. It is the local, not the national union, that is directly represented at the convention of the confederations. It is the local that sets the level of its own dues, although the per capita payments to the national union and the confederation are fixed by those bodies.

Almost every national union (*fédération*) is an industrial, rather than a craft, union. Unions first developed among the skilled trades, and many were craft organizations. Both craft and industrial unions composed the CGT when it was formed, but in 1906, craft unionism was officially condemned by the class-conscious syndicalists, and further craft union affiliations were banned. Most of the national craft organizations were merged into industrial organizations by the end of the World War I. The printing trades have, in each of the national centers, a single national union, which covers all crafts (except the journalists) in printing and publishing. The building trades likewise form a single national union in the CGT, the CFTC, and FO; so do the metal trades, whose unions cover the whole field from basic iron and steel to automobiles and shipbuilding on the one hand, to pots and pans and optical goods on the other. Within these broad jurisdictions, there may be locals organized on craft or on narrower industry lines, as in the building trades, or there may be national and district councils for special problems, as among the railwaymen. Among the few craft unions are the barbers, the jewelry workers, the marine officers, and the ancient and honorable craft of coopers. There are 40 national unions in the CGT. (The American Federation of Labor has 107.)

The CGT carried forward a number of mergers of industrial unions after liberation. Within some of the CGT unions there was a move toward wiping out separate craft locals and merging them in single, department-wide locals. This was soon criticized by the leadership as "excessive centralization." This trend, according to Arrachard, top communist building trades official, had led to "unnatural organizations," which made him think of "the obese who become infirm and impotent." [74] The CGT therefore moved to reconstitute locals along craft or sub-industry lines within some of the big industry-wide unions, notably the building trades.

The chief exceptions to the principle of industrial unionism are the clerical employees of private industry. As in most European countries, the clerical workers (employés, as distinguished from manual workers, ouvriers) are organized into separate unions of considerable importance. In each of the confederations, the clerical workers in government employment have separate national unions for single ministries or groups of ministries, with councils to coordinate their action. The chief organization of teachers is, however, unaffiliated; it left the CGT, but refused to join FO; some of its members also carry FO or CGT cards.

Technicians and lower managerial staff (cadres) have presented a difficult problem of union organization, as they have in most countries. Only under the economic pinch of the depression, and in the political wake of the Popular Front and later of the liberation, did they join the CGT in any large numbers. They have usually felt closer in social and political outlook to their employers than to the general labor unions which have bid for their membership. On the other hand, they have felt a need for organization because their profes-

---

[74] "Pour une Structure Syndicale Plus Efficace," in Servir La France, November-December, 1948, page 42. The woodworkers, he said, lost interest in the union when their locals were merged with locals of the building trades, by whose larger numbers they were swamped. He demolished the arguments made for some mergers in the immediate post-liberation period, to the effect that a new technology of building was making craft lines obsolete, by showing the continued preponderance of small single-craft employers in the building trades. Pages 39–42.

sional and financial opportunities have been sharply restricted by the lack of modernization in industry. The CGC, the *Confédération Générale des Cadres*, became the strongest organization in the field soon after the war, as inflation made worse the position of the *cadres*. It took as its field all technical and managerial personnel except top management, defined as those named directly by boards of directors. In addition, it followed the normal organizational proclivity to organize all those it found organizable, and recruited large numbers of foremen, as well as traveling salesmen and others who were not actually *cadres*.

The general labor confederations have different forms of organization for the *cadres*, who have become more important than ever to them because they lack technical staff for their new functions in the economy. The CGT has compromised between the theory of technicians' "solidarity with the working class" and the fact of technicians' particularism. After the war, it did not revive its special technicians' union, which the communists had always regarded as politically "unreliable"; it recruited the technicians into the unions of their various industries, with an inter-union council to coordinate their group interests, and had a member on the executive board specifically representing them. FO and CFTC have national unions of technicians. Organized foremen are to be found in the industrial unions of all three confederations.

The national union is administered by an executive board (*bureau*) headed by a secretary-general. Ordinarily, the office of union president does not exist. In the CGT, the members of the boards of major unions are usually full-time officers; in many unions, especially in FO and CFTC, some of the board members still work at their trade. These officers are elected by the annual or biennial convention (*congrès*), and come up for reelection at every convention. Tenure has usually been much less solidly established than in American unions. Next to the convention in authority, is the national committee (*comité national*, or *comité fédéral*), which gives representation to different regions and different branches of the industry. In the old days, when the CGT was too poor to pay expenses, and when practically all officials were still working at their trade and found it hard to leave the work bench to travel to meetings, members of the national committees of the unions and the confederation were chosen from among workers in the Paris area. Usually meeting quarterly, the national committee has wide powers of general policy determination and control of elected officials.

The CGT and FO are administered by small executive boards (*bureaux*) of full-time officials (13 in the CGT and 8 in FO); the CFTC is administered by the unwieldy number of 36, most of whom are not full-time. Board members in FO and CGT (*secrétaires con-féderaux*) must give up the national union or departmental federation posts they held before election; therefore, they have no independent base of power to strengthen their hands in dealing with the national unions. A secretary-general is normally the head of the confederation, but in each of the three confederations there has been a variation of this practice. The CFTC made its long-time secretary-general, Gaston Tessier, president; and FO started with Léon Jouhaux as president. In both cases an older leader was honored with the nominal helm, while the operating job was put in the hands of a younger secretary-general. The CGT retains from the 1945–1947 period the anomaly of two secretaries-general.

The convention, ordinarily biennial, is the supreme authority of the confederation. The convention used to be the chief arena of general policy debate in the old CGT. That day has passed; the two conventions since the FO split have ratified the acts of the leadership with the enthusiastic unanimity that has become the mark of big public meetings of the CGT. The conventions of FO have been marked by debate and divided votes, in the traditional style, and articulate criticism of the leadership. Even in FO, however, the conventions are less able than in a slower-moving era to fix policy. They serve rather to give delegates from the locals a chance to let off steam in hard times, and verbalize the traditional distrust of the leadership and the current dissatisfactions of their constituents.

Horizontal organizations

The horizontal groupings of the confederations are the city central (*union locale*) and, much more important, the departmental federation (*union départementale*), which are roughly comparable to A F of L city centrals and state federations or CIO local and state industrial union councils. Between them they have succeeded to the functions of the *Bourse du Travail*,[75] except that of placement. Unlike the old *Bourses*, they are not an independent locus of power or source of labor philosophy. In the democratic confederations, however, some of the departmental federation officials preserve a considerable independence of opinion and action. The city centrals are almost all of minor significance.[76] Departmental federations and city centrals are delegate

---

[75] The *Bourse du Travail* persists as the building occupied by the city central, and in departmental capitals, the departmental federation, usually receiving some municipal and departmental subsidies. The CGT split has caused considerable squabbling, and some litigation, over the uses of these buildings. The CFTC city and departmental offices are, ordinarily, apart from the *Bourses*.

[76] In the Paris region departmental and city organizations are combined in one, which includes Paris and its industrial suburbs.

bodies, with officers elected by annual conventions. In the CGT almost every departmental federation, and many city centrals, have one or a number of full-time officials; in FO and CFTC the number is far smaller. Both FO and the CFTC are developing regional organization to make possible a pooling of services and more effective representation with less overhead. The CFTC has urged weaker departmental federations to group themselves into regional federations. FO has instituted a number of "regional delegates," each covering about half a dozen departments.

Departmental federation officials have a larger role in collective bargaining than city central or state federation officials in American unions. Most employer industrial relations associations are department-wide, and a large percentage of agreements are on that basis. The prefect, the central government's appointed administrator for the department, frequently convokes employers and unions in negotiations, helps settle strikes, and takes a hand in other labor relations questions. The inability of many of the national unions to service their local affiliates means that a considerable responsibility devolves on the departmental official.

Both departmental federations and national unions are represented on the national committee (*comité confédéral national*) of the confederation. This institution has no parallel in American practice. It is composed of one representative, usually the secretary-general, of each national union and of each departmental federation. Thus, it gives a high representation to the horizontal groupings of labor. It provides one more check on the elected officials—although it is a representative body itself composed of elected and normally full-time officials. In the CGT voting in the national committee is, as in the convention, by the number of members represented.[77]

The national committee elects (and may recall) the executive board in the CGT and FO; in the CFTC that is a function of the convention. Between conventions, the national committee has full policy-making powers, and may do anything except revise the constitution. In the CGT the national committee is now only a vestigial remnant of the days when policy was freely debated, and when (until 1946) the federalist principle gave each member of the committee a single vote regardless of the numbers he represented. In FO it retains considerable power. In the CGT now, if there were any overt division, about five

---

[77] The CGT and FO also have an administrative commission, elected by the national committee, to supervise the executive in the implementation of policy between conventions and national committee meetings. With a wide spread of union and area composition, it meets as frequently as once a month. It does not have the power of initiative of the national committee, to which it is responsible.

of the largest unions (metal trades, railwaymen, building trades, miners, textile workers) could control the convention, and these unions plus the Paris region and three or four other big departmental federations could control the national committee.

The formal structure still holds close to the realities of policy determination and action in FO and CFTC. It is, of course, no longer so in the CGT. CGT provisions for local union autonomy from the national office, national union independence of the confederation, frequent elections, and representative body control of elected officers still exist on the books. But communist practice, in the short space of a few years, has mostly pulverized these barriers to centralization, while those who were in overt opposition left the CGT. This is far from signifying that CGT members, or even officials, are all communist or even procommunist.

There is still a widespread distrust of leadership, and particularly of paid leadership, in French unions. To many CGT rank-and-filers, increasingly disillusioned and apathetic in the last few years, their leaders have appeared to be doing better for themselves than for their members. But they have inclined toward an even more jaundiced view of the leaders of other unions and the government officials with whom they hobnobbed. The old anti-authoritarian feelings, kept under control by the leadership of the CGT, are often overt in FO and the CFTC. There are no one-man unions in France. Unions may be run by small cliques or, in the case of the CGT, by a political party. But there is no single boss with a personal machine in control of any union.

Dues—payment and nonpayment

The structure of the democratic labor organizations is hardly adequate to meet the needs of collective bargaining or of organization in a modern labor market, or of representation in the nation's economic decisions. Its inadequacy is all the greater because of the feeble financial nourishment fed into the union organism, and the distribution of what is fed in. Union members nowhere regard the paying of dues as a pleasure, but, passively or actively, in most industrial countries the habit has taken hold. The French worker, according to the well-known jibe of French origin, is ready to die on the barricades, but not to pay dues. "The French labor movement," said the secretary of one of the most active FO departmental federations, "has until this day never been able to introduce in the *mores* a policy of high dues, perhaps for the same reasons for which it has not succeeded in introducing a policy of high levels of consumption and a high standard of living in the working class." [78] Dues are low, even in relation to members' low wages, and they are paid with regularity only in a few unions like those of the government workers and the printers. The French worker assesses himself dues of well under one hour's pay per month, and he is considered in good standing in most unions if, in addition to his yearly dues card, he purchases seven or eight of his monthly dues stamps per year. This is at least as true of the CGT unions as of the more moderate unions.

Of dues paid to locals, a comparatively small percentage goes to the national union, and a very small percentage to the confederation; a comparatively high percentage may go to the departmental federation. The city central usually subsists on contributions voted on an occasional basis. For example, in the CGT the metal workers union is the largest national union, and considers itself the elite. In early 1950, many locals of this union were charging (and not always collecting) 60 francs (then about 17 cents) for the monthly dues stamp, of which 15 francs went to the national union, 12–13 francs to the departmental federation, and 1½ francs to the confederation. The confederation, in addition, was supposed to get 25 francs from the sale of the annual dues card.

Some unions maintain full-time officials on a shoestring budget because officials are detailed to them from the payroll of the government or of nationalized enterprises. A number of union officials are thus able to carry on their work—subject always to the possibility of a change of heart by the ministry or nationalized industry concerned. This recourse was being withdrawn from the CGT, whose unions, notably in the railway and maritime industries, profited from it liberally in the years when the communists were in the government and for a few years after. The CGT has another fruitful recourse. It controls a large number of plant committees, through its predominant position in plant elections. In plants of any size the committees have paid employees for their welfare activities; in the largest plants there may be a dozen or more. On these payrolls the CGT puts many of its own people, with considerable freedom to carry on CGT or Communist Party business.

The low level of union dues has been causing a considerable "examination of conscience" in democratic union circles. In FO this examination has been geared to the need to make the organization less dependent on the good will and financial aid of labor organizations in other democratic countries, as well as more fully independent of the government. FO, as a new organization battling a well-provided and

---

[78] *CGT-FO, IIᵉ Congrès confédéral, Rapports confédéraux,* Paris, October 25–28, 1950, page 70.

intrenched CGT, could hardly have started on dues payments alone. "We must all understand," the deeply respected treasurer of FO told its 1950 convention, "that the hour has come for all our organizations to live only by means of their dues. And we must work to overcome this all too familiar tendency of Frenchmen to hate to pay dues as well as taxes." [79]

All the unions face the need to adapt their finances and organization to operation in an industrial age. French labor is only one of the sections of French society that have to so dramatic an extent refused to recognize these necessities.[80] Higher dues and stricter dues collection are difficult to introduce in a divided union movement. Rival unions, notably the CGT, are ready to offer "cut-rate unionism." With union pluralism the rule, there can be no question of the check-off or the union shop. The only disciplinary action for nonpayment of dues is dropping delinquents from the union rolls, and that carries with it no practical disadvantages to the delinquent member. Low dues, lack of an adequate union bureaucracy, lack of direct and sustained union services to members, the dependence of labor on legislation and on administrative intervention in conflicts—all these create a circle of frustration from which the democratic unions are struggling to free themselves.

Relative strength of the confederations

It would be hard for the various national centers to give valid membership figures even if they were anxious to do so. The very concept of union membership is not a clear one. There is a series of concentric rings of union allegiance and influence, ranging from the members who pay their dues systematically, through those who pay their dues less regularly or only occasionally, but are considered members, to the purely electoral allegiance manifested only on the occasion of shop steward or plant committee voting or social security elections. (It is of course impossible, given the system of collective bargaining, to speak of numbers "covered by contract" of any one union.) Voting the slate

[79] *CGT-FO, II⁰ Congrès Confédéral . . . Rapports Confédéraux,* 1950, page 70.

[80] On this general theme, see *Modern France,* Princeton, 1951, especially essays by John E. Sawyer, on "Strains in the Social Structure"; John B. Wolf, "The *Elan Vital . . .* "; John B. Christopher, "The Desiccation of the Bourgeois Spirit"; Henry E. Guerlac, "Science and French National Strength"; Richard Ruggles, "The French Investment Program"; and David S. Landes, "French Business and the Business Man," all with extensive bibliographies. Also Shepard B. Clough, "Retardative Factors in French Economic Development in the Nineteenth and Twentieth Centuries," *Journal of Economic History,* Supplement VI (1946), pages 91–102; Charles Morazé, *La France bourgeoise,* Paris, 1946, and a number of recent works (in French) by Jean Fourastié.

of the union which appears most advanced is one matter. Joining it and paying dues, or following it on strike, are other matters. Here again appears the divorce between words and actions, between occasional collective affirmation and continuing personal responsibility, that has afflicted the trade union movement.

Both the intensity of interunion competition and the general weakness of labor in the face of employers make for union membership claims to which it is impossible to attach much weight. The best single measure of relative strength and influence can be had from the results of the triennial elections to the quasi-autonomous boards of administration of the general social security system. Three-fourths of their members are elected by the insured employees, the remaining fourth by employers. The election results shown in Table 3 do not include workers in industries, notably mining and railroads, which have special funds under separate administration. (The CGT is strong in these industries.)

TABLE 3

SOCIAL SECURITY ELECTION RESULTS, JUNE, 1950, AND APRIL, 1947

Slate	Number of votes		Per cent of total vote		Per cent of union vote	
	1950	1947	1950	1947	1950	1947
CGT	2,392,000	3,280,000	43.5	59.3	54.4	69.2
CFTC	1,173,000	1,458,000	21.3	26.3	26.6	30.8
FO	833,000		15.2		19.0	
Mutual aid societies* ..	610,000	508,000	11.1	9.2		
Family associations	290,000	288,000	5.3	5.2		
Miscellaneous†	206,000		3.6			
Total	5,504,000	5,534,000	100.0	100.0	100.0	100.0

* FO claimed in 1950 that, since many FO activists have also been active in mutual aid societies, and some appeared on the mutuals' slates, a significant part of the mutuals' vote represented support for FO.
† Includes CTI and other minor unions' slates in 1950.
Source: Based on: *Le Monde*, June 16, 1950.

The CFTC lost somewhat in 1950 as compared with 1947, when it received some of the dissident CGT votes. The CGT-plus-FO vote in 1950, in total numbers and percentage-wise, almost exactly equalled the CGT vote before the split. FO felt keenly its lack of resources in the campaign for the June, 1950, elections. But in this test its means were relatively what they are in other forms of competition for workers' support. The CFTC, like FO, was also able to spend only a fraction of what the CGT spent in electoral propaganda; but its slates had a certain amount of church support. Neither the CFTC nor FO could make promises of social insurance increases as wildly generous, regardless of costs, as the CGT offered the workers. But the results of these elections furnished a broad national gauge of the relative influence of the national centers, rather than a choice for any ephemeral platform of social security administration and benefits.

No nation-wide tabulation of votes is available for the shop steward and plant committee elections. A comparison of recent years' election figures in some of the leading plants showed that, despite its great setbacks in the 1947 and 1948 strikes, the CGT retained its leadership among industrial workers almost everywhere. It was stronger than FO and CFTC combined in mining, steel and metal fabricating, railways, textiles, chemicals, the building trades, gas and electric power, among the seamen and dockers, and in agriculture. FO continued to be strongest in the civil service, and the CFTC in private employment in the white-collar field. The CGT, however, had a considerable following among civil servants, and FO and CFTC had a number of significant minorities among industrial workers.

The great change in French unionism shown by these elections was the emergence of the CFTC as the second largest national trade union center, and the first among the non-communist centers. It has now gained important and apparently solid footholds among industrial workers beyond the heavily Catholic areas of Alsace, the northern textile cities and the west of France. Whatever the limits of expansion of the CFTC in a country whose workers still feel embarrassed in many cities if their fellow-workers see them going to mass, this development gave signs of continuing for some time. Unlike the Catholic unions in other European countries, the CFTC has made clear its independence of the Church and of the Catholic political party, and has shown initiative and militancy equal to that of the other unions. It has a source of recruitment for membership and leadership in the Catholic workers' youth. The CGT has a somewhat comparable source in communist youth organizations. The lack of any effective socialist youth movement is a great handicap to FO in the development of new leadership and following.

It is too soon to tell what the Independent Confederation of Labor, under Gaullist influence, can do, though it has shown strength in some localities. Its development hinges in part on the course of Gaullist political action. There are also several smaller national federations; and a number of unaffiliated unions, notably the teachers' union, which has in times past played a prominent role in French unionism and in politics. The supervisory employees organization, the CGC, as we have seen, is preeminent in its field.

As compared with the year or two after liberation, however, the great fact in 1951 was that several million workers had, after the brief surge of enthusiasm, again dropped out of the labor movement. The CGT had fallen to perhaps somewhat over 2 million members, FO had built an organization of well under a milion, and the CFTC was slightly larger. About half of the industrial workers in the country remained unorganized. The industrial relations and the politics of the country depended to some extent on the unmeasurable action of those whom French unionists ruefully entitled the "organization of the unorganized."

The myth of unity

The French working-class movement has been split into warring groups for most of the decades since the unions and political parties claiming to represent labor were first organized. On the trade union side, there has been unity for only 25 of the 65 years since the first national center was established. On the political side, there has been unity for only 15 years of that period. The reality is thus division and warfare (and indifference) among the workers whom tradition and sentiment would call a single class with a burning identity of interest. So there has grown up an almost mystic belief in "unity." Nor is it entirely sentimental; obviously, disunity has hurt labor in its organizing and its dealing with employers and government. The talk of unity, however, obscures other problems.

On the communist side, "unity" continues to be a main theme of appeal of the CGT leadership to the rank and file of other unions over the heads of their own leadership, particularly FO. On the noncommunist side, and particularly in FO, the theme of unity is a persistent one, corresponding to rank and file demands and hopes. Lengthy bouts of verbalism on unity have inhibited the development of organizational loyalty to the union indulging in them, and put off facing one basic problem: that while disunity is a fact among the organized, half the workers of France are still unorganized. Few, indeed, are the democratic unionists who have the courage and the candor of the officers of the FO Transport Workers' Union, who told the union's 1950 convention, "The division in the trade union movement . . . would be a minor evil if it were not aggravated by the unthinkable indifference of a large number of wage earners toward trade union organization and action." [81] Instead of offering the usual slogans about unity, these FO officials argued, unconventionally, that the best way to help the working class was for FO unionists to organize and build up their own unions.

---

[81] *Force Ouvrière,* November 9, 1950, page 8.

Industrial Relations

Genuine collective bargaining has scarcely been tried in most of French private industry. The brief attempt of 1919 was wrecked by the political struggles within the unions and by employer opposition. The attempt in 1936 was more far-reaching and hopeful, but, again, the period of trial was tragically short. Employer resentment undermined the unions' new rights; union politics brought on the disaster of the 1938 general strike; and unions and employers threw their responsibilities onto government arbitrators rather than bargaining out agreements. The war, the occupation, the Vichy Labor Charter, and the postwar controls halted contractual relations for a decade.

Neither unions nor employers have been prepared for the collective bargaining relationship. "The nature and the character which we attribute to our adversaries helps shape our methods of combat," Maxime Leroy observed many years ago.[82] Their philosophy and structure alike caused the unions to neglect the bargaining function. Like other trade union movements in a position of temporary or chronic weakness, French labor turned to the government for gains it could not achieve by negotiation or economic force. Many of the most important non-wage issues came to be regulated by law: paid vacations, shop stewards, plant committees, social insurance. Despite workers' distrust of government, they wanted government intervention in an impasse, when they were unable to get employers to deal with them, or when they faced the loss of a strike. Their dependence explains some of their resentment of government. And it helps explain why workers do not feel a stronger loyalty to their unions.

Employer attitudes worked against orderly bargaining and union responsibility. In recent years, employers have naturally and correctly pointed to communist leadership of the unions as a barrier to constructive labor relations. But many employers have given the impression of being almost pleased to find communist unions in their path, since that justifies putting off the day of adjustment to real collective bargaining. On the employer side as on the worker side, labor relations still have the character of a class conflict rather than of an economic bargain.

Collective bargaining was slow to resume after the war. Wage bargaining was out of the question in the period of shortages, and the unions sought to solidify their other gains through legislation, not through contract. When the government put through the collective bargaining law of December, 1946, it still kept wages under control. The

---

[82] Maxime Leroy, *La Coutume Ouvrière*, Vol. I, page 18. Paris, 1913.

law, moreover, imposed priorities in agreements, with national agreements required to precede regional, and regional to precede local; and any agreement was subject to government approval; after approval, it was extended to all employers and employees in the trade and area covered. The excessive degree of state intervention, the exclusion of the major issue, wages, and the interminable debates among the unions as to "the most representative organizations" stultified negotiations under the 1946 law. In the three years the law was in effect, only 4 national agreements were signed and approved. Bargaining got under way with a 1950 law decontrolling wages and setting a new legal framework for industrial relations. In 1950 and 1951, the patterns of bargaining were in a state of evolution—to a great extent quite different from that contemplated by the makers of the law.

The collective bargaining law

The basic law of February 11, 1950,[83] envisaged the bargaining parties as "the most representative organizations" of employers and workers. Among employer organizations, the application of this concept raised almost no difficulties, since there was almost no dualism of organization and most employers were affiliated with employer associations. Among the unions, pluralism was the rule. The CGT, FO, and the CFTC were considered nationally "representative" and qualified at almost any level at which they demanded a part in negotiations; the CGC was recognized as "representative" for the technical and supervisory personnel. The effort of the CGT, after liberation, to create a kind of closed shop or, at least, "exclusive bargaining rights" for itself had been doomed to failure by the CFTC's assertion of minority union rights, the CGC's growth, and then the FO split.

The Ministry of Labor and its local or regional representatives at various echelons decide questions of "representativity" and the right to participate in government-convoked negotiations (*commissions mixtes*). The criteria of representativity are in theory the union's: (a) membership, (b) independence, (c) dues, (d) experience and "seniority," (e) "patriotic attitude during the occupation." In most cases it appeared that a union with any showing of strength would be permitted to participate. In the concept of the law, negotiations

---

[83] For a description of the 1950 law in English, see Adolf Sturmthal, "Collective Bargaining in France," *Industrial and Labor Relations Review* (January, 1951), pages 236–248. The text of the law is in *Journal Officiel* (February 12, 1950), with rectifications in *J. O.* (February 22, and March 14, 1950), and with commentary in *France: Documents,* N.S. No. 4 (March, 1950). For a discussion of the law, chiefly juridical, see Paul Durand's articles in *Droit Social* (March, April, and May, 1950),

would normally be launched under the aegis of the government, that is, the Ministry of Labor or its regional or departmental functionaries, or by the prefect. Nothing, however, prevents the parties from beginning negotiations without the benefit of government convocation, or, after convocation by the government, continuing to bargain without the government representatives' presence, as they often do.

The law distinguishes between a full-blown "collective agreement" (*convention collective*) and a simpler "wage agreement" (*accord de salaire*). The collective agreement must contain clauses relating to a large number of issues, in addition to wages: trade union rights, hiring and firing (without "infringing on the workers' free choice of a union"), women's and younger workers' conditions, apprenticeship and vocational training, shop stewards and plant committees,[84] and the financing of social welfare schemes operated by the committees, paid vacations, conciliation procedures for difficulties under the agreement, methods of revision and termination of the agreement. Many of these issues are already rather extensively covered by legislative requirement. In addition, the law lists a number of other issues which *may* be covered by a collective agreement: overtime pay rates and shift rotation, night and holiday work, methods of payment for piece work, and various types of bonuses, pensions, and provisions for arbitration of conflicts.

In scope, a collective agreement may be national, regional, or local. A "plant agreement" may adapt the provisions of such a collective agreement, especially those provisions dealing with rates of pay, to a single plant or group of plants. But in the absence of a nation-wide, regional, or local collective agreement, a plant agreement can cover only wage issues.

Only a full-blown collective agreement is subject to "extension" by the government. Extension covers employers and workers within the industrial and geographic scope of the agreement, but not represented by the parties to the agreement itself. In practice it does not matter whether the worker belongs to a union signatory to the agreement; what is important is whether the employer can be considered bound by the agreement. The process of extension is not automatic; the Minister of Labor (and the Minister of Agriculture for agricultural labor agreements) can use his discretion in extension of all or part of an agreement. Government labor inspectors have the right to check on compliance with the terms of an "extended" agreement. Thus, by the process of extension, the bargaining parties create public regulation of labor conditions.

---

[84] See *infra,* pages 389-393.

Actually, in the first 15 months of the new law, almost all the contracts concluded were essentially wage agreements, and the question of extension hardly arose, since a plant agreement or wage agreement could not be extended. The afterthought in the law that provided that, "pending the conclusion of collective agreements," simple wage agreements might be signed turned out to have great practical importance. The membership of the unions was so dominated by the exigencies of the cost of living that once it obtained wage increases it lost interest in pressing for full collective agreements. The unions were not strong enough to obtain from employers concessions on all the non-wage clauses, such as union activity in the plant, and powers of the shop stewards and plant committees, which the law required for a collective agreement.

The employer attitude on all these "obligatory clauses" was stated by one of its ablest and most reasonable exponents:

> We are now hemmed in by a system of regulation which we owe no doubt as much to the excessive power of government bureaus, encouraged by the war, as to our national mania to legislate on everything and for everybody, and to the competition of our parties in the pursuit of social progress. . . . It would be a strange contribution to the harmonizing of labor conditions in the Europe of tomorrow to pretend to add to the rules of our labor code, considered "untouchable," contractual requirements which would make their weight even heavier. . . . Instead of forcing the parties concerned to build monuments for which they do not have the materials—these having already been employed in the construction of an imposing legislative edifice—logic would have indicated leaving the greatest latitude to the parties concerned so that they might profit by every occasion to build a few more modest but useful structures, and to resume thus the habit of collective bargaining.[85]

Centralization of employer policy

The 1946 law had provided that national industry agreements were to precede regional or local agreements, but the 1950 law set no such priorities. Since the unions had originally wanted nation-wide agreements, the difference was a measure of the revival of employer confidence and the decline of trade union strength in the intervening few years.[86] In almost all industries, employers and employer associations, under the lead of the CNPF, refused to negotiate nationally. They

---

[85] Pierre Waline, "Le Patronat francais et les conventions collectives," *Revue Economique,* February, 1951, Librairie Armand Colin, Paris. Pages 29, 32.

[86] The CGT in fact, though not in public statement, came to favor decentralized bargaining, and would have bargained on a plant basis because it was far better and more widely organized locally than either the CFTC or FO. FO and the CFTC favored nation-wide industry bargaining, by which they could hope to cover up local or regional weaknesses.

insisted on area-wide bargaining, with the region, locality, or, most often, the department as the area.

The determination of employer policy, however, is far more centralized than the bargaining units would indicate, because of the weight of national organization on the employer side, and the weight of one industry in the CNPF. Most of the CNPF heads, including the president and the head of its labor relations department, come from the metal trades. The metal trades set the pattern, by and large, for private industry, and within the metal trades, the Paris region, with a third of the employees in French metal working, sets the pattern.

The record of what happened when the collective bargaining law was passed makes clear why even conservative writers complain that government *dirigisme* (controls) have been abandoned only to make way for employer association *dirigisme*. As soon as the 1950 law was enacted, the unions began to press their demands; wage increases, it was generally admitted, were in order. The CNPF then announced that, if price increases were to be avoided, employers (in industry generally) could grant raises of no more than 5 per cent in the Paris region and 5 to 8 per cent in other regions. The most serious test, and the chief strikes, came in the Paris region metal-working industries. And it was on the basis of the CNPF's 5 per cent figure that the "settlement" was made for the Paris region; an imposed settlement, as, plant by plant, the strikes caved in. The terms of this round of wage increases, in other regions and in other industries, were generally those which had been laid down publicly by the CNPF before the strike movement.

Employers' associations have greater cohesion and far greater means than labor. The national iron, steel, and metal trades group, for example, has some 35 professional people in its labor relations and social insurance departments; and its various regional affiliates, notably that of the Paris area, are well staffed. In 1950 it had 4 high level men whose full time job it was to keep in touch with the regional affiliates on labor relations, wages, and allied questions. Even where the local or regional employer associations are modestly staffed, national employer associations are able, and often anxious, to take a hand in negotiations, if only to protect the rest of the industry from possibly excessive local concessions. Thus the canners' national affiliate in Brittany was told, "At the joint session with the unions, let the specialists delegated from Paris headquarters lead the discussion." Membership in employer associations is far more widespread, more rational, and association discipline much firmer than it ever was before the war. How far the experience of discipline and organization under Vichy was responsible for this change is a matter of conjecture.

Discipline is in some cases reinforced by the threat of economic and social sanctions.

Despite great differences in efficiency and ability to pay among French firms, stated wage rates vary comparatively little within the same industry and area. Area-wide bargaining, rather than single-plant or single-firm bargaining, reinforces a general tendency to gear wage rates to the marginal firm. The employer association protects its marginal members. Unions, because of the fear of unemployment, consciously or unconsciously accept the argument for maintaining the marginal firm in business despite its drag on wage standards and technological progress.

Between employer and labor organizations, the disparity in resources and in coordination is striking. Among the unions, there is a vast disparity between the CGT and its rivals. In the noncommunist unions, discipline is far poorer, channels of communication less developed, and personnel more limited than in the CGT. FO and CFTC have only two or three full-time men each in the offices of major national unions. In many cases, local or department-wide negotiations are carried on by the secretary of the departmental federation. Within a single week, he may have to tackle the problems of metal workers, chemical workers, textile workers, and bank clerks, often with little help from the national offices of the unions concerned. In some departmental federations, FO does not even have a single full-time employee.

Bargaining in nationalized industries

Although there are some forms of collective contract in most industries, a great deal of the most continuous labor relations, in the sense not only of periodic agreements but of consultation in the handling of grievances and the determination of working conditions, takes place in government-owned industries. The nationalization, before the war, of the railroads, potash mines, and aircraft plants, and, after the war, of the coal mining and gas and electricity industries brought into the area of government employment a number of the most active unions, with fairly well developed collective bargaining relations. These relations have continued, although the 1950 collective bargaining law does not apply to the wholly government-owned industries. It does apply to single government-owned enterprises in competitive industries, such as the Renault and Berliot auto and truck works.

In these nationalized industries, management's general relations with the workers are regulated by statute rather than by contract. The statutes for the miners, gas and electric workers, and nationalized bank and insurance company employees were products of the early postliberation period, when labor's political standing was high. Drafted in consultation with the unions, they gave a large role to the unions. Wage scales in these industries are ordinarily promulgated by the government rather than embodied in agreements. But the wage scales represent the culmination of a long process of bargaining, economic and political, rather than simple bureaucratic decision or ministerial fiat.

Although the government as an employer does not ride roughshod over the unions, it is, in the nature of things, not the most satisfactory bargaining partner. The process of government decision is diffuse and laborious, and it has been complicated by the fact of coalition government and the uneasy partnership within the government coalitions. In a period of chronic budget deficits, a central power has been exercised by the powerful Finance Ministry, almost always in the hands of a member of the government least sensitive to labor issues. The visible price inflation has increased workers' dissatisfaction in the face of delays in decision, and placed the more responsible unions at a disadvantage. The inability or reluctance of administrators and ministers to take responsibility, in the almost unceasing negotiations caused by rises in the cost of living, has weakened the authority of management in nationalized industry, and the authority of government in general, with the unions and with the public.

One factor of centralized decision, as we have seen, is the strength of national employer organizations. A second factor is the role of government, which directly influences wage policy and bargaining through (1) its own wage policy and its pattern of dealing with the unions; (2) its determination of the minimum wage; and (3) its fixing of family allowance and social insurance levels, as well as (4) its intervention in conflicts.

As an employer, the government has on its payroll, as civil servants or as workers in industrial enterprises, about one-fourth of all non-agricultural wage-earners. In the first round of 1950 wage adjustments, the government (then headed by Bidault of the MRP) took a general position on "permissible" wage increases similar to that of the CNPF. "Wages are being set by the CNPF, of which the government-as-employer seems a member," bitterly remarked one Catholic union leader. In the second round of 1950 bargaining, the government intervened more vigorously and probably more constructively: first, by its fixing of the national minimum wage; second, by setting a new pattern of negotiation based on the recognition of the political character of the CGT. Without waiting for strikes such as had preceded the spring 1950 adjustments, Renault, nationalized auto works in the Paris suburbs and the country's most important plant, signed an agreement with FO, the CFTC, and the CGC. Although the CGT had more members in the

Renault works than had all the other unions combined, the negotiations and agreement froze out the CGT. The CGT denounced the agreement as a "sell-out," [87] and declared it would not consider itself bound by it. Since the theory and practice of the CGT were that a strike could be called at any time and for any purpose, it would hardly have been more "bound" if it had signed. (It attacked FO and the CFTC for their "betrayal" in agreeing to a four-day strike-notice clause.) The Renault agreement gave a lead to employer associations which resulted in a considerable number of agreements with FO, the CFTC, and the CGC, or with some of them, leaving out the CGT. The pattern, however, was far from uniform; it varied from locality to locality, and the CGT was a party to a number of agreements.

Nothing in the law, despite its discussion of "representativity," requires that agreements include the union which has the majority, or plurality, support within the bargaining unit. Thus, after the long debates over the "most representative" unions, political necessities produced agreements with the numerically least representative unions.[88] After some hesitation, however, CGT unions more frequently took part in negotiations, or added their signatures to agreements negotiated without them.

Minimum wages

In the general low-wage edifice of France, the setting of minimum wages by the government influences pay scales directly and immediately in a way quite different from the effect of federal or state minimum wage determinations in the United States. Each time, new minima have set in motion adjustments all along the line, by collective bargaining or by unilateral action, even in the better-paid industries. The fixing of the first minima, in August, 1950, was followed by a general wage adjustment estimated at about 8 per cent of total direct wage payments. In March, 1951, the general increase was even larger, and corresponded roughly to the 11.5 per cent increase in the minimum for the Paris region.

A major practical effect of the collective bargaining law thus came from the minimum wage provision, although the law was supposed to end the regime of general government wage determination. It had even been hoped that the minimum wage might be set largely by consensus of the parties. The law provided that a national minimum wage

---

[87] The agreement raised the base wage to a higher figure than the CGT had been demanding.

[88] In a period of rising wages, this problem of multi-union bargaining can be by-passed. In a period of falling wages, the excluded unions would be able to capitalize on their opposition.

be set by the Cabinet, on the report of the Ministers of Labor and Economic Affairs; this was to be done in the light of the state of the economy and of the recommendations by the National Collective Agreements Commission. This commission, made up of representatives of employers, unions (CGT, CFTC, FO, and CGC), "family associations," [89] and government, was to recommend "the composition of a typical budget serving to determine the guaranteed minimum national wage for all industries."

The commission did not meet until three months after the law was passed. In the meantime, there had been a first round of modest wage increases and wage accords, regarded by labor as partial and provisional. Now it was argued by the CFTC, and soon generally assumed by labor, that negotiation of "real collective agreements" had to wait until the national minimum was fixed. Employers were content to wait. There was no official cost-of-living index, and price statistics were controversial and incomplete, especially for the provinces. The commission's task was to agree on the composition of a standard minimum budget, and a corresponding monetary sum to recommend to the government as the minimum wage. Since the commission was composed chiefly of employer and union representatives, the bargaining partners were in effect asked to agree, in advance of bargaining, on a figure that might be the key to the ultimate wage negotiations. The idea of an "objective" budget naturally had to be dropped, but not before wrangling over employer objections to this or that clothing or home furnishings item in workers' budgets had stirred old class feelings around the committee tables. Obviously the money figure was the critical one. The committee was unable to muster a majority for any one figure,[90] and at the end of August 1950, with the cabinet again collapsing on the wage-price issue, the government accepted its responsibilities and fixed minimum wages.

The law had spoken of "a minimum." But the government decided that wage zone differentials (largely by size of community), which had existed under wage controls, had to be preserved, although narrowed. Thus, five minima, with an 18 per cent spread, were promulgated, with another lower figure for agriculture.

The government's central role goes beyond its own wage policies as an employer and its minimum wage determination. With the postwar expansion of social insurance and family allowance programs, a great part of workers' income, about one-third of direct wages, is placed

---

[89] The "family associations" are welfare, propaganda and lobbying organizations whose purposes range from protection of the special interests of large families to general consumer defense.

[90] The CGT had come down from its own much higher figure to agree with the CFTC and FO on a single monthly minimum wage demand.

in the area of government decision. It is removed from the area of direct determination by labor and management, and, likewise, from the area of workers' individual effort and output.

The state can also step in at almost any stage of labor negotiations or conflict. The government's original collective bargaining bill called for compulsory arbitration, but the unions insisted on preserving the right to strike. Employers objected generally to government intervention, and they felt that weak and divided unions would get more by government arbitration than by their own economic power. Arbitration was therefore made voluntary. The 1950 law was thought to provide for compulsory conciliation, but its language was unclear. Practice after its enactment has allowed the calling of strikes before conciliation efforts have been exhausted, or even essayed. Formal conciliation machinery consists of a National Conciliation Commission and regional and departmental commissions, with bipartite membership named by the "most representative" unions and employer organizations, plus several government members. The conciliation commissions, where they were set up, played little role in preventing or ending strikes in the first year and a half of the law's functioning. Parties to a conflict can submit to arbitration the questions remaining at issue after failure of conciliation. A National Arbitration Court, composed of high government administrative and judicial officials, was set up to pass on appeals from arbitration decisions.[91]

Beyond the formal procedures specified in the law, there is the long tradition of *ad hoc* administrative intervention in labor conflicts. In many of the important strikes, and many less important ones, since the end of the last century, prefects and subprefects, ministers and even prime ministers have sought to conciliate and even arbitrate. Such intervention has often been successful, but often, too, it has not been accepted.

Plant relations

At the plant level, one finds the least coherent relations between labor and management. There is a multiplicity of competing unions and a high percentage of unorganized workers. There is a profusion of organs for the handling of grievances and a paucity of trained

---

[91] In this the law follows the practice of the similar court set up under the 1938 compulsory arbitration legislation, although it now deals with private arbitration decisions. Such appeals can be taken on legal grounds only. The arbitration court may, on legal grounds, quash a decision and send the case back to the parties, but not decide the issues. Only if the parties go through a second arbitration, and this is appealed, and the appeal is upheld, does the court itself render a decision on the issues.

union officials. Management remains opposed to union activity on a plant basis, and within most industries there has been little chance to develop the experience or even the concept of contract administration or grievance adjustment on a sustained basis.

In plants of any size, each of the three main national centers, CGT, CFTC and FO, generally has at least some membership, as do the CGC and possibly one or two of the minor federations. Even if the CGT were not opposed to the development of peaceful industrial relations, there would be some confusion. With the major union organization preaching class struggle and launching an endless stream of "peace" demonstrations and demands for whatever may be the current communist political issues, confusion has been compounded.

The proliferation of grievance channels has had the twofold effect of complicating labor-management relations and diluting potential worker loyalty to the union. The individual worker does not readily see the union as an institution of protection or service when he has the choice of three, four, or even five channels for adjustment of his grievances. Nominally, the first organized channel is that of the shop steward (*délégué du personnel*). Shop stewards are compulsory, by a law of 1946, in shops of over 10 employees. They are elected by vote of all employees, regardless of union affiliation or lack of it. The unions, however, present the slates of candidates. Within any given department of a plant, a union member often has the choice of taking his grievance to a steward elected from his own department but a member of a different union, or of taking it to a steward who is a fellow-unionist but elected from another department. Many employers are trying to establish the reasonable principle of restricting stewards to handling grievances from within their own departments rather than along the lines of union affiliation.

More efficient and responsible grievance handling is sometimes obtained where stewards put in more time on grievance work. The law requires that the elected shop stewards be permitted 20 hours a month on company time for the duties of that office. A number of stewards, perhaps 5 or 6 of one union, can, with management agreement, combine their aggregate time and "block" it on a single one of their number, so that he has 100 or 120 hours a month for grievance work. In some cases, he may have enough "blocked" time to get full-time pay while putting in full time on grievances and union business.

The plant committees [92] were not designed to process individual complaints, but to consider more generalized issues. The line is obviously hard to draw, and these committees often serve as a channel for individual grievances. As with the shop stewards, the members of

---

[92] See *infra,* pages 389–393.

the committees may also be local union officers. There is often overlapping of personnel between shop stewards and plant committee
members, and the average worker often does not differentiate the two
functions in his mind.

Another possible grievance channel is that of the *Conseil de prud-
'hommes,* a sort of local labor court with an obligation to conciliate
in preference to rendering judgment. The *prud'hommes* may take
jurisdiction over a wide variety of cases arising out of the individual
contract of employment, including disputes over job classification and
dismissals. The *Conseil de prud'hommes* is a bipartite body, its members elected by universal suffrage of employers and workers, the worker
representatives from union slates. In case of failure to agree, the
deciding vote is cast by a justice of the peace.

Still another grievance channel, to be found most commonly in
public utility type enterprises, is the bipartite discipline committee
(*conseil de discipline*), presided over by a management representative.
Its functions are those of review, and its powers usually advisory.
Ordinarily, the committee functions only in the more serious cases
where penalties exceed a certain degree of severity. Discipline committees have been established in some cases by collective agreements
(for example, on the street railways), and in other cases by statute,
for nationalized industries (for example, in the mines).

Grievances may also be taken to the labor inspectors. A single corps
of government labor law inspectors is responsible for compliance with
all labor legislation, ranging from safety and health, night work, and
wage payment to laws on hiring and firing. The inspectors often play
a role in the negotiation of agreements and the enforcement of arbitral
decisions. In certain types of cases, the inspector may have no greater
power than that of remonstrance with management; in other cases,
notably those dealing with discharges, the inspector has wider powers
under agreements and legislation. For some discharges, the inspector
renders an advisory opinion; for others, his consent may be required.

Finally, most employers still leave the door open, and stress that
"the door is open," to individual appeals from their employees. Such
an appeal often goes directly to the top even in a fairly large plant.[93]
Employers, observe two distinguished authorities, are hostile to the
intervention of the bipartite committee or the labor inspector in
matters of discipline. "Personal appearance before the employer would
seem to them the best protection of the . . . worker. It would guarantee

---

[93] Few employers have well-developed personnel departments, and they do not
ordinarily delegate much authority to the personnel departments they have.

that he would not be at the mercy of subaltern personnel, and that he would be able to present his defense before the responsible head of the enterprise." [94]

The recognition of the role of the unions embodied first in the 1936 laws, and then in the postliberation laws, has not yet produced habits of collaboration at the plant level. Rather it has produced an employer stiffening to prevent unions from enjoying any rights beyond those which the law compels. The employer has been forced by law to make place for numerous forms of employee representation and participation. He has sought to restrict that participation to the elected spokesmen of the whole body of his workers, and to keep the unions as such out of the determination of plant conditions and policies. "We want to deal with our own workers; the union as such is not recognized within the plant," is a commonplace employer observation, despite area-wide agreements between employer associations and unions. "Union action should normally not take place at the level of the plant. It should be placed at the level of the corresponding employer associations, that is to say, on the local, regional or national level," the metal trades employers' association has said.[95]

Plant committees

One institution that throws light on labor-management and interunion relations at the plant level is the plant committee (*comité d'entreprise*).[96] Perhaps the one constructive innovation of Vichy was the plant social committees, but these were forbidden to go into economic or financial questions, and, as in the hard times of the occupation their chief concern was with eking out a food supply for the workers, they were dubbed "potato committees." At the liberation, the social committees were swept aside. Plant committees of different types sprang up spontaneously in many parts of the country. Some

---

[94] Paul Durand and André Rouast, *Précis de législation industrielle* (*Droit du travail*), 3rd ed., page 123. Paris, 1948.

[95] *La Discussion du projet de convention collective nationale dans les industries métallurgiques; Etat de la question en avril 1949*, Union des Industries Métallurgiques, page 10. Paris, 1949. This document is perhaps the fullest and best statement of the general employer position on these issues.

[96] The term *"comité d'enterprise,"* like so many of the terms in a foreign social structure, is difficult to translate properly. The American term "labor-management committee" is associated chiefly with the production drive in World War II; those committees were very limited in their aims compared to the French *comités d'enterprise.* The term "works council" would give an inaccurate notion of similarity to the German institution of that name, whose powers in production matters and in layoffs are much broader than those of the French *comités.*

committees dispossessed collaborationist owners, or took over control after their departure, and sought to run their plants. The de Gaulle Government, by an ordinance of February 22, 1945, regularized the situation of the committees already set up, instituted the *comités d'entreprise*, and made them obligatory in all enterprises, private and public, of a hundred or more workers. Their powers, however, were far short of those called for by the programs of the resistance. After complaints by the CGT and the CFTC, the committees were, in 1946, given somewhat wider powers and were extended to all enterprises of 50 or more employees.

The committees, said the preamble of the 1945 ordinance, "must be, above all, the sign of the fruitful union of all elements of production, to return to France its prosperity and its greatness." The committees are joint, but not bipartite. The head of the enterprise or his representative, who presides over the committee, is the only management member. The other members are all elected representatives of the employees, their number determined by the size of the establishment. The method of election compromises between the two possible extremes of making the committees organs of the trade unions, or making them completely independent of the unions. The normal process is election from slates presented by the "most representative" unions. Only if the unions put up no slates, or if their slates receive too few votes, is the field open to individual candidacies.

The original law provided for the election of the whole slate getting the majority, on the theory of trade union unity, a vestige of the resistance, and a theory argued by the CGT. For the first elections, this produced a national agreement between the CGT and the CFTC for joint slates, only partially carried out at the plant level. In 1947, in recognition of the facts of inter-union competition, the law was amended to provide proportional representation when there are competing slates. Elections to the committees now furnish an annual test of strength in most plants; in some (usually smaller) plants, there are formal or informal joint slates.

The committees' powers are sharply divided between what the French call the "social" and the "economic." In the social field, the law gives the committees wide scope, and powers of decision and control. They can run certain types of social welfare schemes such as canteens, cooperatives, vacation camps, and day nurseries, and supervise others, such as housing projects, workers' gardens, and mutual aid activities. They can also supervise apprenticeship and vocational training, and administer plant safety and health committees.

In the economic field, the committees have only consultative powers. They are supposed to be consulted on questions of organization and operation of the enterprise, and, at least once a year, on its plans for the coming year. The committees are to be informed of the concern's profit situation, and they may make suggestions on the disposition of profits. In joint stock companies, they can hire an accountant to examine the books; they are supposed to see all documents submitted to stockholders' meetings and they may have two representatives sit in on meetings of the boards of directors. They also have the right to take up wage questions "in relation to the economic and financial possibilities of the enterprise and to the technical conditions under which it operates." [97]

The committees, however, have had comparatively slight influence; responsible labor leaders themselves confirm this. The chief reasons for this have been: (1) the hostility of many employers; (2) the unpreparedness of labor; and (3) the violent turn in the communist trade union line.

Committees have been set up in practically all large plants, and in a majority of the smaller enterprises covered by the law. But in many plants, especially the smaller ones, the committees have only a nominal existence, and no real independence. While shrewd or progressive employers often work with the committees to good effect in small enterprises,[98] their importance lies in the larger enterprises. Employer hostility has shown itself chiefly to the committees' functioning in "economic" matters. Many employers are happy to see their committees devote their energies to social welfare activities; that leaves them little energy or time to intrude themselves upon matters of production policy or profit distribution.

Some committeemen have felt that running the lunchroom or vacation camp is good training for bigger things to come. But most of the articulate and aggressive committeemen, and union officials, feel that preoccupation with social welfare activities marks a position of inferiority. "All we get to do is to manage the Christmas tree," is a frequent complaint. Or, "We're just lunch peddlers (*marchands de soupes*)." They are likely to feel that the management will not really discuss production, price, or marketing problems with them, and that they are not permitted to see the significant books and documents.

The employer, on the other hand, is likely to feel that the committee is seeing "as much as is good for it to see," or "as much as it can understand." "How can you take up shipbuilding problems if you

---

[97] Ministry of Labor Circular TR80/46 (July 31, 1946), art. II, *Revue française du Travail*, Numero special, 1948, No. 1, pages 62–63.

[98] "I can get the committee to put across a lot of new ideas in the plant far better than I could do myself," remarked the head of an electrical machinery company. In his plant of some 250 workers, moreover, the CGT was the only union effectively organized.

can't even run the canteen?" said the head of a great shipyard (with a long record of labor unrest) to the dissatisfied members of his plant committee. The remark, although sneering, was not easily answered. For although French workers have little confidence in the managerial abilities of their employers, they also know they are not yet ready to furnish that know-how themselves.

No social group would be prepared overnight to supply trained personnel to carry out large responsibilities it had never had a chance to exercise before. The trade unions are especially handicapped in private industry because they have never developed the experience and the officialdom that go with stable membership and large treasuries, or the intimate knowledge of an industry that comes with collective bargaining responsibility.

The CGT unions have had greater resources with which to help out (and keep a check on) the committees. At first they pushed the committees as a means of boosting output, often to the disregard of safety and health. "Win the Battle of Steel so that France May Live!" was the theme of the metal workers' National Conference of Plant Committees early in 1946.[99] In mid-1947 the CGT set its face against these purposes, and sought to use the committees as arms of the local union for wage demands and for political agitation. In the strikes of 1947 and again in 1948, the CGT turned many of the plant committees into strike committees. At the "little convention" of CGT plant committee men, early in 1948, all members "promised to mobilize the committees against the plan of enslavement of the American imperialists."[100] A national conference of committeemen from the metal-working industries called on the committees to fight against "the imposture of the slogan of 'productivity.'"[101] Thus, the CGT cut what possibilities there were of labor-management cooperation through the committees. In some cases, however, habits of cooperation had been built up which resisted the new instructions.

In those enterprises where management and unions have both been in a mood of cooperation, the committees have helped to improve output and productivity, and to give workers a new stake in the production process. They have given workers a measure of training in technical problems, and opened the horizons of many beyond those of their compartmentalized daily jobs. They have substituted workers'

---

[99] CGT, Fédération des Travailleurs de la Métallurgie, *La Bataille de l'acier; Le Comité d'entreprise, organisme de l'avenir. Ière conference nationale des comités d'entreprises de la métallurgie, des 22 et 23 février, 1946,* Paris.

[100] *CGT, XXVIIᵉ Congrès national de Paris . . . 11–15 octobre, 1948. Compte rendu sténographié des Débats,* Paris, 1948, page 262.

[101] *L'Humanité,* April 24, 1950.

management for company paternalism in the case of many social welfare schemes.

The experiment of the *comités d'entreprise*, like most reforms of the postliberation days, has not given the results expected, or feared, in 1945 or 1946. The committees are, after all, only a "mirror of the general psychology," as one observer remarked. In themselves, they "do not create social peace, good understanding between employers and workers. They can only improve relations which are already 'correct.' "[102] The committees themselves could not change the tone of industrial relations, or shift the weight of power in industry. Neither have they destroyed the legitimate authority of management in the plant. It is impossible to say yet that the committees have "worked"; it is too soon to say they can not work. Even under more favorable circumstances, a generation would be needed to tell whether they would work. In the half dozen difficult years since they were first established, they have disappointed the hopes of their advocates and belied the fears of their opponents.

Strikes

In France, the strike is much more than an occasional element in labor relations. French workers have come a long way from the "heroic period" when an observer could say that syndicalism was, after all, only a philosophy of strikes.[103] At no time, of course, are the beliefs or practices of a free social movement anything like uniform. Even in the decades when the syndicalist philosophy was official CGT doctrine, many unions had grave doubts about the virtue of the strike except as a very last resort. But for many workers the strike has great symbolic value; it is the clearest form of direct action, an assertion of militant class-consciousness, valued for its own sake. A moderate FO leader wrote, "It is not so much the union as the strike which creates equilibrium in a capitalistic regime."[104]

To the CGT leaders, strikes offer special possibilities: appealing to the workers in other unions over the heads of their leaders; damaging the economy and increasing the pressures of inflation; making political capital out of economic grievances; deepening the fissures in French society; and training men and cadres for possible tasks of sabotage

---

[102] Pierre Chambelland, *Les Comités d'entreprise*, pages 213–214, 215. Paris, 1949.

[103] F. Challaye, *Syndicalisme révolutionnaire et syndicalisme réformiste*, page 8. Paris, 1909. Cited by Maxime Leroy in *La Coutume Ouvrière*, Vol. II, page 638. Paris, 1913.

[104] Guy Thorel, "La Grève, Fondement du Syndicalisme," *Esprit* (March 1948), page 393.

or revolution. On the other hand, most French workers, whatever the class-conscious language they speak or applaud, are wearying of struggle and skeptical of their ability to sustain long strikes or to win great advantage thereby.

The French Constitution, in an ambiguous phrase of its preamble, guarantees that the "right to strike may be exercised within the framework of the laws which regulate it." The only laws that directly regulate it are the conciliation provisions of the collective bargaining law, the law enacted after the strikes of 1948 barring strikes by police officers and others performing security functions of the state, and the anti-sabotage laws of 1950. The latter were enacted when the communists began public threats of sabotage of the "production, handling, and transport" of military goods, notably American arms shipments to France, and when they began to hold up or sabotage French military goods movements to Indo-China. Otherwise, the government has not proposed any general legislation, implied by the constitutional provision, on the exercise of the right to strike. Beyond its unclear conciliation clause, the 1950 collective bargaining law does not regulate the right to strike, except to settle one issue of long controversy; it provides that going on strike does not break the individual's labor contract with his employer, except in cases of violence or other personal culpability.

Labor leaders have done comparatively little re-thinking of the concepts of the right to strike. That right is claimed and generally recognized, in principle, not only in private but in publicly owned enterprise and even in public administration. The limitation on the right to strike in enterprises where the public health or safety is concerned is not in theory recognized for normal times. The trade unions, as well as the employers' associations, successfully opposed the general compulsory arbitration provisions of the government's collective bargaining bill as presented to the National Assembly, and the attempt by the (less important) upper house of the legislature to write in a public health and safety limitation on stoppages. The right to strike remains, in theory, sacred.

The greatest curb in practice on the freedom to strike is the government's power of requisitioning workers under the National Service Law of 1938. Mobilizing or requisitioning striking workers is an old practice, applied on a number of occasions since 1910 when Briand, with dubious legal authority, as he admitted, mobilized the railway men into the army and broke their strike. The National Service Law provisions were used in 1938 to break the general strike. In early 1950, the government requisitioned a large number of Paris gas and electricity strikers, and, a year later, railway strikers. A significant number of men disregarded the requisitions, and public opinion was far from unanimous against them. In the case of the gas workers, it was held by some of the lower courts that the powers under the 1938 law could be used only in wartime or, at the least, in a state of emergency. On technical grounds, higher authority held that this condition was fulfilled.[105]

The government has another old weapon, that of using troops and police to perform the jobs of men on strike. This it did, for example, in a strike of the Paris garbage collectors in 1950, to the accompaniment of ribald newspaper comments on "troop maneuvers" with pail and brush. In the coal strike of 1948, the troops and police forces not only protected nonstriking miners, but performed safety and maintenance functions in the mines.

Procedures for calling strikes are not regulated by law. Nor do the unions have well-defined practices for strike decisions. A few national unions, notably the printers, have long had requirements (not always enforced) that local unions, on pain of losing strike benefits from the national organization, go through certain prescribed steps of attempting to reach agreement, and obtain the approval of the national organization before calling a strike. In most FO and CFTC unions there are practically no strike funds to use as a means of discipline. Local autonomy in the face of the national union, and national union autonomy in the face of the confederation, are considerable.

As a result of the internal struggle in the CGT centering around the late 1947 strikes, the communist leaders of the CGT ran votes in many industries on the calling or continuance of strikes. They opened the voting to all employees and, wherever possible, took votes by a show of hands in open meeting (a tested communist device, used on many levels of responsibility, to discourage opposition). The anti-communists then in the CGT called, mostly without avail, for secret ballots. In the wave of strikes of early 1950, the CGT again started taking strike votes, sometimes in agreement with other unions. Often, however, it called the men off the job, within single departments of a large plant, as soon as it could claim over 50 per cent in favor of striking. To protect themselves, some employers then asked government labor inspectors to conduct secret strike ballots and count the votes.

The practice of strike referenda, open to all employees, thus seems to have grown up and received general acceptance. The government gives implied sanction to this procedure by permitting labor inspectors to supervise the balloting, and sometimes to intervene in the framing

---

[105] Powers of requisition have occasionally been used against employers. Thus, when the bakery owners of the department of the Gard called a strike for higher bread prices, the prefect requisitioned them and their bakeries.

of questions. There are, however, no legal prohibitions on strikes which dispense with referenda, or ignore their results.

Strike tactics include the usual one of picket lines and mass meetings, often held daily at the plant gate. Strike sabotage is sporadic and comparatively rare in the light of existing social tensions. With the one great victory of 1936 green in memory, the sit-down strike [106] is still popular in many minds. A few sit-downs were attempted after liberation, but in most cases only small groups of strikers rather than masses of men remained in the plants. In the most important instances, the strikers were ejected, without difficulty, by sizeable police operations, and the strikers were too uncertain of themselves to resist seriously.

Violence in strikes naturally varies with the nature of the industry and the community. In mining communities, where the CGT is well-organized and worker solidarity high, it is risky to go through a picket line. In 1947, roving squads of strong-arm men were used extensively by the CGT, and grenades were tossed into the homes of some of the most militant anti-communists who opposed the strikes. Violence against non-strikers, in general, has diminished with the CGT's decline from its postwar peak of influence and assurance, and with firmer measures by government and non-communist unions.

The CGT leaders, in line with the more obvious communist tactics, seek to make martyrs where they can. Considering the extent and bitterness of the 1948 coal stoppage, it was perhaps surprising that only 3 strikers were killed. While no policemen or troops were killed, a number comparable to that of wounded strikers had to be hospitalized. In the 1950 strikes, the communists succeeded in creating one martyr, a building trades worker shot by police in the course of a forbidden protest march in Brest, whose death was immediately laid to "American bullets."

The strikes so frequent among various types of government employees produce their own peculiar tactics, almost as effective as those of the Chinese mail carriers, over a decade ago, who refused to deliver any mail that bore postage stamps. In one customs officials' strike a few years ago, visitors suddenly found they could enter France without any customs inspection or currency control. In a later strike of the same officials, the rules were enforced with almost sadistic zeal. In 1950, Paris traffic policemen demonstrated for reclassification by picking a series of bottleneck points and, for about 15 minutes, enforcing rules with such excessive and literal rigor as to snarl traffic completely.

How is it possible for unions with low dues and anemic treasuries to

---

[106] The French term is, literally, "an occupation strike" (*grève d'occupation*), or the more picturesque "strike on the heap" (*grève sur le tas*).

finance strikes of any duration? The CGT financing must remain something of a mystery. But in its biggest strike since the split, amounts of foreign aid were made public by friend and foe. In the coal strike of 1948, the CGT and the Communist Party press announced contributions from foreign labor movements variously estimated at from 300 to 600 million francs; [107] most of it came from Czechoslovakia. Jules Moch, Socialist Minister of the Interior, described to the National Assembly the various mechanisms of the transfer of funds from behind the Iron Curtain to French communist agencies. This was done largely through the medium of the French *Banque Commerciale pour l'Europe du Nord*, owned principally by two Soviet State banks.[108] FO, which started almost without funds recently, has not accumulated any strike funds. The CFTC has taken the first steps toward building up some modest strike funds at the disposition of the confederation, by a monthly earmarked assessment.

Few striking workers have any cash savings to fall back on. The inflation period has drastically reduced workers' propensity to save. Strikers and their families often go hungry, and strikes often end with the "victory of the baker." French workers pay such a small fraction of their income as rent that the risk of being dispossessed is not great, even if the strike goes beyond the quarterly rent period. Nor do private employers or the government, in coal towns for example, any longer dispossess strikers from company housing. Workers rarely buy either clothing or furniture on the instalment plan, and own almost no automobiles, refrigerators, or other expensive consumer durables, so that there is no danger of the instalment seller's or finance company's recapturing a valued possession. In winter, fuel may be a problem in a long strike. Coal miners on strike, however, would still have stocks of the fuel they receive free.[109] The question resolves itself chiefly into this: how do workers and their families eat during a long strike?

"Solidarity" is the traditional, and still the current, answer of the unionist. The worker who balks at paying modest dues is often prepared to tighten his belt in a crisis to help others on strike. But strike collections and donations cover only a small part of the bill. Another old and dramatic form of solidarity is the moving of numbers of

---

[107] At that time the equivalent of 1.15 to 2.3 million dollars at the "unofficial" (black market) rate of exchange, or 1.4 to 2.8 million at the official rate. Among the contributions announced was one of 10 million francs from the Yugoslav unions, although this was after the Cominform break with Yugoslavia.

[108] Nationalization of banking was limited to the *Banque de France* and the four largest deposit banks.

[109] Coal is provided miners without charge, but is basically part of the wage payment in nonmonetary form.

strikers' children to the country, or to another community where no strike is on. This has the double advantage of freeing strikers from a pressure difficult to resist, and of spreading sympathy.

In this land of class warfare, strikes are to a significant extent financed, not by workers, but by government, by the community, and even by the church and employers. Family allowances continue to be paid to striking workers, and this helps relieve the pressure on the large families who would be worst off. Municipalities, even those under conservative administration, frequently vote cash contributions to strikers and their families, set up soup kitchens, or provide school lunches for strikers' children. Factory lunch rooms sometimes operate during strikes (and sometimes even reduce prices), and factory buying clubs or cooperatives may extend credit. These welfare operations are usually run by the elected plant committees. The employer, private or public, who provides the funds for these welfare schemes, thus, helps subsidize the strike.

Community collections are common. Merchants apparently prefer to give in money or in kind rather than extend credit to strikers. Temporary cooperatives are sometimes set up on the basis of these contributions. In a St. Nazaire shipyard workers' strike, the strike committee (CGT, FO, and CFTC) set up a cooperative to buy and distribute food; within a few days, it was operating branches in no less than 40 of the small communities roundabout, from which workers ordinarily come into war-shattered St. Nazaire. After doing a 40 million franc ($114,000) business, the cooperative dissolved when the strike ended.

The churches also help sometimes, by devoting part, or all, of church collections to the relief of strikers' families. During the 1950 strikes, church collections were widespread, particularly after the French bishops' statement in behalf of a living wage. "Two collections will be taken up this Sunday," was the appeal from the pulpit in an industrial city of Savoy, "one inside the church as usual, and a second one, in front of the church, for the needy families of strikers. Of the two collection plates, the one in front of the church is the more important." [110] The CGT did what it could to make such donations possible by seeing to it that strike relief committees, in the case of joint strike action, were set up in CFTC rather than in its own headquarters.

---

[110] The bishop of Tarbes and Lourdes, who had collections taken up in the churches, wrote in the diocesan bulletin (December 30, 1949), "The suffering which most in the world calls itself to the attention of the observer is incontestably that which weighs so heavily on a significant part of the working class." Cited in "Histoire d'une Grève," *Esprit* (June 1950), pages 1048–1049.

A word about demonstration strikes. These are not restricted to communist action. In late 1949, for example, FO called a nation-wide one day stoppage to press the government into freeing wages for collective bargaining. It also wanted to show workers that it was not a prisoner of the government, and that it was militant enough to know how to strike.[111] The classic demonstration on May 1 has become almost a communist monopoly. In 1950 and 1951, in most cities, only the CGT marched. In Paris, FO contented itself with discreet indoor meetings for its officials and staff. But almost all workers took May Day off, and those who worked collected double time; the day of international proletarian demonstration and protest had become, by French law, a paid holiday.

Unions and Political Parties

France is the country that developed the most extreme philosophy of trade union self-sufficiency and independence of the political parties. But the political party, in the form of international communism, has taken its revenge. All the great shakeups in the CGT, for the past thirty years, have been political in origin. Now the CGT is dominated by a single party, and one far more demanding and disciplined than the warring socialist sects or the unified Socialist Party whose advances the old syndicalists fought off.

To be sure, the syndicalist-led unions, before 1914, did not shun political aims and agitation; they merely shied away from parties and parliaments. They themselves proposed to effect all the political changes which, in other European countries, labor expected from political parties. The French labor movement "has always regarded itself as responsible for the whole universe." [112] From the first moments of World War I, many former revolutionary syndicalists joined the reformists in cooperating with the government. Since then, that has been the position of a large segment of the French labor movement, when the government has known how to permit it to cooperate. The revolutionary spirit, shattered by the events of 1914, was gradually revived by disillusionment with the war and by the illusions of the Russian Revolution. But this current was turned into the communist channel. Too late, the syndicalist revolutionaries saw that the dual labor organization they had done so much to form, the CGTU, was controlled by a political party ready to trample on their libertarian views and able to sweep aside their loose organization.

The communists, however, could not then extend their power from

---

[111] The CGT joined in the strike, but, to the great relief of FO, did not succeed in running away with it or prolonging it beyond the original 24 hours.

[112] Simone Weil, *L'Enracinement,* page 33. Paris, 1949.

the CGTU to the labor movement as a whole. Communist leadership was not yet rooted in the labor movement, and the party was rent by divisions. The Soviet Union, and, hence, the Comintern, were still weak. Europe for a brief period settled down. The French economy succeeded in temporarily stabilizing itself. At that, after the reunification under the Popular Front, the communists were moving toward control of the CGT when the war and their support of the Nazi-Soviet pact drove them underground. It is a sign of their vitality, and of the profound cleavages in French society, that they recovered from that suicidal position, and were able to take over the CGT after liberation. Today, the CGT is heir to the violence and intransigence of syndicalist tradition, though it has lost the humanitarian vision and the originality of thought and independence of action which were the saving graces of syndicalist extremism.

Many of the threads of French labor history run in continuous pattern for fifty or a hundred years. At points, however, the pattern seems suddenly broken, to resume in a new direction. The sweeping success of the communists, after the liberation, is one of those apparent discontinuities. The communists won much of their victory in the CGT in the first months after liberation, as we have seen. While their only potential rivals for mass political support among workers were rejoicing because everybody was "talking socialist," the communists were grasping the realities of power. The basis for this victory, and its continued hold, lay in the unique character of the party the communists had built, and, even deeper, in the dissatisfactions of those to whom they addressed themselves; the swiftness of communist advance after liberation was a reflection of the slowness of the middle classes to assume entrepreneurial or social responsibility in an industrial society.

The Communist Party leadership had undergone a process of selection and toughening in the generation since its early years. It had eliminated those excessively infected with "French individualism," that is, indiscipline to international communist leadership. It had shed most of the middle-class figures inherited from the Socialist Party in 1920, and its leadership was ostentatiously working-class. Many new figures had been attracted to it in the resistance, but the leadership in the party and the CGT was a solidly prewar (but not over-age) leadership that had survived the tests of the Nazi-Soviet pact and the wartime period, in jail, underground or in Russia. The socialists,[113] even more than before the war, were a party of middle-class and professional leadership; and they no longer had the intellectual lights

---

[113] See Henry W. Ehrmann, "The Decline of the Socialist Party," *Modern France,* pages 181–199, for a good brief summary and bibliography.

they had attracted when the party was young. French workers are inclined to forgive a great deal in those they regard as their own, while judging harshly a party of middle-class leadership. While there was not a single manual worker on the Socialist Party's executive committee, the Communist Party could show a high percentage of top leaders of working-class origin and experience at the work bench. For decoration and prestige it also displayed a host of intellectuals and artists. Within the CGT, as well as within the party, communist leaders were tougher and more single-minded, and yet more flexible, than their rivals. And the party's success in the first few years after liberation attracted able young recruits, whom the party could place, train, and advance.

At the top, communist policy in the unions was unified, and geared to party needs. There were no overt disagreements among CGT communist leaders. Among the communists' rivals within the CGT and then in FO, and in the CFTC, dissensions were not only aired, but apparently enjoyed. At the bottom, the Communist Party factory cell was designed for trade union control. The socialists, always parading their public differences, never developed a real "trade union line," and treated the unions as independent organizations. Their attempt to revive their workshop groups (*groupes socialistes d'entreprise*) came to little but talk, and offered no challenge to the communist factory cells.

In tactics, the communists maintained their initiative, despite the dangerous exigencies of Soviet international policy. They abandoned the policy of governmentalism and class collaboration, with its emphasis on production and its throttling of strikes, just in time to escape the outbursts of workers' pent-up wrath. Then, pushing wage demands and reviving the symbols and slogans of class conflict, they managed to keep the tactical initiative even after the launching of the European Recovery Program. Their opponents, prisoners of socialist shibboleths about the character of American capitalism, failed to exploit the turn in communist policy.

The social climate

Tactics and organization alone could not explain the continued hold of the communists on a majority of organized workers. The social climate favored a rebirth of extremism among workers. Even before the war was over, there was a tragic letdown from the high (and, it is now so easy to say, unrealistic) hopes of the resistance and the war. Many Frenchmen spoke of the abortion of the national rebirth (*"la révolution manquée"*), but none more than the workers. The lip service universally paid to labor's efforts in the resistance and reconstruction only underlined for them the contrast between their own conditions and the black market wealth and legal business profits they saw around them. For the first years after liberation, shortages of food and fuel and clothing emphasized the decline of the workers' position relative to that of farmers and manufacturers and middlemen. The war had aggravated the chronic housing shortage and slum conditions in workers' districts, so that even the conservative press echoed Blanqui's cry of a century before, "The housing problem is at the base of all the evils of the social situation." [114]

The institutional reforms first hailed as labor's great gains afforded little satisfaction. Workers "could not eat nationalizations," and they took no pride in what they heard of the management of nationalized enterprises; they identified themselves less and less with the state which owned these enterprises. Plant committees had not greatly changed their relations to their employers. There was a National Economic Council with a trade union leader as its president, but workers could not see that it was doing much of interest to them. The old social enmities, political skepticism and distrust of government flourished again as the government moved to the right and employers appeared to behave as of old. All this undermined the basis of compromise which the democratic unions needed to survive and grow in strength and influence.

The CGT could take an uninhibited counteroffensive in the name of a resentful working class. The handicaps of its Soviet inspiration and control were remote to workers, upon whom weighed more closely the apparent indifference of their government and the "cold intransigeance" [115] of their employers. The communists focused workers' hostilities on more emotionally satisfying targets than their rivals could set up. They alone sounded as if they meant to, and were doing, something about injustice. Even while bidding for the electoral support of farmers and the lower middle class, they were holding out to workers a promise of power and revenge for a century of repeated betrayals.

Interlocking control

The CGT claims to be politically independent. However, almost all the major leaders and most of the minor ones are avowed communists; of the few important exceptions, none has dimmed his standing by publicly opposing any communist policy in the trade union or political

---

[114] *Le Monde,* April 27, 1951.

[115] The phrase is that of the moderate MRP deputy Teitgen, then Information Minister, in a broadcast speech of March 12, 1950.

field. After the war, the CGT changed its statutes to permit members of the confederation's executive board to be members of political party executive bodies, but it still prohibits them from holding political office. The Communist Party makes a show of holding to the old rule of syndicalist nonpolitical virtue. "So that the CGT can group the whole working class, we do not propose to you the candidacies of Benoît Frachon and Gaston Monmousseau," the 1950 party convention was told as the central committee members' names were being presented for its approval; and then: "But we consider them members of the official leadership of our Party." [116] It cost little to exercise such restraint, which could have meaning only when a political party operates half secretly. The Communist Party Central Committee's 30 members (plus the Politburo members) contained, in 1950, eight top CGT leaders, including the heads of the national unions of the building trades, the metal trades, the gas and electric workers, and the railroad men, and the leaders of the departmental federations of the Paris region and Marseille. At the local level, it is hard to say exactly what minority of noncommunists remain in CGT posts. There are still a number, mostly in nonpaid positions. Some, either because of their local following or because of the temporary immunity that goes with noncritical positions, maintain considerable personal independence.

There were no great purges carried out by the Communist Party in the CGT after the immediate postliberation *épuration*. The minority made that, in part, unnecessary by its own withdrawal. There were some shakeups at the local and district levels, notably in the miners' union after the 1948 strike and in the miners' cooperative in 1950, and a number of small local purges, for excessive independence or lack of toughness. But, at least until early 1951, with no significant movements of deviation within the party itself, there were no dramatic purges in CGT ranks.

Rank and file

The degrees of allegiance to the Communist Party shade off from the small hard core of party dependables to the millions who remain in communist-run unions or vote communist. The majority of the CGT's members and their families vote communist, and they constitute the majority of the Communist Party votes. For most of them it is a natural form of occasional protest, and far from representing a deliberate choice in favor of turning France into a Soviet satellite. (Several million farmers and small businessmen have also voted Communist since the liberation.) It is natural because there is, on the left,

---

[116] *L'Humanité,* April 7, 1950.

no other party able to canalize protest. The habit of voting for the "most advanced" candidates, and not quite expecting anything to follow from that vote, of voting "always more to the left, but no further," is a century old; and it is a habit among hard-headed peasants as well as workers.

This voting behavior might seem strange in a land where political discussion is so articulate, and party organization so differentiated. It arises, in part, out of a profound skepticism about the real importance of Parliament.[117] Elie Halévy, discussing the German Social Democrats, noted that in 1912 "four million voters were eager to send to the Reichstag the members of a party whose program was strictly revolutionary." And he commented, "There have never been, in any great country, four million 1evolutionaries."[118] In 1951 five million French voters sent to the National Assembly members of a Communist Party which, unlike the Social Democrats of whom Halévy spoke, meant revolution. Relatively few of these five million voters, even among active CGT members, had any desire for violent revolution. A high proportion of the 700,000 party members the Communist Party claimed in 1950 (and of the smaller number it probably had) were workers. But only a fraction, perhaps under 5 per cent, of the total CGT membership might be reckoned among the hard core of communists who would follow communist instructions in an ultimate crisis.

There are still many rank-and-file members in the CGT who are definitely, even articulately, not communist. The reasons that determine union affiliation are many: union militancy toward the employer, the prestige of shop leaders, local prejudices, habit, and unwillingness to split from the CGT for fear of ostracism or reprisals by CGT members. Remaining in the "old home" of the CGT after the anti-communists split off, does not necessarily indicate a preference for the confederation's party line. Among the rank and file of French labor, there is still a hardy survival of the syndicalist tradition of rejection of all political parties, although it is no longer articulate in the CGT.

FO and the Socialists

"We are not a party like the others," Maurice Thorez repeated

---

[117] All this calls for longer analysis than space permits—and more caution. Even Lord Keynes trod softly on such delicate ground. "If one may ever discuss the political climate of another country . . ." he said in *Essays in Persuasion*, London, 1931. Page 106. (But then went on to prescribe for the French Minister of Finance.)

[118] Elie Halévy, *L'Ere des Tyrannies*, page 175. Paris, 1938.

recently [119] and in no sphere is that truer than in communist relations with the unions. None of the other parties in any democratic country is in aims, structure, or methods able to control the unions as the Communist Party does the CGT. In the CGT, one sees fairly strong unions dominated by a strong totalitarian party; in FO and the CFTC, one sees weaker unions in varying degrees of sympathy for weak parties. A great advance in political thinking of the reformist trade unionists, since the war, has been in the full realization of the difference between action in politics and domination by a political party. Under the influence of old syndicalist doctrine, the two were long confounded and, hence, rejected as evil.

FO is often spoken of as "socialist," in the press and other quarters, where, as in textbooks, a label is handy and must be short. There is no organic connection between the Socialist Party and FO, nor is FO uniformly socialist in leadership or in policy. The Socialist Party has the virtues of its weakness, and its general attitude toward the FO unions is one of equality. FO does not place all its hopes of political action in the Socialist Party. It is close to the socialists because it has a similar constituency, its outlook on the world is similar, and it has no other political resort.

The socialists in turn must be close to FO; the fortunes of their party depend to a considerable extent upon those of a sympathetic noncommunist, nonconfessional trade union movement. The Socialist Party looks wistfully across the channel to the Labour Party-TUC relationship. FO and the Socialist Party are mutually dependent, in part, because both have a very high percentage of their following among civil servants. The socialists, since liberation, have been in a series of repeated crises to avoid alienating this electoral base among the *fonctionnaires*. FO, by the same token, must look to the government, and, within the cabinet and Parliament, chiefly to the socialists, to take the lead in pushing for budgets and legislation on which so many of its members depend.

The FO relationship with the government and with the Socialist Party, which was a member of the postwar government almost all through the period in which the government moved to the right, has been a handicap in appealing to disillusioned workers in difficult times. The motto on the FO banner is: "Against any political control," and FO went to some pains, in its first few years, to establish that it was completely independent of the government. It criticized the government continually for failure to hold the line on prices, for its treatment of its own employees, for not decontrolling wages sooner, for setting minimum wages too low, and for its failure to reform the tax system.

---

[119] *L'Humanité,* April 7, 1950.

Beyond all these specific sins, FO declared, "the cabinets and parliament, by incompetence and impotence, evaded the fundamental problems on which depend the life of the democratic regime . . ." [120]

Socialist support is indispensable for any Third Force, middle-of-the-road government. This might seem to give it, and FO, bargaining power with the other parties who make up the uneasy Third Force coalition. But there has been little room for maneuver. The other parties of the coalition knew that neither the socialists nor FO could afford to wreck the coalition, which would have meant bringing de Gaulle to power. To meet pressures from FO, and to do no more than enable it to hold its own against CGT competition, the socialists brought on five cabinet crises between 1948 and 1951. Each time they returned to cabinet responsibility. Whatever its weaknesses in leadership or vision or dynamism, the Socialist Party's great loss of votes between the 1945 elections and those of 1951 was, in part, the result of sacrificing itself, with scant glory, to the maintenance of the Third Force and the democratic state. And FO, likewise, suffered because its real independence of the government, in a period of chronic crisis and more or less latent civil war, was strictly limited.

There are many others than socialists among FO members. A significant minority consists of politically homeless people of a general left-socialist outlook. Many of them were members of the Socialist Party but dropped out because they felt it was not vigorous enough, or too steeped in the corruptions of office. Others are of the old brand of pure syndicalists or anarcho-syndicalists who, on principle, have no use for political action and, despite all experience, cling to a romantic notion of labor's economic action as the one and sufficient means of social betterment. "It is not by conquest of (political) power that the worker will liberate himself from capitalist exploitation and exploitation by the state . . . it is by the conquest of the shop," declared the secretary of one of the major departmental federations of FO.[121] He called for a labor organization which "would avoid indirect action through official institutions, because that turns the working class from its own effort, the only kind that is effective; and would limit itself to direct action, to the defense of the liberties acquired, and the defense of human personality against invading statism and enslaving totalitarianism." This attitude is a product not only of old tradition but of new disappointment with the liberation, revulsion at the Communist Party, discouragement about the Socialist Party, and

---

[120] "Bases d'un programme economique et sociale," *FO, 2e congrès confédéral, rapports confédéraux* (1950), page 83.

[121] Thevenon, secretary of Loire department federation (St. Etienne), in *Les Cahiers Fernand Pelloutier,* FO Center of Workers' Education (October, 1950), page 4.

alarm at the rightward trend of government. Among many more workers, these factors have produced only political apathy.

The Catholic unions

The importance of Catholic labor thinking on politics is greater than ever before in France, even though most French workers remain anticlerical. Liberal Catholics and Catholic unionists took a significant part in the organizations of the resistance and the liberation, and a number of Catholic trade unionists entered the political arena, while the CFTC made new progress among industrial workers.

The Catholic political parties of pre-World War II days were insignificant. But the Catholic party that sprang up at the liberation, the MRP (*Mouvement Républicain Populaire*), had a lightning rise. In the June 1946 elections, when it still had much of the resistance aura, had not yet broken with de Gaulle, and seemed to many the chief barrier to the Communist Party, it received 5½ million votes. But its decline after 1946 was steep; to the right, it lost most heavily to de Gaulle and, to the left, it lost some of its labor support. Within the party more conservative elements took the helm. No one out of labor's ranks holds a key position in the party, although Bacon, Minister of Labor, was a CFTC activist. The right wing of the CFTC has been close to the MRP. Although a majority of the confederation, it could not swing it to support of the MRP, nor to support of the MRP position in favor of subsidies to church schools; and the CFTC remains politically uncommitted. Its political independence contrasts strongly with the close relations between Catholic unions and Catholic political parties in the other two countries in which Catholic unionism is important, Belgium and the Netherlands.

The left wing of the CFTC has no political home. In its fundamental preferences it is anticlerical and opposed to political party organization (or trade union organization, for that matter) along religious lines. Some of its leaders began an effort, a few years after liberation, seriously and painfully clearing the ground of old prepossessions, to consider the relations between labor and the state, and the forms of political action open to free trade unionists. Unless they found these forms, they thought, the "active noncommunist workers will be able to do no more, in dealing with their government, than forever alternate between the violent momentary reflex of strikes and the disappointments of beautiful, ineffective resolutions." [122] In the light of postwar experience with the futility of money wage increases in an inflationary economy, they have turned to the state, and, hence, to political action, for remedies which cannot be obtained from even the best contractual

---

[122] *Reconstruction,* June-July 1950, page A-3.

relations with employers. "Who will redistribute the national income?" asked a Catholic activist. "The state! It is the only one, despite all the reproaches one can make to it, and God knows there are many." [123] For them, political action does not mean, any more than it does in FO doctrine, a loss of political independence vis-à-vis the parties or the government. "The more trade unionism enters into contact with the state, with politics, the more it must maintain its independence with regard to the groups in political power, or aspiring to power." [124]

The political influence of labor

In 1946, it was possible for Goguel, sober historian of the political parties of the Third Republic, and no labor man, to say, "You cannot revive the bourgeois system of ideas. The common fund of French public spirit from henceforth has to come from the labor movement. . . . It is now up to the working-class elite to constitute the element directing the nation." [125] Labor lost that political momentum and that political prestige, and soon what Goguel called, in the Third Republic, the "party of order" had returned to power, and labor, as part of the "party of movement," felt frustrated and baffled. Labor was unable to give leadership in the critical period after liberation, when other elites had been discredited, because it was disunited, still lacking in qualified men, and too vulnerable to the communist drive for power. Leadership again passed to other groups in French society.

The communists excluded themselves, and, hence, the largest part of articulate French workers, from a share in peaceful political decision by the unbending role of opposition required by Soviet policy. The parties of the right and center acted, most of the time, as if there were nothing they could do to win over the workers. When they talked of combating the Communist Party, it was usually in terms of electoral change, to reduce the number of parliamentary seats which the Communist Party's votes would give it, or in terms of suppression of the Communist Party; rarely was it in terms of meeting the communist appeal to workers. Party programs (including that of the communists) all bid for the vote of the farmers, the multitude of storekeepers, and small and middle-sized businessmen. "Everything happens as if the wage earners were caught between a Right which has no hope of winning them over, and a Left which has no fear of losing them." [126]

---

[123] Marcel Gonin, "Point de Vue d'un Militant sur la Crise Syndicale," *Reconstruction* (February, 1951), page A-4.

[124] *Reconstruction* (April 1950), page B-9.

[125] François Goguel, *La Politique des Partis Sous la IIIe République*, pages 558–559, Paris: 1946.

[126] Pierre Uri, "Scandales de L'Impôt," *Realités* (November 1946), quoted in *Reconstruction* (April, 1950), page B-11.

It was only by parliamentary fits and electoral starts, when crisis threatened or the socialists were once again on the verge of leaving the government, that even the immediate short-run demands of labor got attention from the parties. At other times, labor received chiefly eloquent, general statements about the need of greater social justice.

On the morrow of the 1951 elections, French workers did not see how this greater social justice could be achieved through the forms of political action open to them. The Communist Party was the one which to labor seemed "the least removed from it," in the subtle phrase of Jacques Fauvet.[127] The communists have filled an ideological void, and have obtained an ideological hold which has already shown that it can survive a period of decreasing misery. Democratic trade unionists are perhaps more frustrated than the communists, because they do not enjoy the luxury of opposition. Nor can they look forward, as do hardened communists, to the day when, thanks to the Red Army or a collapse of the French social fabric, power will come to them. Democratic union leaders look forward, if the Soviet drive does not overwhelm them, to a continuing struggle in behalf of a tired working class, against powerful enemies to the right and to the alleged left.

There is, obviously, no single ideal formula of labor-political relations. The British Commonwealth and Scandinavian type of relationship, of unified trade union movements tied in with mildly socialist labor parties, grew uniquely out of conditions in those nations. The American pattern of pragmatic unionism exerting passing pressures on individuals of two heterogeneous, loosely disciplined national parties could be duplicated in no other society. The French syndicalist approach had to be dropped more than a generation ago, as soon as its theory of the relations between labor and the nation met the dramatic test of war. A "New Left" has been talked of, and for labor, in the continental scene, a new political approach would no doubt mean a "New Left." The democratic trade unionists have not yet gone much beyond the phrase and the hope. The existing situation of union-political relations may endure, from year to year, for a long time; it even bears a certain stamp of inevitability. Whether it lasts depends greatly on forces beyond France. Clearly, however, it does not give satisfaction to workingmen or real representation to the interests of labor, and it marks such an estrangement of workers from the national community that, in the absence of social progress, it can hardly even make for political stability.

---

[127] Jacques Fauvet, *Les Partis politiques dans la France actuelle*, page 47. Paris, 1947.

Chapter 6

ITALY——JOHN CLARKE ADAMS

Introduction

With the creation of a constitutional republic after World War II, Italy established a political democracy similar to the American. Millions of Italians are striving to maintain and strengthen this system. Many are working in and through the labor movement, which is an essential element in the struggle. If they fail, the hope that political democracy is an exportable ideal will be gravely shaken. In this light, the struggles of the Italian labor movement take on an importance to Americans beyond that of an idle curiosity over the vicissitudes of a strange and exotic land. They become an indication of the outcome of the struggle of democracy against tyranny throughout the world.

It will be noted that the present study of the Italian labor movement differs in emphasis from that found in most of the companion studies. In countries where conditions are relatively stable, the changes that are likely to occur in the ensuing years can be understood through a knowledge of present conditions. In Italy, conditions are so fluid that a description of how they stand now would ill prepare one to understand them in the years that follow, were that description not accompanied by an account of past events. Only if the Italian labor movement is seen in the perspective of its history can the resultant picture be of any real value to those who seek to understand its present status and future evolution. This is the reason the author has felt called upon to devote about half the space allotted him to descriptions of the historical background of the Italian labor movement.

Origins and History of Trade Unionism

A trade union is a function of the environment, the economic development, and the culture patterns from which it grows. Without a preliminary consideration of these factors, it is difficult to explain certain of the characteristics that distinguish the Italian from other labor movements.

Environment

Geography. The Italian peninsula, shaped like a boot, extends in a southeasterly direction from its base in the European continent into the heart of the Mediterranean. Perhaps because it is so easily distinguished on a map, this peninsula, together with insular Italy, composed principally of the islands of Sardinia and Sicily, is often thought of as containing all of Italy. Actually, continental Italy (90,000 square kilometers, approximately equal to South Carolina) [1] is more than half as large as peninsular Italy (140,000 square kilometers, approximately equal to Georgia) and contains almost a third of the total Italian territory (300,000 square kilometers, approximately equal to Arizona).[2] Except for its northern sections, extending south to Rome, peninsular Italy has been cut off from the flow of ideas and of commerce from continental Europe much as have the countries of the Iberian peninsula. In many respects, peninsular Italy still shows evidence of "backwardness" and of culture traits not derived from the common culture of western Europe. Continental Italy, on the other hand, and the northern extremities of the peninsula have always been in the stream of European intellectual and commercial life and in certain periods of history have been their center.

About 80 per cent of Italy is mountainous and difficult to cultivate. The mountainous region is, for the most part, comprised of the Apennines, a range which extends virtually from the Alps at the north, in a southeasterly direction down the entire peninsula. The Alps themselves form much of Italy's northern border, and the islands of Sicily and Sardinia, comprising insular Italy, are almost entirely mountainous. Italy's major fertile plain is the Po Valley, which lies northeast of the Apennines, principally in continental Italy. It produces most of the country's wheat, corn, and animal products, as well as the rice, sugar beets, and silk. The climate here is similar to that of the American corn belt, but the winters have less snow and are somewhat milder. The climate in the lower peninsula and in Sicily is semi-tropical, with hot, dry summers and mild, rainy winters. Figs, almonds, citrus fruits, and olive oil are produced here in abundance. The land that is not suitable for agriculture is used for sheep grazing.

Italy's many harbors have made her a center of maritime commerce in the Mediterranean. Through their shipping trade, the city-states

---

[1] This includes the regions of Aosta, Piedmont, Liguria, Lombardia, Veneto, Trentino-Alto Adige, and Friuli-Venezia Giulia.

[2] This tri-partite division, although not commonly used today, describes Italy more accurately, on both a geographical and a cultural basis, than other divisions. It was used by Giacomo Durando in his *Della nazionalità italiana*, published in Lausanne in 1846.

of Genoa and Venice, particularly, rose to power and wealth. Genoa is still one of the major seaports of the Mediterranean, while Venice has declined and much of the Adriatic trade has gone to Trieste. In southern Italy, the magnificent natural harbor at Naples is a shipping center, and on the Adriatic side, the seaport of Bari is one of the fastest growing of Italian cities.

Italy has few natural resources. Mineral deposits consist largely of mercury, sulphur, zinc, aluminum, and stone. She has a little poor grade coal and almost no iron. Until recently, Italy had produced no significant amount of oil, but in 1949 deposits were found in the Po Valley, and Italian hopes for greater economic independence soared. The Po Valley also contains quantities of methane gas, which is being used for automobile fuel.

Italy's physical environment is one of the major reasons for her political and cultural disunity and for her inferior economic position. As long as the Mediterranean was the center of the western world, Italy occupied a central position in world affairs, economically and intellectually. Now the peninsula and the islands are off the beaten track and their lack of raw materials and other major attractions to industrial development relegates them to the position of followers.

The Italian labor movement got its start in continental Italy, where Italian industry is concentrated. It followed industry down the peninsula as far as Tuscany, but further south it met with little success. With the exception of its northern extremity, peninsular Italy experienced little of the industrial revolution. The same can be said of all of insular Italy. The economic development of these sections, except in isolated instances, has not reached a state where a strong union movement is feasible.

Demography. Italy is generally considered to be overpopulated, although her population density is lower than that of several other European countries, including Belgium, Holland, and Great Britain. Her territory (116,553 square miles) is about half that of France (212,681), yet it must support some six million more people (Italian population estimated at 47,000,000, French population at 40,500,000). It is difficult to find work for so many people in a country with much infertile land and few natural resources, and, consequently, Italy has a chronic unemployment problem. According to official statistics, Italy's unemployed in 1950 numbered nearly 2 million, almost ten per cent of the total labor force. This figure would be much higher if it were not for the use of such economically questionable practices as the forced absorption of unnecessary workers by industry and agriculture and the avoidance of the use of labor-saving devices. No other country in western Europe has had so serious an unemployment problem in the postwar period.

The unemployment problem is further aggravated by an estimated annual net increase of 400,000, which must be absorbed by the labor market. Italy's high birth rate, however, the cause of this annual increment, is abating. In the industrial centers in northern Italy, deaths exceeded births during the postwar period.

Italy's demographic pressure and consequent unemployment have adversely affected the growth of the labor movement. They are important factors in the low standard of living of the Italian worker, and they have increased the fear of unemployment, which has made job security of such predominant concern to the worker.

Economic system

About half of Italy's 18 million gainfully employed persons, as indicated by Table 1, are engaged in agriculture. About a third (6 million) are employed in industry, and the remaining sixth are employed in commerce, banking, and the professions. The phases of the Italian economic system which offer peculiar problems and seem to merit a brief analysis are agriculture, industry, banking, and the tourist trade, which is of such vital importance to Italy's foreign trade balance.

Agriculture. Despite her nine million farmers, Italy is not self-sufficient in agriculture. This is due in large part to the fact that there are only 1¼ acres of arable land to each farmer. She has exportable surpluses of fruit, cheese, wine, and rice, but she must import other grains. She is also dependent on foreign trade for her sugar, salt, and coffee.

Farming is carried on by various methods. In northern Italy, and particularly in the Po Valley, industrialized farming is practiced extensively. Under this system the men are hired on yearly contracts, and are then free to move on to other employment. Although this practice leads to a floating population, the land is farmed so efficiently that the government is loath to interfere. There are over a million farm laborers and over two million independent farmers, out of a total of almost 4 million people employed in agriculture, in northern Italy. In central Italy, the prevailing farm practice is the *mezzadria* system, under which the owner parcels out the land to the farmers (*mezzadri*) in units which can be farmed by single families. Although this system is similar to sharecropping, it is looked upon in Italy as one of the most equitable farm practices. The arrangements vary with local tradition, but the owner generally supplies the farmer's house, and often the livestock, pays the taxes and upkeep, and divides the produce equally with the farmer. About half of central Italy's million and a half employed agricultural population are *mezzadri*. Of the rest, more than 500,000 own their own land, and more than 300,000 are farm laborers.

TABLE 1

DISTRIBUTION OF THE ITALIAN LABOR FORCE, 1936 AND 1948

(In thousands)

	1936		1948		Change
Population		42,919		46,300	+3381
Total labor force		19,701		20,708	+1007
Less: Unemployed* 706		1482			+ 776
Armed forces 650	1,356	300	1,782		+ 426
	18,345		18,926		+ 581
Productive employment: †					
Agriculture		8,756		9,040	+ 284
Fish and forestry		86		88	+ 2
Mining and quarrying		128		124	— 4
Manufacturing: ‡					
Consumers goods 2383		2343			— 40
Capital goods 1607	3,990	1398	3,741		— 249
Construction.		979		415	— 564
Public utilities		190		184	— 6
Transportation		612		763	+ 151
Trade		1,504		1,910	+ 406
Other services		1,291		1,302	+ 11
Government services		809		1,147	+ 338
Total		18,345		18,714	+ 369

* This includes data for October 1948.
† This distribution of employment does not include October 1948 data.
‡ Includes handicraft employment.
Source: Compiled by ECA Special Mission to Italy and published in *European Recovery Program—Italy, Country Study* (Washington: Economic Cooperation Administration, February, 1949).

In the southern part of the peninsula and in Sicily most of the good land is held in large estates and is farmed by day laborers (*braccianti*), who, unlike the laborers on the industrialized farms of the north, are paid only for the days they work. Southern Italy has about a million of these day laborers. About 750,000 other farm workers, although technically landowners, are forced to hire themselves out to avoid an extreme poverty. There are also a million and a half persons operating their own farms and more than 300,000 *mezzadri*.[3]

The impoverished landowners in the south, who try to cultivate the marginal land, have created a special social problem. These people

[3] Arrigo Serpieri, *La struttura sociale dell'agricoltura italiana, passim.* Roma: Edizioni italiane, 1947.

work long hours to maintain a poor standard of living, and their only satisfaction seems to come from a feeling of superiority to the landless *braccianti*. The antagonism between these two underprivileged groups has led them into opposing camps. The independent owners belong to reactionary anti-labor organizations and, when they dare, the *braccianti* favor communism. The result is sporadic bloodshed.

Industry. Italian industry is centered in the Turin-Milan-Genoa triangle of northwest Italy. Turin is the home of the Fiat works. In nearby Ivrea, the plant of the typewriter monopoly, Olivetti, is located. Genoa is the home of the Ansaldo, the Ilva, and the San Giorgio metallurgical works. Milan, the largest of these cities, is the center of the textile industry and the seat of the Pirelli rubber monopoly and the Montecatini chemical monopoly, as well as the Breda works, where much of Italy's railroad equipment is made.

About a third of the working population engaged in industry is employed in plants that hire ten or fewer workers. In contrast to these numerous small businesses there are giant companies in Italy, some of which, like the Montecatini chemical company and Pirelli, have virtual monopolies. There are few medium-sized businesses to act as buffers between the giants and the midgets. Many of the large plants are, in part, government-owned through IRI (*Istituto ricostruzione industriale*—Institute for Industrial Reconstruction), a government agency established by the Fascists that lends money to insolvent corporations against new stock, which it keeps. In many instances, IRI now has a controlling interest in the larger plants, but it is not its policy to interfere with private management. Most of the large heavy industry plants, except Fiat, are controlled by IRI, but the textile, rubber, and chemical industries are in private hands.

A sketch of Italian economic life cannot be complete without mention of the artisan. The Italian artisan still produces work of high esthetic value, and the goldsmiths, lacemakers, potters, leather workers, and glass blowers, as well as many specialized workers in the textile trade, turn out products which compete favorably on the international market.

Banking. Italy's large banks are also controlled by IRI. One of the major problems faced by Italian industry is the lack of capital. Investors are difficult to find. This situation is due to two major factors. Through a lack of confidence in the Italian economy, many capitalists invest a significant portion of their profits abroad. The government policy of issuing five per cent government bonds makes many investors prefer this type of investment. If the government were willing to subsidize industry with the money it receives from the bond investors, the shortage of capital might be averted.

Tourist trade and emigrant remittances. Italy's great "exports" are the tourist trade and remittances from Italians living abroad. Italy's most valuable resources are the beauty of her land and the beautiful things with which she has adorned it, which bring the foreigner and his gold to Italy, and the filial piety and nostalgia which induce the Italian emigrant to send part of his savings to his relatives in Italy and in many instances to return there when he retires. The Italian economic picture cannot be understood without taking these factors into consideration. Without the foreign currency that these sources bring, the financial condition of Italy, instead of being merely precarious, would be beyond repair.

Distribution of national income. Very little is known about the distribution of income in Italy beyond the obvious fact that the many are very poor and the few are very wealthy. The only available study of this subject was made by a private research organization in Italy in 1949. This study was based on a sampling of only 10,000 families and therefore cannot claim great accuracy. According to these findings, however, about 60 per cent of Italian families had an annual income of 525,000 lire ($832) or less, constituting about 30 per cent of the national income, while 2.5 per cent of the families had incomes of over 1,950,000 lire ($3,040), constituting about 17 per cent of the national income.[4]

Cultural factors

Three other factors, one primarily historical, and the others resulting from typical Italian attitudes, seem of sufficient importance to an understanding of the labor movement to merit attention here. The first is the late development of a political consciousness among the Italian workers; the others are the traditional types of Italian leaders and the Italian custom of expressing grievances and seeking to remedy their causes by public demonstration.

Late development of workers' political consciousness. As a nation, Italy is less than a hundred years old, although the dream of unification inspired Italy's poets and philosophers over the centuries. Dante Alighieri proposed unification in his *De monarchia* (1312–1313), and making explicit the value of unification was the end Niccolo Machiavelli sought to achieve in *The Prince* (1513). It was not until the eighteenth century, however, that plans for unity took a more concrete form in the writings of the Verri brothers, Cesare Beccaria, and the other contributors to *Il Caffè*, and not until the nineteenth century

---

[4] *Bollettino della "DOXA,"* Vol. III (1949), page 183 bis.

that the *Risorgimento*, the resurgence of Italy's dream of national unity, got under way.

The struggle for Italian unity, however, was not a popular movement. Italy's political unification was the work of intellectuals and idealists, drawn mainly from the upper classes.[5] A principal reason for the Italian worker's apathy toward the *Risorgimento* was the diversity of culture among the Italian regions. The language of Dante and the heritage of the Renaissance were shared only by the upper classes. The poor knew only the local community and their loyalties and animosities were reserved to the particular petty state that closed their horizon. The ruling class in Italy had a common language and a common culture at a time when Italian workers from different regions were still unable to communicate with each other. The masses were for the most part illiterate (in some southern provinces they still are) and they had little contact with their brethren in other regions. Even today, when the southern Italian worker goes north, he finds himself in a strange country, where his dialect is not understood and his culture derided.

This lack of political consciousness has affected the Italian labor movement in at least two ways. In the nineteenth century, lack of a common language and wide diversities in culture from region to region were serious handicaps to a national labor movement. In the twentieth century, political consciousness has been gained, but there has remained a hostile attitude toward the government. The Italian worker tends to think of the government as belonging to the *padroni*, the *signori* (the masters, the gentlemen), and not to him. This explains in part his desire for neutrality in World War I and his lack of enthusiasm for fighting on either side in World War II.[6]

Traditional types of leaders. Elizabeth Wiskemann, in her remarkably concise and informative essay on Italy,[7] points out that the Italian national character can be epitomized by two mutually contradictory types: the one, a *naïve* idealist, and the other, a *naïve* cynic; the one a St. Francis, who writes hymns of praise of an awful simplicity and who preaches to birds, and the other a Machiavelli, whose keen and disciplined mind strips reality of the illusory amenities until its naked-

---

[5] Guido De Ruggiero, *Storia del liberalismo europeo*, page 301. Bari: Giuseppe Laterza e Figli, 1945. The point of view that the *Risorgimento* did not affect the mass of the people, nor reflect their views and aspirations, is brilliantly stated by Curzio Malaparte in one of the cleverest of the apologies for fascism, *Italia barbara*. Torino: Gobetti, 1926.

[6] After the Armistice in 1944 many Italian officers were willing to fight with the Allies, but it was difficult to find common soldiers who shared this sentiment. In the Partisan movement behind the German lines, however, all classes joined in the fight for liberation.

[7] Elizabeth Wiskemann, *Italy.* New York: Oxford University Press, 1947.

ness is in itself unreal. The peculiarly direct beauty that pervades Italian culture and the impractical idealism of so many of Italy's great men stem from the first type. Lay saints of a purity and idealism equal to that of St. Francis appear from time to time in Italian politics. The Italian people have an instinctive feeling for leaders of this type, but the Machiavellians in Italy are also held in high esteem, and the practical advantages of their approach, when followed with discernment and sobriety, are considerable. Italy has learned to her sorrow, however, that in politics the complete Machiavellian finds it no easier to attain material success than the complete Franciscan. The blind adherents of Machiavelli—and they are legion in Italy—fail to realize that Cesare Borgia, the man whom the great Florentine political scientist considered the epitome of political guile, was one of history's most patent failures. The favorite son of the reigning Pope, set up under his father's protection as ruler of central Italy, Cesare Borgia could retain his position for only a matter of months after his father's death. The present-day term for the Machiavellian is the *furbo*.[8] The successful *furbo*, however, can deal only with the *fesso*, or "dupe," and the cult of the *furbo* presupposes a world full of *fessi*, who can be misled by the most transparent deceit.[9]

Although Italy has had plenty of *furbi*, one of its most distinctive features has been the number of saintly men who have led its popular movements. Mazzini and Garibaldi stand out in the *Risorgimento*. A later generation brought Turati and Prampolini to the socialist movement. And even among the postwar labor leaders there are many men who have set before the workers an example of personal integrity and idealism worthy of emulation. Unfortunately, however, the kingdoms of this saintly type are certainly not of this world, and the results they can claim in improving the workers' material welfare are meager.

Public demonstrations. Italy has always been a good country for revolutionists, but a poor one for revolutions. The average Italian revolutionist enjoys barking too much to proceed willingly to the more serious business of biting, and the Italian people, as a whole, get enough satisfaction from the oratorical effusions of their protagonists to be themselves content to forego the perils and uncertainties of more decisive action.

---

[8] This term is difficult to translate into English, but "slick operator" gives the general idea.

[9] Francis Marion Crawford remarked that the acumen of a Borgia who put the poison in the cup was less remarkable than the *naïveté* of the victim who put cup to lip. *Salve Venezia*, vol. I, pages 429–430. New York: Macmillan, 1905. The cult of guile, or the cult of the *furbo*, which at one time was prevalent over western Europe (see, for example, *Le roman de Renard*), in modern times has lost ground heavily in northern Italy. It is still a dominant force in the south, however, and one of the principal causes for the "backwardness" of southern Italy.

The Italians have had little experience with democratic elections as a method of changing their government. (Only once in the history of united Italy has the group in power lost an election.) The traditional manner for the Italian people, from the *Renaissance* on, to express dissatisfaction with their lot is to mill around in the central squares of their cities, making and listening to fiery speeches. These demonstrations last from several hours to several days, during which time there may be no casualties. The whole affair is often quite disorganized and generally constitutes no real threat (no "clear and present danger") to the government. If the demonstration is successful, that is, if it appears to represent the "general will" and not merely factional opposition, it is the custom for the government either to resign or to alter its course and personnel in accordance with the wishes of the demonstrators.[10]

The *Risorgimento* used the general technique of the public demonstration, or "row in *piazza*," as a principal means of achieving its ends, and the despotic rule of the various petty tyrants was ended by inspirational speeches, spontaneous uprisings, and general confusion, rather than by the successful conclusion of a coordinated military campaign. Even the fascists' vaunted March on Rome was merely an iteration of an old Italian tradition,[11] to which the king reacted in the traditional manner, when he accepted the resignation of the cabinet and called Mussolini to Rome to head a new government.[12]

The techniques of the *Risorgimento,* having proved successful in the political arena, were adopted by early Italian labor leaders, who in many instances had taken active part in the *Risorgimento.* This appears to be the reason that pamphleteering and inspirational speeches played such an important rôle in the early labor movement and still consume so much of the time of present day Italian labor leaders,

---

[10] This in part explains the frequent communist demonstrations, particularly since May 31, 1947, when the communists were excluded from the government. The De Gasperi government, however, has seldom felt forced to give in to the communist demonstrations because they have usually represented factional, rather than general, disagreement with government policies. There have been exceptions, however, particularly with respect to land reform in the south, where the demonstrators appear to have been allowed to remain on the land which they seized during communist-led popular uprisings.

[11] See George Macaulay Trevelyan, *The Historical Causes of the Present State of Affairs in Italy.* Oxford: Oxford University Press, 1925.

[12] The king's choice was to give in to the pressure of the demonstrators or to sign the decree for martial law presented to him by the President of the Council of Ministers, Luigi Facta. The commanding general, Pietro Badoglio, is said to have given his assurance that the demonstration could be suppressed with little or no bloodshed. Had the king signed the decree, and had Badoglio been able to suppress the revolution, it is probable that Mussolini would never have come to power.

who often seem more interested in putting out a paper few people read than in offering more tangible services to workers.

Another of the favorite techniques of the Italian labor movement is the general strike. As applied in Italy, the general strike is a modification of the "row in *piazza*." It is an essentially harmless act of insubordination by which the people express their disapproval of the government, and, unless it has been accompanied by enough violence to arouse public indignation, its results are often similar to those the strikers' forefathers obtained when they assembled in the central square before the palace of the petty tyrant to demonstrate against the injustices of his rule. The general strike, like the "row in *piazza*," is essentially a democratic procedure, through which the people make known their convictions on important issues. It is not an organized and disciplined procedure, such as the ballot box, but it is one to which the Italians are traditionally inclined.

Even the ordinary strike in Italy bears resemblance to the "row in *piazza*." It is usually in the nature of a demonstration and is of short duration. Rather than an indication of the union's economic strength, it expresses the workers' exasperation with conditions and is often accompanied by the intimidating implication that, should the workers' desires not be satisfied, violence may flare up spontaneously.

The Labor Movement in Prefascist Italy

Before the formation of the CGL

Ideology. From its origin the Italian labor movement had within it the seeds of the basic schism that has impeded its development and thwarted its achievements. Even before there was any significant organization, the Italian labor movement was split at the ideological level between the followers of Giuseppe Mazzini and of Karl Marx.

The first great Italian to influence Italian labor was Giuseppe Mazzini (1805–1872), who, after St. Francis, was perhaps the purest spirit this ancient culture has produced. Mazzini was involved with most of the liberal and radical leaders of his time. Almost none of them agreed with him, but all respected his integrity and the passion with which he devoted his life to the public good. Mazzini's name was an anathema to the conservatives, for he was an uncompromising republican. The radicals were also ill at ease in his presence because of his rejection of materialism and dependence on spiritual and religious values. The Roman Catholic Church reviled him because, with Giuseppe Garibaldi, he had dared to proclaim the freedom of Rome's citizens from the tyranny of the temporal power. And yet this man with whom no one agreed has had, ever since his day, numerous disciples who have been won to him less by the logic of his reasoning than by his vision and his principles.

Mazzini's archantagonist in the European labor movement was Karl Marx. The views of these men were diametrically opposed and they were unable to cooperate over any period of time. Marx's creed was essentially one of justice through revenge and retribution, while Mazzini sought justice through cooperation and understanding. In the words of Nello Rosselli:

> Mazzini's sensitivity was just as delicate as Marx's was dull, heavy, and lacking the genuine sorrow for human suffering that makes the Italian "felt" throughout the world. While Mazzini's theories may be questioned, or even rejected, he is nevertheless understood and beloved. Marx, on the other hand, can only be studied and admired.[13]

It was obvious that men as basically different as Marx and Mazzini could not long cooperate. Marx espoused internationalism and loyalty to a class, not to a country. Mazzini's internationalism was built on a community of nations, each contributing the fruits of its particular abilities to the improvement of the whole. Marx saw the upper classes and the existing social structure as evils that should be eradicated. Mazzini saw evils in the upper classes and in the social structure which he wished to eradicate. Marx considered himself the founder of scientific socialism and was a materialist. Mazzini repudiated Marx's materialism and saw no incompatibility between a desire for the material advancement of the poor and an equally strong desire for their spiritual development.

Into the struggle between Marx and his International and Mazzini for the control of the Italian labor movement, there entered two other figures of importance: Garibaldi and Bakunin. Giuseppe Garibaldi (1807–1882) was an anachronistic knight errant, who devoted his life to fighting to free the oppressed. He was spiritually akin to Mazzini and had a great hold on the popular imagination throughout the world, but his intellectual simplicity and impatient insistence on action made him an unpredictable ally. Garibaldi was leader of the *Mille*, the thousand men who set sail from Liguria to free Sicily and southern Italy from the tyranny of the corrupt Neapolitan monarchy and to surrender all this land to Victor Emmanuel II, thus making real the dream of a united Italy. This expedition was his most glorious exploit. but it was far from his only noble impulse. He had been with Mazzini in Rome in 1848. He had fought for freedom as far from home as

---

[13] Nello Rosselli, *Mazzini e Bakunin, 12 anni di movimento operaio in Italia,* page 146. Torino: Fratelli Bocca, 1927; cited in Humbert L. Gualtieri, *The Labor Movement in Italy,* page 53. New York: S. F. Vanni, 1946.

Uruguay, and he was to suffer defeats from the French when he tried again to free Rome from papal control. Later, however, in France's hour of need, when the Germans again moved westward, Garibaldi offered his services to his long standing enemy, Napoleon III, in the name of that liberty and justice to which his life had been devoted, even though the French had been his enemies and had outraged him when they took over his beloved native city, Nice. His offer of help was accepted and Garibaldi played a conspicuous part in the defense of Dijon.

Mikhail Bakunin (1814–1876) was a charming anarchist with bomb-throwing propensities, quite out of sympathy with both Marx's and Mazzini's views. He, too, was an advocate of direct action, but unlike the simple soldier Garibaldi he elaborated an apology for his point of view.

A crisis in the Italian labor movement occurred in 1871 with the establishment of the Paris Commune. This spectacular achievement attracted radicals of all sorts and was supported by Bakunin, Garibaldi, and Marx, but vigorously opposed by Mazzini, who died the following year, without having regained the prestige he had lost because of his opposition to the Commune. Mazzini's death left the road open to Bakunin and the anarcho-syndicalists, the advocates of direct action, and the Italian labor movement broke with its tradition of peacefulness to agitate for the general strike. The ensuing years marked a repudiation of legalistic methods and an increase in labor violence. By 1874 Bakunin and his friends were ready for the General Strike. On January 25, 1874, a manifesto was secretly printed, reading in part, "The peaceful propaganda of revolutionary ideas must be replaced by a loud, solemn propaganda calling for insurrection and barricades. No effort will be spared to bring about the struggle between the masses and the privileged." [14]

The uprising was planned for August, 1874, but the government seems to have been well informed of the plan and the leaders were caught red-handed and unprepared. During the next year a series of trials was held and the various plotters were sentenced to prison terms of up to ten years. [15] Before the death of Bakunin in 1876 the anarcho-syndicalists had lost their hold on the Italian labor movement.

The collapse of the anarcho-syndicalists left the road open to the

[14] Alfredo Angiolini, *Cinquant'anni di socialismo in Italia*, page 72. Firenze: Nerbini, 1900; cited in Gualtieri, *op. cit.*, page 111.

[15] Many of the defendants, to their apparent chagrin, were acquitted. Errico Malatesta, the famous Anarchist leader, said, "We were acquitted in the face of our explicit declarations of anarchism, collectivism, and revolutionism, because the *bourgeoisie* . . . was not yet alive to the Socialist danger." *Umanità nova,* October 7, 1920, cited in Gualtieri, *op. cit.*, page 114.

legalitarians, represented by Enrico Bignami, who felt that political action was advisable. When the new electoral law of 1882 gave a large number of laborers the right to vote, a Labor party (*Partito operaio*) was formed. This party repudiated Bakunin. Its leader, Costantino Lazzari, later became general secretary of the socialists. Repressive measures against the Labor Party were taken by the government, and, although its membership is said to have risen to 30,000 in three years, it had passed out of existence by 1888.

Four years later the Socialist Party was formed, following by one year the first publication of Italy's foremost socialist magazine, *Critica sociale*. Italy's great socialist leader, from the party's inception until its dissolution under fascism, was Filippo Turati (1857–1932). With the advent of Turati the incipient Italian labor movement came full circle. Like Mazzini, Turati was more an evangelist than a politician, and his results were in the inspirational, rather than in the practical, field. Also, like Mazzini, Turati was on the extreme right of the labor movement because he distrusted violent and vengeful tactics and believed progress resulted from cooperation, compromise, and patient determination.[16]

The Turati policy met its first grave difficulty in the labor field over the general strike of 1904, which badly split the Italian socialists. This strike does not appear to have been consciously instigated to the degree that the earlier anarcho-syndicalist attempts had been. It was in part the spontaneous reaction to widespread exasperation, kindled by the killing and wounding of some striking farmers by the police. The left wing of the party under Arturo Labriola, however, supported the strike wholeheartedly and was instrumental in initiating it. The right-wing majority, headed by Turati, disapproved of the strike, but supported it, once under way, in order not to aggravate the party split. The strike was a failure and the public reaction against labor was unfavorable.

Organization. Despite the vicissitudes of labor leadership in nine-

---

[16] "Turati will not be recorded in Italian history as a figure possessing the quality of a statesman, but of a great party leader and a crusader of a new social order. Rather than a clever politician, he was a poet whose policy found its driving power in a mind overflowing with inspiration but with a limited fund of political wisdom." Gualtieri, *op. cit.*, page 306.

Typical of the position of men like Mazzini and Turati is the statement of another great Italian political "evangelist," Camillo Prampolini, the socialist leader from Reggio Emilia, a friend and contemporary of Turati. This statement appears on the masthead of *La giustizia,* the weekly socialist organ Prampolini published in Reggio Emilia. "Poverty is not born of the evil of capitalists, but of the bad organization of society, of private property; therefore we preach no hate against the rich or their class, but rather the urgent necessity of a social reform based on collectivism." This is a far cry from the class hatred preached by Karl Marx and many of his followers.

teenth century Italy, a steady growth in trade u.iionism occurred. These unions were primarily local in character and then loosely federated on a national or semi-national basis. They were, in part, fraternal and protective associations, bargaining agencies, and cells for the propagation of political and economic dogmas. During the nineteenth century, however, there was little or no central supervision of these organizations, and the affiliation of the various units was often a tenuous one, based on the momentary prestige of a leader.

Even before unification, "leagues of resistance" (*società di resistenza*) were established, the original function of which appears to have been to resist wage decreases. An early league of this nature was formed by the Turin printers in 1848, which in that same year negotiated the first collective agreement in Italy;[17] but these leagues did not become prominent until the decade 1870–1880. Among the oldest of the national unions is that of the printers, established in 1872, although it claims a direct link with the 1848 Turin league of resistance. By 1880 the printers' union was strong enough to hold its first strike in Milan. In this strike, which lasted three and a half months, the printers succeeded in winning a wage increase that netted them a fraction over six cents per thousand letters. In 1890 they negotiated their first collective agreement for an entire region (Veneto).[18]

Around 1890, another type of labor organization called the labor chamber (*camera del lavoro*) [19] started to grow in northern Italy. The labor chamber was an attempt to unify the labor movement at the communal, or, in Italy, often the provincial level. Central offices were established for all the affiliated labor organizations. Mutual aid was offered and common programs adopted. Among the more important functions of these organizations was that of employment agencies. The first labor chambers were established in 1891 in Turin, Milan, and Piacenza, and others followed quickly. In 1893 a convention of labor chambers was held, at which a national program was outlined. By 1896 there were 14 labor chambers in operation,[20] the largest at

---

[17] Rinaldo Rigola, *Storia del movimento operaio italiano,* pages 9 ff. Milano: 1947.

[18] T. Bruno, *La federazione del libro nel suo primo cinquantennio di vita,* pages 17, 38–39, 69–70. Bologna: Cooperativa Tipografica Mareggiani, 1925.

[19] This name is equally infelicitous in English and Italian, and according to Sacco comes from the official jargon of the Kingdom of Piedmont. The name Chamber of Commerce, however, has now been universally accepted for the analogous organization representing the merchants. The labor groups are called *Bourses du travail* (labor exchanges) in French, and there were those who wanted to use the term *Borse del lavoro* for their Italian counterparts. Italo Mario Sacco, *Storia del sindacalismo.* 2ª edizione accresciuta. Torino: Società Editrice Internazionale, 1947.

[20] A fifteenth, in Genoa, was in formation, and a sixteenth, in Padova, had been dissolved by government order.

Bologna, with 16,594 persons enrolled, the smallest in Piacenza, with an enrollment of 851. The other cities in which these organizations were in operation were Brescia, Cremona, Florence, Milan, Monza, Naples, Pavia, Parma, Rome, San Pier d'Arena, Turin, and Venice.[21] Although the labor chambers were socialist-dominated, they performed a recognized public function, and all fourteen in operation in 1896 received public subsidies, usually from the municipality, sometimes from the province; and, in two instances each, from the local Chambers of Commerce and from the national government. Besides cash subsidies, some communal governments supplied the labor chambers with headquarters. In 1895, these labor chambers found work for nearly 20,000 people.[22]

Another type of organization appearing in nineteenth century Italy was the *fascio*. This word, which means "bundle," was the one later adopted by the fascists in establishing their *Fasci di combattimento* (Combat Bundles or Units), from which they later derived the words "fascist" and "fascism." The original *fasci*, inspired by the Paris Commune, were radical societies whose members were recruited from the working class. The first *fascio* appears to have been founded in Catania in 1891 by Giuseppe De Felice Giuffrida. The movement spread quickly over Sicily and, to a lesser extent, the mainland. Most of the *fasci* were affiliated with the Socialist Party, although their programs were considerably more revolutionary than Turati's. Particularly in Sicily, their activities led to violence, and strong repressive measures were taken against them by the Italian government under Francesco Crispi, including an order for the dissolution of the Socialist Party.[23] The intemperance of the government and the threat to civil liberties that this action constituted caused a strong public reaction against the government on the part of all liberal and democratic elements. After this scare, however, the Socialist Party resolved to disaffiliate all groups and, thereafter, to rely exclusively on individual membership. From this time on the labor movement in Italy was officially independent of the Socialist Party.

Formation of the CGL

In the twentieth century the loosely federated local unions lost their autonomy, and four national labor confederations arose. These

---

[21] From Angiolo Cabrini, *Le camere del lavoro in Italia*. Genova: Federazione Socialista Ligure, 1896; table reproduced in Sacco, *op. cit.*, page 426; Osvaldo Gnocchi Viani, *Dieci anni di camere del lavoro*, page 22. Bologna: Libreria Treves di Luigi Beltrami, 1899.

[22] Gualtieri, *op. cit.*, pages 167–168.

[23] Caspare Nicotri, *Storia della Sicilia nelle rivoluzioni e revolte*, pages 183–200. New York: Italian Publishers, 1934.

organizations became known as the "red," "yellow," "white," and "black" confederations, in accordance with the political complexion of their adherents.

The first and most important of these was the "red" CGL (*Confederazione generale del lavoro*—General Confederation of Labor), formed October 1, 1906. This was a Socialist organization, although independent of the party. Cooperation between the Confederation and the party was difficult because the two organizations were frequently controlled by different factions of the party. Although new factions were continually springing up in both the CGL and the party, the basic cleavage was between the reformists, under Turati, and the revolutionists, under such men as Arturo Labriola and Enrico Leone. At the Socialist Party congresses of 1904, dominated by the Revolutionists, the Labriola-Leone faction succeeded in calling a general strike, the major result of which was that the socialists lost the subsequent national election. After the party congress at Rome in 1906, Turati returned to power, and two years later, at the congress of Florence, the party expelled the revolutionist leaders. In 1912, however, the tables were turned, and a faction of the reformists, led by Leonida Bissolati, that had favored the Italo-Turkish war of 1911, was expelled from the party by the resurgent revolutionists. To make the accusation against Bissolati and his fellow socialist deputies, the revolutionists chose a then unknown youngster from the Romagna, Benito Mussolini, who had just been freed from a five-months' prison sentence for his violent antimilitarist actions.[24] The Bissolati group was soon joined by other right-wing Socialist leaders and together they formed the *Partito socialista riformista* (Reform Socialist Party). The creation of this second socialist party, led by men of wide popularity, was a further blow to the CGL.

In spite of the fact that the CGL was almost constantly disturbed by the factional strife within the Socialist Party, it was in many respects the least politically-minded labor confederation that Italy has ever had. Under the leadership of Rinaldo Rigola (1907–1918) and Ludovico D'Aragona (1918–1925), serious efforts were made to build up a strong union movement pledged to gradualism and working within the law. Violent and illegal methods were frowned upon. Under this leadership, the CGL grew from 190,000 members in 1907 to a peak of 2,200,000 members in 1920. During all this period the CGL tried to create labor unity on a nonpolitical basis, but its numerous politically-

---

[24] Interesting accounts of this period of the Socialist party can be found in Angelica Balabanoff, *My Life as a Rebel*. New York: Harpers, 1938, and Ivanoe Bonomi, *Leonida Bissolati e il movimento socialista in Italia*. Roma: Cogliati, 1929, or Edizioni Sestante, 1945.

minded adherents blocked its efforts. Desperate attempts in this line were made by Rigola at the Confederation's congress at Mantua in 1914 and again in 1920, but with little effect.[25]

TABLE 2

MEMBERSHIP IN THE GENERAL CONFEDERATION OF LABOR

Year	Number of members
1907	190,422
1908	258,515
1909	292,905
1910	302,400
1911	383,770
1912	309,671
1913	327,312
1914	320,858
1915	233,863
1916	201,291
1917	237,560
1918	249,039
1919	1,150,062
1920	2,200,100
1921	1,128,915
1922	401,054
1923	211,016
1924	201,049

These figures indicate the number of members according to the number of full-year dues paid.

Source: *Almanacco socialista, 1931,* edito dal Partito socialista italiano, Sezione della Internazionale operaia socialista, Parigi, p. 138.

Not all the organized workers, however, belonged to the CGL. In 1912 the left-wingers who had been responsible for the general strike eight years previously formed the USI (*Unione sindacale italiana—* Italian Syndical Union). The philosophy of the USI was derived mainly from French revolutionary syndicalism. (See Chapter 5.) Its main strength was found among the railroad workers, who had left the CGL in 1911, and some of the labor chambers, particularly the one in Parma, transferred their allegiance from the CGL to the USI.[26] At its second congress in Milan in 1913 the USI claimed over 100,000 members, and in spite of the fact that it expelled its right wing during

---

[25] For a detailed account of the labor movement and the CGL in their early years see *Origini, vicende e conquiste delle organizzazioni operaie aderenti alla Camera del Lavoro di Milano.* Milano: Ufficio del lavoro della Società Umanitaria, 1909. Also see Sacco, *op. cit.,* pages 228–231, 236; Giuliano Mazzoni, *La conquista della libertà sindacale,* pages 83–84. Roma: Edizioni Leonardo, 1947. Strike statistics from 1878 to 1923 are analyzed in *Annuario di statistiche del lavoro, 1949,* pages 374–388. Roma: Rassegna di statistiche del lavoro, 1949.

[26] Biagio Riguzzi, *Sindacalismo e riformismo nel parmense.* Bari: Giuseppe Laterza e Figli, 1931.

the war for favoring intervention on the side of the *Entente,* by 1919 it had grown to a claimed membership of 500,000.

The Catholic labor movement got under way after the encyclical *Rerum Novarum* was issued in 1891, and according to one authority, in that same year there were 80,000 Catholic workers enrolled in Catholic labor organizations. By 1911 the claimed membership had risen to 104,614. 33,402 of these were textile workers, and 37,148 were farmers. About half of the membership came from Lombardy, and about 20 per cent from Veneto. There were 374 associations in all, and two national federations, one for the textile workers and the other for the railway workers.[27] In March, 1918, the Catholics founded the CIL (*Confederazione italiana dei lavoratori*—Italian Confederation of Workers). This was formed of 10 national unions and 25 labor chambers that the Catholics had already established.

The CIL was related to the Catholic *Partito popolare* in much the way that the CGL was related to the Socialist Party. For Marxist economics and philosophy, stressing class struggle, internationalism, and materialism, the Catholic organizations substituted a theory of class collaboration, based in part on the writings of Giuseppe Toniolo,[28] the Italian Catholic labor theorist, and in part on the writings of the French Catholic theorists, particularly La Tour du Pin.[29] The desire of these Catholic theorists was to return to something similar to the medieval gilds. Labor unions were to be treated as natural and spontaneous institutions, which the state should recognize and to which it should grant legal personality. The Catholic union, however, would represent not merely its active members but all the workers in a given occupation. According to this theory, representation by a union is similar to representation by a city council. The one results inevitably from employment in a specific occupation; the other results inevitably from residence in a specific locality. In neither case is voluntary or active participation necessary. Catholic labor theory also favored profit-sharing by the workers through the ownership of stock, and it stressed the religious and moral duties of the labor movement, along with its economic functions.[30] In 1921 the CIL claimed 1½ million members, including 130,000 textile workers. This union benefited from capable leadership during its short life under its secre-

---

[27] Sacco, *op. cit.,* pages 221–222; Giorgio Candeloro, *Il movimento sindacale in Italia,* page 81. Roma: Coltura Sociale, 1950.

[28] Luisa Riva Sanseverino, *Il movimento sindacale cristiano,* page 210 ff. Roma: Cesare Zuffi, 1950.

[29] René Charles Humbert, Marquis de la Tour du Pin Chambly la Charce, *Vers un ordre social crétien. Jalons de route, 1882–1907.* Paris: Librairie Plon, 1929.

[30] Riva Sanseverino, *op. cit.,* pages 348–386; Sacco, *op. cit.,* pages 168–182, 223–228, 385–386; Mazzoni, *op. cit.,* pages 84–86.

taries, Corazzin, Giovanbattista Valente, Giovanni Gronchi,[31] and Achille Grandi.[32]

A fourth union, the UIL (*Unione italiana del lavoro*—Italian Labor Union) was formed in Milan in May, 1918, by the nationalists expelled from the USI shortly before. This group was composed of opportunists whose philosophy was more Nietzschian than Marxist. Its spiritual leader, Filippo Corridoni, was killed in the war. The men who lived to head the movement were Edmondo Rossoni and Alceste De Ambris.

The doctrine of the UIL was national syndicalism. Its basic premise was that the nation was more important than the class, and that collaboration among the various classes of a nation was preferable to, and more feasible than, class collaboration among workers of different nations. National syndicalism denied the existence of neither classes nor class interests, but believed they should be subordinate to the interests of the state.

The tendencies of this theory toward fascism are clearly apparent. In their early years neither fascism nor national syndicalism had definite philosophies, but it was obvious from the start that the two movements could get along together. By 1922 the nationalist and anti-Marxist tendencies in the UIL were sufficiently crystallized, so that when it received an invitation to meet with the "red" union, which at that time, like all socialist unions in Europe, had international affiliations, the UIL declared that international unions were an absurdity so long as there were "have" and "have not" nations, that the UIL was unwilling to deny the principle of nationalism, and that it would not submit to control by a political party, but wished to preserve its liberty and autonomy.[33]

Even with four distinct and competing confederations in existence, some cooperation might have been effected if the unions had been willing to concentrate their efforts in the labor field. Instead, a further cleavage resulted in 1920 over a political issue. In that year the Italian poet Gabriele D'Annunzio led a group of unemployed ex-soldiers who were not yet reacclimated to civilian life on a comic opera expedition

[31] Gronchi held an undersecretaryship in Mussolini's first cabinet. He was a member of the Popular (Catholic) party, which at that time was supporting the Fascists. After the liberation (1945), Gronchi held various ministerial posts and, in 1948, became President of the Chamber of Deputies. He is the nominal head of the Christian Democratic elements that are dissatisfied with the leadership of Alcide De Gasperi.

[32] Grandi represented the Catholic faction as one of the three general secretaries of the postfascist labor union, CGIL, from its inception in January, 1945, until his death in the summer of 1946.

[33] Sacco, *op. cit.*, page 233; Mazzoni, *op. cit.*, pages 87–88; Herbert W. Schneider, *Making the Fascist State*, pages 138–164. New York: Oxford University Press, 1928.

to seize Fiume, which the Allies had made a free city. This action was deplored by the CGL and the USI as well as by the labor organizations in other countries, but was vociferously supported by the UIL.

Labor union recognition. Labor unions were frowned upon by the petty states set up in Italy after the Congress of Vienna. After the unification of Italy the medieval gilds were expressly abolished by the law of May 29, 1864, but mutual aid societies among the workers were permitted to continue. In 1883, San Giuliano, better known to Americans as the Italian Foreign Minister at the outbreak of World War I, presented a bill to legalize unions. He argued that prohibition of labor unions and of strikes had been less unfair in a past age, when wages and basic prices were fixed by government order, than in 1883 under a liberal regime. The bill was defeated 121–117.

Unions were legalized, by implication at least, by the Italian Criminal Code of 1890. Article 165 of this Code provided for punishment of anyone who, by violence or threats, impeded the freedom of industry or of commerce, and the following article provided for punishment of anyone who, by violence or threats, provoked or prolonged a strike or lockout for the purpose of altering existing wage scales. The maximum punishment was 20 months' imprisonment and a 3000 lire fine for followers, and 36 months' imprisonment and a 5000 lire fine for leaders.[34] The fact that unions were legal, so long as they did not use violence and threats, although not specifically stated in the Criminal Code, was taken for granted by the Deputies in the debates on the Code itself.[35]

No further legislation concerning the right to organize was passed in Italy before the fascist period, although several bills on this subject were presented in the Chamber of Deputies. The worst, perhaps, was presented in 1899 by the Pelloux Ministry. This bill copied German legislation of the period and would have given the police the right to dissolve any organizations which threatened public order. Although the Chamber rejected the bill, the government issued a decree with the same provisions. The *Corte dei conti* [36] later declared this decree *ultra vires,* and the Court of Cassation [37] declared it null. A few years later, in 1902, Minister of Justice Cocco Ortu presented a bill authorizing the unions registered with the Labor Office of the Ministry of Agriculture, Industry, and Commerce to take part in negotiations for collective agreements and granting registered unions the right to sue and be sued and to own property. The bill, however, was not passed.

---

[34] In 1890, 5000 lire was worth about $1000.

[35] Mazzoni, *op. cit.,* page 149.

[36] The functions of this body are roughly equivalent to those of the office of the Controller General in the United States.

[37] The highest tribunal of Italy's regular judicial system.

In the same year, another Deputy, Alessio, presented a bill to give legal personality to unions representing farm workers. This also failed to pass:

Three decrees in the prefascist period recognized the *de facto* existence of unions. The first, issued in 1904, gave certain labor unions the right to select some of the members of an institution called the Superior Labor Council. The second, issued in 1918, authorized the prefects to consult with management and labor organizations before selecting labor judges. The third, in 1920, authorized management and labor associations to assist in the selection of representatives on the Administrative Council of the National Social Security Institute (*Cassa nazionale per le assicurazioni sociali*).

Conciliation and arbitration

The first law setting up conciliation proceedings was that of June 15, 1893, establishing the *Collegi dei probiviri*. This law resulted from the proposals of a Royal Commission of Inquiry on strikes. The term *Collegi dei probiviri*, taken from the French *Conseil de prud'hommes*, translated literally, means "Colleges of Honest Men." These "colleges" were groups of three or more men chosen for their honesty and impartiality as mediators or arbitrators in labor disputes. The men did not necessarily have legal training and the procedure before them was informal. The Italian deputies were guided by the successful French and Belgian experiments in this field and the practice of private bodies which had been functioning in Italy for some time. One of the earliest of these private Italian *Collegi dei probiviri* was functioning in the silk industry at Como in 1878.

The Italian law empowered the Minister of Justice and the Minister of Agriculture, Industry, and Commerce to set up *Collegi dei probiviri* for each industry, or group of industries, in each locality where the industries existed. The president of each board was a judge, or a private citizen with the qualifications necessary to be a Justice of the Peace (*conciliatore*). The other members were equally divided between labor and management representatives. In mediation cases the board consisted of at least three members; in arbitration cases, of at least five. There were no sanctions against parties who refused to attend the proceedings before these boards.

The next important general legislation on the subject was a war measure making arbitration compulsory in all disputes on economic or disciplinary questions in industries subject to the regulations concerning the war mobilization of industries.[38] The list of affected in-

---

[38] Royal Decree of June 26, 1915.

dustries increased steadily during the war, and later agricultural disputes were also included. The institutions to which the arbitral power was granted were the seven Regional Committees of Industrial Mobilization and a Central Committee of Mobilization at Rome, the latter acting as an appeals board.

In the following year, arbitration commissions for white-collar workers in private industry were set up. At first these commissions were concerned only with disputes arising out of recall to military service, but their competence was later extended. A commission was set up in each province, consisting of a president chosen by the president of the provincial court (*tribunale*) from among the judges of the court and of eight members, four representing management and four representing employees. Two representives each, of management and workers, were regular members of the commission, and the others were alternates.

With the Decree of October 13, 1918, the competence of the commissions was extended to all types of labor disputes, either of a judicial nature over the interpretation of an existing agreement, or of an economic nature over the determination of a new agreement. Under this law, if the attempt at conciliation failed, the commission was required to give a judgment that was in effect legally binding, since individual contracts that set conditions less favorable to the workers than those contained in the judgment were null and void.[39]

During this period of early development the Italian labor movement gave some indication of the direction in which it was heading. The political influences which predominated in the early years have yet to be eradicated. The habit of working through legislation rather than through direct negotiations with management had already been acquired, and the tendency of labor to dissipate its power by splitting into factions often more mutually antagonistic than united against management was already apparent. Despite these disruptive tendencies in the labor movement, the pre-fascist period witnessed the rise of the CGL, a labor organization, that had at its peak over two million members and that had won the loyalty of its members and the respect of its adversaries during a quarter century of steady growth. Debilitated by the bad habits the Italian labor movement had acquired in its infancy, the CGL was soon to succumb to fascism.

[39] International Labor Office, *Conciliation and Arbitration in Industrial Disputes,* pages 425–428. Geneva, 1933; Luigi De Litala, *Diritto processuale del lavoro,* pages 36–44. Torino: UTET, 1936; Nicola Jaeger, *Le controversie individuali del lavoro,* pages 12–15. Padova: CEDAM, 1934; Ubaldo Prosperetti, "La giurisdizione del lavoro," *Atti della Commisione per lo studio dei problemi del lavoro,* Vol. II. *L'ordinamento del lavoro nella legislazione comparata.* Roma: U.E.S.I.S.A., 1946, pages 331–332.

The Labor Movement in the Fascist Period

Fascism results from economic crisis, a decline in parliamentarianism, and the threat of Communism. In its origins it is a *petit-bourgeois* movement with a muddled programme, composed of a mixture of quasi-radical reforms and ultra-nationalism. The inconstancies of this curious medley of contradictions, frequently referred to as National Socialism, are overlooked or forgotten in the worship of a blindly followed leader whose word is the final dictum on all matters. Fascism comes to political power by finally gaining the support, at first surreptitious, of large-scale capital interests, which see in it a potent weapon for the defense of the status quo. To begin with, it amply justifies the hopes and expectations of this group, whose backing made its ascent to power possible. In so doing, however, it abandons the progressive planks of its earlier platform and ruthlessly suppresses the elements which advocated them.[40]

Fascism might never have taken hold in Italy if the labor movement had not split apart and if its leaders had not become more concerned with internecine strife than with the protection of labor interests. At the same time, fascism had a peculiarly pernicious influence on labor organizations, acting as a fifth column within the labor ranks, attracting many members of the working class with its promise of quasi-radical reforms and its gaudy creed of nationalism, thus further dividing the already divided ranks of labor and making them even less able to act with unity and decision.

The corporate system

Fascist labor policy was a combination of national syndicalism and Catholic labor theory. The national syndicalists supplied the enthusiasm. They had only the vaguest platform, and this was based in good part on the extravagant Constitution of the *Reggenza* of Carnaro, which Gabriele D'Annunzio wrote during the Fiume incident.[41] The contributions of D'Annunzio lay more in window dressing than in substance. He was responsible for what Charles E. Merriam calls the *miranda* of power,[42] the things to be looked at in the potpourri that became the corporate system. The national syndicalist leaders were

[40] Lorne T. Morgan, "The State and Economic Life in Fascist Italy," *University of Toronto Quarterly*, Vol. IX (1940), page 428.

[41] The best account of D'Annunzio and Fiume in English is found in Giuseppe Antonio Borgese, *Goliath*, pages 90–93, 112–113, 150–168. New York: Viking Press, 1937. The Constitution of Fiume is translated into English in Odon Por, *Fascism*, pages i–xxi. London: Labour Publishing Company, 1923. The original Constitution and many speeches that D'Annunzio made at Fiume are found in Gabriele D'Annunzio, *Per la più grande Italia*, Milano: Instituto nazionale per la pubblicazione di tutte le opere di Gabriele D'Annunzio, 1923.

[42] Charles Edward Merriam, *Political Power*, pages 102–113. New York: McGraw-Hill Book Company, Inc., 1934.

trained in the use of violence and adept at arousing an emotional response from their followers,[43] but they lacked an organizational plan and a plausible goal for the labor movement.

The plan and the goal were supplied by the Catholics. The Catholic influence came in part from the theorists of the Catholic confederation, CIL, and in part from Alfredo Rocco, a distinguished law professor and a leading figure in the Nationalist Party. Rocco in turn was heavily indebted to Catholic labor theory.[44] The resulting fusion of national syndicalist extravagance and Catholic labor theory was the corporate system (also called corporative system, gild system, corporate state, and so forth).[45]

The establishment of the corporate system was a far cry from the economic policies of the earlier fascists.[46] As late as September, 1922, one month before the March on Rome, Mussolini delivered a speech at Udine pledging a swift return to the economics of Adam Smith. He advocated selling the railroads and other government services on the theory that trade was beneath a government, just as in an earlier tradition, a trade had been beneath a gentleman.[47]

Organization

The unions under fascism. The corporate system was organized as follows: although *de facto* unions were allowed, the government recognized one union and a corresponding employers' unit for each locality and each trade or industry. It also recognized associations for professional men and artists, for which there were no corresponding employer associations. The recognized unions were empowered to negotiate collective labor agreements that applied to all workers in

---

[43] Harold Dwight Lasswell and Renzo Sereno, "Governmental and Party Leaders in Fascist Italy," *American Political Science Review,* Vol. XXXI (1937), pages 914–929.

[44] Alfredo Rocco, "Crisi dello Stato e sindacati," *Politica,* VII (1920), pages 1–14. For an analysis of Rocco's character and influence, see Herman Finer, *Mussolini's Italy,* page 236. New York: Henry Holt and Company, n.d.

[45] The Italian terms are *stato corporativo* and *sistema corporativo.* The noun *corporazione* means, among other things, "gild," and the English translation "corporate" or "corporative" is probably the work of a careless journalist. The use of the word "state" in place of "system" is confusing in both languages, as the term "corporate state" means nothing more than a state that has instituted a "corporate system."

[46] In 1932 Italo Balbo, the Number 2 fascist, referred to the corporate system as "our confused idea of '21." *Atti del II convegno di studi sindacali e corporativi,* Vol. III (Roma, 1932), page 20. Even this relatively modest statement was a gross exaggeration.

[47] Luigi Einaudi, *La condotta economica e gli effetti sociali della guerra italiana,* page 414. Bari: Giuseppe Laterza e Figli, 1933.

the field, whether or not they were members of the contracting associations. Strikes and lockouts, except in rare instances, were prohibited, and whenever collective labor agreements could not be reached by negotiation between the parties, various institutions attempted conciliation. If these attempts failed in turn, a new collective agreement was drawn up and imposed on the parties by a specially constituted labor court. In the event of a disagreement over an existing collective agreement, the same court was empowered to interpret the agreement after various attempts at conciliation had proved unsuccessful.

The local unions combined, as did the employers' associations, to form two types of secondary associations. The one type was national in scale and was composed of the various provincial unions pertaining to a single trade or industry (e.g., the provincial textile unions formed the National Federation of Textile Workers). The other type combined all the unions within a large economic category and within the same province (for example, the textile workers' union of Brescia and the Brescia metallurgical workers' union were joined with the other industrial workers' unions to form the Provincial Union of Industrial Workers of Brescia). The federations and the provincial unions, the two types of secondary association, joined together to form the tertiary association, the confederation, whose members were all the provincial unions and the federations. There were nine confederations in all, one each for management and labor interests in industry, agriculture, commerce, and banking and insurance, and a ninth for professional men and artists.[48]

The corporations. Alongside the unions and employers' associations, which represented the contrasting interests of labor and management, a series of corporations (gilds) was set up, to deal with the economic interests shared by capital and labor, such as increased production, lowered production costs, national planning. Each of the twenty-two corporations represented an entire industrial cycle. For example, the wood corporation (*Corporazione del legno*) was intended to represent the lumber interests, the cork industry, the furniture industry, and the commercial establishments selling their products, and contained representatives of the various workers' groups concerned, such as lumberjacks, carpenters, wood carvers, tree surgeons, and clerks in furniture stores. In addition, fascist hierarchs were appointed members of each of the corporations, who, all too aptly, were to represent the consumers' interests. Although labor ostensibly had equal representation with management in the corporations, all members of the corporations were

---

[48] Edmondo Rossoni created and headed a super-confederation composed of the four workers' confederations, but this organization was soon abolished.

appointed by the fascist government, and labor had no influence over the appointments.[49]

Labor policy in practice

Nonrecognized unions. If one stuck closely to the letter of the law, there was nothing obviously undemocratic in this system.[50] Rival, nonrecognized unions were permitted, and the recognized unions were democratically controlled by officers whom the members elected. The fascist practice, however, was far from democratic. An elementary text in corporate law, more honest than some, had this to say for the unrecognized, or *de facto,* unions:

> The system adopted by the law of April 3, 1926, is based on the principle of the recognition of a single association per category and of the free existence of *de facto* unions, which latter, however, are under the control of the State. This control is exercised by the prefect through his right of inspection, of revocation and annulment of the acts of the union, of dissolving its councils and committees, of liquidating its assets. . . .[51]

Selection of union officials. The statement that union officials were to be popularly elected gave an equally fallacious impression. The elections were by acclamation, and only one candidate ran for office. This was the candidate chosen by the Fascist Party.

Since the fascist labor unions were not controlled from below, they functioned as organs of the government, from whence came their directives. The labor leaders were creatures of the Fascist Party, to which they owed their position and future advancement, and their prime concern was to please the party. What the workers thought was of little immediate importance to them.[52]

Collective agreements. The major work of the unions was the draw-

---

[49] For an account of the theory and early practice of the corporations, see Giuseppe Bottai, *Il consiglio nazionale delle corporazioni.* Milano: Mondadori, 1932. For a list of the corporations as finally set up, see Giovanni Salemi (ed.), *Codice corporativo e del lavoro,* pages 210–287. Padova: Cedam, 1943.

[50] For an exposition of the point of view that the corporate system will inevitably lead to totalitarianism, see Gaëtan Pirou, *Essais sur le corporatisme.* Paris: Librairie du Recueil Sirey, 1938.

[51] Ernesto Fodale, *Corso di diritto corporativo,* pages 73–74. Firenze: Casa Editrice Poligrafica Universitaria dell'Dott. Carlo Cya, 1933.

[52] "The corporative system was unworkable since the syndicates and corporations were organized not as self-governing associations but as government departments under a new central agency, the Ministry of Corporations. The officers of the syndicates were not elected by and responsible to the members of the syndicates but appointed by and responsible to the government. Negotiations between officers of two syndicates became negotiations between two government officials who were equally subject to the directions and orders of their common superiors, especially the Minister of Corporations." Max Rheinstein, "Methods of Wage Policy. II," *The University of Chicago Law Review,* Vol. VI (1939), page 74.

ing up of collective labor agreements. These were usually negotiated on a national scale between the representatives of the unions and of the employers' associations. These latter were somewhat less under fascist control. The secretaries of the employers' organizations were, for the most part, career men who did not expect other, and better, political jobs. They were better prepared and more eager to protect the employers' interests than their adversaries were to protect labor interests.[53] If any snags were hit, or if the fascists had a new policy they wanted to put into effect, however, the negotiations were soon taken out of the hands of the unions and employers' associations. Whenever the parties failed to agree, the dispute was taken to the Ministry of Corporations for conciliation, where much of the effective work in labor policy was done. A group of capable career officials, trained in the intricacies of collective labor agreements, carried out this work. As career officials of the Ministry, they were in a position to know the latest government policies, and, as technicians, they knew how to put the policies into effect. Rarely did the labor representatives hold out for greater benefits than those suggested by the officials at the Ministry of Corporations.[54]

The national collective agreements usually contained the regulations for apprenticeship, hours of work, holidays, vacations, grounds for dismissal, disciplinary procedures, overtime pay, and seniority. Much of the material in the national agreements, however, was merely a rehash of previously existing legislation.[55] Wages were usually determined by supplementary provincial labor agreements, in part because the cost of living varied considerably in the different provinces. (Milan and its environs had the highest cost of living, and the island of Sardinia the lowest.) In some instances questions other than wages were determined at the provincial level, and in others the entire agreement was negotiated there. The negotiators of the supplementary provincial agreements, however, were primarily concerned with the inclusion in the agreement of minor local usages, usually to the

---

[53] In 1936 there was a startling contrast between the industrialists' confederation, *Confindustria,* and the Confederation of Industrial Workers. *Confindustria* had a staff of competent full-time lawyers at its national headquarters in Rome, while the Confederation of Industrial Workers had the assistance of a single part-time lawyer who commuted weekly from Turin.

[54] After the establishment of the corporations in the middle thirties, the conciliatory efforts were made by the interested corporations, rather than by the Ministry of Corporations, but the change was a formal one, since the work was carried on by the same technicians under a new guise.

[55] The 48-hour week and the 8-hour day were established by Royal Decree-Law of March 15, 1923, No. 692. The Sunday rest was established by the law of February 22, 1934, No. 340. Sanitation provisions were established by Royal Decree of April 14, 1927, No. 530/809, and Royal Decree of July 27, 1934, No. 1265. See *Codice corporativo* 2087–2194.

advantage of the workers, and they were ever mindful of the general policies of the Fascist Party as shown in the latest collective agreements.[56]

In the few instances when collective labor agreements were not reached after the conciliatory efforts of the Ministry of Corporations officials, the disputes were taken before the labor courts. These courts were established in each of the appellate court districts and were composed of three appellate judges and two experts. The experts were selected by an extremely complicated process. The persons chosen usually turned out to be government officials or professors with technical knowledge in the field where the dispute lay. Before adjudicating a case the labor courts made an attempt to conciliate the dispute and a representative of the prosecuting attorney's office also suggested what he thought would be an equitable settlement. Only on the failure of these attempts was adjudication resorted to. Labor courts were one of the most vaunted of the corporate institutions. In practice, however, they had virtually no work to do in the field of collective disputes, adjudicating a total of less than two disputes a year and conciliating about the same number. About half of these were on questions of interpretation rather than economic disputes over the formulation of new collective agreements.[57]

The fascists abolished the arbitration boards in 1928 and gave

[56] *Codice corporativo, 1194–1220,* and Pelio Marrani, *Il contratto collettivo di lavoro.* Padova: CEDAM, 1935; also G. Lowell Field, *The Syndical and Corporative Institutions of Italian Fascism,* pages 96–117. New York: Columbia University Press, 1938. Over 2,000 collective agreements of national scope were published in pamphlet form in Milan by L. di G. Pirola. A complete list of collective agreements in the commercial field was compiled by Giuseppe Grillo and published under the title *I contratti collettivi di lavoro nel settore commerciale,* Vols. I–VI. Roma: Signorelli, 1937–1942; Vol. VII. Roma: Eredi Giovanni Artero, 1943.

Regarding the juridical nature of the collective agreement, see John Clarke Adams, *Sulla natura del contratto collettivo.* Roma: Diritto di lavoro, 1937.

[57] For the laws see *Codice corporativo,* 2420–2438. For legal theory see Alessandro Rosselli, *La magistratura del lavoro.* Padova: CEDAM, 1934, and Piero Calamandrei, "La natura giuridica delle decisioni della magistratura del lavoro," in both Piero Calamandrei, *Studi sul processo civile,* Vol. III, pages 141–157. Padova: CEDAM, 1934, and *Recueil d'études sur les sources du droit en l'honneur de François Gény.* Tome III. Paris: Librairie du Recueil Sirey, n.d. The latter edition also contains a French translation. For the practice see John Clarke Adams, *The Judicial Settlement of Labor Disputes in Fascist Italy* (unpublished thesis, University of Chicago, 1940), abstracted as "The Adjudication of Collective Labor Disputes in Italy," *Quarterly Journal of Economics,* Vol. LVI (1942), pages 456–474; G. Lowell Field, *op. cit.,* pages 118–125; L. Rosenstock-Franck, *L'économie corporative fasciste en doctrine et en fait,* 2nd ed., pages 186–202. Paris: Librairie Universitaire J. Gamber, 1934. The major documents of one of the few important and complex controversies adjudicated by the labor courts have been collected by the Confederation of Industrial Workers in *La controversia collettiva dei tessili serici lombardi.* Roma: Società editrice Il lavoro fascista, 1934.

authority over individual labor disputes to the regular courts. Even individual labor disputes, however, could not be heard by the courts until attempts at conciliation had been made through the unions. Often the unions themselves took the disputes to court when efforts at conciliation had failed.[58] A large number of the labor disputes to reach the courts were over severance pay. The Italian law gave high severance pay, particularly to white collar workers. The often considerable sum involved, and the fact that the discharged worker had free time on his hands not available to the worker on the job, are probably the explanations for the preponderance of cases of this type. The decisions of the courts in individual labor disputes were on the whole favorable to labor, and the Fascist statistics show millions of lire annually awarded to workers through conciliatory and judicial procedures.[59]

Conclusion

The corporate system was the negative aspect of fascist labor policy. It was the method by which the fascists prevented an organized labor

---

[58] *Codice corporativo*, 2397–2419; Luigi De Litala, *Diritto processuale del lavoro*. Torino: UTET, 1936; Nicola Jaeger, *Le controversie individuali del lavoro*, reprinting of 3d ed., Padova: CEDAM, 1934; Luisa Riva Sanseverino, *Corso di diritto del lavoro*, 3d ed., Padova: CEDAM, 1941; Field, *op. cit.*, pages 125–133. The labor courts also served as a valuable experiment in judicial procedure for Italy, as the ordinary civil procedure was somewhat simplified before the labor courts, and some of these reforms found their way into the new Italian civil code. See Piero Calamandrei, "Le controversie del lavoro e l'oralità," in Piero Calamandrei, *Studi sul processo civile*, Vol. IV, pages 1–14. Padova: CEDAM, 1939; and Piero Calamandrei, *Delle buone relazioni fra i giudici e gli avvocati nel nuovo processo civile*. Firenze: Felice Le Monnier, 1941.

[59] *Annuario statistico italiano 1939—XVII*. Roma: Istituto Poligrafico dello Stato G. C., 1939. Page 221 gives an average of over 45,000,000 lire annually from 1935 to 1938 recuperated for industrial workers alone. Only 6,500,000 of this was gained through court action. The rest resulted from conciliation. These figures probably exaggerate the workers' gains. If one takes into consideration the number of small and essentially fly-by-night concerns in Italy, the following case, known to the author, is presumably not atypical. The man in question was a sound technician in a small movie company. The hours in this industry are long and irregular, and a large portion of the total remuneration is for overtime pay. This employer, though never openly refusing overtime pay on principle, never got around to paying it to the sound technician, who, after many months, quit the job and took the dispute to his union. The union's attempt at conciliation failed, and it agreed to go to court on his behalf. The employer used all the dilatory tactics at his command, but judgment was finally given against him for the overtime pay. He waited until the last day permitted under the law to appeal the case, and after he had again delayed proceedings as long as possible, the labor court, which also had appellate jurisdiction over individual labor disputes, sustained the judgment of the lower court. When the worker then went to collect, he found the employer had gone bankrupt, and all the worker could get was a lien on second-grade sound equipment, which, for want of a better alternative, he loaned back to the same ex-employer, who was starting up business again under a new name.

opposition, but it was not destined to play a prominent part in the positive labor legislation of the fascist period. This legislation will be discussed in the following chapters, since, as it was "nonfascist" (that is, not part of the corporate system), it was not abrogated on the fall of fascism, and is, largely, still in effect.

The major and almost sole aim of the fascist leaders was the preservation and enjoyment of their power. They were opposed to a free labor movement because they wanted no competition from the leaders of such a movement, and they were not eager to give power even to the fascist-controlled unions. Instead, they tried to win labor support by making labor dependent directly on the fascist government. Wages were kept low through state-controlled collective agreements and on occasion were lowered further by the government's deflationary measures decreeing general wage cuts. The result was that a worker, unable to live on his wages, was dependent on the aid he received through fascist legislation. In this way his loyalty tended to switch from his employer to his government. The government gave him a considerable degree of job security when his most pressing fear was losing his job. It also gave him benefits in the way of family allowances, old age pensions, unemployment insurance, and so forth, and through the *Dopolavoro* (the "after-work" recreation agency) it gave him cut-rate entertainment. The Fascist Party and the fascist government were the hands that fed him, but even if the costs, material and moral, are not taken into consideration, the hand-outs were pitifully meager.

There is one thing the fascists did not do, however (and in this they differed from the Nazis) : by and large they did not kill the enemies of fascism, including the leaders of the free labor movement. Some of these were imprisoned, some of them fled abroad, and others were exiled to remote sections of Italy by the process known as *confino;* but when fascism fell, many of them were able to start rebuilding a free labor movement in Italy.

Postwar Trade Union Structure and Organization

Unity

The free labor movement got under way in southern Italy with Allied guidance. Antifascist labor leaders were brought together in Bari in 1944, and the CGIL (*Confederazione generale italiana del lavoro*—Italian General Confederation of Labor) was formed in January, 1945, in Naples. The leaders of the CGIL had one boast in this early period. They represented a united labor movement, a fusion of the "red," "white," and "yellow" unions of the prefascist period.

These leaders represented the various antifascist parties. The confederation was headed by three general secretaries, representing the Christian Democrat, the Socialist, and the Communist Parties, respectively. The men primed for these posts in 1944 were three prefascist labor leaders, Achille Grandi, Bruno Buozzi, and Giovanni Roveda. Of these, only Grandi, the Christian Democrat representative, was selected in Naples. He was a saintly old man dying of cancer, who had been an active and respected labor leader in the textile industry in north Italy preceding fascism and the last general secretary of the "white" CIL. During the postfascist period, however, his ill health made him ineffective. The socialist leader, Buozzi, was expected to become the top man in the Italian labor movement. He had been a leading figure in the socialist labor movement before fascism and had been an active and prominent *émigré* during fascism. Unfortunately, he was killed by the Germans just before they evacuated Rome. He was replaced by Oreste Lizzadri, a Neapolitan who had lived in Rome during fascism, managing a vineyard in Frascati, and who had displayed considerable courage in the Resistance movement, but had little reputation as a labor leader. Roveda was left behind the lines as a partisan leader in Turin, and the communist general secretaryship of the CGIL fell to a southern Italian, Giuseppe Di Vittorio, who had had experience in the prefascist period in the syndicalist labor movement.[60] Other parties, too, were represented in the CGIL. The most important of these was the *Partito d'azione* (Action Party), composed of noncommunist antifascists who wished to participate actively in the partisan movement, and who were displeased with the ineffectiveness and negative attitude of the other antifascist parties, such as the socialists and the republicans. The almost legendary leader of the Action Party was Ferruccio Parri, the gentle and kindly high school teacher who, before the enormity of fascism, rose to become the commanding general of the entire partisan movement. As a result of Di Vittorio's machinations at the Naples congress, the Action Party was relegated to a position of inferiority in the labor movement, on a par with the republicans and the anarcho-syndicalists, each of which, for the support of the CGIL, was given token representation in its national council.

The CGIL was not only founded from above by the antifascist parties with the help and support of the Allies, but it was placed virtually in

---

[60] It is reported that Di Vittorio, one of the most capable of the communist leaders, had wanted the editorship of *L'unità,* the communist daily, but that the inner clique of the party did not want to entrust a comparative outsider with this job. In appointing him to the labor post, where they felt relatively weak, they planned either to get rid of Di Vittorio or gain control of the CGIL. In a little over two years, Di Vittorio managed to get a clear communist majority in all the directive offices of the CGIL,

a vacuum. The labor movement in Italy has always been a preponderantly north Italian phenomenon. The CGIL in 1944 had little contact with the north. Moreover, the labor laws under which it was to operate were fascist laws, and it was not immediately clear which, if any, of these were still operative. The new confederation could expect eventually to receive some of the capital of the defunct fascist organizations, but this was not immediately forthcoming. Even the buildings formerly occupied by the fascist unions were for the most part requisitioned by the Allies. Temporarily, the CGIL's only means of support was membership dues, but the majority of the prospective members were behind the German lines, and those in southern Italy often needed more than their wages for food alone.

The structure of the CGIL was based on the double hierarchy common to the fascist and prefascist unions. Each of the national federations, as well as the provincial labor chambers, was headed by a group of secretaries representing the major parties. Usually there were three, but, frequently, a fourth secretary was added, representing the Action Party, or, particularly in Emilia Romagna, the Republican Party. Nominally, the various secretaries of the CGIL or of its component parts had equal authority. In most cases, however, there was a dominant personality who controlled. Often this dominant personality was a communist. Communist labor leaders tended to be superior for several reasons. The Communist Party was the only antifascist party to remain organized in Italy during fascism. Its leaders were tested men of proven worth. Socialist and Christian Democrat labor leaders had served little or no apprenticeship before their appointments. Perhaps more important in turning the scales in favor of the communists was the relative economic security of communist labor leaders. If the union could not support them, the party would, and no matter what happened, they were still better off than they had been under fascism. Socialist and Christian Democrat labor leaders during Mussolini's rule had for the most part been nonfascist rather than antifascist, and many of them, particularly the socialists, had lived well as commercial agents, traveling salesmen, and the like. These people suffered financially from the fall of fascism, and were often unwilling to sacrifice the economic security of their families by devoting their full energies to the labor movement. Therefore, when there was work to be done, it was often a communist who did it. When there was a business trip to be taken, it was usually a communist who took it, traveling on party funds when the union coffers were empty. In this way the communist labor leaders were not only more active, but they had the best contacts with Rome and with each other.

Communist control at the top level was further encouraged by the personalities of the general secretaries. Neither the Christian Democrats nor the Socialists were able to find a secretary who could stand up to Di Vittorio, whose forcefulness of character and physical endurance were too much for whoever was chosen. The easygoing Lizzadri, a left-wing socialist whose political philosophy seemed to be that the Socialist Party could conquer the Communist Party only by fusion with it, was replaced in 1947 by Fernando Santi, a labor leader of promise, who has been as unable to take a stand against the compelling will of Di Vittorio as was his predecessor. The Catholics fared little better. Grandi, who was in the hospital more than he was out of it until his death in 1946, was succeeded by Giuseppe Rapelli, another capable man with a good background in union work, who retired with a nervous breakdown after some months of attempting to cope with his communist colleague. His successor, Giulio Pastore, kept his health and succeeded in remaining firm before the persuasiveness of Di Vittorio, but this firmness led only to splitting the confederation.

The first national congress of the CGIL after the unification of Italy and the termination of hostilities was held in Florence in June, 1947. By that time the confederation had a claimed membership of over five and a half million. Not even Di Vittorio himself, however, could know the actual number. Since the annual dues to be paid in to the CGIL were extremely low, any labor chamber was able to pad its membership by paying in extra dues, amounting to a few cents per hypothetical member. The additional votes obtained in this manner would help assure election of candidates acceptable to the party in control of that particular labor chamber. It is certain that practices of this kind went on, and since the communists were in control of the majority of the labor chambers, they were the group which stood most to gain thereby.[61]

Division

The municipal elections of 1945 and 1946, as well as the elections for the Constitutional Assembly in the latter year, showed that Italy had only three parties with mass appeal—the Communist, the Socialist, and the Christian Democracy. So long as these parties were cooperating in the government, labor unity could also be maintained. When, however, the communists were forced out of the government in 1947, it

[61] It is estimated that about 80 per cent of the provincial labor chambers were in Communist hands in June, 1947. The Christian Democrats had a majority in intensely Catholic Bergamo, whereas the Socialists and Republicans had pluralities respectively in Salerno and Ravenna. These latter provinces, however, are of minor significance in the labor movement.

was obvious that unity in the labor movement was at an end, since the Communist Party, assuming the position of the major opposition party, thereafter opposed the labor policies of the Christian Democratic government. No institution of such an essentially political nature as the CGIL could remain united under these conditions.

The creation of the CISL. The split which occurred in 1948 [62] was, in some respects, overdue and, in others, premature. The Christian Democrat labor leaders had shown great forbearance in remaining so long, at least technically, the colleagues and allies of those who wished to overthrow the Christian Democratic government and cast Italy's lot with Moscow. Their patience, however, might have been better rewarded had they been able to wait a little longer and take the socialist elements of the CGIL along with them.[63]

In 1947 the Catholics had about 15 per cent of the voting strength in the CGIL. Christian Democratic sentiment was strongest in the textile industry and among white-collar workers. The first of these groups is composed primarily of women, who are traditionally more under the domination of priests than are men. The Catholic preference of the second group can be explained psychologically as an attempt on the part of these workers to disassociate themselves from the pro-communist manual laborer.

The organization of the new Christian Democratic labor confederation, called the LCGIL (*Libera confederazione generale italiana dei lavoratori*—Free Italian General Confederation of Workers) was facilitated, both by the tradition of the prefascist "white" (Catholic)

---

[62] Previous to 1948 several attempts had been made to create unions outside the CGIL, but none of these could be termed successful, at least on a national scale. These unions were of two types. Some were the brain children of impecunious agitators, often with anarcho-syndicalist leanings, who were more pamphleteers than true labor leaders. Their main interest and sole ability was that of publishing a weekly paper of little literary or news value. The other type was anticommunist and employer-controlled, often headed by experienced ex-fascist labor leaders. Such unions made little headway in the north, but had some success among the fascist-ridden government offices, where there is little sympathy with democracy, and less with communism, and in some of the poorer southern agricultural communities, where the employer-controlled union was the only effective employment agency for the farm laborers. One of the organizations, the CSIL (*Confederazione sindacale italiana dei lavoratori*—Italian Workers' Syndical Confederation), whose officers were almost entirely high-ranking fascists, is reported to have been financed by Confindustria, but in 1948 neofascism had little or no appeal for the Italian laborer. The few people reached by these organizations were of little interest or importance to the CGIL, and the defection of the Catholic labor movement was the first split of any significance in the labor ranks.

[63] One of the major tragedies of postwar Italy is that international events forced Italian liberals to choose between the clericals and the communists at a time when the advisability of choosing the former, however distasteful the choice, was not yet apparent to many of them. The consequence was that in many cases the better elements in Italy have become confused, disunited, and ineffectual.

confederation and by the existence of the postfascist ACLI (*Associazioni cristiane dei lavoratori italiani*—Italian Catholic Workers' Association). This latter organization was established to do welfare work among the workers and was technically separate from the Christian Democratic labor movement, the Christian Democratic party, and the Catholic Action (the official political propaganda institution of the Roman Church). The ACLI has branches throughout Italy, where workers may go for advice and assistance. No money or other direct charity is given them, but they are helped in filling out the complicated forms necessary for the receipt of government aid, and in some sectors vocational training and employment service are provided. Giulio Pastore, the head of the LCGIL, was national secretary of the ACLI and the president of its social services section before he became Christian Democratic secretary of the CGIL.

In the following year, 1949, as was also inevitable, the labor leaders representing the other government parties (the Republican Party and the right-wing socialists [PSLI][64]) found they could no longer remain within the CGIL. Although these parties were in the government coalition with De Gasperi's Christian Democrats, many of their leaders and adherents were strongly anticlerical. For this reason, although the LCGIL was willing to receive non-Christian Democratic elements, the Republican and PSLI labor leaders were hesitant to join them. The Republican party polled its organized workers and found they were almost unanimously in favor of leaving the CGIL and equally strongly opposed to joining the Catholics. The PSLI leaders reached the same conclusion without the help of a popular vote, and so the vice secretaries of the CGIL representing the PSLI and the Republicans formed a third union, the FIL (*Federazione italiana del lavoro*—Italian Labor Federation), which sought the affiliation of those workers who were both anticlerical and anticommunist. The FIL was not very successful in this endeavor. Under some pressure and friendly advice from anticommunist labor sources in the United States, the FIL leaders joined the LCGIL in April, 1950, and the union changed its name to the CISL (*Confederazione italiana sindacati lavoratori*—Italian Confederation of Workers' Unions). The new organization is ostensibly independent of Christian Democrat con-

---

[64] The PSLI (*Partito socialista dei lavoratori italiani*—Italian Workers' Socialist Party) split from the old United Socialist Party (*Partito socialista italiano di unità proletaria*—PSIUP) in January, 1947, when the procommunist faction, headed by Pietro Nenni and Lelio Basso, took over control. The major faction which left with Saragat was known as the Friends of the *Critica Sociale* (*Amici della Critica sociale*). They were carrying on the reformist tradition of Filippo Turati. At this time the Nenni-Basso procommunist faction and the many moderates who remained in the old Socialist party, PSIUP, changed the party name to Italian Socialist Party (*Partito socialista italiano*—PSI).

trol, but its leadership and its membership are still predominantly Guelph; Giulio Pastore of the LCGIL became general secretary of the CISL, and two of the secretaries, Luigi Morelli and Roberto Cuzzaniti, were also Christian Democrats. The other three secretaries were the two secretaries of the FIL, Giovanni Canini and Enrico Parri, and the head of a small independent union. The meager forces of the FIL, however, did not follow their leaders in their hegira, and the Republicans repudiated the move, expelling Parri from the party for failing to carry out a program of independence from the Communist and Catholic unions that had been overwhelmingly approved by the Republican workers.

The creation of the UIL.[65] Later in 1949, most of the remaining socialist labor leaders left the CGIL, including the socialist national secretaries of most of the big unions.[66] This group, under the political leadership of Giuseppe Romita, Luigi Carmagnola, and the novelist Ignazio Silone, sought to join the PSLI and the FIL. These hopes proved illusory at that time because of personal rivalries and because no agreement could be reached on the political question of whether the proposed coalition should support the government or should form a loyal (i.e., democratic) opposition. The Romita-Carmagnola-Silone group, therefore, formed a third Socialist Party, the PSU (*Partito socialista unitario*) and, joining forces with the Republicans and right-wing Socialists who had refused to merge with the Catholic-dominated CISL, formed a third labor union, the UIL, under the leadership of Italo Viglianesi, former national secretary of the CGIL chemical workers' union, FILC. The UIL opposed the CGIL on nationalist and democratic grounds and the CISL on anticlerical grounds.

On May 1, 1951, after months of negotiations, the PSU and the PSLI united, forming the PS-SIIS (*Partito socialista—Sezione italiana dell'- internazionale socialista*—Socialist Party—Italian Section of the Socialist International). The UIL has had the full support of the small Republican party and of the Romita socialists in the PS-SIIS. Ex-PSLI Socialists continued to be found in all three unions.

It is doubtful that these newly created and frequently reorganized confederations have had a great effect on the CGIL. During the period of their formation, the CGIL lost heavily in membership, but the losses seem due more to popular disapproval of the CGIL's policy than

---

[65] The reader should not be surprised to find that with the plethora of unions in Italy, new combinations of appropriate initials were finally exhausted. The new UIL *(Unione italiana dei lavoratori*—Italian Workers' Union) should be distinguished from the pre- and profascist UIL *(Unione italiana del lavoro)*.

[66] Among the group were the national secretaries of FIOM (metal workers), FIOT (textile workers), and FILC (chemical workers) as well as the two socialist vice secretaries of the CGIL, Enzo Dalla Chiesa and Renato Bulleri.

to any positive attraction the new unions exercised. By the fall of 1950, the estimated membership of the CGIL was 3,500,000, of the CISL, 800,000, and of the UIL, 200,000.[67]

The federations and the labor chambers

Each of the rival confederations is composed of national industrial unions, usually called federations, and of city centrals, usually with province-wide jurisdiction, called labor chambers.[68] Both the CGIL and the CISL have established complete sets of federations and labor chambers, although some of the CISL organizations exist in little more than name. The UIL, which came on the scene later, and which, at its inception, had little financial backing, is not so completely organized, although by the end of 1950 it had established local organizations in most of the provincial capitals, and federations in the major industries.

The federations. The federations vary greatly in both potential and actual size. Some industries are highly organized; others only partially so. In most industries, three federations, representing the three confederations, are competing for the workers' support, although except for the elementary school teachers and possibly the textile workers, where the CISL is strong, the CGIL federations are the largest.

Accurate statistics on the number of workers in the various industries and the number already organized are unobtainable. Table 3 gives approximate figures for the larger groups.

The largest and most active unions in Italy include the FIOM (*Federazione impiegati operai metallurgici*—Federation of Clerical and Manual Metal Workers), the FIOT (*Federazione impiegati operai tessili*—Federation of Clerical and Manual Textile Workers), the FILC (*Federazione italiana lavoratori chimici*—Italian Federation of Chemical Workers), the SFI (*Sindacato ferrovieri italiani*—Italian Railway Workers' Union), *Confederterra* (*Confederazione italiana lavoratori della terra*—Italian Farm Workers' Confederation),[69] and the government workers' union.[70] All these federations are members of

---

[67] The claimed membership of these unions was much higher. The CGIL claimed almost 5,000,000, the CISL claimed 1,800,000, and the UIL 400,000.

[68] Each confederation uses a different term for "labor chamber." The CGIL's word is *Camera del lavoro,* the UIL uses *Camera sindacale,* and the CISL, faithful to the tradition of the prefascist "white" confederation, CIL, uses the term *unione.* To avoid confusion all these organizations will in these pages be called labor chambers.

[69] *Confederterra,* nominally a "confederation," is a federation composed of various farm workers' groups which are equivalent to "sub-federations."

[70] The building trades claim over 350,000 organized workers in their CGIL union (see Table 3). This would make them the third largest union in claimed membership. The membership is probably grossly exaggerated, however. In Italy this is a difficult field to organize, as many of the workers are unskilled, much of

the CGIL, but all are experiencing competition from noncommunist federations.

The metallurgical industry has traditionally been a center of left-wing activity and is one of the most highly organized. The occupation of the factories that the FIOM carried out in 1920 marked the climax of prefascist union activity, and in the postfascist period the FIOM has been strongly communist. The importance which the communists give to the FIOM is shown by the fact that their most experienced labor

TABLE 3

NUMBER OF WORKERS EMPLOYED AND ORGANIZED IN INDUSTRIES EMPLOYING
100,000 OR MORE PERSONS IN 1949

Industry	Organizable workers, according to CGIL*	Claimed membership in CGIL federation*	Number of workers employed 1949†
Farm laborers	2,035,521	993,262	2,355,000
Tenant farmers	1,787,601	512,510	
Heavy industry	750,000	609,094	844,500
Textiles	600,000	357,174	659,900
Govt. workers (except R.R. workers and school teachers)	275,000	105,413	579,942
Construction	650,000	364,554	542,000
Food preparation (except fishing)			384,500
Local govt. agencies	240,000	111,769	348,000
Woodcutters and woodworkers	100,000	64,092	220,000
Chemical (incl. rubber)..	240,000	162,429	218,500
Railroad workers	185,974	129,702	185,973 (1948 figure)
Streetcar workers, bus and truck drivers	130,000	77,468	177,000
Clothing (except hats) ..	200,000	88,393	159,550
Elementary school teachers			149,936 (1948 figure)
Printers and papermakers	110,000	83,364	119,250
Miners and stone quarriers	90,000	50,143	108,000

N. B.—There were approximately 2 million unemployed in Italy. About 300,000 of these were farm laborers and about 100,000 were in heavy industry.
Sources: * *Guida del lavoratore, 1950.* Modena: INCA, Camera Confederale del Lavoro, 1950, pages 33–35.
† *Annuario di statistiche del lavoro,* ed. *Rassegna di statistiche del lavoro.* Roma, 1949, pages 27–31, 64–65, 70.

leader, Roveda, was appointed its responsible secretary in 1946. He has also served as president of the metal workers' international organization affiliated with the WFTU. Unemployment is particularly heavy in this sector, and there is consequently much labor friction. Both the CISL

the work is seasonal, and most of the contractors hire only a few workers and often treat them well, particularly in the postwar period, when there was so much to rebuild. For these reasons this federation has been one of the least active in the post fascist period.

and the UIL have competing organizations in operation, but, as yet, they represent only minority groups in this field.

The textile industry is another of the highly organized industries. The FIOT, run by the communist Teresa Noce, wife of the party leader, Luigi Longo, has lost heavily in the last few years and the Catholics claim that their rival federation has surpassed it in membership. The relatively poor showing of the FIOT may be in part ascribed to the unpopularity of Noce, who is international president of the WFTU textile workers, in part to the stronger Catholic influence among the women textile workers, and in part to the relative prosperity of Milan and its environs, where the textile industry is centered.

The third of the three major industrial unions is the FILC. Although communist influence was strong in this union, it was under the efficient control of a young socialist, Italo Viglianesi. Viglianesi has since become the principal organizer of the UIL.

As in many other countries, the railway workers in Italy are a law unto themselves. Their history has been one of eccentric activity rather than cooperation with the confederations, and, to a greater degree than the other federations, their loyalty has been to their own group rather than to the confederation. Before fascism the SFI bolted from the CGL to the USI. In the postfascist period there has been a small but active republican and anarchist minority, which is now operating a rival union affiliated with the UIL.

The union which claims the largest membership of all is *Confederterra*. It is, however, more loosely organized and less effective than the federations mentioned in the previous paragraphs. Like the other unions, it is meeting competition from the CISL and the UIL.

Although the government workers are less highly organized than the railway workers and the industrial groups mentioned above, their union has been among the most active in postwar Italy. Its strength lies primarily among the lowest paid categories of workers, such as the doormen and the cleaning women. For the most part, the white-collar workers either belong to the competing CISL and UIL federations or are unorganized.

The headquarters of most of the federations are in Rome, although Rome is not an industrial city. (Only the government workers and the printers have a high percentage of their members employed in Rome.) A few of the larger federations, however, maintain their national headquarters in the north, in the center of their particular industry. The headquarters of FIOM, for instance, are in Turin, and those of FIOT and FILC are in Milan.

Alongside these major federations in the CGIL there are some smaller and more highly organized unions where, by and large, politics have played a smaller role. Although in the CGIL many of these unions were not under Communist control, now that the Catholic workers have been withdrawn from these unions and rival Catholic federations set up, the non-Communist leaders of these federations are required to rely more heavily on Communist support to maintain themselves in power. Among the unions in this group are the printers', the electrical workers', the seamen's, and the port workers' federations.

The printers' union has one of the longest traditions in the Italian labor movement. It has been functioning on a national scale for over a half century, and staged some of the earliest successful strikes recorded in Italy. It is a closely knit association composed primarily of skilled workers conscious of their worth. This union is not large enough to have great political importance, and the parties, therefore, have not felt impelled to interfere with it. The printers, for their part, although the communists have a majority in the union, have been sufficiently conscious of their vested economic interests to prevent the union from becoming a sounding board for the vagaries of the political parties competing for the labor vote.[71]

The electrical workers' union, like the printers' union, is small and mainly composed of skilled workers. In the prefascist and postfascist periods, it has enjoyed the capable leadership of Vasco Cesari, who, although an anticommunist (PSLI socialist), has succeeded in relegating politics to a secondary position in his union. It was this union, for instance, which negotiated the first postfascist national collective agreement. Because of the compactness of the union, the high percentage of skilled workers in it, and the relative prosperity and lack of competition among the employers, it has been possible for this group to secure working conditions superior to those of most other categories of Italian workers.

In their efforts at organization, the seamen have had the advantage of the ministrations of one of Italy's most prominent labor leaders, Captain Giuseppe Giulietti. Ostensibly a republican, and elected as a republican deputy in 1948, he has flirted with fascism and communism as it has suited his own, and his seamen's, interests. Giulietti was one of the first Italian labor leaders to attempt to put a union on a strong economic footing. With the establishment of his seamen's cooperative he succeeded in placing himself not only at the head of a union, but of a large fund of money, devoted to the protection of the union members. By the single-minded attention he devoted to the welfare of seamen, including Giulietti, he built up the only union in Italy which has con-

---

[71] For an account of the activities of the first fifty years of the printers' union, see the anniversary volume by T. Bruno, *La federazione del libro nel suo primo cinquantennio di vita*. Bologna: Cooperativa Tipografica Mareggiani, 1925.

tinued unimpaired under essentially the same management for much
of the prefascist, fascist, and postfascist periods. Giulietti may be
criticized for placing the interests of the seamen above the interests of
the country at large, but he can claim a certain superiority over most
other Italian labor leaders in that he has never sacrificed the interests
of the men he represents to the aspirations of any political party, and
in exchange the seamen have uniquely honored him by electing him
their national secretary for life.[72]

Because of their peculiar legal status, the longshoremen in Italy are
a special case. Their organization is more like a medieval gild than a
modern union, and in consequence it operates differently from the
other Italian unions. Longshoremen are divided into companies
(*compagnie*), of which there is one or more in each port, and it is
illegal for any extraneous person to work as a longshoreman. In this
situation, the companies have a virtually unbreakable monopoly of one
of Italy's more flourishing trades. It is not surprising, with this closed
corporation, that the Italian longshoremen are more conservative than
those of most other countries. As long as the skilled and experienced longshoremen are organized and the present system is in effect,
there is little likelihood that the present monopoly will be broken. The
head of the longshoremen's union, Marino De Stefano, is one of the
few Italian labor leaders who lack political backing. He originally
belonged to the Action Party. When it split in 1946 he attempted to
form a workers' party in southern Italy and in this way get himself
elected deputy. The attempt was a failure, and since then, with the
aid of communist support, he has prospered as a union leader.

The labor chambers. The provincial labor chamber is the local headquarters of the labor movement, and whatever labor activity goes on
in the locality is likely to be centered there. Within its walls are the
local offices of the national federations, and it is there that the local
labor leaders are found. In industrial cities like Milan and Turin the
labor chambers seem more active than the confederation headquarters
in Rome. In sleepy provinical towns there is little activity at the
labor chamber.

Financial structure. The strength and importance of labor unions
cannot be measured in membership alone. Dues are paid annually to
the confederation by the individual workers. The annual membership
dues for the CGIL were 150 lire (less than 25 cents) in 1951, of which
100 went to the CGIL and 50 to the labor chamber. Dues in the UIL
and CISL were similar. Assuming the membership estimated *supra*
(page 447), the annual income from dues of the CGIL, the CISL, and

---

[72] An interesting account of an early meeting between Giulietti and Mussolini
is related in Angelica Balabanoff, *My Life as a Rebel*, pages 109–111.

the UIL for 1950 would be about $525,000, $120,000, and $30,000 respectively. Additional monthly dues totaling about 100 lire are paid by the individual members to the labor chambers, local unions, and federations.[73] None of this money, however, goes to the confederation. A typical labor chamber, that of Florence, exacts 30 lire a month. The dues are generally paid by the acquisition of stamps, which are attached to the union membership card. The check-off system is not general. It cannot be assumed, however, that the labor chambers and federations succeed in collecting every month from all the affiliated workers, as it is easier to collect an annual payment from a worker than it is to collect continuous payments from him throughout the year. An optimistic estimate is that half the so-called *organized* workers make regular monthly payments.

Without the leadership and organization that money can buy, the most highly representative of unions "is but a fond thing, vainly invented." The Italian unions are not financially independent; without exception they must seek outside and seldom disinterested economic assistance. This poverty and its consequences are perhaps their major weakness.

Legal Status, Functions and Achievements of Trade Unions

The legal status of Italian trade unions is not clearly defined. The Italian Constitution, promulgated January 1, 1948, contains several articles that deal with labor and union activities, but like other parts of the Italian Constitution, these articles are attempts to compromise the incompatible and perhaps essentially antithetical concepts of a free labor movement and stringent government supervision in the interests of conformity.

Chapter 14 of the Constitution, which deals with economic relations, contains in its early articles many provisions that are generic to Western democratic principles, although some of them may not appear sufficiently basic or definite to merit constitutional standing, and others might be considered more fittingly placed in the preamble of a constitution than in the substantive law of its corpus. The first type includes statements on child labor (minimum age will be determined by statute), annual paid vacations, and the right of emigration. The second type gives Italians rights to adequate social security benefits and to vocational training,[74] rights that under present conditions are not realizable.

---

[73] At a time (1946) when the CGIL farmers' union, *Confederterra*, boasted of 2 million members, it spent 15 per cent of its annual budget for the acquisition and maintenance of a single automobile at national headquarters.

[74] See Articles 36, 37, and 38.

The Constitution states that trade union organization is free and that no other obligation, but compulsory registration, can be required of unions by law. Registration, however, will not be granted unless the union constitution is democratic. Registered unions gain legal recognition, and have the power to negotiate and sign collective labor agreements that will cover all workers and employers in the particular industrial field.[75]

Although these provisions have not been implemented as yet by legislation, the general Christian Democrat views on these matters are well known, and the broad outline of what the eventual legislation will be can be fairly safely surmised. Three successive Christian Democrat Ministers of Labor, Amintore Fanfani, Achille Marazza, and Leopoldo Rubinacci, have prepared enabling legislation for the constitutional provisions on labor. Nothing officially is known about the first two proposals, however, since they were not presented in Parliament. The Marazza proposal was approved in principle by the Italian Cabinet on May 9, 1951, and at that time the newspapers gave an indication of its contents.[76] The Rubinacci proposal was printed in one of the financial papers in November, 1951,[77] and presented to the Chamber of Deputies early in December. This proposal would require a minimum membership (at least 10 per cent of the average number of employed workers in the industry) and a degree of democratic control before unions could be registered, and would permit the registration of competing unions. It would give legal validity throughout the industry to collective agreements signed by representatives of over 50 per cent of the organized workers in the industry and of over half the recognized unions.

Employers' associations

The major labor function of the confederations and of their component parts is to negotiate collective labor agreements with the various employer organizations. It should be noted that Italian labor does not customarily deal with single employers. The normal practice is to deal with an organization representing an entire trade or industry. It seems advisable, therefore, at this point to describe the structure of the employers' associations.

Confindustria. *Confindustria* (*Confederazione generale dell'industria italiana*—General Confederation of Italian Industry) is almost the sole agency with which Italian labor bargains in the industrial sphere. This organization has no rivals in its field. It is wealthy and staffed

---

[75] Article 39.

[76] See, for example, *Il corriere della sera* of May 10, 1951.

[77] *24 ore*, November 21, 1951.

with trained and efficient personnel. It has accomplished what the various labor confederations have sought to accomplish and what their internecine squabbles have prevented them from realizing. *Confindustria* was founded in 1919 as the result, in part, of the cooperation and coordination necessary in the war economy. In 1926 it became a public institution within the fascist corporate system, representing all management interests in industry. Membership was still voluntary, but dues were assessed on members and nonmembers alike, and the collective agreements entered into were mandatory on all, regardless of membership. In spite of this drastic change, similar to that forced on the unions, *Confindustria* suffered considerably less than did labor, as its directors and staff remained virtually the same as before. In 1934, with the advent of the corporations, *Confindustria* had to meet a more serious challenge. Under the new set-up, most of its authority was to pass to the secondary vertical federations, which were directly represented in the various corporations. *Confindustria* weathered this storm also, maintaining its position of superiority and continuing to direct the operations of the federations from behind the scenes.[78] After liberation *Confindustria* resumed its private character and now, as before fascism, it represents only its members.

In its prefascist, fascist and postfascist manifestations, *Confindustria* has retained a basic structure similar to that of the Italian labor confederations, resting on a double hierarchy of vertical and horizontal organizations. In 1950 dues were paid for 2,353,055 workers, out of a labor force in industry of over 3,000,000 employed workers.[79]

Other employer associations. Alongside *Confindustria* there exist organizations of agriculturists and merchants, which operate similarly to *Confindustria*, although neither is so strong nor so well staffed. The agriculturists' association appears to represent the more reactionary of farm landowners and has poor relations with the farm workers' unions. In both commerce and agriculture, the general weakness of the employers' and the workers' organizations limits the effectiveness of the collective agreements they may reach, and requires a greater degree of government intervention through legislation than is the case in the industrial field. Because of the relative unimportance

---

[78] The headquarters of *Confindustria* are in one of the two Venetian palaces on the Piazza Venezia in Rome, and its front windows look directly on to the balcony of the other from which Mussolini used to expostulate. One day in 1936, when Mussolini was at the height of his popularity, an American student asked one of the magnificently uniformed messengers at *Confindustria* if they were not awed by the august presence so near them. The messenger replied, "My dear sir, we were here before he came, and we expect to be here after he goes." They are.

[79] *Annuario 1951*, page 278. Roma: Confederazione generale dell'industria italiana, 1951.

of these organizations, the examples given in the following pages will deal with *Confindustria* and not with the agriculturists' or merchants' organizations.

Means

The principal means through which the unions operate are collective agreements, conciliation proceedings, labor legislation, and labor conflicts.

Collective agreements. The collective agreement in the postfascist period, as under fascism, is usually national in scope. The actual negotiations are generally carried on by representatives of the opposing national federations and by representatives of the labor confederations and the employers' organizations involved. The national agreement usually covers questions of general working conditions, such as hours, overtime, seniority, and disciplinary measures. The national agreement may later be supplemented by a local agreement, which may include local practices and deal with technical questions of classification, beyond the competence of the less specialized negotiators in Rome. One of the major differences between the collective agreement under fascism and at the present time is that then the agreement applied to entire industries, while the present agreements appear to be enforceable only against the signatories.[80]

In negotiating with *Confindustria* or with the organizations of the agricultural employers or the commercial employers the labor confederations are at a disadvantage because of their lack of unity. It is the general practice, however, for the same agreements to be signed by representatives of all three confederations.[81] There is likely to be little difference in the demands of the three confederations in the strictly labor field. They all want substantially the same benefits for the workers. Their differences are more over political policies than labor policies.

The whole structure of the collective agreement, however, is in some

---

[80] According to Article 39 of the Constitution, collective agreements signed by "registered" unions and employer associations may be given, by law, validity over an entire field of industry. By December, 1951, however, no legislation had been passed implementing this constitutional provision.

[81] For instance, an industry-wide collective agreement raising the wage differentials between skilled and unskilled workers and between the various grades of white-collar workers was reached December 8, 1950, between *Confindustria* and the three confederations (CGIL, CISL, and UIL) "under the auspices and with the assistance of the Ministry of Labor." The relative importance of the confederations was shown in this agreement by the fact that the CGIL was represented by three officers, Di Vittorio, Santi, and Renato Bitossi; the CISL by two, Pastore and Morelli; and the UIL by Bulleri alone. See *Notiziario dell'associazione degli industriali della provincia di Venezia,* Vol. VI (1950), pages 181–184.

danger of being undermined by Article 36 of the Constitution, which reads in part, "The worker has a right to remuneration in proportion to the quantity and quality of his work, and in any case sufficient to assure him and his family a free and decent life." This constitutional provision apparently empowers any worker to question the validity of the wage provisions in any collective agreement before the courts and empowers the judges to alter the terms of a collective agreement whenever in their opinion the worker's remuneration is insufficient. The situation created by the inclusion of this provision in the Constitution may prove to be confusing if the judges avail themselves of the power to make exceptions to the wage provisions in the collective agreements. It would be difficult to remove this portion of Article 36 from the Constitution by an amendment, since few members of Parliament would care to vote against the proposition that an honest worker should be paid a living wage.

Conciliation. Neither the amateur labor courts (*Collegi dei probiviri*), nor the professional labor courts (*Magistrature del lavoro*) are operative in the postfascist period. Conciliation, in a different sense, however, is a common practice. In this sense, it refers to the custom of taking disputes to higher authorities for settlement. When an agreement cannot be reached between a factory committee and management over the dismissal of a worker, the local union officials and the local organization of *Confindustria* are called in. Disputes of a more general nature are often taken to Rome, where they are handled by the labor confederations and *Confindustria*. If the dispute is of sufficient importance, the government often intervenes through the Ministry of Labor, and through its good offices attempts to reach a solution satisfactory to the parties.

Two 1950 agreements on dismissal of workers in industry set up conciliation procedures. The first agreement, signed in April, dealt with general layoffs, and the second agreement, signed in October, with individual dismissals. Neither accord mentions arbitration.[82]

Labor legislation. Labor legislation plays a particularly important rôle in Italy, since without government intervention labor and management are often unable to protect their interests. There are a large number of small concerns, often employing only a handful of workers, which are not affiliated with *Confindustria* and are therefore not obligated by the terms of the agreement signed with *Confindustria*. These businesses are so small and scattered that it is not feasible to make separate collective agreements with every one of them. On the

---

[82] The Rubinacci proposal for implementing Article 39 of the Constitution (see *supra*, p. 453) includes a provision requiring conciliation of collective labor disputes of an economic nature before calling a strike.

other hand, the number of these small establishments may be such that it is not possible to maintain collective agreements with the major industries unless they are brought into line. For this reason *Confindustria* is often as eager as labor to see much of the collective agreement translated into legislation so that it may be enforced against the unaffiliated competitor who otherwise would be able to undercut its members; and therefore it is to the mutual benefit of *Confindustria* and labor that the unorganized worker does not lose, and the unaffiliated employer does not gain, by continuing to follow employment practices less favorable to the worker than those established by the collective agreement.

Labor conflicts. The postwar period has been one of continual labor conflict. Strikes, generally a criminal offense under fascism and consequently infrequent,[83] became an everyday occurrence in the postfascist period. Unfortunately, complete and accurate statistics are lacking in this field, and one is obliged to rely on the fragmentary information available from the Ministry of Labor and *Confindustria*.[84]

Many of the postfascist strikes were of a political nature, but because this type of strike received more attention in the press, the larger number of economic strikes is sometimes overlooked. Few Italian strikes, however, have been of long duration. Of the 585 strikes [85] taking place in the first half of 1949, as reported by *Confindustria*, 216 lasted half a day or less, and only 130 were of over a week's duration. The average number of hours lost by the 2,090,467 strikers was about 14. Over 25 per cent of the strikes taking place in this period were in the metal trades, where over a third of the hours were lost (10,287,437 out of 28,310;785). Of the 177 strikes affecting more than a single plant, 2 were general strikes, and only 7 others affected an industry on a national scale. The three longest of these national strikes appear to have lasted about a week.[86]

In the first years after liberation, when the workers had regained the right to strike, which they had lost under fascism, they were eager to avail themselves of this right on little or no provocation. Later, and particularly after the CGIL got into the habit of calling communist-

---

[83] 134 strikes were reported by the Ministry of Justice in 1942. In most of the other years of the fascist period fewer than 100 strikes were reported each year. *Annuario di statistiche del lavoro, 1949,* page 388.

[84] The confederations' lack of statistical information of this kind is remarkable. On one occasion a high official of the CGIL requested the author to ask *Confindustria* how many strikes had occurred in a certain industry because he was embarrassed to ask directly, and the CGIL had no records of its own.

[85] If the workers stop working for less than an hour, the action is considered an "agitation" and not a strike. There were 200 "agitations" reported during the first six months of 1949.

[86] *Annuario di statistiche del lavoro, 1949,* pages 392–394.

inspired political strikes, from which the workers gained no benefits
to compensate for the loss of pay incurred, enthusiasm for striking
waned and the CGIL, with its prestige weakened, was less successful
in getting a high percentage of workers out on strike.

There was much bitter discussion during the Constitutional Convention concerning the right to strike. As with so many other parts of
the Constitution, the result of the discussion was a not very meaningful compromise that reads in its entirety: "The right to strike is
exercised in accordance with the laws that regulate it." [87] The
Rubinacci proposal covers this matter also. It forbids strikes over the
interpretation of collective agreements, but permits economic strikes
over the formulation of new collective agreements after conciliation
has failed. Even public service workers will be permitted to strike.[88]

Achievements

In the labor field, the efforts of the confederations have been primarily directed toward improving the workers' standard of living. To
a lesser degree, the confederations have been interested in job security
and in workers' participation in management. The Italians have made
progress with respect to wages, but they have done little to reduce the
work week or to eliminate child labor. They have advanced far in the
direction of job security, but workers' participation in management
is little beyond the paper stage. An elaborate social security system
has been set up, but the benefits are inadequate. There is also a government program for adult vocational training. The following paragraphs
will attempt to summarize present working conditions in Italy with
respect to each of the above factors.

Standard of living. The wage picture in Italy is complicated by a
number of factors. The basic wage is often only a small part of the
worker's cost to the employer or of his take-home pay. To his basic
wage are added various supplements for seniority, family allowances,
cost of living allowances, overtime, Christmas bonus, and so forth,
while from this total are then deducted various taxes paid directly
to the government by the employer.

The early postwar trend in wages was toward blanket increases to
meet the steady rise in the cost of living. This meant that lira differences in wages between skilled and unskilled workers remained
constant while the real differences decreased considerably. By January of 1947 there was an average of about fifty lire (less than ten
cents) a day difference in the total pay of the S and M class [89]

---

[87] Article 40.
[88] Rubinacci bill, articles 26–35, as reported in *24 ore*, November 21, 1951.
[89] Italian manual workers are generally classified in four major groups, which

workers.[90] The injustices of this situation were somewhat alleviated, however, by the fact that in many economic sectors there was a shortage of skilled workers, who could therefore demand more than the minimum wage set by the collective agreements and existing legislation.

By several agreements culminating in the agreement of December 8, 1950, the minimum wage differential between skilled and unskilled workers rose to 25 per cent of the unskilled worker's wage.[91] The minimum differential between the wages of the highest and lowest class of white-collar workers is 110 per cent.[92]

Postwar Italy has experienced a plethora of cost of living allowances, some on a continuing basis and others granted as one-time payments. In 1945 these various bonuses were combined into a single cost-of-living allowance (indennità di contingenza). Eighteen months later, when the Italian government freed the price of bread, a "bread bonus" was established as a supplementary cost of living payment.

The new variable cost-of-living allowance was established as a concession to labor in an agreement between Confindustria and the CGIL on December 6, 1945,[93] that froze the basic wage. Commissions were set up in each province to determine the actual cost of the basic supplies needed by a typical family. The figures for four provinces (Milan and Turin, where living costs were high, and two others, Rovigo and Mantova, where the cost of living was relatively low) were then averaged, and that average was assigned a cost of living allowance of 100 lire a day. The cost of living allowance received by the workers in the various provinces was proportionate to the average cost of living in the four selected provinces, with the further proviso that no allowance should be more than 107 or less than 85 lire for the initial month. The cost of living was to be redetermined monthly in each province, and male workers were to receive twice the percentage increase in the cost of living (1.75 for women).[94]

By 1948 this allowance was, in some cases, well over 50 per cent of

---

for brevity can be called S, Q, C, and M classes, the S class (operai specializzati) representing the most highly skilled workers, the Q and C classes (operai qualificati and operai comuni or manovali specializzati), semiskilled workers, and the M class (manovali) unskilled workers.

[90] Compendio statistico italiano, 1947–48, page 138. Roma: Istituto Poligrafico dello Stato, 1948.

[91] For the purpose of determining this differential the wage, excluding family allowances, but including a total cost of living allowance of 600 lire, is considered.

[92] The 1950 differentials for manual laborers are about half the 1948 differentials, while the differentials of the white-collar workers are about 75 per cent of the prewar figures. Notiziario dell'associazione degli industriali della provincia di Venezia, Vol. VI (1950), page 183; and Confindustria, Annuario, 1949, page 615.

[93] This agreement was extended to southern Italy by the agreement of May 23, 1946.

[94] This was later changed to 2.3 for men and 2 for women.

the worker's total pay. When, however, toward the end of 1947 the cost of living became somewhat stabilized in Italy, it was necessary to make provision for what would happen to the cost of living allowance should there be sizable decreases in the cost of living, and in an agreement of November 28, 1947, it was determined that there would be no reduction in the cost of living allowance for industrial workers for the first 8 per cent decrease, whereas for the next 4 per cent the decrease would be 1.2 per cent, and for the following 8 per cent decrease the reduction in the cost of living allowance would be 4 per cent.[95] This agreement embodied a principle, strongly supported by the CGIL, that real wages in Italy were low, and that a disproportionate decrease in the cost of living allowance to the advantage of the worker was a method of increasing real wages in a way that was not heavily burdensome on industry.

A new basic agreement on cost of living allowances in industry was reached between *Confindustria* and the three confederations on March 21, 1951. According to this agreement the cost of living is redetermined six times a year. The determination is made by a specially created national commission composed of representatives of labor and management and is no longer entrusted to the provincial authorities. The figures for April-May, 1951, show the minimum cost of living allowance for the industrial laborer over 20 years of age as 618 lire a day.

The *indennità caropane*, or bread bonus, was established by decree, May 6, 1947. By August 1, 1948, this bonus was 20 lire a day for ordinary workers, rising to 30-60 lire for persons doing particularly heavy work, with the 60-lire bonus going exclusively to miners and lumbermen.

A peculiarity of the Italian wage structure is the Christmas bonus (*tredicesima mensilità*—thirteenth month payment). Before Christmas each year, Italian firms are required to pay an extra month's (25 working days) salary to office workers and one month's (200 hours) wages to manual laborers. Workers also receive two weeks (12 working days) paid vacation, and about 16 paid holidays, of either a religious or a patriotic nature.

Italian workers' wages are further supplemented by family allowances, paid according to the number of dependents for whom each worker is responsible. They were instituted by the fascists in 1934 as a compensation for a reduction in hours. The costs of these allowances are borne by management. The money is paid to the INPS (*Istituto nazionale della previdenza sociale*—National Social Security Agency), from which the employer receives credit against future disbursements for the actual family allowances he pays his employees. In this way the

---

[95] Confindustria, *Annuario 1949*, pages 618–623.

number of dependents his employees may have is immaterial to the individual employer. The average monthly payment to a manual worker in 1949 was 2,803.12 lire, and to a white-collar worker 2,449.23 lire.[96] In the case of the manual worker, the average family allowance payment was about 12 per cent of the wage.

During the inflationary postwar period it was natural that monetary wages should rise fast, and by August, 1948, the index of manual industrial workers' monetary wages had risen to 5,315 (1938 figures equaled 100). In real wages, the high through 1948 was an index of 113.5 for July. (Breaking this figure down by sex, the men's real wages were still slightly below the 1938 figure, while the index for women was almost 150.)

The 48-hour week was established by law in 1923.[97] In 1937 a maximum workweek of 40 hours was established, although many exceptions were permitted.[98] In 1941, the 40-hour week was suspended and 48 hours again became the practice.[99] In 1949 and 1950 about 60 per cent of industrial workers worked more than 40 hours a week and the others were divided about equally between those who worked exactly 40 hours and those who worked less. With real wages as low as they are, the workers are generally eager to work additional hours, and the trade unions are hard put to it to protest against a procedure of which the workers approve, in spite of Italy's 2 million unemployed.

Child labor. As may be expected in a poor country with an inadequate school system, there is a good deal of child labor in Italy. Accurate postwar statistics are not available on this question. The Ministry of Labor has counted over 100,000 persons under 18 years of age employed in industry in March, 1949, but this census does not include workers in establishments employing less than 10 persons nor workers in the building trades. In the plants where the census was taken, 6.2 per cent of the workers were found to be under 18 years of age. The occupations in which the highest percentages of minors were employed were unwinding silkworm cocoons (21 per cent), candy making (14.2 per cent) and silk weaving (13.2 per cent). According to the available statistics in the postwar period, however, there was a notable and steady decline in the number of employed minors in industry from a total of 140,757 counted in September, 1947, to 105,440 counted in March, 1949. This corresponded to a percentage drop from 7.9 to 6.2.[100]

Job security. Job security is a primary problem in any country with a low standard of living and chronic unemployment. Two major

---

[96] *Rassegna di statistiche del lavoro,* Quaderno III (April, 1950), page 51.
[97] Royal Decree-Law of March 15, 1923, No. 692.
[98] Royal Decree-Law of May 29, 1937, No. 1768.
[99] Royal Decree-Law of March 20, 1941, No. 125.
[100] *Annuario di statistiche del lavoro, 1949,* pages 48, 49, 51.

methods have been used in Italy to increase job security. One is the establishment of high severance pay for workers, particularly white-collar workers, and the second consists of various methods of freezing employment.

The basic legislation on job security was passed in the early years of fascism and applied to white-collar workers only.[101] The most important benefit guaranteed under this law, however, is severance pay, consisting of (1) notice and (2) severance pay proper. Notice varies from fifteen days for the lowest class of white-collar workers with five years or less seniority, up to four months for the highest classes with over ten years' seniority. Severance pay consists of a half month's salary at the current rate for every year of service. At death, the employee's family receives the equivalent of the severance pay which would be due him on dismissal.

As a further job security measure, the law requires all employers to give six months' sick leave to employees with ten years or more seniority. Other employees are granted three months. During the first third of this sick leave, the white-collar worker receives his full salary, and for the remainder, half his salary. If the illness continues beyond this period, the employer may discharge the employee, but must give him severance pay. For the purposes of this law, pregnancy is counted as an illness.

Each white-collar worker is also entitled by law to a paid vacation, the duration of which is based on seniority and which, by 1950, averaged about a month.

Severance pay, sick pay, and paid vacations have also been granted manual workers under fascist and postfascist collective agreements, but the terms have been much less advantageous. In the fascist period, typical severance pay for a manual worker was two days per year, instead of the 15 days per year accorded a white-collar worker.

A more direct method of gaining job security for the Italian worker was the freezing of employment, put into effect in northern Italy immediately after liberation. This law was never operative for the south of Italy. The original decree-law, freezing employment, was issued November 9, 1945, and was to be in effect until September 30, 1946, but in practice it continued beyond that date. Under this law management was forced to maintain all its workers on its payroll, even if they could not be gainfully employed. Since many concerns were in no financial condition to meet this burden, the government lent them the money to pay the wages of their superfluous, nonworking employees. The result was rather like a dole with many of the administrative

---

[101] Royal Decree-Law of November 13, 1924, *Disposizioni relative al contratto d'impiego privato.*

costs borne by industry rather than by the government. In 1946, the CGIL was opposed to the unfreezing of employment, and in the ensuing years compromises were reached at the local level, by which management agreed to keep on decreasing numbers of superfluous employees. This problem was most acute in the metallurgical industry, and there the final unfreezing did not occur until 1950, when management felt strong enough to disregard labor protests and rid itself of the burden of unproductive workers.

A procedure of perhaps more lasting importance, relating to job security, was agreed to by *Confindustria* and the CGIL on August 7, 1947. This agreement set up new procedures for the reduction of personnel. Management agreed to consult with the factory committees (*commissioni interne*) whenever it felt called upon to reduce its personnel, and when agreement could not be reached with the factory committees, management further agreed to consult with the union. If, after three weeks of negotiation, agreement could not be reached, management then reserved the right to act unilaterally. The result of this procedure has been that the factory committees have often had the final word as to who would be dismissed, and this has increased the job security of workers in good standing with, and of the same political persuasion as, the workers' representatives on the factory committees. The power and the intransigence of factory committees vary greatly. In general, however, particularly in the smaller plants, and where management has shown an inclination to explain its position to labor, the factory committees have been cooperative.

Participation in management. Italian labor has sought participation in management through two types of organization: factory committees (*commissioni interne*) and labor-management councils (*consigli di fabbrica or consigli di gestione*).[102] Factory committees were first established in Italy in the early years of the century. They were originally little more than grievance committees, concerned with matters of factory discipline. Their institution, although voluntary and sporadic, tended to become more common, particularly after World War I. With the rise of fascism, however, they disappeared. In 1943, in Rome, *Confindustria* signed an agreement with the labor leaders Buozzi, Roveda, and Quarello creating factory committees in all establishments employing over 20 workers. These committees were given the functions of acting as liaison between the unions and the workers, seeing that the collective agreement was scrupulously carried

---

[102] The term *consigli di fabbrica* (factory councils) was used in the period after World War I, while the term *consigli di gestione* (management councils) is the one used after World War II. In these pages both terms are translated "labor-management councils."

out, attempting to mediate individual labor disputes, negotiating local collective agreements, expressing their opinion on the factory rules and regulations, and making suggestions of a technical nature to improve the efficiency of production.[103] It has been previously noted that the factory committees were later given partial authority over dismissal of workers.

Agitation for labor participation in management got under way at the close of World War I, particularly in the metallurgical industries. The most spectacular attempt at labor control of management, at this period, was made at the Fiat works in Turin, where in 1920 the workers actually took over the management of the plant. The ensuing violence was so serious that the President of the Council of Ministers, Giovanni Giolitti, intervened, and peace was reestablished between *Confindustria* and the "red" union, the CGL, with the understanding that negotiations would be entered into between the parties for the establishment of labor-management councils. After over a month of fruitless negotiations, *Confindustria* and the CGL issued a statement on October 29, 1920, that their views on this subject could not be reconciled. Both parties then proceeded to draft legislation on the subject which would be acceptable to them. These drafts were publicized in November. During the same month the "white" union, the CIL, offered a third draft, embodying its pet principle of profit-sharing, by which a certain percentage of the profits would go to the workers as stock dividends, and labor participation in management would eventually be proportionate to labor's capital holdings. On February 8, 1921, the president of the Council of Ministers presented a fourth bill, which would establish workers' industry-wide control committees (*commissioni di controllo*). No government action was taken, however, and the whole matter was dropped.[104]

In a final effort to gain popular support, Mussolini's Social Republic of Salò offered the workers virtual control of the industries that employed them through the establishment of labor-management councils.[105] The establishment of these labor-management councils, however, took place in the fall and winter of 1944–45, and, consequently, they had little chance to function before liberation.

With liberation came further confusion when the newly formed

---

[103] *I consigli di gestione,* Vol. II, pages 65–66. Roma: *Confindustria,* 1947.

[104] *I consigli di gestione,* Vol. II, pages 8–10, 28–46; Silvio Bacchi Andreoli, *I consigli di fabbrica in Europa,* pages 89–131. Roma: Associazione fra le società per azioni, 1945.

[105] See the proclamation of the Fascist Republican Party, November 18, 1943; the plan approved by the Council of Ministers of the Fascist Republican Party, January 11, 1944; Legislative Decree of the Fascist Republic, February 12, 1944, No. 375; all cited in *I consigli di gestione,* Vol. II, pages 67–71.

labor-management councils first assumed real power and the heads of many of the larger industries were dismissed. The new organizations took over in difficult and troubled times, and it is not surprising that they had little success. In most cases the former managers were back in authority a year later, and in those relatively few cases in which the former director's political past made him unacceptable, trained administrators replaced the improvised heads chosen by the labor-management councils, and control of the business returned to the owners and their representatives.

In spite of this initial failure, the labor-management councils were not abolished. Although they did not spread further south or to smaller concerns, the ones already created continued in existence. As after World War I, the functions, structure and even existence of the labor-management councils became a political question. The parties from the extreme right to the anticlerical center of the republicans opposed them, while the communists and socialists vociferously supported them. *Confindustria* remained adamant and refused to give the *de facto* organizations the powers and privileges they demanded. The President of the Council of Ministers, Alcide De Gasperi, like his predecessor, Giolitti, stalled for time; and meanwhile, the Minister of Labor, Ludovico D'Aragona, former secretary of the CGL, drafted legislation making labor-management councils obligatory. Shortly thereafter, the Minister of Industry and Commerce, Rodolfo Morandi, a young socialist, presented a more radical draft that was adopted by the government in place of the D'Aragona draft. History repeated itself and the Constitutional Assembly took no legislative action. Italy again proved herself to be too traditional and conservative a country to accept such a large measure of socialism.[106]

The committee of the Assembly which was writing the Constitution, however, proposed the following article on labor-management councils for inclusion in the new Constitution: "The State assures the right of the workers to participate in the management of the concerns which employ them. . . ." This provision, which management found somewhat alarming, was considerably watered down when the article was debated by the Assembly. One of the major points of conflict was over the desire of the Christian Democrats to include one of their favorite ideas, that of giving special stock dividends to employees, thus making them co-owners. The socialists and communists were strongly opposed to this, on the grounds that it would upset the class consciousness of the masses and that it might make the workers partially responsible before the law in case the concern went bankrupt. It was the com-

---

[106] *I consigli di gestione,* Vol. I, pages 146–171; Vol. II, pages 12–25.

munists' contention that the workers should share in the management without assuming any responsibility for management. Finally, a compromise article was suggested by Giovanni Gronchi and accepted by the Assembly. This article reads: "With a view to the economic and social advancement of labor, and in harmony with the requirements of production, the Republic recognizes the right of workers to collaborate in the management of business enterprises in the ways and within the limits established by law." [107]

Social security. Social security legislation in Italy gives the worker much protection on paper, as the coverage is wide. The benefits, however, are quite inadequate, and in some cases are ridiculously small.

Under the social security system, almost all contributions are made by the employer. In the exceptional cases in which the worker pays, the employer is obliged to deduct the contributions from the worker's wage. Most contributions are made by buying social security stamps, which the employer puts in the worker's social security book (*tessera*). This booklet is kept by the employer until the employee leaves or is dismissed, at which time it is given to the worker, who presents it to his next employer. Disbursements to the insured are made either directly by government agencies or by the employer, as is the case, for instance, with family allowances. The employer, however, is never reimbursed directly for the payments he makes to his workers. He is merely credited with these sums against future payments.

In September, 1950, the total social security payments by management in industry averaged 37 per cent of the manual worker's wages and 23 per cent of the office worker's salary. Workers' payments averaged less that 2 per cent of their pay.

The social security system is administered through a series of public agencies, three of which merit attention here. The numerous other agencies are concerned with special categories of persons who are not covered under the general social security laws. Many of these special agencies are concerned with government workers, who receive outright pensions from the government that are not administered by the regular social security agencies.

The INPS (*Istituto nazionale della previdenza sociale*—National Social Security Agency) is the major agency in the field of social security. It was established in 1898 as an agency for old age and disability pensions for manual workers. It is managed by a president, who is assisted by a board of governors and a board of auditors. Both boards are composed of civil servants of the Ministry of Labor and of workers' and management representatives. For almost a quarter of a

---

[107] Vittorio Falzone, *Costituzione della repubblica italiana,* pages 40–41. Roma: Colombo, 1948.

century insurance with this agency was voluntary. The first compulsory insurance (for old age and disability) was instituted by law in April, 1919. The agency went through a basic reorganization in October, 1935.

The major types of insurance administered by the INPS are (1) disability, old age, and survivors' insurance, (2) unemployment insurance, and (3) tuberculosis insurance. The INPS also administers the family allowance system.

Disability, old age, and survivors' insurance was made obligatory in 1919. A voluntary system was set up in 1898 and is still in force for those who do not fall under the obligatory provisions. Insurance is obligatory for men between 15 and 60 years of age and women between 15 and 55 who receive salaries and wages, except for government employees and tenant farmers. Insurance for the self-employed is voluntary. The estimated coverage for 1942 was 7,687,000 persons.[108]

Unemployment insurance is obligatory for industrial, commercial, and banking and insurance workers between the ages of 14 and 60; the range is 14 to 55 if they are women. Farm laborers, government employees, domestic servants, and some other groups are excluded. It is estimated that 5,320,000 are covered.[109] The cost of this insurance is borne entirely by the employer.

Tuberculosis insurance first went into effect on July 1, 1928. Its coverage is considerably greater than that of the two types of insurance discussed above. Agricultural workers, including tenant farmers, and certain government employees, such as elementary school teachers, are covered. The insurance also extends to the spouses, minor children, and minor dependent siblings of the insured. The total number insured in 1942 was 19,305,000. Contributions for this insurance are paid entirely by the employer. The major payments are for care in tuberculosis sanatoriums. The number of persons cared for in sanatoriums in 1948 was 105,938, and the average stay was 139 days.[110]

The INAIL (*Istituto nazionale per l'assicurazione contro gli infortuni sul lavoro*—Workmen's Compensation Agency) was established in 1935 and modified in 1949. Originally the insurance it administered covered only industrial workers, but in 1943 it extended coverage to farmers. It is estimated that 3,013,047 industrial workers were covered by this insurance in 1948, as well as a large but indeterminate number of farm workers.[111] The contributions are paid entirely by the em-

[108] *Rassegna di statistiche del lavoro.* Vol. III (April, 1950), page 22.
[109] *Ibid.*, page 34.
[110] *Ibid.*, pages 39–40.
[111] *Ibid.*, pages 62–63.

ployer. The payments made to industrial workers are two thirds of the wages for the duration of temporary disability, and for permanent disability, a lump sum of 120,000–180,000 lire, depending upon the percentage of permanent disability. Additional payments are made for dependents of the permanently disabled. The dependent survivors of workers killed in industrial accidents receive a cash payment of 8,000 –16,000 lire, depending on their relationship to the deceased worker, and a percentage of two-thirds of his salary, which ranges from 50 per cent for the widow to 20 per cent for each child.

The INAM (*Istituto nazionale per l'assicurazione contro le malattie*—National Health Insurance Agency) was created in 1943. Previous to this date, health insurance was regulated by collective agreements, which, under fascism, applied to all workers and employers. Since 1943 the compulsory health insurance now administered by the INAM covers practically all workers, except government employees. The dependents of insured workers are also given medical care, and the insured worker receives a portion of his wages when unable to work because of illness.[112]

The contributions are paid entirely by the employer and range from 5 per cent of the total wage paid manual workers in industry to 3 per cent of the salaries of clerical workers in industry and banking. For farm workers, a sum is paid for each day's work, ranging from 6.13 lire for tenant farmers to 25 lire for day laborers.

In 1948, 14,248,600 persons were covered by INAM insurance. About 5 million of these were workers who had a right to payments, usually 50 per cent of the daily wage, for days absent from work because of illness. In 1948, almost half (49.8 per cent) of the workers entitled to benefits claimed them, and 45 per cent received benefits. The average number of work days missed annually by these persons was 19.1.[113]

Commencing in 1951, pregnancy was considered an illness, and was compensated for through INAM. Additional contributions, up to .5 per cent of wages, were paid by the employers to meet the additional costs. At the same time the marriage and birth benefits, previously paid by INPS, were discontinued, and the money collected for them was turned over to a government-operated agency for the care of orphans. The workers lost little by this change, as the maximum payments under the old system were about $2 for a marriage, about 60

---

[112] Tenant farmers and most clerical workers do not receive insurance for working days lost. Most clerical workers receive sick leave with pay, depending upon seniority. (See *supra*, p. 462).

[113] *Rassegna di statistiche del lavoro*, Vol. III (April, 1950), pages 73–74, 76.

cents for post-third children, and a smaller amount for the first three children.

The social security picture in Italy is typical of the high ideals and the poor practical results in a country where men's aspirations run beyond their pocketbooks. The general coverage is good, but the system is hopelessly bogged down by an unnecessarily complicated administration and needs a general overhauling to reduce its present high administrative costs. In 1945, these costs rose to 13.18 per cent of the disbursements.[114] Until such time as the Italian economy can afford greater benefits, it might be wise to eliminate certain types of insurance that require in administrative costs more than their total value. It cannot be of any particular help to a person hospitalized with tuberculosis to know that each of his children is receiving 8 lire a day from the INPS when the price of a daily newspaper is 20 lire. The government is planning a thorough reorganization of the social security system to achieve greater integration and efficiency. Italian bureaucrats, however, are adept at resisting reform, and it may be some time before the Italian system can be put in operation on a more rational basis.

Ideological Influences

Perhaps the major tragedy of the Italian labor movement is that it has rarely had a common policy. It has, in its ranks, purists and intransigents, whose energies have been more often directed toward the purging of dissident elements than to reaching compromise goals through cooperation. For this reason, although ideological influences were a factor leading to the unification of Italian labor, they have also been powerful as a dividing and destructive force.

As the sentiment of national unity in Italy penetrated to the lower classes, and Italian labor grew slowly conscious of a common bond, it might have been possible to create a movement representing the common interests of Italian labor. There was a strong class consciousness in Italy, based on antagonism against the *padroni* and *signori,* and the labor movement would have coordinated and strengthened this class consciousness had it succeeded in remaining united. Before fascism the labor movement, through the CGL, got off to a good start. It built up strong unions, particularly in the northern industrial centers, and developed successful cooperatives, especially in Emilia. At the same time, it trained men to serve as labor and political leaders. This united union was soon disrupted by internal strife of a political

---

[114] *Annuario di statistiche del lavoro, 1949,* pages 262–264.

nature and by the rise of competing unions representing other political faiths.

For a brief period during, and immediately after, World War II, unified action on the part of labor was possible. In northern Italy, before liberation, a united free labor movement was working underground with the partisan resistance movement. The labor activities behind the lines consisted of slowdowns, plant destruction, hiding of strategic materials, and general sabotage. This work was not only valuable to the Allied cause; it gave the workers an opportunity to cooperate for a common end.

After liberation, cooperation continued as long as the communists remained in the coalition government, but as soon as the communists became the major opposition party, a common labor policy was no longer possible within the CGIL.

An examination of the ideological influences on the labor movement entails an analysis of the Italian political parties and the party system, of the influence exerted by the parties on the labor movement, and, finally, of the internal politics in the confederations.

Structure of Italian political parties

The present Italian party system resembles both the multi-party system of France and the traditional Italian type of two-party system. In Italy a political party is not merely a group of men who want to hold public office, or who expect to receive favors if certain men hold office. It is a group of people who think alike. It is a club, a church, a fraternal organization. The Italian worker has a choice of several political parties which purport to represent his special interests: the Republican Party, whose Bible is Mazzini, the Socialist Parties, each of which interprets its Marxian Bible differently, and the Communist Party, whose pope is Stalin.[115]

All the political parties which have been competing for labor votes must share responsibility for the factionalism which has made a unified policy impossible, but a large share of the blame must be borne by the socialists. Italian labor's major tragedy has been the failure of Italian socialism. Italian socialism has tried to reconcile antithetical and incompatible elements, which have done little but vitiate its strength. The philosophy of right-wing socialists, like Turati and Prampolini, was based on a compassionate understanding of human

---

[115] In a speech at the Republican Party convention at Bologna in 1948 the party secretary, Randolfo Pacciardi, spoke of the collected writings of Mazzini as the "Bible." Giuseppe Saragat and other prominent Socialists cite the works of Marx in their addresses as if they were quoting Scripture. The infallibility of Stalin is about the only constant feature in the tortuous and changing communist doctrine.

beings, including capitalists, that to left-wingers was incomprehensible and aggravating. On the other hand, the bull in the china shop tactics of their bomb-throwing antagonists to the left were incompatible with the doctrines of the right-wing socialists and esthetically distasteful to them.

Most of the positive results the socialists have achieved can be attributed to right-wing influence. Left-wing movements such as those of Bakunin, Labriola, and Leone previous to World War I and, later, of the communists, are not interested in achieving positive results under the present economic system, and, as long as the system persists, serve merely as destructive influences. Right-wing socialism, however, has taken root only in certain sections of Italy. Milan [116] and the surrounding industrial suburbs have always been its Italian headquarters. It was never able, however, to contain the exuberance of the more impulsive elements in the socialist movement, and its strength was being constantly sapped by deserters to the left and occasionally even by deserters to the right, such as Bissolati and Bonomi.

To a lesser extent, the Catholic parties (the pre-Fascist *Partito popolare* and the present Christian Democracy) have also had a disrupting influence on Italian labor. The extremism of the left-wing socialists, as well as the anticlericalism of all socialists, caused the clericals to create a labor movement of their own, thus further splitting the labor ranks, in spite of the fact that on purely labor problems there was little difference between the Catholic and the Marxist positions.

The republican followers of Mazzini are primarily a middle class party. Although the strength of the party itself is concentrated in Tuscany and the former papal states, where anticlericalism is strong, its labor strength is limited to the Romagna and a few communities in southern Italy and Sicily. In these communities there is little but political factionalism that separates the republican from the right-wing socialist.

The ideological picture was further cluttered after the outbreak of World War I by the advent of national syndicalism, at once anti-Marxist, anti-Mazzinian, and anti-Catholic. Although national syndicalism was not essentially a labor ideology, it appealed to the working classes and attacked all existing labor ideologies, and, therefore, played an important part in the debilitation of the labor movement that preceded its submission to fascism.[117]

---

[116] In the municipal elections of 1945 and 1946 almost all north Italian cities gave majorities to the communist and left-wing socialist parties. Milan alone has maintained its anticommunist mayor, Antonio Greppi, formerly affiliated with the PSLI and later with the PSU.

[117] In the fall of 1950 the neofascist M. S. I. (*Movimento sociale italiano*—Italian

Behind the façade of the French multi-party system lies the traditional Italian system of two antithetical parties. Classically, these were the Guelphs and the Ghibellines. The old Guelphs were the party which supported the papal claims to temporal power, and the Ghibellines were the protagonists of the temporal supremacy of the Holy Roman Emperor in Germany. The neo-Guelphs of today are still the papal party, while the successors of the Ghibellines, the communists, look to Moscow instead of to Germany. In Italy, the two antagonistic parties do not have similar platforms, as they do in Great Britain and the United States, and the tradition of a loyal opposition is lacking. In the latter countries, the more conservative party espouses a platform that its leaders feel is radical enough to be acceptable to 55 per cent of the voters, and the more radical party espouses a program that it believes conservative enough to elicit roughly the same number of votes.[118] In Italy, the party programs tend to mutual antithesis, with the result that peaceful change from one to the other appears almost an impossibility.

There is another sense in which the Italian multi-party system resolves itself into a two-party system, and this is in the division between the ruling classes and the laboring masses. The strong class consciousness of Italian labor places it naturally in the opposite political camp from that of the *padroni* and the *signori*. Since these latter groups are identified with government and authority, the labor policy is, traditionally, a policy of opposition. A political party claiming to espouse labor interests must run a serious risk of being called traitorous if it joins the government, which, to the essentially anarchistic Italian, is an enemy. This state of affairs gives the Communist Party, as the most intransigent of opposition parties, a considerable influence over labor. The counter-propaganda against the communists is that they are representatives of foreign imperialism, and essentially indifferent to the welfare of Italian labor. A struggle within the Italian working class results from this conflict. As workingmen, Italians are traditionally against the government and drawn toward the Communist Party. As patriots (and patriotism, although not associated with the government, is strong in Italy), they are against foreign

---

Social Movement) formed another labor confederation apparently modeled after the national syndicalist movement of the prefascist era. This confederation is called CISNAL (*Confederazione italiana sindacati nazionali lavoratori*—Italian Confederation of National Workers' Unions). For the present the CISNAL is of no importance, and it is not likely to become so in the foreseeable future.

[118] It appears that an Italian was one of the first to appreciate the political stability that such a two-party system affords, but his country has never enjoyed such a system. See Vittorio Alfieri, *Della tirannide*, Book I, chapter 11, quoted in Guido DeRuggiero, *Storia del liberalismo europeo*. 3d ed., page 300. Bari: Giuseppe Laterza e Figli, 1945.

influence and recede from it. From this point of view, the Communist Party must take the major share of the blame for the present split in the labor movement.

Political control of unions

The Italian confederations are required to espouse the political platform of the party with which they are affiliated.[119] In all three of the confederations, the relation of the labor leaders to the political parties is one of subordination. In every case the political leaders dominate, and the labor leaders have a secondary position. Whenever there is a difference of opinion on labor matters between the political leaders and the labor leaders within a party, the latter must give in, resign their positions in the labor movement, or risk expulsion from the party.

The political control of the Communist Party over the policies of the CGIL has been the most flagrant example of the abuse of a labor union for political purposes. The splits which have occurred in the CGIL since 1947 and the creation of rival confederations are direct results of the communist policy of making a political tool of the CGIL, converting it into a major instrument in the communist opposition to a Christian Democratic government. In assenting to this misuse of his union, Di Vittorio showed himself first a communist and second a labor leader.

Di Vittorio's action was all the more remarkable as he was shown to be second only to Togliatti in popular following among communist candidates in the elections of 1946 and 1948. This might lead one to suppose either that Di Vittorio would have considerable influence in party policies or that he would be in a position to act with considerable independence. In spite of his popularity with the voters, however, Di Vittorio is still a second rater in party councils and has followed a party line which must be personally distasteful to him. Even after Togliatti was sent to Russia on leave in 1950, the triumvirate which took over temporary control of the Communist Party, consisting of Luigi Longo, Pietro Secchia, and Umberto Terracini, contained no labor leaders.[120]

---

[119] An example of this was reported in the *Corriere della sera* for July 2, 1950, where it was stated that the CGIL endorsed the Communist Party's stand condemning American "aggression" in Korea, while the CISL officially approved of the UN action.

[120] Longo is generally considered the party's hatchet man and military genius. He was the chief communist officer of the Italians who fought against the Spanish rebels, and had the same position with the partisan forces in Italy. Secchia is the party's administrative secretary and of its leaders is considered the most subservient to Stalin and the Cominform. Terracini is one of the party's outstanding intellectuals.

Perhaps the most extreme example of party domination is the expulsion of most of the socialist labor leaders from both the CGIL and the Socialist Party (PSI). Their crime was refusal to hew to the Communist Party line. Since this group was a clear majority of the PSI labor leaders, it would seem that their point of view should have had some influence with the party; but the political leaders chose to follow the communists, and the views of the labor leaders were overridden. It is also significant that in spite of this experience, the expelled socialist labor leaders, instead of creating a labor union independent of political influence, sought party backing (of the PSU and the republicans) for the new union, UIL, that they established.

The influence of the Christian Democracy and the republicans over their union leaders has been effective, if somewhat less spectacular. Catholic labor leaders such as Rubinacci, Baldelli, Rapelli, and Carcano have lost their influence in the Catholic labor movement, not through the vote of the Catholic workers, but through lack of confidence in them on the part of the party's political leaders.[121] The republican labor leaders, Enrico Parri and Appio Claudio Rocchi, were expelled from their party for joining the Catholic-dominated CISL, after the organized workers who were members of the party had voted against the merger.

The PSLI seems to have exerted less influence over its labor leaders, probably because it has been unable to make up its mind on a labor policy. When Canini, the PSLI vice secretary of the CGIL, left the Confederation, however, this action was taken after party consultation and approval.

Union politics

Each of the three major labor movements in Italy, regardless of protestations of independence, is dominated by a political party, and two of them are each supported by another party with less labor influence. The CGIL is a communist union, with left-wing socialist (PSI) support. The UIL is a democratic socialist (PS-SIIS) union, with republican support. The CISL is Christian Democratic, with the halfhearted support of the right wing of the PS-SIIS. Thus, not only is the labor movement split three ways, but the socialists, who in other countries of western Europe are a bulwark of the democratic labor movement, are now supporting three distinct confederations.

Within each of the confederations there are factions striving to alter the established policy and direct it to other purposes than those

---

[121] Senator Rubinacci has made a come-back as Minister of Labor. Baldelli was sent to the Italian Embassy in Argentina. Rapelli is a deputy, and Carcano has returned to private business

of the dominant political group with which the union is affiliated. So far these attempts have had little success.

Within the CGIL the struggle is between the policy determined by the Communist Party and a policy of more direct assistance to CGIL members, which it is believed Di Vittorio and most of the other CGIL leaders prefer. This is a latent, not an overt, struggle, however, and communist policy still prevails. Fernando Santi, the top socialist (PSI) in the CGIL, has been relegated to the politically innocuous duties of running the confederation's social services, and representing it at the ILO, and thus, little active opposition can be expected from the socialist forces still affiliated with the CGIL. Of considerably more importance is the split within the communist ranks, brought into the open with the resignations from the party in January, 1951, of the "Titoist" Deputies Valdo Magnani and Aldo Cucchi. There is widespread sympathy within the Communist Party for Magnani and Cucchi's action, as many Italian communists resent Russian influence. It is likely, however, that the majority of the pro-Western, anti-Russian wing will continue to serve the Communist Party. Magnani and Cucchi are relatively young (under 40) and apparently have private incomes. They can afford to take chances which their older, poorer, and perhaps wiser colleagues must wistfully refuse.

In the CISL the struggle is more open. The general secretary, Pastore, is pledged to the furtherance of an apolitical union, and members of the FIL have been admitted to the confederation's councils in subordinate positions. Pastore, however, has not felt obliged to resign his seat in parliament in the interest of the independence of his confederation.

There are two minority factions in the Christian Democratic labor movement. One is led by Giuseppe Rapelli, the former Christian Democrat secretary of the CGIL, and is reported to have the backing of Gronchi and Rubinacci. Rapelli believes that it is difficult to combine clericals and anticlericals in the same labor movement and that it would be better to have an out-and-out Catholic labor confederation collaborating with a democratic socialist labor confederation, such as the UIL.

The other faction in the CISL is allied with the followers of Giuseppe Dossetti, a professor of canon law at the University of Modena and a Christian Democrat deputy. Dossetti's group is composed of left-wing fanatical Catholics, who favor social reform and oppose the moderation of the party leader, Alcide De Gasperi. This group is trying to take over the CISL as a means of increasing its power and prestige within the Christian Democracy. It has recruited many able young men for the CISL from ACLI, the Catholic workers' assistance organization. The aims and the ideals of Dossetti and his followers are hardly compatible with those of the few right-wing socialists and republicans who came over from the FIL, and should this group succeed in impregnating the CISL with their brand of Roman Catholicism, it will have even less chance of gaining wide mass support.

For the moment the UIL seems to suffer less from political influence than its competitors, perhaps because its political backers have less influence to assert. The national leaders of the UIL are members of the PS-SIIS, but in some of the provincial centers, particularly in the Romagna and in southern Italy, the organization is predominantly republican.

The Future of Trade Unionism

As long as Article 39 of the Italian Constitution is not implemented, the Italian labor movement is, in many respects, in a state of suspended animation. During this interim period, it is more than rash to predict the road the Italian labor movement will follow and to what degree its progress will be satisfactory.

The Italian unions are operating in relative freedom, with little legal power and few legal liabilities. This is rather the climate of the American labor movement. But between the Italian and American scenes there is one vast difference, and that is money. American unions are often wealthy; Italian unions are always poor. American unions do not need the cloak of governmental power to function effectively. Perhaps the Italian unions do.

Beyond the problems of the Rubinacci bill and its enforcement lie other basic problems that by now must be evident to readers of this chapter. They include the political orientation of the labor movement, the lack of democratic leadership in the unions, the weak position of the entire Italian economy, and the precarious state of union finances.

Italian labor is now in the position of trying to support three mutually antagonistic labor unions, the CGIL, the CISL, and the UIL. Few Italians, either in or out of the labor movement, fail to see the evil of the present situation, but, unfortunately, it is not one that can be easily remedied. The split in the labor movement is basically a political split, and it will not be remedied until there is political unity among the labor parties, or until the opposition parties are obliterated. It is conceivable that, in time, a united Socialist Party could gain for itself, and the union it represented, a sufficient majority of the labor support to function effectively alongside small communist and Catholic labor groups, much as the British labor movement is not seriously impeded by the handful of British communists. This possibility is remote and, therefore, the unity which Italian labor enjoyed, by compulsion under fascism and voluntarily under the coalition government of the immediate postfascist period, is not likely soon to be regained.

Democracy is the soil in which a free labor movement is supposed to grow best. In some respects, however, the Italian labor movement is not free. There is little democracy in the selection of the union leaders. The labor rank and file can hardly look upon them as their choice. The leaders are chosen by the parties, and their first loyalty is to the parties.

In the case of all three confederations, power is placed in the hands of national organizations and policy is determined according to political exigencies. To be sure, the major parties interested in the labor movement purport to represent the masses, but in practice it is often the tail that wags the dog; it is the union that obeys the party. At times it would appear that the workers sense this inferiority of the unions to the parties and resent it. This reaction seems particularly evident with respect to the political domination of the Communist Party over the CGIL and, as was suggested above, it appears that this use of the labor movement for purely political purposes and to the immediate detriment of the interests of the union members is a principal cause for the decline in that confederation. Often, however, the party seems to have a stronger appeal to the worker than the union, and membership in the union follows party preference.

The Italian labor movement is faced with certain grave economic problems which it must help solve. Under fascism, Italy experimented with an autarchic economy, and, in consequence, built up, particularly in the heavy industry sector, many uneconomic industries which require constant government subsidizing. Italy must also cope with a chronic unemployment problem. The attitude of the labor movement will be an important factor in handling these problems. Labor, at present, is opposed to abandoning the uneconomic metallurgical industries and is also opposed to the installation of labor-saving devices or other efficiency methods reducing man-hours in industry and thereby increasing unemployment. The position of labor on these questions is easy to understand, and it is difficult to see how a labor movement could react otherwise. Unfortunately, however, labor's position is not a remedy, but rather an insistence upon maintaining the *status quo* with respect to these problems. The Italian economy is in no financial condition to withstand serious drains of this kind for an indefinite period.

A solution for the unemployment problem, which has labor's partial support, is emigration. With unemployment chronic in Italy and

shortages of manpower common in other European countries, internal
European migration would seem to be a mutually satisfactory arrangement. Most of Italy's unemployed, however, are unskilled laborers,
often farm laborers, and shortages in the other countries are often
most acute among skilled laborers. There are further problems of a
financial nature concerning payments to the workers' families, and in
the early agreements worked out after World War II there was often
much dissatisfaction on both sides. One of the more successful agreements reached was that with Belgium for miners, but, even here, the
agencies that Italy used for recruiting proved inadequate, and middle-
aged, underfed Sicilian barbers, quite unaccustomed to heavy work or
rugged climate, were transported to Belgium and expected to work in
the mines. The basic problem with the emigration agreements arranged
through the Italian government has been that for political reasons the
government has had to select workers from all parts of the country,
while many European countries prefer to employ only northern Italians,
whose culture is more similar to that of the receiving countries and
who are more likely to understand other languages. Switzerland, for
instance, has preferred not to sign such a treaty with Italy, but to
take on individual workers, particularly from the contiguous regions
of Lombardy and Piedmont. Many of these workers are so successful
in Switzerland that they remain there and become Swiss citizens.[122]

The future of the labor movement in Italy is also dependent upon
the economic stability of the unions. By and large, the unions lack
funds. Membership dues are ridiculously low, and a union movement
cannot be strong or independent until it has more money at its disposal. It is not likely, however, that, so long as labor is as divided as it
is today, the Italian workman will have sufficient faith in his union to
care to pay higher dues.

Since membership dues are insufficient to meet expenses, aid must
be sought elsewhere. With the aid come external guidance and control,
and a more or less voluntary acceptance of an ideology. Although
most of the political parties are themselves poor, the parties have
patronage, and many an Italian labor leader supports his family on
money obtained through the party as a party official, a member of
parliament, or the holder of some public office. In some cases, the
Italian unions have gone to other groups for financial aid. The
American Federation of Labor, for instance, has been active in the
Italian labor field. It gave financial support to the FIL and was

---

[122] The ability of the Italians to assimilate in Switzerland is shown by the fact
that over 25 per cent of the Italian-speaking Swiss are foreign-born. John Clarke
Adams *et al., Foreign Governments and Their Backgrounds,* page 300. New
York: Harper, 1950.

instrumental in the formation of the CISL. One of the causes of the slow start of the UIL was its lack of money. By the end of 1950, however, it too seemed to have found financial backing.

Even with financial aid from external sources, the unions are too poor to finance a strike of long duration, and so labor is tempted to resort to threats of violence as a means of bringing a labor conflict to a speedier solution. In postfascist Italy little violence and bloodshed have been connected with labor disputes. The fear of violence, however, is always present. Labor does not resort to open threats. Its policy is one of intimidation, and it is eager to avoid the overt acts which would turn public opinion against it. The usual technique is for the labor leader to inform management that unless the workers' demands are met, the union cannot be responsible for what may happen. It is not of great practical importance whether or not the labor leader is telling the truth when he makes such a statement, although many times the danger of violence is probably real and beyond the control of the union. It is, nevertheless, an indubitable fact that the fear of personal injury and damage to the plant often causes management to consider the demands of labor more seriously than the impoverished finances of the unions and their consequent inability to prolong a strike would merit.

It was, I believe, Don Marquis who remarked after "investigating" the police systems of various American cities that, for the most part, he found them "honeycombed with honesty." The Italian labor movement also has its encouraging side. In the field of labor relations there have been no irreconcilable differences among the various Italian labor movements other than those of a political origin. Italian labor may not be unified, but it is fully aware of itself and its problems. It has a well-developed class consciousness, common ideals, common heroes, common songs. Only when it tries to act is it overcome by problems of coordination.[123] As has been pointed out above, a few unions have shown considerable cohesiveness and *esprit de corps* and have built up a tradition of loyalty. In time, other unions may acquire these traits. The progressive forces, however, are struggling against a system basically inimical to them. Their persistence in these troubled times attests to the latent vitality of the labor movement, but they cannot be expected to prosper so long as the conditions under which Italian labor now operates prevail.

---

[123] There is an old Florentine saying: "One Italian, an artist; two Italians, an orchestra; three Italians, confusion."

Chapter 7

RUSSIA—ISAAC DEUTSCHER *

Trade Unions under Tsardom

This chapter attempts to describe and analyze trade unions under the Soviet regime and their place in the labor policy of the Soviet government. A retrospective summary of trends in Russian trade-unionism before the Bolshevik revolution may help the reader in approaching the subject.

One of the striking features of the Russian labor movement before the revolution of 1917 was the relative insignificance of the trade unions. In part, this was due to the fact that Russian industry was still very young and that the mass of industrial workers consisted of recently proletarianized peasants. The trade unions of western Europe had behind them the long tradition of medieval guilds, whose descendants in a sense they were. No such tradition existed in Russia. More important still, up to the beginning of this century trade union organization was as strictly prohibited and persecuted by tsardom as was any form of political opposition. In suppressing trade unionism, tsardom unwittingly put a premium upon revolutionary political organization.[1] Only the most politically-minded workers, those prepared to pay for their conviction with prison and exile, could be willing to join trade unions in these circumstances. But those who were already so politically-minded were, naturally enough, more attracted by political organizations. The broader and more inert mass of workers, who were inclined to shun politics but would have readily joined trade unions, were not only prevented from forming unions but were also gradually accustomed to look for leadership to the clandestine political parties.

---

* This chapter is an adapted and abridged version of my *Soviet Trade Unions,* written for and published by The Royal Institute of International Affairs, London. I wish to express my thanks to the publishers of the original book for their very kind permission to include the abridged version in this publication.

[1] In 1902 Col Zubatov, chief of the Moscow political police, sponsored closely-supervised trade unions designed to compete with the revolutionary organizations. These police-sponsored trade unions were no substitute for real ones; and they were soon infiltrated by the revolutionaries.

"The most characteristic feature in the history of our Trade Unions," says Stalin, "is that they have emerged, developed and grown strong only after the party, around the party and in friendship with the party." This view, somewhat over-simple, is, nevertheless, essentially correct. Whereas in Britain the Labour Party was created by the trade unions, the Russian trade unions from their beginning led their existence in the shadow of the political movement. Although sporadic economic associations of workers occurred as early as in the eighties and even seventies of the last century, it is, broadly speaking, true that the political organization, more specifically the Russian Social Democratic Workers' Party,[2] and not the trade unions, held the birthright in the Russian labor movement.

Lenin on trade unions

Revolutionary socialist politics did not, however, gain ascendancy over the economic movement without some struggle. In 1899 a group of socialists, who were soon labelled "Economists," set out to dispute the supremacy of revolutionary politics. For a short time they did so with some success; they found strong support even among underground circles of socialists. But their success was shortlived. By 1903, when the Social Democratic Party held its second Congress, at which it split into Bolsheviks and Mensheviks, the influence of the "Economists" had already waned. Among the Social Democrats who preached the primacy of revolutionary politics, the young Lenin played a very prominent role. In his polemical writings against the "Economists" he first developed his views on trade unionism, views which he was to hold, in almost unmodified form, up to 1917. Even after 1917 his approach to trade unions was in the main governed by the broad view of the inter-relationship of economics and politics, class, party and trade unions, which he had expressed in those early polemics. It is therefore worthwhile briefly to survey Lenin's ideas on the subject:

When . . . the first International was formed, the question of the significance of the Trade Unions and of the workers' economic struggle was
raised at its first Congress in Geneva in 1866. The resolution of that Congress underlined with precision the significance of the economic struggle,
warning socialists and workers, on the one hand, against overrating its importance (which was characteristic for the English workers at that time) and,
on the other, against underrating it (which was characteristic for the French
and the Germans, especially the followers of Lassalle). The resolution recognized that Trade Unions were not only legitimate but necessary as long as

---

[2] The Russian Social Democratic Party was formed at the turn of the century;
it was the mother-party of Menshevism (moderate socialism) and Bolshevism
(communism).

capitalism existed; it recognized them to be extremely important in the organization of the working class in its daily struggle against capital and for the
abolition of wage labor. The resolution also stated that Trade Unions ought
not to pay their attention exclusively to "the direct struggle against capital,"
that they ought not to keep aloof from the political and social movement of the
working class. They ought not to pursue "narrow" objectives, but they ought
to strive for the general emancipation of the oppressed millions of the working
people. . . . The conviction that the single class struggle ought necessarily
to unite the political and the economic struggle has become part and parcel of
the international social democratic outlook.[3]

The attitude of the "Economists" was by no means uniform or clear-
cut. Some of them were opposed to the creation of a political Social
Democratic Party; others merely urged the party, then in its first
formative period, to base its policy exclusively or primarily on the
immediate economic interests of the workers. Against this Lenin argued
that (a) the party should, of course, base its activity *inter alia* on the
workers' immediate economic interests, and (b) that those interests
formed a highly inadequate basis for the party's policy as a whole:

> For the socialist the economic struggle serves as the basis for the organiza-
> tion of workers in a revolutionary party, for the consolidation and develop-
> ment of the class struggle against the whole capitalist system. But if the
> economic struggle is regarded as something self-sufficient, then, there is nothing
> socialist in it. And in the experience of all European countries we have had
> many not only socialist but also anti-socialist Trade Unions.
> "To assist in the economic struggle of the proletariat" [this was what the
> "Economists" wanted]—is the job of the bourgeois politician. The task of the
> socialist is to make the economic struggle of the workers assist the socialist
> movement and contribute to the success of the revolutionary socialist party.[4]

The entire Leninist conception of proletarian class struggle was
implied in this deliberately paradoxical epigram. Lenin saw the working class as a heterogeneous mass consisting of the most diverse
elements and representing the most diverse levels of "class-consciousness." Various groups of workers are immediately interested merely
in securing their own, narrow, material advantage. They may try to
secure it against the interests of other groups of workers, an attitude
characteristic of craft trade unionism. Other groups may try to secure
immediate advantages at the expense even of their own long-term
interests. Sections of the working class thus try to assert themselves
against the rest of the class; and at times even the whole working
class sacrifices its collective and permanent interests for the sake of
meretricious and transitory benefits. It was true in Lenin's view, as

---

[3] Lenin, *Sochinenya* (Works), 4th ed., Vol. IV, pages 158–159.
[4] *Ibid.*, Vol. IV, page 270.

Marx had pointed out, that modern industry tended to organize the proletariat for class struggle, to shape its collective mind and to form its revolutionary will; but it was also true that the unity of the working class was being constantly disrupted by centrifugal forces, that its class consciousness was constantly disintegrating and that its collective will was being dissipated in the pursuit of the most diverse and contradictory objectives.

This dialectical contradiction between the unifying and the disruptive tendencies formed the background against which Lenin viewed the respective roles of various labor organizations, and analyzed the relative antagonism between trade unionism and political socialism. It was, he said, the peculiar task of the Socialist (and later of the Communist) Party to unify the proletariat for the pursuit of its corporate and permanent interest—the overthrow of capitalism and the establishment of socialism. To this objective the party had to subordinate the sectional or temporary interests of the working class. It was, on the other hand, inherent in trade unionism that it should devote its energy to the workers' sectional and temporary advantages.

From this fundamental difference in the functions of trade union and party followed the profound differences in the outlook and structure of the two organizations. The trade union tended to embrace the bulk of the working class. It was a mass organization *par excellence*. The party, on the other hand, ought to embrace only the most advanced, class conscious, and disciplined elements of the class. It was, or should be an *élite* organization, for only such an *élite*, closely knit and politically trained, could be the unifying and leading factor in the life of the working class. In this sense the Socialist Party was the "vanguard of the proletariat."

At first sight this conception resembled various older theories of "active minorities" or groups of revolutionary initiative, of which Blanquism had been the best known in Europe. Lenin was, indeed, charged with following in the footsteps of Blanqui and expounding the idea of a revolution accomplished by a small minority. The resemblance, he replied, was superficial. Blanqui believed in revolution accomplished by a conspiratorial *élite*, without the participation, and regardless of the attitude, of the majority of the nation. Not so Lenin. His *élite* or the proletarian vanguard, organized in the party, was not called upon to make the revolution by itself. Its task was to persuade, prepare, and organize the vast majority of the nation for the upheaval. Socialist revolution could win and succeed only if it was approved and supported by the majority; but that majority had to be enlightened and guided by a class-conscious Marxist minority. In periods of reaction or slow social development the party might be isolated from the working class. But in the process of revolution it would assume the actual leadership of the broadest masses of the working people.

In the light of this conception, the relationship between party and trade unions could not be free from some dualism. The Marxist vanguard must not turn its back upon the trade unions. Since its purpose was to influence and lead the mass of the workers, it had, on the contrary, to turn to the trade unions, in which that mass was organized; but it could turn to them only in the sense in which the leader turns to the led. In no circumstances could it place itself on an equal footing with the trade unions—this would amount to a renunciation of its own peculiar mission. It was the task of the party to see to it that the struggle for "bread and butter," led by the trade unions, should not deflect the workers from, but that it should prepare them for the revolutionary transformation of society. As long as the trade unions were willing to be guided along that path, their role was, from the party's viewpoint, progressive. As soon, however, as they proclaimed their "neutrality" in politics, or, what was worse, the primacy of their narrowly economic pursuits, the party inevitably came in conflict with them, for the trade unions were now in fact reconciling themselves with the existing social order. From the Marxist viewpoint, their struggle for "bread and butter" could, anyhow, not be effective in the long run, for even if they succeeded in obtaining higher wages or better labor conditions for their workers, the share of the working class in the national income was in the longer run bound to decline as long as capitalism existed.

Lenin emphasized another crucial difference between party and trade unions. The trade union is strictly a workers' organization, whereas the party concerns itself with the condition of all social classes. The central figure in the Social Democratic Party is not and should not be the man with the outlook of a trade union secretary but the tribune of the people.

. . . the "Economists" always lapse from Social Democracy back into *Trade Unionism*.[5] The political struggle waged by Social Democrats is far more extensive and complex than the economic struggle of the workers against the employers and the government. Similarly, the organization of a Revolutionary Social Democratic Party must inevitably *differ* from the organizations of the workers for economic struggle. A workers' organization must in the first place be a trade organization; secondly, it must be as wide as possible; and, thirdly, there must be as little clandestinity about it as possible. (Here and farther I have, of course, only autocratic Russian in mind.) On the contrary,

---

[5] Lenin uses the English expression "trade unionism" in the Russian text to denote the negative aspects of the trade unionist's attitude. In this pejorative sense the English expression has ever since been used by Russian Bolshevik writers.

the organization of revolutionaries ought to embrace first of all and mainly people for whom their revolutionary activity is their [main] occupation. . . . In view of this common characteristic of the members of such an organization, *every distinction between workers and intellectuals ought to vanish,* not to speak of distinctions between occupations. . . .[6]

Trade unions in the 1905 revolution and after

The supremacy of revolutionary politics over trade unionism became apparent in the first Russian revolution of 1905. The tsarist autocracy was greatly weakened; and the trade unions, for the first time enjoying full freedom of organization, gained considerable membership. Nevertheless, their role in the turbulent strike movement of that year was only secondary. In St. Petersburg, the capital and the centre of the revolution, they were completely overshadowed by a new institution that had spontaneously sprung into being—the Council of Workers' Delegates, the first Soviet in history. So, incidentally, were also the political parties, some of which, especially the Bolsheviks, were at first vaguely opposed to the Soviet. It was this Council of Workers' Delegates that actually inspired the great general strike of November 1905, which, together with the December rising in Moscow, marked the culmination of the revolution. Even the campaign for the eight hour day was proclaimed primarily by the Soviet.

The auxiliary role of the trade unions was emphasized in a resolution adopted by a Congress of the Russian Social Democratic Workers' Party (April and May 1906), at which Bolsheviks and Mensheviks reunited into a single party. The resolution stated that "in the atmosphere of a revolutionary epoch the trade unions, apart from defending the economic interests of the workers, draw the working class into direct political struggle and assist in its broad organization and political unification."[7] The Congress obliged all members of the party to join trade unions and participate in their work; and it pronounced itself in favor of setting up "nonparty" trade unions. At the same time the Congress rejected any notion of political neutrality of the unions. At this Congress the Bolsheviks insisted that the party ought to do its utmost to secure its actual leadership in the nonparty unions, whereas the resolution adopted spoke vaguely about the need for an "organic connexion" between party and unions.

The relationship between party and trade unions underwent some change after 1906, in the years of counter-revolution, under the so-called regime of June 3. For quite a few years the political parties

[6] *Ibid.,* pages 421–422.
[7] *V.K.P. (b) o Profsoyuzakh* (All-Union Communist Party on Trade Unions) 2nd ed. (Moscow, 1940), pages 12–13.

were wrecked and demoralized by defeat. The Mensheviks never succeeded in reconstituting a solid clandestine organization; the Bolsheviks did so only slowly and with great difficulty. The regime of June 3 did not spare the trade unions either. Many unions were banned; their members were severely punished for participation in strikes or other economic activity. But some trade unions were allowed to exist under close police supervision. This soon gave rise to hesitation in the ranks of the Social Democratic Party. The so-called "Liquidators" among the Mensheviks (those who were prepared to give up clandestine political organization) were inclined to confine themselves to such forms of activity as were tolerated by the government. They were consequently ready to accept virtually nonpolitical trade unions. At the London Congress of the party, in 1907, an attempt was made to revise the party's attitude toward trade unions. A motion tabled at the Congress stated that "the premature establishment of an organizational connection [between the Social Democratic Party and the Trade Unions] may result . . . in separation and alienation between the political and the economic organizations of the proletariat. . . . On the other hand, as experience has shown, the Trade Unions which are neutral *vis-à-vis* the parties have, in the overwhelming majority of cases, adhered to a class policy and have not held aloof from the general proletarian movement." [8] The practical conclusion was that the Social Democrats should give up their aspiration to lead the trade unions wherever their insistence on this threatened to weaken the unions. This attempt to revise the party's attitude brought forth a sharp protest from Lenin. The Congress was unable to reach a conclusion; and four resolutions submitted on the matter were not put to the vote.

Soon afterwards, the joint Bolshevik-Menshevik Central Committee of the party restated its attitude in a manner which, on the whole, conformed with Lenin's attitude. The idea of neutral trade unions was once again ruled out of court. The party was, on the other hand, warned that it should not try to impose itself upon the unions; it should rather secure its influence by way of solid propaganda and organization; and it should exercise that influence so as not to weaken the unity of the trade unionists in their economic struggle. Acknowledging that the tsarist government had succeeded in routing many or most of the trade unions, the Central Committee pointed out that this was due to the fact that the unions had failed to build up strong nuclei within the factories and the workshops. To withstand further repression they should be firmly anchored in the factories and workshops.

---

[8] *V.K.P. (b) v Rezolutsiyakh* (Resolutions of the All-Union Communist Party) 5th ed. (Moscow, 1936), Vol. I, pages 116–117.

The Social Democratic Party, on the other hand, ought to form its own nuclei within those wider trade union nuclei in the factories.[9]

This resolution, endorsed by both Bolsheviks and Mensheviks in February 1908, suggested the pattern for the so-called "fractions" and cells that later were to become characteristic for the communist method of organization. At the bottom of the organizational pyramid there is the broad mass of workers, many of them inert or backward; the more advanced or active part of that mass is organized in trade unions and leads the rest, especially in times of economic conflict with employers and/or with the government; within the trade union the most politically minded and organized elements form the party cell, which should, thanks to its moral authority, superior experience and skill, guide the trade unions directly or indirectly; the activities of the party cells in their turn are guided and coordinated, directly or indirectly, by the leadership of the party. Thus the leadership of the party should be able to exercise—through a whole series of intermediate links—its influence upon the broadest masses. (At a later period the trade unions were to be called the "transmission belts" between the party and the main body of the working class.)

In subsequent years this scheme of organization could not be put into operation on any wide scale. The labor movement was in a state of depression until roughly 1912, when a political revival manifested itself in many strikes. This revival was for a time interrupted by the outbreak of World War I.

Trade Unions and the Revolution

The effect of the revolution that took place in February 1917 was in one way similar to that of the revolution of 1905: the newly won political freedom favored the rapid growth of the trade unions. In 1905 the trade unions counted 250,000 members. During the first months of 1917 their membership rose from a few scores of thousands to 1.5 million. These numbers reflected the general urge of workers to use the newly won freedom of organization.

The practical role of the trade unions in the revolution did not, however, correspond to their numerical strength. It was even less significant than in 1905. For one thing, in 1917 strikes never assumed the scale and power they had in 1905. The economic ruin of Russia at war, the galloping inflation, the scarcity of consumers' goods, and so on, made normal "bread and butter" struggle unreal. In addition, the threat of mobilization hung over would-be strikers. The working class was in no mood to strive for limited economic advantages and partial

---

[9] *V.K.P. (b) o Profsoyuzakh*, pages 30–31.

reforms. The entire social order of Russia was at stake. Even more than in 1905 the trade unions were now overshadowed by the Soviets, and at no significant turn of the revolution did they come to the fore.

As in all labor organizations, so in the unions the extreme and the moderate parties—Bolsheviks, Mensheviks, and Social Revolutionaries —confronted one another in a ceaseless and intense struggle for influence. At first the trade unions, like the Soviets, were dominated by the Mensheviks, who nominally favored the unions' political neutrality. On behalf of the Labor Ministry of the Kerensky Government, Maisky (the future Soviet ambassador in London, then still a Menshevik) claimed to guide the trade unions in this spirit.[10] Actually, under Menshevik leadership the trade unions supported the Kerensky Government and its war policy. The Menshevik advocacy of neutrality was mainly a form of their opposition to the growth of Bolshevik influence in the trade unions.

As they were preparing for the seizure of power, Lenin and his followers tried to approach the trade unions from a new angle and to define their role in the Soviet system. The central economic idea that Lenin then expounded was "workers' control" over industry. This did not yet amount to wholesale socialization or nationalization of the economy. "Workers' control" was to be a sort of dual control of employers and workers over industry, a condominium in which the workers were to train themselves for future exclusive management and in which they were progressively to widen the sphere of their responsibility. Lenin did not envisage any prolonged collaboration between the classes; and his "workers' control" can therefore not be compared with, say, the British joint production committees. "Workers' control," on the contrary, provided the framework for the struggle between capitalists and workers in a transition period, at the end of which the former were to be expropriated. The trade unions were expected to play their part in establishing "workers' control."

A resolution of the Bolshevik Central Committee, passed some time before the October revolution, contained the following scheme of the control:

For such control it is necessary: (1) that in all important establishments there should be secured for the workers a majority of not less than three quarters of all votes. It is thereby obligatory to draw into participation the industrialists who have not deserted their businesses and the educated technical and scientific personnel; (2) that the factory committees, the central and local Councils of Workers', Peasants', and Soldier's Delegates and the Trade Unions should obtain the right to participate in control, that all commercial

---

[10] 1. *Vserossiiskii Syezd Profsoyuzov* (First All-Russian Congress of Trade Unions), (Moscow, 1918), page 10.

books and bank accounts should be opened to them and all data obligatorily supplied to them; and (3) that representatives of all influential democratic and socialist parties should obtain the same rights.[11]

From these terms it is clear that the dual power of capitalists and workers in industry was designed to end in the complete elimination of the former—very few capitalists could be expected to reconcile themselves to a situation in which at least three-quarters of the controlling votes belonged to the workers.

Another significant point is the order in which the various labor organizations participating in "workers' control" were enumerated: the factory committees came first, then the Soviets, and only in the last instance the trade unions. This order corresponded to the actual importance that the three types of organization had in the economic upheaval, as distinct from the political revolution in which the Soviets came first.

The factory committees constituted the most direct representation of the workers and employees of any factory and workshop. They were the primary and basic units of organization, much narrower than the trade unions or the Soviets, but of much greater weight in the establishment of workers' control. The struggle for that control was waged within every factory or workshop of any significance, and its immediate purpose was control by the workers "on the spot." At this stage the Bolsheviks appeared as adherents of the most extreme decentralization of economic power, which gave their Menshevik opponents the opportunity to charge them with abandoning Marxism in favor of anarchism. Actually, Lenin and his followers remained firm upholders of the Marxist conception of the centralized state. Their immediate objective, however, was not yet to set up the centralized proletarian dictatorship but to decentralize as much as possible the bourgeois state and the bourgeois economy. This was a necessary condition for the success of the revolution. In the economic field, therefore, the factory committee, the organ "on the spot," rather than the trade union, was the most potent and deadly instrument of upheaval. Thus the trade unions were relegated to the background not only by the Soviets but also by the factory committees.[12]

---

[11] *V.K.P. (b) o Profsoyuzakh*, page 62.

[12] At the first All-Russian Conference of Factory Committees, which opened a few days before the October revolution, Schmidt, the future Commissar for Labor in Lenin's Government, stated: "At the moment when the factory committees were formed the Trade Unions actually did not yet exist, and the factory committees filled the vacuum." Later on, after the trade unions gained in strength, "control from below" was exercised by the factory committees. See *Oktyabrskaya Revolutsiya i Fabzavkomy* (The October Revolution and the Factory Committees) (Moscow, 1927), II, page 188. Another speaker stated at the

Another body that stole the trade unions' thunder was the Workers' Section of the Soviet. This consisted of those members of the Soviet who had been directly elected in factories and workshops. The Workers' Section often held meetings and conferences independently of the Soviet as a whole and its decisions on matters of labor policy were accepted as authoritative by the workers.

After the October revolution

This multiplicity of overlapping organizations gave rise to much confusion and friction soon after the October revolution. Having assumed power, the Bolsheviks were anxious to bring some order out of the revolutionary chaos. The old machinery of the state had been crushed, and the economy of the country had lost any sign of coherence. Centralization of political power and of economic control was now indispensable if the newly formed Soviet Government was to survive. At their first attempts at central control over industry, the Bolsheviks came into conflict with the factory committees, on which they had so strongly relied prior to the revolution. The anarchic characteristics of the committees made themselves felt: every factory committee aspired to have the last and final say on all matters affecting the factory, its output, its stock of raw materials, its conditions of work, etc., and paid little or no attention to the needs of industry as a whole. A few weeks after the upheaval, the factory committees attempted to form their own national organization, which was to secure their virtual economic dictatorship. The Bolsheviks now called upon the trade unions to render a special service to the nascent Soviet State and to discipline the factory committees. The unions came

conference: " . . . the growth of the influence of the factory committees has naturally occurred at the expense of centralized economic organizations of the working class such as the Trade Unions. . . . This, of course, is a highly abnormal development which has in practice led to very undesirable results . . ."(*Ibid.* page 190). Against this an anarchist speaker argued: "The Trade Unions wish to devour the factory committees. There is no popular discontent with the factory committees, but there is discontent with the Trade Unions. . . . To the workers the Trade Union is a form of organization imposed from without. The factory committee is closer to them. . . . Anarchists think that they should set up and develop the cells of future society. . . . The factory committees are such cells of the future. . . . They, not the state, will now administer. . . ." (*Ibid.* page 191). The anarchist influence in the factory committees was fairly strong at that time, but the antagonism between Bolshevism and anarchism was still largely hidden. In the first half of 1917 the Mensheviks, dominating the trade unions, tried in vain to bring the factory committees under control. The Bolsheviks then juxtaposed the factory committees to the trade unions and so they had some common ground with the anarchists. (*Ibid.* page 104). The Bolshevik attitude changed later in the year when, having gained the decisive influence in the trade unions, they sought to subordinate the factory committees to the trade unions.

out firmly against the attempt of the factory committees to form a national organization of their own. They prevented the convocation of a planned All-Russian Congress of Factory Committees and demanded total subordination on the part of the committees. The committees, however, were too strong to surrender altogether. Toward the end of 1917 a compromise was reached, under which the factory committees accepted a new status: they were to form the primary organizations upon which the trade unions based themselves; but by the same token they were, of course, incorporated in the unions. Gradually they gave up the ambition to act, either locally or nationally, in opposition to the trade unions or independently of them. The unions now became the main channels through which the government was assuming effective control over industry.

This was roughly the situation when the first All-Russian Congress of the Trade Unions assembled in Moscow in the second week of January 1918.[13] The trade unions had asserted themselves against the factory committees, but in other respects their position had not been clearly defined. Not only did the spokesmen of the various parties— Bolsheviks, Mensheviks, Social Revolutionaries, and Anarchists— advance conflicting views; but also within the ranks of Bolshevik trade unionists there was as yet little agreement on the principles of the new trade unionism.

Debates at the first Trade Union Congress

The issue before the Congress was in the words of Mikhail Tomsky, the leading Bolshevik trade unionist, whether "the trade unions should tie their fortunes to those of the Soviet Government or whether they should remain independent organs of economic class struggle." Tomsky's own answer was clear enough, if only general in character:

Even before the October revolution the general condition of industry compelled the Trade Unions to give up strike action. . . . Now, when the proletariat has assumed the political and economic leadership of the country and removed the *bourgeoisie* from the management of industry, the struggle of the workers for the improvement of their position has naturally had to take on new forms, the forms of an organized action, through the Trade Unions and through various regulating bodies, upon the economic policy of the working class as a whole. The sectional interests of groups of workers have had to be subordinated to the interests of the entire class.[14]

[13] This was the first fully-fledged Trade Union Congress in the whole history of Russia. In 1905 and 1906 and then in the summer of 1917 only conferences of active trade unionists but not of elected delegates took place.
[14] See Tomsky's Preface to *1. Vserossiiskii Syezd Profsoyuzov.*

Against this the Mensheviks advocated the independence of the trade unions. Their argument was put briefly by Maisky:

> Comrades, although other views are now popular among many workers, we still think that our revolution remains, as we used to say, a bourgeois revolution, and that the Trade Unions have therefore to perform their customary jobs. . . . I suppose that capitalism will unfortunately very soon reassert itself with all its might and power. I think therefore that if capitalism remains intact, the tasks with which Trade Unions are confronted under capitalism remain unaltered as well.[15]

This argument was in line with the traditional Menshevik view that the Russian revolution could not, because of Russia's backward outlook, be socialist in character, and that it could only usher in a bourgeois-democratic republic. What was implied even in this Menshevik argument was that if, contrary to the Menshevik forecast, the revolution should develop along socialist lines, then there was no reason for socialists to insist on the independence of the trade unions— their task would then be to assist the government in the transformation of the economic and social system. In theory, there was no difference between the Bolsheviks and the Mensheviks on this crucial point. The role of the trade unions was seen by both to be secondary, and the discussion centered primarily on the prospects of the revolution.

Those who foresaw a restoration of capitalism and thought that the Bolshevik regime would prove an historical episode, thought it unwise for the trade unions to give up their independence during that episode —the trade unions, they said, must be ready to face a restored capitalism. This view was shared by some Bolsheviks such as Ryazanov and Lozovsky, the future leader of the Profintern, the Red Trade Union International. But the majority took the socialist character of the revolution for granted; and they were concerned with defining the status of the unions in the new regime rather than with perparing them for the contingency of a counter revolution. The question that Zinoviev, on behalf of the party, put before the Congress seemed to most delegates to admit one answer only: "I ask you," said Zinoviev, "why and from whom do you need independence: from your own government . . . ? The Trade Unions have already issued decrees on requisitions and on many other measures of prime importance, decrees which are normally issued only by the state administration." [16]

Thus, at this stage, the official Bolshevik view was that the trade unions should be subordinated to the government, since they themselves acted as part of the administration. But did this mean that the

---

[15] *1. Vserossiiskii Syezd Profsoyuzov*, p. 11.
[16] *Ibid.* page 75.

trade unions should be completely absorbed by the administration, that they should be "statified"? [17] If so, how were bodies that counted three million members [18] to be fitted in with the machinery of the new state? What was to be their relationship with the Soviets, that backbone of the new republic? Lozovsky described to the Congress the constant friction between Soviets and trade unions that had developed in the few months since the revolution.[19] The Soviets demanded that the trade unions should take their orders from them. The All-Russian Central Council of Trade Unions (ACCTU) protested against this and impressed upon its branches that they did not come under the Soviets and that they should not allow the latter to interfere with the direction of the economic struggle. Although they accepted subordination to the government as a matter of high policy, the Bolshevik trade unionists jealously guarded the prerogatives of their organization. At the same time the Central Council of the Trade Unions was gaining considerable influence inside the new governmental machine. The Central Council of Trade Unions was, immediately after the revolution, accorded thirty-five seats, from one-fourth to one-third of all seats on the Central Executive Committee of the Soviets, the highest legislative and executive body during the intervals between the All-Russian Congresses of the Soviets.[20] The trade unions were also invited to send their delegates to most of the other newly formed governmental bodies. The Central Council of Trade Unions was often prevented from accepting such invitations by shortage of personnel and it passed on the invitations to the central committees of particular trade unions.

In spite of all this, Lozovsky objected to Zinoviev's description of trade unions as "organs of governmental power": ". . . the Trade Unions would . . . lose very much. . . . What would it mean for them to become 'organs of state power'? This would mean that the decisions of the Trade Unions would be carried out by compulsion . . . that they would not be connected with the activity of the mass of productive workers." [21] Coercion, Lozovsky went on, would take the place of spontaneous class solidarity. Under full socialism the statification of the trade unions would probably be justified, but Russia would

---

[17] This is a literal translation of the Russian word used throughout this controversy, for which there is no suitable English equivalent.

[18] *Ibid.* page 29.

[19] *Ibid.* page 31.

[20] *Ibid.* page 35. The Central Executive Committee of the Soviets consisted of 101 members in November 1917, immediately after the revolution. Through co-optation and additional elections their number grew to 200 in the course of 1918.

[21] *Ibid.,* page 97.

become socialist only after the revolution had won in the west, and until then the trade unions should not allow themselves to be absorbed by the state.[22] This division between adherents and opponents of statification cut across normal party divisions: some Left Social Revolutionaries advocated the incorporation of the trade unions by the state more categorically than did the Bolsheviks.[23]

The resolution adopted by the Congress reflected, at least in part, this conflict of views. It rejected political neutrality of the trade unions as a "bourgeois idea," for "there is and there can be no neutrality in the great historic struggle between revolutionary socialism and its opponents." The trade unions pledged their support to the government in all essential matters:

> The centre of gravity of Trade Union work must now shift to the organizational-economic sphere. . . . The Trade Unions ought to shoulder the main burden of organizing production and of rehabilitating the country's shattered productive forces. Their most urgent tasks consist in their energetic participation in all central bodies called upon to regulate output, in the organization of workers' control, registration and redistribution of labor force, organization of exchange between town and countryside, in the most active participation in the demobilization of industry, in the struggle against sabotage and in enforcing the general obligation to work, and so on.

The mere enumeration of these functions showed the trade unions as most important props of the new regime. Yet the Congress of the Trade Unions could not bring itself to declare that the trade unions would at once form part and parcel of the new administration—it spoke about their statification in vague and conditional terms:

> *After they have fully developed* the Trade Unions should, in the process of the present socialist revolution, become organs of socialist power, and as such they should work in coordination with, and subordination to other bodies in order to carry into effect the new principles. . . .
> The Congress is convinced that in consequence of the foreshadowed process, the Trade Unions will inevitably become transformed into organs of the socialist state, and the participation in the Trade Unions will for all people employed in any industry be their duty *vis-à-vis* the state.[24]

The resolution implied that in the nearest future the trade unions would be hybrid organizations, performing many vital functions for the state, but remaining outside the formal framework of the governmental machine. Two general principles seemed to have been accepted: (a) that in a socialist economy the state would completely incorporate

---

[22] *Ibid.*, page 197.

[23] *Ibid.*, page 128.

[24] *Ibid.*, page 364 ff.

the trade unions, and (b) that socialist economy was not yet in existence and the trade unions still had a role of their own to perform. But the main specific questions concerning that role were left open. The Congress could not make up its mind, for instance, on whether the unions should continue to resort to strike action in defense of their members. A motion, tabled by Tsyperovich, a prominent Bolshevik trade unionist, which answered the question in the affirmative, was rejected.[25] On the other hand the Bolshevik Party with its fresh memories of its own pre-revolutionary activity was not ready to come out explicitly against strikes.

A number of administrative functions ("state-functions" as Lenin put it) were transferred to the trade unions. A decree issued in December 1917 entrusted the unions with the administration of all social insurance schemes, even though this might as well have been the job of the newly formed Commissariat of Labor, which it indeed became somewhat later. The Commissariat of Labor and the trade unions overlapped from the beginning, although Schmidt, the head of the Commissariat, was appointed on a proposal of the trade unions and was himself a trade unionist.

The trade unions further formed "control-distributive commissions" whose task it was to exercise direct and indirect control over industry, through so-called *local control commissions* elected by workers in the workshops. The control-distributive commissions were half elected by the factory control commissions and half appointed by the trade unions. At that time, we know, the Soviet Government was not yet committed to immediate and wholesale socialization of industry. But privately owned factories were under workers' control, which, since the relegation of the factory committees, was carried out by the control-distributive commissions of the trade unions. A resolution on this subject stated *inter alia* [26] that "it was the task of workers' control to put an end to autocracy in the economic field just as an end has been put to it in the political field." Industrial management by committee as opposed to individual management was now the characteristically revolutionary feature of economic policy.

All forms of economic organization were in utter flux, however; and so the prerogatives of the trade unions could not be clearly defined. More important still, the whole concept of workers' control over industry (with private ownership still tolerated) was soon to be abandoned, under the pressure of civil war; and the trade unions had to adjust themselves to the needs of a new situation.

---

[25] *Ibid.,* page 367.
[26] *Ibid.,* pages 369–372.

Trade unions in the civil war

When civil war flared up in 1918 the Bolsheviks possessed little
more than the rudiments of an administrative machine of their own.
The old army had disintegrated and a new one had to be formed. No
governmental organization existed capable of recruiting men for the
Red Army and of ensuring supplies. The Soviets were unwieldy and
the party itself had too many tasks to cope with. The trade unions,
whose nominal membership grew to 3.5 million in the first year of the
fighting, transformed themselves into organs of civil war. It was
mainly through them that the government assessed and mobilized
manpower. The Central Council of the trade unions issued weekly
progress reports on this work, and most trade unions formed special
supply services for the Red Army. As the civil war dragged on the
trade unions called up and armed 50 per cent of their own members.

The unions assumed an entirely new and enormous responsibility
when the government, afraid that privately owned industry would
not work for the needs of the Red Army, speeded up the process of
total socialization, at first as a matter of military, rather than of
economic, policy. Workers' control, in the sense given to it in 1917,
came to an end. Unexpectedly for both the Bolshevik Party and the
trade unions, the "state functions" of the latter expanded with
enormous rapidity, even though the administration of social insurance,
at this stage more nominal than real anyhow, was transferred back
from the trade unions to the Commissariat of Labor in December 1918.

In line with this development the second All-Russian Congress of
Trade Unions (January 1919) placed more emphasis than did its
predecessor on the "state functions" of unions. The Congress sanctioned
the arrangements under which the unions had become at once military
recruiting offices, supply services, punitive organs, and so on. Tomsky
had no hesitation in stating: "At this moment when the Trade Unions
regulate wages and conditions of labor, when the appointment
of the Commissar for Labor, too, depends on our Congress, no strikes
can take place in Soviet Russia." [27] Addressing the Congress, Lenin
spoke about the "inevitable statification of the Trade Unions" and
illustrated his point by saying that a Supreme Council of National
Economy had just been set up primarily by the trade unions to direct
the entire economy of the republic. "It is not enough to proclaim the

---

[27] 2. *Vserossiiskii Syezd Profsoyuzov,* page 96. This change in the trade unions,
even though it had been caused by the civil war, did not fail to provoke ferment
in the Bolshevik Party. At the second Trade Union Congress, Lozovsky, having
left the party, spoke as an independent "internationalist" against Bolshevik policy
in the unions, *ibid.* page 37.

dictatorship of the proletariat . . . it is necessary that the Trade Unions merge with the organs of state power and that they take over the entire large scale economic construction. . . ." It was possible to argue over the pace of the merger, and Lenin held it to be a mistake to try to effect it "at a single stroke." But the general trend of the development was—in Lenin's view—beyond dispute.[28]

It would, nevertheless, be wrong to describe Lenin at this stage as an advocate of statification *tout court*. His view on the new trade unions was part of a wider conception of the Soviet State. He saw the trade unions as being incorporated by the state; but at the same time he expounded his ideas about the "withering away" of the state. The state was gradually to cease to be a distinct administrative machine separated from, opposed to, and elevated above the people. Every shepherd, "every cook" was to learn the business of government so that there should be no need for a special body of civil servants. The trade unions were to educate the mass of the workers in the arts of administration. "We must ever more broaden," these were Lenin's words, "the participation of the workers themselves in the direction of the economy. . . . If we fail to convert the Trade Unions into organs educating the masses, on a scale ten times larger than at present, for the immediate participation in the direction of the state, then we shall not achieve our objective in building communism." [29]

However, the "withering away" of the state, for all the doctrinal importance attached to this point, was a matter of the future, whereas the merger of trade unions and the administration was of urgent practical significance. But the mode of the merger was not clear. Were the trade unions to absorb the state or *vice versa?* So far this question had not even been posed: and the two variants of the merger were often confused. Sometimes the claim of the unions to dominate a particular branch of the administration was openly recognized, as in the case of the Commissariat of Labor. At the second Congress of the Trade Unions Schmidt thus described the relationship between his Commissariat and the trade unions:

The role of the Commissariat . . . should be to give obligatory effect to the recommendations and plans worked out by the Trade Unions. Moreover, not only must the Commissariat not interfere with the prerogatives of the Unions, but even the organs of the Commissariat . . . should, as far as possible, be formed by the Trade Unions themselves. Here, at the centre, we act consistently upon this principle. Not only does the All-Russian Central Council of

[28] *Ibid.,* pages 31–32.
[29] *Ibid.,* page 33. The same idea was expressed in the debate by Ryazanov: "But our ideal is not further statification but the de-statification of the entire social life." *Ibid.,* page 39.

the Trade Unions propose the candidate for the post of the People's Commissar for Labor—the Trade Unions have also organized the entire leading team [Collegium] of the Commissariat.[30]

Yet, so complete a subordination of a governmental department to the unions was exceptional. At this stage a conflict that was to loom large in Soviet labor policy began to cast its shadow ahead. The Supreme Council of National Economy had begun to function. This was the nucleus of the new economic administration that gradually extended its control over the whole field of industry through the so-called *Glavki*, the managements of national industrial trusts. The trade unions had to be reorganized so that their vertical structure should correspond to that of the industrial administration. The apparatus of the Supreme Council of National Economy was, as we know, set up in cooperation with the trade unions, but it soon acquired an identity of its own. More and more the trade unions and the Supreme Council of National Economy (VSNKh) came into conflict. The VSNKh was inclined to regard the Unions as its auxiliaries, whereas at least some trade unionists held that the actual direction of industry was a prerogative of the unions. The conflict was aggravated when the VSNKh secured the cooperation of a number of technical specialists and old-time economic administrators, upon whom many trade unionists habitually looked with the utmost distrust. Here was clearly a great and dramatic conflict in the making.

"Point Five" of the 1919 Program

An attempt to give a new programmatic definition to the position of the trade unions was made by the Communist Party at its eighth Congress, in March 1919, when the party discussed and adopted a new program.

In its "Economic Section" (Point 5) the new program of the party stated:

The organizational apparatus of socialized industry ought to be based, in the first instance, on the Trade Unions. These ought progressively to free themselves from craft-like narrowness and transform themselves into large associations based on production and embracing the majority of the toilers in any branch of industry. . . .

Participating already, in accordance with the laws of the Soviet Republic and established practice, in all local and central organs of industrial administration, *the Trade Unions ought in the end actually to concentrate in their hand all the administration of the entire national economy.* . . . The par-

---

[30] *Ibid.,* page 47. The Congress adopted a special resolution urging close cooperation between the provincial branches of the two bodies, for in the provinces their relations had by no means been smooth.

ticipation of the Trade Unions in economic management . . . constitutes also the chief means of the struggle against the bureaucratization of the economic apparatus . . . (My italics. I. D.).[31]

This paragraph, the famous Point 5 of the Party Program, was to be invoked in later years by Bolshevik groups advocating the economic supremacy of the trade unions in the Soviet State. "Point 5" was, in the interpretation of those groups, the Magna Charta of the new trade unionism. And indeed, the view that "the Trade Unions ought in the end actually to concentrate in their hands all the administration of the entire national economy" savored of syndicalism, to which the Bolshevik Party, as a whole, had always been opposed. Lenin and the other Bolshevik leaders would soon have to do a lot of explaining away in order to invalidate this promissory note that the party so solemnly handed to the trade unions. The 1919 Program, however, contained also other clauses that may be said to have canceled out "Point 5" and limited, at any rate for the immediate future, the prerogatives of the trade unions by making labor policy a responsibility of the Soviets as well as of the unions:

Moreover, the Soviet government . . . has established in the Code of Labor Laws . . . the participation of labor organizations in the solution of problems of employment and release of labor . . . [it has established] state-regulated wages on the basis of tariffs worked out by Trade Unions . . . and organs for the assessment and distribution of the labor force, organs which are attached to Soviets and Trade Unions and are obliged to provide work for the unemployed.

Other points of the Program also dealt with the role of the trade unions. "Point 6" stated: "The next task of the economic policy of the Soviet government is . . . maximum utilization of all available labor force, its correct distribution and redistribution as between various geographic areas and various branches of the national economy, a task which [the Soviets] can accomplish only in close cooperation with the Trade Unions." "Point 7":

In view of the disintegration of capitalist organization of labor, the productive forces of the country can be rehabilitated and further developed and the socialist method of production can be enhanced only on the basis of comradely discipline among the toilers and of an utmost expansion of active citizenship. . . . The attainment of this objective requires stubborn and systematic work for the re-education of the masses, which has now been made easier because the working masses see that the capitalists, landlords, and merchants have in fact been eliminated. Through their own experience the masses arrive at the conviction that the standard of their well-being depends exclusively on

---

[31] *V.K.P.* (*b*) *o Profsoyuzakh,* page 95.

their own disciplined work. In the creation of a new socialist discipline the main role falls to the Trade Unions. Abandoning old clichés . . . the Trade Unions ought to adopt and try out in practice . . . labor accountancy, norms of output, responsibility [of workers] before special comradely workers' courts, etc.[32]

In "Point 8" the Program urged the unions to impress upon the workers the need to work with, and learn from, bourgeois technicians and specialists and to overcome the "ultra-radical" distrust of the latter. The workers, it was stated, could not build socialism without going through a period of apprenticeship to the bourgeois intelligentsia. On social policy the Program stated *inter alia:* "Striving for equality of remuneration for every kind of work, striving for full communism, the Soviet Government cannot set itself the task of bringing about that equality now, immediately, when only the first steps are being made in the transition from capitalism to communism." Payment of high salaries and premiums to bourgeois specialists was therefore sanctioned. This was, according to an expression used by Lenin, the ransom that the young proletarian state had to pay the bourgeois-bred technicians and scientists for services with which it could not dispense. Wages to manual workers, however, were still regulated in a more or less egalitarian spirit.[33]

Although the Program and many other resolutions tried to clarify the position of the unions, the trade unions, the Supreme Council of National Economy, the Commissariat of Labor, and the multiple organs of the soviets continued to overlap and clash with one another. The more confused their mutual relations, the more strongly did the Communist Party insist on its own supreme control over all those bodies. This was exercised through the system of party cells inside the trade unions.

The eighth conference of the party (December, 1919) worked out a statute that defined rigidly the rights and prerogatives of the cells.[34] The general idea of the statute was not new—it dated back to pre-revolutionary schemes of organization. What was new was the elaborate detail of the scheme calculated to secure for the party a leading role in every organization. These were the main provisions:

(*a*) Wherever at least three members of the party belonged to a trade union, they were obliged to form a cell (*fraktsya*—fraction) that was to take its orders from the corresponding regional or local party committee outside the trade union.

(*b*) If, inside a trade union, members of the party formed a fairly

[32] *Ibid.*, page 102 ff.
[33] *Ibid.*, pages 95–102.
[34] *Ibid.*, pages 109–110.

large group their *fraktsya* elected a bureau that was in charge of the entire party work inside the union.

(c) The *fraktsya* enjoyed autonomy *vis-à-vis* the party hierarchy in matters concerning the internal affairs of the *fraktsya;* but in case of a conflict between it and the party committee outside the trade union, the party committee had the last word. The party committee also had unrestricted right of appointment and dismissal: it could send any communist, even if he was not a member of the trade union, to serve on the communist *fraktsya* inside the trade union; and it could order any communist to leave any office in the trade union to which he had been elected.

(d) The *fraktsya* proposed its candidates to trade union offices in agreement with the local, regional, or central committee of the party.

(e) The *fraktsya*, or its bureau, discussed and took preliminary decisions on every issue that was expected to be placed on the agenda of any trade union body. Communist trade unionists were obliged to vote unanimously at the general meeting of the trade unions in accordance with decisions taken inside the *fraktsya,* but they were free to oppose those decisions during the preliminary discussion inside the *fraktsya.*

This system ran through the entire structure of the trade unions, from factory committee at the bottom to central committees of the trade unions and to the All-Russian Central Council of the Trade Unions at the top.[35] The communist trade unionist was thus a communist first and only then a trade unionist, and by his disciplined behavior he enabled the party to lead the trade unions.

Individual management and labor armies

The ninth Congress of the party (March–April, 1920) and the third All-Russian Congress of the Trade Unions (April, 1920) marked a new turn. The Bolshevik leaders then hoped that the civil war was at an end and that they would soon be free to turn toward the peaceful reconstruction of Russia's ruined economy. This hope was deferred, for the Russo-Polish war and the campaign against General Wrangel were still ahead. Nevertheless, the ninth Congress of the party sanctioned certain preparations for the transition to peace. The measures adopted were, as later developments showed, not always well suited to smooth that transition. The Bolshevik leaders were not fully aware of the vastness of the devastation and the chaos left behind by the civil war. Nor did they make sufficient allowance for the weariness of the urban

---

[35] This system of cells was built up in every nonparty organization, not only in the trade unions.

working class and the discontent of the peasantry. By inertia they carried on with the system of military communism established during the civil war. The main features of this were: conscription of all available man-power and wealth; socialization of all industrial property; prohibition of private trade; compulsory direction of labor; strict rationing of consumers' goods; payment of wages in kind; and requisitioning of agricultural produce from the peasants (in lieu of taxation). The ninth Congress foreshadowed the continuation and extension of these methods in time of peace. Two new measures stood in the center of debate: (a) the introduction of individual management in industry in place of management by committee, prevalent hitherto; and (b) further militarization of labor and formation of labor armies.

The substitution of individual for collective management in industry met with considerable opposition inside the trade unions, and its actual realization was delayed until 1922. The motive for this reform was economic expediency. Management by committee was found to be inefficient; the need for greater industrial discipline had become painfully obvious; and greater efficiency could be secured by individual management. It is enough to recall that only recently the trade unions had proclaimed an end to "economic autocracy in industry" to understand why the return to individual management could not but be decried by many trade unionists as the reappearance of that autocracy, even though the present managers were not the old industrialists or their nominees but directors appointed by the proletarian state. The authoritative spokesmen of the party—Lenin, Trotsky, and Bukharin—met the objections to individual management with the argument that the standing of the working class, as the ruling class in the Soviet Republic, was not involved in this controversy over individual or collective management. The working class, they stated, would through its representative organs merely delegate its power of economic disposition to industrial managers: "Individual management does not in any degree limit or infringe upon the rights of the [working] class or the 'rights' of the Trade Unions, because the class can exercise its rule in one form or another, as technical expediency may dictate. It is the ruling class at large which in every case 'appoints' persons for the managerial and administrative jobs." [36]

A resolution submitted by Trotsky and adopted by the Congress of the party did in fact allow the trade unions to exercise a very strong influence upon the appointment of industrial managers. The organization of industrial management "should be carried out by agreement between the organs of the Supreme Council of National Economy

---

[36] *Ibid.,* page 128.

and the corresponding organs of the Central Council of the Trade Unions." [37]

Four types of industrial management were provided for:

(*a*) Intelligent and energetic trade unionists might be appointed to posts of industrial managers. This was the most favored variant, but the difficulty was that few trade unionists with managerial abilities were available.

(*b*) Bourgeois technicians or specialists might be appointed to managerial posts. A manager of this category was supervised by a trade unionist commissar, in the same way in which the military specialist in the Army was supervised by the political commissar, who could veto his orders.

(*c*) Alternatively, a bourgeois technician could be appointed as manager with two trade unionists as assistant managers, who could, however, exercise no veto over his decisions. (This was apparently the case when the bourgeois technician was beyond suspicion of hostility toward the Soviet regime.)

(*d*) Management by committee was left in existence if the work of the managerial team had been satisfactory, but even then the powers of the chairman of the team were extended.

Meanwhile it was the task of the trade unions to train their advanced members for managerial responsibilities. Special trade union training centers were set up for this purpose.

The labor armies represented an even more fundamental issue of economic and labor policy affecting the trade unions. The originator of the labor armies was Trotsky, but at that time (1920) his scheme had the backing of the entire party leadership.[38] It arose empirically, in connection with the planned demobilization of the Red Army. Toward the end of the civil war transport was completely paralyzed, because of the destruction of rolling-stock and railway lines. It was impossible to release the soldiers and send them home. Entire divisions and armies wasted their time in inactivity, while industrial and in part agricultural production were at a standstill. It was then decided to employ idle detachments in coal-mining, timber-felling, harvesting, and so on. Later the government proceeded to mobilize civilian labor as well—it was only a step from the employment of armed forces as labor battalions to the organization of civilian labor into military units. In the aftermath of the civil war, amid its appalling

---

[37] *Ibid.*, page 117.

[38] In later years it became the fashion to decry the labor armies and to suggest that Trotsky exclusively was responsible for them. Yet Stalin himself served as the chairman of the Ukranian Council of the Labor Army, while Trotsky, as chairman of the Council of Labor and Defense, headed the all-Russian organization.

misery and complete breakdown of labor discipline, the government hoped to break in this way what looked like a hopeless economic deadlock.[39]

At the third Congress of the Trade Unions Trotsky defended the labor armies. His most vocal, though not the only, critics were the Mensheviks, who still enjoyed some freedom of expression and argued that militarization of labor would lower and not raise productivity, for high productivity could be obtained with free labor only. The central point in Trotsky's counter-argument was the denial of any real difference between voluntary and compulsory labor:

Let the Menshevik speakers explain to us [these were Trotsky's words] what is meant by free, noncompulsory labor. We have known slave-labor, serf-labor, compulsory regimented labor in the medieval crafts, and the labor of free wage-earners which the *bourgeoisie* calls free labor. We are now heading toward the type of labor that is socially regulated on the basis of an economic plan, obligatory for the whole country, compulsory for every worker. This is the basis of socialism. . . . The militarization of labor, in this fundamental meaning of which I have spoken, is the indispensable, basic method for the organization of our labor forces. . . . If our new form of organization of labor were to result in lower productivity, then, *ipso facto*, we would be heading for disaster. . . . But is it true that compulsory labor is always unproductive? . . . This is the most wretched and miserable liberal prejudice: chattel-slavery, too, was productive. Its productivity was higher than that of slave-labor, and in so far as serfdom and feudal lordship guaranteed the security of the towns . . . and of peasant labor, in so far it was a progressive form of labor. Compulsory serf-labor did not grow out of the feudal lords' ill-will. It was a progressive phenomenon. . . . The whole history of mankind is the history of its education for work, for higher productivity of labor. This is by no means so simple a task, for man is lazy and he has the right to be so. . . . Even free wage-labor was not productive at first . . . it became so gradually after a process of social education. All sorts of methods were used for that education. The *bourgeoisie* at first drove the peasant out to the high roads and grabbed his land. When the peasant refused to work in the factories, the *bourgeoisie* branded him with hot iron, hanged, or shot him and so forcibly trained him for manufacture.[40] . . . Our task is to educate the working class on socialist principles. What are our methods for that?

They are not less varied than those used by the *bourgeoisie*, but they are more honest, more direct and frank, uncorrupted by mendacity and fraud. The *bourgeoisie* had to pretend that its system of labor was free and it deceived

---

[39] In his report to the third Congress of the Trade Unions, Rykov, then chief of the Supreme Council of National Economy, stated that because of lack of fuel not a single furnace was in operation in the entire Donetz Basin. The output of the Donetz coal mines was only about 300,000 tons a month, about 10 per cent of prewar output. The entire output of the steel industry was less than 5 per cent of prewar output. Only 6 per cent of all textile spindles were in operation. *3. Vserossiiskii Syezd Profsoyuzov*, page 80.

[40] Trotsky obviously referred here to the English "enclosures" of the early period of capitalism.

the simple-minded about the productivity of that labor. We know that every labor is socially compulsory labor. Man must work in order not to die. He does not want to work. But the social organization compels and whips him into that direction. The new, socialist order differs from the bourgeois one in that with us labor is performed in the interest of society, and therefore we need no priestly, church-like, liberal, or Menshevik recipes for raising the labor energy of the proletariat. . . . The first way of disciplining and organizing labor is to make the economic plan clear to the widest masses of the toilers. When we transfer a worker from one spot to another, when we call up the peasant for labor duty, those called up should first of all be convinced that they are not being called up for nothing, that those who have mobilized them have a definite plan, that a necessary economic job must be performed at the spot where the labor force has now been placed. . . .

Wages, under present conditions, must not be viewed from the angle of securing the personal existence of the individual worker; they should above all serve to evaluate what that individual worker contributes to the workers' republic. Wages should measure the conscientiousness, usefulness, and efficiency of the work of every laborer. As long as we are poor, as long as we do not have enough food to satisfy minimum needs, we cannot distribute it equally to all workers, and we shall allocate consumers' goods . . . to essential workers. . . . We are obliged to act in this way for the sake of the country's future and in order to save the working masses.[41]

This is, as far as we know, the frankest statement of what may conditionally be termed a totalitarian labor policy, perhaps the only attempt at a sociological and philosophical justification of such a policy that has ever been made in Russia or elsewhere. Trotsky proclaimed the unrestricted right of the proletarian state to use the labor power of the nation in the way it considered proper and the duty of the trade unions to concern themselves with the worker as a producer and not as a consumer. The trade unions ought to discipline the worker, to raise his efficiency, to get him interested in the management and organization of industry rather than to defend his claims to higher wages and better working conditions. All these would no doubt become available with the growth of the national income earned by the socialized economy, and therefore the trade unions should preoccupy themselves with the *national* income rather than with the *individual* incomes of the workers. In view of all this—such was Trotsky's as yet unspoken conclusion—the trade unions, in their old form, had played out their role. As producers' organizations they would have little in common with the old trade unions, except the name.

In making his striking statements, Trotsky elevated an expedient to a principle, and, as so often happens, made an ideological virtue out of a bitter necessity. His immediate purpose was to justify the labor armies and to prove the inescapable need for them. He could

---

[41] *Ibid.*, pages 87–96.

have easily done this on the ground that the labor armies were a desperate emergency measure, without necessarily proclaiming the unlimited right of the state permanently to conscript labor and without declaring militarization of labor to be of the essence of socialist planning. In later years Trotsky himself became the strongest critic of a labor policy of which he had unwittingly been an inspirer. Trotsky's philosophy of labor came to underlie Stalin's practical labor policy in the thirties, although Stalin and his adherents would, for obvious reasons (and for one special reason to be discussed later), never admit it. Moreover, in Stalin's practice Trotsky's theory was not only embodied, but also exaggerated and brutalized *ad absurdum*.

From a Marxist viewpoint, Trotsky's argument contained a half-truth only. Marxist economic theory, like any other sociological theory, does in fact stress the social necessity of labor. "Man must work in order not to die" remains true under any social system. In this broad sense it is, of course, true that all labor is compulsory. But here the real problem only begins. Marx and his followers devoted their main attention to the differences of form that this compulsion of labor took under different social systems; and to these "differences of form" they attached the greatest importance. In a society based on slave or serf labor the compulsion was direct and legal. It manifested itself in a social, political, and economic relationship under which the producer himself and/or his product or part of his product were owned by the slave-owner or the feudal lord. In the capitalist order the compulsion became indirect and purely economic. The wage-earner is legally and politically free. He *must* sell his labor power because, unlike the artisan or the peasant, he does not own his means of production, and because he must earn his living. Marx, bitterly as he criticized the capitalist order, repeatedly stressed the "progressive" implications of this change from direct to indirect compulsion. That labor is free under capitalism is an illusion, but that illusion (and the modern worker's "formal "freedom on which it is based) has nevertheless heightened the self-confidence of the worker and helped to develop his mental faculties and human dignity. Without it the growth of modern industry and the consequent struggle of the working classes for socialism would hardly have been possible.[42]

---

[42] In a famous footnote to *Capital* Marx wrote: "This is one of the circumstances that makes production by slave labor such a costly process. The laborer here is, to use a striking expression of the ancients, distinguishable only as *instrumentum vocale,* from an animal as *instrumentum semi vocale,* and from an implement as *instrumentum mutum.* But he himself takes care to let both beast and implement feel that he is none of them, but is a man. He convinces himself with immense satisfaction that he is a different being, by treating the one unmercifully and damaging the other *con amore.* Hence the principle, universally applied in this method of production, only to employ the rudest and heaviest

All Marxists, including the Bolshevik leaders, had hitherto taken it for granted that in comparison with capitalism socialism would ease, and not aggravate, the compulsion of labor and that it would thereby powerfully stimulate its productivity. What Trotsky now dismissed as a "wretched and miserable liberal prejudice"—the view that compulsory labor was relatively unproductive—belonged in fact to the essence of Marxism. His statement—one of the exaggerations and over simplifications of military communism—reflected no doubt the strains and stresses of the civil war; but it also suggested a continuation of the methods of war communism into peace.[43]

Throughout 1920 the trade unions were in a ferment. Opposition groups appeared at almost every level of the organization. In the latter part of the year, after the conclusion of the Russo-Polish war, the repressed discontent broke into the open. The trade unions reacted against the interference of the party in their affairs, and they protested against the appointment and dismissal of trade union officials by the party. The All-Russian Central Council of the Trade Unions split into two factions: one acted on the principle enunciated by Trotsky that the trade unions should view their tasks in the "productionist" and not "consumptionist" spirit, while the other faction, headed by Tomsky, insisted on the need for the trade unions to resume, in some measure, the defense of the interests of their members. In this conflict the Politbureau repeatedly intervened, first in favor of Trotsky (August, 1920), then against him, until in November he was forbidden to debate the issue in public.[44]

The *cause célèbre* in this controversy was the *Tsektran* or the Central Committee of Transport. This body, headed by Trotsky, was formed at a time when the Russian railways had almost ceased to function, and its task was to revive the transport system. Endowed with wide emergency powers, Trotsky dismissed the leadership of the trade union of railwaymen, proclaimed a state of emergency in transport, militarized labor, and rapidly brought the railways into some

---

implements and such as are difficult to damage owing to their sheer clumsiness. In the slave states bordering on the Gulf of Mexico, down to the date of the civil war, ploughs constructed on old Chinese models, which turned up the soil like a hog or a mole, instead of making furrows, were alone to be found." (Karl Marx, *Capital,* Vol. I, page 178, n. 1. London: G. Allen and Unwin, Ltd., 1938.)

[43] Trotsky, however, was justified in claiming that he had urged the Politbureau to end military communism as early as February 1920 but that his advice had been rejected. He revealed this at the tenth Congress in the presence of Lenin and other Bolshevik leaders, without being contradicted. (*10. Syezd RKP (b)*, pages 191–192.) Since it had been decided to continue with military communism, militarization of labor was inescapable; and Trotsky drew the conclusions of a decision taken against his advice.

[44] *Ibid.*, pages 214–215.

working order. The feat was hailed, but Trotsky, carried away by his success, intimated that a "shake-up" in other trade unions, similar to that which had taken place in the railwaymen's union, was needed, to replace "irresponsible agitators" by production-minded trade unionists.[45] This brought the trade unions to their feet and at the fifth trade union conference (November, 1920) Tomsky openly attacked Trotsky.

The Central Committee of the party, to which the dispute was referred, was itself divided on the issue. A resolution on the *Tsektran* adopted at a plenary session of the Central Committee was in part a rebuff to Trotsky. It ordered the disbandment of the so-called political departments in transport and called for the democratization of the trade unions and for a stop to the practice of appointing from above officials who should be democratically elected to their posts. But on other essential points the Central Committee backed Trotsky: "The party ought to educate and support . . . a new type of Trade Unionist, the energetic and imaginative economic organizer who will approach economic issues not from the angle of distribution and consumption but from that of expanding production, who will view them not with the eyes of somebody accustomed to confront the soviet government with demands and to bargain, but with the eyes of the true economic organizer." [46]

However, the debates in the Central Committee revealed so profound and many-sided a division of opinion among the Bolshevik chiefs that it was decided to put the whole matter to public debate. Extremely turbulent and confused, the debate lasted throughout the whole winter of 1920–21; it culminated in the tenth Congress of the party (March, 1921), one of the most dramatic assemblies in the history of Bolshevism.

The trade union controversy at the Tenth Party Congress

In the course of the pre-Congress discussion a great number of factions and groups emerged, each with its own views and "theses" on trade unions. The differences between some of those groups were very subtle indeed, and nearly all groups referred to so many common principles that sometimes the object of the debate seemed almost unreal. However, as the controversy unfolded various groups merged with one another, and in the end only three resolutions were put before the Congress. One motion, put forward by Trotsky and Bukharin, urged the complete "statification" of the trade unions. A motion emanating from the so-called Workers' Opposition (its leader

---

[45] *Ibid.*, page 214.

[46] G. Zinoviev, *Sochinenya* (Moscow, 1924–6), Vol. VI, pages 599–600.

was the former Commissar of Labor, A. Shlyapnikov) demanded the transfer of the entire economic administration to the trade unions. These were the two extreme attitudes. Lenin, backed by nine other members of the Central Committee, tried to strike a balance between the extremes—his set of resolutions was commonly referred to as the "Platform of the Ten."

The views of Trotsky-Bukharin.[47] Trotsky now drew the logical conclusion from his previous statements on labor policy: "The transformation of the Trade Unions into Production Unions—not only in name but in content and method of work as well—forms the greatest task of our epoch." [48] The educational work of the trade unions—Trotsky's motion went on—should be focused on the participation of the workers in organizing industry. Their struggle for better living conditions ought to be carried more and more into the sphere of economic organization, and should be directed, for instance, towards raising the productivity of consumers' industries. ". . . the Union ought to embrace all workers . . . from the unskilled ones to the most qualified technicians, all subordinated to the regime of the proletarian class organization. The Union ought permanently to assess its membership from the angle of production and it should always possess a full and precise characterization of the productive value of any worker. . . ." [49] It is necessary that the working masses be fully aware that their interests are best defended by those who raise the productivity of labor, rehabilitate the economy, and increase the volume of material goods available. It was from this viewpoint, too, that

[47] The "Trotskyist" motion was signed by the following members of the Central Committee: Trotsky, Bukharin, Andreev, Dzerzhinsky, Krestinsky, Preobrazhensky, Rakovsky, Serebriakov. (Dzerzhinsky was the founder and head of the Cheka, later G.P.U. and M.V.D. Andreev is still a member of Stalin's Politbureau. All the other signatories were "purged" in the 1930s.) Among prominent Bolsheviks who backed it were Pyatakov, F. Kon, Larin, and Sokolnikov. In the motion submitted to the Congress Trotsky's view appeared in a diluted form. In the pre-Congress discussion he had urged full and immediate statification of the trade unions, but then he softened his attitude, in part under the influence of Lenin's severe criticism and in order to facilitate coalition with Bukharin's so-called "buffer group," which had taken an intermediate position between Lenin and Trotsky.

[48] *10. Syezd R.K.P.* (b), page 454.

[49] The Trotskyist motion, of course, presupposed compulsory membership of trade unions, which had actually been in force throughout the period of military communism. In practice, the workers and employees of a factory "collectively" adhered to a union, and the individual worker or employee had no right to secede. This explained the phenomenal growth of the trade union membership during the civil war. According to figures given by Zinoviev at the tenth Congress the membership was 1.5 million in July 1917, 2.6 in January 1918, 3.5 in 1919, 4.3 in 1920 and 7 million in 1921. Another reason for this expansion in membership was the inclusion in the trade unions of all employees, civil servants, and professional men who had not been organized before the revolution. (*Ibid.,* pages 187–188

the election of the leading bodies of the trade unions should be organized.

Trotsky's motion further asserted that: (a) the statification of the trade unions had in actual fact already been carried very far; (b) the workers' share in organizing the national economy was insufficient; (c) the gradual transfer of the economic administration to the trade unions, which the party program of 1919 had promised, presupposed "the planned transformation of the Unions into apparatuses of the workers' state." This, however, was to be achieved gradually, and not by a single juridical act. For the present, it was proposed that the trade unions and the economic administration should be overhauled so that their leading bodies, the Praesidiums of the Central Council of the Trade Unions and of the Supreme Council of National Economy, should have between one-third and one-half of their members in common. This was to put an end to the "alienation" or antagonism between the trade unions and the economic administration, an "alienation" on which Trotsky's motion dwelt with considerable emphasis. The Central Council of the Trade Unions and the Supreme Council of National Economy were to hold joint sessions periodically. Personal union was also to be établised between the two organizations in their lower grades. No doubt was left, however, that the trade unions should be subordinate to the economic administration, although it was proposed that they alone should be in charge of distribution and protection of labor and of regulation of wages and working conditions. The Commissariat of Labor, hitherto in charge of those matters, was to be disbanded altogether. It was further proposed that the unions should settle conflicts between the economic administration and the workers, acting as a sort of an arbitration body directly responsible to the government.

Finally, the position of industrial managers was at least in part to be determined by their standing with the trade unions. Bourgeois technicians and administrators who had become full members of a union were to be entitled to hold managerial posts, without supervision by commissars; those who were only candidates to trade union membership could hold managerial posts but were to be supervised by commissars; and, lastly, politically unreliable persons could serve only as assistant managers on probation.

The wage policy of the statified trade unions should be guided by two principles: (a) shock competition (udarnichestvo) between workers at production; and (b) the leveling out of wages, at least in so far that premiums for high output should be paid out only after a real minimum wage had been secured to all workers. In this respect Trotsky had shifted his ground since the third Congress of the Trade

Unions, where he had more emphatically favored differentiation of wages.

The Workers' Opposition. The motion of the Workers' Opposition was labeled by its opponents as syndicalist or anarcho-syndicalist. Explicitly or implicitly, it postulated the domination of the trade unions over the state, the abolition of the normal economic administration, and its substitution by the trade unions.

The Workers' Opposition referred, of course, to "Point 5" of the 1919 program and charged the leadership of the party with violating its pledges toward the trade unions. "In practice the leadership of the party and the governmental bodies have in the last two years systematically narrowed the scope of trade union work and reduced almost to nil the influence of the working class associations in the soviet state." [50] The participation of the trade unions in industrial management meant in practice that the unions were used by the economic administration merely as reference bureaus or advisory bodies. Conflicts between trade unions, party committees, and the economic authorities had piled up dangerously; and—the Workers' Opposition claimed—the party and the economic authorities, having been swamped by bourgeois technicians and other nonproletarian elements, displayed outright hostility toward the trade unions, a hostility that reflected "bourgeois class hatred of the proletariat."

The remedy for all these evils was "the concentration of industrial management in the hands of the Trade Unions." The transition to the new system should begin from the lowest industrial unit and extend upward. At the factory level the factory committee should regain the dominant position it had had at the beginning of the revolution.[51] This demand, it will be remembered, had been raised by anarcho-syndicalist elements in 1917, when it was bitterly opposed by the Bolshevik-led trade unions. To some extent, therefore, both Lenin and Trotsky were justified in describing the attitude of the Workers' Opposition as anarcho-syndicalist.

The Workers' Opposition proposed the following specific measures: the nominal parity of representation of trade unions and of the economic administration in various controlling bodies should be abolished in favor of predominantly trade union control. "Not a single person is to be appointed to any administrative-economic post without the agreement of the Trade Unions." Candidatures proposed by the latter should be binding on the economic authorities. Officials recommended by the trade unions were to remain accountable for their conduct to the unions, who should also have the right to recall them

---

[50] *Ibid.,* page 360.
[51] *Ibid.,* pages 361–362.

from their posts at any time. This program culminated in the demand that an "All-Russian Producers' Congress" be convened to elect the central management of the entire national economy. National congresses of separate trade unions were similarly to elect managements for the various branches of the economy. Local and regional managements should be formed by local trade union conferences, while the management of single factories was to belong to the factory committees, which were to remain part of the trade union organization.

Last but not least, the Workers' Opposition proposed a radical revision of the wage policy in an extremely egalitarian spirit: money wages were to be progressively replaced by rewards in kind; the basic food ration was to be made available to workers without any payment; the same was to apply to meals in factory canteens, essential travelling facilities, and facilities for education and leisure, lodging, lighting, and so on. No attempt was made to explain how this program of full communism, theoretically designed for an economy of great plenty, was to be made to work amid the utter poverty of Russian society after the civil war. The only specific palliative suggested was that factories should run their own auxiliary farms to secure the supply of food to their workers.[52]

"Platform of Ten." The motion tabled by Lenin was the most elaborate and carefully balanced of all the resolutions placed before the Congress. Its polemic edge was directed primarily against the Workers' Opposition and only in the second instance against Trotsky—both Lenin and Trotsky made a common front against the Workers' Opposition. The Leninist motion began with a verbal reaffirmation of the principles embodied in "Point 5" of the 1919 program, promising the transfer of all economic administration to the trade unions. "The present situation," the motion went on, "urgently requires that the Trade Unions should take a more direct part in the organization of production not only through detailing their members to work in the economic administration but through the whole of their own machinery as well." But, apart from this, the whole tenor of the motion suggested the need for the strictest subordination of trade union policy to the government. Nevertheless, the idea about the statification of the trade unions was described as erroneous on the ground that statification would not help

---

[52] Before the Congress another opposition group, the so-called Group of Democratic Centralism or *Decemists* (Bubnov, Sapronov, Ossinsky, and others), advocated similar views. At the Congress, however, the *Decemists* withdrew their "Theses" and stated that they would not take part in the "shadow-boxing" over the trade unions, for the real problem was how to bring the party back to democratic ways. Compared with this the position of the trade unions was a secondary issue.

to improve Russia's economic position and that trade unions absorbed by the state would not be able to perform their proper functions.[53]

What were these functions? The trade unions were to provide a broad *social* base for the proletarian dictatorship exercised by the party. The need for that base was dictated by the peasant character of the country. The ruling class, the proletariat, was in a minority, which had to be effectively organized in order to be able to keep under steady political influence the vast peasant majority. The trade unions were, or should be, the broadest voluntary organization of industrial workers. Absorbed by the state they would become a mere bureaucratic machine. The trade unions were further to be the "school of communism" for their seven million members. Again and again it was pointed out that the Communist Party had only half a million people in its ranks, a minority within the proletarian minority. The communists must not attempt to impose themselves as the government's nominees upon the trade unions. Instead, they should strive to be accepted by the mass of the trade unionists as its leaders on the strength of their merits and qualities of leadership. Only then could they hope to turn the trade unions into schools of communism for the entire working class.

Trotsky had insisted that the militarization of labor was in the long run essential for the socialist reorganization of economy. Against this the Leninist motion stressed that militarization could not be regarded as a permanent feature of socialist labor policy. The proletarian dictatorship must use persuasion as well as coercion, and it ought carefully to balance the one against the other. Coercion was peculiar to the state, even though the state, too, must, wherever possible, try to attain its ends by persuasion. As a social organization, distinct from the state, the trade unions were in their real element when they worked through persuasion, even though in exceptional cases they, too, might use coercion. It was normal for the state to appoint officials from above.

The reorganization of the Trade Unions from above would be utterly inexpedient. The methods of a workers' democracy, severely curtailed in the three years of the most savage civil war, ought to be re-established, in the first instance and on the widest possible scale, in the Trade Union movement. It is necessary that the leading bodies of the Trade Unions should in actual fact be elected and broadly based.[54]

The methods of coercion and command that had been used to such salutary effect in the Red Army during the civil war must not be extended to the field of economic policy.

[53] *V.K.P.* (*b*) *v Rezolutsiyakh,* Vol. 1, page 381.

[54] *Ibid.,* page 382.

A similar balance, it was further stated, ought to be struck between the productionist and the consumptionist viewpoints. The trade unions were to take part in the working out of economic plans; they were to propose candidates for administrative-economic jobs, although their proposals were to have the strength of recommendations only; they were to inspect, through specialized departments, the work of the economic administration, to keep account of industrial manpower and its distribution; they were to work out norms of output, this being their exclusive prerogative.

In view of the fact that the working out of norms of labor . . . has been concentrated in the Trade Unions . . . and that the protection of labor . . . ought to be entirely transferred to the Trade Unions, the Congress considers it necessary that the departments for wage-rate fixing and protection of labor attached hitherto to the Commissariat of Labor . . . should be wound up and transferred to the All-Russian Central Council of Trade Unions.[55]

As "schools of labor discipline" the trade unions were to establish "comradely" disciplinary courts for trying offenders in open session. In addition, trade union "plenipotentiaries" were to supervise labor discipline in the factories and to supply daily reports to the trade unions.

In regard to wages, the Leninist motion, too, declared the leveling of wages to be the ultimate objective, but, more emphatically than the Trotskyist motion, it rejected the extreme egalitarianism of the Workers' Opposition. Wage policy was to be designed so as to "discipline labor and increase its productivity." Workers' emulation for higher output, so Lenin argued against Trotsky, could not be squared with equality in consumption. Since wages were paid in kind as well as in money, this implied the need for a differential rationing system to be worked out and put into effect by the joint efforts of the trade unions, the food offices, and the industrial managements.

These then were the three motions that competed for acceptance. Comparison tends, up to a point, to obscure rather than throw into relief the issue with which the Congress tried to come to grips, because, for tactical reasons, the authors of every motion incorporated passages from their opponents' motions and thereby blurred the real differences. Nor did the Congress try to solve the problem of the trade unions only —in this debate the entire structure of the Soviet regime was at stake.

Proletarian dictatorship, proletarian democracy, and trade unions

The complete ruin of Russian industry and the virtual dispersal of the industrial working class formed the background to this con-

---

[55] *Ibid.*, page 385.

troversy. At the fourth Congress of the Trade Unions (May, 1921) Miliutin, *rapporteur* of the Supreme Council of National Economy, stated that the output of metal was only 4 per cent of prewar, while the volume of consumers' goods was only 30 per cent. The cities were depopulated, Petersburg having less than three-quarters of a million inhabitants and Moscow only slightly more than a million. The industrial workers were fleeing from the town into the countryside; those who stayed behind produced very little and spent most of their time trading on the black markets.[56] The disorganization of the entire economy and the demoralization of the working class were further illustrated by statements, made at the fourth Congress of the Trade Unions, that workers in factories were stealing 50 per cent of the goods produced and that the average worker could pay with his wage only one-fifth of his cost of living, being compelled to earn the rest by illicit trading.[57] Bukharin, addressing the Congress on behalf of the party, stated: "The fundamental danger which now confronts us is that chaos is washing away the strength of the proletariat as a class in action. . . . If this class becomes demoralized and hollowed out from inside, the problem is really very grave. . . . The workers become petty traders." [58] In the days of the tenth Congress of the party, popular discontent flared up in the armed risings of Kronstadt, Tambov, and other places in which disillusioned Bolsheviks, as well as anti-Bolsheviks, took part. For the first time the Bolshevik regime, having emerged triumphantly from the civil war, was really isolated, lacking support from the mass of the people.

Hitherto, the entire Bolshevik conception of the Soviet regime and of the place of the trade unions in it had been based on the premise that at least the industrial working class stood solidly behind the revolution and would continue to do so. Now, three and a half years after the October revolution, this premise was disproved by the facts. The crisis that ensued was reflected in the trade union debate. Hitherto, the Bolshevik Party had taken it for granted that proletarian dictatorship and proletarian democracy (as distinct from formal or bourgeois democracy), far from contradicting one another, were identical, or at least complementary: the dictatorship was suppressing the resistance of landlords and capitalists, but it was based on freedom of expression inside the working classes. Now a conflict arose between proletarian dictatorship and proletarian democracy. In the trade unions, that broadest mass organization of the proletariat, this was felt most acutely. The Workers' Opposition was the mouthpiece of that same popular discontent that had led even Bolsheviks to join

---

[56] *4. Syezd Profsoyuzov*, pages 72–77.

[57] *Ibid.*, page 119.

[58] *Ibid.*, page 22.

in the Kronstadt rising. The emergence of that opposition inside the ruling party was itself a measure of the social disorganization in the background. It represented a revolt inside the trade unions against dictation by the party and by the economic administration. In quasi-anarchist fashion it evoked the principle of proletarian democracy against the dictatorship.

Most Bolshevik leaders were dimly aware of the symptomatic significance of the Workers' Opposition. But they held that the Opposition expressed the demoralization of the working class, the psychology of the workingman turned into the black marketeer and incapable of any constructive attitude toward the new state. They were determined to maintain the proletarian dictatorship, of which they considered the Bolshevik Party to be the trustee, even though for the moment it lacked the democratic support of the proletariat; and they hoped that with economic recovery and political stabilization the dictatorship would soon be able to base itself, once again, on proletarian democracy.

This then was the issue that underlay the controversy over the trade unions. The Workers' Opposition argued in fact against the dictatorship of the party when it demanded that the entire management of the national economy be transferred to an All-Russian Congress of Producers. Shlyapnikov, the leader of the Opposition, stated:

> We ought to shift the center of our attention to the factories and workshops. There we ought to start with the organization of our economy. . . . At present communists are thrown out of the factory committees. The factory committees, which form the basis of our Trade Unions, acquire a nonparty outlook because the rights that we [the party] leave to our Trade Unions and party cells are negligible.[59]

The spokesmen of the opposition blamed both Lenin and Trotsky as "economic militarizers" and complained that for all their differences of views they had in fact made common cause against the proletarian rank and file. On the other side, Zinoviev, who throughout these debates acted as Lenin's mouthpiece, used the following significant argument against the Workers' Opposition's demand for a Producers' Congress:

> At this Producers' Congress which you want to be convened at this great moment [Zinoviev was referring to the Kronstadt rising still in progress] the majority will consist of nonparty people. A good many of them will be Social Revolutionaries and Mensheviks. Should we hand over everything to them?

---

[59] *10. Syezd R.K.P. (b)*, pages 213–214.

To whom is it not clear that to put the question thus would be to stake the head of the entire proletarian movement?

Trotsky put the issue with even greater bluntness:

> The Workers' Opposition has come out with dangerous slogans, making a fetish of democratic principles. They place the workers' right to elect their representatives—above the party, as it were, as if the party were not entitled to assert its dictatorship even if that dictatorship temporarily clashed with the passing moods of the workers' democracy.
>
> It is necessary to create among us the awareness of the revolutionary historical birthright of the party, which is obliged to maintain its dictatorship, regardless of temporary wavering in the spontaneous moods of the masses, regardless of the temporary waverings even in the working classes. This awareness is for us the indispensable unifying element. The dictatorship does not base itself at every given moment on the formal principle of a workers' democracy, although the workers' democracy is, of course, the only method by which the masses can be drawn more and more into political life.[60]

In conclusion, Trotsky suggested that the party should, for the time being, cease to advocate and practice proletarian democracy, and that, instead, it should concentrate on building up a "producers' democracy." A regime based on publicly owned industry, producing not for profit but for the satisfaction of social needs, was, by definition, proletarian, even though the working class was temporarily in virtual opposition to it. The regime represented the general interest of the proletariat, as distinct from sectional or temporary benefits. The state (or the party) had therefore the right to impose its policies upon the working class. This determined the attitude of the party toward the trade unions. The latter ought to be made to serve the workers' state; they were not entitled to confront that state with traditional claims and demands.

At this point begins the real difference between Trotsky and Lenin. Taking up an argument that had first been advanced by the Menshevik Martov in 1918, Lenin now dismissed as a false syllogism the view that the trade unions had nothing to defend against the workers' state. The Soviet state of the day, he said, was not a workers' state. It was a state of workers and peasants; and in addition it had been "bureaucratically deformed." The position was therefore more complex than Trotsky (or Bukharin) had described it. The workers were, of course, bound in duty to defend that state, and this must determine the attitude of the trade unions toward it. The unions should not indulge in systematic opposition; they must adopt a constructive attitude toward the state. But the workers were still bound to defend themselves from the state, because: (a) its policy might at times be the resultant

---

[60] *Ibid.*, pages 190–192.

of conflicting pressures from peasants and workers, and (*b*) arbitrary bureaucratic acts might necessitate such defence on the part of the workers. The trade unions should therefore have a measure of autonomy *vis-à-vis* the government. Nor should adherence to the trade unions be made compulsory for the workers, as Trotsky had suggested. "First of all," Lenin again pleaded, "we ought to try and prevail by persuasion and only then by coercion." [61] Lenin as much as Trotsky, however, insisted on the "revolutionary historical birthright of the party" and on the need for the trade unions to accept the party's guidance. The difference was one of emphasis: Trotsky dwelt more on the party's supremacy, whereas Lenin placed the greater stress on the democratic, voluntary, educational character of the trade unions.

The difference was one of precept, not of practice. Immediately, the party leadership, as a whole, was determined to overrule the trade unions. This was soon illustrated by a striking incident, when the Central Committee of the party demoted the most prominent Bolshevik trade unionist, Tomsky, from the trade union leadership. Such demotions were later to occur with some frequency; and the procedure adopted was as follows: the decision of the Central Committee of the party about the dismissal of, say, Tomsky, was conveyed not strictly to the All-Russian Council of Trade Unions (of which Tomsky had been the chairman) but to the communist *fraktsya* or cell within that council. The members of the *fraktsya* were bound by the statutes of the party to act on instructions from the Central Committee. The *fraktsya* then placed a proposal for a change in the leadership before the plenary session of the Trade Union Council. The nonparty members of the council might insist on retaining Tomsky as leader of the trade unions, but they could hardly carry the day. The entire *fraktsya*, including Tomsky, would vote for the proposal embodying the party's instruction. In this way the party could almost always impose its will. [62]

For all that, Lenin's insistence on relative autonomy for the trade unions was not without significance. In the combination of coercion and persuasion that Lenin envisaged, he aimed at progressively reducing the share of the former and increasing that of the latter. He hoped that economic recovery would enable the ruling party to reinfuse proletarian democracy into the proletarian dictatorship and to restore a wide measure of free expression of working-class opinion. Whether this was practicable or not is a different question—there were enough

---

[61] *Ibid.,* p. 208.

[62] One of the charges made against Lenin and Trotsky by Shlyapnikov was that they systematically abused the *fraktsyas* inside the trade unions to overrule the opinion of Bolshevik trade unionists. *Ibid.,* page 212.

symptoms already to show that *ce n'est que le provisoire qui dure*. But in his motion on the trade unions Lenin was anxious to underline the provisional character of the curtailment of workers' rights.

His motion was accepted by an overwhelming majority at the Congress. For it there voted 336 delegates as against 50 who voted for Trotsky's motion and only 18 for the Workers' Opposition. The actual division of opinion was deeper and wider than the vote suggested. The Leninist attitude, because of its moderate and inconclusive character, was acceptable to various groups in the party: to the economic administrators who wished for greater submission on the part of the trade unions, and to trade unionists anxious to obtain more elbow room. Whatever the motives, the view that the trade unions should not be swallowed up by the state but that they should voluntarily cooperate with it obtained the sanction of the Congress. Since this view was associated with Lenin's name and since Lenin himself never revised it (a year later illness removed him from the stage), it became part of the Leninist orthodoxy, which came to be established after his death, that the trade unions should remain a nongovernmental, a nonstate organization. This could have some reality, in the long run, only if the state had become more democratic, if the idea at least of proletarian democracy had made genuine progress. This was not to happen. As we shall see later, in practise Trotsky's formula, after its author had been expelled from the party and from Russia, came to govern the position of the trade unions in later years, in the period of planned economy. To all intents and purposes the unions then became part of the governmental machinery. In theory, however, Lenin's formula, unrevised, was to remain in force.

The New Economic Policy

Transition to NEP

The controversy at the tenth Congress was based on the assumption of a totally state-owned and state-managed industry. The problem whether the trade unions should or should not form part of the state was so acute precisely in this context. Yet at the same Congress Lenin initiated the New Economic Policy (NEP), which introduced a mixed, socialist-capitalist economy. Soon afterwards, private capital, Russian and foreign, was readmitted into industry and commerce, while the state retained its "commanding posts" in large-scale industry. This change was bound to create a new situation for the trade unions.

The first consequences of NEP for the unions became apparent when their fourth Congress was convened in May, 1921. Curiously enough, only the faintest echo of the recent stormy debates was heard at this national gathering of trade unionists. The Bolsheviks, having decided the issue at the Congress of the party, did not reopen it before the trade union forum. For them the matter had been settled; all members of the party, whatever their private views, had now to vote unanimously for the official resolutions. This circumstance again indicated to what extent matters of vital importance to the trade unions were now settled outside the unions. The non-Bolshevik groups at the fourth Trade Union Congress tried to provoke discussion, but with little effect. The Left Social Revolutionaries, who as a party had been banned but were still allowed to act as a group at the Trade Union Congress, demanded, like the Workers' Opposition in the Bolshevik ranks, complete trade union control over industry. The Mensheviks, on the other hand, denounced the extent to which the statification of the trade unions had, regardless of Bolshevik resolutions to the contrary, already taken place; and they pressed for complete separation between trade unions and state, on the ground that under the NEP the workers would be compelled to defend themselves against private and state capitalism. The Menshevik motion also demanded free elections, freedom of speech, and freedom of action for all socialist parties in and outside the trade unions.[63] All these motions were, of course, voted down by the Bolshevik majority.

The main issue confronting the congress was the role of the trade unions in a mixed capitalist-socialist economy, even though the extent to which capitalism would be readmitted had not yet become clear. A motion submitted by the Central Council of the Trade Unions anticipated not only the defense of workers against small capitalists but also the formation of special organs through which the trade unions would exercise control over privately owned industry, a reminiscence of the "workers' control" of 1917.[64] The prevailing attitude seems to have been that the trade unions would adopt a dual attitude, a productionist one in state-owned industry and a consumptionist one toward private employers. But it was already pointed out by delegates that such a dual attitude might be untenable: if the trade unions succeeded in raising wages and improving conditions in private industry, workers would rush from governmental to privately owned factories.

The implications of NEP became much clearer the following year, at the eleventh Congress of the party, in March 1922, and at the fifth Congress of the Trade Unions in September. The eleventh Congress of the party reasserted the main principles of the Leninist resolution

---

[63] *4. Syezd Profsoyuzov*, page 69 ff.
[64] *Ibid.*, page 66 ff.

passed by the tenth Congress. But it also introduced a few essential correctives, which further curtailed the influence of the trade unions. True enough, it was now re-emphasized that the unions ought to support the claims of labor in private and leased enterprises and also in such socialized concerns where workers suffered from bureaucratic encroachments.[65] The Congress did not ban strikes, but appealed to the trade unions to refrain from calling them: "Neither the Communist Party, nor the Soviet Government, nor the Trade Unions can forget and conceal from the workers . . . that strike action in a state with a proletarian government can be explained and justified exclusively by bureaucratic deformations of that state and by remnants of capitalism. . . ."[66] If mistakes of the economic administration, backwardness of certain groups of workers, provocation by counter-revolutionary elements, or imprudence on the part of the trade unions led to labor conflicts in state-owned enterprises, the unions were obliged to do their utmost to bring them to an end. In private industry they were apparently to allow labor conflicts to run their spontaneous course. But contrary to what the previous Congress had said on the matter, the party now resolved that "the Trade Unions should not assume directly any functions of control over production in private businesses and in businesses leased to private hands."[67] The Bolsheviks were anxious to enlist the assistance of private capital in the reconstruction of Russia; and no capitalist, at any rate not one who remembered "workers' control" in 1917, was willing to open a business in which the trade union would be the master.

More important still was the decision of the eleventh Congress finally to eliminate the trade unions from participation in actual industrial management. Individual management instead of management by committee was now to be firmly established. Managers alone were to be responsible for fixing wages and rations and for the distribution of working clothes to workers, though they should do this in accordance with collective agreements concluded with trade unions. The Leninist resolution adopted by the previous Congress had made all these the joint responsibility of trade unions, food offices, and industrial managements.[68]

---

[65] *V.K.P. (b) o Profsoyuzakh*, page 165.

[66] *Ibid.*

[67] *Ibid.*, p. 168.

[68] Hitherto the trade unions had been in charge of the distribution of some consumers' goods. Since wages were often still paid in kind and not in money, it was a matter of some importance who fixed rations for various categories of workers. At the fourth Congress of the Trade Unions it was stated that seven categories of rations were in existence and that the differences between them were very considerable.

These reforms deepened a split in the Central Council of Trade Unions. Tomsky, opposed to the reforms, was temporarily removed from work at the council and ostensibly sent on a mission to Turkestan. Andreev, who had backed Trotsky in the trade union debate and consistently represented the productionist viewpoint, took Tomsky's place. When Tomsky and his adherents protested that the trade unions had been reduced to impotence, the productionists replied that this was not so, because the trade unions were expected to supply an ever-growing contingent of industrial managers from their members.[69] This was true enough. But those who shared Tomsky's viewpoint argued that, although many individual trade unionists had become industrial managers, the trade unions, as bodies, were losing influence, especially as the workers promoted to managers tended to lose touch with their original unions. The party then urged the new worker-managers to remain good trade unionists. This was no more than a *pium desideratum*. The worker promoted to manager gradually became accustomed to approach his problems from the managerial and not the trade unionist angle. The trade unions were once again offered the consolation that they would participate in over-all economic planning and advise the government which factories should and which should not be handed over to private capital. The pill was hardly sweetened.

The new economic course was justified on grounds of expediency. But there was more to it than that. The party was now engaged in building up, on the basis of its monopoly of power, the monolithic state.[70] The subordination of the trade unions was a prerequisite as well as one of the results of that process. Yet this whole development was still in one of its initial phases. Nominally, the party still insisted on the need for the trade unions to keep the balance, so subtly drawn by Lenin, between the various aspects of their activity: persuasion and coercion; defense of the material interests of the workers and pressure on the workers for higher productivity; the need to take into account the moods of the rank and file and the need to resist those moods,

---

[69] (1) The Trade Unions take part in the formation of all economic and state authorities . . . putting forward their own candidates . . . [but] the power of decision belongs exclusively to the economic authorities. . . . These take into account the opinions on all candidates expressed by the corresponding Trade Unions. (2) One of the most important tasks of any Trade Union is the promotion and training of administrators from among workers . . . . If at present we have only tens of really competent industrial administrators [drafted from Trade Unions] and hundreds of more or less competent ones, we shall very soon need hundreds of the former category and thousands of the latter." (*Ibid.*, page 168.)

[70] It was not pure coincidence that on the day after the conclusion of the eleventh Congress of the party, which adopted these resolutions, Stalin was appointed General Secretary of the Central Committee.

when from an economic viewpoint they were not sound. "These contradictions," stated the eleventh Congress, "are not accidental and they cannot be removed in the course even of a number of decades." [71] The aforementioned contradictions will inevitably give rise to conflicts, lack of harmony, friction, and so forth. A higher authority . . . is necessary to settle such conflicts at once. Such an authority is the Communist Party and the international association of the Communist Parties of all countries, the Comintern." [72] This curious phrase meant that the trade unions had the right to appeal from the Soviet Government to the Russian Communist Party and from the latter to the Communist International. They never were to make use of this right. In later years, after Stalin had firmly established himself in power, the very idea of such an appeal would have seemed wild, not only because the Comintern was completely in the hands of the Russian party, but because the mere thought of such an appeal smacked of treason.[73] Meanwhile, it was significant that the Bolshevik leaders still anticipated that within the framework of the single-party state, now taking shape, the trade unions would for a long time to come (for a "number of decades") maintain their relative autonomy and, consequently, their dual attitude toward the state.

Nevertheless, the eleventh Congress made another long step toward the complete destruction of the democratic constitution of the trade unions. It resolved that the secretaries and chairmen of the central committees of the unions must be long standing members of the party, men who had belonged to it before the revolution. Similarly, the chairmen, secretaries, and members of the leading regional trade union bodies had also to be party members of at least three years' standing.[74] The Congress, at the same time, adopted one more of a series of resolutions in favor of normal elections in trade unions; but it did not say what should happen if in normal elections other than party members were elected. In practice, elections were already rigged to such an extent that the dilemma could hardly arise.

The productionist viewpoint found eloquent expression in the resolutions of the twelfth Congress of the party (April, 1923), the first Congress in which Lenin did not participate:

Aiming by all means at an improvement in the condition of the working class, the state authorities and the Trade Unions ought to remember that a prolonged and all-round improvement is possible only on the basis of an

---

[71] *V.K.P. (b) o Profsoyuzakh*, page 171.

[72] *Ibid.*, page 172.

[73] This was how the appeals of the Trotskyist Opposition from the Russian party to the Comintern were in fact treated.

[74] *Ibid.*, page 173.

expanding, that is profit-bearing, industry. . . . To keep in operation businesses with low employment or to keep employed in any factory a number of workers which does not correspond with the actual productivity of that factory is a wasteful and irrational form of social security and is therefore detrimental to the working class interests of to-morrow. The saddling of industrial enterprises with all sorts of overhead costs . . . disrupts the possibility of correct calculation and imposes . . . upon the state expenses which it is not at present in a position to bear. Arbitrary . . . "grants" by trusts represent nothing else but wastage of governmental property and should be punished by law.[75]

The appointment, transfer, and replacement of the economic personnel is the responsibility of the leading economic authorities—a necessary condition for the genuine management of industry. . . . The recommendations and testimonials of the Trade Unions should be attentively taken into account, but they can in no case lift the responsibility [for taking decisions] from the corresponding economic authorities, to whom the existing legislation leaves complete freedom of choice and appointment.

The economic administrator is always confronted with two dangers: (a) the danger that his exacting demands may antagonize the workers, their representative bodies, the local branches of the party and Soviet institutions; and (b) the danger of taking in matters of production, wages, and so forth, the line of least resistance and of sacrificing thereby the profitability of the business, and consequently its future. It goes without saying that the manager of a Soviet factory ought to show the greatest attentiveness to the material and spiritual needs of the workers, to their feelings and moods. But at the same time he must not lose sight of his supreme duty toward the working class, as a whole, a duty which consists in raising productivity of labor, lowering costs of production and increasing the volume of material goods available to the proletarian state. Trade Unionists and party members ought to cooperate in every way with the Soviet manager for this purpose. Attentiveness, determination and discrimination are the indispensable qualities of the Soviet manager. But his best testimonial is the favorable balance sheet of the business.[76]

Trade unions under NEP

The further evolution of the trade unions was bound up with two factors: (a) the general economic situation and the changing social structure of Russia; and (b) the political evolution of the regime, that is, the progressive crystallization of the single-party system.

The mixed economy of NEP existed from 1921 till roughly the end of 1928, when the first Five-Year Plan was initiated. The effect upon the trade unions of the partial readmission of capitalism was not as far-reaching as had been expected. In industry, capitalist enterprise regained relatively little ground. Foreign concessionaires were less interested in investment in Russia than Lenin and his colleagues had hoped. Private enterprise was strong only in trade and, of course, in

---

[75] *Ibid.*, pages 175–176.
[76] *Ibid.*, pages 186–187. The author of this resolution was Trotsky.

farming. At the height of NEP only 16.6 per cent (1.6 out of 9.6 million) of the total number of wage- and salary-earners were employed in the private sector of the economy, not counting individual farmers. However, although the state employed four-fifths of the mass of wage-earners, the circumstance that a fraction of the working class was again employed by private capital could not but affect in some degree the outlook of the trade unions as a whole. In relation to private employers the trade unions preserved their independence and made demands on behalf of the workers. This alone tended to give them some independence in relation to the state as well, altogether apart from the fact that, in virtue of the resolutions of the last three party Congresses, the state was committed to respect their relative autonomy. The trade unions could not adopt a totally productionist attitude in governmental factories and a totally consumptionist one in private industry. Throughout the years of NEP their policy was the resultant of the two attitudes.

One of the dominant economic features of this period was mass unemployment. Due to a combination of industrial underemployment and agricultural overpopulation, it persisted throughout the NEP. At the height of NEP about two million people were without jobs, a very large number for a country in which total industrial employment was only 1.2 million in 1920 and 2.1 million in 1925.[77] The problem with which Russia had to contend in the next decade—that of securing, under conditions of full employment, a steady supply of fresh labor to an expanding industry—did not yet arise.

Direction of labor that had been part and parcel of military communism was no longer needed—it was, in fact, abandoned in February, 1922. The "reserve army of unemployed," to use the Marxian term, performed in the Russian economy of the twenties the same function that it performs in any capitalist economy: it pressed upon the wages and living conditions of the employed workers. Throughout most of this period real wages were considerably below the pre-1914 level, which was understandable in view of the disastrous impoverishment of the country. Fear of unemployment prevented workers from demanding higher wages and from pressing the trade unions to stake out claims on their behalf, claims that might have brought the unions into conflict with the employer state. In 1924, only 24,000 workers

---

[77] Latent agricultural overpopulation was reflected in the steady growth of seasonal employment of peasants outside farming:

Peasants seasonally employed in industry

1923–1924	1.7 million	1927–1928	4.0 million
1926–1927	3.2 million	1928–1929	4.3 million.

Bolshaya Sovetskaya Entsiklopediya S.S.S.R. (1948), page 1124.

went on strike in state-owned industry; in 1925—34,000; in 1926—33,000; in 1927—20,000; and in 1928 even fewer than 20,000. This is not to say that labor conflicts in milder form were not widespread. By the end of NEP, at the eighth Congress of the Trade Unions (December, 1928) Schmidt, the Commissar for Labor, stated that in the previous few years industrial conflicts had involved nearly 2.5 million workers annually. But as the workers were wary of resorting to strikes, most conflicts were settled by arbitration.

The attitude of the trade unions toward private industry fluctuated and was ambiguous. At the beginning of NEP and up to the middle twenties, private employers were often able to offer better conditions of labor than those prevailing in state-owned industry. Private capital re-entrenched itself in consumers' industries, the produce of which was in very heavy demand. The profits of private industry were sufficiently high to make it worth while for employers to raise wages.[78] The trade unions witnessed the paradox that small capitalist businesses compelled the proletarian state to compete with them in the improvement of labor conditions.[79] But this could not, of course, last very long. In the middle twenties, state-owned industry was rehabilitated and reached the prewar level of output; and private industry was quickly losing the advantages it had enjoyed. The normal antagonism between employer and trade union returned. However, the government, determined to speed up economic recovery, did not want to see the working of private industry interrupted by strikes. The private employers certainly worked for their profit, but the output of their factories, it was pointed out, was essential to the economic balance of the proletarian state. The trade unions, therefore, often adopted the "productionist" attitude even in private industry.[80] But equally often, compelled to tread warily in state-owned industry, they compensated themselves by excessive militancy toward private employers, until they (that is, trade unions) were curbed by the government. Between these two extremes the unions wavered.

The NEP period saw the introduction of a mass of progressive labor legislation. But the trade unions did not regain real freedom of action, in spite of the relative liberalism in the government's

---

[78] This caused the fifth Congress of the Trade Unions to complain that heavy industry was at a disadvantage in its competition with light industry and to ask the government to protect heavy industry against unfair competition.

[79] In 1922 wages in state-owned industry were increased by 100 per cent, but the increase was soon swallowed up by monetary inflation.

[80] At the Seventh Congress of the Trade Unions (December, 1926) Dogadov, one of the prominent leaders of that period, complained about a "deviation" in the trade unions which consisted in the treatment of private businesses on an equal footing with the socialist ones. (7. *Syezd Profsoyuzov*, page 84.)

economic policy. This became striking after the recovery of industry was more or less complete. In March, 1927 the Central Committee of the party ordered a large-scale release of redundant labor from state-owned industry.[81] The release was explained on the ground that industry was already fully utilizing its old plant and that expansion was now possible only through technical rationalization, higher efficiency, and construction of new plant. The trade unions were asked not only to agree to the release of redundant labor, but also to work out higher norms of output and to cooperate with the economic administration in the processes of rationalization. The Commissariat of Labor was to shift the released workers to new places of employment. This, of course, implied a degree of direction of labor. But for some time yet this implication was to be devoid of practical significance, because industry was still developing too slowly to require and absorb the redundant labor. The resolution of the Central Committee brought forth a vehement protest from the opposition led by Trotsky, Zinoviev, and Kamenev. One of the charges leveled against the economic administration and the trade unions was that in the scheme for rationalization the emphasis was not on higher technical efficiency but on exacting more physical exertion from the workers.[82] The trade unions, nevertheless, responded to the appeal of the Central Committee, although they did so half-heartedly and not without provoking protests from the ranks.

In their attempt to balance between the state and the workers, between the economic administration and their own rank and file, the trade unions most often inclined toward the state and the economic administration.[83] Nevertheless, they were in almost constant conflict with everybody: the state, the economic administration, the party, and their own rank and file. At the fifth Congress of the Trade Unions Tomsky related with melancholy irony:

. . . at every congress, conference, meeting, wherever four people assembled, the first and the most important point on the agenda is the problem of our mutual relations. . . . If you ask any branch, sub-branch, or responsible official for a report or an organizational plan, you may rest assured that three-quarters, or at best a good half of that report will be devoted to the problem of our mutual relations.[84]

[81] V.K.P. (b) o Profsoyuzakh, page 310.

[82] L. Trotsky, The Real Situation in Russia, page 44. London: Allen & Unwin, 1928.

[83] Some parallel might perhaps be drawn between the position of the Soviet trade unions in those years and the attitude of the T.U.C. toward Mr. Attlee's government in 1945–1951, but it would be wrong to overlook the differences in the economic and social background, since even under the NEP, more than 80 per cent of the Soviet workers were employed in the socialist sector of the economy.

[84] 5. Syezd Profsoyuzov, page 118.

The fourteenth Congress of the party (December, 1925) thus rebuked the trade unions:

> It is necessary to fight against that deviation which takes the form of a strange bloc of some Trade Unionists and Trade Unions with the economic authorities, a bloc based on uncritical wholesale approval and defence . . . before the workers of all measures and proposals emanating from the economic administration. This transforms the Trade Unions into an appendage and political department of the economic administration and leads them to forget what is their main function.[85]

At the same time the Congress rebuked the unions for meddling with the business of the economic administration; it also remonstrated with the economic administration for dealing with the workers behind the back of the trade unions. At a Congress of the Trade Unions, Dogadov charged the Supreme Council of National Economy with trying to decree industrial wages without any reference to the unions. Other delegates stated that collective bargaining had become a mere sham.[86]

The extent to which the trade unions' influence was diminishing can be seen in their changing attitudes toward governmental arbitration in labor conflicts. In the opening years of NEP it was thought almost impossible that compulsory arbitration should be imposed upon the unions. At the fifth Trade Union Congress (1922) Schmidt, the Commissar for Labor, reported on a governmental decision investing powers of arbitration in his Commissariat. The Commissar himself, as we know, was appointed on the proposal of the Central Council of Trade Unions and could, in principle, be dismissed by that council. Even so, the idea that he should act as an arbiter, independently of the unions, still shocked many trade unionists. And so Schmidt told the Congress that the decree on compulsory arbitration had been passed by the government against his opinion and that he would in practice interpret it in favor of the unions.[87] Compulsory arbitration, he stated, would be applied in individual conflicts only, where no collective agreement was involved, and in cases of flagrant violation of labor legislation. If there must be arbitration, then it should be carried out not by a branch of the administration but by a special chamber, and in no case should the trade unions be denied the right to call strikes.[88] On behalf of the trade unions, Tomsky then spoke

---

[85] *V.K.P.* (*b*) *o Profsoyuzakh,* page 271.

[86] *7. Syezd Profsoyuzov,* page 86 and *passim.*

[87] In later years no member of the Soviet Government would have dared to reveal his disagreement with the government. Schmidt remained Commissar for Labor six years longer.

[88] *5. Syezd Profsoyuzov,* page 87.

in favor of local arbitration commissions, composed of trade unionists and representatives of factory managements, and of the advisability of their referring conflicts to the local branches of the Commissariat of Labor. The trade unions, he added, would call strikes only in extreme cases.[89] Another leading trade unionist, Rudzutak, the future vice-Premier, declared that the unions would suppress unauthorized strikes, but they would insist that in all strikes backed by themselves the demands of the workers must be met, and that the administrative organs that provoked strikes must be held responsible for this and the guilty officials must be dismissed, as a matter of principle. Some speakers at the Congress demanded that full powers of arbitration should be vested exclusively in the trade unions, but this was resisted by the government. The debate, on the whole, revealed how relatively great was still the strength of the trade unions.

Three years later, in December, 1925, the fourteenth Congress of the party adopted another resolution on compulsory arbitration that showed to what an extent the position of the trade unions had in the meantime changed.[90] The resolution asserted that it had become customary for the party committees, instead of the branches of the Commissariat of Labor, to arbitrate in labor conflicts. The Congress urged that this practice be discontinued. Yet the habit of those concerned to refer their conflicts to the party committees, and not to the trade unions or the Commissariat of Labor, reflected the real relationship between the respective institutions. The Congress further gave the economic administration the right to ask for compulsory arbitration and it strengthened the influence of the industrial managements in local arbitration committees. This was a far cry from Schmidt's assurance that compulsory arbitration would not be used against trade unions. The Trotsky-Zinoviev opposition commented on this reform that it ". . . reduced to nothing the collective contract itself, changing it from a two-sided act of agreement into an administrative organ. . . . The past years have been characterized by a sharp increase in labor conflicts, most of them being settled by compulsory rather than by conciliatory measures." [91] The opposition pressed for the annulment of the rights just given to the industrial managements. The trade union leaders, including Tomsky, still endorsed the extension of the prerogatives of the industrial managers, but two or three years later Tomsky and his adherents were to repeat, almost literally, Trotsky's and Zinoviev's criticisms and demands.

[89] *Ibid.*, page 105 and *passim.*

[90] *V.K.P. (b) o Profsoyuzakh,* page 272 ff.

[91] L. Trotsky, *The Real Situation in Russia,* page 49. London: Allen & Unwin, 1928.

Planned Economy

In the years 1925–27 the Soviets reaped the fruits of NEP; but the Bolshevik Party was divided by a bitter controversy, in which the trade unions were anything but disinterested spectators. Trotsky, Zinoviev, and Kamenev demanded that private enterprise be curbed with a stronger hand than hitherto, and that the government should embark upon more rapid industrialization and upon gradual collectivization of farming. The opposition, at the same time, criticized the "bureaucratic centralism" of the regime and demanded a return to "proletarian democracy," in which the trade unions would once again be free to defend the workers against the managements.

In those years the ruling group in party and government still consisted of a coalition of the so-called "right wing" of the party, which was in principle opposed to the demands of the opposition, and of the center, led by Stalin, which wavered between the opposed wings but for the time being stuck to the coalition with the right. The ruling circle favored a continuation of NEP and was reluctant to embark upon rapid industrialization and collectivization. It is difficult to say exactly what was the attitude of the mass of trade unionists, since they never had the chance to speak their minds frankly. The whole dispute was conducted under immense administrative pressure against the opposition. The leadership of the trade unions, however, sided unequivocally with the right wing of the party and resisted demands for rapid industrialization. Tomsky, still the most authoritative leader of the unions, was one of the three chiefs—the other two were Bukharin and Rykov—of the right-wing Bolsheviks. At the Congresses of the Trade Unions which took place in this period the Trotsky-Zinoviev opposition (or the "joint opposition" as it was officially called) still had a few spokesmen, but the overwhelming majority of delegates, who may or may not have faithfully reflected the mood of the rank and file, voted for the official party line, as represented by Tomsky.

Transition to planned economy

This lack of enthusiasm for industrialization displayed by the trade union leadership may appear puzzling. The trade unions, so it might seem, should have grasped how much they stood to gain from a policy that promised to increase the numbers of industrial workers and, generally speaking, to add weight to the industrial and trade unionist elements. Trotsky, Zinoviev, and Kamenev therefore charged the trade union leadership with lack of imagination and "bureaucratic conservatism," charges that are so often leveled by the political sections of the labor movements against the chiefs of the trade unions in other countries as well. And indeed, the economic policy advocated by the opposition, and later applied with extreme brutality by Stalin himself, did involve enormous uncertainties and risks, which a cautious, more or less honest but narrow-minded and already routine-ridden trade union officialdom wished to avoid. But, altogether apart from this, Tomsky and his adherents had their specific reasons for viewing with anxiety the prospects of rapid industrialization.

It was, or it must have been clear to them that this would be, accompanied by a further considerable increase in the powers of the economic administration as against the trade unions. For all the readiness of the unions, and of Tomsky personally, to cooperate with and to submit to the government and the Supreme Council of National Economy, there was almost permanent friction between them, friction that was not necessarily harmful—it had in theory been accepted as part of the normal processes of proletarian democracy—and that was inevitable as long as the trade unions enjoyed a modicum of autonomy. The trade union leadership clung to that modicum of autonomy.

Planned industrialization implied direction of labor. When the issue was posed in the middle twenties, it was a theoretical point only, in view of the large unemployment still existing. But it was not difficult to foresee that with expansion of industry unemployment would vanish, and that the next problem would be how to secure additional labor. The trade union leaders must also have been aware that rapid industrialization demanded the expansion of producers' industries, in the first instance. The individual worker was immediately interested in the development of consumers' industries, and the union leaders tended to voice his consumptionist bias. Apart from such strictly trade unionist considerations, Tomsky and the right-wing Bolsheviks were apprehensive of the ruthlessness with which the new policy, if adopted, was likely to be sponsored.

Tomsky gave all these reasons for his opposition in a speech at the eighth Congress of the Trade Unions (December, 1928). Stalin had just fallen out with the right wing of the party and sponsored the first Five-Year Plan; and this was the last time that Tomsky appeared at a Congress as the recognized leader of the trade unions. He revealed that industry had been troubled by many unofficial strikes, which had been due to the "Trade Unions paying inadequate attention to the needs of the masses, to their being detached from the masses and showing contempt for the small matters of the workers' life." [92] He demanded real elections in the unions, implying that hitherto

---

[92] 8. *Syezd Profsoyuzov*, page 24 and *passim*.

elections had been rigged. The rank and file, he went on, were afraid of speaking their minds, because critics were sure to be labeled Mensheviks or counter-revolutionaries.[93] The friction between the trade unions and the economic administration had been getting worse. The economic administration had been pressing down the level of wages and failing to observe collective agreements. It was the industrial managements rather than the unions that needed more discipline. Tomsky said:

> There should be no friendship between the economic administrator and the Trade Unionist, when it comes to carrying out the collective agreement—both sides must fulfil their commitments. . . . Very often pathetic things are concealed behind planning. Planning is often understood in this way: "Talk according to plan, do not say a word that is not according to plan."[94]

Factory meetings were convened only three times a year; even so they were regarded as a nuisance by industrial managers. The resolutions of the party which had urged systematic education of workers in the administration of the national economy had not been honored. Planned economy, Tomsky argued just as Trotsky had done some time earlier, could not properly function without some freedom of discussion, for only through discussion was it possible to correct mistakes and bring precision into the plans. He did not discard the productionist attitude in principle, and he repeated emphatically that the trade unions need not be ashamed of pressing workers for higher productivity, but this pressure "must take civilized forms. . . . This means that you and we have left behind the period of military communism, when . . . in some Trade Unions they set up jails (that is, for their undisciplined members). This, of course, was no civilized form of action, when Trade Unions together with managers imposed disciplinary punishment upon the workers."[95] Tomsky was supported

---

[93] *Ibid.,* page 38.

[94] *Loc. cit.*

[95] *Ibid., pages* 42, 44, and *passim.* The Webbs attributed to Tomsky the view that "It was not for the Trade Unions to press for improvements in factory technique, even if these would lead to increased productivity," and described him as an advocate of an "anarchic scramble after rises in wages . . . irrespective of their effect on the required universal increase of industrial productivity. . . . " (Sidney and Beatrice Webb, *Soviet Communism,* p. 131. London: Longmans, 1944.) This is, of course, an uncritical repetition of the official distortions and charges directed against Tomsky. Another echo of an official legend is the Webbs' assertion that the purpose of the anti-Tomsky purge in the trade unions was to remove uncooperative persons "not sprung from the manual labour class" (*op. cit.*). Whether any of the disputants was of working-class origin was completely irrelevant to this controversy, but what the Webbs apparently did not know is that for many years Tomsky had been the only authentic worker among the members of the Politbureau.

in the debate by other spokesmen, among them by the representative of the most important trade union, that of the metal workers, who spoke about the disregard shown for the needs of the consumers.[96]

The case for rapid industrialization was made by Kuibyshev, Ordzhonikidze, Zhdanov, and other leaders of the Stalinist group. Kuibyshev acquainted the Congress with one of the early variants of the first Five-Year Plan and made a striking comparison between the productivity of the American and the Russian workers. He said that whereas the output of one American worker at the furnace was 3,300 tons of steel per year, the output of the Russian worker was only 330 tons, exactly one-tenth. This comparison provided an index of Russian industrial backwardness.[97] The country could not overcome that backwardness as long as it was satisfied with industrialization "at the snail's pace," advocated by right-wing Bolsheviks. According to another spokesman, the Five-Year Plan provided for a 95 per cent increase in productivity of labor, which in the case given by Kuibyshev would still have left Russian productivity at one-fifth of the American. The economic administration could not but press for higher output; and—this was the unspoken but obvious conclusion—it could not be very selective about the forms of that pressure.[98]

Dramatic as was the controversy on the floor of the Congress, the real fight took place not there but at a closed session of the communist *fraktsya*, that is, at a conference of the communist delegates to the Congress. The *fraktsya* followed the Politbureau's instruction not to re-elect Tomsky as chairman of the Central Council. The Stalinist group in the trade union leadership was strengthened by the election of Kaganovich to the council—Kaganovich was the main driving power behind the subsequent purge in the unions. The nominal successor to Tomsky as chairman of the council was Shvernik, who was later to become President of the U.S.S.R. Schmidt, the Commissar for Labor, who was inclined toward the right-wing Bolsheviks, announced at the Congress his resignation from the commissariat.[99]

---

[96] *8. Syezd Profsoyuzov*, p. 96.

[97] *Ibid.*, page 373 and *passim*.

[98] Kuibyshev denied the statement made by Tomsky's adherents that the government had started the new policy of industrialization with a cut in the social services.

[99] It was during this debate that A. Zhdanov, then known only as one of the leaders of Communist Youth, moved into the limelight. He was "in the front line" of the attack against the right-wing Bolsheviks. It was he who from the floor of the Congress demanded Tomsky's dismissal. Yaglom, the editor of *Trud*, the official organ of the trade unions, in the course of a turbulent exchange spoke about Zhdanov's "Hottentot morals," while Tomsky spoke of Zhdanov as a "good but superficial man" wasting his considerable talents in the wrong causes. (*Ibid.*, page 177.)

The eighth Congress of the Trade Unions, and even more so the sixteenth conference of the party, which took place four months later, in April, 1929, opened a new chapter in the history of the trade unions and indeed of the Soviet regime at large.[100] A long series of controversies had been brought to an end. After the Trotskyist opposition, the group of Bukharin, Rykov, and Tomsky was silenced. Henceforth, no open discussion of policy would be permitted. The totalitarian state with its rigid uniformity and absolute discipline, under a single leader, had taken final shape. True enough, the clauses of the old Leninist resolutions of 1921 and 1922, which guaranteed the trade unions their relative freedom, were never declared null and void, for the regime, professing a strict Leninist orthodoxy, could not openly discard a principle established by Lenin himself. But the relative autonomy of the trade unions could have no meaning when no institution and no organization whatsoever could maintain even a shred of independence vis-à-vis the state. To be sure, the single-party system had been in existence at least since the end of the civil war—all opposition parties had been suppressed by then. Yet in the early twenties the Bolshevik leaders were still inclined to regard that suppression as an emergency measure to be reversed as soon as the regime regained enough stability to tolerate organized opposition. And in those years Mensheviks, Social Revolutionaries, and other anti-Bolshevik groups still enjoyed some freedom of expression and organization inside the trade unions, even though their parties had been banned. In the middle twenties the open controversies inside the ruling party continued to prevent the regime from acquiring the monolithic outlook. Thus, although the basis for the totalitarian state had been laid during and after the civil war, it took nearly a decade before the edifice grew up. In the course of that decade the trade unions availed themselves of such margins of freedom and relative independence as there were. Now, toward the end of the twenties, those margins vanished.

Trade unions and planned economy

Toward the end of 1928 the first Five-Year Plan was proclaimed.

---

[100] A resolution of the sixteenth conference stated *inter alia:* ". . . in Trade Union problems Bukharin, Rykov and Tomsky are prepared to oppose in the most dangerous fashion the Trade Unions to the party, actually aiming at the weakening of party leadership in the Unions, blurring defects in the work of the Unions, defending craft trends and the manifestations of bureaucratic ossification in parts of the Trade Union machinery, and presenting the party's struggle against these defects as a Trotskyist 'shake up' of the Trade Unions. . . . " Referring to Tomsky's demand for freedom of expression, the resolution stated: "The party . . . rejects with determination such 'freedom' of criticism which the right elements demand in order to defend their anti-Leninist political line." *V.K.P.* (*b*) *o Profsoyuzakh,* page 389.

Unlike previous plans, emanating from the *Gosplan,* the central planning authority, which were no more than loose prognostications, this Plan had the character of a law, enforced by the government upon the whole country. Planning included labor policy, and consequently the activity of the trade unions was now strictly confined within the limits set to it.

The problem with which the planners had to contend over the greater part of the period under discussion was the extreme shortage of industrial labor, especially of skilled labor. In an effort to overcome this, the government gradually worked out a very wide assortment of methods, in the application of which the trade unions played a crucial part.

As stated before, direction of labor was abolished in 1922; and up to World War II it was never *nominally* reenacted. In actual fact, however, more and more elements of compulsory direction were introduced in the course of the three prewar Five-Year Plans (1929–1941). Moreover, some of the forms of direction of labor were much more drastic than any of those that had been associated with militarization of labor during the civil war. The notorious mammoth forced labor camps that came into existence during the thirties are a case in point. From a legislative viewpoint, the fact that the Soviet Government, in spite of such drastic and brutal practices, up to World War II never claimed for itself over-all powers of direction of labor, represents a curious anomaly. For this the Leninist orthodoxy, to which Stalinism had committed itself, was responsible: Lenin had dismissed compulsory direction of labor and the use of the trade unions for this purpose as unjustifiable in a socialist regime, under normal conditions. This principle came to be enshrined in the party tradition, and to it the Stalinist regime had to pay its tribute. In theory, labor remained "free." Elements of direction and compulsion were introduced on an increasing scale, but in a way that should not openly clash with precept. Thus, a wide discrepancy arose between precept and practice, a discrepancy that was entirely lacking in the labor policy of military communism, including Trotsky's militarization of labor. Under military communism the powers of the government and the limits to which it went to enforce them were at least known, and they were the object of discussion and criticism. This alone provided a safeguard against gross abuses, a safeguard that has not been available to the Russian workers under the evasive policies of the thirties, forties and early fifties.

Given the purposes of national policy that the Soviet Government had set itself when it embarked upon rapid industrialization, a degree of direction of labor was almost inevitable. At the beginning of the first Five-Year Plan this need was in part revealed and in part veiled by the fact that, while industry was already experiencing an acute shortage of labor, the labor exchanges still registered more than a million unemployed. In December, 1929 the Central Committee of the party instructed the Central Council of the Trade Unions to find out "within the shortest possible time what were the needs for skilled labor in various branches of industry and transport and in the various regions of the country . . . and to find out what were the changes in the composition and training of labor caused by the reconstruction and rationalization of industry." The trade unions were also expected to help in the ". . . working out of a system of measures guaranteeing the timely and full supply of skilled labor. . . ." [101] The Commissariat of Labor and the trade unions were further instructed to check the registered unemployment and to find out how much of it was real and how much illusory. In the course of 1930, unemployment virtually disappeared, and the government was confronted with a new problem: how to expand industry rapidly, while the actual industrial labor force of the nation was already fully employed. There was, first and foremost, the question of how to increase the total labor force, and then— the more specific issue: how to increase the supply of skilled labor.

Industrial recruitment. The solution to the first problem lay in transferring the surplus manpower of an overpopulated countryside into the old and new industrial centers. This had been, broadly speaking, the main source from which other countries in the process of industrialization had drawn their manpower. But in those countries masses of migrant peasants were drawn in by the *laissez-faire* mechanism of supply and demand on labor markets; and the unregulated, "spontaneous" supply of labor dictated up to a point the rhythm of industrialization. Other circumstances being equal, scarcity of labor slowed down industrialization, whereas an overabundant supply speeded it up, at the expense of the living standard of the working population. The Soviet Government was determined itself to dictate the tempo of industrialization, which it could not do unless it regulated the transfer of the rural surplus population into industry. This was arranged in the following way: industrial managements concluded annual agreements with the managements of collective farms, under which the latter were obliged to supply specified numbers of their "redundant members" to the factories, mines, and so forth. Through this "organized intake" of labor, industry received between 1.5 million and 2 million new workers annually, throughout the prewar Five-Year Periods. Thus was made possible a phenomenal influx of the rural population into the cities and towns of the Soviet Union, an influx for which hardly a single

---

[101] *V.K.P. (b) o Profsoyuzakh*, pages 459–468.

historic precedent can be found; it involved 24 million people between 1926 and 1939.[102]

The contracts between factories and collective farms were to be strictly voluntary. This they were, in part. Rural overpopulation was only too real, and it became even more pronounced when the collective farms were mechanized and much more new labor was "set free." That the great mass of raw peasants had no need to wander helplessly in search of work in remote cities, that it had no need to experience the lot of migrant peasants exposed to the horrors of early capitalist industrial revolutions, might have been of obvious social advantage. From this angle, the Soviet Government could make a very strong case for the "organized recruitment" of peasant labor.[103] On the other hand, there was massive compulsion. The individual peasant singled out as redundant by the chairman of the collective farm had no choice but to leave; he was as good as expropriated; and he had to go to the factory or mine to which he was directed, although once there he was, as a rule, free to change his job.

A much more rigid method of "organized intake" was enforced shortly before the German invasion of Russia, when the government considered it necessary to increase even more rapidly than hitherto the reserves of industrial manpower. Under the decree on the State Labor Reserves, of December 2, 1940, chairmen of collective farms were obliged to call up for the labor reserves specified numbers of young men. The quotas were fixed at 20 boys between 14–15 years and two between 16–17 for every 100 members of any collective farm aged between 14 and 55 years.[104] In proportion to the young members of the collective farms the number of those called up was, of course, very high; and the method of recruitment resembled the manner in which Russians had been called up for the army a hundred years before under Tsar Nicholas I.

In this "organized intake" of peasant labor the trade unions played, and still play, an important auxiliary role. The contracts with the collective farms are signed by the industrial managements. But the trade union, or more strictly the factory committee—its basic unit— acts as a sort of recruiting agent. Like every recruiting agent, it tries

---

[102] The total growth of the urban population in the same period, including the normal increase in the town-dwelling population, amounted to nearly 30 million.

[103] This does not apply, of course, to the forced labor camps, among the inmates of which political offenders or suspects formed a very high, perhaps the highest, proportion. But the forced labor camp is a monstrous excess, not the typical form of Soviet direction of labor. The typical form is precisely this "organized intake" of peasant labor, on the basis of contracts between the industrial concerns and collective farms.

[104] *Pravda,* October 3, 1940.

to make the industrial job as attractive as possible in the eyes of the recruit. But, unlike the recruiting agent of the early capitalist industrial revolution, it continues to watch and, within limits, protect the recruit at the factory. The trade union is, in part or entirely, responsible for inuring the newcomer to labor discipline and imparting to him the habits and rudimentary skills of the industrial worker. It sees to it that the wages of the recruit, however low he may be in the scale, should, at any rate, not be lower than those paid to any worker of no higher skill and diligence. Nominally, the trade unions are also jointly responsible for the housing of the new workers, which in most cases was and still is abominable; and they are actually responsible for such matters as the protection of their labor, social insurance, and so forth. By standards of old-time trade unionism, the functions of the Russian trade unions are highly mixed. No self-respecting union in the capitalist countries would act as the recruiting agent for the industrial management; but, on the other hand, few trade unions have ever concerned themselves with the raw industrial recruit (as distinct from the skilled or half-skilled and settled worker) as the Soviet trade unions have.

The organized transfer of the rural surplus population to the industrial centers solved the one great problem, without which rapid industrialization would have been impossible: it supplied industry with an almost automatically expanding reserve of manpower. But it did not solve another no less vital problem—it did not secure stability of employment. Over many years Soviet industry suffered from the so-called "fluidity of labor," the real scourge of the Russian economy in the thirties. Indeed, the effect of industrialization was greatly diminished by that fluidity. Workers refused to stay on their jobs; they constantly shifted from mine to mine and from factory to factory. This peculiarly Soviet phenomenon affected, as we shall see later, skilled as well as unskilled labor, but it was most characteristic for the millions of peasants drawn into industry. The causes and effects of "fluidity" and the problems that it created for the trade unions are not difficult to gauge. In general, the poor living conditions, and quite especially the desperate shortage of housing in the cities and towns, which had been unprepared for the formidable influx of a new population, made for instability of labor. Workers moved from place to place in search of better living conditions. There was also the lack of industrial tradition and discipline in the proletarianized peasantry. All the habits of settled industrial life, regulated by the factory siren, that had in other countries been imparted to the working class over generations, often with the help of ruthless legislation—all those habits were conspicuously lacking in Russia. The peasant, who had been accustomed to work in his field according to the rhythm of nature, to toil from sunrise to sunset in the summer, and to sleep through most of the winter, had now to be forced and conditioned into an entirely new routine of work. Against that he revolted and restlessly shifted from place to place. The threat of unemployment, which so often prevents a worker from leaving even the most unsatisfactory job, was absent. The fears that the *laissez-faire* mechanism of supply and demand of labor normally produced and impressed upon the mind of the worker were not there to chain the Soviet worker to the bench; and new fears were not yet substituted for the old ones. On the other hand, the Soviet worker was not free to struggle for the improvement of his living conditions as the worker in other countries had struggled under the leadership of the trade unions: he could not strike. The Soviet trade union firmly discouraged strikes, and behind the union stood the political police. Fluidity of labor was the substitute for strikes. The workers did not now coalesce to down tools. Instead, the individual worker or millions of workers individually downed tools and left their places of work to hire themselves elsewhere.

The effect of fluidity was to hamper the acquisition of industrial skill by the new worker, to disturb the functioning of industry, and to make the very basis of planning uncertain. The fact that throughout the thirties fluidity was the central point of every discussion on labor policy, the subject of innumerable exhortations, instructions, and decrees, shows to what extent this spontaneous and unforeseen process obstructed the working of the planned economy. The resulting confusion was, up to a point, inevitable in the circumstances, but it was made even worse than it need have been by inconsistencies of policy and a neglect of consumers' needs, that only an autocratic administration could afford.

Direction of labor was at first confined to the initial stage of supplying labor to industry, that is, to the transfer of people from the countryside to the industrial centers. At the next stage direction ceased, or at any rate ceased to be effective. Here is a brief survey of the measures taken by the government and the trade unions to overcome fluidity. The government was first alarmed by this development in the latter part of 1930. On September 3, the Central Committee of the party dealt with it in its message on the third year of the first Five-Year Plan.[105] It appealed to the trade unions (and to other organizations) to take specific measures against fluidity. It proposed that workers drafted into industry should accept the obligation to remain in their factories for specified periods, that special incentives be offered to those who honored the obligation, and that notorious "de-

---

[105] *V.K.P. (b) o Profsoyuzakh,* page 506.

serters from production" be placed under boycott by the trade unions and other bodies. At the same time it was decided to abolish the labor exchanges that had apparently facilitated "desertion," by enabling any worker who had left his job to register for unemployment assistance and to find a new job.

A few weeks later, in October, 1930, the Central Committee, realizing that exhortation was not enough, proposed specific incentives and deterrents calculated to ensure stability of labor. Workers who stayed on the same job for two years were to receive somewhat longer holidays than others; and the penalty imposed on "deserters" and absentees was the loss of the right to industrial employment for six months.[106] The incentives were still feeble. The deterrents would have been all too powerful had it not been for the endemic character of fluidity; industrial managers, chronically short of labor and desperately anxious to reach their targets of output, were certain to disregard the sanctions decreed and to give a job to any "deserter" from another factory who applied for one. Incidentally, the same instruction by which "deserters" were deprived of the right of employment urged the Central Council of Trade Unions to see that no administrative pressure or compulsion should be exerted in order to make workers enter into obligations for long-term employment. This injunction once again illustrated the dilemmas of an administration that was compelled by policy and circumstance to resort to direction of labor and yet was anxious to maintain the appearance that it was not doing so.

At the beginning of the second Five-Year Plan (1933), fluidity of labor was as widespread and severe as ever, even though sanctions introduced in the meantime included the denial to "deserters" of ration cards, living quarters, and so on. A resolution issued under the joint authority of government and party, and signed by Molotov and Stalin on April 8, 1933, indicated the extent of the trouble in the coal industry of the Donetz Basin, on whose output depended the fulfilment or nonfulfilment of the Five-Year Plan. The resolution stated that:

. . . according to the information of the statistical offices, 423,000 workers and employees left the mines in 1932. During the same period 458,000 workers and employees entered employment. In January of 1933 alone, 32,000 left and 35,000 workers and employees entered employment. This means that a considerable part of workers and employees, if not the majority, drifts restlessly from mine to mine, from the mines into the countryside, and from the countryside into the mines rather than work. . . . It goes without saying that in view of such fluidity it is impossible to assimilate, if only in a half-satisfactory manner, the new technique and to master the new machines. Yet the mastery

106 *Ibid.*, page 516.

of the new technique is the key to the rise of the entire coal industry of the Donbas.[107]

[The disorder indicated] would not have taken place, if the managers of the pits . . . had given effect to the law against loiterers and absentees and deprived them of their ration cards and the right to living quarters.[108]

Five years later, at the beginning of the third Five-Year Plan (1938), the same disorder was still plaguing Soviet industry. New and more drastic measures were taken to tie the worker to his workshop, and these were enforced directly by the trade unions. The whole system of social insurance was remodelled so as to help to promote stability of labor; and, as the trade unions had (in 1933) been made responsible for the administration of the social insurance funds, they were the chief executors of the new policy.

A decree of December 28, 1938, signed by Stalin (for the party), Molotov (for the government), and Shvernik (for the trade unions) embodied the following provisions:[109]

The workers' right to a holiday with pay after five and a half months' employment was abolished; henceforth holidays were to be granted only after eleven months of uninterrupted work.

Notorious "loiterers" and absentees were to be unconditionally dismissed from jobs.

"A worker or employee guilty of coming late to work without a valid reason, of leaving for lunch too early or returning too late, of leaving the factory or office before time or idling during working hours is liable to administrative prosecution: to be rebuked or rebuked with notice of dismissal; to be transferred to a job with less pay for three months; or to be altogether transferred to a lower grade. A worker or employee guilty of committing three such offenses in one month, or four in two consecutive months, is dismissed as . . . an offender against the law of labor and labor discipline." [110] Industrial managers failing to impose the prescribed punishments were themselves made liable to dismissal or prosecution.

The payment of insurance allowances to workers temporarily incapacitated was, under the same decree, made dependent on the length of time during which the person concerned stayed in his or her job.[111] Only after six years of permanent employment was 100 per cent of the wage or salary to be paid to the incapacitated; 80 per cent was paid after three to six years; 60 per cent after two to three years;

---

[107] *Ibid.*, page 545.

[108] *Ibid.*, pages 546–547.

[109] *V.K.P.* (*b*) *o Profsoyuzakh*, pages 594–601.

[110] *Ibid.*, page 596.

[111] The sanctions did not, of course, apply to workers who changed jobs by order or permission of their superiors.

and only 50 per cent if the worker or employee had stayed in his job less than two years.[112] (These allowances were paid to members of trade unions. Nonmembers received only 50 per cent of the appropriate rates. Thus, although membership of the trade unions was, in accordance with the Leninist principle, nominally voluntary, it carried with it substantial material benefits, and nonmembership entailed equally substantial loss.)

Pensions for permanent invalids were also graded in relation to the length of employment. In addition to the basic pension, bonuses were granted to invalids with satisfactory employment records. To give one example, invalids of the "first category" (that is, those who had been employed in mines, underground, or in harmful occupations) received 10 per cent over and above the pension after 3–5 years of permanent employment in one concern, 20 per cent after 5–10 years, and 25 per cent after more than 10 years.[113] Since all these measures were certain not only to reduce fluidity of labor, but also to reduce the sum total of pensions paid out by the trade unions, the latter were instructed to use the saved money for building additional houses for workers.

Perhaps the most drastic provision of the decree was that people who had left their jobs without permission or had been guilty of grave offenses against labor discipline were "liable to compulsory administrative eviction [from their dwellings] within ten days, without any living quarters being provided for them." [114] Since houses, as a rule, belonged to municipalities or other public corporations, the evicted offender had practically no chance to obtain new quarters. Often this entailed deportation to a forced labor camp. The fear of the forced labor camp now came to play the role that the fear of unemployment had played under capitalism—it helped to maintain labor discipline. This stage, however, was reached only in the latter part of the thirties, when mass deportation of political suspects, too, became a normal practice. Yet even now the theory that workers were not tied to their workshops was not abandoned. The decree just quoted states *inter alia* that workers desiring to leave their jobs ought to give one month's notice of their intention, as if they had still been free to carry out such an intention. More curiously still, some of these legislative measures were introduced by the government allegedly in response to demands from the trade unions themselves.

Training of labor. With the progress of industrialization and the

---

[112] In the coal industry allowances were more liberal. Coal miners received 100 per cent after two years, and 60 per cent after less than two years of permanent employment.

[113] For a more detailed scale of bonuses see *V.K.P.* (*b*) *o Profsoyuzakh,* page 599.

[114] *Ibid.,* page 598.

enforcement of draconic legislation, fluidity of labor tended to weaken, if not to disappear altogether. In the late thirties complaints about fluidity became less frequent, and after World War II they became rare. A considerable proportion of the 20 millions or so of the industrial proletariat already consisted of people who had acquired, if only recently, the habits and outlook of industrial workers, and were capable of imparting these to newcomers from the countryside.[115] Government, industry, and trade unions had also acquired considerable experience in handling the influx of new and raw labor. In addition, the recruits now drafted into industry were no longer quite the same raw, backward *muzhiks* of the early thirties, who had never handled a machine. The mechanized collective farm became the first training ground for industrial workers. Thus the most painful phase of the industrial revolution, and some of its ugliest repercussions in labor policy, should have been largely left behind.

For the history of the Soviet trade unions and labor policy the period of the initial accumulation of industrial skill in the rapidly growing working class presents enormous interest. The problem was first tackled on a fairly large scale toward the end of 1929, when the trade unions, jointly with the Supreme Council of National Economy and the Commissariat of Education, started experimental factory schools, where cadres of skilled workers were trained without interrupting normal work at the bench. From this developed the system of *fabzavuchi*, the factory school which played an important role in later years. At the same time, the Central Committee of the party decreed that the technical colleges and schools should have at least 70 per cent of workers among their pupils.[116] The Central Council of Trade Unions organized general educational courses—it was essential for industrialization that the general standards of education be raised. The cost of these courses was borne by the trade unions, whose revenue was assured—the economic administration deducted two per cent of workers' wages as membership fees for the unions.[117] The trade unions were also responsible for choosing from among the workers candidates for technical schools of all grades. They distributed scholarships among their advanced members who had shown diligence and technical ability and displayed initiative at so-called "factory produc-

---

[115] The total number of workers and employees was approaching 30 million before World War II (it was about 33 million in 1949), but it has never been stated how many of these were manual workers and how many were office employees. Indirect indications suggest that industrial workers formed about two-thirds or slightly more of the total.

[116] *Ibid.*, page 450.

[117] In the late thirties the membership fee was reduced to one per cent of wages.

tion meetings." As the rapidly expanding industry badly needed managerial personnel the Central Council of the Trade Unions was also asked to submit a list of 1,500–2,000 of its ablest organizers for promotion to managerial posts.

A year later, in 1930, economic development was so severely impeded by the shortage of skilled labor that trade unions were ordered to prepare, within twenty days, a practical plan for the training of labor in 1931. It was estimated that the additional demand for skilled labor in the basic industries alone would amount to 1.3 million men in the course of that year. These were trained in the *fabzavuchi* and technical schools in a manner that was of necessity extremely hasty and superficial. At the same time the trade unions helped the Commissariat of Labor to comb out unessential industries for skilled labor, which was to be directed to essential industries. The trade unions further established a permanent register of skilled workers, which enabled them to respond instantaneously to the demands of the economic administration for labor. The pressure under which industry was working was illustrated by the fact that the Central Committee of the party now prohibited the promotion of skilled workers to administrative posts, the prohibition being valid for two years. Industrial managers were made liable to prosecution for obstructing or delaying the transfer of skilled workers, for the improper use of skilled labor, for luring workers and technicians from other undertakings by offers of higher wages, and for employing more workers than was allowed by governmentally fixed standards.[118]

Along these and similar lines the program for training labor developed throughout the thirties. It culminated in the 1940 decree on State Labor Reserves, which ordered *inter alia* that a high proportion of those called up for industrial labor be directed to training schools. In the same year 1,500 such schools, training 800,000 pupils, were opened; and for the following years the program provided for the training of one million apprentices annually. This system worked throughout the war. It will be remembered that the State Labor Reserves consisted of boys in their middle teens. When war broke out the following year, these were too young to be called up for the forces, but vast numbers of them had already received sufficient training to fill gaps in industrial manpower caused by the mobilization of the older age-groups. It was to a large extent with the help of that juvenile labor that Soviet industry kept its wheels turning during the war.

"Socialist emulation." In its striving for higher efficiency Soviet

---

[118] *V.K.P. (b) o Profsoyuzakh,* page 515.

industry gradually came to rely upon "socialist emulation" and upon an elaborate system of incentive wages.

At the beginning of 1929 the sixteenth party conference initiated "socialist emulation" *en masse*. The idea dated back to the first years of the Soviet regime. The sixteenth conference, in fact, recalled the following words from a resolution adopted by the ninth Congress of the party (1920):

> Every social system . . . has had its own methods and ways of labor compulsion and education for labor in the interest of the exploiting classes.
>
> The Soviet order is confronted with the task . . . of developing its own methods, designed to raise the intensity and efficiency of labor on the basis of a socialized economy and in the interests of the whole people.
>
> On a par with the propaganda of ideas, which should influence the mind of the toiling masses, and with repressive measures, used against deliberate idlers, drones, and disorganizers, emulation is the most powerful means toward raising productivity of labor.
>
> In capitalist society emulation has had the character of competition and has led to the exploitation of man by man. In a society in which the means of production have been nationalized, emulation in labor ought, without impinging upon the solidarity [of workers] only to raise the sum total of the products of labor.
>
> Emulation between factories, regions, shops, workshops, and individual workers should be the object of careful organization and attentive research on the part of the Trade Unions and the economic administration.[119]

A serious ideological dilemma was implicit in this idea of emulation. It will be noted that the resolution just quoted stressed that the workers' emulation in production should not "impinge upon their solidarity." This proviso implicitly referred back to Marx's theory of the development of the modern industrial working class, given in his *Misère de la Philosophie* and in other writings. Marx distinguished two historic stages, not strictly separated from one another but rather overlapping, in the evolution of the proletariat. In the first, the outlook of the working class is characterized primarily by individualistic competition between its members. In the workshop and factory, members of an immature working class compete with one another for jobs, better wages, and so forth. They have not yet learned to act in solidarity. They are still opposed to one another and only individually opposed to their employers. In the next phase, marked by the emergence of trade unions and other class organizations, competition between individual members of the working class tends to give place

---

[119] *Ibid.*, page 414. The author of this resolution was Trotsky, although the same idea was frequently expounded by Lenin. There was a touch of irony in the fact that Trotsky's words, without the authorship being mentioned, were approvingly quoted in the solemn message of the sixteenth party conference only a few weeks after the Politbureau had expelled Trotsky from Russia.

to their solidarity *vis-à-vis* the capitalists. This supersession of competition by solidarity reflects the growing maturity of the proletariat, enables it to overcome centrifugal tendencies in its own midst and to act as a class. This broad view of the evolution of the working class, which became part and parcel of the socialist and communist outlook, presupposed, of course, that in a socialist regime competition between individual members of the working class would tend to disappear, making room for full solidarity, first of the workers and then of all members of a classless society.

No wonder that in the first Bolshevik appeals for socialist emulation mental reservations could be read between the lines. Emulation was "not to impinge upon solidarity." Emulation may take various forms: there ought to be emulation between factories, regions, shops, and workshops; that is, between collectives; but, in the last instance, it should also develop between individual workers. Its purpose was to be "only to raise the sum total of the products of labor." Who will produce more and better? But already behind these first appeals there loomed the tricky question whether those who produce more and better should also receive higher rewards. At first the dilemma presented itself in the dimmest of forms; and the answers were tentative and at times self-contradictory. One answer, formulated by Lenin, was that if there was to be competition, that is, inequality in production (if some people were to produce more than others), then there must also be inequality in consumption. Otherwise there would be no incentive to higher production. The "levellers" (among whom Trotsky might be classed only with the strongest of qualifications) argued in favor of "shock methods" in production and equality in consumption. But in those early years all Bolshevik leaders were "levellers" in the sense that, even when they admitted the need for differential wages in the period of transition to socialism, they still saw in the gradual equalization of wages the *sine qua non* of socialist labor policy.

This egalitarian frame of mind was still quite strong when, in 1929, the sixteenth party conference, already under Stalin's exclusive leadership, launched its full-scale campaign for "socialist emulation." The conference still appealed, mainly if not exclusively, to the communist idealism of the working masses rather than to their *immediate* interests. It stated that "the Trade Unions and the economic organs ought to adopt a broad system of incentives." [120] But the incentives proposed were mainly of a moral character, designed to spur the worker's ambition and to stir his imagination.

The names of the best workers, best specialists, best economic administrators

---

[120] *Ibid.,* page 415.

and agronomists, the names of factories and mines and of the best Soviet and collective farms ought to become known to the entire country. . . . The heroic traditions of the past years have been preserved and enriched by the working class of our country. The Leninist idea of "the organization of emulation on socialist principles" finds an evermore practical realization. The principles of a communist attitude toward labor begin to strike ever deeper roots. . . .[121]

The emphasis so far was on emulation between collective bodies rather than individual workers. Material rewards were to be given primarily to collective bodies, factories, regions, and so on. The emulation took the form of factories challenging one another to raise and improve output. These practices tended all too quickly to become stale routine or unproductive pageantry, and the trade unions were urged to take care of the economic realities behind the reports on emulation.

In 1930–1931, the emphasis shifted to emulation between individual workers and to individual material rewards for records achieved in production. The shock-worker, the industrial record-man, became in a sense the central figure of Russian society. The trade unions proclaimed an All-Union Day of the Shock-Worker (or the *udarnik*) on October 1, 1930. In this movement there was undoubtedly a strong streak of idealism. The young worker was encouraged in the hope that a few years of unsparing exertion on his part would transform the whole country, modernize it, and make it into a "Socialist America." The trade unions displayed much initiative and shrewd propagandist techniques in promoting emulation. At the same time the shock-worker was given a privileged position. In the factories special canteens and restaurants were opened exclusively for the *udarniki;* and they were immeasurably better supplied than the canteens for ordinary workers. Better living quarters, facilities for education and rest, better supplies of rare consumer goods, and so on were reserved for shock-workers and their families. Socialist emulation began most drastically to "impinge upon solidarity"; and soon a radical revision of wage policy followed.

Wage policy. Very early in the NEP period the Soviet Government enunciated the principle that the national wage bill must be closely related to the size of the national income, or rather, to its most important co-determinant—efficiency of labor. This rule was, in general terms, laid down by the twelfth Congress of the party (1923). In a more specific and emphatic form it was reiterated by a plenary conference of the party's Central Committee in August, 1924, in connection with a curious situation that had arisen in Russian industry. According to a statistical calculation, the correctness of which was

[121] *Ibid.,* pages 415–416.

not generally accepted, industrial wages had risen by 90 per cent between October, 1922 and January, 1924. During the same period, output per man-day had risen only by 23 per cent. As, in consequence of the civil war, the standard of living of the Russian workers had been depressed far below any essential minimum, the Central Committee put up with this disproportion between the rise of wages and improvement in industrial efficiency. But with the evident, if still incomplete, normalization of the economy, this state of affairs could not continue. Henceforth, it was stated, productivity of labor must rise more quickly than wages.

It is not possible to make any precise comparison between the trends in wages and industrial efficiency during subsequent years. The official statistical indices were not very reliable and were hotly disputed. In the middle twenties the Trotskyist opposition asserted that, while the government claimed that industrial wages had risen to the prewar level, real wages were actually less than two-thirds of what they had been before 1914. The opposition concluded that the wage policy of 1924 should be reversed, and that wages should be increased at least at the same rate at which productivity of labor was rising. Against this, the official spokesmen advanced the argument, which has since become something of an axiom, that, if industry was to expand, productivity of labor must rise more quickly than wages so as to create a sufficiently wide margin of resources for capital investment.

The entire wage policy of the prewar Plans was based on this principle, which did not, of course, meet with any open criticism or opposition on the part of the trade unions. The sixteenth party conference, when it launched the first Five-Year Plan, foreshadowed an over-all rise in the productivity of industrial labor by 110 per cent. Wages were to rise by 71 per cent over the same five-year period.[122] In 1930 alone, the increase in productivity was planned to be 25 per cent, while the rise in nominal wages was to amount to 9 per cent and in real wages to 12 per cent. Similar proportions were characteristic for all prewar Plans. (The first postwar Five-Year Plan, however, provided for an increase in wages by 48 per cent and in productivity by only 36 per cent above the 1940 levels.)

The size of the national wage bill was, and still is, as strictly planned as were the targets of output, the rates of capital investment, the proportions of expansion between heavy and light industry, and so on. Theoretically, the planned wage bill represents only another name for the mass of consumer goods that the plan allocates to the industrial population; that is, the *real* wage bill. An increase in the national wage

---

[122] *V.K.P.* (b) *o Profsoyuzakh*, pp. 393–395.

bill without a corresponding increase in the volume of consumer goods must, of course, lead to inflation. The Soviet trade unions understood and accepted this maxim from their earliest years; they had learnt their lesson from the depreciation of the rouble in World War I, during the revolution, the civil war, and the early twenties. As, under the Five-Year Plans, the output of consumer industries was rigidly fixed in advance, the trade unions were left with no scope for bargaining over the national wage bill, even if they had wanted to bargain.

This statement needs perhaps to be qualified. In theory, the trade unions exercise their influence at the very top of the governmental pyramid, at the stage when the Politbureau, the government, and the planning authorities still discuss the main features of any Five-Year Plan. It is impossible to say whether, or to what extent, they have ever pressed for higher wages (that is, for an increase in the targets of output set for consumer industries) before any plan has been accepted. We do not know, in other words, to what extent the trade unions have ever acted as a pressure group on the highest level of the administration. What is certain is that they could not act as pressure groups or bargain at the medium and lower levels. Once the national plan had been adopted and broken down into regional plans the trade unions could not and would not ask for any revision of those of its features that dealt with wages and conditions of labor. No trade unionist would take upon himself the odium of trying to upset the plan.

This is not to say that wage policy has always worked smoothly and efficiently, "according to plan." We have seen how the fluidity of labor threatened to disturb the working of the planned economy. Other spontaneous reactions on the part of this or that section of the population to certain features of governmental policy had similar upsetting effects. The entire wage policy of the first Five-Year Plan, for instance, was based on an anticipation of a cheapening of consumer goods. Hence the rises in nominal wages were, as a rule, planned to be lower than those in real wages. (For instance, in 1930 nominal wages were to rise by 9 per cent and real wages by 12 per cent.) This anticipation did not come true. The revolt of vast sections of the peasantry against collectivization, the mass slaughter of cattle, and the resulting scarcity of goods caused a steep rise in the prices of nearly all unrationed goods and often made it impossible for the government to supply the rationed goods. Thus, whatever the rise in the nominal wages, real wages went down, although it is not easy to say by just how much. The fact is that throughout the first Five-Year Plan the "scissors" between the ever-rising nominal wages and the declining real wages grew ever wider. The gap was considerably narrowed in the second and third Five-Year Plans, when the supply of food and other consumer goods became more abundant.

So far we have seen how the *national* wage bill has been related to *national* efficiency. The next step was to correlate *individual* wages and *individual* efficiency.

Before the period of planned economy, in the twenties, two major reforms of wage policy had been carried out. The first, based on resolutions of the fourth Congress of the Trade Unions, took place in 1921–22. The scale of wages then introduced comprised seventeen grades, nine for manual workers and eight for clerical employees. The proportion of the lowest to the highest wage was 1 to 3.5. The main differentiation was between the two broad categories of skilled and unskilled labor. The differences in wage rates paid for various grades of skill were relatively slight; and additional rewards showed a decreasing progression in the higher grades. Thus, for instance, while a man in the third grade of skill earned 25 per cent more than one in the second grade, the worker of the eighth category earned only 10.5 per cent more than his colleague in the seventh grade. This decreasing scale of additional rewards is now retrospectively denounced as a manifestation of *uravnilovka*, the condemned egalitarian heresy. Yet throughout the twenties this scale of wages was considered to be an excess of bourgeois inequality surviving in the proletarian state. The leadership of the trade unions was on this ground denounced as the mouthpiece of a new labor aristocracy by the Trotskyist opposition; and it met the opposition's criticisms with shamefaced embarrassment, admitting that the differences in wages were too great and ought to be reduced. At the seventh Congress of the Trade Unions, in December, 1926, Tomsky, then still an all-powerful member of the Politbureau, on the one hand opposed the demands of his critics for a general rise in wages but, on the other, conceded the need for equalization.[123] In the middle twenties the discrepancies in wages were in fact slightly reduced.[124]

The second tariff reform, carried out in 1927–28, was calculated to give further satisfaction to the demand for more equality. Graduations between the earnings of the skilled and unskilled workers were lessened. "The higher the tariff grade of the worker the smaller was

---

[123] 7. *Syezd Profsoyuzov*, page 49 and *passim*. Tomsky told the Congress that well-wishing foreign visitors had been shocked by the differences between the earnings of skilled and unskilled workers in Russia. At that time, such criticisms coming from foreign visitors, mostly communists, still made their impression on the Russian Communist Party.

[124] See Dogadov's statement in *8. Syezd Profsoyuzov*, page 87. In 1926, the highest wage paid, say, in railway workshops, was only 53 per cent above the lowest, while in engineering the highest wage was 128 per cent above the lowest.

his additional reward," says a recent critic of the reform. An attempt was also made to limit the application of piece-rates.

It is interesting to note that the egalitarian trend found a consistent and early critic in Stalin himself who already in 1925 admonished the fourteenth Congress of the party: "We must not play with the phrase about equality. This is playing with fire." [125] But a drastic practical reaction against the egalitarian trend was initiated by Stalin only in the middle of 1931, in one of his famous speeches to industrial managers. "In a number of enterprises," Stalin then said, "the wage rates have been fixed in such a way that there is almost no difference between skilled and unskilled labor, between heavy and light labor. This leveling causes the unskilled worker to be disinterested in the acquisition of skill." [126] He blamed the fluidity of labor on the 1927–28 wage scales, saying that there would have been little of it if workers had been given the chance to improve their skills and raise their wages by staying in their jobs.

Soon afterward the national wage structure was radically remade. A many-sided differentiation of wage rates was introduced, as between entire industries, geographical regions, and categories of skill. The differentiation as between industries was calculated to promote heavy industry. Thus, coal miners, who under the old scale held the fourteenth place with regard to rates, were promoted to the fourth place in 1935, and to the second in 1937. Oil workers moved from the eighth to the first place; iron and steel workers from the ninth to the fifth, and so on. The light industries were put at the bottom of the scale. Geographical differentiation of wages was designed to encourage the migration of workers to new industrial centers in the Urals and beyond, where they could get higher wages than elsewhere. In this way the wage policy was turned into a direct instrument of national policy aiming at the development of heavy industry and the industrialization of the eastern provinces.[127] The nationally planned demand for certain categories of goods led to a deliberate raising of wages in the industries producing those goods. Planning thus performed "in an organized manner" the function that the mechanism of wages performed "blindly and spontaneously" in a *laissez-faire* economy, where, too, the demand for goods codetermined the level of wages and its fluctuations.

---

[125] J. Stalin, *Sochinenya* (Moscow, 1947) vii, page 376.

[126] J. Stalin, *Voprosy Leninizma* (*Problems of Leninism*) 11th ed., page 334.

[127] In June 1931, the Railwaymen's Trade Union was ordered to work out, in cooperation with the Commissariat of Transport, special wage rates for railwaymen employed on the eastern and far northern lines. *V.K.P.* (*b*) *o Profsoyuzakh*, pages 534–535. Similar measures were adopted after World War II, when industrial wages in the east were, in many cases, fixed 50 per cent higher than in the west.

The central feature of the reform, initiated in 1931, consisted, however, in the differentiation of individual wages. It is significant that since that reform no comprehensive statistics of wages have been published, except for claims about periodic rises in the national bill of nominal wages and in the average wage, claims that cannot be translated into terms of real wages because the publication of price indices has also been discontinued. In the total of the national wage bill the earnings of industrial workers and of office employees are lumped together. The distribution of incomes between these two categories has not been disclosed. The withholding of these statistical data from publication is primarily a matter of social policy; although the regime has openly conducted a systematic campaign against "levellers," a frank disclosure of the real differences between the earnings of various categories of workers and employees would almost certainly have caused considerable ideological embarrassment—it would show how far the pendulum had now swung in the direction of inequality.

Another guiding principle of the new policy was to extend piece-work to as wide a field of industry as possible. This met with some opposition, ineffective, of course, in the trade unions, already purged of Trotskyist and Tomskyist elements. Even the Commissariat of Labor had its hesitations; and its organ *Voprosy Truda* stated that "the development of technique, the increasing role of transport and electricity . . . narrow the field of industry where piece rates are applicable." [128] Through a number of instructions from the Central Committee of the party the new policy was, however, enforced. Thus, a resolution of July 7, 1931 instructed the Central Committee of the Miners' Trade Union and the managers of the coal mines of the Donetz to do away "within two months" with the equalization of wages and to transfer 85 to 90 per cent of the underground staffs and 70 per cent of all other workers to piece-rates. The trade unions were rudely reminded that they had merely a consultative voice in fixing new wage scales: the same instruction stated that the Norms and Conflicts Commissions (RKK), which were to fix the new rates, should be placed under the leadership of the pit managers. Similar instructions were issued to every major branch of industry with the result that, whereas before the reform 57 per cent of the total of man-hours worked were paid in piece-rates, the percentage of man-hours so paid rose to 75 in 1937.[129]

Simple piece-rates were, however, not considered to be powerful enough as incentives to higher production; and so-called "progressive

[128] Quoted from *Pravda* of July 7, 1931, which attacked the Commissariat of Labor for this statement.

[129] *Bolshaya Sovetskaya Entsiklopediya, SSSR,* page 1117.

rates" were introduced. Simple, that is, equal, piece-rates were paid for output up to fixed norms. Output above the norms was paid according to a new scale of rates increasing with the output. Thus an instruction of March 29, 1940 on wages in the Donetz coal mines, signed by Stalin and Molotov, ordered, apart from a 100 per cent increase in normal rates for coal miners, the following progressive piece-rates: a coal miner who produced 10 per cent more than his norm received double the normal rate for output above the norm. One who produced, say, 20 per cent above the norm was paid treble rates for output above the norm.[130] Where the introduction of piece-rates was technically impossible, time bonuses served to stimulate intensity of labor. "Brigade piece-rates" were a special form of payment introduced in industries where the output of the individual worker could not be measured in piece-rates but the output of a whole team lent itself to such measurement. The total output of the team was paid in piece-rates; and then the members of the team divided the collective wage among themselves according to their qualifications and the time worked by every member. This form of payment was not encouraged, however, because it was found that the teams of workers showed a "deplorable" bias towards egalitarianism.[131]

The eventual result of these many-sided and thorough-going changes in the national structure of wages, carried out through the trade unions, can be seen from the following figures: on January 1, 1938, 43 per cent of all Soviet workers and employees were paid simple piece-rates. Progressive piece-rates were received by 32 per cent. Of the 25 per cent who were still paid time-rates, 9 per cent received bonuses in addition to their basic wages. Only 16 per cent of all workers and employees continued to receive old-fashioned, ordinary time wages.

Stakhanovism. "Socialist emulation" thus became uninhibited competition between individual workers for higher output and higher

---

[130] *V.K.P. (b) o Profsoyuzakh*, pages 654–665. John Scott in his *Behind the Urals* (London: Secker & Warburg, 1942) gives the following scale of progressive rates for metal workers in Magnitogorsk in the middle thirties:

Production in Percentages of the Plan per Month	Payment in Percentages of Basic Rates First Group	Second Group
less than 100	75	75
100	100	100
101–120	130	120
121–130	170	150
131–150	200	180
151 and upwards	300	250

To the first group belonged the highly skilled technical personnel, while the second comprised foremen and skilled personnel of a lower category.
[131] *Bolshaya Sovetskaya Entsiklopediya, SSSR*, page 1115.

wages. The trade unions spurred on that competition. In the early thirties the form of emulation they favored was *udarnichestvo* or shock-work. Since 1935 Stakhanovism has taken its place.

The difference between the two "movements" is one of degree. The emulation in output associated with the Stakhanov method has been more intense and brutal than the older system of shock-work. It has also spread over a wider field of industry. It was with the development of Stakhanovism that the differentiation of wages was greatly intensified and made common.

The transition from the one method to the other was connected primarily with the abolition of food rationing in 1934 and with the government's attempt to stabilize the rouble. In the first years of the planned economy, up to 1934, money wages were of little significance, because the rouble had been depreciated. The industrial system was based mainly on wages in kind; and the differentiation of wages expressed itself, as under military communism, primarily in a differential rationing system. This included various categories of canteens, restaurants, and shops for the various categories of workers. The differences between the nominal piece-rates were not very great. High rates paid in worthless currency were poor incentives to higher production. The shock-worker was not interested in saving money for future purchases. All this changed at a stroke with the abolition of rationing and the stabilization of the rouble. The nominal piece-rates acquired real value; and the progressively growing rates paid for output above norm represented steep increases in the purchasing power of the worker who had earned them.

The scope for differentiation of wages now became incomparably wider than hitherto. As long as wages in kind predominated it was very difficult to give different rations to unskilled and semiskilled workers, or to devise any elastic system of rewards for various categories of skilled workers. A differential rationing system may comprise five, six, or, at the most, seven categories of rations; the gradations in skill and productivity are much more numerous; no rationing system can do full justice to their subtlety and variety.

Even differential rationing has, therefore, a faint flavor of *uravnilovka*, the egalitarian heresy, while the piece-wage paid in stable money is completely free from it. To quote Karl Marx: "Since the quality and intensity of the work are here controlled by the form of the wage itself," [132] the piece-wage automatically registers the slightest difference in the quality and intensity of the work performed. Marx goes on to say:

---

[132] Karl Marx, *Capital,* 1, page 564.

The wider scope that piece-wages gives to individuality tends to develop on the one hand that individuality, and with it the sense of liberty, independence and self-control of the laborers, on the other their competition one with another. Piecework has, therefore, a tendency, while raising individual wages above the average, to lower this average itself. . . . Piece-wages is the form of wages most in harmony with the capitalist mode of production.[133]

Marx held that the "sense of liberty and independence" that piece-work gave to the workers was largely illusory; the competition between them was more real. This, however, has not prevented the Soviet Government and the Soviet trade unions from hailing piece-wages as the form of payment most in harmony with the socialist mode of production. It is in Stakhanovism that the piece-wage has achieved its supreme triumph.

The origin of that "movement" goes back to a production record achieved by a coal miner named Alexei Stakhanov, who was reported to have produced 102 tons of coal in one shift, fourteen times as much as the norm, on August 31, 1935. The limelight of trade union propaganda was at once turned upon him. Workers all over the country were called on to imitate him. The fact, however, that Stakhanov gave his name to this "movement" was as much accidental as the "movement" itself was carefully staged.

The actual achievements of Stakhanovism have been the subject of much controversy. While Soviet propagandists have proclaimed Stakhanovism to be a peculiar feature of socialist organization of labor, many critics have dismissed it as sheer bluff. As far as one can judge from Soviet reports and eye-witness accounts of independent foreigners, Stakhanovism has greatly helped to raise industrial efficiency from the extremely low level at which it stood when the experiment was started. It seems that the Central Committee of the party was essentially right when, in December 1935, it stated that:

The Stakhanov movement signifies a new organization of labor, the rationalization of technological processes, the correct distribution of labor in production, the freeing of skilled workers from second-rate preparatory work, the better organization of work sites, the securing of the rapid increase of labor productivity and of a considerable growth in the wages and salaries of workers and employees.[134]

This statement implicitly explains how the production records were achieved and it also allows us to distinguish between the startling façade of Stakhanovism and the reality behind it. By the middle thirties, it will be remembered, the technical equipment of Russian

---

[133] *Ibid.*, pages 566–567.
[134] *V.K.P. (b) o Profsoyuzakh*, page 579.

industry had been modernized and greatly expanded. Yet, because of obsolete methods of work and extreme shortage of industrial skill, the coefficient of utilization of the new equipment was still extremely low. Moderate improvements in the organization of labor were able to yield and did yield quite abnormal, spectacular rises in productivity. This was the indubitably progressive facet of Stakhanovism. The records of individuals were usually followed by a general raising of the average norms of output, endorsed by the trade unions; and the new norms were fixed halfway between the old ones and the Stakhanovite records.[135]

In part, however, the production records claimed were publicity stunts. The old norms of output made allowance for the time that the worker spent on the maintenance of his tools, on the preparation of the work site, and other auxiliary functions. The Stakhanovite was, as a rule, freed from all auxiliary work, which other people had to do for him so that he might concentrate on the actual output. This was, of course, part of the "correct distribution of labor," which demanded that the skilled worker should not waste his time on jobs requiring no skill. But the final production record resulted most often from the work of a whole team and not of the individual Stakhanovite, who as a rule claimed it for himself.

It is often asked just how great has been the inequality to which Stakhanovism has led. How does that inequality compare with differences in incomes in other countries? Only a very general answer to these questions can be given, because of the fragmentary character of the information available. In spite of the sustained campaign against "levellers," which has been going on since 1931, the inequality of incomes in the Soviet Union has hardly achieved anything like the discrepancy between the incomes of, say, big shareholders and unskilled laborers in any other country. Briefly, the inequality *between classes* is less than elsewhere. But the inequality *inside* the working class, between various groups of workers, has certainly been much greater than in any other country. This contention can be illustrated by the following data given by *Pravda* toward the end of 1935, shortly

---

[135] The new norms were fixed by industrial managers and technicians to the exclusion of the factory committees and the trade unions who now acted as mere publicity agents for Stakhanovism. (*Ibid.,* pages 581, 583–588 and *passim.*) This can be seen, *inter alia,* from the instructions of the Central Committee of the party, issued in December 1935, about the revision of norms that was to be carried out in all industries in 1936. The instructions contained detailed descriptions of production conferences called for this purpose. In every case, the participants mentioned were only "managers, chief engineers, shop managers, foremen and prominent Stakhanovites"—no representatives of trade unions or factory committees were included.

after Stakhanovism had been launched. An ordinary non-Stakhanovite coal miner doing auxiliary work underground earned 170 roubles per month. The wage of a non-Stakhanovite coal miner was 400–500 roubles. The monthly earnings of a Stakhanovite were more than 1,600 roubles.[136] It will be interesting to compare these figures with data obtained in 1948 by a delegation of foreign trade unionists on a visit to Russia. Thus, in 1948, the basic pay of a coal miner amounted to as much as 2,000 roubles per month, that of an auxiliary above ground worker was 250 roubles, one-eighth of the coal miner's wage. Since the early thirties wage policy in the coal industry has fluctuated, now reducing the discrepancy and now widening it even more; but on balance the trend has been toward more, and not less, inequality. In 1948 there were twelve categories of wages in the iron and steel industry, eight in machine building, but only six in industries producing consumer goods. In addition to higher wages Stakhanovites enjoy important privileges: free sojourns in rest homes and sanatoria owned by the trade unions; the right to have home tutors for their children without payment, free medical help at the Stakhanovite's home, and a number of other services that have raised the Stakhanovite's standard of living far above that of the ordinary worker.[137] Stakhanovism has made of Russia an almost classical country of a labor aristocracy; and the trade unions, in so far as they play any role as a labor organization, have been converted into strongholds of that workers' aristocracy.

In its first years, Stakhanovism met with considerable resistance on the part of the lower ranks of trade union officials, who, willingly or unwillingly, became the mouthpieces of discontent among the rank and file. This opposition could not become vocal, but it was widespread, intense, and, for a time, dangerously effective.

This is not to say that the workers' reaction to Stakhanovism was uniformly or even predominantly hostile. It was mixed. Some sections of the working class received with satisfaction the opportunity of improving their lot through better and more diligent work. The appeal to the worker's individualism was especially effective because an inherited peasant individualism was still strong in the Soviet working class.[138] But, as in any competitive system, so in Stakhanovism the number of those who were beaten at the competition was greater than

---

[136] *Pravda,* November 16, 1935.

[137] *Trud,* November 1 and 2, 1935.

[138] The biographies of Stakhanov, himself, and of other celebrated Stakhanovites are highly instructive. Most Stakhanovites were young workers in their twenties or early thirties who had left the countryside only a few years before.

the number of those who benefited from it. Those who suffered from Stakhanovite methods were, of course, opposed to them, and they were branded as "backward elements" by their own trade unions. No doubt there was no lack of such "backward elements" opposed to technical innovations and rational organization of labor. But among the discontented were also workers whom ill-health or age had made unfit for the exertion now required to earn a minimum wage. Among those opposed to Stakhanovism was the cadre of industrial workers who had been brought up in class consciousness and class solidarity and taught to regard equality as the ultimate goal of socialism—the good communists of the preceding era, now denounced as "petty bourgeois" levellers. This last category of workers was strongly represented among the lower and middle officials of the trade unions.

The opposition to Stakhanovism, with all the mixed motives behind it, formed the background to the violent campaigns against "saboteurs and wreckers" that were conducted in the middle thirties. Press reports in 1935 and 1936, abounding in much realistic detail and circumstantial evidence, offered some insight into the character of that "sabotage." Contrary to later claims, made during the famous purge trials of the old Bolshevik guard, these reports presented the "wrecking" and "sabotage" not as the result of any political plot, but as the spontaneous and, at times, Luddite-like resistance of workers to new methods of labor. Attacks by workers on Stakhanovites, attempts to intimidate them and prevent them from assisting the industrial managers in raising average norms of output, occurred quite frequently. Lower trade union officials were sometimes implicated in such attempts.[139] In some cases Stakhanovites were assassinated. Much more often workers damaged, put out of order, or concealed the Stakhanovite's tools so as to disorganize or delay his work.

The party's reaction to this resistance was determined but not immediately effective. "In some enterprises," so Zhdanov stated in November, 1935, "the Stakhanov movement has met with resistance. . . . The party will not shrink from any measures that will help it to sweep away all the resisters from the victorious path of the Stakhanovite movement."[140] But in the following year, and even the year after, innumerable resolutions acknowledged the continuance of the opposition to Stakhanovism and the ambiguous attitude of the trade unions on the spot. A typical resolution of April, 1937, signed by Stalin and Molotov, asserted that previous instructions on Stakhanovism had not been obeyed, that differential wage rates had not been introduced,

[139] *Trud,* November 3, 1935.
[140] *Pravda,* November 13, 1935.

and that trade unions and even party committees had refused to expose "wreckers." [141] Nevertheless, Zhdanov's threat that the "party will sweep away all the resisters" was eventually carried out. During the great purges of 1937–38 the trade unions were among the chief victims. After the purges were over, in March, 1939, Shvernik announced at the eighteenth Congress of the party that "the composition of the Trade Union committees in factories and other establishments was changed to the extent of 70–80 per cent and of the central committees to the extent of 96 per cent." [142] The opposition to Stakhanovism seems to have been largely overcome since then, and Stakhanovism, that mixture of progressive rationalization and old-time sweated labor, has come to be accepted as the peculiarly Soviet style of labor.

Trade unions and social insurance. As the trade unions, unable or unwilling to defend the workers, tended to become merely vestigial institutions, new functions were transferred to them, presumably in order to justify their continued existence. In 1933 the Commissariat of Labor was officially abolished and its functions and funds were transferred to the trade unions. The main consequence of this reform was that the trade unions were charged with the administration of social insurance.[143] The Department of Social Insurance in the Central Council of Trade Unions was the body directly responsible for this new and vast field of work and for the utilization of social insurance funds. Branches of that department were set up at every level of the trade union machinery. Every factory committee formed its council for social insurance; and at the lowest level special insurance delegates were attached to every shop committee. In 1948, altogether about one million active trade unionists performed the functions of insurance delegates. Their task has been to regulate locally all matters concerning invalid pensions, sickness benefits, and so forth. The trade unions also took over the management of holiday resorts, sanatoria, and rest homes.[144]

This transformation of the trade unions into a social insurance

---

[141] *V.K.P.* (*b*) *o Profsoyuzakh,* pages 590–593.

[142] See his statement in *The Land of Socialism,* page 405. Moscow: Foreign Languages Publishing House, 1939.

[143] The trade unions thereby came into possession of very considerable assets. The funds of social insurance amounted to 10.4 billion roubles under the first Five-Year Plan and to 32.5 billion under the second. They amounted to 61.6 billion roubles under the 1946–1950 Five-Year Plan.

[144] Before World War II they owned 853 sanatoria and rest homes capable of accommodating 161,000 persons. Many of these establishments were destroyed during the Nazi invasion. The 1946–1950 Five-Year Plan provided for their reconstruction and expansion.

organization has had its undoubted advantages. It has given a very broad basis to the entire system of social insurance. The voluntary unpaid work of one million insurance delegates in factories and work-shops must have lowered the cost of social insurance and brought its administration closer to the working masses. On the other hand, the entire system of the social services has been used as an instrument for raising the productivity of labor. We have seen how the rates of sickness benefits and invalid pensions were graded so as to serve that purpose. The number of sanatoria, rest homes, and similar establish-ments has been rather limited in relation to needs, and so, practically, they have been accessible only to the high administrative and technical personnel and to Stakhanovites.

These two purposes of the 1933 reform, that of giving the system of social insurance a broad unbureaucratic base in the trade unions and that of harnessing the entire system to the government's economic policy, have not always been compatible. The insurance delegates in the factories were not always inclined to give the Stakhanovites priority in the benefits and the facilities that they, the insurance delegates, administered. Here, too, the government, assisted by the Central Council of Trade Unions, waged a stubborn fight against the instinctive egalitarianism of rank-and-file trade unionists. In April, 1939, the seventh plenary session of the Central Council of Trade Unions adopted the following characteristic resolution:

The most important means toward strengthening labor discipline has been the improvement in the functioning of state social insurance and the elimina-tion of abuses in that field. Yet many factories and local committees have offended against the decision of the government, the Central Committee of the Party and the Central Council of Trade Unions . . . by the incorrect alloca-tion of relief for temporarily incapacitated workers. . . . The factory com-mittees have not paid attention to the entries in the labor cards, on the basis of which they should ascertain how long the applicant for relief has been permanently employed at a given factory or institution. The plenary session condemns these anti-state activities of the factory and local committees which offend against the decision of December 28, 1938, fixing the rates of relief under the social insurance scheme.

The central committees of the Trade Unions are hereby reminded of their duty to improve the work of the councils and commissions of social insurance, to establish permanent control over the correctness of the allocation and pay-ment of allowances to temporarily incapacitated workers and to charge with responsibility those guilty of offending against the scales of allowances fixed by the government, the Central Committee of the Party, and the Central Council of the Trade Unions. . . .

The Praesidium of the Central Council of Trade Unions is instructed to consult the People's Commissar for Health of the U.S.S.R. about further im-provements in medical services for workers and employees and about the measures that are being taken by the People's Commissar for Health against doctors who admit idlers and malingerers to hospitals.[145]

Since 1933 the trade unions have also been responsible for protection of labor. The central committees of the trade unions maintain technical inspectorates that employ several thousand full-time industrial inspectors. In addition, part-time voluntary workers act as inspectors in factories and shops. They check, at least in precept, how the industrial managements utilize government funds allocated for labor protection.[146] The manner in which these funds are to be used is the subject of special agreements periodically concluded between industrial managements and factory committees. At the lowest level, in the shops, one worker in every group of trade unionists is the inspector responsible for protection of female and juvenile labor and for observing the length of the working day,[147] for arranging holidays, and so forth.

The trade unions have also been made responsible for welfare and a number of auxiliary functions designed to improve the workers' standard of living within the limits set by the Plan and the fixed fund of wages. It is in these fields that the unions have found some compensation for the loss of their bargaining power over wages. Since the grave food crises of the early thirties it has been a common practice of Soviet factories to develop their own auxiliary farms and vegetable gardens. This practice was further developed during World War II, and it then helped to keep the industrial population supplied with food. The trade unions have assisted in the organization and running of the auxiliary farms. They have also controlled the work of the so-called "Workers' Supply Departments," factory canteens and cooperative shops. One of many characteristic resolutions states, for instance, that the chairman of any factory committee (that is, the chief trade union organizer on the spot) is personally responsible for any malpractices in the cooperatives and food supply centers. "The Trade Union officials who carry out this control ought to have some knowledge of bookkeeping and to be able to analyse the calculation of prices so as to know how and where malpractices occur." [148] Similarly, the trade unions check on how funds allocated for housing of workers

---

[145] See Appendix in N. Shvernik, *O Rabote Profsoyuzov v Suyazi s Resheniyami XVIII Syezda V.K.P. (b)* (Trade Union Activities in connection with the Decisions taken by the Eighteenth Congress of the All-Union Communist Party) (Moscow, 1939), pages 90–91.

[146] In the 1946–50 Five-Year Plan about 5 billion roubles have been allocated for labor protection.

[147] The working day was seven hours before the war and was raised to eight hours in 1940.

[148] *V.K.P. (b) o Profsoyuzakh*, page 577.

are used, on the quality of the houses built, and so on. Since World War II letters and articles by trade unionists have frequently appeared in the press censuring industrial managers and even ministers for .neglecting to carry out housing programs.

Finally, the trade unions have taken an active part in *Ossoaviakhim* and other paramilitary organizations; and the very strong sports organizations of the trade unions have been useful auxiliaries of the Armed Forces.[149]

Machinery and Organization of Trade Unions

The organization of the trade unions has undergone many changes since the revolution. The second Congress of the Trade Unions adopted the "production principle," which required that all workers and employees of any enterprise, regardless of their craft or trade, be members of the same union. The workers and employees, say, of a machinery plant, no matter what their individual occupation, joined the trade union of the metal workers. The seventh Trade Union Congress (1926) adopted the rule "one economic organ—one union." This was designed to adjust the structure of the trade unions to that of the economic administration so that one commissariat should, as far as possible, deal with only one union, and *vice versa*.[150] Subsequently the number and organization of trade unions varied in accordance with changes and reforms in the economic administration. In 1930 there existed only 23 national trade unions. Since then their number has steadily grown with the multiplication of economic commissariats (or, later, of ministries). In 1931 there already existed 45 national trade unions; in 1934—154; in 1939—168; in 1944—176; but in 1949, after several mergers there existed only 67 national trade union organizations.[151]

The membership of the trade unions has steadily grown, with the exception of a short period in the early twenties when there was a considerable decline during the transition from military communism to NEP. A noteworthy feature in the organization of the unions has been the so-called "single membership card": a member of any union, when he changes his occupation, becomes automatically a member of any other union, without paying a new entrance fee. This principle underlines the organic unity of the entire movement and its freedom from sectional or craft divisions.

The accuracy of the membership statistics cannot be ascertained.

---

[149] It is claimed, for instance, that in World War II the trade unions trained two million skiers for the Red Army.

[150] *7. Syezd Profsoyuzov*, page **43**.

[151] *Trud,* May **23**, 1949.

The following table gives the official claims of membership in various years between 1917 and 1948:

June, 1917	1,450,000	1925	6,950,000
January, 1918	2,532,000	1926	8,768,000
January, 1919	3,639,000	1928	10,995,000
April, 1920	4,326,000	1933	17,126,000
July, 1921	8,400,000 [152]	1940	25,000,000
January, 1922	6,700,000	1947	27,000,000
September, 1922	5,100,000	1948	28,500,000

In 1918–22, under military communism, membership was "collective" and compulsory. The workers and employees of any business joined the trade union as a body; and the individual worker or employee had no right to contract out. With the transition to NEP, the principle of voluntary and individual membership was adopted, primarily on Lenin's insistence. This caused the spectacular decline in membership in 1921–22, even though the transition to voluntary membership was only gradual. In the twenties, the voluntary character of the organization was real enough, although adherence to the trade union did, of course, secure advantages for the worker. In precept, the principle of voluntary organization has been preserved until now. But the material advantages of membership have grown so enormously that one wonders how it is that only 90 and not 100 per cent of the total number of workers and employees is claimed to belong to the trade unions. It will be remembered that the worker who does not belong to a union receives only 50 per cent of the sickness benefits paid to the trade unionist.

In the early years the trade unions organized, almost exclusively, the manual workers. As a matter of principle they refused to admit the higher technical personnel, and they were not overanxious to organize civil servants. Soon after the revolution, professional people and clerical employees were drawn into the movement, and trade unions of teachers and of the "medical and sanitary personnel" were formed. Later, the higher technical and administrative personnel were also organized, including industrial managers, whose standing in relation to the workers approximated that of employers.[153]

---

[152] This was the figure given by Andreev at the fifth Congress of the Trade Unions. (5. *Vserossiiskii Syezd Profsoyuzov,* page 41) *Bolshaya Sovetskaya Entsiklopediya* gives the membership for May, 1921 as only 6.5 million, nearly 2 million less than the figure given by Andreev. Similar discrepancies occur between figures for other years as well. Thus the Encyclopaedia claims a membership of more than 9.5 million for 1926, whereas the number given at the fifteenth party conference was less than 8.8 million. See *V.K.P. (b) o Profsoyuzakh.* p. 239.

[153] The inclusion of managers in the trade unions was justified by the familiar argument that they, and the economic administration at large, represented the

The massive vertical structure of the trade unions rests upon the *fabzavkom* or the factory committee, its basic unit. The factory committees, as we know, aspired to independence from the unions and even tried to act as their rivals in the early days of the revolution. This aspiration was completely defeated, and, after a complex evolution lasting nearly two decades, the factory committees took up a position in which they seem closer to the administration and the industrial managements than to the workers.

The factory committee is elected at a general meeting of all trade unionists in any factory, mine, or office. In precept, the general meeting is the sovereign master of the factory committee; in actual fact, the committee takes its orders and instructions from the trade union hierarchy, the party, and the management rather than from its electors. In the intervals between the general meetings—according to the rarely observed statutes the factory committees ought to be elected every year—the factory committee represents the trade union on the spot and is represented by its chairman.

The factory committee works through the following specialized commissions:

(a) The Council of Social Insurance.
(b) The Wage Commission.
(c) The Commission for Labor Protection.
(d) The Commission for Cultural and Educational Activities.
(e) The Housing Commission.
(f) The Commission for Workers' Supplies.
(g) The Commission for Workers' Inventions and Rationalization.
(h) The Commission for Gardening and Auxiliary Farming.
(i) The Commission for Assistance to Servicemen's Families.[154]

Apart from these permanent bodies, temporary commissions may be

proletarian state and were therefore, by definition, not opposed to the workers. "As, in the U.S.S.R.," says the *Great Soviet Encyclopaedia*, "there do not exist, and cannot exist, any class antagonisms between workers and economic administrators, and as the parties to any collective agreement are representatives of the same class and pursue the common objectives of developing socialist production and raising the material and cultural level of the toilers, the essential purpose of any collective agreement is at present: to secure the fulfilment and overfulfilment of production plans, to further higher productivity of labor, to improve the organization of labor and to raise the responsibility of the administration and Trade Unions for the material and cultural well-being of the workers. . . . " (*Bolshaya Sovetskaya Entsiklopediya, SSSR,* page 1758). This view does not quite tally with Lenin's insistence on the need of the workers to defend themselves against the state, in so far as that state is "bureaucratically deformed" and is not a proletarian state *tout court,* but a state of workers and peasants.

[154] This branch of the factory committee has been in existence only since World War II.

set up to deal with special tasks. The factory committee also participates in the important RKK (*Rastsenochnaya Konfliktnaya Komisya*), the Norms and Conflicts Commission, which deals with complaints from workers and managers. The factory committee is represented in the RKK on a basis of parity with the management; but as a rule the manager, or his appointee, presides over the RKK.

Within the limits set by government labor policy, the functions of the factory committee are manifold and important. Since 1948 the factory committee has concluded collective agreements. But its initiative in this field has been limited, because the local collective agreements must be strictly modelled on the central collective agreement concluded for a whole industry between the ministry in charge of that industry and the central committee of the corresponding trade union. The local collective agreement can, at best, introduce only very minor variations in the general norms of output and productivity, wages, and so on. The role of the factory committee is more important in the fields of labor protection, in providing for industrial safety, and in a large variety of welfare activities.

In most industrial concerns the factory committee is the basic but not the lowest unit of the organization. Below it is the shop committee, which is elected in any shop employing at least one hundred workers. The structure of the shop committee is closely modeled on that of the factory committee; nearly all the commissions of the factory committee, listed above, have their counterparts in commissions of the shop committee. The lowest link in the organization is the so-called *"Profgrup,"* a group of trade unionists consisting of twenty members and usually comprising a brigade or a team of workers employed in a particular sector of the shop. It is through joining the *Profgrup* that the worker usually becomes a member of the trade union. The *Profgrup* elects its own insurance delegate and its own "inspector" for labor protection, and one or two other functionaries. The organizer of this smallest unit is called the *Profgruporg;* and he represents his team *vis-à-vis* the industrial management and the trade union hierarchy. The organizer is elected at a meeting of the members of the *Profgrup*.

Periodical production meetings are one of the vital functions of the factory committees. At these meetings, the fulfilment of the collective agreement by workers and managements should be checked once every three months. Special production meetings are convened from time to time to encourage workers' inventions and projects for rationalization of labor. Workers are expected to communicate their observations and suggestions about possible improvements in machinery, organization of labor, handling of materials, and so forth. The observations and suggestions are collected, sifted, and classified by the special commission of the factory committee that deals with such issues. The industrial managers have special funds at their disposal from which premiums are paid to worker-inventors. Like so many ideas in Soviet trade unionism, this imaginative scheme for the accumulation and utilization of the mass inventiveness of producers has, in practice, often been marred by official routine: at the production meetings the customary long-winded, monotonous speeches, followed by unanimous adoption of official resolutions, have often swamped any businesslike discussion of projects for rationalization of labor. Very often, too, the production meetings have been used merely for the whipping up of the crudest forms of competition between the workers.

Above the factory committee there are the town, regional, republican, and central committees of the various trade unions, all elected by secret ballot.[155] At the top of the entire organization there is the All-Union Central Council of the Trade Unions. Re-elected at the tenth Congress of the Trade Unions in April 1949, it consisted of 175 members and 57 alternate members. The Central Council in its turn elects a smaller body, the Praesidium, to act as its executive.

As in all Soviet institutions, so in the Soviet trade unions the organization is in theory governed by the principles of democratic centralism, which require that all directing bodies be regularly elected in accordance with statutes but that they should, in the intervals between elections, be the real masters of the organization, with a claim to absolute discipline on the part of the membership. In practice, bureaucratic rather than democratic centralism prevails. The power of the center is practically unlimited, and the statutory provisions about the responsibility of the trade union officials to their electorate are disregarded. This has been strikingly illustrated by the fact that no less than seventeen years elapsed between the ninth Congress of the Trade Unions, which took place in 1932, and the tenth Congress, convened in April, 1949. In violation of all statutory regulations the Central Council of the Trade Unions did not even bother to go through the formal motions of an election over all these years.

The Tenth Trade Union Congress

It is not very clear why, after an interval of seventeen years, a Trade Union Congress was convened in 1949. There had been no apparent reason for this sudden return to half-forgotten "parliamentary" procedures. Nothing startling happened during the Congress; no new

---

[155] As an exception, insurance delegates and inspectors for labor protection are elected in open ballot.

policy was announced; nor was any fresh light shed on the evolution of the trade unions since the Congress of 1932. The chairman of the All-Union Central Council, V. V. Kuznetsov, did not in his report even attempt to review the trends or discuss the changes in Soviet trade unionism between the two Congresses. The newly adopted statute did not alter the structure of the organization, except in one point to be discussed later. Finally, the election of the new All-Union Central Council brought little or no change in the leadership. The only hypothetical explanation for the calling of the Congress is that the regime may have been anxious to revive, within limits prescribed by the single-party system, some of the formal democratic practices that had been suspended in connection with the political convulsions of the thirties and World War II.

A significant sidelight on the character of the trade union leadership was given in the report of the Mandate Commission on the composition of the Congress. The delegates to the Congress represented, to a greater extent than is true of such gatherings outside Russia, the trade union hierarchy rather than the rank and file. Only 23.5 per cent of all delegates were workers. 43 per cent were full-time trade union officials. 39 per cent were members of the Central Committees of the Trade Unions in control of the sixty-seven national organizations. 9.4 per cent of the delegates came from the technical intelligentsia (compared with only 2 per cent at the previous Congress). Twenty-odd per cent of the participants, at the most, were trade union officials of medium or low rank.[156] Eighty-five per cent of all delegates had some governmental award, the distinctive mark of a member of the "labor aristocracy." Seventy-one per cent of the delegates had secondary or higher education; only about twenty per cent had received not more than elementary education. (At the ninth Congress, sixty per cent had only elementary education.) Seventy-two per cent were either members of the Communist Party or had applied for membership. (A striking feature was the very active participation of women: nearly 40 per cent of the delegates were women, compared with only 18 at the previous Congress.)

These data reflect the dominating position held inside the unions by the officials and the "labor aristocracy" and also the higher educational standards attained by these groups since the early thirties.

Some significance may be attached to one postwar development that was not, however, discussed in any real sense by the Congress, namely, the resumption of collective agreements between trade unions and industrial managements. This practice, too, had been discarded

---

[156] *Trud*, April 23, 1949.

since the early thirties. In February, 1933 collective agreements were formally abolished by government decree; but even before that, under the first Five-Year Plan, they had tended to become meaningless. What used to be their central feature—the settlement of wage claims and of conditions of labor—was directly regulated by the government. Since 1947, however, collective agreements have been revived ("on Comrade Stalin's demand," as V. V. Kuznetsov stated at the tenth Congress [157]) in order "to stimulate the fulfilment and overfulfilment of the economic plans." The explanation explains nothing, for the government must have been equally anxious to "stimulate the fulfilment of economic plans" in the thirties. when collective agreements were declared to be no longer needed. It can only be surmised that in this instance, too, the government has been anxious to give its labor policy some democratic appearance, possibly in order to calm a postwar *malaise* in the working class.

The renewal of collective agreements gave rise to a faint controversy in the press over their scope and meaning, but it has been commonly agreed that the contracts are not meant to settle wages and conditions of labor, which continue to be regulated by the government. Where collective agreements do include clauses on wages, such clauses do not embody the results of any collective bargaining; they merely incorporate passages from governmental decrees and instructions.[158] In view of this, the discussion over the meaning of the collective agreements concerned only minor legal points. The "contracts" nominally impose obligations upon both managements and workers, but such obligations arise out of the economic plan and would have existed no matter whether a collective agreement was concluded or not.[159]

The total exclusion of wage policy from trade union activity is seen

---

[157] *Trud,* April 20, 1949.

[158] "The present-day collective agreement usually includes norms regulating the remuneration of labor (rate systems, with coefficients and grades, progressive scales, and so forth). These norms, however, are not the result of the collective agreement contract. They originate from the appropriate state authorities. The inclusion of such norms in collective agreements is intended . . . to facilitate the mobilization of manual and office workers in campaigns for the plan . . . ," states Professor V. M. Dogadov in an article on the subject, the English translation of which appeared in *Soviet Studies,* Vol. I, pages 79–84. Oxford: Blackwell, 1949.

[159] In the article just quoted, V. M. Dogadov cites the following excerpt from a collective agreement concluded in an ordnance factory: "Open hearth furnace No. 5 is to be made automatic . . . capital repairs are to be carried out at electrofurnace No. 1 . . . a school for young workers is to be built with accommodation for 600 pupils; a building for a polyclinic serving the workers of the factory is to be built; one five-story building, three two-story buildings, and three three-story buildings with a total living space of 6,000 square meters are to be built and put into use. . . . " Other collective agreements do include some provisions about conditions of labor, but only, to quote Dogadov, about "isolated, individual matters."

from the fact that in the main report to the Congress—the report by
V. V. Kuznetsov that covered more than four full pages in *Trud*—only
the smallest paragraph was devoted to wages. The Congress was given
not a single piece of information about the structure of wages, their
purchasing power, and so on.[160] The resolutions of the Congress were
equally uninformative, but they contained the characteristic statement
that "it is necessary henceforth, too, to wage the struggle against
uravnilovka. . . . ," that is, against egalitarian attitudes.[161] Since
after all the official anathemas hardly anybody would now have dared
to advocate egalitarianism, this statement merely means that the
government regards further differentiation of wages, that is, the further
growth of inequality, as necessary and that the trade unions accept this
view.

A noteworthy change in the organization, carried out in 1948 (again
"on Comrade Stalin's initiative"), is the formation of provincial,
regional, and town Councils of Trade Unions. The representatives of
all trade unions of any province or locality sit on these councils. Until
1948, the trade unions were organized, almost exclusively, along vertical
lines. The local and provincial bodies of any union were connected with
the higher and lower links in their own hierarchy. No solid horizontal
organization existed to coordinate the activities of various trade unions
on a local scale. Thus, the coal miners' union in any locality had
hardly any stable links with the union of the steel workers or with
that of the textile workers in the same place. Its official intercourse
was confined to that with other bodies in the national Coal Miners'
Union, whose central committee, in its turn, was subordinated to the
All-Union Central Council. This scheme of organization was characteristic of the overcentralization of the trade unions. The local and
provincial councils now set up have introduced an element of horizontal
organization that should allow various trade unions on the spot to
concert their activities. This reform, too, seems to have been dictated
by a desire to weaken somewhat the rigidity of the vertical organization, or at least to give the rank and file the impression of relaxation.

All these reforms—the convening of the Congress, the revival of
collective agreements, and the setting up of local trade union councils
—may add up to a degree of democratization, but will hardly affect
the functions and character of the organization as a whole. Somewhat
more emphasis than usual was placed on internal democracy in the
trade unions and also on the right of the worker to lodge complaints
against the management. On the other hand, the newly adopted statute

---

[160] Kuznetsov stated *inter alia* that the value of social insurance and health
services amounted to one-third of the national wage bill.

[161] *Trud*, May 11, 1949.

fixes the terms for which the various trade union bodies are to be elected in a manner calculated still further to enhance central control over the entire organization. Thus the Central Council of the Trade Unions is elected for four years. The central committee of any trade union is elected for two years only; so are the regional, provincial, and republican councils. Finally, the primary organizations, the factory committees, are elected for one year only. The higher the trade union authority, the greater is its statutory stability and, therefore, also its power over subordinated bodies.

The reports given at the tenth Congress leave no doubt about the broad scope of trade union activity in the fields of social insurance and welfare. For that the trade unions have built up a vast and, in many ways, highly impressive organization.

At the base of the organization there were in 1949:

(a) one million voluntary organizers of trade union groups—*prof-gruporgi;*

(b) more than 1.2 million voluntary insurance delegates and inspectors of labor; [162]

(c) more than one million members of the wages commissions;

(d) more than two million rank-and-file trade unionists active in welfare commissions;

(e) altogether more than nine million "activists," that is, members voluntarily engaged in part-time work for the unions. The number of "activists" amounts to one-third of the total membership.

In 1948, more than two million production meetings were reported to have taken place, at which four million suggestions for the rationalization of labor were made.

The mass of voluntary unpaid part-time workers has been a highly important characteristic of the unions—it has a strong flavor of that "production-democracy" that was juxtaposed to political democracy in the debates of the early twenties. S. Gorbunov, chairman of a shop committee, in one of many typical utterances on this subject, said:

I cannot imagine how we, the leaders of a Trade Union, engaged in intensive productive work all day long, could achieve anything without the backing of this broad mass of activists. Seven people have been elected to our shop committee, but in their work they have been assisted by 230 activists. About one hundred people are members of the various commissions of the shop committee. We have 26 group organizers, 52 social inspectors and insurance delegates.[163]

---

[162] The All-Union Central Council has five research institutes and twelve laboratories working on improving protection of industrial labor. They are managed by the Department for Protection of Labor of the All-Union Central Council. The central committees of the individual unions, too, have their specialized research institutes and laboratories.

[163] *Trud,* April 19, 1949.

It is largely through this vast mass of "activists" that the trade unions have been able to assist in the training of new workers—under the 1946–50 Five-Year Plan, nearly fourteen million workers underwent some degree of retraining, while nearly eight million received full-time training.

Road to Serfdom?

In this survey of their development, the Soviet trade unions are seen as an organic part of the social fabric of the Soviet Union. Only in the context of the broad changes that have transformed Soviet society in more than three decades since the revolution can the role and functions of the trade unions be understood.

It is only proper to ask what, if any, moral of international significance can be drawn from this survey. One conclusion frequently drawn is that in a planned economy there is little or no scope for normal trade union activity, especially for the defense of the workers' interests against the employer-state. Most admirers of the Soviet Union, as well as its opponents, seem to agree on this. In addition, the opponents of planned economy and socialism will see in the story of the Soviet trade unions a confirmation of their view that public ownership and economic planning drive the nations that have chosen these forms of social organization, or upon whom these forms have been imposed, along the "road to serfdom."

At first sight, the story of the Soviet trade unions appears to justify such a conclusion. The Soviet trade unions have often been used by the employer-state as an instrument of coercion against the working classes. As the organization designed to forge the workers' solidarity in their struggle for better living conditions, they have suffered complete atrophy. As bodies entrusted with the management of social insurance, and as welfare institutions they have certainly performed, and are still performing, very useful services; but these, whatever the official Soviet theory may be, they have performed as subsidiaries of the state administration, not as autonomous social bodies or working class organizations in the accepted sense.

Yet, on closer analysis, the story of the Soviet trade unions does not really support such sweeping conclusion. For what emerges from this survey is that the peculiar role that the Soviet unions have come to play has been conditioned not so much by the needs of planned economy as such as by the application of planning to an extremely low level of economic and cultural development, the level at which Russia stood until recently and, in so many respects, still stands.

The essential condition, according to Marxist theory, in which planning can yield the fruits expected from it is that it should be applied to an economy of plenty and not to one of scarcity. All socialist advocates of planning, including the Bolsheviks, once used to argue that planned socialist economy could effectively begin only from, roughly, that level of industrial and cultural development that the older capitalist nations had already attained. At that level, it was argued, planning is both necessary and possible. It is *necessary*—in order to protect society from the wastefulness and moral degradation that result from recurring slumps, mass unemployment, social tension, mass neuroses, and military conflicts. It is *possible,* because the high output of material goods, and the accumulation of industrial-administrative skill and experience and, last but not least, of civilized habits of life enable society to advance in a civilized manner toward economic equality and rational social organization. When the experiment in planned economy was begun, Russia was, and up to a point still is, far below the level at which such results could be expected.

The function of the Russian planned economy was primarily to carry out an industrial revolution such as the older capitalist countries had gone through long ago but in different social forms. This industrial revolution, which elsewhere, either under the *laissez-faire* system or under bourgeois protectionism, extended over the lifetime of several generations, was, in Russia, compressed within little more than one decade, the last before World War II. Within that decade were also compressed all the horrors that attended earlier industrial revolutions. In a nation whose large-scale industry produced only 3–4 million tons of steel and only 30 million pairs of shoes for a population of 150 million (to take only two striking indices of Russian poverty toward the end of the twenties) no real movement toward equality, promised by the revolution, could take place. In a nation that had accumulated less industrial and administrative skill and experience than had any medium-sized European country, in a nation, furthermore, burdened with the oppressive traditions of inefficient autocracy at its top and of illiteracy and a barbarous way of life below, the arrears in economic and cultural development were so enormous, and the lack of civic responsibility in rulers and ruled alike was so baffling that the techniques of economic planning could be developed only in the crudest and most ruthless forms. This basically determined the place of the trade unions in Soviet labor policy.

In spite of the handicaps under which planned economy has been tried out in Russia, it has enabled that country to become a great industrial power within a very short time. But it would be rash to deduce from this that the peculiarly Russian features of labor policy, the features that have, in fact, more than a flavor of revived serfdom about them, are inherent in planned economy or, more specifically, in socialist planning. There is no reason to assume that in any society that already has at its disposal a more or less modern apparatus for industrial production and substantial reserves of trained manpower planned economy would reproduce the worst aspects of the Russian experiment. The amount of ruthless coercion that has gone into the making of the Russian industrial revolution is explained mainly by the rulers' determination to overcome at any cost and within the shortest time the prodigious difficulties involved in the mobilization, training, and education of many millions of raw, undisciplined peasants. In a more highly developed economy with a disciplined and civilized industrial working class such methods would be not only superfluous—they would also be positively incompatible with an orderly planned economy. It is therefore reasonable to think that the planners would not feel themselves tempted to resort to them.

Within a planned economy, developing on a relatively high industrial and cultural basis, considerable scope should be left for trade union activity. In Russia, no bargaining was really possible between management and workers because of the extreme scarcity of all material resources. In a country producing, say, only one pair of shoes per year for every third citizen, the worker could not effectively bargain over whether his wages should enable him to buy only one or two pairs of shoes per year. The trade unions could not adopt a "consumptionist" attitude in any circumstances, although they need not have gone to extremes of anti-consumptionism. But in any economy possessing its safety margins in material wealth a degree of bargaining between management and workers would not only be compatible with planning but also essential to its effectiveness. Here the worker may try to improve his standard of living without necessarily upsetting the balance of the plans or seriously hampering capital investment. Here the planners should be in a position to plan the distribution of the national income with a flexibility of which the Russians could not even dream. The freedom of bargaining may, of course, have to be restricted occasionally; but this need not be the rule. The question of how often the need to restrict such freedom would arise depends on how wide or narrow are the safety margins of any national economy at any time. On the other hand, it must be expected that in the east, especially in a communist China, which even today is more backward than was pre-revolutionary Russia, the main features of the Russian system will be reproduced, if rapid industrialization is attempted.

Nor is this merely a matter of the industrial resources with which a country embarks upon planned economy. Social custom and habit and the peculiarities of native civilizations play their part. The traditional outlook of any nation permeates the fabric of any new social organization that nation may adopt and lends to it its own color. Soviet Russia, with its public ownership and planned economy, has absorbed the still fresh traditions of tsarist autocracy and serfdom. It was not planned economy that drove Russia on to the "road of serfdom"—the fact that Russia had hardly ever left that road for any length of time vitiated her planned economy. In countries with a deep-rooted tradition of liberty, the social and cultural climate should help evolve methods of planning so efficient and humane that by comparison the Russian experiment would appear what historically it is—the first barbarously clumsy and costly, and yet profoundly significant attempt of a nation to master the "blind forces" of its economy.

SELECTED BIBLIOGRAPHY

Great Britain

Barou, N., *British Trade Unions*. Gollancz, London, 1947.

Bell, J. O. M., *Industrial Unionism: A Critical Analysis*. University of Glasgow, Glasgow, 1949.

Chang, Duck Soo, *British Methods of Industrial Peace*. Columbia University Press, New York, 1936.

Citrine, Norman A., *Trade Union Law*. Stevens, London, 1950.

Clegg, H. A., *Industrial Democracy and Nationalisation*. Blackwell, Oxford, 1951.

Cole, G. D. H., *A History of the Labor Party from 1914*. Routledge and Kegan Paul, London, 1948.

——, *British Working Class Politics*. Routledge and Kegan Paul, London, 1941.

—— (editor), *British Trade Unionism Today*. Gollanz, London, 1939.

Goodrich, Carter L., *The Frontier of Control*. Harcourt, New York, 1920.

Knowles, K. G. J. C., *Strikes—A Study in Industrial Conflict*. Blackwell, Oxford, 1951.

Milne-Bailey, W., *Trade Unions and the State*. Allen and Unwin, London, 1934.

——, *Trade Union Documents*. Bell, London, 1929.

Ministry of Labour and National Service, *Industrial Relations Handbook* (1944), Supplement No. 3: "Joint Consultation in Industry." His Majesty's Stationery Office, London, 1950.

Political & Economic Planning, *British Trade Unionism*. London, 1948.

Richardson, J. H., *Industrial Relations in Great Britain*. International Labor Office, 1933.

Sharp, I. G., *Industrial Conciliation and Arbitration in Great Britain*. Allen and Unwin, London, 1950.

Webb, Sidney and Beatrice, *History of Trade Unionism*. London, 1920.

——, *Industrial Democracy*, London, 1920.

Scandinavia

Bruun, Henry, *Den Faglige Arbejderbevegelse i Danmark*. Copenhagen, 1944.

Bull, Edvard, *Arbeiderklassen i Norsk Historie*. Oslo, 1947.

Casparsson, Ragnar, *L O Under Fem Årtionden*. Stockholm, 1947.

De Samvirkende Fagforbund, *Under Samvirkets Flag*. Copenhagen, 1948.

Galenson, Walter, *Labor in Norway*. Cambridge, 1949.

——, *The Danish System of Labor Relations*. Cambridge, 1952.

Heckscher, Eli F., *Svenskt Arbete och Liv*. Stockholm, 1941.

Hovde, Bryn J., *The Scandinavian Countries*. Ithaca, 1948.
Illum, Knud, *Den Kollektive Arbejdsret*. Copenhagen, 1939.
Lindbom, Tage, *Den Svenska Fackföreningsrörelsens Uppkomst*. Stockholm, 1938.
Norgren, Paul, *The Swedish Collective Bargaining System*, Cambridge, 1941.
Nørregaard, Georg, *Arbejdsforhold Indenfor Dansk Haandverk og Industri*. Copenhagen, 1943.
Ousland, Gunnar, *Fagorganisasjonen i Norge*. Oslo, 1949.
Petersen, Erling, *Norsk Arbeidsgiverforening 1900–1950*. Oslo, 1950.
Robbins, James J., *The Government of Labor Relations in Sweden*. Chapel Hill, 1942.
Tingsten, Herbert, *Den Svenska Socialdemokratiens Ideutveckling*. Stockholm, 1941.
Westerståhl, Jörgen, *Svensk Fackförenings-Rörelse*, Stockholm, 1945.

Australia

Fitzpatrick, Brian, *A Short History of the Australian Labor Movement*, Melbourne, 1944.
Foenander, Orwell, *Industrial Regulation in Australia*. Melbourne, 1947.
———, *Solving Labour Problems in Australia*. Melbourne, 1941.
———, "The Commonwealth Court of Conciliation and Arbitration," *Quarterly Journal of Economics* (August, 1949), Vol. 63, p. 408.
Hancock, W. K., *Australia*. London, 1930.
McCawley, T. W., *Industrial Arbitration*. Brisbane, 1924.
McLaurin, W. R., "Compulsory Arbitration in Australia," *American Economic Review*, Vol. XXVIII (March, 1938).
Metin, A., *Le Socialisme sans Doctrines*. Paris, 1901.
Reddaway, W. B., "Australian Wage Policy, 1927–37," *International Labour Review*, Vol. 37, p. 314.
Ross, L., "Australian Labor and the Crisis," *Economic Record*, Vol. VIII (1932), p. 204.
———, "Socialism and Australian Labor," *Australian Quarterly*, Vol. XXII (1950), p. 21.
Sutcliffe, J. T., *A History of Trade Unionism in Australia*. Melbourne, 1921.

Germany

Bebel, August, *My Life*. Chicago, 1913.
Böhme, Theodore, *Die Christlich-nationale Gewerkschaft*. Stuttgart, 1930.
Fiedler, Johann, *Die Konzentrationsbewegung der Gewerkschaften*. Leipzig, 1924.
Göhre, Paul, *The Evangelical-Social Movement in Germany*. London, 1898.
Guillebaud, C. W., *The Works Council*. Cambridge, 1928.
Kautsky, Karl, *Die Politsche Massenstreik*. Berlin, 1914.
Legien, Karl, *Die deutsche Gewerkschaftsbewegung*. Berlin, 1911.
Luxembourg, Rosa, *The Mass Strike*. Detroit (no date).
Mayer, Gustav, *Johann Baptist von Schweitzer und die Sozialdemokratie*. Jena, 1909.
Mehring, Franz, *Geschichte der Deutschen Sozialdemokratie*. Stuttgart, 1896.
Nestriepke, S., *Die Gewerkschaftsbewegung*. Leipzig, 1921–1923,

Perlman, Selig, *A Theory of the Labor Movement*. New York, 1949.
Reich, Nathan, *Labour Relations in Republican Germany*. New York, 1938.
Stern, Boris, *Works' Council Movement in Germany*. Washington, 1925.
Sturmthal, A., *The Tragedy of European Labor*. New York, 1951.
Taft, Philip, *Movements for Economic Reform*. New York, 1950.
Wunderlich, Frieda, *German Labor Courts*. Chapel Hill, 1947.

France

Bothereau, Robert, *Histoire du Syndicalisme Français*. Paris, 1945.
Chambelland, Pierre, *Les Comités d'entreprise, fonctionnement et résultats pratiques*. Paris, 1949.
Clark, Marjorie R., *A History of the French Labor Movement (1910–28)*. Berkeley, 1930.
Colton, Joel, *Compulsory Labor Arbitration in France, 1936–1939*. New York, 1951.
Dehove, Gerard, *Le contrôle ouvrier en France*. Paris, 1937.
Dolléans, Edouard, *Histoire du Mouvement Ouvrier, 1830–1936*, 3d ed. Paris, 1948.
Dolléans, Edouard, and Michel Crozier, *Mouvements ouvrier et socialiste, Chronologie et bibliographie: Angleterre, France, Allemagne, Etats-Unis (1750–1918)*. Paris, 1950.
Dubreuil, Hyacinthe, *Employeurs et salariés en France*. Paris, 1934.
Duchemin, René P., *Organisation syndicale patronale en France*. Paris, 1940.
Durand, Paul, and R. Jaussaud, *Traité du Droit du Travail*, two volumes. Paris, 1947–50.
Durand, Paul, and André Rouast, *Précis de Législation industrielle (Droit du Travail)*, 3d ed. Paris, 1948.
Duveau, Georges, *La vie ouvrière en France sous le second empire*. Paris, 1946.
Ehrmann, Henry W., *French Labor: From Popular Front to Liberation*. New York, 1947.
Halévy, Daniel, *Essais sur le mouvement ouvrier en France*. Paris, 1901.
Hoog, Georges, *Histoire du Catholicisme social en France, 1871–1931*. Paris, 1946.
International Labour Offices, *Labour-Management Cooperation in France*. Geneva, 1950.
Jouhaux, Léon, *La CGT, ce qu'elle est, ce qu'elle veut*. Paris, 1937.
———, *Le syndicalisme et la CGT*. Paris, 1920.
Lagardelle, Hubert, *Le socialisme ouvrier*. Paris, 1911.
Laroque, Pierre, *Les rapports entre patrons et ouvriers*, Paris, 1938.
Lefranc, Georges, *Histoire du syndicalisme français*, Paris, 1937.
———, *Les expériences syndicales en France de 1939 à 1950*. Paris, 1950.
Leroy, Maxime, *La coutume ouvrière*, two volumes. Paris, 1913.
———, *Les techniques nouvelles du syndicalisme*. Paris, 1921.
Levasseur, Emile, *Histoire des classes ouvrières et de l'industrie en France, de 1789 à 1870*. Paris, 1903.
Lorwin, Lewis L., *Syndicalism in France*. New York, 1914.
Louis, Paul, *La condition ouvrière en France depuis cent ans*. Paris, 1950.
———, *Histoire du mouvement syndical en France*, two volumes. Paris, 1947–48.

Marchal, André, *Le mouvement syndical en France*. Paris, 1945.

Montreuil, Jean (Georges Lefranc), *Histoire du mouvement syndical en France, des origines à nos jours*. Paris, 1947.

Moon, Parker T., *The Labor Problem and the Social Catholic Movement in France*. New York, 1920.

Netter, F., *Notions essentielles de sécurite sociale*. Paris, 1951.

Philip, André, *Trade-unionisme et syndicalisme*. Paris, 1936.

Picard, Roger, *Le syndicalisme durant la guerre*. Paris, 1927.

Rosmer, Alfred, *Le mouvement ouvrier pendant la guerre: De l'union sacrée à Zimmerwald*. Paris, 1936.

Saposs, David J., *The Labor Movement in Post-War France*. New York, 1931.

Sorel, Georges, *Reflections on Violence*. Glencoe, Illinois, 1950.

Thorel, Guy, *Chronologie du movement syndical ouvrier en France, 1791–1946*. Paris, 1947.

Vignaux, Paul, *Traditionalisme et syndicalisme, essai d'histoire sociale (1884–1941)*. New York, 1943.

Villey, Etienne, *L'organisation professionnelle des employeurs dans l'industrie française*. Paris, 1923.

Weill, Georges, *Histoire du mouvement social en France, 1852–1924*. Paris, 1924.

Zirnheld, Jules, *Cinquante années de syndicalisme chrétien*. Paris, 1937.

Italy

Angiolini, Alfredo, and Eugenio Ciacchi, *Socialismo e Socialisti in Italia*. Firenze, 1919.

Bruno, T., *La federazione del libro nel suo primo cinquantennio di vita*. Bologna, 1925.

Cabrini, Angiolo, *Le camere del lavoro in Italia*. Genoa, 1896.

———, *La Legislazione Sociale, 1895–1913*. Rome, 1913.

Candeloro, Giorgio, *Il movimento sindicale in Italia*. Rome, 1950.

La CGIL dal Patto di Roma al Congresso di Genova, Vol. I and III (Vol. II not published). Rome, 1949.

Confederazione generale dell'industria italiana, *I consigli di gestione*. Rome, 1947.

Field, G. Lowell, *The Syndical and Corporative Institutions of Italian Fascism*. New York, 1938.

Gnocchi Viani, Osvaldo, *Dieci anni di camere del lavoro*. Bologna, 1899.

Gualtieri, Humbert L., *The Labor Movement in Italy*. New York, 1946.

Haider, Carmen, *Capital and Labor under Fascism*. New York, 1930.

Michels, Roberto, *Proletario e Borghesia nel Movimento Socialista Italiano*. Turin, 1908.

———, *Storia Critica del Movimento Socialista Italiano*. Firenze, 1926.

Rigola, Rinaldo, *Storia del movimento operaio italiano*. Milan, 1946.

———, *Rinaldo Rigola e il movimento operaio nel biellese*. Bari, 1930.

Riguzzi, Biagio, *Sindicalismo e reformismo nel parmense*. Bari, 1931.

Riva Sanseverino, Luisa, *Il movimento sindicale cristiano*. Rome, 1950.

Rosenstock-Franck, L., *L'économie corporative fasciste en doctrine et en fait*. Paris, 1934.

Rosselli, Nello, *Mazzini e Bakunin*. Turin, 1927.

Schneider, Herbert W., *Making the Fascist State*. New York, 1928.

Zibordi, Giovanni, *Saggio sulla storia del movimento operaio in Italia*. Bari, 1930.

Russia

Aleksandrov, N. G. (editor), *Sovyetskoye Trudovoye Pravo* (*Soviet Labor Law*). Moscow, 1949.

Antoshkin, D., *Professionalnoye Dvizheniye v Rossii* (*The Trade Union Movement in Russia*). Moscow, 1925.

Bergson, Abram, *The Structure of Soviet Wages*. Cambridge, 1944.

Bienstock, G., S. Schwartz, and A. Yugow, *Management in Russian Industry and Agriculture*. New York, 1944.

Dallin, David, and Boris Nicolaevski, *Forced Labor in Soviet Russia*. New Haven, 1947.

Dunn, R. W., *Soviet Trade Unions*. London, 1928.

Gordon, Manya, *Workers Before and After Lenin*. New York, 1941.

Hubbard, L. E., *Soviet Labor and Industry*. London, 1942.

International Labor Organization, *The Trade Union Movement in Soviet Russia*. Geneva, 1927.

Lozovsky, A., *Handbook on the Soviet Trade Unions*. Moscow, 1937.

Miller, Margaret, *Labour in the USSR*, British Association for Labour Legislation. London, 1942.

Rashin, A. G., *Formirovaniye Promishlennovo Proletariata v Rossii* (*Formation of the Industrial Proletariat in Russia*). Moscow, 1940.

Rolnikas, Michel, *Les Syndicats Professionels en U.R.S.S.* Paris, 1936.

Romanov, F. A., *Rabochi i Professionalnoye Dvizheniye* (*Workers in the Trade Union Movement*). Moscow, 1949.

Shelymagin, I. I., *Fabrichno-Trudovoye Zakonodatelstvo v Rossii* (*Factory Legislation in Russia*). Moscow, 1947.

Turin, S. P., *From Peter the Great to Lenin: A History of the Russian Labor Movement*. London, 1935.

INDEX

INDEX

DATE DUE

NOV 20 79			
NOV 13 79			
GAYLORD			PRINTED IN U.S.A.